Inheritance and Originality

Wittgenstein, Heidegger, Kierkegaard

STEPHEN MULHALL

CLARENDON PRESS · OXFORD

2001

OXFORD

UNIVERSITY PRESS

Great Clarendon Street, Oxford OX2 6DP

Oxford University Press is a department of the University of Oxford.
It furthers the University's objective of excellence in research, scholarship,
and education by publishing worldwide in

Oxford New York

Athens Auckland Bangkok Bogotá Buenos Aires
Cape Town Chennai Dar es Salaam Delhi Florence Hong Kong Istanbul
Karachi Kolkata Kuala Lumpur Madrid Melbourne Mexico City Mumbai
Nairobi Paris São Paulo Shanghai Singapore Taipei Tokyo Toronto Warsaw
and associated companies in Berlin Ibadan

Oxford is a registered trade mark of Oxford University Press
in the UK and certain other countries

Published in the United States
by Oxford University Press Inc., New York

British Library Cataloguing in Publication Data
Mulhall, Stephen, 1962–
Inheritance and originality : Wittgenstein, Heidegger, Kierkegaard / Stephen Mulhall.
p. cm.
Includes bibliographical references and index.
1. Wittgenstein, Ludwig, 1889–1951—Contributions in methodology. 2. Heidegger, Martin,
1889–1976—Contributions in methodology. 3. Kierkegaard, Søren, 1813–1855—Contributions
in methodology. 4. Methodology—History—19th century. 5. Methodology—History—
20th century. I. Title.
B3376.W564 M79 2001 190—dc21 00-068832
ISBN 0-19-924390-5

Library of Congress Cataloging in Publication Data

1 3 5 7 9 10 8 6 4 2

Typeset in Times
by Best-set Typesetter Ltd., Hong Kong
Printed in Great Britain by
Biddles Ltd., Guildford & King's Lynn

What we inherit from the past is now a cultural obsession; and the nature of inheritance itself informs our most compelling fictions.

Adam Phillips, *Darwin's Worms*

It is very unhappy, but too late to be helped, the discovery we have made that we exist. That discovery is called the Fall of Man.

Ralph Waldo Emerson, 'Experience'

Just as the Virgin was called to offer herself entirely as human being and as woman that God's Word might take flesh and come among us, so too philosophy is called to offer its rational and critical resources that theology, as the understanding of faith, may be fruitful and creative. And just as in giving her assent to Gabriel's word, Mary lost nothing of her true humanity and freedom, so too when philosophy heeds the summons of the Gospel's truth its autonomy is in no way impaired. Indeed it is then that philosophy sees all its enquiries rise to their highest expression. This was a truth which the holy monks of Christian antiquity understood well when they called Mary 'the table at which faith sits in thought'.

John Paul II, *Fides et Ratio*

CONTENTS

List of Abbreviations   x

Introduction

Modernist Origins: Reading Stanley Cavell's *The Claim of
Reason*   1

First Paragraph: Integrity and Reflexivity   2
Second Paragraph: Texts and Problems   6
Third Paragraph: Writing, Speech, and the Human Voice   9
Fourth Paragraph: Modernism   11
  Fragmentation   13
  Amentia   16
  Myth   18
  Song   21

Fifth Paragraph: Approaching the Hermeneutic Circle   23

Part One

Wittgenstein's Vision of Language: Reading the *Philosophical
Investigations*   27

Opening: Quotation   29
Pictures, Paradigms, and Conversion   36
The Shopkeeper and the Shopper   43
The Builders   52
Games and Board Games   58
Language-Games   61
Expanding a Language-Game: Diachrony and Synchrony   66
The Natural History of Speech   70
Games and Language   75
Family Resemblance   81
Subliming the Logic of our Language   87
Criteria, Essence, and Context   93
The Circumstances of Speech: Normal and Abnormal   97
Rules: The Normal, the Natural, and Knowing how to Go On   102
Reading: An Interpolation   106
Rules: Intuitions, Decisions, and Judgements   112
Rules: The Machinery of Symbolism   118
Rules: Individuals and Communities   122

Rules: Fantasies, Myths, and Symbols   135
The Paradox of Aspect-Dawning   153
Dissolving the Paradox   157
Aspects of Meaning   163
Aspects of the Inner   171
Reinheriting the Idea of Grammar   174

Part Two

Heidegger's Vision of Scepticism: Reading *Being and Time* and
What is Called Thinking?   183

Opening: Quotation   185
The Meaning of Being: Genus and Species   196
The Structure of Questioning   198
The Priority of Dasein   202
Dasein, Time, and History   208
Phenomenology: Appearance and Reality   211
Everydayness: The Average, the Primitive, and the Theological   215
The Cartesian Subject: Inviting Scepticism   218
Questions of Method: Construction and Hyphenation   223
Dasein's Worldliness   226
The Worldhood of the World   229
World, Language, and Discourse   234
Scepticism: The Scandal of Philosophy   237
Average Everyday Being-with-Others: The 'They'   243
Being-in: Thrown Projection   248
Moods: Deconstructing Kant   252
An Uncanny Emblem of Being-in-the-World: Anxiety   256
A Sceptical Mood   262
The Ontological Myth of Care   265
Conscience: The Silent Call   272
Locating the Voice of Conscience   276
The Voice of Philosophy's Conscience   278

* * * * *

Before the Beginning: A Word-Chain   286
Heidegger's Most Thought-Provoking Thought   292
Transition: Thinking and Teaching   295
Nietzsche: The Blossoming of Scepticism   300
Thinking, Language, History   307
Parmenides' Words   310
The Draw of Paratactic Reading   313
The Horizon of Christianity   318

Part Three

Kierkegaard's Vision of Religion: Reading *Philosophical
Fragments, Fear and Trembling,* and *Repetition*   321

The Self-Assessments of Johannes Climacus   323
Subverting Descartes: Thought and Existence   329
Subverting Descartes: Creation and Dependence   332
Subverting Descartes: Metaphysics and Difference   334
Subverting the Subversion: Socratic Origins   338
Logic, Poetry, and Theology   346
Appendix and Interlude: Caption and Performance   348
Teacher and Teaching: Owning Indebtedness   351

* * * * *

De Silentio, by Johannes Climacus   354
Abraham without Words   356
Abraham's Words: Saying Nothing?   359
Language and the Literal   364
De Silentio: Philosopher or Poet?   368
Language and the Figurative   370
Abraham's Posterity: Parable and Prefiguration   376
Ethics and Faith: After Abraham, After Hegel   380

* * * * *

Constantius, by Johannes Climacus   388
Prologue: Citation, Question, and Genre   390
Theatricality and Selfhood   392
Farce and Selfhood   395
Repetition as Farce: Doubling, Dynamism, and Therapy   399
Therapy Transposed: Writing and Reading   403
Job's Testament: The Whirlwind's Nature   405
Christ's Testament: Prodigal Forgiveness   409

Concluding Dogmatic Postscript

Biblical Origins: Hereditary Sin and the Body of the Victim   415

Acknowledgements   439
Bibliography   441
Index   445

LIST OF ABBREVIATIONS

AT   V. Hearne, *Adam's Task* (Heinemann: London, 1986)

BT   M. Heidegger, *Being and Time*, trans. J. Macquarrie and E. Robinson (Blackwell: Oxford, 1962)

C   Augustine, *Confessions*, trans. H. Chadwick (Oxford University Press: Oxford, 1991)

CA   S. Kierkegaard, *The Concept of Anxiety: A Simple Psychologically Orienting Deliberation on the Dogmatic Issue of Hereditary Sin*, trans. R. Thomte and A. B. Anderson (Princeton University Press: Princeton, 1980)

CHU   S. Cavell, *Conditions Handsome and Unhandsome* (University of Chicago Press; Chicago, 1990)

CR   S. Cavell, *The Claim of Reason* (Oxford University Press: Oxford, 1979)

CUP   S. Kierkegaard, *Concluding Unscientific Postscript to the Philosophical Fragments*, trans. H. V. and E. H. Hong (Princeton University Press: Princeton, 1992)

F   J. W. Goethe, *Faust Part Two*, trans. P. Wayne (Penguin: London, 1959)

FCM   M. Heidegger, *The Fundamental Concepts of Metaphysics*, trans. W. McNeill and N. Walker (Indiana University Press: Bloomington, 1995)

FT   *Fear and Trembling*, in S. Kierkegaard, *Fear and Trembling & Repetition*, trans. H. V. and E. H. Hong (Princeton University Press: Princeton, 1983)

IEA   S. Cavell, 'The *Investigations*' Everyday Aesthetics of Itself', in S. Mulhall (ed.), *The Cavell Reader* (Blackwell: Oxford, 1996)

LW   L. Wittgenstein, *Last Writings on the Philosophy of Psychology*, i and ii, trans. C. G. Luckhardt and M. A. E. Aue (Blackwell: Oxford, 1982, 1992)

MLBJ   H. Fingarette, 'The Meaning of Law in the Book of Job', in S. Hauerwas and A. MacIntyre (eds.), *Revisions* (University of Notre Dame Press: Notre Dame, 1981)

MLR   G. P. Baker and P. M. S. Hacker, 'Malcolm on Language and Rules', *Philosophy*, 65 (1990)

MWM   S. Cavell, *Must we Mean what we Say?* (Cambridge University Press: Cambridge, 1969)

OED   *Oxford English Dictionary*

PF S. Kierkegaard, *Philosophical Fragments*, trans. H. V. and E. H. Hong (Princeton University Press: Princeton, 1985)

PI L. Wittgenstein, *Philosophical Investigations*, trans. G. E. M. Anscombe (Blackwell: Oxford, 1953)

POP S. Cavell, *A Pitch of Philosophy* (Harvard University Press: Cambridge, Mass., 1994)

PP S. Cavell, *Philosophical Passages* (Blackwell: Oxford, 1995)

R *Repetition*, in S. Kierkegaard, *Fear and Trembling & Repetition*, trans. H. V. and E. H. Hong (Princeton University Press: Princeton, 1983)

RGN G. P. Baker and P. M. S. Hacker, *Wittgenstein: Rules, Grammar and Necessity* (Blackwell: Oxford, 1986)

RPP L. Wittgenstein, *Remarks on the Philosophy of Psychology*, vol. i, trans. G. E. M. Anscombe, vol. ii, trans. C. G. Luckhardt and M. A. E. Aue (Blackwell: Oxford, 1980)

S Plato, *Sophist*, trans. N. White (Hackett: Indianapolis, 1993)

SRL G. P. Baker and P. M. S. Hacker, *Scepticism, Rules and Language* (Blackwell: Oxford, 1984)

SW S. Cavell, *The Senses of Walden* (North Point Press: San Francisco, 1981)

TSW F. Nietzsche, *Thus Spake Zarathustra*, trans. R. J. Hollingdale (Penguin: London, 1961)

WB R. Rhees, 'Wittgenstein's Builders', in his *Discussions of Wittgenstein* (Routledge & Kegan Paul: London, 1970)

WCT M. Heidegger, *What is Called Thinking?* (Harper & Row: New York, 1968)

WLR N. Malcolm, 'Wittgenstein on Language and Rules', in his *Essays on Wittgensteinian Themes* (Cornell University Press: Ithaca, NY, 1996)

INTRODUCTION

Modernist Origins:

Reading Stanley Cavell's *The Claim of Reason*

[Despite] Cavell's philosophical and literary gifts [*The Claim of Reason*] as it stands is a misshapen, undisciplined amalgam of ill-sorted parts . . . [It] is a worthwhile book, but it could have been much better had it been pruned of dead-wood and over-exuberant foliage. The need for trimming can be illustrated by the very first sentence . . . The exasperated reader might well put the book down and go no further.

(Anthony Kenny, *Times Literary Supplement*, 16 April 1980)

These words, it seems to me, give us a particular picture of the essence of philosophical writing—of what it is for such writing to be well shaped and disciplined, for its parts to form a genuine whole, for its sections and sentences to have neither too little nor too much vitality. But do they—in developing that metaphor of vegetable life perhaps a little too exuberantly, and amalgamating it perhaps a little too forcibly with another, more metallic or mechanical, one—observe the canons of propriety they deploy in criticism of another's words? They certainly do not take the picture to which they officially cleave as open to question—as if the matter of philosophical form has been forgotten, or is capable at any moment of being passed over, even when the text we are reading all but explicitly aims to provide an occasion for us to question the obviousness or self-evidence of our picture of that matter. But since, to those in the grip of the picture, such texts are rather more likely to occasion exasperation, how might such all but inevitable circuits of mutual misunderstanding be disrupted? How might a text such as *The Claim of Reason*[1] be understood as attempting to initiate such disruption? Since any such purposes can be effective only if those who encounter this text choose to stay with its orderings of words, we must first ask how it aims to justify or reward such a choice—how its opening encounter with its readers is designed to attract rather than repel them. But where and how does this text conceive that its readers

[1] (Oxford University Press: Oxford, 1979); hereafter *CR*.

are to approach it? How are we to let this book teach us, this or
anything?

FIRST PARAGRAPH: INTEGRITY AND REFLEXIVITY

We might, provisionally, begin at the beginning. After all, the book's
Emersonian epigraph tells us that 'truly speaking, it is not instruction
but provocation, that I can receive from another soul'; and the opening
sentences of *The Claim of Reason* are certainly among its most
provocative.

If not at the beginning of Wittgenstein's later philosophy, since what starts philosophy is no more to be known at the outset than how to make an end of it;
and if not at the opening of *Philosophical Investigations*, since its opening is
not to be confused with the starting of the philosophy it expresses, and since
the terms in which that opening might be understood can hardly be given along
with the opening itself; and if we acknowledge at the commencement, anyway
leave open at the opening, that the way this work is written is internal to what
it teaches, which means that we cannot understand the manner (call it the
method) before we understand its work; and if we do not look to our history,
since placing this book historically can hardly happen earlier than placing it
philosophically; nor look to Wittgenstein's past, since then we are likely to
suppose that the *Investigations* is written in criticism of the *Tractatus*, which is
not so much wrong as empty, both because to know what constitutes its criticism would be to know what constitutes its philosophy, and because it is more
to the present point to see how the *Investigations* is written in criticism of itself;
then where and how are we to approach this text? How shall we let this book
teach us, this or anything? (CR 3)

From such provocation, what instruction?

First, that *The Claim of Reason* is, above or at least before all, a
reading of the *Philosophical Investigations*, a response to that highly
unusual text. Second, that any such reading should begin by reflecting
upon its own beginnings; it originates in its responsiveness to the issue
of its own origin, in a capacity to regard the proper place and manner
of its own commencement as a genuine question. (Here, the form of the
first sentence—with its seemingly endless series of clauses deferring
completion in favour of reiterated beginnings—enacts its content.)
Third, that the series of clauses through which this question is articulated also constitutes a provisional answer to it. The fourth clause
asserts the futility of beginning from the historical context in which the
Investigations was written and is read; the fifth and first clauses deny

that earlier points in Wittgenstein's philosophical development can provide a useful opening; the second warns against assuming that the opening of the *Investigations* contains everything needed to comprehend its own philosophy; and the third suggests that the book's substance is inseparable from its form. Taken as a whole, they tell us that we must avoid treating the *Investigations* as a part of a larger whole, or treating any of its parts as more important than the whole they make up, or treating its manner or method as if it were not integral to its work. In short: if we are to read it properly, we must read it whole.

A further implication is that, properly read, the *Investigations* will give us everything we need to answer the external and internal questions that have just been rejected as inappropriate approaches to that text. For Cavell, it is fundamental to the work of the *Investigations* that it simultaneously provide the terms in which its readers can understand its work (and so its manner or method), the terms in which it will criticize itself and other philosophies, and the terms in which it might be related to its personal and historical context. And by linking these apparently separate issues in a single sentence, as if they add up to a single, complete thought, he further implies that the terms needed to comprehend them will turn out to be, if not identical, then internally related. Each budget of terms will form part of a larger lexicon; understanding the work of the *Investigations* appears inseparable from understanding its parts, its manner, and its context.

If, however, Wittgenstein's text must provide its readers with the terms in which to read it, that responsibility must have priority; the first aim of its teaching must be to teach the terms in which its teaching can alone be taken up. The consequent paradox is evident. If only the book as a whole can teach us the terms in which to understand its teaching, how can we learn which terms those are? It would seem that, if we are to learn anything from this book, we must first understand it. It is to this paradox, the apparent burden of *The Claim of Reason*'s first sentence, that its second sentence is a response: 'How shall we let this book teach us, this or anything?' What does this second sentence have to teach us?

First, it is a response to the book's previous sentence—as if this text's progress will be determined as much by Cavell's responses to the *Investigations* as by the *Investigations* itself. Second, it does not directly answer the preceding question, but rather restates it—as if this investigation neither begins nor ends with theses but is rather a matter of continuously renewed questioning, as if this sentence itself constitutes a new beginning to the investigation, as if every sentence in this book aspires to be a new beginning (and so, a new end). Third, it restates the question by reformulating it; it drops the first sentence's unquestioning reliance upon the idea of an approach to the *Investigations*, and shifts from active to passive mode. It thereby asks whether this idea of an approach (as opposed, say, to a mode of reception) is prejudicial—whether the sense of paradox which the first question generates is a function not of the task it describes but of the present description of it.

Before we follow out these implications, however, we need to register a further range of significance in Cavell's second sentence. For it is my guiding intuition that *The Claim of Reason*'s characterizations of the text to which it is a response are also self-characterizations, and so that their opening instructions concerning how (and how not) to read the *Investigations* apply also to readers of the book whose opening they constitute. This does not mean that I take *The Claim of Reason* to be a mechanical reiteration of the teachings and methods of the *Investigations*, as if Cavell's response to this text is to ventriloquize its voice. My claim is rather that the various extensions and denials of Wittgenstein's voice to which Cavell is driven by the need to investigate his own pre-occupations in his own way are compatible with his continuing to look to its general form or manner, and in particular its tendency to embody self-characterizations within its orderings of words, as exemplary for the present of philosophy (see *CR*, p. xv).

On this reading, the opening sentence of *The Claim of Reason* tells us that its fundamental task is to begin providing the terms needed to understand its teaching, terms which will also make sense of this book's modes of self-criticism, its criticism of earlier texts by Cavell, and its criticism of other philosophers, as well as its historical placement. This text cannot therefore be understood by approaching it via these contextual and intra-textual matters; it must rather be taken as a whole, and it can only be so taken if its manner or method is seen as internal to its work. This means that the paradox apparently involved in understanding the *Investigations* seems equally applicable to *The Claim of Reason*: if only the work as a whole can provide the terms needed to comprehend it, then it seems that only those who already understand it can come to understand it. Where and how, then, are we to approach this text?

The second clause of the book's first sentence appears to intensify our difficulties here. For it claims that we should not regard the opening of the *Investigations* as an approach to the book as a whole, 'since its opening is not to be confused with the starting of the philosophy it expresses, and since the terms in which that opening might be understood can hardly be given along with the opening itself' (*CR* 3).

Does it not then follow that approaching *The Claim of Reason* through its opening violates the book's proffered terms for understanding itself?

An external ground for questioning this inference appears in Cavell's 'Notes and Afterthoughts on the Opening of Wittgenstein's *Investigations*'.[2] They contain a late version of a set of lecture notes through which Cavell has repeatedly introduced his students to Wittgenstein's thought, and they begin precisely with the opening sections of the *Investigations*; indeed, Cavell claims that 'what's left of these opening lectures in *The Claim of Reason*, or epitomized there, is its paragraph-length opening sentence' (*PP* 126)—which suggests that *The Claim of Reason* implicitly opens, not with its famous discussion of Wittgenstein's notion of a criterion, but with a compressed response to the *Investigations*' famous opening. Since, however, this line of thought might seem to violate another of our present text's opening instructions—that which forbids utilizing texts other than *The Claim of Reason* as part of an approach to it—I will not pursue it. I want instead to propose two other ways of responding to our difficulty. The first is to suggest that the second clause of the opening sentence does not guide its readers away from beginning their encounter with *The Claim of Reason* with its opening, but guides them away from thinking that its opening is a way to approach *The Claim of Reason*; in short, that what we are here being warned off is the idea of there being 'an approach' to this, or any other such, text. I will return to this.

The second response is to suggest that beginning with the opening of *The Claim of Reason* need not involve either confusing that opening with the starting of the philosophy it expresses, or assuming that the terms in which it might be understood can be given along with it. We might, for example, think that the book's opening offers some guidance for interpreting both itself and the book it initiates, without assuming that it offers *all* the guidance we shall need; on the contrary, when we do move beyond its opening paragraph, we shall find that further, vital specifications of how *The Claim of Reason* should be read appear regularly throughout this text. Similarly, we can begin a reading of *The Claim of Reason* with its notorious opening sentence without confusing that opening with the starting of the philosophy that the book expresses; we might, for example, think that its philosophy starts before that opening—with the epigraph to the part of the book in which this opening chapter appears, with the title, subtitle, and epigraph of the book itself, or with its foreword. The fact that my reading begins by

[2] In Stanley Cavell, *Philosophical Passages* (Blackwell: Oxford, 1995); hereafter *PP*.

passing over these elements does not entail that it must overlook the instruction they contain; a reading of a text might as properly go on from the point at which it begins by going backwards as by going forwards. Mine will do both.

SECOND PARAGRAPH: TEXTS AND PROBLEMS

Shall we go on? The third sentence of the book's opening chapter, the opening sentence of its second paragraph, runs as follows: 'I will say first, by way of introducing myself and saying why I insist, as I will throughout the following pages, upon the *Investigations* as a philosophical text, that I have wished to understand philosophy not as a set of problems but as a set of texts' (*CR* 3). This sentence has been taken to establish two conclusions. First, that this is where Cavell first appears in person in *The Claim of Reason*;[3] and second, that in doing so he asserts that *The Claim of Reason* as a whole is predicated upon an understanding of philosophy as a set of texts rather than a set of problems.[4] Both are based on misconstruals of the sentence.

The first conclusion is doubly erroneous. The pronoun which appears for the first time in this paragraph is the first-person *singular*—the first paragraph is studded with instances of the first-person plural, and as always, 'we' includes both speaker and addressees. And the explicit deployment of the first-person singular pronoun is anyway not needed for an author to leave his personal mark on a sentence. On the contrary, if any sentences of philosophical prose fit the aphorism 'Le style c'est l'homme même', it is surely those opening *The Claim of Reason*; they perform as full an introduction to their author's philosophical personality as might be desired. What the shift from 'we' to 'I' rather implies is Cavell's sense of isolation, his sense that he cannot even hope (and perhaps does not even wish) that the idea he will advance is something with which others already, unknowingly, agree.

The second conclusion registers the contrastive force of the 'but' in Cavell's sentence, but not the presence and the tense of the verb 'to

---

[3] 'Before introducing himself in *The Claim of Reason* thus reserving the first-person pronoun for his second paragraph, Cavell insists that his reader enter the text through a labyrinthine first sentence of two-hundred and sixteen words' (Michael Payne, 'Introduction', *Bucknell Review*, 32 (1989)).

[4] 'Why an interest in texts over problems? . . . the problems of philosophy for Cavell are secondary to the contributed texts of philosophy' (Richard Fleming, *The State of Philosophy* (Bucknell University Press: Lewisburg, Pa., 1993)).

wish'. This sentence does not say that Cavell understands philosophy not as a set of problems but as a set of texts; it does not even say that he wishes so to understand philosophy; it says that he has so wished. The past tense strongly implies that this wish is one by which he is no longer possessed, or at least with which he is no longer comfortable as it stands—that it is something from which he has attained, or wishes to attain, a certain perspective; without entirely wishing to spurn it, he harbours a certain suspicion about it. We might feel that this suspicion is also registered in his description of himself as 'insisting' upon the *Investigations* as a philosophical text. In the *Investigations* itself Wittgenstein is always suspicious of interlocutors who are led to insist on something; and Cavell maintains this wariness throughout *The Claim of Reason*. We might therefore ask ourselves: when Cavell insists that the *Investigations* is a philosophical text, who does he take himself to be informing, and of what? How or why might anyone think otherwise?

These suspicions are clarified in the following sentence. 'This means to me that the contribution of a philosopher—anyway of a creative thinker—to the subject of philosophy is not to be understood as a contribution to, or of, a set of *given* problems, although both historians and non-historians of the subject are given to suppose otherwise' (*CR* 3–4). Here, the stress falls not upon the idea of problems but upon their *givenness*. Cavell is not proposing a view of philosophy as a set of texts rather than problems (a proposal requiring a suspiciously simple opposition between problems and texts), but rather opposing the presumption that philosophical problems can be thought to form a *given* set or list. The implication is that if we properly acknowledge the obvious fact that philosophers typically contribute to their subject by means of texts, then we will question the idea that we can define a distinctively philosophical problem by pointing to, or by enumerating, a given set of features. For Cavell, what a distinctively philosophical problem might be is itself a philosophical problem, and one of its most fundamental ones.

This idea harks back to his first sentence's emphasis upon the idea that the terms of criticism and self-criticism that a philosophy deploys are definitive of it. For they crystallize that philosophy's understanding of what it is for a position or statement to be philosophically problematic or questionable; and on Cavell's view, to elaborate terms of criticism is precisely the work of philosophical texts. To characterize philosophical texts by their shouldering of such burdens is bound to unsettle given philosophical conceptions of the nature of a text, as well as the idea that which texts count as philosophical can be specified by a given list—in terms of what one might call a canon (one from which literary texts, for example, are excluded). In other words, Cavell's investigation aims to question our conception of philosophical problems as given by questioning our conception of philosophical texts as given; so, for him, the concept of a philosophical problem and that of a philosophical text are not so much opposed as internally related.

All this preliminary unsettling induces the first intervention of many from his interlocutor (or the first intervention from one of his many interlocutors)—a signature effect of this text. '—And is the remark about texts and not problems itself to be taken as a philosophical text? It seems argumentative or empty enough, since obviously not all texts are philosophical ones, but only those that precisely contain problems of a certain sort!' (*CR* 4)

Cavell's response is a straight-faced, even stuffy, reply to the first rather than the second of its sentences; he simply points out that the shortness of his own remark is no bar to its being counted as philosophical. This is hardly calculated to satisfy the interlocutor: for it responds to what is (clearly?) a piece of sarcasm disguised as a query as if it were a genuine question, and leaves entirely unaddressed the substantive (argumentative?) points contained in the second sentence. In so far as it does, however, it brings into question the interlocutor's standing conceptions of what a well-directed philosophical intervention, and what a satisfying philosophical response to it, might be. It implies, for example, that the sarcastic query is a more genuinely philosophical intervention than its argumentative follow-up, more genuinely deserving of a philosophical response. Why? Because it at least takes the form of an attempt to apply the (argumentative?) content of Cavell's third sentence to itself, to test its consistency with or responsiveness to itself—to measure its self-consciousness or reflexivity. The implicit instruction here is that no text that fails to measure up to the claims it advances can count as genuinely philosophical—that a philosophical text is one whose form and content are mutually attuned from top to bottom.

In reality, however, Cavell does not overlook his interlocutor's second sentence. For he immediately develops the theme of the length of philosophical texts into what he calls a budget of philosophical genres or paradigms, within which he remarks: 'Some philosophers are able to make about anything into a philosophical text, like a preacher improving upon the infant's first cry; while some people are not even able to start a quarrel with God' (*CR* 4). Here Cavell implicitly denies that he is endorsing what the interlocutor thinks his earlier remark about texts and problems commits him to—the idea that all texts are (at least potentially?) philosophical ones. For him, someone who treats anything and everything as a philosophical text is no more a genuine philosopher than someone who improves upon an infant's first cry is properly preaching; both, in their eagerness to extend the reach of their responses, have exceeded their grasp of what might merit or require such a response. Of course, it also implies that those who find nothing to be worthy of a philosophical response have equally lost touch with the point of philosophy; it has gone dead for them, receded from their grasp. In this sense, Cavell has no quarrel with his interlocutor's second remark; since he does not wish to assert what the interlocutor denies, he need not oppose that denial.

He cannot, however, simply refuse to satisfy the interlocutor's wish for an argument, because of the way the interlocutor formulates the denial. The interlocutor does not say: 'Not all texts are philosophical ones', but rather: 'Obviously not all texts are philosophical ones'; and the criterion invoked for this obvious distinction is the fact that a text contains problems of a certain sort. That 'obviously', paired with the assumption of a standing sense of what sort of problems are distinctively philosophical, conflicts with Cavell's view that whether a text is one to which a philosophical response is appropriate, or (if you prefer) one that raises problems of a sort requiring a philosophical response, is not given or obvious, but is rather to be discovered through individual acts of what one might call philosophical criticism. After all, as we shall see, the whole of the *Investigations* can be thought of as a philosophical response (to a preacher's response) to an infant's first utterances, its first cry for language (and we might ask whether Wittgenstein thinks that Augustine was (philosophically?) wrong because he improved upon that cry, or because he improved upon it in the wrong way); and the whole of *The Claim of Reason* might be thought of as attempting not to start (or to transcend) a quarrel with God.

THIRD PARAGRAPH: WRITING, SPEECH, AND THE HUMAN VOICE

Still within the first of Cavell's overtly self-introductory remarks, he devotes his third paragraph to a further specification of what he wants from the idea of a new emphasis upon (or an emphasis upon a new conception of) philosophical texts.

A measure of the quality of a new text is the quality of the texts it arouses. That a text may exist primarily in an oral tradition would not counter my thought here. Though the fact that it exists primarily in an oral tradition may determine the size or shape of its response, i.e., of an acceptable contribution to its text. I may say that while Wittgenstein's philosophizing is more completely attentive to the human voice than any other I think of, it strikes me that its teaching is essentially something written, that some things essential to its teaching cannot be spoken. This may mean that some things he says have lost, or have yet to find, the human circle in which they can usefully be said. (CR 5)

Clearly, Cavell's concept of a text does not signify writing as opposed to speech. Nevertheless, from the third clause of his opening sentence his emphasis upon philosophical texts has hung together with an emphasis upon the essential contribution made to philosophical work by philosophical writing, its manner, and its method; and he states that some things essential to the teaching of the *Investigations* (and thus, according to my intuition, to *The Claim of Reason*) cannot be spoken. However, this assertion is multiply qualified. First, since Cavell also regards the *Investigations* as fundamentally attuned to the human voice, its writtenness appears not in opposition to that voice but as essential to its proper expression; if anything, what this remark opposes to the voice is not writing but speech. And second, Cavell's own (admittedly tentative) gloss on his claim that some things essential to Wittgenstein's teaching cannot be spoken bargains away the necessity of that 'cannot'; he suggests that the context in which it might be spoken may be absent only at present.

Here is a concrete instance of his methodological claim that essence is expressed by grammar, and so must be understood as a function of the embodiment of the language it articulates in a form of life, which means in the particular arrangements of a human community. This Wittgensteinian conception implies that essence and necessity ultimately rest upon the responses that are normal and natural to human beings, and so that what is necessary can be subject to alteration, to the forces (however vast, unintended, and slow-moving) of contingency. With respect to the particular essences and necessities in question here, Cavell's second qualification shows that, for him, both the essential connection between Wittgenstein's teaching and writing, and the essential opposition between that teaching and speech, are a function of the prevailing forms of human community to which that teaching is addressed. It suggests, in other words, that in another human community, or in this one under another dispensation of culture, what must now be written could usefully be said—that the human voice could reappear in both oral and written texts.

FOURTH PARAGRAPH: MODERNISM

Why, then, must that teaching—both Wittgenstein's and that of *The Claim of Reason*—be written under the present dispensation of culture? Cavell devotes his fourth (entirely parenthetical) paragraph, still within the first of his overtly self-introductory remarks, to a reformulation of and response to this question.

(If one asks: When *must* a work, or task, be written, or permanently marked?, one may start thinking what makes a work, or task, *memorable*. And of course the answer to this alone should not distinguish philosophy from, say, music or poetry or early astronomy or ruler and compass proofs in geometry (or, I wish I knew, what level of logic?). Poetry (some poetry) need not be written; novels must be. It seems to me that a thought I once expressed concerning the development of music relates to this. I said ('Music Discomposed', pp. 200, 201) that at some point in Beethoven's work you can no longer relate what you hear to a process of improvisation. Here I should like to add the thought that at that point music, such music, *must* be written. If one may speculate that at such a stage a musical work of art requires parts that are unpredictable from one another (though after the fact, upon analysis, you may say how one is derivable from the other), then one may speculate further that Beethoven's sketches were necessary both because not all ideas are ready for use upon their appearance (because not ever ready in any but their right company), and also because not all are usable in their initial appearance, but must first, as it were, grow outside the womb. What must be sketched must be written. If what is in a sketch book is jotted just for saving, just to await its company, with which it is then juxtaposed as it stands, you may say the juxtaposition, or composition, is that of the lyric. If it is sketched knowing that it must be, and gets in time, transformed in order to take its place, you may say that its juxtaposition, or composition, is essentially stratified and partitioned; that of the drama; the drama of the metaphysical, or of the sonata. Here are different tasks for criticism, or tasks for different criticisms.) (*CR* 5–6)

I want to concentrate on the instructions this paragraph contains for reading the *Investigations*, and so for reading *The Claim of Reason*; we have, after all, been told that the form of both texts is internal to their work, and the most fundamental fact about their form—more fundamental than any fact about *how* they are written—is *that* they are written. According to the paragraph's opening sentence, one reason for thinking that a certain teaching must be written is the idea that it would otherwise be impermanent, that its oral expression or marking would not ensure that it remained open to remarking. Presumably, then, in the present state of human (philosophical) culture, if this teaching were not written, it would be forgotten; it is written in the name of a past or future human circle, of a kind that our present circle cannot recall or create (remember or re-member). But why is our present human circle unable to preserve this teaching in the absence of its written record? Cavell offers an analogy, recalled from his earlier writings, to develop this theme. It will help our understanding of what is to come if I recall some sentences from that essay, in which he describes Beethoven's earlier work.

One can hear, in the music in question, how the composition is *related* to, or could grow in familiar ways from, a process of improvisation; as though the parts meted out by the composer were re-enactments, or dramatizations, of successes his improvisations had discovered—given the finish and permanence the occasion deserves and the public demands, but containing essentially only such discoveries . . . Somewhere in the development of Beethoven, this ceases to be imaginable.

Why might such a phenomenon occur? . . . The context in which we can hear music as improvisatory is one in which the language it employs, its conventions, are familiar or obvious enough (whether because simple or because they permit of a total mastery or perspicuity) that at no point are we or the performer in doubt about our location or goal; there are solutions to every problem, permitting the exercise of familiar forms of resourcefulness; a mistake is clearly recognizable as such, and may even present a chance to be seized; and just as the general range of chances is circumscribed, so there is a preparation for every chance, and if not an inspired one, then a formula for one. But in the late experience of Beethoven, it is as if our freedom to act no longer depends on the possibility of spontaneity; improvising to fit a *given* lack or need is no longer enough. The entire enterprise of action and of communication has become problematic. The problem is no longer how to do what you want, but to know what would satisfy you. We could also say: Convention as a whole is now looked upon not as a firm inheritance from the past, but as a continuing improvisation in the face of problems we no longer understand. Nothing we now have to say, no *personal* utterance, has its meaning conveyed in the conventions and formulas we now share . . . our choices seem to be those of silence, or nihilism (the denial of the value of shared meaning altogether), or statements so personal as to form the possibility of communication without the support of convention—perhaps to become the source of new convention . . . Such, at any rate, are the choices which the modern works of art I know seem to me to have made. (*Must we Mean what we Say?*[5] 200–2)

Add to this, as Cavell immediately does, the thought that at such a point such music must be written, and the work of the writing of the *Investigations* and *The Claim of Reason* appears as essentially modernist. Their teaching is triply devoid of memorability. Its parts or elements can no longer be read as re-enactments or memorials of insights

    [5] (Cambridge University Press: Cambridge, 1969); hereafter *MWM*.

originally discovered by improvisation; this is because neither writer nor readers possess a common fund of agreed conventions which they might call upon or recall to control their sense of what a philosophical problem is, what might count as its solution, what resources might be used to discover those solutions, and what might count as a mistaken resolution; and the absence of such familiar landmarks or reference points puts the direction of any exercise of philosophical thinking, and so the tasks of predicting or recalling its progress, in the absence of a permanent record of it, essentially beyond us. In these conditions philosophical teaching must be written, and written in face of the thought that the entire enterprise of creative thinking has become problematic, that thinkers in the present circumstances of human culture lack any grasp of what they want of thinking, let alone how to achieve it. In short, there are no given philosophical conventions; the present philosophical task is continuously to improvise them, and to do so through the writing of texts that offer statements so personal as to permit communication without convention, or the origination of new conventions.

One might say that, in citing the work of his earlier self to introduce and justify the sense in which he thinks of *The Claim of Reason* as essentially modernist, and hence to encapsulate what is attained in, and what is unattained but attainable from, his present situation (thus presenting this new beginning as indebted to that old beginning, as if no such beginning can be truly new), Cavell shows the reflexive inflection of his earlier comment on Descartes's method (placed in his budget of philosophical genres)—that its value lies in showing that and how 'one could, truly and legitimately, *use oneself* (clearly and distinctly) in arriving at [philosophical] conclusions so strange and so familiar' (*CR* 4). But there is much more instruction to be derived from the fourth paragraph of the book than has hitherto emerged.

Fragmentation

To begin with, Cavell's discussion of later Beethoven emphasizes that writing produced in the condition of modernism, being essentially unmemorable, will have parts that are unpredictable (although not retrospectively underivable) from each other. Lacking obvious valencies or lines of development, their mode of composition will essentially be that of juxtaposition, and their writers will require a sketchbook, an album for sketches of ideas; for some ideas arrived at under these conditions will require preservation until their right company emerges or is arranged, and others will require evolution or transformation before finding their place. The former invite the lyric mode of composition, the latter invite the dramatic. I take it that these concluding parenthetical remarks further specify Cavell's sense of the philosophical significance of Wittgenstein's modes of composing the *Investigations*, and of his prefatory characterization of his book as an album of sketches. But I also take it that they have a reflexive application. What instruction, then, do they offer concerning the composition of *The Claim of Reason*?

The book consists of four parts, involving respectively—or so the book's subtitle appears to suggest—a reading of Wittgenstein, an exploration of scepticism about the external world, a set of forays into moral philosophy, and an examination of relations between scepticism about other minds and tragedy. But the book might be otherwise decomposed or dismembered. As the foreword makes clear, it was supposed to be a revision of Cavell's 1961 Ph.D. dissertation; and although we are told that 'it is no more properly speaking a revision than its predecessor was properly speaking a dissertation' (*CR*, p. xi), we are also told that the book could not have appeared had Cavell not decided that the central two-thirds of that dissertation—with its original structure and ideas and prose broadly intact—could be included within it (*CR*, p. xv), so the concept of 'revision' must be understood as being itself revised rather than jettisoned. This provides a second way of distinguishing its parts. Parts II and III constitute the concluding, more or less heavily edited, two-thirds of the dissertation (with part III containing the most thesis-bound chapters in the book); part I comprises original dissertation material interspersed with more recent passages; and Part IV, which begins from thirty pages of lecture notes deriving from the period after submitting his dissertation, is otherwise made up of writing more recent than anything Cavell had published in 1979.

Given this, would we want to say that *The Claim of Reason* is a lyric or a dramatic composition? Were its elements fully formed on their first appearance and written down only to await their right company; or were they preserved so that they might grow outside the womb, to allow the transformations through which they might find their proper place? On the one hand, parts II and III appear as reduced but otherwise unaltered from their original appearance in Cavell's dissertation. Their pairing is intended to facilitate comparisons and contrasts between epistemological and moral debates (*CR* 250), and so amounts to juxtaposing independently establishable sketches of two modes of claim assessment; and the reader's sense of shock in making the transition from part III to part IV, thereby encountering prose of a very different range, complexity, and intensity, indicates that parts III and IV appear to be at best related by juxtaposition—with neither adapting to or accommodating the specificities of the other's style and substance. On the other hand, Cavell's description of the dramatic mode of composition as 'essentially stratified and partitioned' seems an apt characterization of *The Claim of Reason* as a whole: it is partitioned into four portions, and multiply stratified by its shifting periods of composition and its alterations of textual *telos*. Moreover, part I has been heavily revised, parts II and III have at least been edited in order to take their place in this company, and part IV is itself composed of passages that progress by constant self-revision or evolution (I will come back to this).

I take it, then, that the question of this book's composition concerns both its structural integrity as a whole and the nature of its parts or elements; and that our answer to it depends upon whether we read those parts as prefabricated units or as organically premature—as building-blocks or body parts. The fact that the textual indications point to two different answers shows, I believe, not that we can read *The Claim of Reason* either as a lyric or as a dramatic composition, but rather that we must read it as both. Think of this as the book's theory of itself—a theory of itself as composed of fragments or as fragmentary. We might here recall Friedrich Schlegel's aphorism (the 24th Athenaeum Fragment[6]): 'Many works of the ancients have become fragments. Many works of the moderns are fragments right from their beginning', and understand this theory as both a confirmation and a further specification of *The Claim of Reason*'s understanding of itself as a modernist work. If we focus on the dramatic aspects of the book's composition, its fragments will appear as both embryos and members—each is capable of further growth (even if outside the womb), but each thereby grows towards taking its place as a member of, to re-member, a larger organic whole. But there remains the undeniable sense that this book does not quite achieve such wholeness, that it remains somehow fragmentary, its members never shaking off the aura or memory of dismemberment, perhaps because they aren't meant to do so (since such a coming to term would undercut their claim to fragmentariness, and so betray that aspect of their author's modernist purpose). We might then ask why this air of the embryonic is internal to the book's work; and if we now try thinking of its fragmentariness in lyric terms—in terms of building-blocks rather than body parts—we will start thinking of the book as an edifice arising from ruins, and of its material as stones, slabs, pillars, and blocks strewn along the ground.

[6] See *Lucinde and The Fragments*, trans. P. Firchow (University of Minnesota Press: Minneapolis, 1971).

Such an image recalls the work of the builders at the opening of the *Investigations*; it also recalls Wittgenstein's interlocutor's sense that philosophy as he practices it destroys everything that is important, 'as it were all the buildings, leaving behind only bits of stone and rubble' (*Philosophical Investigations,*[7] 118), against which Wittgenstein claims that he is only 'clearing up the ground of language' on which structures of air, philosophical houses of cards, once stood. So is a modernist philosophical text engaged in destruction or reconstruction, or both, or neither? Is destroying structures of air true destruction? Is clearing up the ground of language on which they stood a form of construction or of reconstruction, or a preparation for (re)construction? What are the materials for such a project, and what does it aim to build? From what we have learned so far, we might say: the birth or rebirth of a new human circle, which means a new dispensation of culture, one which dispenses with the present illusion of human cultivation in the name of a possibility of genuinely creative thought, of a form of life in which thinkers (which means language-users, which means all human beings) can discover genuine satisfaction, in which the fragments of past communities of meaningful thought and value can be used in the reconstruction of new but personally authorized conventions. In such a circle what Wittgenstein and Cavell hope to teach can indeed be usefully said; but since the texts they now write are written in the name of that future possibility and in the shadow of the present actuality, on a ground where construction is possible but only with the ruins of the past and amid the ruination of the present, they must take on a form that is both dismembered and embryonic, a half-built edifice whose form acknowledges both its origin in ruins and the completion it foreshadows.

Amentia

One such acknowledgement of past and future, one edification aimed at by Cavell's textual edifice, is embodied in its questioning of the boundaries between the work of philosophy, on the one hand, and the work of politics and morality on the other. This is effected by *The Claim of Reason*'s juxtaposition of Wittgenstein's philosophical method with the myth of the social contract in chapter 1 of part I, and by its positioning of part III's chapters on morality between the book's most extensive discussions of the encounter between Wittgenstein's thought and that of scepticism. In part III's critique of Rawls, for example, Cavell attributes to his thought an intimate relation to the rationalization of

---

[7] Trans. G. E. M. Anscombe (Blackwell: Oxford, 1953); hereafter *PI*.

modern society; he identifies in it a perspective in which 'all human relationships are pictured as contractual rather than personal, within which
one's commitments, liabilities, responsibilities are from the outset
limited, and not total, or anyway always being in the process of being
determined' (*CR* 299). This envisions human culture as external to its
members, as an exoskeleton within which individuals relate through
roles or offices, their flesh-and-blood specificity as persons, their capacity and freedom to determine (perhaps revolutionize) their relations with
others, left unacknowledged or unsatisfied. It is opposed by the social
contract theorists, who act upon the intuition that we are always already
implicated in the arrangements of our society, that this is undeniable if
we are to continue claiming a voice in it, but that its range and depth
is a matter of our personal responsibility—of what we are prepared to
be responsible for.

These political and moral matters connect with Wittgenstein's philosophical method through many ideas—including that of the represen-
tativeness of the human voice, Cavell's sense that to speak is to be able
to speak not just to but for others and to have others speak for you;
the idea that the extent of the community thereby constituted is open
to individual determination; the idea that modes of self-knowledge can
subserve self-education and cultural criticism. Most fundamentally,
however, it relies upon Cavell's reading of Wittgensteinian criteria as
showing that statements of fact and judgements of value rest upon the
same capacities of human nature—that only a creature that can judge
of value can state a fact (*CR* 14–15). Further on in part I, he reformulates this as the claim that 'what can comprehensibly be said is what is
found to be worth saying' (*CR* 94), which he thinks of as requiring an
aesthetics and an economics of speech.

In the former case we follow the fact that understanding what someone says is
a function of understanding the intention expressed in his or her saying it, and
then the fact that one's intention is a function of what one wants, to a perspective from which responding to what another says is to be seen as demanding a response to the other's desire. When in earlier writing of mine I broach
the topic of the modern, I am broaching the topic of art as one in which the
connection between expression and desire is purified, [in which] nothing secures
the value or the significance of an object apart from one's wanting the thing to
be as it is. A strictness or scrupulousness of artistic desire thus comes to seem
a moral and intellectual imperative. About the latter case ... if we formulate
the idea that valuing underwrites asserting as the idea that interest informs
telling or talking generally, then we may say that the degree to which you talk
of things, and talk in ways, that hold no interest for you, or listen to what you
cannot imagine the talker's caring about, in the way he carries the care, is the

degree to which you consign yourself to nonsensicality, stupify yourself . . . I think of this consignment as a form not so much of dementia as of what amentia ought to mean, a form of mindlessness. It does not appear unthinkable that the bulk of an entire culture, call it the public discourse of a culture, the culture thinking aloud about itself, hence believing itself to be talking philosophy, should become ungovernably inane. (*CR* 94–5)

Here, the Wittgensteinian philosopher's responsiveness to those moments when our speech stupefies itself (when we find ourselves meaning something other than we took ourselves to be saying, or meaning nothing intelligible at all) is interpreted as a response to moments when our speech loses touch with comprehensible human desires and interests; and this amentia or inanity is read as exemplary of a possibility that our present culture faces or has already actualized. In this light, philosophy becomes the education of grown-ups; its task is that of turning its interlocutors away from mindlessness, and towards a form of life in which they might become genuinely interested. Texts written in this spirit ask for a species of conversion or rebirth, and attempt to effect it by forcing their readers to acknowledge themselves as internally split—fixated upon spurious forms of culture, but attracted to a new circle of possibilities. Hence the connection, mooted in the foreword, between modernist philosophy and esotericism (*CR*, p. xvi); hence also Cavell's future interest in moral perfectionism.[8]

Myth

A second line of edification proposed by the construction of this textual edifice is effected by Cavell's placing his most recent writing in part IV, which encourages us to think of it as the future foreshadowed in (that is, unpredictable from but retrospectively derivable from) the book's preceding and originating parts—the fragments of his dissertation. Thematically, it draws upon, develops, and reworks material from the other three parts; and in terms of his philosophical development, it is only at the centre of part IV that Cavell hears himself using his own voice (a voice that is at once an extension and a denial of Wittgenstein's (see *CR*, p. xv)) to say something 'fairly continuously at the right level' for thinking about the problems that sparked his original interest in Wittgenstein, the shifting focus of his dissertation, and his continuing concerns in philosophy (see *CR*, p. xiii). Accordingly, anyone interested in the mode of composition of *The Claim of Reason* must be con-

---

[8] See *Conditions Handsome and Unhandsome* (University of Chicago Press: Chicago, 1990).

cerned with the mode of composition of its culminating portion; and here too the foreword has more than autobiographical value.

There, Cavell offers the following account of the composition of part IV:

What emerged . . . was something I more and more came to regard, or to accept, even to depend upon, as the keeping of a limited philosophical journal. Writing it was like the keeping of a journal in two main respects. First, the autonomy of each span of writing is a more important goal than smooth, or any, transitions between spans (where one span may join a number of actual days, or occupy less than one full day). This ordering of goals tends to push prose to the aphoristic . . . Second, there would be no point, or no hope, in showing the work to others until the life, or place, of which it was the journal, was successfully, if temporarily, left behind, used up. (CR, p. xix)

I note the implication that this part of *The Claim of Reason* conforms to both the lyric and the dramatic modes of composition we have applied to the book as a whole—its entries are at once autonomous building-blocks juxtaposed with one another, and yet each is responsive to conclusions formed in earlier entries (there are real transitions between them, as Cavell's note on the overlapping ranges of the subtitles he assigns to their various phases makes clear; see CR, p. viii). I note also certain ideas of temporality and progress—the dailiness or diurnality of the journal form (and name), the idea of entries as records of past inhabitations and experiences, but as allowing new inhabitations and new experience (so that their composition amounts to the remembering of a journey, the using up of nostalgia in the name of the future). I note finally the idea of the aphorism as a paradigm for prose produced under such pressures—an idea that Cavell has recently argued is as applicable to the *Investigations* as it is to this part of his text, and internal to its modernist work[9] (we shall return to this).

Two other passages offer further instruction in reading part IV. The first ends the fourth paragraph of the book, and claims that one possible dramatic mode of composition is that 'of the sonata' (CR, p. 6). Sonata form classically involves the exposition, development, and recapitulation of a theme or themes. Such a model might well be applied to *The Claim of Reason* as a whole, since the themes picked out by the book's subtitle as 'Wittgenstein', 'Scepticism', and 'Morality' are laid out and developed in each of parts I, II, and III (one might even argue that they are all laid out in part I), and are then recapitulated in part IV. But the model clearly applies to part IV itself. Its themes—the

---

[9] See 'The *Investigations*' Everyday Aesthetics of Itself', in S. Mulhall (ed.), *The Cavell Reader* (Blackwell: Oxford, 1996).

relations between body and mind, self and society—receive an initial exposition in the opening thirty pages, which derive from Wittgenstein's remarks on private languages and seeing aspects; the opening discussion of the parable of the boiling pot might even be read as an epitome of the argumentative substance Cavell derives from material relating to the private diarist, and Wittgenstein's aphorism that the human body is the best picture of the human soul might be read as its recapitulation. Then the multiple implications of that aphorism are variously developed (by means of arguments, narratives, science fiction, and literary criticism, each instance of which is aphoristically epitomized); and the whole is then recapitulated in the concluding reading of *Othello*.

Can the motley of writing modes to which Cavell resorts in the development sequence of part IV be more precisely characterized? Instruction emerges in the passage which bridges the gap between the opening discussion of Wittgenstein and its development, in which Cavell explicitly denies that Wittgenstein's (and so his) aphorisms are to be understood as metaphorical—certainly not when the idea of 'metaphor' in play is reductive, one which pictures metaphorical meaning as reducible to, exhausted by, paraphrase. Instead, Cavell suggests the following paradigm: '[Such] remarks . . . may be looked upon as myths, or fragments of a myth . . . I should imagine that a reason one feels certain remarks about the soul to be metaphorical is that one does not want, or know how, to speak of them as mythological' (*CR* 364). What might it mean to regard them as mythological? I assemble a list of distinctive features mentioned in succeeding pages. Myths are the subject of interpretation and argument; they will generally deal with origins that no one can have been present at; they are open to continuation, which can be thought of as revision; a false myth is not just untrue but destructive of truth; when the mythology and actuality cease to coexist harmoniously, then you have stopped living the myth.

Cavell's view is that our myths of the soul and the actuality of which they are mythological expressions (which in this case means our sense of ourselves, and our lives, as embodied individuals in community with others) have come apart, and that we consequently find ourselves burdened with fragments of myths which we have stopped living, or with fragments of false myths—myths that are destructive of the truth of our nature, myths that cannot or should not be thought of as humanly liveable. These are the materials with which the Wittgensteinian philosopher finds the ground of language strewn; they are the fragments from which a properly responsible modernist philosophy must construct its criticism of present human culture, and attempt to reconstruct a humanly inhabitable form of life.

Wittgenstein's expression 'the human body is the best picture of the human soul' is an attempt to replace or reinterpret these fragments of myth. It continues to express the idea that the soul is there to be seen, that my relation to another's soul is as immediate as to an object of sight, or would be immediate if, so to speak, the relation could be effected. But Wittgenstein's mythology shifts the location of the thing which blocks this vision.

The block to my vision of the other is not the other's body, but my incapacity or unwillingness to interpret or to judge it accurately, to draw the right connections. The suggestion is: I suffer a kind of blindness, but I avoid the issue by projecting this darkness upon the other. (*CR* 368)

This interpretation of Wittgenstein's myth-fragment or aphorism exemplifies the way in which Cavell takes mythological uses of words to invite accounts of why they seem to epitomize or give expression to (to construct) a truth, or to destroy it; and by giving an account of why a given word is or is not the word I want—of whether or not it gives expression to a genuine human desire or interest or response—I make it possible to move away or to move on from those words, probably to some others. Cavell points out parenthetically that 'The willingness and the refusal to exchange one word or expression for another, as well as the usefulness or futility in doing so, are themes running throughout the *Investigations*' (*CR* 363). This same willingness or refusal is the engine of part IV of *The Claim of Reason*. It moves from one aphoristic myth-fragment to another, constantly purifying their responsiveness to human desires and assessing their proper modes or rates of exchange, and thereby exemplifying at once an aesthetics and an economics of speech; and by forming itself from fragments of myth and aphorism, it can never itself be other than fragmentary or embryonic in form—thus continuing in philosophy one line of the modernist impulse in modern human culture.

Song

I said earlier that the reading of *Othello* with which the fourth part of *The Claim of Reason* concludes might be thought of as a recapitulation of its themes, and so of the themes of the book. Certainly, its brief pages employ every term that has accrued mythic significance in the pages preceding it (as Cavell has pointed out elsewhere[10]). But might its own conclusion be thought of as epitomizing that recapitulation? This question of endings seems appropriate as a way of turning this Introduction towards its conclusion; so let us recall how that concluding paragraph runs:

[10] See S. Cavell *Disowning Knowledge* (Cambridge University Press: Cambridge, 1987), 11–12.

So here we are, knowing they are 'gone to burning hell', she with a lie on her lips, protecting him, he with her blood on him. Perhaps Blake has what he calls songs to win them back with, to make room for hell in a juster city. But can philosophy accept them back at the hands of poetry? Certainly not as long as philosophy continues, as it has from the first, to demand the banishment of poetry from its republic. Perhaps it could if it could itself become literature. But can philosophy become literature and still know itself? (*CR* 496)

We might begin by pointing out that the question with which this conclusion concludes is genuine. Cavell is not certain that a philosophy which became literature could still know itself—know itself, that is, to be still a version or revision of philosophy (any more than it would be knowable to itself as literature); if anything, he has implied that such self-knowledge requires relationships with disciplinary others that maintain a relative autonomy, a separate identity. He is, however, certain that philosophy should not continue to banish poetry from the just city, the future human circle. So what are we to make of the possibility that Blake—of all the writers Cavell might cite—can make room for such an acknowledgement of literature? Cavell earlier asserted that his convictions about the meaning of certain Blake poems go so deep, and are therefore so personal, that he is not at present willing to talk about them—that their meaning is something he might want us to know, but not by his telling us (*CR* 360). Perhaps those poems are what Cavell here calls 'what Blake calls songs'—perhaps including songs of innocence and experience, of the marriage of heaven and hell, of a prophecy concerning America. Perhaps they might form the basis of future philosophical conventions.

I cannot explore these possibilities here; but I can point out that the only explicit quotation from Blake in this book (*CR* 471) comes from none of these sources, but rather from his 'Gnomic Verses or Epigrams' (or aphorisms?), and might stand as literature's revisioning of Wittgenstein's myth-fragment about the human body and the human soul:

> What is it men in women do require?
> The lineaments of Gratified Desire.
> What is it women do in men require?
> The lineaments of Gratified Desire.

Blake's verse thus introduces the question of sexual difference, and Cavell's emphasis upon what Blake 'calls songs' connects with this. For it reminds us of the pervasive insistence of analogies, examples, and analyses of music in this text; and this in turn connects with a possibility I left unexplored when examining *The Claim of Reason*'s mode of composition. I suggested that it is both lyric and dramatic; but I omitted to mention that the *OED* recognizes a mode of composition that it calls 'lyric drama'—namely, opera. As Cavell has recently emphasized, opera distinctively focuses upon the relation between the human voice and the human body,

> a relation in which not this character and this actor are embodied in each other but in which this voice is located in—one might say disembodied within—this figure, this double, this person, this persona, this singer, whose voice is essentially unaffected by the role.
>
> A Cartesian intuition of the absolute metaphysical difference between mind and body, together with the twin Cartesian intuition of an undefined intimacy between just this body and only this spirit, appears to describe conditions of the possibility of opera. (*A Pitch of Philosophy*,[11] 137)

Is this singer's body the best picture of her soul? Her voice certainly is: as Cavell later says, 'surely the operatic voice is the grandest realization of having a signature, of an abandonment to your words, hence of your mortal immortality' (*POP* 144); and as he further claims, opera's all but overwhelming subject is the singing of women, and how this singing might be suffocated or stopped. This revision of the myth of the soul suggests that it is the female registers of the human voice to which Wittgensteinian philosophy is intended to be attentive, and that we might think of the manner or method of its work, its aphorisms unfolding fragments of myth as part of a lyric drama, as an aria or song.

FIFTH PARAGRAPH: APPROACHING
THE HERMENEUTIC CIRCLE

But we cannot quite yet bring this Introduction to a close; for we have not yet completed our reading of the opening of *The Claim of Reason*. We have so far only interpreted the first of the two self-introductory remarks Cavell offers before embarking on his opening interpretation of Wittgenstein's notion of a criterion; and the second of these remarks provides his solution to the paradox that emerged in the first paragraph of the book.

> But I was supposed to be saying something more, having said something first, by way of introducing myself, and concerning how we should approach

[11] (Harvard University Press: Cambridge, Mass., 1994); hereafter *POP*.

Wittgenstein's text. Accordingly, I will say, second, that there is no approach to it, anyway I have none. Approach suggests moving nearer, getting closer; hence it suggests that we are not already clear or close enough; hence suggests we know some orderly direction to it not already taken within it; that we sense some distance between us and it which useful criticism could close. (*CR* 6)

Our paradox was: if the terms needed to approach a book can only be learned from the book itself, how can we ever begin to learn from it, this or anything? It can now be seen that the misunderstanding here arises from our having recourse to the idea of there being an approach to the text—for that places us entirely outside the text, and makes the text entirely opaque to us. The reality is that anyone capable of opening its covers is already close enough to learn from it—in part because no reader can begin a text entirely without a range of relevant capacities and experiences, or a basic orientation towards it (without the resources or prejudgements bequeathed to them by their life and traditions); in part because to begin to read it is to begin to learn from it, which includes beginning to learn how to read it. Texts are not monolithic, essentially unarticulated units, that must either be completely understood or completely unintelligible; they are articulated wholes. Accordingly, the reader's preliminary orientation allows her to work through the various parts of a text, to draw provisional conclusions from them that occasion revisions to her sense of its overall shape, which in turn deepens her capacity to learn from its parts, and so on. A text can teach its readers how to read it because the mutual implication and relative autonomy of parts and whole creates a play of meaning that invites initial interpretation and can reward progressively deeper readings.

Some texts are produced under conditions which entail that the reader's preliminary, tradition-grounded, orientation cannot be trusted, and so they must bear most of the responsibility of establishing the terms on which they can be understood. In these cases, nothing outside the text itself will provide an opening; only directions already taken within them will help. They cannot give their readers everything they need for deeper understanding at the outset; but they can give them enough to go on further, where they can be given more. I find Stanley Cavell's book to be such a text, and I find in its depiction of these conditions of its own composition a recognizable portrait of the philosophical culture I inhabit. Hence I think of the opening of this text (I mean this present text, mine, in its attempts to open up the opening of Cavell's text, and hence to open up the terms in which it invites its readers to move further into what follows from that opening) as simultaneously opening up the terms in which its readers might fruitfully begin to follow out the sequence of readings of various texts by Wittgenstein, Heidegger, and Kierkegaard that are to come, and from which a deeper understanding of those initial terms can alone be secured. And of course, each reading aims to show that the words of each of those texts open themselves in new ways to readings that are receptive to the words with which they open.

PART ONE

WITTGENSTEIN'S VISION OF LANGUAGE

Reading the
Philosophical Investigations

OPENING: QUOTATION

1. The first of Wittgenstein's philosophical remarks (as he characterizes the prose of the *Philosophical Investigations* in its preface) is a citation (a re-marking) of some remarks by Augustine. How remarkable is this? Readers accustomed to contextualizing Wittgenstein's text as inheriting the philosophical tradition of Frege and Russell are likely to find Augustine's words (particularly when detached from their textual and cultural context) utterly unremarkable, and hence to find Wittgenstein's citation of them utterly remarkable. Why choose to cite a handful of sentences relating Augustine's brief and apparently casual reminiscences of an early stage of his initiation into language, rather than sentences from other authors (perhaps even other sentences from the same author, perhaps even from the same text) whose interest in language is more self-evidently philosophical in their sophistication and relevance? Other readers, perhaps led by Wittgenstein's citation to recall Augustine's towering influence on Western culture and the complexity with which his *Confessions* weaves together its autobiographical, spiritual, and metaphysical themes, might rather find remarkable the assumption that the sole proper context for Wittgenstein's text, and hence for his conception of the tradition of philosophizing he wishes to inherit, is the work of Frege and Russell. Does Wittgenstein's citational gesture support one of these apparently opposing responses more than the other, or does it rather invite his readers to recognize that both lines of response are at once justified and partial—let us say, worth questioning?

Certainly, beyond or before any significance we might attach to what Augustine actually says in this passage, we can say that Wittgenstein's remarkable willingness to cede his own opening to another's words, and so to present his own first words as responding to them, implies a conception of philosophy as essentially responsive and dialogical.[1] For him, philosophy is not self-generating or self-supporting, not a matter of advancing one's own views or constructing one's own account of a particular topic; it is rather something that is called for or awakened by certain kinds of words.

But which kinds of words call for philosophy? If Wittgenstein finds that it is awakened by the spiritual autobiography of a fourth-century Christian bishop, and by specific words from its opening chapters that are not self-evidently offered either as direct contri-

---

[1] As Stanley Cavell points out in 'Notes and Afterthoughts on the Opening of Wittgenstein's *Investigations*', *PP*.

butions to a philosophical enterprise, or in a spirit recognizably related
to that which animates such enterprises (then or now), then we cannot
say in advance that any aspect of human culture and experience exceeds
Wittgenstein's conception of philosophy's reach; if philosophy must
always speak second, it can be called upon to speak by anyone.

But how is philosophy to speak, if and when it does? What kind of
attention does it give to the kinds of words that awaken its interest?
In this first section of the *Investigations* Wittgenstein offers three
paragraphs in response to Augustine's words; he begins by claiming to
locate in them what he calls a 'picture of the essence of human
language', and ends by painting a picture of what he calls one of the
'ways that one operates with words'. Again, we cannot properly understand this response without examining the substance of Augustine's
remarks; but it is surely already worth remarking that its culmination
lies in the telling of a story—in recounting a narrative of our life with
words against which Augustine's narrative of his induction into that life
might be measured and held to account. In other words, Wittgenstein
stakes his philosophical claim against Augustine in recognizably literary terms. By asking his readers to compare Augustine's memoir of
childhood with his own sketch of a shopping trip, he asks them which
tale, and hence which teller of tales, they trust—who is the more reliable narrator.

2. Before moving on to consider Wittgenstein's direct response to
Augustine's quoted words, it is worth asking whether we can assume
that his interest in the text from which they are cited is restricted to that
part of it reproduced in the quotation. It might seem obvious that we
can; what, after all, is the point of quoting from another text if not to
distinguish that part of it which has a bearing on one's own concerns
from those parts of it which do not? But such a conclusion overlooks
an essential ambivalence in any act of citation. When a writer quotes a
passage from another text, that gesture necessarily implies that something about the passage quoted is relevant to its new context; but since
any cited passage, in presenting itself as a citation and thus as an ordering of words dislocated from another text, necessarily brings traces of
that context with it into its new location (traces symbolized by the
bracketed or footnoted reference to its original source that scholarly
convention attaches to it), the quotation marks which demarcate it point
us towards the uncited stretches of that original text even as they fence
us from it.

For example, anyone familiar with the *Confessions* as a whole might well question whether that text is self-evidently not, and not intended to be, a contribution to a recognizably philosophical enterprise. After all, the final four of its thirteen books concern themselves in detail with the nature of memory and the human mind, time and the creation of the universe—metaphysical issues that seem rather obviously to invite philosophical attention. On the other hand, the first nine books of the *Confessions* are preoccupied with what appear to be very different matters—with Augustine's tale of his own life up to the moment of his religious conversion and the death of his mother—and Wittgenstein's citation comes from the first of those nine autobiographical books. Does that not simply confirm that he is deliberately avoiding the more obviously philosophical interest of the later books?

Such a reading is defensible, but it depends upon attending to (rather than ignoring) the place of the quoted passage in its original context, and upon a particular reading of its relation to that context; and that reading is contestable. For example, rather than accepting the idea of a radical discontinuity in the *Confessions* between nine autobiographical books and four metaphysical ones, we might argue that Augustine deliberately sited his metaphysical questionings at the end of his text in order to present them as the culmination of the preceding nine books of autobiographical exercises, in order to imply that those questions somehow emerged from (were invited or made unavoidable by) those exercises—as if autobiography necessarily tended towards the metaphysical, or had revealed itself to him as having an ineliminably metaphysical and hence philosophical dimension. Since Wittgenstein was at least as capable of seeing such possibilities of significance in Augustine's text as anyone else, we must leave open the possibility that his choice of a passage from book I is in fact intended to signal an interest in (at least one version of) the idea of the autobiographical as a means of access to, or a medium of, the philosophical. Nevertheless, since most philosophers would regard the autobiographical (with its unremitting interest in the person of the author) as self-evidently, even inherently, non-philosophical, we might view this claim as inflecting rather than contradicting the thought that Wittgenstein's citation signals his sense of philosophy as responsive to the apparently non-philosophical.

3. Suppose we remain for a little longer within the paths opened up by an inclusive rather than an exclusionary reading of Wittgenstein's gesture of citation. What other aspects of Augustine's text, of the broader context of the passage Wittgenstein actually quotes, might have struck him as pertinent to his concerns? To begin with, Augustine's

manner of developing the philosophical from the autobiographical implies not only a general sense of the self's exploitation of its own resources as essential to making philosophical and spiritual progress, but also a more specific sense that such progress requires an adequate conception of memory and of time (the topics of the first two of his last four books). Of course, these two phenomena are not simply matters of metaphysical substance; they necessarily constitute the medium of any essentially autobiographical enterprise. It is as if Augustine is moved to examine them philosophically because of their role in shaping the form of his previous nine books of narrative, as if he thinks of himself as committed (by his commitment to recounting his autobiography) to giving an account of the conditions for the possibility of such a narrative—its intention to recall events as ordered in time, to comprehend the self by remembering its history. Such commitments (call them transcendental) are hardly unrecognizable to philosophers; and the particular enabling conditions that Augustine explores, as well as his sense of the peculiar difficulties their exploration poses, are surely no less central to (even if differently conceived in) a conception of philosophy such as Wittgenstein's. Indeed, one of Wittgenstein's few other direct quotations from the *Confessions* refers us to Augustine's remark about time (that we know what it is when no one asks us, but no longer know when asked to give an account of it; *Confessions*,[2] xi. xiv), and adapts it to give a general characterization of philosophical problems, and of his own method as a matter of reminding us of what we already know (*PI* 89)—in other words, of remembering what we should say when, recalling the contexts (the social and temporal circumstances) of speech.

To those familiar with Augustine's text, finding it cited at (as?) the very beginning of Wittgenstein's text is also likely to remind them of Augustine's own pervasive concern in the *Confessions* with the question of beginnings. Most immediately, of course, he is concerned to narrate his conversion from Manichaean and sceptic to Christian, his own new beginning; but it is striking that the stance in which he represents himself at the end of his text as exemplary of his new state, the mode through which he presents his metaphysical discussions of memory, time, and creation in books x–xiii, is that of a reader—a reader of the opening lines of the first book in the most famous book of all, the account of the world's beginning as presented in the biblical book of Genesis and as misunderstood by the Manichaeans with whom Augustine had previously associated himself.

[2] Trans. H. Chadwick (Oxford University Press: Oxford, 1991); hereafter C.

In fact, the autobiographical books of his text present him primarily or at least pervasively as a reader throughout—moving from his youthful love of literature, through his adult employment as a teacher of liberal arts, and his being profoundly influenced by the example of Bishop Ambrose reading (his exegetical motto: 'The letter kills, the spirit gives life'; C VI. iv), to the act of reading the New Testament in the garden (in response to the oracular words 'Tolle lege'), which seals his culminating conversion experience. It is as if his conversion is emblematized in a reorientation of his capacities as a reader, in his finding a new beginning, in finding a new way to read or interpret beginnings—from a Manichaean focus upon the idea of a single, correct interpretation of the Word to a discovery of the possibility of allegory, and hence of the idea that a text may have more than one meaning, that its words can go forth and multiply in its readers, so that all good readings need not conflict with one another, as if verifiable only by falsifying all other interpretative possibilities.

If, however, Augustine's self-presentation as reader is the culminating portrayal of his new beginning within the text of the *Confessions*, the most immediate and pervasive exemplification of his spiritual reconstitution lies in the text of the *Confessions* itself, composed as it is from the post-conversion perspective that it aims at once to portray and illustrate, to speak about and to show in its manner of speaking. In other words, the full fruition of that conversion lies in the mode of writing that Augustine's newly discovered mode of reading engendered—the mode of writing that issued in the *Confessions* itself. It is, then, no surprise, to discover that the *Confessions* begins by making an issue of its own beginning. More specifically, the first five sections of book I form a kind of prologue to the text as a whole, by means of which Augustine defers the question of where his autobiographical story can and should begin in favour of asking how—in what manner or form—it should be recounted. For at the outset of his text he presents his writing task as one of addressing God, thus enacting the commitment with which the course of his narrative will culminate, that of allowing his reconstitution around a relation to God to find expression in every aspect of his life: and this creates a number of difficulties for him. For example, how can he tell this tale to someone who already knows everything there is to know about its subject? Why should this being care about anything Augustine has to say? How can or should Augustine direct his words to a being who is omnipresent, and thus occupies the position of addresser as well as addressee? And how might his narrative be given the only form which properly acknowledges the relative status of its author and its reader as creature and Creator respectively—that of prayer and praise?

Part of Augustine's answer to this last question is that an autobiographical text recounting how one lost individual was helped to recognize his status as God's creature and to reorient his life around that recognition, would necessarily constitute a prayer of thanks and praise to his Creator and Saviour. Hence the deferred beginning of the autobiographical element of the *Confessions* is in one sense the true beginning of the *Confessions* as a whole: his account of the original constitution (the birth and development) of his old self is designed to provide the proper context for recounting its reconstitution (its rebirth), and is therefore central in any assessment of how that reconstitution is to be understood.

Sections vi and vii of book i begin that account by recounting Augustine's birth and infancy; but he finds even his birth a questionable marker for his own beginning (being unwilling to exclude existence prior to birth), and his account of these phases is based only on others' accounts of it and on his own later observations of other infants. Only in section viii does he make the transition from infancy to boyhood (that is, from speechlessness to speech), and enter upon the first phase of his existence of which (Augustine declares) he is capable of giving a genuinely autobiographical account, one that is not only by and about himself but also told from his own perspective upon himself—that is, based on his own memory. It follows, of course, as Augustine himself recognizes, that his account of the transition itself cannot be, but can at most bring us to the threshold of the, genuinely autobiographical; for a memory incapable of reaching beyond boyhood cannot grasp its own emergence from infancy.

Can it be accidental that Wittgenstein chooses to restrict his quotation from the *Confessions* to Augustine's account of that transition—to the very sentences from section viii of book i in which the text's autobiographical impulse begins to emerge, thereby acknowledging its indebtedness to the consideration of formal or stylistic (that is, non-autobiographical) questions from which it emerges, and hence implying both the essential indeterminacy of its own origin and the inextricability of its content from its manner or mode? If not, then what degree of indebtedness to Augustine does Wittgenstein mean his gesture to acknowledge? In fashioning so questionable a beginning to his own text, Wittgenstein plainly shares Augustine's sense of beginnings as questionable, as posing a problem. And if, thus encouraged, we take his preface to the *Investigations* as being as much part of its opening work as is Augustine's 'prologue' to his autobiography proper, we will see further grounds for thinking that Wittgenstein equally shares Augustine's more general concern with style or form as a pressing issue.

In his preface Wittgenstein finds it necessary to account for the tone and structure of his own orderings of words, and to do so not only in highly figurative but in essentially autobiographical terms—suggesting that their capacity to make their readers struggle results from a long struggle on his part to recognize that their unfinished or disorganized appearance was in fact their proper and final form. He explains that they are essentially remarks, an album of sketches of landscapes; he claims that they would have been crippled if welded together into a more conventional whole, one which organized them against their natural inclination; he emphasizes that they are designed to stimulate his readers to thoughts of their own; he connects their power to illuminate the darkness of our time and our minds with their apparent poverty; and he implies that such originality as they possess lies not in their content so much as in the stamp that they bear as a result of these constraints, the impress of his solution to the problem of style.

Augustine's sense of the problem of style was in important part shaped by his sense of the difficulties created by the nature of the recipient of his remarks. Abstracting for the moment from the specifically theological cast of those difficulties, one might think of this as Augustine's awareness that the relation of his writing to its reader is an undismissable issue for him. Anyone familiar with Wittgenstein's characterizations of his own philosophical method as not informing us but reminding us of something, as recalling us to what we always already knew, as relying on no expertise, will see that he faces a structurally similar series of questions—concerning how he can, and can want to, tell us what we already know, how he can expect us to care about what he tells us, how he can redefine the differences and similarities between himself as writer and us as readers without invoking or implying differences in knowledge or expertise. The more or less obvious peculiarities of tone and style in Wittgenstein's writing can thus appear as reflecting not only the distinctive inclination of his thoughts and the specific cartography of their journeyings, but also the particular work they are intended to perform on their readers (as opposed to the particular, divine status of Augustine's intended auditor). It would seem to follow that if our readings of Wittgenstein make no effort to come to terms with the form as well as the content of his writing, if we do not allow the unique stamp his sentences bear—their appearance of poverty and provisionality, their following out of inclination rather than the dictates of a system, their rootedness in self-examination, their flights of figuration—to stimulate us to thought, then we will utterly miss their point.

PICTURES, PARADIGMS, AND CONVERSION

4. The various ways in which the *Investigations* can be seen to be in implicit dialogue with dimensions and themes of the *Confessions* that are articulated outside the specific passage Wittgenstein quotes from Augustine's text will continue to emerge as this reading develops. For the moment, however, we should suspend our interest in the inclusive reading of Wittgenstein's citational gesture, and return to an exclusionary reading of its significance—to the paths he opens up more explicitly in his response to the specific substance and tone of the words of the *Confessions* that he chose to begin his text by reproducing.

Augustine's tale is intended to depict his acquisition of language, and so necessarily incorporates a depiction of what is thereby acquired. Wittgenstein begins his response to Augustine by claiming that this gives us a picture of the essence of human language—that individual words name objects, and sentences are combinations of such names. Then a pause—signalled by a long dash—as if it isn't yet clear exactly what should be said about this picture. Then he further remarks that a particular idea of language is rooted in it: the idea that every word has a meaning correlated with it, and that this meaning is the object for which the word stands.

This second remark amounts to a further citation, this time of Wittgenstein's own previous philosophical remarks. Those of his readers familiar with his early work will note the kinship between this idea of language and the picture theory of meaning developed in the *Tractatus Logico-Philosophicus*, which portrays all propositions as ultimately composed of simple names whose meaningfulness is determined by the nature of the simple object for which each name stands. Presenting that theory as rooted in Augustine's picture of language implies that Wittgenstein sees philosophical criticism as a form of self-criticism—that his interlocutors are not giving voice to thoughts or impulses from which he can dissociate himself. Since, however, he does not exactly emphasize the source of this idea of language in the present context, his reason for citing it appears to lie more in the light it casts upon the general notion of an 'idea', and so upon the general notion of a 'picture' to which he links (and thus distinguishes) it.

It should be clear from what we have already noted that Augustine's picture of language and the Tractarian idea of language are distinct. I can picture all words as names without endorsing the idea that the meaning of a word is the object it names—and I would be well advised to do so; for the claim that the word 'table' names a particular type of object looks a lot more defensible than the idea that such an object (or type of object) is the meaning (as opposed to the referent) of the word 'table'. Annihilating the referent or bearer of a name does not annihilate its meaningfulness; 'Mr. N. N. is dead' makes perfect sense (*PI* 40).

It should, however, be equally clear that Wittgenstein takes Augustine's picture of language and the Tractarian idea of language to be linked; the extremity of the Tractarian idea would, after all, only look tenable if its author's starting-point is something like the Augustinian picture. Wittgenstein's image or figure for that link is 'rootedness'—the idea is rooted in the picture, the picture is the soil from which the idea grows. This tells us that the idea is logically secondary to the picture, that it depends upon it for its existence and flourishing; and just as soil is not typically nutritious for only one plant or type of plant, so a picture can and does nourish a range of related ideas (hence the unimportance of the specifically Tractarian slant of the particular idea Wittgenstein mentions). Since, however, soil is not a kind of plant, neither can pictures be thought of as just another kind of idea or set of ideas; and since the specific example of an idea that Wittgenstein cites in this paragraph is a theory, we can reformulate this last point by saying that a picture is not itself a theory or set of theories (philosophical or otherwise).

Wittgenstein's image of 'rootedness' rather suggests that it is a pre-theoretical framework or orientation, providing that without which a certain kind or range of theorizing would not be possible: a particular conceptualization of the area of investigation, a specific set of theory-building tools or components, a conception of what problems such a theory should be addressing, a conception of what a good solution to those problems would look like, and so on. Those familiar with Kuhn's vision of scientists in normal phases of their discipline as united by a shared but taken-for-granted *paradigm* of what good scientific work amounts to may see a useful analogy here between the notion of a paradigm and that of a picture (particularly when the philosophizing that grows out of Augustine's picture sees itself as essentially continuous with science).[3]

---

[3] See G. P. Baker and P. M. S. Hacker, 'Augustine's Picture', in their *Wittgenstein: Understanding and Meaning* (Blackwell: Oxford, 1980), 14.

Since any given picture can find expression in a wide range of specific ideas or theories, Wittgenstein's philosophical responsiveness will not be restricted to philosophical theories of language that bear the traces of Augustine's picture. Not to *philosophical* theories, because theories of language produced in other disciplines (linguistics, literary criticism, and so on) can also be rooted in Augustinian thinking; and not to theories of *language*, because Augustine's picture of language can inflect theories about non-linguistic phenomena (if an experimental psychologist thinks of 'pain' as the name of a psychological or mental thing, her laboratory set-ups will be informed by that assumption). In all these cases, however, the primary focus of his response will be the picture in which these various theories are rooted; the logical priority of pictures over theories or ideas entails their methodological priority.

This means that Wittgenstein's terms of philosophical criticism cannot be those appropriate to ideas. Theories can be criticized with respect to the accuracy of their descriptions of data, the validity of their reasoning, the correctness of their predictions, and so on; but if Wittgenstein's concern is with the way such theories manifest their authors' commitment to Augustine's picture, such terms of criticism would be futile and inappropriate. Any such theory could be altered to accommodate an inaccurate observation, an invalid line of reasoning, or a falsified prediction without losing its rootedness in Augustine's picture. In fact, part of the point of Wittgenstein's image of 'rootedness' is precisely to imply that any specific alterations in a theorist's work—in the content of her theory, in what she takes to be a serious problem and what a serious solution to it, in any decision she may take about jettisoning one theory in favour of another—will be implicitly shaped by the picture which governs her attitude to the phenomena under examination. Loosening the grip of a picture means effecting a shift in a person's sense of what matters to her intellectual project; it requires not that she respond to criticism, but that she be responsive to a reorientation of her interests. It asks, in short, for conversion.

5. What terms of criticism might effect a conversion, a turning away, from Augustine's picture (itself, of course, embedded in a tale of conversion—of its effects and of how to effect it)? Wittgenstein offers the following initial response: Augustine does not speak of there being any difference between kinds of word—and this is because he was thinking primarily of nouns and proper names, secondarily about terms for actions and properties, and assuming that all other kinds of word will accommodate themselves to this approach.

Does this amount to the accusation that Augustine has produced a faulty generalization—that he has offered a description of language that applies happily to nouns and proper names, less happily to verbs and adjectives, and is inapplicable elsewhere? If so, Wittgenstein would in effect be treating Augustine's picture as a theory, by subjecting it to a perfectly standard criticism of theories of any kind. But what he actually says is that Augustine's picture will *seem* unproblematically correct to someone who has nouns on her mind; he does not say, and it does not follow from what he does say, that the picture is applicable even to that kind of word. His point is diagnostic rather than critical; he is addressing the question of the likely grounds for a person's attraction to Augustine's picture, not that of the picture's applicability to any given region of language.

Furthermore, Wittgenstein has no objection to statements such as ' "table" is the name of a piece of furniture', ' "pain" is the name of a sensation', or ' "five" is the name of a number'; as he elsewhere acknowledges (see *PI* 10), they can usefully remove mistaken ideas about how words are used, perhaps in those attempting to learn English—pointing out, for example, that 'table' is not a number-word, or that 'five' does not signify a piece of furniture (see *PI*, bottom of p. 14). His criticism is not directed at that form of utterance, but at the way in which its employment can lead its users (as he claims it led Augustine) to overlook differences between kinds of word.

The most obvious purpose of Wittgenstein's story of the shopping trip is to bring out the full implications of this criticism; so we should examine the applicability of Augustine's picture to the three words that story highlights: 'apple', 'red', and 'five'. We might perfectly legitimately explain the meaning of the first word by saying that ' "apple" is the name of a type of fruit', and reinforce the explanation by pointing to the contents of the grocer's apple drawer. If, however, we then go on to use the same form of explanation with respect to 'red' and 'five', it will be difficult to avoid assuming that the same ways of supplementing the explanation will also hold good. How, though, after declaring that ' "red" is the name of a colour', might we point to its referent? We can, of course, point to a red object—the very same apple, perhaps—but how can we point to its colour (as opposed, say, to its shape or the type of fruit it instantiates)? What, if anything, makes our pointing a pointing to its colour? Such pointing can then seem a very difficult thing to do, as if we need to isolate or dig just under the apple's skin with our pointing finger; and we might even begin to wonder how we earlier succeeded so effortlessly in pointing to the apple *qua* instance of a type of fruit.

Nevertheless, perhaps recalling the grocer's method of ensuring that he gets the right kind of apple from his drawer, we may suddenly realize that pointing to a colour is in fact unproblematic under the right circumstances—when, for example, we are asked to point out one specific colour amongst a range of others on a colour chart; in short, we point to an object's colour by pointing to another object with the same colour (*CR* 74–6). So someone in the grip of Augustine's picture can think of the colour patch aligned with the word 'red' on the grocer's chart as its referent, as that which is designated by the word. We might accept this, although it means accepting a significant disanalogy with the case of 'apple', where no such chart seemed necessary; but what about 'five'? To what might we point to elaborate the claim that ' "five" is the name of a number'? Pointing to the number instantiated by the group of five apples in my shopping bag seems even more difficult than pointing to their colour; the grocer wields no number table in the way he uses his table of colours, and even if we imagine one—say a chart aligning numerals with groups of strokes—it doesn't seem to supply us with numbers in the way a colour chart supplies us with colours. (Aren't the strokes just another system of numerals? Where are the numbers themselves?)

Wittgenstein does not suggest that these questions cannot be answered. Philosophers of mathematics have sometimes done so by choosing to regard numbers as entities existing in a logical realm outside space and time, of which number-words are the names; and they have tried to accommodate the new problems that such a strategy throws up (for example, explaining the relation of this realm to our ordinary world, our capacity to grasp its entities and their relations with one another, and so on). However, the basic point of the shopping trip story already seems clear enough. As we find ourselves building more and more elaborate epicycles into our theory to cope with the apparent differences between kinds of word that the story emphasizes, as every proposed solution to a problem generates several more problems of its own, Wittgenstein hopes that we might consider stepping back from our guiding, pre-theoretical assumption that all words are of the same kind, that all name things and so must show the same kinds of links with objects and activities in the world. Such problem-proliferation is, after all, one of the features Kuhn categorizes as indicative of the breakdown of a normal phase of science, a sign that a research community's guiding paradigm is no longer capable of generating fruitful theory-construction.

In Wittgenstein's terms, applying the Augustinian template for language across the board forces us to distort the everyday facts of language use in increasingly extreme ways, to elide or repress the very different kinds of ways in which words are used rather than reflecting proper attention to those differences. If, however, we try to avoid such distortions by jettisoning more and more of the substance of that form of description—so that, for example, we preserve the ' "*x*" names "*y*" ' paradigm but no longer require that *y*s be the kind of things we can point to—then our continued use of the paradigm across the board will eventually tell us nothing whatever about a word's kind of employment, its role in language and human life; it will be an empty form, to which we can regiment every such description only by evacuating them of content. It would be like saying that all tools serve to modify something (*PI* 14); assimilating a ruler, a glue-pot, and nails to this paradigm would require intellectual gymnastics (e.g. 'nails modify the solidity of wood') of a kind which distorts the facts about tool use and empties the descriptive form of the content it requires to be usefully applicable even to hammers and saws.

The problem with Augustine's picture is therefore not that it makes a substantial claim about language as a whole which turns out only to be true of some subset of language. It is rather that it makes what appears to be a substantial claim about language as a whole which turns out to lack any substance whatever. If the Augustinian's claim that all words are names employs the word 'name' in its ordinary sense, then it has a plain content, but it is also so self-evidently false that it makes little sense to imagine it being advanced by mistake (as if she might simply have failed to notice the obvious differences between proper names and other types of word); whereas if her words are read as advocating the introduction of a regimented form of description of word-meaning, then it fails to advance a substantive claim at all.

The Augustinian can, of course, use her form of words in either of these two ways; but for Wittgenstein, her attraction to those words actually depends upon her wishing to use them both ways at once, to make a substantive claim which all words can be seen to satisfy—and that she cannot do, for 'all words are names' cannot be both a proposal for adopting a certain form of description and a substantive descriptive claim at one and the same time. She has, then, in a very clear sense, become confused about the significance of her utterance, has lost control over her words; but it would not quite be right to say that she is talking nonsense. It is more that she has suffered a hallucination of sense; she has maintained her conviction of saying something self-evidently true only because her utterance hovers between two very different possibilities of sense or meaning without ever actualizing either.

Once the necessity of separating out those two possibilities is made clear to her, she will see that there is nothing here to be said—no claim of the kind she took herself to be making; and then her attraction to this form of words will wither away, her interests will undergo a reorientation. She will, in other words, have begun to turn away from the picture which fascinated her.

6. Turning away is always a turning towards; we undergo conversion from something to something else. In Kuhnian terms, a loss of confidence in one paradigm heralds a period of crisis in the discipline concerned that can be overcome only by its practitioners converging upon a new paradigm within which to reinstitute their normal practice of problem-solving and theory-building. What, then, is the paradigm or picture to which Wittgenstein wishes to attract us? Here the most pervasive opposition between Augustine's tale and Wittgenstein's story appears to come into focus; for it seems undeniable that the critical force embodied in the details of the shopping trip depends upon the way in which Wittgenstein's narration focuses upon how words are used in the wider context of human practical activity.

  Is this, then, the alternative picture we seek—the notion that meaning is use? In one sense, the answer must be 'Yes'; the differences between kinds of word, and Augustine's elision of them, are highlighted by Wittgenstein's tale purely because it emphasizes how differently its key words are used. However, Wittgenstein also explicitly denies that this focus on use is an answer to the question of what a word's meaning consists in. For when his interlocutor presses that question with respect to the word 'five', his response is to say that 'No such thing was in question here, only how the word "five" is used.' This suggests that Wittgenstein is not proposing that we picture meaning as use, but rather that, if we answer the question of how a word is used, then we will have no inclination to inquire about, or to attempt to picture, its meaning. Talk of use is an alternative to talk about meaning, not an extension or refinement of it.

  We might say: the conversion he seeks is a turning away from certain types of question as well as certain types of answer to those questions, a turning away from the impulse to theorize about meaning as well as from certain families of theory about meaning. Here, a disanalogy with Kuhnian paradigms and the 'paradigm' of 'meaning as use' emerges, and with it a fundamental danger inherent in the very idea of comparing Wittgensteinian pictures and Kuhnian paradigms—the danger of assuming that Wittgenstein's conception of philosophical practice aligns it, as oppposed to rendering it discontinuous with, scientific enterprises.

For Wittgenstein's proposed alternative to Augustine's picture is not something that will allow normal (that is, quasi-scientific) philosophical techniques of problem-solving and theory-building to continue in more fruitful and progressive directions; it is rather designed to render such techniques uninteresting or pointless, to establish an orientation in which they will no longer appear to attract or satisfy us. If, then, Wittgenstein's emphasis on use is a paradigm, it is the paradigm to end all theoretical paradigms; it may not spell the end of philosophy, but it aims to break the spell of philosophy as theory.

THE SHOPKEEPER AND THE SHOPPER

7. But of course, the deeper or more pervasive the picture from which one is attempting to induce conversion, the more difficult it is to succeed in the endeavour; and Wittgenstein's interlocutor is plainly far from convinced by his counter-tale. For the shopkeeper's behaviour doesn't relieve her of the desire to raise philosophical questions about word-meaning, but rather intensifies it. ' "But how does he know where and how he is to look up the word 'red' and what he is to do with the word 'five'?" ' There's no problem with 'apple', of course; mastering that word appears unproblematic, just as it would to someone taking nouns and proper names as their paradigm for words. So these questions emerge from an Augustinian perspective, and show how that picture shapes the interlocutor's response to the narrative that is designed to undermine it. Paradigms are not easily overthrown.

Which makes the abruptness of Wittgenstein's response to these questions even more remarkable: 'Well, I assume that he *acts* as I have described. Explanations come to an end somewhere.' Even if we accept Wittgenstein's unsupported emphasis here upon the weaving of words into practical activity, how exactly does this answer the interlocutor's questions? To be sure, explanations cannot go on indefinitely; but then the critical issue is determining where and when they can and should stop—and this cannot be done merely by flatly asserting that a terminus has been reached. On the contrary: the fact that the interlocutor is plainly not content to stop here surely shows that the matter cannot simply be foreclosed in this way.

Suppose we stay with the interlocutor's (surely legitimate) sense of dissatisfaction for a moment, and reconsider the statement that actually unleashes her questions—Wittgenstein's rather breezy claim about his shopping trip story that 'It is in this and similar ways that one operates with words.' The implication is that this story is a paradigm of the ordinary—an everyday tale of buying and selling. But I don't recall ever attempting to buy apples by mutely presenting my shopping list to the shopkeeper. Nor have I ever gone shopping in a grocery store where the shopkeeper kept his fruit in drawers, employed a sample chart when selecting among them by colour, and counted aloud as he deposited each apple in my bag. The staff in a hardware store have often counted out nuts and bolts from their drawers for me; others (maybe the same staff in the same store) have often selected a can of paint for me with the help of a colour chart; but to transfer and amalgamate familiar elements of other kinds of shopping trip into a trip to the grocer is not to construct a familiar tale of our commerce with apples. For Wittgenstein to present such a surreal transposition as an unremarkable example of the way we 'operate with words' places our conception of everyday human transactions under intolerable strain. Surely nothing could be more extraordinary than this scene of supposedly ordinary life.

It is therefore hardly surprising that Wittgenstein's interlocutor should respond to the tale with a flurry of questions; but it is far from clear that her questions are provoked by the real extraordinariness of that narrative. For her doubts about whether the shopkeeper actually understands the words 'red' and 'five' are not awakened by any specifically odd detail of what he says and does with his tables and his chants, any more than her certainty that he understands the word 'apple' is shaken by the oddness of his apple-storing techniques. The cast of her questions rather takes it for granted that nothing behavioural can settle the issue of understanding even in principle; only a transition to the entirely separate realm of the inner can give her the reassurance she craves. But by picturing human behaviour and human mental life as essentially unrelated to one another, and so placing the minds of others beyond her reach, she ensures that the general reassurance she seeks (as opposed to the specific kinds of reassurance we all seek when faced by behaviour that is specifically ambiguous, suggestive of duplicity, and so on) will prove unattainable. In this sense, the interlocutor's scepticism is produced by the picture of inner and outer that she brings to the story, not by anything specific to Wittgenstein's telling of it. And that picture not only prepares the ground for both behaviourism and dualism—opponents whose agreement on a distorted map of the terrain creates their quarrel over it; it also has a clear kinship with Augustine's picture of language. For if all words are names, and the word 'understanding' obviously does not name a specific piece or kind of behaviour, then it must be the name of a specific, inner phenomenon. 'Where our language suggests a body, and there is none: there, we should like to say, is a *spirit*' (*PI* 36).[4]

However, even if the interlocutor's questions are remarkably insensitive to the surreal details of Wittgenstein's tale, the tale turns out to be remarkably sensitive to the details of those questions. For the interlocutor's sceptical anxiety about the shopkeeper clearly implies that if we could establish the presence of an internal, mental procedure or mechanism of understanding in him—if, for example, we could show that he was able to use the word 'red' to discriminate between apples because he had internally correlated the word 'red' with a mental image of red, and that he could count the apples in the drawer because he had internally correlated the sequence of number words with sequences of imagined units or strokes—then we could overcome our scepticism about whether his public behaviour was indeed a manifestation of genuine understanding. But then, what the interlocutor imagines must be going on inside anyone who does genuinely understand the meanings of words would be nothing more than an internalized version of the public processes of correlation and comparison that the shopkeeper goes through in Wittgenstein's story; and this immediately raises a number of problems.

First, if the public, externalized versions of such procedures were not in themselves enough to establish the presence of understanding to the interlocutor's satisfaction, why should their inner counterparts? The sheer fact of their interiority is surely not enough to show that the procedures and mechanisms embody understanding, and yet there appears to be no other difference, for example, between a mental image of red and a sample of red on a colour chart. This is the real force of Wittgenstein's seemingly brusque response to his interlocutor's questions. She is happy that explanations should come to an end when we reach internal procedures and mechanisms, but these differ in no significant respect from the external procedures and mechanisms about which she claimed to have real doubts; so either those doubts apply to the internal as well as the external procedures and mechanisms, or our explanations can perfectly well stop in the public realm, to which Wittgenstein's tale so noticeably restricts itself.

[4] Although, to be fair to Augustine, Wittgenstein's diagnosis of the error he finds in the *Confessions*' account of language-acquisition is also to be found in the *Confessions*; in book VII, for example, he diagnoses the deepest root of his Manichaeism as his inability to conceive of anything real, and particularly anything spiritual or non-physical, except on the model of material substance: 'I thought simply non-existent anything not extended in space or diffused or concentrated or expanding . . .' (*C* VII. i). This is, in part, why his post-conversion mode of reading characterizes itself as open to non-literal, figurative, or allegorical dimensions of meaning in a text.

The second problem is this. If Wittgenstein's shopkeeper's way with words strikes us as surreal and oddly mechanical, to the point at which we want to question the nature and even the reality of his inner life, and yet his public behaviour amounts to an externalized replica of the way we picture the inner life of all ordinary, comprehending language-users, then our picture of the inner must be as surreal, as oddly mechanical, as Wittgenstein's depiction of the outer. What the story shows is that the interlocutor's imaginings would have us zombies inside as well as out; her supposed solution to her sceptical problem is in fact a further, deeper expression of her scepticism. In other words, Wittgenstein's tale is not a depiction of ordinary life, but a realization of one of our fantasies of it: the drawers and tables of his grocer's shop reflect the architecture and furnishings of the mental theatre we attribute to ourselves, and the robotic, chanting shopkeeper is the homunculus who occupies its stage.

It follows that if we, as readers, happily accept Wittgenstein's invitation to regard this oddly mechanical tale as an episode from ordinary life, and proceed to berate his interlocutor for failing to do likewise, then we are participating in the very confusions that we are so quick to condemn in others. Our eagerness to rebut our opponents implicates us in their errors. This suggests more than the need for humility. It warns us not to think of the interlocutory voices in Wittgenstein's text as somehow other than our own (or, indeed, his own); the impulses to which they give utterance are to be found in us as well, and they are voiced in Wittgenstein's text at least in part in order to invite us to acknowledge their more or less repressed presence in us. And it further warns us that what Wittgenstein means by 'the ordinary'—whether with respect to language or to life—is not necessarily either obvious or ordinary. On the contrary, it may prove as difficult to achieve an understanding of that conception as it is to understand his later philosophy as a whole. In particular, it may not pick out a common or neutral domain immune to philosophical distortion or colonization; the shopkeeper's tale rather suggests that the realm of the ordinary can prove vulnerable to philosophical depredations as well as providing a means of overcoming them.

8. In accounting for the extraordinariness of the shopkeeper's behaviour and environment in Wittgenstein's tale, we seem to have passed over the behaviour of the shopper. To recall: Wittgenstein begins his narrative by telling us 'I send someone shopping. I give him a slip marked 'five red apples'. He takes the slip to the shopkeeper, who . . .'.

I remarked earlier that I don't normally do my shopping by mutely handing over my shopping list to the shopkeeper. I have suggested that we do not typically think of shopping lists as made for use as an alternative to speech, but rather as employed in conjunction with further words, for example as an aide-memoire for conversational exchanges with shopkeepers. Are there, nevertheless, ways of imagining Wittgenstein's scene as ordinary or everyday?

One way would be to imagine the shopper as going about his business in a foreign country whose language he does not speak, and who is thereby constrained to take down instructions from a native. This would make of him a concrete instance of the general condition which Wittgenstein later claims is implicit in Augustine's picture of language learning, in which it is 'as if the child came into a strange country and did not understand the language of the country; that is, as if it already had a language, only not this one' (*PI* 32). Could we then think of the shopping tale as Wittgenstein's anticipatory way of bringing this aspect of Augustine's thinking back down to earth, recalling us to our ordinary experiences of foreignness to words and reminding us that they constitute one of a variety of everyday ways of using language? But if the shopping tale is, as its context suggests, intended as an emblematic counter to Augustine's distorted picture of language use in general, then this reading of it would have Wittgenstein repeating Augustine's error— presenting our relation to words in a foreign language as exemplary of our relation to words per se.

Another approach would be to imagine the shopper (and the elder who sent him) as mute, without the ability to speak. Since there is no necessity to think of their muteness as a loss (no need to imagine that they once possessed the capacity to speak and then were deprived of it), why should their way of using the shopping list be thought of as anything other than ordinary for them? After all, such perhaps untypical ways of operating with words can achieve their goal (the shopper will get the apples for his elder), and their success depends upon exploiting perfectly ordinary aspects of the powers of words; ordinary words, we might say, just are so made as to be usable in such ways.

A further way of imagining Wittgenstein's scene as ordinary emerges if we ask whether its specific details can be seen as responding to specific details of Augustine's autobiographical narrative. Looking at that passage in the light of its fictional counterpart, the following matters stand out. Augustine's world of words contains no writing: every linguistic transaction is a speech-act, unlike the shopping trip, where the characters exchange words presented as marks on paper and speech is reserved for monologue. Further, the narrator of Augustine's tale appears to understand others, and definitely understands himself, in terms of the mind–body dualism parodied in Wittgenstein's story; he talks of himself as training his mouth to form signs with which to speak his mind, as if his body were one more instrument at his disposal—as if his mind and all its states floated within his body as his brain floats within his skull. Perhaps most strikingly, however, Augustine's story primarily has to do with the acquisition of language; its protagonist is himself as a child learning to speak, whereas Wittgenstein's emphasis appears to be on the use of language in adult life.

Both sides of this last contrast need qualification, however. First, there is far more learning than teaching in Augustine's tale.[5] The child is clearly working hard to learn the language of his elders—observing their utterances and movements, grasping the connection between sounds and objects with the help of facial expressions and intonation, and then employing those connections for its own purposes. But this enormous expenditure of effort (an expenditure which, when one stops to think about it, takes suspiciously adult, theoretical forms) is called for because the child's elders appear to be making no effort to teach him. It is as if the child acquires language despite the indifference of his elders, as if he is forced to pick it up by stealth—to steal it rather than being gifted with it, inheriting it.

And what of Wittgenstein's tale? In section 5 of the *Investigations*, after referring to the shopping trip story as an example of the phenomena of language in primitive kinds of application, Wittgenstein says that 'a child uses such primitive forms of language when it learns to talk'. With this in mind, if we ask ourselves again in what kinds of uncontroversially ordinary circumstance we might expect to find someone wordlessly handing over to the shopkeeper a shopping list itself handed to him by another person, I believe we might answer: when observing a young child sent on an errand. (And thinking again about the fairy-tale quality of the shopkeeper's surreal arrangements and actions, quite as if he is inhabiting or acting out a child's fantasy of a grocer's shop, we might further ask: is the child's parent actually sending him to the local store, or rather participating in a game the child is playing with a friend, one pretending to be the customer and one the shopkeeper?) Whether or not the shopkeeper is a grown-up, however, if we imagine his customer as a child, then Wittgenstein's tale can be taken as directly (if not explicitly or even exclusively) telling a counter-narrative about the acquisition of lan-

---

[5] See Cavell, 'Notes and Afterthoughts', *PP* 169.

guage; for this child's elders are fully engaged in the task of handing on the inheritance of language, and their favoured form for this teaching or training is that of encouraging the child to play a part in their life with words.

Can we say that a child sent on such an errand is really or properly buying groceries? Discussing a number of parallel examples (including one in which a child asks to pay for the groceries, takes the money from its parent's hand, and gives it to the shopkeeper), Stanley Cavell suggests that to describe the child that way is to describe him as if he were an adult, or at least master of that adult activity.

You *and* the child know that you are really playing—which does not mean that what you are doing isn't serious. Nothing is more serious business for a child than knowing it *will* be an adult—and *wanting* to be, i.e. *wanting to do the things we do*—and knowing that it can't really do them yet. What is wrong is to say what a child is doing as though the child were an adult, and not recognize that he is still a child playing, above all growing. (*CR* 176)

I think we can say that Augustine describes himself as a child who is already an adult, even if in miniature; he may expand, but growing larger is not always growth. It is as if he writes knowing that he cannot have grown into adulthood in the face of his elders' failure to acknowledge his desire to do so, in the absence of their responsive, welcoming recognition of him as a child, and so as someone who will be an adult, and who must therefore play at being an adult; and yet, since he *is* now an adult, telling his tale of unacknowledged childhood, he must always already have been one. Wittgenstein's child is growing towards language, and so towards adulthood; like Augustine's child, he has the desire for growth, but unlike him he also has its necessary condition—that of his elders' desire to reciprocate his desire, and their willingness to play.

The contrast implies that Augustine's child will struggle to inherit a willingness to play with words, or any sense that human life with language is playful rather than sheer hard labour. And since his words are stolen, his right to them unacknowledged by others, they will (for him) always ultimately belong to his elders, be their private property; so his way with them will inexorably, fearfully repeat their ways, devoid of any sense that there is enough flexibility (enough play) in human language and culture for him to find his own way within it.

These speculations are confirmed by the ways in which Augustine continues the tale of his life into boyhood, in the remainder of book I of the *Confessions*. For there we find him recalling that his continued impulses towards play rather than study met with continued repression by his elders, through the repeated meting out of punishment (*C* I. ix); and his general authorial commentary on his schooldays shows the long-term success of that repression. For, speaking as the adult who developed from such instruction, he condemns his stubborn childish preference for the playfulness of literature over the rules of grammar (*C* I. xiii); and by more or less clearly associating literature (in both content and form) with self-indulgence, the temptations of the flesh and sinfulness, and grammar with austerity, self-discipline, and an earthly image of divine authority (*C* I. xvi–xix), he thereby dissociates playfulness from the essence of language in an essentially Manichaean way. This gesture sets the fundamental tone of Augustine's account, even though he admits at one point that he learned Latin quickly and easily 'from my nurses caressing me, from people laughing over jokes, and from those who played games and were enjoying them' (*C* I. xiv), even though his conversion is signalled by words seemingly overheard from a children's game (*C* IX. xii), and even though the mode of reading that emblematizes that conversion revels in the allegorical play of the divine Word. We might think of this as indicating the incompleteness of Augustine's conversion—a conclusion entirely in keeping with his conception of conversion as always essentially incomplete, endlessly in need of repetition and renewal (as his account in book x of the self's essential unknowability to itself, the depths of its motivations so labyrinthine and unsurveyable that regression is always possible, would lead us to expect).

Augustine's tale thus manifests the schizophrenia or hypocrisy he attributes to the elders whose teaching he has internalized—their capacity to pass over the essentially playful, self-indulgent, and sinful nature of their own activities when condemning that same nature in their young charges, their praise for poems about adultery modulating into condemnations of adulterous practices, their criticism of the mote of incorrect speech intimately juxtaposed with their endorsement of the beam of capital punishment. In this respect, the child who fathers the narrator of this tale is himself made in the image of its fathers, and grows to recount his own past in a manner that reiterates the worst of his culture rather than remaking it in the more humane image that his words elsewhere recognize and aim to attain. In Wittgenstein's child human culture finds an independent life, an unpredictable future—he and his culture can grow and develop together; in Augustine's child human culture is haunted by its past, and doomed to repeat it—its future is foreclosed.

The notion of desire offers one further dimension of comparison between Augustine's and Wittgenstein's tales. For of course, Augustine's child not only possesses the desire for language and the adulthood it emblematizes; he also plainly thinks of language *as such* as an instrument for the communication and satisfaction of desire, and depicts the adult world into which that language is woven as pervaded with desire—as a realm in which human beings struggle to seek and have what they want, and to reject or avoid what they do not want. Interestingly, Wittgenstein's tale does not appear desirous of rejecting or avoiding this implication of Augustine's narrative. Wittgenstein's child is, after all, playing at shopping; he acts as a messenger for one elder's linguistic expression of desire to another, he will (presumably) act as a messenger for the other's attempt to satisfy it—and one of our earliest stories (a story from the book with which Augustine ends the *Confessions* by occupying himself) links apples with desire. On the other hand, the very concreteness of Wittgenstein's tale militates against its reliance on desire being taken as a figure for the whole of the adult realm into which the child is being invited; the matter-of-factness of the adult exchange he facilitates, the downbeat sense it creates that the elder's investment in his desire for an apple allows for the possibility of the shopkeeper's inability to satisfy it, lacks the background sense (perhaps metaphysical, perhaps spiritual) of a world of unceasing, desirous struggle conjured up so effectively by Augustine—a world of original sinfulness delivered over to its own reproduction, as children imbibe their elders' enacted conception of words as instruments of self-satisfaction.

It is as if Wittgenstein wishes to drive a wedge between Augustine's sense of a fundamental connection between language and desire, and his vision of human beings as driven and mastered by the need to submit the world to their will. He offers no criticism of the former: indeed, since his tale variously implies that the inheritance of language is emblematic of human maturation, that this inheritance depends upon the child's willingness to desire it and to accept it as the medium for expressing his own desires, and that play is the primary mode of its acquisition, his narrative invites the conclusion that to acquire language is to participate in the play of human desire. But by implicitly dissociating himself from Augustine's vision of human beings as given over to the urge to remake the world in their image, he also implies that human desire is distinguishable from, say, need or fixation—that properly human growth should take us past an inability to accept the world's independence from our will, beyond a fixation on satisfying the relentlessly needy ego.

THE BUILDERS

9. One would not have to endorse every aspect of the readings developed in the preceding pages to appreciate that Wittgenstein's words are treacherous from the very beginning. Their innocent limpidity conceals a complexity of purpose and a writerly sophistication that cannot be treated as detachable from the philosophical insights they are designed to convey. The first section of the *Philosophical Investigations* is thus enough on its own to confirm that we cannot hope to understand this text if we do not achieve an understanding of its distinctiveness as prose, as a piece of writing; but the second section of the book drives home the lesson of the first even more forcefully.

Wittgenstein begins again by rephrasing his critique of Augustine's picture: one might say that it forms part of a primitive idea of the way language functions, or that it is an idea of the way a primitive language functions. The first formulation suggests that the natural languages with which we are familiar function in a more sophisticated and multifaceted way than Augustine's picture allows for; the second suggests that Augustine's picture would fit a more primitive language than the ones with which we are familiar. Neither formulation implies that Augustine's picture applies to some portion or subset of our language—that it is a faulty generalization; but the second does imply that we can imagine something that we could justifiably call a language (however primitive) and for which the description given by Augustine is right. Wittgenstein's following paragraph takes up this creative or literary challenge by recounting a story that he appears to think will fit Augustine's bill—the tale of the builders.

Notoriously, many of Wittgenstein's readers have found it difficult to obey his concluding instruction to 'Conceive this as a complete primitive language.' To be sure, his depiction of the two people using their four words to facilitate their building work with blocks, pillars, slabs, and beams supplies a context of practical activity, a speech community, a vocabulary, ways of using that vocabulary, and criteria for understanding utterances which employ it. On the other hand, as Baker and Hacker point out, what is described has no syntax, contains no rules for forming either simple or complex sentences and so no logical connectives, is incapable of expressing generality, and has only one (imperative) mood, which makes it impossible to speak of truth or falsity with respect to utterances in the 'language'.[6] Furthermore, as Rush Rhees

---

[6] See *An Analytical Commentary on Wittgenstein's* Philosophical Investigations, vol. i (Blackwell: Oxford, 1980), 26.

emphasizes, those who use it can interact 'linguistically' only by exchanging orders during the performance of their task; they do not, it appears, either plan for or reminisce about that task with this vocabulary, and there seems to be no possibility of even primitive versions of what might be called conversation, in which topics are discussed and interchanges of opinion (driven by previous contributions to the conversation and by the nature of its subject) take place. Moreover, the immediate context in which orders are exchanged is not located in any wider cultural or social context, in which the vocabulary employed in the building process is interwoven with other words and other activities, including ones related to a range of recognizably human interests and concerns (eating and drinking, art and worship, friendship and enmity, birth and death).[7]

Call these worries about content and context respectively. At various later points in the text Wittgenstein confronts a number of them directly. For example, the importance of a distinction between words and sentences is investigated in sections 19 ff.; and the significance of the builders being restricted to the issuing of orders is raised and dismissed in sections 18 ff. It is also worth noting that there is a difference, for Wittgenstein, between imagining the builders' language as complete, and imagining it as their whole language, or as the whole language of their tribe; the latter possibility is only raised in section 6, and is presented there as a further exercise of the imagination (although one that Wittgenstein thinks we can perform). This suggests that the decontextualization of the builders' language in section 2 ought not to be read as showing that Wittgenstein wishes to deny that it has (and must have) a wider social and cultural context—'to imagine a language means to imagine a form of life' (*PI* 19)—but only as showing that he wishes to leave the question, and the precise details of any such context, temporarily open.

As readers and thinkers, we are strongly tempted to assume that a detailed examination of the various strands of this complex pattern of objection and response will reveal a definitive answer to the question of whether or not the builders have a language. But the very fact that the pattern is one of objection and response—that there are things to be said on both sides of the question—ought to make us question this assumption. Perhaps Wittgenstein's primary reason for telling this tale is not to underwrite one particular answer to the question he poses, but rather to reveal how much complexity any answer to it must

[7] See 'Wittgenstein's Builders', in his *Discussions on Wittgenstein* (Routledge & Kegan Paul: London, 1970).

accommodate, and thus to suggest that the real confusion here is to think that a single, determinate answer is necessarily always available. After all, despite his concluding instruction, Wittgenstein portrays the builders' supposedly linguistic activities in strikingly cautious terms; he talks of their utterances as 'calls', and of their vocabulary as meant 'to serve for communication', or as a 'system of communication' (phrases that we might more happily apply to exchanges between non-human animals). This hardly suggests a narrator at ease with his own directions for reading; it suggests rather a desire on his part to engender a salutary discomfort in his audience.

In effect, Wittgenstein has constructed a fictional context of a particular sort, and invited us to project our concept of a language into that context; and we have responded by trying to gauge the degree to which the builders' exchanges resemble those we engage in with our ordinary, natural languages. But our attempt has revealed that the kinds of consideration (what Wittgenstein will later call 'the criteria') by reference to which we judge that resemblance are multiple and complex, that the significance of any given criterion being satisfied or not satisfied in any given case is contestable, and so that the degree of resemblance needed to ground the projection of the concept of a language into this (or any) context is importantly open to individual judgement. It follows that what counts as the proper response to Wittgenstein's invitation is similarly open to individual judgement—that the meaning or grammar of the word 'language' is not such as to determine impersonally or objectively that the builders definitely do, or that they definitely do not, possess a language. Our grasp of the criteria for the term offers us guidance, and determines what kinds of consideration will be pertinent to the question at stake; but the responsibility for judging whether or not the absence of certain criteria, or the presence of what are at best analogues or primitive versions of them, are enough for us to withhold the word in this case ultimately rests with the individuals invited to project those criteria into this imagined context.

We can think of this as a lesson about the nature of criteria and grammar as such, and of our responsibility in determining the limits of their appropriate projection. Wittgenstein's literary exercise invites us to recognize how our life with words is open-ended or undefined in front, how our inheritance of language not only allows us to find our own way of going on with words, but deprives us of the opportunity of sloughing off that responsibility onto others (whether the elders we once knew or those who are now our fellows), or onto our words themselves—as if they come to us pre-programmed with every possible inflection of significance that any new or newly imagined context might call forth. The spare, suggestive tale of the builders shows that the word 'language' is as flexibly inflexible as any word in our language, and so just as capable of revealing us (revealing our own commitments and interests) to others and to ourselves. For in exploring which aspects of the tale make us reluctant to think of the builders as using a language and which encourage us to do so, we establish what we take to be truly significant in our concept of a language, and so illuminate our sense of its significance in our lives. If, for example, we give weight to the worry about content, and deny that the builders possess a language because their calls lack syntax, rules for sentence-formation, and logical connectives, then we declare that *those* are the features we take to lie at the heart of language; but if we accept that they possess a language because there are criteria for understanding their utterances which are woven into a shared practical activity with a recognizable human purpose, then we declare that *those* are features we take to be central to language. And in so far as Wittgenstein appears to be urging us, however cautiously, to view the builders' activities as inviting the projection of the concept of a language, then we must conclude that there is something about the ways in which the builders' calls resemble the words of our natural languages that he takes to be of fundamental importance.

Nevertheless, we need to remember that Wittgenstein's primary reason for telling his tale is to provide a context for which Augustine's description of language is right. This means that, in so far as we resist his instruction to think of the builders as possessed of a language, we are condemning Augustine rather more than Wittgenstein—refusing to concede to Augustine even the little that Wittgenstein is prepared, with qualifications, to offer.

10. But in offering this concession, what exactly does Wittgenstein take himself to be conceding? At the beginning of section 2 he gives a dual characterization of Augustine's picture—as a primitive idea of language, and as an idea of a primitive language. This suggests that what allows him to overcome his natural reluctance (evinced in his cautious talk of 'calls' and 'systems of communication') to project the concept of language into this imagined context is its being paired with and inflected by the concept of the 'primitive' (a concept very likely to be called up in Augustine's thinking, however subliminally, by his focus on the inheritance of words in childhood). It is the primitiveness of the builders and their calls that at once resists and invites (or at least tolerates) the projection of our concept of a language; so it is that aspect of Wittgenstein's tale with which we need to come to grips.

Stanley Cavell has suggested that at least three main interpretative possibilities open up from this concept of the primitive, from its criteria or grammar.[8] The first can be summarized by saying that Wittgenstein's builders strike us as not quite or fully human, as permanently cut off from full membership of the human race—in short, as primitive human beings, a species of Neanderthal. This is not simply because they have only four calls or words: in this respect they resemble young children, and *they* do not give the impression that their primitive understanding of their words is permanent. Why? Because a child will experiment with its words, excitedly repeating them, trying them out in new contexts, putting them together, and so on; it will use them imaginatively. By contrast, the places of the builders' words in their activities are more or less unvarying, they evince no capacity or willingness to construct combinations of words, no desire to experiment or play with their words, to go on with them into new contexts; they appear to be completely lacking in imagination. We might say that the child has a future with its words, whereas the builders have none; but words without a future—words which contain no possibility for their users of playful, creative repetition, of projection into new contexts—are not obviously words at all.

Another way of taking the primitiveness of the builders offers less resistance to the idea that they have a language. It involves taking seriously the suggestion that this system of communication is designed for a building site. In such a context, with huge amounts of noisy activity, transport, and machinery as a permanent background, the kind of vocabulary outlined by Wittgenstein would have a perfectly obvious point, allowing the builders to communicate the bare minimum of information needed to accomplish their task with the least likelihood of misunderstanding. Here, we might say, the language is primitive but the people who use it are not; on the contrary, their deployment of it indicates a highly sophisticated response to the environment in which they are operating. If we encountered such a system of communication on a real building site, would we hesitate to say that the builders were using a language?

Perhaps not; but we might nonetheless hesitate to make the same claim about Wittgenstein's builders. True, he does not explicitly say that his building site is not part of the familiar, modern urban scene; but he does deliberately leave any such wider context unspecified in section 2, and at the beginning of section 6 he explicitly claims that this system

---

[8] See 'Declining Decline: Wittgenstein as a Philosopher of Culture', in S. Mulhall (ed.), *The Cavell Reader* (Blackwell: Oxford, 1996).

of communication could be the whole language of the builders' tribe. This implies that, unlike builders on a modern, urban site, these builders do not deploy different vocabularies or modes of speech outside the building site; they simply teach their children the vocabulary they will need for the site. If our modern builders had no alternative to the system they deploy on their site, if it exhausted the linguistic possibilities available to them, we would surely be right to resist thinking of that system as a language; but since section 2 leaves the wider context of their activities unspecified, we cannot regard such resistance as our only interpretative option here.

A third possible way of understanding the primitiveness of the builders is as an allegory of the way people in modern culture in fact speak. If we accept for a moment that it is an essential part of Wittgenstein's challenge to us as readers to fill in the unspecified wider context of the builders' lives, then we can imagine that their unvarnished, almost psychotically functional deployments of their words constitute a microcosm of their ways with words off the building site at least as easily as imagining that they stand in sharp contrast to that broader linguistic reality. The idea here is not that their vocabulary might constitute the whole language of their society (the elaboration invited in section 6), but that their orientation to their words exemplifies that of their culture as a whole. We can, in other words, take them as non-primitive human beings in the surroundings of a developed culture who nonetheless find themselves speaking primitively—in more or less simplified expressions of more or less uncultivated, fixated desires. Here the culture as a whole must be thought of as pervaded by debilitating noise and distraction, as a collectivity that is stupefying itself by the poverty of its practices and conceptions, stultifying the human imagination and depriving itself of a future.

This projection of Wittgenstein's tale certainly calls for a more extended use of the imagination than the previous two—or rather, it calls for its extension into a different, more figurative dimension. But allegorical or parabolic uses of language are perfectly everyday tools of the storyteller's trade; and Wittgenstein's earlier tale of the surreal shopping trip also invites us to consider some rather reductively utilitarian operations with words as emblematic of ordinary linguistic life —indeed, once the builders' activities are modified (as in section 8) to include numerals and colour samples, the two stories appear pretty much convergent, providing a composite or binocular sketch of the same cultural landscape. It is also worth recalling that Augustine's post-conversion mode of reading embodies a new capacity to perceive an allegorical dimension in the book of Genesis, and to see that such dimensions of meaning are not in competition with more literal or non-figurative ones.

In inviting such an understanding of his builders, Wittgenstein thereby suggests that Augustine's description of the language he acquired can be seen as fitting our life with words as it really is—that the way we inhabit our language (just like that of Augustine's elders) is more primitive than our official idea of it may suggest, and so that it positively invites the construction of pictures such as Augustine's. In this sense, his primitive philosophical conception of language does not misrepresent our present language and form of life; it mirrors them back to us, or at least prophesies the future towards which our present needy, fixated life with words now asymptotically tends (encouraged, amongst other things, by the dissemination of impoverished philosophical conceptions of that life). And our resistance to that conception will then amount to a repression of knowledge of our true state—a refusal to let Augustine's tale teach us what we have or may become.

GAMES AND BOARD GAMES

11. Once again, only a fixated need for determinacy—what Augustine would call a Manichaean or pre-conversion orientation to the literal— would suggest that we must choose one of these interpretations of the builders over the others. The very sparseness of Wittgenstein's tale suggests that it is meant to invite a number of non-exclusive interpretations, each with its own particular edification. He thereby underlines his sense of the flexibility of the grammar of words—the fact that the capacity of words like 'language' and 'primitive' to fit new contexts is limited not so much by a predetermined structure of grammatical rules, but by the imaginations of those who use them. And this in turn suggests that the philosophical method exemplified in his telling of this tale is as dependent upon imagination as are the modes of language that the method aims to characterize—hardly a surprising conclusion, since that method relies upon exactly the same capacity that it takes to be central to our mastery of ordinary language: the ability to recall and project criteria.

Nevertheless, in section 3 of the *Investigations* Wittgenstein is concerned to emphasize one particular moral of the reading lesson that section 2 aims to impart. He appears to claim that the tale of the builders shows that Augustine's description of language is appropriate for a narrowly circumscribed region of language use, but not for the whole of what he was claiming to describe. But doesn't this precisely imply what we have earlier denied—namely, that Augustine is guilty of the perfectly familiar philosophical error of propounding a false generalization? Wittgenstein's immediately subsequent analogy suggests that this would be an over-hasty conclusion.

He compares Augustine's description of language to someone who says: 'A game consists in moving objects about on a surface according to certain rules'—to which he responds by saying: 'You seem to be thinking of board games, but there are others. You can make your definition correct by expressly restricting it to those games.' As with Wittgenstein's initial response to the opening citation from Augustine, this rejoinder is a diagnostic speculation about what might have led the definer to make his claim, not an admission of its accuracy with respect to the particular examples he has in mind. For of course, if the definition is expressly restricted to board games, then it loses even the appearance of being a definition of games as such. It would then begin to tell us what board games have in common with one another (what leads us to group chess with draughts), as we might specify what card games have in common (what leads us to group poker with gin rummy); but neither tells us what leads us to group board games and card games together—what makes board games and card games *games* (nor could they, if—as Wittgenstein later argues—there is no such thing as a property or properties common to all games). But of course, his interlocutor understood herself to be contributing to just such a project with her original definition. So once the explicit restriction is introduced into her definition, she will find herself correctly defining something other than she took herself to be defining; she will be defining an adjective rather than a noun—what makes a game a *board* game, not what makes a board game (or any other type of game) a *game*.

This is why Wittgenstein says that such reformulated definitions are only appropriate 'for a narrowly-circumscribed region, not for the whole of what you were claiming to describe'. It is natural to assume that, since the region remains a part of the whole from which it has been excerpted, a characterization of that region will at least contribute to a characterization of the whole—natural, but entirely wrong. For the characterization of the region may in fact articulate what differentiates it from the whole, what makes it a distinct region.

The person offering the original definition took herself to be offering a definition of one particular concept, but finds that she must either regard her definition as so self-evidently false that it makes little sense to think of it even as a wildly mistaken definition of that original concept at all (did she simply overlook the differences between board games and card games?), or else regard it as a definition of a different concept altogether. Taken as an attempted definition of the essence of games, her words comprehensively fail to apply even to board games; but taken as an attempted definition of the essence of board games, what they define will not be what she intended them to define. Either way, her words will not and cannot say what she originally took herself to mean by them; she has lost control of them, suffered a hallucination of sense that was generated by her hovering between two possible meanings that her words might have without ever actualizing either. Once these two readings are clarified and separated from one another, she is at perfect liberty to deploy either of them; but of course, that same clarificatory process will in all likelihood deprive those words of the attraction they once had for her. Once again, the philosophical confusion is not that her words are overly general, or that they mean nothing; the point is rather that, of all the many things that her words might mean, none will convey what she took herself to mean by them.

This is why, with respect to Augustine's picture of language, Wittgenstein's first remark in section 3 is: 'Augustine, we might say, does describe a system of communication; only not everything that we call language is this system.' Recall Cavell's three readings of Wittgenstein's claim that the builders have a complete, primitive language. It might be the language of primitive human beings, and so at best an animal-like system of communication rather than a human language; or it might be something used on a modern building site, and so function as a skeletal system of communication that forms part of a wider human language; or it might be an allegory of human language in its modern, impoverished state, and so serve to characterize our natural language as if it had become no more than a primitive, subhuman system of communication. In all three cases Augustine's picture—although intended to capture the essence of language—in reality depicts a system of communication; he intends to assert obvious truths about humans and their words, but he ends up portraying creatures and calls which have never attained, or have been deprived by specific circumstances of, any genuinely human significance.

In that case, however, none of Cavell's three ways of imagining a context for Wittgenstein's sketch permit us to think that Augustine's picture correctly describes a region or subset of human language. According to the first reading, Augustine is not describing a *language* at all; according to the third, he is not *describing* a language, but allegorizing its degeneracy. According to the second, he *is* describing a system of communication that forms part of a natural language; but it is the *primitiveness* of such systems that his words characterize, the adjective rather than the noun—he is highlighting what makes such primitive (parts of) language *primitive* rather than what makes them *language*, what distinguishes such parts of a natural language from its other parts rather than what relates them to that larger whole. As we saw earlier, if we do take such parts of language entirely on their own, narrowly circumscribed terms, isolating them from their broader context of linguistic and cultural practice, we deprive ourselves of any reason to think of them as language; we are left instead with Cavell's first scenario, that of the primitive human beings, within which the builders' calls appear as an animal-like system of communication.

As with the putative definition of games, the Augustinian's form of words has spun out of her control. It is intended to be a definition of the essence of language, but as such fails even to apply to the narrowly circumscribed region of systems of communication whose contemplation or imagination may subliminally have prompted them; and if those words are appropriately reformulated so as to characterize the essence of systems of communication, then they will not define what their proponent originally intended them to define. So it is not that Augustine's words are overly general, or that they mean nothing; there are various things that they might be taken to mean, but the process of clarifying and disentangling these possibilities is likely to deprive the Augustinian's words of the attraction they once held. Augustinians can maintain the conviction that there is something they have it at heart to say only by hovering between two of the many things their words might mean without committing themselves to either; they thereby induce a hallucination of meaning, an illusion of sense. It is illusions of this kind that Wittgenstein aims to dispel, by encouraging us to turn away from the pictures which turn us towards them; and in doing so, he takes on the obligation to account for the fact that we, who are otherwise at home in our natural language, can come, under the pressure to philosophize, to fall prey to such profoundly uncanny self-deceptions.

LANGUAGE-GAMES

12. In drawing an analogy between mischaracterizing language and mischaracterizing games, section 3 of the *Investigations* implicitly introduces one of Wittgenstein's fundamental comparative gestures, a movement of thought made all but explicit four sections later in his coinage of the term 'language-game'. His sense of a kinship between language

(or languages) and games, of the openness of these concepts to fruitful hyphenation, pervades the *Investigations* as a whole, and has generated great anxiety among some of his most perceptive commentators. But before I can address that anxiety directly, we must determine whether the means for allaying much of it are not already to be found strewn amidst the early sections of the book, in passages where the idea of a 'language-game', and what soon comes to be known as the builders' language-game, undergo reciprocal elaboration.

Why, to begin with, do the calls of the builders call forth Wittgenstein's coinage only retrospectively, in section 7 rather than at their initial fabrication in section 2? What happens in the intervening sections to motivate the shift from the idea that those calls constitute a 'complete primitive language' to the idea that they constitute a 'language-game'? The answer lies in section 6, which effects a double alteration in Wittgenstein's original tale: it asks us to imagine the language of section 2 as the whole language of a tribe, and to further imagine that the elders of that tribe utilize their vocabulary not only in calls made during the building process but also in training their children to use and respond to those calls.

It is striking that Wittgenstein does not appear to think of these alterations as expansions of the language sketched in section 2: the term 'expansion' is elicited only by the addition of new vocabulary to the builders' repertoire, as imagined in section 8. Apparently he thinks of what is involved in instructing children in the language (the teacher pointing to objects, directing the child's attention to them, and uttering the appropriate call; the child repeating the call after the teacher utters it; the child uttering the appropriate call when the teacher points to a given object) as processes 'resembling language' (*PI* 7)—that is, as not being full or proper uses of words. They are preparatory to genuine language use rather than fully fledged instances of it; they establish associations between words and things for the child, but the child has not yet begun to use the calls to say or do something—to express its own desire for a stone or to act upon another's expression of that desire. Hence Wittgenstein's denial, in section 6, that such instruction is a species of ostensive definition (since the child cannot ask for the names of the stones, does not even know what a name is). He regards it instead as ostensive teaching—a kind of training rather than a kind of explanation (see *PI* 5); it helps to bring about linguistic understanding in human beings, but is not itself an exercise of that understanding (except for the teacher).

Imagining the complete primitive language of the builders in section 2 as the whole language of a tribe does not, then, require an expansion of the language of section 2. But it does involve an expansion in our conception of the context of the builders' calls; it asks us to introduce a conception of the linguistic community whose system of communication those calls constitute. And, for Wittgenstein, this expansion inevitably requires that the old vocabulary be directed to a new kind of use—that of training the children of the tribe. But then it appears that thinking of a system of communication as the whole language of a tribe immediately introduces the thought of passing on that system to a new generation; the idea of a linguistic community is not separable from the idea of that community's capacity to reproduce itself over time by ensuring the effective inheritance of its words.

When Wittgenstein introduces the term 'language-game' in section 7, immediately after imagining the kinds of linguistic instruction mentioned earlier, it is to this new or renewed focus on the figure of the child that he is responding.

We can also think of the whole process of using words in (2) as one of those games by means of which children learn their native language. I will call these games 'language-games' and will sometimes speak of a primitive language as a language-game.

And the processes of naming the stones and of repeating words after someone might also be called language-games. Think of much of the use of words in games like ring-a-ring-a-roses.

I shall also call the whole, consisting of language and the actions into which it is woven, the 'language-game'. (*PI* 7)

Plainly, the term 'language-game' primarily signifies a certain kind of game—a game with words of the kind Wittgenstein imagines as central to the linguistic instruction of children. In this respect, language-games resemble language but are not fully fledged instances of it; the weight of the hyphenated term falls on its second element rather than its first. Utilizing this first sense of the term, Wittgenstein allows that the 'complete primitive language' he invents in section 2 can be seen as itself a kind of game with words. (He thereby explicitly characterizes the language of section 2 in virtually the same terms that Rush Rhees employs in the belief that he is thereby revealing an aspect of the builders' primitive language which escaped Wittgenstein's attention and which subverts the point of its construction—'Wittgenstein has described a *game* with building stones'.)[9]

Meeting the challenge issued in section 6 of imagining the complete primitive language of section 2 as the whole language of a tribe thus

---

[9] See 'Wittgenstein's Builders', *in Discussions of Wittgenstein*; hereafter WB.

leads Wittgenstein to see not only that the idea of whole languages generates the idea of language-games as their means of (re)production, but
also that the particular language he imagined could be seen as itself a
language-game, and hence presumably as resembling language rather
than exemplifying it. At the same time, however, he tells us that he will
sometimes speak of a primitive language as a language-game—a remark
which reasserts the original claim of section 2 that the builders' calls
can be conceived as a complete (even if a primitive) language, and which
thereby introduces a second and opposite sense of the term 'language-
game', one in which the weight falls on the first of its two elements and
according to which language-games are (primitive) exemplifications of
language and not just analogues or essential preliminaries to it.

Once again, it seems worth while resisting any initial impulse to
attempt to defuse or reconcile these opposing senses of Wittgenstein's
coinage—whether by allowing one of its elements definitively to eclipse
the other, or by sharply distinguishing one sense from the other (as if
the term as Wittgenstein introduces it hides a damaging ambiguity).
Instead, we might rather interpret its hyphenation to indicate an
intended equality or mutuality between its two elements, and so a
complementarity underlying its two directions of signification. On this
reading, the very point of the term 'language-game' lies in the double
implication that its duality opens up; it allows Wittgenstein to imply
that language both generates and is engendered by playing games with
words—that play is not only our route into the inheritance of language
but also an essential dimension of the language we thereby inherit. In
other words, Wittgenstein's coinage is designed explicitly to crystallize
something left implicit in the counter-tale of the shopping trip in section
1—to reveal the playfulness of language as well as (or rather, by underlining) its origination in play.

13. Suppose, however, that we do take seriously the invitation that
Wittgenstein's concept of 'language-games' appears to extend; what
exactly might be the consequences of introducing a notion of play into
our understanding of language? Looked at from this perspective,
Wittgenstein's discussion of ostensive teaching in section 6 is pregnant
with implication. For the first attempt to grasp the point of ostensive
teaching that he imagines his reader making involves the idea that establishing an association between a word and a thing is a matter of having
an image or picture of the thing come before the child's mind; and
Wittgenstein gives expression to this idea in the following way. 'I can
imagine such a use of words (of series of sounds). (Uttering a word is
like striking a note on the keyboard of the imagination.)' (*PI* 6). The

air of Augustinian fantasy in this haunting image is confirmed by its being released by the bracketed equation of words with series of sounds—an equation prepared for in section 4, in which Wittgenstein's first general diagnosis of Augustine's confusion is rephrased (for the third time) as an attempt to picture language as if it were a script designed to describe patterns of sound (thus sounding a Derridean note, and not for the first time). But the keyboard image of ostensive teaching pictures the teacher as tuning the child's imagination, preparing her for playing (the child figured not as pianist but as piano)— as if to learn to speak is to learn to play upon, and be played upon by, others, as if the aim of teaching is to establish exactly the same imaginative associations in every speaker, to transform children into adults whose play of mind is structured so as precisely to mirror those of their elders.

To this image of language as fixated or frozen play Wittgenstein opposes the following counter-image: ' "I set the brake up by connecting up rod and lever."—Yes, given the whole of the rest of the mechanism. Only in conjunction with that is it a brake-lever, and separated from its support it is not even a lever; it may be anything, or nothing' (*PI* 6). We can think of this as a counter-image of play if we recall that properly functioning mechanisms require some degree of play among their parts (some give-and-take or flexibility in their relations with one another, a kind of constrained or directed freedom); this play facilitates and partly constitutes the work of the mechanism, and its point or purpose is given not by any single correspondence between a handle (or switch or pedal) and an image in its user's mind but by the mechanism's general structure and by its relation to its environment. More generally, a properly functioning mechanism which requires a brake-lever (a car? a train?) must be one that is designed to be controlled by its driver's desires and interests, to give her the freedom of road or rail, the capacity for self-directed, independent movement. It is an image of empowerment, of the play of language as facilitating its user's journey into her own future.

This sense of openness to futurity plainly enters into the significance of the term 'language-game' from its very introduction, in the sense that language is the end-point of language-games, that playing games with words opens us to a future with language; but the second aspect of the term, reversing its polarity in the light of Wittgenstein's counter-image of play, would suggest that language-games also embody the future of language, that the growth or development of language—its aliveness— lies in the play of words, in our ability to be energized by and to direct the constrained freedom of their play with one another and with our actions in the world. In section 7 this notion of play appears in the figure of weaving, with the third and final introductory sense of the term 'language-game' that is implicit in Wittgenstein's concluding remark that he will also 'call the whole, consisting of language and the actions into which it is woven, the "language-game"'. Through the interplay of warp and weft in a loom, a fabric emerges; language extends itself in similar ways, at once growing from and growing through the interactive shuttling of words and world.

EXPANDING A LANGUAGE-GAME: DIACHRONY AND SYNCHRONY

14. Again, however, the words Wittgenstein interweaves with his figure of weaving embody an interesting ambiguity; it is left unclear whether 'the whole' to which he refers is 'the whole process of using words in (2)', or 'the whole language of a tribe' as imagined in section 8. Each, of course, is a whole in the sense that it is a self-contained instance, rather than an incomplete fragment, of linguistic activity; in particular, the language imagined in section 2 does not, on Wittgenstein's view, stand in need of completion by the contextual expansion he imagines in section 6. Nevertheless, there is a sense in which the language of section 6 accommodates an idea of wholeness which the complete primitive language of section 2 lacks—an idea of the four calls as the whole language of a tribe, as a system of communication for a linguistic community; and once that idea of wholeness appears, the completeness or self-containedness of the builders' calls comes under extreme pressure. It immediately secretes the idea of linguistic instruction and generational inheritance, or more broadly the idea of reproduction; and this in turn invites (without necessitating) what Wittgenstein is prepared to call expansion—a form of growth that is not simply a contextual broadening, or a simple self-replication, but a complication or blossoming of content along a natural developmental trajectory, a maturation.

For after the new wholeness of the language in section 6 is christened a 'language-game', its strictly finite vocabulary and menu of possible speech-acts suffers an expansion commensurate with a sequence of rapidly introduced complications in the behaviour and world that its users are conceived to inhabit. In section 8 the builders acquire a series of numeral-letters, some indexicals, and a set of colour samples (thus pushing their linguistic practices beyond the level achieved by the shoppers of section 1); in section 15 they acquire tools, together with marks which are impressed on those tools and used to refer to them; in section 21 they extend their repertoire of speech-acts to include questions about and reports on the location, number, and colour of their stones, as well as orders concerning their relocation; in section 27 the language-game of ostensive definition (as opposed to those of ostensive teaching) makes its appearance; and in sections 41 and 42 the builders respond to circumstances which might either deprive their words of meaning or inspire a joke. This constitutes their final appearance in this opening sequence of the book (in effect, the *Investigations* then begins again in section 46 by reapplying the method, and thus reproducing the structure, of its own opening—Wittgenstein quotes the *Theaetetus'* account of names, and responds by imagining, in section 48, a new language-game for which that account is really valid).

Staying within the first application of this method, the arc of development undergone by the builders beautifully displays Wittgenstein's double sense of the discontinuities and continuities of language and life. On the one hand, each episode of the story has its own integrity or wholeness—as if each were a tale told about a different tribe. Each aspires to make sense on its own terms, and inspires and guides philosophical reflection on the real importance of distinguishable aspects of language use whose absence from the primitive language-game of section 2 has troubled so many philosophers—differences in kind between words, the labelling function of names, the difference between words and sentences, the differences between kinds of sentence and speech-act, and so on. On the other hand, each episode also reads perfectly naturally as a further stage in the development of a single tribe—a kind of mythical history of its growth into fully human language use and form of life. Each alteration can be taken as an expansion or complication called forth by existing purposes and circumstances, or by plausible expansions or complications of them; and the final two stages appear as a kind of culmination of this dialectic between words, deeds, and world, in which the language runs up against its own limits, turns back on itself, and attains a new perspective on those limits.

The penultimate episode (section 27) sees training superseded by teaching, thereby marking the child's taking on a properly autonomous role in language—attaining the capacity to ask for the names he wants rather than having associations between names and things drilled into him, and thus becoming capable of using language to give expression to his desire to use language. But this is not all: according to

Wittgenstein, being able to name something hangs together being able to invent new names for things—he cites as an example a child's ability to give names to its dolls. In such a case, however, the child is not only going on with an established practice of naming—which would be the case if, having seen people being given names, he then goes on to give new names to new people; he is also adapting the practice of naming to a new context—one in which names are attached to dolls rather than people, to beings that do not (for example) speak or act independently of him, and so in which the names (once conferred) can and must be used in very different ways. There is, in short, no practice of giving names to things that is independent of the kinds of things being named; there is no single, context-invariant use to which 'names' are put. It follows that learning to give names to things involves not only learning how to go on with a given practice but also how to transform it—how to project it into contexts which call for its creative adaptation.

The final episode further develops this last capacity for creative projection. Drawing upon the introduction of proper names for tools in section 15, section 41 asks us to imagine what will happen if builder A asks builder B for tool N when the tool of that name is broken, or when (because of a change of names of which the speaker is unaware) there is no longer any tool marked with that name.

What is B to do when he is given it?—We have not settled anything about this. One might ask: what *will* he do? Well, perhaps he will stand there at a loss, or shew A the pieces. Here one *might* say: 'N' has become meaningless; and this expression would mean that the sign 'N' no longer had a use in our language-game (unless we gave it a new one) . . . [e.g.] B has to shake his head in reply if A gives him the sign belonging to a tool that is broken. (*PI* 41)

Here, we might say, the users of a language-game run up against (at least a version of) the distinction between sense and nonsense whose putative absence so troubled some readers of section 2 (with respect to which an analogue of this case, involving orders relating to broken stones, can be imagined without adding proper names to the builders' vocabulary). Criteria for using words cannot anticipate all eventualities, and so make possible meaninglessness as well as meaning. However, on Wittgenstein's account, a meaningless word or utterance is simply one to which no use has yet been given, although such an assignment could perfectly well be made. In short, nonsensicality occurs not because we violate established criteria for the use of words, but because we have not yet established criteria for their use in the relevant context; a meaningless utterance is one to which no sense has yet been given, not one which cannot have meaning because of the sense that it (or its component terms) have already been given. And in section 42, Wittgenstein reiterates his sense of our freedom to make the meaningless meaningful in a new register.

> ... has a name which has *never* been used for a tool also got a meaning in that game?—Let us assume that 'X' is such a sign and that A gives this sign to B— well, even such signs could be given a place in the language-game, and B might have, say, to answer them too with a shake of the head. (One could imagine this as a sort of joke between them.) (*PI* 42)

Here, the threat of meaninglessness as our criteria run out is obviated by the inventiveness of wit or humour; a loss of correspondence between utterance and world is taken as an opportunity to indulge in a certain playfulness with words and so with the world to which they refer—an overcoming of any fixation on purely representational modes of speech. Taken together with section 27, the two parts of this final episode thus appear to imply that fully human language use is inherently and playfully self-aware—a matter of being able to see that words form part of the world to which words refer, to recognize where established ways of using words have run out, and to improvise ways of getting beyond such impasses along routes of shared human responses.

If we step back for a moment and look at the sequence of expansions of the language of section 6 as a whole, then there seems no necessity to choose which of the two ways of interpreting it (as a sequence of discontinuous tales, or as episodes in one continuous tale) is the right one, the one Wittgenstein intended. Since his presentation of the sequence calls for both readings with equal plausibility, it is worth considering what might be learned from keeping both readings in mind throughout. Most fundamentally, such an interpretation would teach us that the integrity of any given language-game is always provisional, always open to further expansion, and that no particular expansion of a language-game is ever necessary, ever more than simply natural. For Wittgenstein, each state of a language is circumscribed, self-contained, an unbroken circle; but around every such circle another circle can be inscribed, and will be inscribed (but need not be). We might think here of the concentric rings marking the maturation of a tree; Wittgenstein offers the image of a city.

> ... ask yourself whether our language is complete;—whether it was so before the symbolism of chemistry and the notation of the infinitesimal calculus were incorporated in it; for these are, so to speak, suburbs of our language. (And how many houses or streets does it take before a town begins to be a town?) Our language can be seen as an ancient city: a maze of little streets and squares,

of old and new houses, and of houses with additions from various periods; and this surrounded by a multitude of new boroughs with straight regular streets and uniform houses. (*PI* 18)

The bracketed question draws out one of the morals encoded into a discontinuous or synchronic reading of the expansion of the builders' language-game. Each episode adds to the original tale an element of the structure or content of natural languages whose absence had raised doubts about the linguistic nature of the builders' calls, and the sequence of such episodes suggests the folly of looking for one such element as marking *the* threshold between animal noises and words; the distinction is real, but there is no sharp and single boundary, any more than there is to mark when a village becomes a town (although, of course, such a threshold could be constructed). However, the final image of the ancient city shifts our focus to a more continuous or diachronic reading of Wittgenstein's sequence. It says that language is something we inhabit, a fundamental mode of human dwelling in the world; its structures pre-exist us and will survive our departure, but they are nevertheless a human edifice and subject to a variety of unpredictable but retrospectively comprehensible modes of alteration, extension, and expansion in response to human needs and purposes (what else might the builders be building, with their pillars and slabs and beams, if not a village or a town?). Most fundamentally of all, therefore, language is essentially historical; it grows and develops through time, and its present state always carries traces of its past. From which it follows that the peculiarities of its synchronic structures—the differences between modern suburbs and ancient quarters, the grafting of modern additions onto ancient structures—can best be understood through diachronic spectacles, as fundamentally historical phenomena. In other words, to see language aright is to see that it must be viewed synchronically and diachronically at one and the same time.

THE NATURAL HISTORY OF SPEECH

15. This idea of growth, of the naturalness and the inherent historicality of growth in language, is registered in the fourth and final sense of the term 'language-game', as Wittgenstein introduces it in section 23.

But how many kinds of sentence are there? Say assertion, question and command?—There are *countless* kinds: countless different kinds of use of what we call 'symbols', 'words', 'sentences'. And this multiplicity is not something fixed, given once for all; but new types of language, new language-games, as we may say, come into existence, and others become obsolete and get forgotten. (We can get a *rough picture* of this from the changes in mathematics.)

Here the term 'language-*game*' is meant to bring into prominence the fact that the *speaking* of language is part of an activity, or of a form of life. (*PI* 23)

Here, we first see the term 'language-game' extend itself beyond primitive languages, the games of ostensive training, and the broad relation between words, actions, and world to find application to distinguishable sectors of fully fledged natural languages; the concept can be used as an analytical map of the mazes of ancient cities (its discriminations relative to our classificatory purposes rather than to any ultimate truth about urban geography), not just to invoke their primitive village origins and analogues, or their rootedness in the requirements of human practical activity in the world. But the aspect of the city of language which elicits this fourth sense of the term is not so much its existing array of regions as its capacity for constructing new ones. It marks the depth of Wittgenstein's perception that language is and must be open to the future; no given state of language, no determinate array of modes of language use, can be regarded as final or total, established beyond the sway of changing human needs and interests or new circumstances, outside the medium of time and history. On something like the contrary, speaking a natural language involves not only mastering countless different kinds of use of words and sentences, but also cultivating the capacity to create and make sense of linguistic innovation—to follow words into a future more various than, although informed by, their history.

We might see this notion of innovation as conveyed by the refraction of the three earlier senses of the term 'language-game' into its fourth—as what Wittgenstein is here drawing out of his previous emphasis upon the play of words, upon their interplay with one another and with the world. At the same time, however, this sense of the unpredictable burgeoning of a natural language modifies any desire we might have to conclude from the fourth sense of the term 'language-game' that Wittgenstein takes speaking a language to be purely a matter of mastering a number of language-games. Since it is primarily *new* uses of words and sentences that call forth the application of the term 'language-game' to the structure of natural languages, we must rather conclude that, for Wittgenstein, being able to speak a language depends not so much upon mastering any specific language-game (or set of language-games) with words as upon maintaining the desire to develop existing games in new ways and to create new games. Beyond knowing how to play this game and that game, learning to speak depends upon our inhabiting a language (and so, its history) in such a way that its improvisations, both the future trajectories of its present ways with words and the growth over time of new ways that are grafted onto the old stock, appear entirely natural.

If we reformulate this as the thought that speaking involves conjoining the natural and the historical, that speech embodies and is embodied in the natural history of its speakers, then we arrive at the words of section 25:

It is sometimes said that animals do not talk because they lack the mental capacity. And this means: 'they do not think, and that is why they do not talk.' But— they simply do not talk. Or to put it better: they do not use language—if we except the most primitive forms of language.—Commanding, questioning, recounting, chatting, are as much a part of our natural history as walking, eating, drinking, playing. (*PI* 25)

The passage tells us that, as Cavell has put it, talking is the human form of life; but it also tells us that such facts of human natural history are not subject to philosophical accountings, are neither in need of nor open to the provision or uncovering of foundations. It is not that human beings talk because they think; they simply talk. Doing things with words is as natural to us as—and naturally interwoven with—the distinctively human ways of eating and drinking, walking and playing. (And if we ask ourselves how the distinction between the natural history of human beings and animals might best be articulated, what most fruitfully emblematizes the kinship and difference between human and non-human animals that Wittgenstein marks from the outset of his book of tales by implying that human maturation moves from subjection to training (*Abrichtung*, a term which invokes the training of animals) to making requests for definitions, then it is worth recalling that Wittgenstein most commonly figures words as tools and handles—as in sections 6, 11, 12, 14, 15, 16, and so seemingly endlessly on. Both modes of imagery invite us to ask whether humanity rests in, or grows from, the human hand with its opposable thumb, and our consequent ability to take a grip on the world as well as to let it slip through our fingers. Stanley Cavell has taken further steps with these questions in a number of places.[10])

If, however, the ability and the desire to do things with words is beyond further philosophical explanation, if the impulse to give linguistic expression to ourselves is as natural as the impulses of self-preservation, perambulation, and play, then it may nonetheless prove to

---

[10] See 'Declining Decline', in Mulhall (ed.), *The Cavell Reader*, 329.

be an explanatory terminus for other phenomena. To see what this last claim might mean, we must take the double hint of Wittgenstein's characterization of the things we do with words as 'language-games', and his listing of play together with talking, eating, and walking as given aspects of human natural history, and follow up his discussion in section 31 of how ostensive definition might contribute to someone's coming to grasp how to play chess.

> I am explaining chess to someone; and I begin by pointing to a chessman and saying: 'This is the king; it can move like this . . . and so on.'—In this case we shall say: the words 'This is the king' (or 'This is called the "king"') are a definition only if the learner already knows what a piece in a game is. That is, if he has already played other games, or has watched other people playing 'and understood'—*and similar things*. Further only under these conditions will he be able to ask relevantly in the course of learning the game: 'What do you call this?'—that is, this piece in a game.
>
> We may say: only someone who already knows how to do something with it can significantly ask a name. (*PI* 31)

We can teach someone how to play chess by identifying which chess pieces are which and explaining how they move in the game; but he will learn something from our explanation—he will learn the game of chess—only if he already knows what a piece in a game is. Note that Wittgenstein does not say: 'only if he already knows what a piece in *the game of chess* is'; the knowledge presupposed by attempted ostensive definitions of chess is not (or not only) a knowledge of the grammar of chess pieces, of the kinds of role pieces happen to have in that particular game, but rather a knowledge of the grammar of pieces in a game, of the kinds of role pieces generally have in the playing of games that involve pieces, and so a knowledge of what it is to play a game. Only someone who appreciates what playing is, for whom the playing of games forms part of his natural history or form of life, can significantly ask (and so usefully be told) how to play a particular game.

With this analogy in mind, we can approach the putatively parallel case of language (emphasized by Wittgenstein's section 31 comparison of the shape of chess pieces with the sound or shape of words) by looking at his treatment of 'describing' in section 24. There he reminds us of how many different kinds of thing are called 'descriptions'—descriptions of the position of a body in Cartesian space, of facial expressions, of sensations of touch, of a mood; and this reminder itself recalls section 23's open-ended list of the variety of language-games or kinds of use of words. By analogy with the chess learner, someone could learn how to play one specific language-game of description only if he knew what kinds of thing we call descriptions, what it is to describe something (as opposed to, say, testing a hypothesis or making up a story)—and so, only if describing is a part of his natural history, one aspect of his life with words. This aligns describing with commanding, questioning, recounting, and chatting; and of course, philosophical accounts of each of these modes of language use could be constructed along similar lines. One might say that knowing how to give orders or ask questions is a matter of knowing how to do specific kinds of things with words, and that that ability presupposes a more general or basic awareness of what it is to do things with words—in short, of what it is to speak.

And with this, we can return to Wittgenstein's preferred discourse of language-games. Once again on analogy with the chess learner, we can say that, for Wittgenstein, learning which words are which in a particular language-game presupposes not just a knowledge of the particular posts at which the words of this specific game are to be stationed, but also a knowledge of what kinds of role words generally have in the playing of language-games, and so a knowledge of what it is to play a language-game. In short, only someone who knows what it is to do things with words, only someone for whom speaking or talking forms part of his natural repertoire, can significantly ask (and so usefully be told) how to do something particular with words. When Wittgenstein tells us that 'to imagine a language is to imagine a form of life' (*PI* 19), he means 'a form of life with language'; what has to be accepted—the given, so one could say—is that human forms of life are forms of life with words (see *PI* 226).

This conclusion crystallizes a central moral of the gradual expansion of focus that is effected during the course of the first movement of Wittgenstein's text—the way in which an initial handful of words becomes embedded in a more differentiated vocabulary, which becomes embedded in a more complex array of sentences, speech-acts, and practical activity within increasingly complex worlds, which is in turn framed against a sketch of the natural history of human beings. It is as if our desire to imagine those initial, truncated calls as words can truly be satisfied only by imagining a progressively broader and more complex setting for them, and ultimately only by bedding them down in the linguistically inflected repertoire of human natural history. (We might here recall Wittgenstein's comparison of words with the handles in the cabin of a locomotive (*PI* 12): the handle of a brake-lever is what it is not just because of connections effected in the engine, but because that engine powers the locomotive of a train that runs together with other trains on a system of tracks, signals, and stations in accordance with timetables that integrate it with other forms of transport and with the desires and necessities of everyday human life.) The lesson of these unstoppable literary expansions is that what makes a word a word is not its individual correspondence with an object, or the existence of a technique of its use considered in isolation, or its contrasts with other words, or its suitability as one component of a menu of sentences and speech-acts; it depends in the last analysis upon its taking its place as one element in one of the countless kinds of ways in which creatures like us say and do things with words. Inside that unsurveyably complex context, individual words function without let or hindrance, their ties to specific objects beyond question; but outside it, they are nothing but breath and ink, not even the sounds or shapes of words.

GAMES AND LANGUAGE

16. At the same time, however, this moral also gives us a perspective on a deep anxiety about Wittgenstein's deployment of the analogy between language and games to which Rush Rhees gives powerful expression in the following passage: 'I have wanted to say that learning to speak is not learning *how* to speak or how to do anything. And it is not learning the mastery of a technique . . . it is not like learning the meaning of this or that expression . . . not like going on with the use of any particular expression or set of expressions, although of course it includes that' (WB 82). The general thrust of these words might perhaps be summarized as follows. Rhees believes that Wittgenstein intends to utilize the idea of 'mastery of various language games' as part of a general explanation or philosophical account of what it is to master a language, or to speak—to suggest that learning to speak is a matter of learning to play various games with words; and he regards this suggestion as distorting the true nature of human speech.

We shall return in a moment to the question of what Rhees actually takes to be the true nature of human speech. But we can already appreciate that the analogy we have just seen Wittgenstein draw between playing games and speaking a natural language runs directly counter to Rhees's interpretation of Wittgenstein's intentions. His discussion of ostensive definition in learning chess implies that mastery of specific language-games presupposes that speaking—the general impulse and capacity to do things with words—is part of the natural repertoire of human beings, and so lies beyond the reach of any philosophical accounting of the kind Rhees imagines. Wittgenstein's talk of language-games is therefore not an attempt to reduce speaking to the ability to play a number of specific games with words; it is rather an attempt to show that being able to talk (and so being able to say specific things) is a matter of being able to play games with words—being able to appreciate the play and interplay of words with one another and with the world, to accommodate the interplay of the human capacity to talk with the human capacity for play.

17. Rhees's seminal article makes a number of other criticisms of Wittgenstein's analogy between using language and playing games. One of them emerges from the following passages:

If there were someone who could not carry on a conversation, who had no idea of asking questions or making any comment, then I do not think we should say he could speak. Now one reason why a conversation is not like playing a game together is that the point of the various moves and counter-moves is within the game. Whereas we may learn from a conversation and from what is said in it.

I want to contrast (a) the external relations of the moves in a game, and (b) the internal relations of the remarks people make to one another. 'Internal relations' has a technical sense, so it may be misleading. But it does suggest 'connexions of meaning', and this is the point here. It cannot be reduced to connexions in a game.

The point about chess, for instance, is that the pieces are furnished to you—you do not have to find them or decide what they shall be. (WB 80, 81)

The precise import of these passages may be unclear, but their general thrust seems evident. Rhees is struck by a number of important disanalogies between speaking and playing games—disanalogies which might well seriously distort our understanding of what it is to talk, and to learn to talk. In particular, he takes it that games are not only rule-governed but rule-bound; the pieces of the game and their legitimate uses are fixed in advance of any particular game, and determine the moves that can be made by the players, and the kind of course that the game may take. These rules make the game what it is; but they also keep the game external to the players and to the ordinary business of living—the game does not have anything to do with, it does not get its sense from, what happens in the rest of the players' lives. Further, in knowing how to play a game (or a number of games), there is no such thing as growth in understanding—the kind of understanding that can develop only in time, through the acquisition of experience, and that is manifest in coming to see the point of saying things, the sometimes entirely surprising ways in which remarks hang together with one another in relation to the subject of the dialogue and with other aspects of the life of those engaging in the conversation. It is this dialogic dimension to speaking which Rhees takes to be occluded by Wittgenstein's general tendency to talk of language-games, and so to think of speaking as a matter of playing games with words.

However, the value of the analogy between language and games obviously depends upon which aspects of playing games are held to be analogous to speaking a language; and this question is critically affected by which kinds of games we take to be exemplary of games-playing in general. It seems clear from Rhees's remarks that when he thinks of games he has such things as ring-o'-roses or pass the parcel in the forefront of his mind, or at least that much of what he says about other games (such as chess)—and in particular, the way he views the role of rules in such games—is shaped by reference to such primitive instances of games-playing. And this seriously distorts his sense of the particular aspects of games in which Wittgenstein might actually be interested.

It is worth noting, for example, that when Wittgenstein does actually talk about how rules function in games, he appears to have a remarkably pluralist picture of the matter. In section 31, he tells us that

One can also imagine someone's having learnt the game without ever learning or formulating rules. He might have learnt quite simple games first, by watching, and have progressed to more and more complicated ones . . . we shall only say that [an ostensive definition] tells him the use [of a chess piece], if the place is already prepared. And in this case it is so, not because the person to whom we give the explanation already knows rules, but because in another sense he is already master of a game. (*PI* 31)

Here, there seems to be at least an implication that mastery of a game is not always a matter of mastering (and hence submitting to being mastered in one's play by) definite rules. In sections 53 and 54 Wittgenstein further tells us that 'what we call a rule of a language-game may have very different roles in the game'; and by asking us to recall 'the kinds of case where we say that a game is played according to a definite rule' (among which he includes cases in which 'a rule is employed neither in the teaching nor in the game itself; nor is it set down in a list of rules'), he also invites us to recall that there are kinds of case where we would say that a game is *not* played according to definite rules— perhaps because the game is not rule-governed, perhaps because the rules governing it are not definite (definitively formulated, fixed, and unequivocal).

These remarks may induce some initial disquiet with Rhees's comments; but we need to get down to particular cases. Take the game of ring-o'-roses: about this, virtually everything Rhees claims is true—the game is not just rule-governed but rule-bound, with every legitimate move dictated in advance, and no room for any exercises of skill or talent, or for the development of understanding. (Even here, however, once we are reminded of the game's possible roots in the period of the Black Death and its aftermath, we might at least hesitate to claim that its structure and satisfactions bore no relation to the rest of human life.) But matters are significantly different if we focus on a more complex game such as chess—one of Wittgenstein's favourite examples. In particular, this game is governed but not bound by rules; or more precisely, we can (following Cavell[11]) distinguish a number of different types of rules by which the game is governed. There are, in fact, at least four: defining rules ('A bishop moves along the diagonal'), regulating rules ('When a player touches a piece, she must either . . .'), principles ('Develop your pieces as early as possible'), and maxims ('Develop knights before bishops'). The first (and perhaps the second) type of rule tells us what must be done if we are to play the game at all; the third and fourth types tell us how we ought to play the game, what is involved in playing the game well. Both kinds of rule are essential to mastery of the game—someone who knows the defining rules of chess but lacks any grasp of its strategic and tactical principles does not know how to play chess. But the principles of the game obviously do not dictate every move that is made—a sufficiently competent player can break them if she sees a more efficient or elegant way of achieving her goal; and neither do its defining or regulating rules—for not all, and not even most, of the actions which take place in playing a game are determined or required by its defining rules. Every move must of course be in accordance with those rules; but they do not prescribe her every move—leaving her with no licit alternative.

This is why such games (competitive games of skill) can and must be practised. But it has far more significant consequences, as Cavell spells out:

Part of what gives games their special quality . . . is that within them what we *must* do is (ideally) completely specified and radically marked off from considerations of what we ought to (or should not) do. It is as though within the prosecution of a game, we are set free to concentrate all of our consciousness and energy on the very human quests for utility and style: if the moves and rules

---

[11] See *CR* chs XI and XII.

can be *taken for granted*, then we can give ourselves over totally to doing what will win, and win applause. (CR 308)

Perhaps the fullest expression of the way games permit the achievement of freedom through subjection to law is to be found in competitive team games such as football. To be sure, even in such contexts the end of the players' endeavours is fixed in a way that does not hold in ordinary discourse or conversation; their aim is to score more goals than the opposing team—to win. But the actions that, say, the players of Manchester United take in pursuit of this aim are not bound by rules; they must accord with the defining rules of the game, but within the space those rules mark out their moves are not fixed or determined. On the contrary, their achievement as players is precisely to combine the fullest possible development of certain strategic skills with the capacity to innovate, to produce the most unexpectedly efficient and unprecedentedly elegant means towards the end to which they have given themselves over. At their best, such players construct unremitting patterns of quick passing, searching runs off the ball, closing down space in the opposition midfield, speedy deployment of the offside trap—all the principles that practice can make perfect; but those patterns are there precisely to provide the conditions for their own disruption—by the mazy runs of Giggs, by Solskjær's instinctively predatory shots on goal from any angle, by Beckham's capacity to execute passes that no one else even sees as possible. When such a team meets another of equal talent, and both perform to their fullest potential—perceiving the strengths and weaknesses of one another's tactics, improvising responses to those tactics, and then to those responses, with certain fluctuating one-on-one contests emerging as pivotal—then the image of a conversation seems invited rather than negated by the resulting passages of play.

What, then, of Rhees's claim that the rule-governed nature of games forbids the growth of understanding, and separates the game from the players and from their ordinary lives off the field? It seems plain that, over a career, a player's understanding of the game of football can deepen and broaden, and that what he proves capable of doing on a football pitch—particularly under the most intense pressure—can expand both his fellow players' and the spectators' understanding of what is possible in football, and so what it might mean to play the game and to play it well. But perhaps the kind of understanding of which Rhees speaks is not an understanding of the game being played (although, if playing the game really is like a conversation, its primary subject would of course be the nature or essence of the game itself), but of life beyond the game. Then it may be worth pointing out that, as

Cavell has argued, in playing games we discover how particular combinations of spatial, physical, and temporal constraints reveal the limits
of certain human capacities; without them, and without those dedicated
to their specific exploration, we would not have known those limits, or
the possibilities they determine—we would not have known certain distinctively human limits.[12]

Or we might ask just how game-specific are the qualities of character needed for achieving excellence in any given game. It is a com-
monplace that, beyond the talents that distinguish footballers from
good cricketers or good marathon runners, they have certain physical
and spiritual virtues in common—athleticism, intellectual acumen,
perseverance, self-command, honesty with oneself and one's team-
mates, courage, and so on. A sportsman's ability to develop those
excellences is surely not entirely separable from growth in their understanding of themselves as persons, and of the relation of those character traits to problems of life outside the sporting arena. The thought
here is not that pre-eminent sportsmen are more virtuous on or off the
pitch than less talented people; it is rather that the qualities and achievements that human beings celebrate in sport themselves illuminate and
perhaps alter our sense of human excellence more generally, that sporting quests are part of the human quest for self-development and self-
understanding.

The natural emergence of such concepts as 'spiritual qualities',
'virtue', and 'quest' in gaming contexts is far from coincidental. It is,
for example, what leads Alasdair MacIntyre to ground his account of
the virtues in a conception of the goods internal to practices, and to
deploy as a central example of such practices the game of chess.[13] Mac-
Intyre's account foregrounds the fact that participation in particular
practices (roughly, complex forms of human cooperative activity) makes
it possible for human beings to achieve goods that cannot otherwise be
attained (unlike money or fame), on condition that they develop the
specific excellences necessary to do so. Chess, for example, is not simply
a means of amusement, but a context within which certain particular
refinements of the intellect and the will can alone be developed, with
the help of less context-specific excellences such as truthfulness, courage,
honesty, and so on. Both the individual participant's understanding of
the practice's requirements, and that of the practice's most capable expo-
nents, presuppose development over time; ultimately, for MacIntyre, a
practice or set of practices forms the core of a human tradition, and is

---

[12] See CR 120.   [13] See *After Virtue* (Duckworth: London, 1981).

possessed of a history within which its conception of what excellence within the practice might consist in alters and deepens (or declines) over time, through the experience of contesting and refining its core conceptions and achievements.

MacIntyre's (Aristotelian) name for the excellences that such traditions make possible and presuppose is 'virtues'; and his choice of that term is intended precisely to suggest that morality can be perceived as involving far more than promise-keeping and categorical imperatives— that living the good life for human beings certainly involves questions of how to treat one's neighbour, but that the excellences of character which must be brought to bear on such questions can themselves be developed, studied, and celebrated in contexts that are not obviously moral in nature. In this respect, the artificiality of the spaces or conditions within which games are played, which Rhees takes as a sign of their separateness from human life, is precisely what makes possible the internal relations between the excellences that games are designed to cultivate and celebrate, and the kinds of problems in life with which Rhees thinks that the essentially dialogical character of human speech is primarily concerned. Once again, then, the views that Rhees feels compelled to develop in opposition to Wittgenstein's analogy between speaking and playing games are in fact the ones that can perfectly naturally be developed from that very analogy. As so often in philosophy, the example is everything.

FAMILY RESEMBLANCE

18. Perhaps the most famous dimension of Wittgenstein's comparison between language and games lies in the discussion that inaugurates the third phase or chapter of the *Investigations* (after he has reapplied the method of section 2 to the *Theaetetus* account of names and simples, imagining a language which serves to describe combinations of coloured squares), a discussion inaugurated by an interlocutor's accusation that Wittgenstein has so far failed to confront the very question that gave him so much pain in earlier years—that of specifying the essence of language. Wittgenstein's response is disarming. 'And this is true.—Instead of producing something common to all that we call language, I am saying that these phenomena have no one thing in common which makes us use the same word for all,—but that they are *related* to one another in many different ways. And it is because of this relationship,

or these relationships, that we call them all "language"' (*PI* 65). The analogy he chooses to illustrate this kind of relatedness is, of course, that of games. He claims that there is in fact no quality or property that is common to all the various things we call games, and in virtue of which we apply the same term to each one, but rather a complicated network of overlapping and criss-crossing similarities, sometimes very general, sometimes very specific. 'I can think of no better expression to characterize these similarities than "family resemblances"; for the various resemblances between members of a family: build, features, colour of eyes, gait, temperament, etc. etc. overlap and criss-cross in the same way.—And I shall say: "games" form a family' (*PI* 67).

It is worth noting just how little Wittgenstein is actually claiming here. He says that some concepts (two in particular) have a family resemblance structure, not that many, most, or all concepts do, nor that many, most, or all concepts must. In other words, the image of family resemblance is not an answer to the question that the interlocutor raises, but an attempt to deflect or derail it by displaying its indebtedness to a tendentious presupposition. For accusing Wittgenstein of a failure to tell us what the essence of language is, what is common to everything that we call 'language', makes sense only if the application of this particular concept is determined by the presence or absence of a specific common feature or property; if, in fact, close attention to how the term is used suggests that its application is not so determined, then the accusation of failure is misdirected. What Wittgenstein detects in his interlocutor's impatience is the influence of a false necessity—a misplaced sense of what must and what cannot be the case with respect to the use of a particular word, and with respect to the nature of words or human language more generally. His image of family resemblance is designed to break up that false sense of necessity, to liberate us from one picture of language by providing us with another.

Another of Rush Rhees's grounds for objecting to Wittgenstein's comparison of language with games arises at just this point.

Suppose you say that 'speaking' covers a family of related cases, just as 'game' does. And suppose you then say that language—or the language we speak—*is* a family of language games. Here you would not be saying simply that the games are various instances of what we call language; but that *a* language is a family of language games: that this is the kind of unity a language has. (WB 71)

As Rhees himself sometimes recognizes, however, this speculative interpretation attributes rather more to Wittgenstein than the relevant texts justify. To begin with, it is at best misleading baldly to state that

Wittgenstein thinks of language-games as 'various instances of what we call language'—as if they are obviously central and unproblematic examples of the application of that term. After all, 'language-game' is precisely a technical term, a coinage that registers on its very face that the term 'language' is here undergoing a kind of transformation or creative projection—even though its transformative coupling with the term 'game' is certainly intended to cast light on the nature of language 'proper'. What Wittgenstein in fact calls 'language-games' are either primitive forms of linguistic activity, the kinds of games we play when teaching children to speak, or analytically separated fragments of ordinary language. In the first and second cases the primitiveness of the phenomenon is explicitly acknowledged to problematize the applicability of the term 'language', and in the third case it would surely be more natural to talk of language-games as (artificially segregated) *parts* of language, not instances of it.

Furthermore, and more importantly, it is not at all obvious that the key purpose of the image of family resemblance is to claim that 'a language is a family of language-games'. Here, Rhees appears to run together the idea of language-games and the idea of family resemblance in a manner that Wittgenstein's texts do not license. Plainly, if both 'language' and 'game' are family resemblance concepts, then so must be the concept of a 'language-game'; so we can legitimately say that the various examples (and presumably the various senses) of 'language-games' form a family. It is also true that one of Wittgenstein's uses of the term 'language-game' is as an analytical tool to apply to the structure of a natural language; but in this respect, it means only that we can for certain purposes treat portions of that language as self-contained practical operations with words. As he puts the matter in section 130: 'The language-games are rather set up as *objects of comparison* which are meant to throw light on the facts of our language by way not only of similarities, but also of dissimilarities.' There is plainly no ontological claim here, no implication that the language really consists of, or is constituted by, a number of such components; the method of language-games involves imaginative construction rather than modelling to a first approximation, and it comes with a clear warning to attend to the dissimilarities which inevitably result from applying such a method. There cannot, accordingly, be any necessity to think of a language as comprising a family of language-games.

Certainly, Wittgenstein never *says* that a language is a family of language-games, or indeed a family of anything. And when he says that the concept 'language', just like the concept 'game', is a family resemblance concept, that means that the various things we call 'language' or 'languages' form a family, not that any one such thing, any particular instance of what we might call language, is made up of elements which themselves form a family. The most natural way to take his claim is made explicit in a much later remark. 'I want to say: It is *primarily* the apparatus of our ordinary language, of our word-language, that we call language; and then other things by analogy or comparability with this' (*PI* 494). In other words, the family resemblance structure of the term 'language' will have such phenomena as natural languages (English, German) and their analytically separable parts (our language for colour of shape, the Inuit language for types of snow) among its central cases; but it will also include real and imagined instances of more or less primitive languages, of artificial languages (Esperanto, BASIC II), of systems of communication used by animals or children, of non-linguistic modes of signification (clothes, music), and so on. It is these various instances that form a family—not the various components into which we might wish to divide any single instance. Once again, then, there seems no reason to think that this specific use of the analogy between language and games must lead to the trouble that Rhees fears.

19. One of Bede Rundle's recent criticisms of the idea of family resemblance may, however, appear more formidable. Focusing primarily on the concept of 'game' rather than that of 'language', he argues that no concept could possibly have the kind of structure that the idea of 'family resemblance' invokes. For according to that notion, two items could fall under the same concept and yet have no features whatever in common, without the concept being ambiguous or lacking in unity of meaning; but 'if we had two games which really did have nothing of relevance in common, then we should surely be prepared to say without further ado that the common description could not apply to both univocally . . . if a term behaved as Wittgenstein considers "game" to behave, then . . . we should simply have to ascribe more than one meaning to that term'.[14]

Rundle's sense of necessity here clearly reflects his view that he is simply reminding us of the grammar of our concept of 'univocity'; any situation in which a word applies to two items that have no common feature is one in which the criterion for that word's having different meanings has been satisfied. But in reality, this necessity appears false or misplaced; for he fails to distinguish between a case in which two such instances were linked by a chain of overlapping resemblances that

[14] See *Wittgenstein and Contemporary Philosophy of Language* (Oxford: Blackwell, 1990), 49–50.

passes from one to the other via intermediate cases, and a case in which no such chain is to be found. The latter case would clearly make the concept of univocity inapplicable; but is the same so obviously true of the former case?

Let us take, as an example, the word 'picture', which we use to denote abstract paintings, representational paintings, and films (i.e. motion pictures). Although abstract paintings and films each have something in common with representational paintings, there seem to be no features common to a Jackson Pollock canvas and a projected image of Humphrey Bogart; and yet we have no inclination to say that the word 'picture' has one meaning when used in a conversation about *Casablanca* and another when the talk turns to 'Lavender Mist'. To be sure, if someone were to invent a language-game from scratch in which a single term were to be used so as to pick out such seemingly diverse items, we might find the point of the practice rather puzzling; but if we see its structure as the result of a process of historical development, the puzzle dissolves. In the case of 'picture', the original focus on representational painting naturally licenses an extension of the term's use to photographs (understood as another sort of representation) and thence to motion pictures; and developments in painting also made natural a different extension of the term to include canvases of a non-representational sort.

In other words, the key to dissolving Rundle's puzzle is to see language in its historical dimension. A purely synchronic perspective on a family resemblance structure will make it almost impossible to understand how or why a univocal concept can be forged through a chain of overlapping resemblances; but when it is seen as the outcome of diachronic filiation, as emerging in response to technological and artistic changes in human forms of life and along routes of shared natural reactions, then it becomes the very reverse of surprising—not perhaps predictable, but certainly retrospectively comprehensible. And this failure to see the diachronic in the synchronic is not just a failure to absorb one of the key lessons of Wittgenstein's notion of a language-game; it is also a literary failure—a failure properly to take account of the implications of the imagery Wittgenstein deploys in attempting to make this point. For of course, family resemblances hold not just across space but across time; a son inherits his father's build, a daughter her grandmother's eyes—and even when the similarity holds between two members of the same generation, say a brother and sister, it holds because they share a common ancestor, from whom their distinctive gait or temperament is derived (whether by nature or nurture).

It is, in fact, difficult to think of a more appropriate figure than that of a family to capture Wittgenstein's sense of the embeddedness of language in time and worldly circumstance, its rootedness in the complex interplay between nature and culture (as ties of blood are legally or ceremonially bound into those of other families, their intermarriage bequeathing new possibilities of resemblance and difference to their offspring), its dependence upon the bedrock of natural history. And of course, such graftings and renewals produce an inherently unpredictable distribution of resemblances; we cannot tell which offspring will resemble which parent, and in which respects. In this way, the notion of family resemblance encodes the ideas of innovation and generation, of futurity and openness, that we have seen to be central in Wittgenstein's general working out of his comparison of games with language, and in particular in his emphasis upon the play and interplay of words with one another and with their world.

The discussion of family resemblance makes this point explicit in the very long section 79, which investigates the meaning of the name 'Moses'. Setting aside for the moment the important worry about whether it ever makes sense to talk of proper names as having a meaning other than a purely etymological one (a worry that might in large part be defused by noting that the whole discussion is framed in terms set up by Russell and never explicitly endorsed by Wittgenstein), it seems plain that the main purpose of Wittgenstein's lengthy remarks is to drive home the fact that the word 'Moses' does not have a fixed meaning.

Has the name 'Moses' got a fixed and unequivocal use for me in all possible cases? Is it not the case that I have, so to speak, a whole series of props [i.e. beliefs about his activities and accomplishments] in readiness, and am ready to lean on one if another should be taken from under me and vice versa? . . .

And this can be expressed like this: I use the name 'N' without a fixed meaning. (But that detracts as little from its usefulness, as it detracts from that of a table that it stands on four legs instead of three and so sometimes wobbles.) (*PI* 79)

The furniture imagery is taken further in section 80, where Wittgenstein points out that our understanding of the word 'chair' does not encompass rules for every possible application of it (e.g. when what appears to be a chair repeatedly disappears and then reappears—it looks right, but could we sit on such a thing?). The general point, however, is clear: when we know how to use words, we do not know in advance precisely what we will do with them when we encounter new circumstances and situations; our grasp of their meaning does not and could not budget for every possible turn that our life with those words might take. And that flexibility or tolerance, the temper of our words, is not only not a flaw in them, but something without which they would not be what we mean by 'words'—units of meaning that can be seen to recur across time and history, and so in unpredictably new circumstances. The equivocal rhythms governing the recurrence of family resemblances conjure up a similar vision of the improvisatory interplay of culture and nature; and so does Wittgenstein's idea of playing games itself—a point that he deliberately underlines.

Doesn't the analogy between language and games throw light here? We can easily imagine people amusing themselves in a field by playing with a ball so as to start various existing games, but playing many without finishing them and in between throwing the ball aimlessly into the air, chasing one another with the ball and bombarding one another for a joke and so on. And now someone says: The whole time they are playing a ball-game and following definite rules at every throw.

   And is there not also the case where we play and—make up the rules as we go along? And there is even one where we alter them—as we go along. (*PI* 83)

An analytical eye might find some illumination in artificially distinguishing certain segments of these people's play from other segments, and considering those segments as forming a family. But Wittgenstein's tale as it stands primarily emphasizes the seamless but unpredictable fluidity of their actions, the diachronic process of play rather than its synchronic phases: and they certainly don't move on from one to another mode of activity with their ball in any way that the notion of family resemblance could hope to capture. Wittgenstein's point is rather that their play involves moves within each phase of play, shifts between phases of play, and the creation of new modes of play; and that, although some aspects of their activity might involve the following or the creation of rules, these should not be thought of as fixed, unequivocal, behaviour-determining norms. Rather, their actions are primarily shaped by the ebb and flow of shared, natural inclinations, interests, and desires. His implicit claim is that exactly the same is true of speaking, of the unpredictably interwoven modes of talk that make up the human form of life. As parables go, it is difficult to imagine one more attuned to Rush Rhees's vision of what is involved in speaking a language.

SUBLIMING THE LOGIC OF OUR LANGUAGE

20. In section 89 Wittgenstein suggests that his examination of family resemblance involves us in a problem: 'In what sense is logic something

sublime?' But this question itself raises the question of what Wittgenstein might mean here by 'sublime'; and the ensuing sections offer little in the way of direct explications of that apparently technical term. Instead, they are crowded with imagery and metaphor—interlinked chains of figuration that attempt to capture our sense of the peculiar character, the queerness, of logic. We must therefore follow out the logic of those chains.

The first link in the first chain is that of depth. '. . . logical investigation . . . seeks to see to the bottom of things . . . It takes its rise . . . from an urge to understand the basis, or essence, of everything empirical' (*PI* 89). Once a picture of essence as the basis or foundation of the empirical arises, we will inevitably 'feel as if we had to penetrate phenomena' (*PI* 90); and any analysis we might make of the language in which we talk about phenomena will be treated as if 'our usual forms of expression were, essentially, unanalysed; as if there were something hidden in them that had to be brought to light' (*PI* 91). We thus picture essence as 'something that lies within, which we see when we look into the thing, and which an analysis digs out' (*PI* 92). Consequently, the form our problem now assumes is '*the essence is hidden from us*' (*PI* 92). We might think of this as the sublime understood as the subliminal—that which lies below the threshold of ordinary awareness.

But the sublime also contains the idea of sublimation or refinement—the process of extracting a substance from a solution, separating it out in solid form by (for example) heating the solution beyond a certain threshold. Wittgenstein hits off this idea by talking of our trying 'to purify, to sublime, the signs' of our language (*PI* 94). He elaborates by saying that logic 'is prior to all experience, must run through all experience; no empirical cloudiness or uncertainty can be allowed to affect it—It must rather be of the purest crystal. But this crystal does not appear as an abstraction; but as something concrete, indeed, as the most concrete, as it were the *hardest* thing there is' (*PI* 97). Here, the priority of logic to the empirical or phenomenal realm which it nevertheless informs is pictured as the pollution or dilution of logic by the world of everyday experience; we must distil its crystalline forms from the impurities in which it is suspended.

But the idea of the sublime, as the notion of refinement implies, also embodies a notion of sublimity—a sense of exaltation or excellence, of being elevated to or beyond a certain threshold. That which is sublime produces an overwhelming sense of awe and reverence; Romanticism interprets it as a matter of standing at the very limits of human experience, being made aware of the finitude of human understanding and thereby of that which passes beyond it. Wittgenstein's chain of imagery incorporates this idea of sublimity when he tells us that 'The ideal, as we think of it, is unshakeable. You can never get outside it; you must always turn back. There is no outside; outside you cannot breathe' (*PI* 103). The semi-colon of that last sentence marks a critical metaphorical shift, delineating the boundary at which our idea of the ideal as an uttermost limit transmutes into an idea of the ideal as a limitation, as fencing us off from something—even if only a void inimical to human life and its conditions. Is there no outside, or just no outside for us (living, breathing creatures)? A little earlier the limits of logic conjured up an image of a man locked up fast in a room (*PI* 99); his imprisonment is unbreachable, but it can be imprisonment only if it deprives him of a life outside the room's walls. The same ambivalence reappears later, when Wittgenstein pictures us as imagining 'that we have to describe extreme subtleties, which in turn we are after all quite unable to describe with the means at our disposal. We feel as if we had to repair a torn spider's web with our fingers' (*PI* 106). Are the subtleties of logic beyond description, or just beyond our present means, or even our utmost powers, of description? For Wittgenstein, our sense of the sublimity of logic takes us 'on to slippery ice where there is no friction and so in a certain sense the conditions are ideal, but also, just because of that, we are unable to walk' (*PI* 107). The purity and emptiness of the void makes it humanly uninhabitable; but ice is, after all, not nothing, not a void—it merely refuses human locomotion.

Throughout this third chain of images, the sublime appears as antithetical to the human, threatening suffocation, muteness, and paralysis; but its threshold also appears as a barrier or constraint, an unshakeable prison wall or a clinging web—quite as if the very inhumanity of the sublime seduces us, as if transcending the human condition amounted to an infinitely desirable purification or refinement of ourselves. Wittgenstein's other two chains of imagery also advert to ideas of imprisonment; for the sublime understood as the subliminal, and the sublime understood as sublimation, ask us to think of logic as hidden or imprisoned in the empirical or the ordinary, as needing to be dug or crystallized out of the circumstances of ordinary human life. But if we think of logic as imprisoned in the ordinary, and ourselves as imprisoned by logic, then we must think of ourselves too as imprisoned in the ordinary; so attempting to dig logic out from the everyday will at once symbolize and realize our attempts to enact our own freedom from ordinariness. For if we penetrate the hiddenness of logic, if we bring it back into our grasp, then we at least bring within our view that which it places beyond our grasp; we surely cannot bring the limits of human reality into focus without at least glimpsing the sublimely icy vacuum that lies beyond that threshold. And by the same token, if we can over-come the idea of logic as imprisoned in the ordinary, we might thereby overcome our sense of our own sense of imprisonment in the everyday. If we can overcome our sense of the sublimity of logic, then we might cease to picture logic as liminal, and so as demarcating that which is within from that which is beyond human experience. Would this be empiricism or realism in philosophy? Could such a distinction even be articulated in terms of a conception of experience from which the picture of inner and outer has been removed?

21. In what way does this diagnosis of our sense of the sublimity of logic arise from the previous discussion of family resemblance? How does that discussion precipitate the articulation of just these fantasies of purity and penetration? Wittgenstein's implied answer to this question brings out a further consequence of those fantasies.

> We see that what we call 'sentence' and 'language' has not the formal unity that I imagined, but is the family of structures more or less related to one another.—But what becomes of logic now? Its rigour seems to be giving way here.—But in that case doesn't logic altogether disappear?—For how can it lose its rigour? Of course not by our bargaining any of its rigour out of it.—*The preconceived idea* of crystalline purity can only be removed by turning our whole examination round. (*PI* 108)

The idea of family resemblance subverts the idea of rigour that is embodied in our sense of the crystalline purity of logic—subverts it, of course, in the name of a reconception of logical rigour, not a rejection or dissolution of it. As we saw earlier, Wittgenstein suggests that, once we sublimate logic from its empirical context, it appears as the hardest, most concrete thing there is—its rigour a kind of super-rigidity (*PI* 97). It is as if we picture ourselves as having extracted the skeleton of an animal. The creature's bone structure happily supports the mass of the body in which it is ordinarily embedded, because it is itself supported by the surrounding tissue; but when that flesh falls away, the skeleton will collapse unless pinned and wired. So when we try to imagine logic outside its empirical contexts, and hence as entirely self-supporting, we can preserve our conviction in its rigour only by picturing it as a super-latively rigid mechanism or structure, as having a hyperbolic exactness of definition. And when we then contemplate our ordinary life with words, which we know to be in order as it is since those words have sense (*PI* 98), we think of that order as a logical skeleton underpinning our ordinary life from within, an underlying mechanism empowering the everyday—but with the hyperbolic rigidity we take ourselves to have discovered that it must have.

It is worth noting here that we will not have overcome the impulse to sublime logic simply by returning it to its empirical contexts and attributing its rigidity to the support of those contexts; for if we picture this return as a matter of restoring the independent, hidden framework of the empirical, then we continue to think of essence as prior to or independent of the empirical, as subliminal and so as a candidate for sublimation. After all, we could imagine logic as something extractable from the ordinary, as open to study outside that context and hence as hyperbolically rigid, only if we already pictured logic as the skeleton of the ordinary, as the hidden armature of its flesh and blood. So attempts to counter the subliming of logic by arguing that its rigidity in reality derives from its being embedded within the body of the ordinary will actually reaffirm the deeper picture which permits the hyperbolicized picture of logic's rigidity, and so will amount to maintaining the sublimation of logic. True desublimation requires that logic be thought of not as separable from, and not as suspended in, the empirical but as ultimately indistinguishable from it—as pervading our life with words rather than existing as a separable element within it which makes that life possible. We will return to this.

However, my immediate concern is with our hyperbolic sense of the rigidity of logic. For from that perspective, the informal unity of family resemblance concepts will appear vague and indefinite, and will therefore threaten to bargain away the rigour of logic entirely.

'But still, it isn't a game, if there is some vagueness *in the rules*'.—But *does* this prevent its being a game?—'Perhaps you'll call it a game, but at any rate it certainly isn't a perfect game.' This means: it has impurities, and what I am interested in at present is the pure article.—But I want to say: we misunderstand the role of the ideal in our language. That is to say: we too should call it a game, only we are dazzled by the ideal and therefore fail to see the actual use of the word 'game' clearly.

We want to say that there can't be any vagueness in logic. The idea now absorbs us, that the ideal *'must'* be found in reality. Meanwhile we do not as yet see *how* it occurs there, nor do we understand the nature of this 'must'. We think it must be in reality; for we think we already see it there.

The strict and clear rules of the logical structure of propositions appear to us as something in the background—hidden in the medium of the understanding. (*PI* 100–2)

This is why Wittgenstein's earlier discussion of family resemblance concentrates so intensively on the question of whether a family resemblance concept is vague, inexact, or indefinite. For the overlapping structures of family resemblance most fundamentally offend against the assumption that 'if anyone utters a sentence and *means* or *understands* it he is operating a calculus according to definite rules' (*PI* 81). In other words, this conflict brings to the surface a set of fantasies about the meaningfulness of words as dependent upon the existence of rules for every possible context of their application (*PI* 80), rules which stop up all the cracks through which doubt might conceivably creep in (*PI* 84), rules whose exactness is thought of as absolute—and thus as entirely independent of any human goal or purpose (*PI* 88). Once again, of course, Wittgenstein's aim is not to deny that language-games have rules, or to demonstrate that their logic is imprecise or inexact; he wants rather to remind us that judgements about exactness are empty if they remain entirely unrelated to specific human goals or purposes, and that, when family resemblance concepts are so related, they can be seen to have all the precision for which we could intelligibly wish. By going on to locate these fantasies of precision as expressions of a deep desire to sublime the logic of our language, Wittgenstein is therefore offering a further diagnosis of their nature and their source, and a further indication of what we must avoid if they are to be overcome.

22. What, then, does it take to overcome our sense of logic as sublime? Wittgenstein famously tells us that 'the axis of reference of our examination must be rotated, but about the fixed point of our real need' (*PI* 108). According to the terms laid out in the chains of imagery preceding this image, the fixed point of our examination is an idea of logic as relating to the essence of everything empirical ('we too in these investigations are trying to understand the essence'; *PI* 92); and since our subliming of logic pictures it as hidden beneath, as needing extraction from, and as pointing beyond, the empirical or the phenomenal, we might say that the axis of reference of our examination hitherto has been vertical—penetrating beneath and pushing beyond a threshold. So, rotating our axis of reference would turn it towards the horizontal—towards a desire to stay with the surface we have hitherto wished to dig up or demolish, to attend to the logic of language as that is manifest in the empirical contexts within which our life with words is lived.

On this account, then, essence is 'something that already lies open to view and that becomes surveyable by a rearrangement' (*PI* 92); it emerges through 'talking about the spatial and temporal phenomenon of language, not some non-spatial, non-temporal phantasm' (*PI* 108). Our investigation aims not at penetrating phenomena, but 'towards the *"possibilities"* of phenomena. We remind ourselves . . . of the *kind of statement* that we make about phenomena' (*PI* 90). And while these grammatical investigations of essence may involve substituting one form of expression for another in order to remove misunderstandings, they entirely eschew the idea of 'a state of complete exactness', of unearthing 'a *single* completely resolved' form that is thought of as hidden within our everyday expressions (*PI* 91).

Wittgenstein's counter-concepts of family resemblance and grammatical investigation must therefore be careful above all to avoid similarly subliming our sense of the rules governing our uses of words. Or to put matters the other way round: if our accounts of those counter-concepts result in a picture of the grammar or the criteria of words as liminal and as superlatively rigid, as the a priori armature of the ordinary, then they too must be counted as further expressions of the fantasy they aim to contest.

CRITERIA, ESSENCE, AND CONTEXT

23. These remarks may help to give us a general sense of what Wittgenstein imagines to be entailed by adopting a horizontal rather than a vertical axis of reference in our investigations; but what might this look like in practice, and in detail? Initial examples can be found if we look back beyond the explicit discussion of how we sublime logic, beyond even the explicit introduction of the idea of family resemblance, to the point at which Wittgenstein first deploys his notion of the sublime—in section 38, when he turns to discuss indexicals such as 'this' and 'that'.

If you do not want to produce confusion you will do best not to call these words names at all.—Yet, strange to say, the word 'this' has been called the only *genuine* name; so that anything else we call a name was one only in an inexact, approximate sense.

This queer conception springs from a tendency to sublime the logic of our language—as one might put it. The proper answer to it is: we call very different things 'names'; the word 'name' is used to characterize many different kinds of use of a word, related to one another in many different ways;—but the kind of use that 'this' has is not among them. (*PI* 38)

As Wittgenstein goes on to spell out later in the same section, this queer conception evinces all the hallmarks of our subliming tendency: naming, understood as one aspect of the logic of our language, 'appears as a *queer* connexion of a word with an object', because the philosopher is trying 'to bring out *the* relation between name and thing by staring at an object in front of him and repeating a name or even the word 'this' innumerable times. For philosophical problems arise when language *idles'*. The philosopher has extracted naming from its contexts in our everyday life with words, and hence arrived at the idea that naming is a single, unique, and superlatively definite kind of relation between word and thing—a hidden connection of crystalline purity against which our ordinary practices of naming appear as impure, cloudy, and inexact.

What Wittgenstein calls 'the proper answer' to such subliming is to recognize the multiplicity of things that we call 'names', the many different kinds of use to which we put names—uses which are themselves related to one another in a multiplicity of ways. The idea of family resemblance is already at work in the background here; it is the singularity of this fantasy of naming—the idea that any word deserving the title of 'name' must manifest a single, highly specific character—to which we must be most fundamentally opposed, and we effect that opposition by reminding ourselves that names form a family. The language-game for describing coloured squares which Wittgenstein introduces in section 48 (reiterating the method of section 2) is designed to demonstrate that fact.

Our language-game (48) has *various* possibilities; there is a variety of cases in which we should say that a sign in the game was the name of a square of such-and-such a colour. We should say so if, for instance, we knew that the people who used the language were taught the use of the signs in such-and-such a way. Or if it were set down in writing, say in the form of a table, that this element corresponded to this sign, and if the table were used in teaching the language and were appealed to in certain disputed cases.

We can also imagine such a table's being a tool in the use of the language. Describing a complex [array of squares] is then done like this: the person who describes the complex has a table with him and looks up each element of the complex in it and passes from this to the sign . . .

If we call such a table the expression of a rule of the language-game, it can be said that what we call a rule of a language-game may have very different roles in the game. (*PI* 53)

There is no single common feature of these various imagined uses of signs that might be held to justify our calling them all 'names'; not every method of teaching their use need employ a table, and not every use that is taught by means of a table need involve the continued employment of a table (Wittgenstein emphasizes in particular that not all names presuppose the highly precise sign–object correspondences for which tables are most appropriate; *PI* 54). Nevertheless, there are plainly specific respects in which one use of a sign as a name may resemble other such uses—the specific employment of a table being one of them; and it is clear when certain uses of signs (say, the use of the word 'this') fall outside this family. In short, the concept of a name is held together by a number of overlapping resemblances, not by a single, pure essence that must be hidden behind this multiplicity and dug out from it; and we can remind ourselves of this by broadening our investigation, by staying on the surface and describing or extrapolating from what is to be seen there—in short, by understanding language as a spatial and temporal phenomenon, by treating logic as an aspect of human forms of life with words.

Other early examples of this anti-subliming strategy are scattered throughout the early pages of the *Investigations*; but perhaps the clearest and most illuminating of them occurs during Wittgenstein's discussion of ostensive definition, when he is contesting his interlocutor's idea that directing one's attention to the colour of an object (as opposed, say, to its shape) is a single, specific sort of act.

But do you always do the *same* thing when you direct your attention to the colour? Imagine various cases. To indicate a few:

'Is this blue the same as the blue over there? Do you see any difference?'—
You are mixing paint and you say 'It's hard to get the blue of this sky.'
'It's turning fine, you can already see blue sky again.'
'Look what different effects these two blues have.'
'Do you see the blue book over there? Bring it here.'
'This blue light-signal means . . .'
'What's this blue called?—Is it "indigo"?'

You sometimes attend to the colour by putting your hand up to keep the outline from view; or by not looking at the outline of the thing; sometimes by staring at the object and trying to remember where you saw that colour before.

You attend to the shape, sometimes by tracing it, sometimes by screwing up your eyes so as not to see the colour clearly, and in many other ways. I want to say: This is the sort of thing that happens *while* one 'directs one's attention to this or that.' But it isn't these things by themselves that make us say someone is attending to the shapes, the colour and so on. Just as a move in chess doesn't consist simply in moving a piece in such-and-such a way on the board—nor yet in one's thoughts and feelings as one makes the move: but in the circumstances that we call 'playing a game of chess', 'solving a chess problem', and so on. (*PI* 33)

Once again, while there are a number of overlapping similarities that obtain between the individual instances of 'attending to the colour' on Wittgenstein's list, there is no single common feature—no unique, underlying essence available for analytical extraction. But Wittgenstein also asserts that we judge any specific pattern of sayings and doings to be an instance of attending to the colour of something *only in certain circumstances*—that just as moving a chess piece on a board constitutes making a move only in a particular context, so turning to look at a bookcase constitutes attending to the colour of its books only in a particular context.

But just what are these circumstances? Once again, we can begin to construct a list of examples: we might say, for instance, that turning to look at a bookcase constitutes attending to the colour of its books when it is done in response to someone's request to bring the blue book over to her, or when it is followed by your saying, 'Look how beautiful the blue binding of that book is in the sunlight', or when you then pick out two of the books and ask which is royal blue, and so on. In other circumstances (if we imagine different things happening before and after the action (*PI* 35), give it a different history or narrative context), the same turn and gaze might give us grounds for judging that you were attending to the shape of the books, or to the proportions of the wall against which the bookcase rests, or that you were attempting to avoid seeing what was going on through the window, and so on. In other words, the same action is a criterion for different things in different circumstances; and of course, the significance of the relatively local circumstances to which we have hitherto restricted ourselves will itself alter (and perhaps entirely dissipate) if we alter our conception of the broader context—perhaps by imagining a world in which specific colours and shapes always go together, or in which no other questions have ever or will ever be asked, or in which the room and the things and people in it appeared only the previous instant and will vanish the next.

This suggests that the enterprise of restoring logic to its empirical contexts must not restrict itself to an unduly narrow conception of those contexts; part of what determines the logic of a particular language-game is its relation with the logic of other language-games, and ultimately its role in the complex articulations of human forms of life. But the issue that concerns us at present is that these indefinitely extendable lists—of the kinds of circumstance in which turning and looking would be a criterion for one kind of thing, of those in which it would be a criterion of something very different, and of the various kinds of thing for which (given the right circumstances) it can be a criterion—comprise individual items, specific scenarios, that are perfectly definite in themselves, and that can be added to in perfectly definite ways; and yet there are no obvious recipes or concise formulae lying to hand for their construction and expansion. Anyone who knows how to talk knows how the lists might be extended, and reveals in the exercise of that knowledge how demanding and exact the criteria which inform those extensions really are; but if someone were to ask, 'In what sorts of circumstance is turning and looking at the books a criterion of attending to their colour?', we could not specify a particular *sort* of circumstance—we could only answer by offering some examples together with a similarity rider, and perhaps by evaluating further examples that our questioner may bring up.

As Wittgenstein is at pains to emphasize, it is not that such explanations gesture towards a kind of understanding that is beyond explicit articulation; they simply exhaust our understanding of the terms explained (*PI 75*). The reality of the situation is that criteria are plainly not algorithms that generate these series of examples as if they were functions generating values for certain arguments; and yet our criteria-based judgements about the significance of specific patterns of behaviour in specific contexts, and our criteria-based imaginings of the ways in which different contexts and different utterances and actions might accommodate one another, are equally plainly as rigorous and precise in their unfolding as any that algorithms might demand. Wittgenstein's point is that understanding the logic of our language in terms of grammar and criteria does not bargain away its rigour and precision, but rather attempts to turn us away from our preconceived idea of how that rigour and precision must be understood—to reveal that there are modes of exactness that can match that of the algorithmic without sharing its apparent abstraction from the particularities of space and time, its turn towards what we might be inclined to call the eternal and the a priori. A grammatical investigation, just like the ability to speak which such investigations track, relies upon our capacity to place words in, and follow them through, the endlessly varying contexts of their use; and it reveals that multiple networks of circumstance-dependent criteria can nevertheless give precise and rigorous expression to the essence of things.

THE CIRCUMSTANCES OF SPEECH: NORMAL AND ABNORMAL

24. It should be clear from the foregoing that Wittgenstein's long and much-studied discussion of rule-following (stretching from section 143 to section 243 and beyond) can be taken to have a double purpose. It is designed at once to explore what a desublimated understanding of the role of rules in language might amount to, and to trace the implications of such an understanding for our grasp of what Wittgenstein himself might mean by a grammatical or criterial investigation of our

life with words. It asks, in short, what his conception of the grammar of words implies for his conception of the nature of philosophy. However, before he broaches this topic explicitly, Wittgenstein provides a kind of prologue—a mini-grammatical investigation with an important moral for those who wish to interpret what is to come.

Beginning at section 138, he asks how it is possible to grasp the meaning of a word in a flash, a moment of inspiration, when what one thereby understands is the use of the word—something that extends through time. How, in short, can what is present to us in an instant fit (or fail to fit) a use? Wittgenstein attempts to disabuse us of the idea that this 'fitness' is a matter of forcing a particular use upon us; having the picture of a cube come before your mind when someone says the word 'cube' might well suggest a certain use or method of projection to us, but it could perfectly well be applied in other ways—to triangular prisms rather than cubes, say. And the same argument applies to any mental representation of a given method of projection—any such schema could also be applied in a number of different ways.

In attacking the idea that pictures (whether mental or physical) force a particular use upon us, Wittgenstein is careful to say that he is not denying that the application of a picture or a word can come before our minds, be grasped in a flash; he is rather trying to clarify the application of these expressions. In doing so, he claims that there are (at least) two different kinds of criteria we use when deciding whether we should say that the method of application or meaning that I intend has come before another's mind—'on the one hand the picture (of whatever kind) that at some time or other comes before his mind; and on the other, the application which—in the course of time—he makes of what he imagines' (*PI* 141). This plainly implies that mental pictures are candidates for criteria, that their presence or absence at least sometimes governs what we might say about someone's understanding (something that those who assume all Wittgensteinian criteria to be external or outer might wish to consider). But more importantly, Wittgenstein goes on immediately to draw the following moral:

Can there be a collision between picture and application? There can, inasmuch as the picture makes us expect a different use, because people in general apply *this* picture like *this*.

I want to say: we have here a *normal* case, and abnormal cases.

It is only in normal cases that the use of a word is clearly prescribed; we know, are in no doubt, what to say in this or that case. The more abnormal the case, the more doubtful it becomes what we are to say. And if things were quite different from what they actually are—if there were for instance no characteristic expression of pain, of fear, of joy; if rule became exception and exception rule; or if both became phenomena of roughly equal frequency—this would make our normal language-games lose their point.—The procedure of putting a lump of cheese on a balance and fixing the price by the turn of the scale would lose its point if it frequently happened for such lumps to suddenly grow or shrink for no obvious reason. (*PI* 141–2)

Applying these remarks to the case of the cube picture, the implication is that the criterial roles of picture and application work perfectly well in normal circumstances, because people in general apply certain kinds of picture in certain kinds of way. In abnormal circumstances, in which people don't all apply the same kinds of picture in the same kinds of way, those criteria could come into conflict—it would then be doubtful what we are to say about whether the right application has come before the person's mind. In other words, these criteria do what they do only in certain circumstances—but in this case, it is not that the criteria which determine that we should say one thing in one kind of context determine that we should say something else in another kind of context; it is rather that in abnormal circumstances these criteria no longer determine what we are to say—in such circumstances they come into conflict, which means that the use of the phrase 'the application came before his mind' is no longer clear.

In effect, Wittgenstein is saying that our practice of using words, our agreement in criteria, is attuned to what people normally do, or perhaps to what normal people do. Normal human behaviour, very general facts of human nature and of nature taken more broadly, form part of the context in which our normal practices of employing words, our normal language-games, have point or purpose. If these very general facts were to change, that point, says Wittgenstein, would be lost.

25. However, as Cora Diamond has emphasized,[15] this claim of Wittgenstein's can be taken in two very different ways. The third sentence of section 142 ('if things were quite different from what they are . . . this would make our normal language-games lose their point') might naturally be taken to imply that abnormal circumstances, in stripping a language-game of its point, would render it useless but leave the game itself (its basic structure or identity) essentially intact. In circumstances where people no longer applied certain kinds of picture in the same kinds of way, there would be no point in employing our concept of 'the application coming into his mind'; and in circumstances where lumps of cheese placed on scales grow or shrink for no obvious reason, there

---

[15] 'Rules: Looking in the Right Place', in D. Z. Phillips (ed.), *Wittgenstein: Attention to Particulars* (Macmillan: London, 1989).

would be no point in employing our normal concept of weight. Nevertheless, both concepts could be articulated, could be grasped or understood, in those very different circumstances. On this interpretation, Wittgenstein is aiming to reconceive the relation between language and its empirical circumstances, to free us from the idea that words are indebted to reality for their meaningfulness in favour of the idea that reality gives point to their use—that natural regularities condition the utility rather than the possibility of meaningful speech.

However, when Wittgenstein actually discusses the abnormal lumps of cheese example, he talks not of our practice of weighing being rendered pointless, but merely of 'the procedure of putting a lump of cheese on a balance and fixing the price by the turn of the scale' losing its point. In other words, he eschews the concept of weight entirely in describing our normal behaviour in the context of that abnormal situation—quite as if the abnormality has deprived him of that concept altogether, rather than simply removing the point of employing it. This suggests that Wittgenstein's aim is not to reconceive the relation between language and its empirical circumstances, understood as two analytically separable or externally related phenomena, but rather to deny their distinctness. On this interpretation, Wittgenstein is claiming that our concepts would not be the concepts they are in such abnormal circumstances—that whatever talk of 'an application coming before his mind' or of 'weighing the cheese' in such circumstances might mean, it does not mean what it means in normal circumstances.

As Wittgenstein's careful phrasing allows, people might put the strange lumps of cheese in their scales, and read off a number from the dial, and exchange coins for cheese in accordance with that number, but they could not on that basis alone be said to be selling cheese by weight. Their practice is undeniably similar in those ways to our normal practice of weighing, but it will also be dissimilar to it in a number of more or less obvious ways. We can see this by asking how Wittgenstein's vignette is to be filled out: for example, how do these people react to a lump of cheese shrinking or expanding while on the scales (which reading fixes the price?), and how are the shopkeeper's payments to his cheese suppliers fixed (by a calculation with scales on departure from the warehouse, on arrival at the shop, or at the moment of sale?)? These shoppers will also have a very different relation to recipes (how can one be sure of getting enough cheese for a meal for four people, and how might recipes be written to take account of the nature of this cheese?), to dieting (how do they determine how much cheese they have eaten?), to allotting money for housekeeping, and so on. Will their economic arrangements be such as to allow stockpilers of cheese to make a killing by selling when their cheese stocks have randomly grown? Much will also depend upon whether we imagine that all foodstuffs are subject to such random changes in size, or all goods stocked by shops, or all physical stuffs.

Whatever the specific answers we give to these questions, however, the fact that the questions even arise with respect to the people we are imagining makes it clear that and how their procedure of fixing the price of cheese by the turn of a scale differs from ours; for it is part of our normal concept of an object's weight that the results of weighing an object on one scale will be matched by the results of weighing it on other scales at other times—and this comes out in the fact that the questions I have just elaborated simply would not arise in the context of our life with this procedure. This makes it manifest how different their life with this procedure is from our life with it—how different the connections are in their lives between this procedure and a ramifying array of other procedures, patterns of behaviour, and ways of living.

To formulate this point as the claim that the existence of those normal connections is a condition for the possibility (rather than simply a condition for the utility) of our normal concept of weight would be radically misleading, for it would maintain the very assumption that Wittgenstein is most concerned to bring into question—the assumption that words and the circumstances of their use are analytically separable, that we could intelligibly isolate the concept from its wider context and ask ourselves whether that concept could exist without those conditions. Wittgenstein's point is rather that that web of connections, that ramifying array of ways of living, just *is* what is involved in having our normal concept of weight. As one element in that web of connections, our procedure with the scales is indeed a method of weighing; but in the absence of that web it might mean anything or nothing— and it will only mean something specific in so far as it is taken as occupying some particular position in a particular form of life. It is not that having a complex life with concepts of weight is one thing, and having concepts of weight is another; it is rather that having that complex life just *is* having that concept, and not having that complex life (would not make it impractical, and not make it impossible, to have that concept, but) would *be* not having that concept.

We can think of this as a further implication of Wittgenstein's hostility to subliming the logic of our language, and of what is involved in overcoming that tendency by rotating the axis of our examination—by staying with descriptions of the surface of our lives with words rather than attempting to dig beneath or decompose that surface. If we think of the grammar of one of our ordinary words as the framework for a

technique which can, even in principle, be isolated from its position in our general life with that and other words, then from Wittgenstein's perspective, we are continuing to treat the logic of our language as something that might be dug or crystallized out from the general stream of life within which alone it has the meaning it does. That broader context is not something that conditions grammar; for this implies that the relevant words could be said to have the grammar they have, to mean what they mean, or indeed to mean anything at all, if considered in isolation from the form of life of which they are a part. Without that context, we have a procedure with noises and behaviour; but we do not have a grammatical technique—we do not, in short, have words.

RULES: THE NORMAL, THE NATURAL, AND KNOWING HOW TO GO ON

26. Section 143 introduces the example of rule-following around which Wittgenstein's long discussion will spiral—that of one person ordering another to write down series of numbers according to a specific formation rule. He begins by asking how the pupil gets to understand the rule, and at once is eager to stress that the efficacy of any explanation offered by the teacher depends on the reaction of the pupil (*PI* 145). She may, for example, be required to copy series of numbers written down for her by the teacher: 'And here already there is a normal and an abnormal learner's reaction.—At first perhaps we guide his hand in writing out the series 0 to 9; but then *the possibility of getting him to understand* will depend on his going on to write it down independently' (*PI* 143). Likewise for further stages in the teaching process: the pupil may write numbers at random, or make infrequent mistakes in the order, or make systematic mistakes—and although we might be able to wean her away from some of them (particularly, thinks Wittgenstein, in the last case), our pupil's capacity to learn may come to an end at any of these points; for if he responds abnormally to a given explanation, his responses to any further explanation we can offer might be similarly abnormal, and then we will not be able to get beneath that divergence to establish communication.

Bearing in mind the strange lumps of cheese, we might say: if such abnormal reactions were to become the norm, then our normal concept of explanation would lose its point—not because our normal reactions are a condition for the utility of that practice, or even a condition of its possibility, but rather because the drilling and copying procedures which, in the context of a broader web of normative practices and attitudes of the kind familiar from our own lives, count as explanatory would have no such significance in the context of the kinds of practices and attitudes one imagines Wittgenstein's 'abnormal' people as having developed. Thus, his deviant pupil immediately implies a general dependence of the normative upon the normal and the natural, or more precisely a general interweaving of the normative, the normal, and the natural.

27. Wittgenstein moves on. 'Now, however, let us suppose that after some efforts on the teacher's part he continues the series correctly, that is, as we do it. So now we can say he has mastered the system.—But how far need he continue the series for us to have the right to say that? Clearly you cannot state a limit here' (*PI* 145). If we understand anything about judging another's understanding of a rule, then surely we know when to say that the pupil's sequence of applications shows that he has mastered the rule. But we can see at once that our understanding is not capturable by the specification of a limit—a specific number of applications; in some circumstances one or two successful steps would suffice, in others one or two dozen would not, and although we might illustrate this circumstance-dependence with concrete examples (varying the age of the pupil, his experience with other mathematical rules, our trust in his teacher, and so on), we have no handy algorithm for generating these examples. In other words, our concept of understanding is in these respects precise, but not mathematically precise, even when the understanding under judgement is mathematical understanding; the pupil's application of the mathematical rule is still a criterion of understanding (*PI* 146), but the application of that criterion is not akin to that of an algorithm.

Wittgenstein is thus centrally concerned to contest the idea that this absence of a specific limit is to be explained as showing that the pupil's ability to apply the rule correctly is not a criterion of his understanding at all, but rather a manifestation or symptom of it. This involves picturing understanding as a state that is the *source* of the correct use (*PI* 146), as if the pupil's ability to apply the rule were something he derived from his understanding in the way we can be said to derive a series from its algebraic formula. The problem is that, as we saw earlier, a formula— just like a picture—can be variously applied or interpreted; so we return once again to the fact that only the derivation of the right series can determine whether or not the pupil understands the rule—in other words, that his application of the rule is still a criterion of understanding.

The interlocutor's immediate objection to this conclusion is that it appears to misinterpret the pupil's relation to his own understanding. For he surely does not have to wait to see how he applies the rule in order to know whether he understands it; and more particularly, we commonly experience a sudden dawning of understanding—expressed in such phrases as 'Now I can go on!', or 'Now I've got it!'—before making any attempt to demonstrate that understanding in action. Wittgenstein has no wish to deny either claim; but he is concerned to contest certain interpretations of how the words 'Now I understand' actually function. For there is a strong temptation to think that they report or describe something or things that happen to us at the moment of the utterance—a specific experience or event or process that *is* the understanding we claim to possess.

To be sure, a number of specific things may and often do happen when we suddenly understand, and their occurrence may well be what leads us to claim that we understand. We may have tried various formulae on the numbers our teacher has written down until one fitted, or recognized a pattern in the differences between those numbers, or experienced mild tension and a number of vague thoughts before the problem resolves itself, or simply continued the series without hesitation. However, there is no single, specific experience that is common to all cases of sudden understanding, and no such experience guarantees an access of understanding in any particular case; for example, the right formula might occur to us and we nevertheless not understand. So 'Now I understand' cannot simply mean 'The formula occurred to me' or 'My feeling of tension has dissipated'.

It is tempting to respond by saying that 'Now I understand' must therefore refer to a process that occurs behind or beneath the various familiar phenomenological accompaniments of understanding. Here the subliming process is in full swing: unable to find the referent of 'Now I understand' amidst the coarser, more readily visible aspects of our mental life, we posit the existence of hidden referents buried beneath the surface of our consciousness—failing to see that phenomena inaccessible to consciousness could hardly form the basis of our claims suddenly to understand something (*PI* 153). Once again, we need to shift the axis of our examination from the vertical to the horizontal:

If there has to be anything 'behind the utterance of the formula' it is *particular circumstances* which justify me in saying I can go on—when the formula occurs to me.

. . . what I wanted to say was: when he suddenly knew how to go on, when he understood the principle, then possibly he had a special experience . . . but for us it is *the circumstances* under which he had such an experience that justify him in saying in such a case that he understands, that he knows how to go on. (*PI* 154, 155)

The particular circumstances Wittgenstein has in mind are that the pupil has learned algebra, had used such formulae before success-fully, had made good on such claims to understand these kinds of rule formulations before, and so on (*PI* 179). In such circumstances, circumstances which serve to establish a connection between think-ing of a formula and actually continuing the series, the occurrence of the formula in his mind gives him the right to claim to know how to go on; but that does not of course mean that 'Now I can go on' amounts to a description of that empirical connection or those circumstances —as if it really means 'I have an experience which I know empirically to lead to the continuation of the series' or 'I have successfully made such derivations before'. Those circumstances 'constitute the scene for our language-game' of expressions of sudden understanding (*PI* 179), but they are not its subject. The words 'Now I can go on' do not describe that scene, any more than they describe a mental state (whether conscious or unconscious); they are more akin to a signal which we judge to be rightly employed by what the signaller then goes on to do.

And this conclusion returns us to the point Wittgenstein first made in sections 141–2, with respect to pictures and their application. For if what we might call normal circumstances were to change (if, for example, people regularly began to think of the right formula and then fail to derive the correct series from it) then 'Now I can go on' would not have the significance it now has, that of being one criterion for attributing understanding to the speaker; for that significance depends upon the general fact that most people to whom the correct formula occurs can go on to apply it correctly. If that correlation breaks down, if what we ordinarily call 'accompaniments of understanding' no longer in fact accompany understanding, then uttering the signal 'Now I can go on' in the usual way and attributing authority to those signals in the usual way would become pointless; and that means that such utterances would no longer be signals of the sudden accession of under-standing. It is not that playing our ordinary language-game of under-standing would become pointless; it is rather that the behaviour which under ordinary circumstances counts as claiming to understand and as acknowledging such claims would no longer do so. People could utter the words 'Now I understand', but their utterances would not be claims to understanding.

READING: AN INTERPOLATION

28. In summarizing this aspect of Wittgenstein's investigation, it is worth remarking that I have, in effect, edited out a long stretch of his text. His rejection of the idea that what justifies the use of 'Now I understand' is a contemporaneous psychological occurrence (whether conscious or hidden), and his counter-claim that it is rather justified by the circumstances of the utterance—his signature shift from a vertical to a horizontal axis of investigation—are in place by sections 154–5. But he does not then actually specify what those circumstances are. Instead, he 'interpolate[s] the consideration of another word, namely "reading"' (*PI* 156), into which he then interpolates a consideration of the word 'derivation' (*PI* 162), which itself leads into a consideration of the words 'influence' and 'guidance' (*PI* 169), before we return to our point of departure at section 179, where the circumstances to which Wittgenstein had first referred twenty-five sections earlier are at long last specified. In other words, the critical clarification that his readers are impatiently awaiting does not emerge until we emerge from the interpolation itself.

To be sure, Wittgenstein explicitly claims to introduce this long interpolation as a way of clarifying what he means by that reference to circumstances; but although the central lesson of the interpolation does indeed involve the concept of circumstance-dependence, it does not do so in the sense in which that concept has just been invoked with respect to rule-following. The central lesson is summarized in section 164, where Wittgenstein is commenting on his example of someone who derives his cursive copy of a printed text by consulting a table which correlates printed letters with cursive letters:

In [that] case the meaning of the word 'derive' stood out quite clearly. But we told ourselves that this was only a quite special case of deriving; deriving in a quite special garb, which had to be stripped from it if we wanted to see the essence of deriving. So we stripped those particular coverings off; but then deriving itself disappeared.—In order to find the real artichoke, we divested it of its leaves. For certainly [the first case] was a special case of deriving; what is essential to deriving, however, was not hidden beneath the surface of this case, but this 'surface' was one case out of the family of cases of deriving.

And in the same way we also use the word 'to read' for a family of cases. And in different circumstances we apply different criteria for a person's reading. (*PI* 164)

The criteria for 'deriving' and for 'reading' are circumstance-dependent in the sense that there are no criteria common to all exam-

ples of deriving or reading, but rather different criteria in different circumstances—in other words, that 'reading' and 'deriving' are family
resemblance concepts, structured like an artichoke rather than, say, a
peach or an avocado. But although Wittgenstein holds this to be true
of sudden understanding as well, it is not the point that he offers to
clarify at the beginning of section 156. The claim he makes in sections
154–5 is that certain circumstances, certain general facts of nature, are
what justify someone in signalling the sudden advent of understanding.
As section 179 eventually makes clear, these circumstances are among
the general facts of nature which constitute the scene or setting of our
language-game of understanding: the functioning and significance of
that language-game depend on their obtaining, and would be obviated
in their absence. This is not a point about family resemblance, but one
about normality and abnormality: Wittgenstein is not emphasizing that
there are different criteria for understanding in different circumstances,
but rather that our practice of employing two different kinds of criteria for understanding only hangs together within the broader context
or circumstances of normal human behaviour. So the point that Wittgenstein's interpolation illustrates is not the point that it was introduced to
clarify; the interpolation repeats a different point, and defers a proper
understanding of the point that is really at issue.

How, as readers of Wittgenstein, are we to understand this? What
lesson are we to derive from it? How should it guide or influence our
understanding of him as a writer? We might, of course, take it that sections 156 to 178 really are no more than they claim to be—an interpolation rather than a further step in the progress of Wittgenstein's
investigation; from which we might conclude that properly structuring a philosophical elucidation of a given concept is not one of
Wittgenstein's strengths as a writer. But we might instead ask ourselves
whether it is significant that the terms we naturally employ in posing
the questions raised by this interpolation—reading, derivation, guidance, influence—are the very ones under examination in it; from which
we might rather conclude that it is one of Wittgenstein's concerns as a
writer to ask his readers to reflect upon what being influenced or guided
by, what deriving lessons from, a writer such as himself can require—
what this writer thinks reading can be.

Is the contemplation of such a possibility excluded by Wittgenstein's
opening declaration that he is 'not counting the understanding of what
is read as part of "reading" for the purposes of this investigation: reading is here the activity of rendering out loud what is written
or printed; and also of writing from dictation, writing out something printed, playing from a score, and so on' (*PI* 156)? Surely no

conception of what reading might aspire to can require an utter lack of understanding of what is read; surely that lack is motivated rather by the desire to find a way of casting light on understanding by studying a phenomenon which, although related to it, does not presuppose it.

This conclusion would be more convincing if it were not more or less obvious that Wittgenstein does not live up to his opening declaration in the ensuing discussion. To be sure, certain stretches of it heighten that original emphasis upon reading taken as a mechanical process of rendering out loud what is written: in section 156 he compares such a process to the behaviour of a reading-machine, and by the next section this apparently casual metaphor has generated the surreal tale of our using human or non-human creatures as reading-machines. However, in the very same sections he also talks of 'reading' as a word whose 'use in the ordinary circumstances of our life is of course extremely familiar to us', and of someone learning to read his native language through 'one of the kinds of education usual among us'; but of course our ordinary education, and our ordinary uses of the word 'reading', precisely draw together learning to read and learning to understand what is read. The rest of his discussion is shadowed by this opening oscillation: when he later talks of the characteristic experiences of reading (*PI* 159), of reading the numbers off the dial of a watch (*PI* 161), and of the familiarity of the words we read (*PI* 167), it is never absolutely clear whether these discussions refer to forms of mechanical reading or of the more familiar, comprehending kind.

I want to suggest that this unclarity is instructive—that it is, in fact, a lesson in how to read Wittgenstein with understanding. For oddly mechanical pictures of our ordinary ways with words have been threaded through the *Investigations* from the beginning, with its opening portrait of the robotic shopkeeper and the primitive builders. I suggested there that those portraits could be read both as primitive pictures of civilized human behaviour, and as pictures of the primitive forms of behaviour to which civilized human beings are presently reduced. Exactly the same double aspect can be seen in these pictures of mechanical reading. On the one hand, Wittgenstein is implying that his interlocutor's immediately preceding emphasis upon understanding as an inner state from which comprehending behaviour flows is a primitive conception of understanding; his own talk of reading-machines amounts to a figurative externalization of that conception of the inner— and as with the shopkeeper, if we find the behaviour of the reading-machines oddly devoid of understanding, then we should ask ourselves why we take an internalized version of the same mechanical model to exemplify the essence of understanding. At the same time, however,

Wittgenstein's repeated refusal clearly to separate his vision of human reading-machines from his invocation of the ordinary Englishman's ability to read invites us to consider whether the attractions of the primitive picture of understanding as a mechanism are not in part based on the degree to which our ordinary ways with words in reality verge upon the mechanical, the thoughtless, the unreflective and slavish reiteration of others' words. In this sense, Wittgenstein's interpolation embodies a portrait of the kinds of reading to which he expects that his own words might be subjected; but he offers it in the hope that we might recognize a version of ourselves in it, and utilize that recognition to overcome it, to read otherwise.

29. What, then, might the structure of Wittgenstein's interpolation about reading have to teach us about how to read otherwise—how to read that interpolation, and hence how to read Wittgenstein's philosophical writing more generally? What we can see within that interpolation, beyond the oscillation between mechanical and comprehending reading, is a struggle between two models of reading the word 'reading'. The first looks for the single, hidden essence of the word: it looks for a core of significance common to all instances of the word's use, a core that might itself be summed up in a kind of definitional equivalence between 'reading' and another word—this is what forces the investigation on from 'reading' itself to 'derivation' (which is presented as a definition of 'reading' at section 162), and then on in turn to 'guidance' and 'influence' (section 170). The second model cuts across the penetrative, vertical axis of the first (what Augustine might call its Manichaean one-dimensionality): it stresses the multiplicity and circumstance-specificity of our criteria for 'reading', for 'derivation', and for 'guidance', and the familial links between these putatively synonymous words—their synchronic filiation serving to blunt or diffuse our impulse to line them up as proxies or substitutes for one another. This second model finds its apotheosis in Wittgenstein's comments on the concept of 'guidance', and in particular the idea of our course being guided by something or someone.

Imagine the following cases:
  You are in a playing field with your eyes bandaged, and someone leads you by the hand, sometimes left, sometimes right; you have constantly to be ready for the tug of his hand, and must also take care not to stumble when he gives you an unexpected tug.
  Or again: someone leads you by the hand where you are unwilling to go, by force.

Or: you are guided by a partner in a dance; you make yourself as receptive as possible, in order to guess his intention and obey the slightest pressure.

Or: someone takes you for a walk; you are having a conversation; you go wherever he does.

Or: you walk along a field-track, simply following it.

All these situations are similar to one another; but what is common to all the experiences? (*PI* 172)

The implied answer to the immediate question is of course: nothing—just what one would expect by this stage in Wittgenstein's reiterative discussion of family resemblance structures. There is no essence, no single, underlying core to the business of offering guidance to another—whether we think of that other as another adult, or as a child looking for initiation into mathematics and language more generally, as is the case with the pupil whose vicissitudes form the overarching narrative framework of Wittgenstein's investigation. Against that framework, however, and thinking back to the double aspect I claimed to detect in many of Wittgenstein's earlier imaginary tales, then we might be struck by the possibility of interpreting Wittgenstein's sheaf of examples in diachronic as well as synchronic terms.

In other words, as well as stressing the sheer, context-dependent variety of what we might call guidance, section 172 might simultaneously be read as a compressed genetic account of how someone, anyone, first learns how to construct an arithmetical series. First, the pupil feels as if he is being dragged blindfold through alien terrain; then the blindfold is removed but his progress remains reluctant and coerced; then he gives himself over entirely to the example his teacher sets—and this transforms the landscape into the scene for a reciprocal dialogue between more or less equals, which culminates in his being able to find and keep to the familiar human paths through the terrain of numbers without either explicit external direction or conscious self-admonition.

There is, on this reading, no need to regard either the synchronic or the diachronic way of reading the idea of guidance as prior to its counterpart, although each may temporarily eclipse the other or be eclipsed by it; their complementarity or internal relation figures Wittgenstein's sense that our capacity properly to inhabit the variegated landscape of numbers and words is dependent upon a continued openness to the anxieties and exhilarations, the imaginative openness and receptivity, of childhood.

In thus portraying the course into which the grammar of the word 'guidance' guides us, however, Wittgenstein can be interpreted as simultaneously providing a portrait of grammatical guidance, of the course of guidance that grammar as such, grammar in general, can supply—a portrait of the grammatical investigator's shifting and various relations to grammar.[16] This portrait tells us that grammatical guidance can as easily be experienced as a disorienting and coercive master as it can a natural path through the landscape of our lives; that whatever our experience of it, we end up going where grammar takes us; and that we can best maintain our own autonomy within such a relationship by remaining receptive to its smallest inflections. Above all, perhaps, it tells us that the normativity of grammar, its modes of governance of our lives with words, are as individually concrete and as collectively various as the ways in which one human being can guide the course of another.

30. A further level of implication opens up if we entertain the interpolation's provisional equation of guidance with derivation, and hence with reading. For it is then difficult to avoid the impression that this section of Wittgenstein's text is also a kind of compendious self-portrait—an album of pictures of its relations with its readers. It successively pictures the reader either as disoriented and under compulsion, or as intensely receptive to suggestion, or as somewhere in between—engrossed in a dialogue with the text, or in unruffled accommodation with its twists and turns. And the overarching idea that this is a family of cases of guidance, and hence of reading, further suggests that no one case should be regarded as more paradigmatic or exemplary than any other—that at various times this text's author will resemble a captor, a parent, a dancing partner, a sociable host, and a pathbreaker, and that its reader must be prepared to adopt or find herself adopting any or perhaps all of the necessary complementary postures at any given time.

Take, for example, our experience of the interpolated passage itself. The artfully artless smoothness of Wittgenstein's transitions from understanding to reading to deriving to guidance and back to understanding soon dissolves, leaving us with the feeling of having been compelled to go in directions we have not chosen through a landscape we cannot survey. But if we allow ourselves to be guided by what may appear to be faint or trivial traces in the text, if we question it about the disorientations it induces, we will find that it is responsive to that questioning, and that it aims thereby to reposition us as genuine partners in the

[16] Henry Staten, in *Wittgenstein and Derrida* (Blackwell: London, 1984), suggests a similarly reflexive reading of these examples of guidance, but develops his argument in a rather different direction from my own.

grammatical investigations that it recommends and enacts. It is worth recalling, after all, that just before Wittgenstein interpolates his discussion of reading, he has challenged us to respond to the disorienting remark about the circumstance-dependence of saying 'Now I can go on': 'ask yourself: in what sort of case, in what kind of circumstances, do we say, "Now I know how to go on", when, that is, the formula *has* occurred to me?' (*PI* 154). It may be that, by deliberately interrupting himself and thereby deferring his own elaboration of his remark, Wittgenstein aims to wean us away from the habit of expecting books to spare us the trouble of thinking, and to stimulate us to thoughts of our own. A true conversation, like an elegant dance, requires two equal partners—and the receptivity that can see how an interpolation about reading might seek to offer guidance on how to read interpolations.

RULES: INTUITIONS, DECISIONS, AND JUDGEMENTS

31. In section 185 Wittgenstein returns to the story of section 143. Thus far, he has employed that tale to emphasize the embeddedness of the normative within the natural, the circumstance-dependence of the criteria for understanding, and the absence of a sharp threshold for understanding—there can be no (non-stipulative) identification of 'the point' in a series of 'successful' applications of a rule at which understanding begins (*PI* 157) or is incontestably present (*PI* 145). In section 185 the first and last of these points are reiterated in a manner that raises new questions about the relationship between a rule and the sequence of its correct applications.

The pupil, moving on from the sequence of natural numbers, and having passed various tests of his ability to develop series of the form '+n' with numbers below 1,000, reveals with respect to numbers above 1,000 a natural inclination 'to understand our order [e.g. "Add 2"] with our explanations as *we* should understand the order: "Add 2 up to 1,000, 4 up to 2,000, 6 up to 3,000 and so on"' (*PI* 185). Since the same divergence of response will attend any attempt we might make to illustrate that or explain why his number sequence above 1,000 is the wrong one, do we want to say that he cannot understand the function of addition (and then perhaps separate him out and treat him as a lunatic, as Wittgenstein contemplates in the *Blue Book*)? Or is his mistake so systematic as to tempt us to say that he has simply understood wrong, and to try weaning him away from his error—say, by teaching our rule as an offshoot or variant of his (*PI* 143)? Is there a specific point in the teaching process, or a specific mode of divergence, which marks the limits of the pupil's intelligibility to us (and hence ours to him, and so ours to ourselves); or would stipulating such a limit simply mark the extent of our power over him (and so his power over us—the power to induce anxieties about our own intelligibility that our exercise of power over him hopes to mask)?

However we imagine the tale of the teacher's response to her pupil unfolding beyond this point, Wittgenstein's interlocutor quickly makes us aware of the anxieties that the tale thus far induces in him. He takes its implication to be that 'a new insight—intuition—is needed at every step to carry out the order "+*n*" correctly' (*PI* 186). We can intuit only what is already there, something given prior to our intuition of it; so this remark declares the interlocutor's sense that the steps of the series exist independently of any and every would-be rule-follower. Such a picture would assuage any anxiety that we might arbitrarily be imposing our own purely personal conception of correctness upon the deviant pupil; if the picture of intuition is correct, the imposition is essentially impersonal, itself authorized by the rule and its sequence of applications. But, as Wittgenstein points out, the deviant pupil undercuts this picture: for if he takes himself to be going on in exactly the same way after 1,000, if he regards his sequence of applications as simply continuing the pre-1,000 sequence, if he talks of this as what his intuition tells him to do, how exactly can our intuition about the matter claim authority? Talk of intuition presupposes an independent determination of correctness, and so cannot be employed to make that determination; but it is this prior question of what makes one way of going on correct and another incorrect that Wittgenstein's tale raises.

Wittgenstein then suggests that it 'would almost be more correct to say, not that an intuition was needed at every stage, but that a new decision was needed at every stage' (*PI* 186). Almost more correct: and so, not quite more correct, in fact no more correct than talk of a new intuition at every stage—which would mean that it was entirely question-begging, assuming the very thing that is at issue here. How, exactly? Because it invokes the idea that a *new* decision is needed at every step? Or because it invokes the idea of a *decision* at all? A decision (as the word's etymology suggests) concludes matters, cutting off a chain of reasoning, of considerations for and against a given plan of action—cutting free the action decided upon from the factors supporting or subverting it. It thus invokes the idea of a considered, a justified, or reasoned choice—in the extreme, it implies that every step chosen is taken only after explicit deliberation. But no such deliberative processes interpose themselves when, in everyday life, we add two numbers together; we do not typically have to stop and think about what the right answer might be. And if we are pressed retrospectively to justify our answer, what considerations might we invoke? What factors speak for or against deciding that $1,000 + 2 = 1,002$? Are they the same as or different from those speaking for or against deciding that $1,002 + 2 = 1,004$ (or that $100 + 2 = 102$, or that $10 + 2 = 12$)? If any steps are immediate, surely these are. Anything offered in their support, as licensing these steps, stands as much and as little in need of support as the steps themselves— which is, after all, the central point of Wittgenstein's depiction of their (and hence our) powerlessness in the face of the pupil's deviant responses.

If, in the face of this pupil, we discard the idea of considerations speaking for or against our steps but retain the idea of them being ours to choose, then the only apparent alternative to intuitionism about rules collapses into what one might call existentialism: the idea that rule-following is a matter of arbitrary choice, of the utterly unjustified exercise of the individual will—as if every step taken creates the way it purports to follow, and hence requires a renewed exercise of the will, a new choice. Hence, Wittgenstein warns us against thinking that decisionism is any more correct than intuitionism. But why, then, is it *almost* more correct? Perhaps because the concept of a decision also carries with it the idea that something remains to be taken—a step, more specifically a step into action—and by someone in particular, whether the specific individual to whom the teacher's order is addressed, or any specific individual who has decided to guide her action by that rule, and hence must now go on to apply it, to make a judgement about how to go on with it, how to do what it requires. If this is true of any given step in following a rule, it must be true of every such step: hence the idea of a *new* decision—the idea that every step in the following out of a rule, in the application of a given normative technique to particular situations, involves or is a matter of personal judgement, a step in the unfolding or production of a rule's extension that has to be taken by the individual rule-follower. If talk of decisions invokes this idea of judgement, it can dispense with the idea of choice—thus dispensing with the idea that steps cannot be deliberate without being the result of deliberation (an explicit or implicit weighing of alternatives), or that each step creates its own correctness (although not, of course, dispensing with the idea that we can choose whether or not to follow a rule). What such talk then retains is the idea that rules do not, as it were, contain their own applications—that individual rule-followers must act upon their judgements about how to apply them from case to case.

However, even Wittgenstein's highly hedged talk of new decisions makes his interlocutor feel that he risks losing something that talk of intuition at least purports to hold fast—our belief that we do know in advance what the pupil should do at every stage of the rule's expansion, that we know from the outset what we meant him to do at each stage. Wittgenstein once again admits the justice of such beliefs, but tries to ward off misleading interpretations of them. In particular, in section 187 he warns against taking such claims to mean that the teacher must have explicitly considered each step in the sequence when she first ordered the pupil to produce it—even though it is clear that the teacher, if asked at that point what number comes after 1,000, would have said, '1,002'. But this is no more paradoxical a conjunction than claiming that, although I would have jumped into the water after my friend if he had fallen in while we were strolling by the river, I did not explicitly think of so doing at the time—when he didn't actually fall in, and when nothing in our deeds, words, or thoughts actually raised that possibility.

The fact that the teacher was capable from the outset of saying immediately what number results from adding two to any given number in the natural number sequence does not entail that she must already have worked out what number results in every such case; it means exactly what it says—that she could have done so, that she possessed the means to do so. That is just what is meant by saying that she knows how to add two; since that rule can be applied to any number in the endless sequence of natural numbers, then her ability to apply it must be an ability to apply it correctly to any number in that sequence—but to be able to deal with an open-ended sequence of such cases is not to have already dealt with them.

Having worked to distinguish his account of rules as having to be applied, their extensions unfolded or produced in the judgement and the practice of those who follow them, from the idea that they have to be invented or created, Wittgenstein is now working to distinguish this idea of production from that of reproduction. Our ability to apply a rule is an ability to say what results from its application in an indefinite sequence of specific cases, but that ability is not a matter of retracing steps that have always already been taken even before we actually do take them. But this attempt once again makes Wittgenstein's interlocutor anxious; for he takes it to imply that how the rule is to be applied in those hitherto unconsidered cases is left entirely undetermined—at the mercy of the arbitrary human will—when the truth of the matter is that the rule determines how it is to be applied. But Wittgenstein takes his interlocutor to be asserting something that he does not wish to deny; more precisely, he takes it that the interlocutor is suffering a hallucination of sense—that the question he frames for Wittgenstein is either not the question he thinks he is posing or not a question at all.

With respect to the case of adding two, with x as the number to which the rule is to be applied and y as the result of so applying it, the interlocutor must be imagined as asking (see section 189): 'But *are* the steps then *not* determined by the algebraic formula "$y = x + 2$"?' But what exactly is the idea of determination that is here invoked? It might be used to contrast one kind of algebraic formula against another—those which do determine a single number y for any given x (e.g. $y = 2x$) as opposed to those which do not (e.g. $y \neq 2x$). But $y = x + 2$ plainly falls into the former category; for anyone who understands the formal difference between determinate and indeterminate formulae just outlined, our formula is plainly determinate. Alternatively, the interlocutor's words might be used to ask whether people faced with this formula all unhesitatingly work out the same value for y, as opposed to each unhesitatingly working out a different value for y, or all reacting with uncertainty. Once again, however, the answer in our case is obvious; for us, this formula completely determines every step in our application of it.

Of course, Wittgenstein's interlocutor takes himself to be asking another question altogether—a question about the link between the rule-formulation and its sequence of correct applications that is prior to the question of whether the form of the rule is determinate, or whether a given group of people can all apply it unhesitatingly. He is asking whether the rule determines what counts as applying it correctly; but in so asking, he presupposes that anything other than a positive answer would make sense. What, however, is the alternative to saying that the rule determines its own extension? Is that not simply a way of reminding us what a rule—as opposed, say, to a matter of taste or purely personal preference—actually is? Only someone unaware of what a rule is could treat this as a real question. In a sense, of course, the interlocutor does think of his question as more rhetorical than real: he poses it precisely because he thinks that Wittgenstein's attempt to avert a metaphysical conception of a rule's capacity to determine its extension subverts that capacity itself. But this leads him to insist upon the connection between a rule and its extension, to propound it as if it were a hypothesis or claim which someone might intelligibly oppose or doubt, and which it might therefore make sense to assert—as if it might come as news to, or provoke a controversy with, anyone who grasps what rule-following actually is.

Of course, there are those who might wish to oppose this insistence with another—those who perhaps feel that talk of a rule determining its own extension omits the vital determining role played by individual participants in the rule-following practice. They might, for example, attempt to insist that a teacher introducing a rule-formulation to her pupil determines how that pupil should go on by performing an act of meaning—hooking herself and so her pupil onto the line of one particular sequence of applications by running through that sequence in advance (*PI* 190). Wittgenstein gives exactly the same kind of uninsistent response to this opposing insistence. He points out that the question 'How did you mean it?', directed at someone who utters a particular rule-formulation, amounts to asking, 'Of what rule is that formula the expression?' If, for example, by the '$x!2$' in $y = x!2$, you meant x squared, then you get one value for y; if you meant $2x$ instead, then you get another. In short, how you meant the formula determines the steps of its extension in advance because it determines which rule the formula is meant to formulate, and the rule determines its own extension. No putative act of meaning determines what are the right values for y; what determines that is whichever rule we are supposed to be applying to generate y. It is not the way the formula is meant that matters, but rather which formula is meant—that is, which rule the formula formulates. Once again, intimations of metaphysical mysteries dissolve into platitudes—into assertions that are not obviously worth asserting.

We have here a signature effect of Wittgensteinian philosophical responsiveness. Wittgenstein does not assert that his interlocutor's questions are nonsensical—unintelligible, a violation of the bounds of sense. Rather, he claims that it is not clear offhand what we are to make of them, and offers a number of possible ways in which they might be taken. However, each such way would leave it unclear why the interlocutor would want to pose the question. With respect to the intuitionist, for example, on the two most obvious ways of taking it, his question emerges as one the answer to which is so obvious that it is difficult to see why it was worth posing; and on his preferred way of taking it, it turns out not to be a real question at all, and not a claim upon which one might wish to insist in the teeth of real or imagined opposition, but at best a grammatical reminder. And once these various possible ways of making sense of his words are disentangled, it is not clear that the interlocutor will continue to be attracted by any of the indefinitely many things that he could mean by his words.

RULES: THE MACHINERY OF SYMBOLISM

32. In effect, then, Wittgenstein has been trying to find a way between intuitionism and decisionism about rules, to find a position that is capable of acknowledging both the impersonal authority of normativity and its dimension of personal judgement without denying or exaggerating either facet of the phenomenon. Nevertheless, a certain amount of common ground has appeared in the mythologies developed by both intuitionists and decisionists; for despite their disputes, both parties appear eager to imagine rules as containing their own applications in a way that forecloses the future. Whether they think it comes about through an insight into the rule itself or through an act of meaning or will, both think of rules as anticipating reality; the pattern of their future uses is predetermined in some peculiar way, the steps they require of us always already taken, and so our grasp of rules is pictured as a kind of clairvoyance—an intuition of the future in the present.

This comes out most clearly in Wittgenstein's discussion of the machine-as-symbol (*PI* 193–4). A machine can be said to determine or embody its own future movements, in the sense that anyone who understands its construction can predict how its parts will move and interact. But of course, whether those empirically predetermined movements actually take place depends on other things—for example, on the parts of the machine not bending, breaking off, melting, and so on; so in this sense, the machine does not anticipate the future. If, however, we employ the machine symbolically—for example, specifying a particular arrangement of its parts as that which they will take up after two complete turns of its main cogwheel—then we do not mean by that 'whatever arrangement happens to emerge from two turns of the cogwheel' even if, say, the teeth of the cogwheel shear off during the second turn; we mean 'the arrangement its parts are designed to take up at that stage in its action'. It is then very tempting to interpret the machine-as-symbol's immunity to empirical distortion as proof that the movements of its parts are contained in it far more determinately than in the actual machine: 'As if it were not enough for the movements in question to be empirically determined in advance, but they had to be really—in a mysterious sense—already *present*' (*PI* 193).

The movements are already present in the sense that what counts as the correct sequence of the machine's movements is not empirically or experimentally established, or capable of being altered by how its parts actually interact; but this sense of presence is nevertheless mysterious to us, in that we know that the machine-as-symbol does not actually move—that the successive arrangements of its parts have to be derived from their initial arrangement. The ideally rigid machine can only move in one specific way, but this absolutely determinate possibility of movement is still a possibility, not the movement itself. So we think of the ideal machine as containing possibilities of movement just as actual machines do; and we think of its ideality as meaning that the unfolding of those possibilities is more inexorable than is the unfolding of an actual machine's empirical possibilities. To grasp the symbolic significance of the machine is thus to grasp how the future must be, not how it might be or ought to be; the machine-as-symbol reduces the gap between present and future to vanishing-point.

In this respect, the machine-as-symbol is not just one example of the many ways in which human beings formulate rules, and then misunderstand their own practices with them; after all, a symbolically employed machine is hardly an everyday instance of a rule-formulation. Wittgenstein's choice of example rather suggests that our misconceptions of rules in effect mythologize them as machines—as a kind of self-defining super-mechanism that contains their own (and so, our) future. This mythology in effect writes us as rule-followers out of the scene, as if following a rule were a matter of switching on a mechanism and sitting back to watch what emerges from its workings—as if the sequence of its correct applications were something to which we are fated, not something to be worked out. Or perhaps we might say: this myth pictures us, in so far as we are followers of rules, as ourselves mechanical—as perfect automata or robots, mechanically transforming orders into actions, free even of the degree of play (e.g. between pin and socket; *PI* 194) to be found in real machines, and hence utterly devoid of freedom, imagination, and judgement.

We might also say that, just as a symbolically employed machine is like the first in a series of pictures that we learn to derive from it (*PI* 193), so Wittgenstein's use of a machine to symbolize rule-following invites us to draw certain consequences from that figurative choice—to derive a series of pictures (the effacement of individual judgement, the occlusion of futurity by fate, ideally rigid robots) from that first picture by following out its mythological logic. He also thereby invites us to see this picture of rules as itself part of a larger series of pictures developed in the *Investigations*—a chain whose earlier links include the oddly mechanical shopkeeper, the builders, the sublimers of logic, and the human reading-machines. Of the present link in this chain, Wittgenstein comments that it pictures rules in the way in which primitive human beings might picture the expressions of civilized men (*PI* 194). In thus recalling his earliest invocation of the figure of the primitive (*PI* 2), he reminds us that this comment can be taken in more than one way: it might mean that these are primitive pictures of the genuinely civilized, or (since the primitives who produced these pictures are also the civilized men they depict) that they picture a civilization that has become genuinely primitive—its inhabitants and their practices reduced to the merely mechanical, expressive only of more or less primitive interests and desires, devoid of genuine individuality. The links between these series of symbols may not be as incontrovertible as those connecting the successive states of a machine-as-symbol, but neither are they merely empirical—the shadow of a chain of purely personal associations (whether Wittgenstein's or his reader's); for the idea of 'the mechanical' has a grammar whose demands unfold as precisely and rigorously in its figurative employments as they do in any of its modes of use.

Of course, none of this means that Wittgenstein has any wish to deny that we can grasp the whole use of a formula, or a word, in a flash— or that in such cases the future use of the rule is present to us in some sense, a sense very different from that of empirical predetermination. He is concerned to remove the air of queerness with which his interlocutor surrounds these ideas, or rather to suggest that this atmosphere is itself illusory—a creation of the interlocutor's desire to construct a conception of normativity as anticipating reality in an absolute or unique way. For the interlocutor, of course, to question this absolute conception of normative determination amounts to questioning the very possibility of normativity; if a rule does not contain its own applications in a super-empirical sense, then 'how can a rule shew me what I have to do at *this* [or any] point? Whatever I do is, on some interpretation, in accord with the rule' (*PI* 198). Without absolute predetermination, only arbitrary acts of individual will could fix normative standards, and that amounts to the absence of normativity.

Wittgenstein begs to differ:

Let me ask this: what has the expression of a rule—say a sign-post—got to do with my actions? What sort of connexion is there here?—Well, perhaps this one: I have been trained to react to this sign in a particular way, and now I do so react to it.

But that is only to give a causal connexion; to tell how it has come about that we now go by the sign-post; not what this going-by-the-sign really consists in. On the contrary; I have further indicated that a person goes by a sign-post only in so far as there exists a regular use of sign-posts, a custom. (*PI* 198)

Wittgenstein's interlocutor continues to search for the essence of normativity, for the hidden core of which guidance consists. Wittgenstein suggests instead that the right direction of investigation is horizontal rather than vertical: the expression of a rule and the sequence of its correct applications hang together only within a certain context—that of a regular use of the expression of the rule, a custom. Training pupils to react to expressions of a rule in certain ways and not in others, teaching them to adapt what they do and say in specific ways to such signs, encouraging them to respond with a given pattern or sequence of actions—these are not an inessential outer layer of the phenomenon of normativity, a genetic or causal narrative whose structure presupposes the connection between rule and applications that is at issue, but rather the medium through which that connection is established and maintained. Only in that kind of context can there be 'a way of grasping a rule which is *not* an *interpretation*, but which is exhibited in what we call "obeying the rule" and "going against it" in actual cases' (*PI* 201); and there must *be* such a way, since if normativity were entirely determined by individual interpretation, any conceivable course of action could be made out to accord with a given rule, and so there could be no such thing as normativity. To put the matter the other way round: talk of competing interpretations of a rule makes sense only if there already is a rule about which competing interpretations might be advanced, so those interpretations can hardly be invoked to establish its existence.

In effect, then, the notion of a custom or practice or institution signposts Wittgenstein's path between intuitionism and decisionism about rules. The sense of ideal inexorability that grounds the supermechanical picture of rules is itself brought back to the empirical ground of our practice of inexorably treating certain sequences of applications as correct and others as incorrect; but the fact that the practice is ours, one thread in the tapestry of our form of life, does not prevent us from distinguishing actually obeying a rule from merely thinking that one is obeying it, and so does not amount to picturing the sequence of correct applications of a rule as generated by arbitrary fiat at each stage of its unfolding. Wittgenstein thereby relocates normative or logical determination within the realms of time, history, and society, without conflating it with empirical determination. For on the one hand, we could not talk of rules (and mathematical rules in particular) as determining their correct applications in the lives of a group of people who respond to the order 'Add 2' by expressing confusion, or by each reacting in a different way but with perfect certainty. For them, we might say, the order 'Add 2' does not determine every step from one number to the next, as it does for us (*PI* 189)—and that in itself gives us reason to judge that 'Add 2' does not give expression to our arithmetical function of addition. On the other hand, we can distinguish between normatively and causally determined behaviour: using a signpost to guide our journey is not like using an automatic pilot—in the former case, we employ a technique and can make a mistake in doing so; in the latter, we engage a mechanism, and the mechanism can malfunction. Our normative practices are what they are only against the background of certain very general facts of nature; but what counts as obeying a rule neither is itself a fact of nature, nor is it determined by a fact of nature.

RULES: INDIVIDUALS AND COMMUNITIES

33. This brings us to a question that has dominated commentary on Wittgenstein's conception of rule-following for a number of years.

Is what we call 'obeying a rule' something that it would be possible for only *one* man to do, and to do only *once* in his life?—This is of course a note on the grammar of the expression 'to obey a rule'.

It is not possible that there should have been only one occasion on which someone obeyed a rule. It is not possible that there should have been only one occasion on which a report was made, an order given or understood; and so on.—To obey a rule, to make a report, to give an order, to play a game of chess, are *customs* (uses, institutions).

To understand a sentence means to understand a language. To understand a language means to be master of a technique. (*PI* 199)

Wittgenstein's answer to his own question makes clear the centrality of a multiplicity of occasions to his concept of a practice or custom. Without a patterned sequence of applications of a rule, the context of the human behaviour under judgement would not be sufficiently complex for it to be capable of manifesting a distinction between applying the rule correctly as opposed to incorrectly, and more generally of manifesting the kind of explanatory, justificatory, corrective activity that is integral to our sense of what normativity involves. But this is only a partial answer to the original question, or rather an answer to one part of that question; it tells us that 'obeying a rule' is not something that someone could do only once, but it does not tell us whether or not 'obeying a rule' is something that one person could do. In other words, Wittgenstein appears to avoid committing himself on the self-posed question of whether or not rule-following is possible only in the context of a community of rule-followers.

This apparent reticence has not been shared by Wittgenstein's commentators; on the contrary, much of the now voluminous secondary literature on this topic focuses upon precisely this question—but it is divided (far from evenly) between two possible answers to it. On the one hand, there are those, such as Norman Malcolm, who argue that Wittgenstein argues that no sense can be made of the idea of following a rule except against a context of communal agreement over what counts as correctly applying that rule. On the other, there are those, such as Baker and Hacker, who argue that Wittgenstein argues that, although any technique of rule-following must be shareable with others, it need not be actually shared—that the existence of a community of practitioners is not intrinsic to the concept of a normative practice as such. Since the leading representatives of these conflicting schools of interpretation have engaged in detailed criticism of one another, it may prove illuminating to examine their exchanges.[17]

This disagreement has two focal points: the first involves how to understand the relation between a rule and its extension, the second how to construe the solitariness of an isolated would-be rule-follower. Under the first heading, Malcolm is suspicious of Baker and Hacker's claim that 'the rule and nothing but the rule determines what is correct' (i.e. which acts are in accord with it and which are not) (*RGN* 171).

> . . . Wittgenstein remarks [in MS 165, unpublished] that 'a rule is not an extension. To follow a rule means to form an extension according to a "general" expression'. Which is to say that the applications of a rule (its 'extension') are not given with the rule, but have to be *produced*; the extension has to be *constructed*. This point sets the stage for the hard question—what *decides* whether a particular step taken, a particular application made, is or is not in accordance with the rule? This question is not answered by the declaration that a rule is 'internally' related to the acts that accord with it. (WLR 148)

Why not? Because the truth it embodies—that, roughly speaking, there is no understanding a rule without knowing what counts as applying it correctly—provides no answer to the question posed in section 185.

> It would seem that different people, with similar training and equal intelligence, *could* form *different* extensions in accordance with the same general expression. They could go on differently. Indeed, that *could* happen—and sometimes does happen. But if such divergence became frequent, then the understanding of what rules are, and what following a rule is, would have disappeared. The fact that almost everyone does go on in the same way, is a great example of a

---

[17] In 'Wittgenstein on Language and Rules' (in his *Essays on Wittgensteinian Themes* (Cornell University Press: Ithaca, NY, 1996), hereafter WLR, Norman Malcolm criticizes G. P. Baker and P. M. S. Hacker's account of rule-following, as presented in *Wittgenstein: Rules, Grammar and Necessity* (Blackwell: Oxford, 1986), hereafter *RGN*; Baker and Hacker reply to those criticisms in 'Malcolm on Language and Rules', *Philosophy*, 65 (1990), hereafter MLR.

'form of life', and also an example of something that is normally hidden from us because of its 'simplicity and familiarity'. (WLR 152)

Only this framework of quiet agreement, claims Malcolm, allows us to distinguish one pattern of applications as correct and others as incorrect; in the absence of that framework, no such distinction could be made, and that would amount to there being no such thing as following a rule.

In response, Baker and Hacker argue that the question posed in section 185 could be taken seriously by someone who accepts their claim about the internal relation between a rule and its applications only if she fails to distinguish between a formula and the rule it formulates.

The rule '+2' would not be what it is, viz. the rule for the series of even integers, if '1,002' did not follow '1,000' in its application (if the intension of 'even integer' is given, then so is its extension, even though the intension neither is nor 'contains' the extension!) . . . A sign is only the expression of a rule if it is taken together with its method of projection . . . The claim that if a rule is given then so is its extension is tantamount to the claim that the identity of a rule (as opposed to the identity of a sign or formula) is logically dependent upon the identity of its extension. (MLR 171)

For Baker and Hacker, if the 'general expression of the rule' that Malcolm mentions is considered apart from a particular method of projection, then indeed it offers us no guidance as to how to apply it—but that is because it then amounts to a mere sign or formula; only taken together with a method of projection is it really the general expression *of a rule*, and then it does precisely determine how we should go on with it.

Unfortunately, this grammatical reminder will not necessarily remove Malcolm's qualms. For even granted that a rule is given only if there exists a practice of employing a rule-formulation (a 'general expression') in accordance with a specific method of projection, there remains a sense in which for him it is seriously misleading to say that when a rule is given, so is its extension. For of course, the extension of a rule such as 'Add 2', being non-finite, is always open to further development, and hence not only is not given but cannot be given in its entirety; its users will accordingly always face the problem of determining how their given practice of applying this rule, their given method of projection, is itself to be projected beyond its present reach. And if this problem arises with respect to going on with a given way of going on with a rule, there seems no way of preventing it from arising within that given way of going on. For any step within a given segment of a rule's extension (whether or not that extension is non-finite), being distinct from its predecessors, goes beyond them; hence, taking any such step involves taking a given method of projection further, projecting it beyond its previous reach. The question that Wittgenstein's example starkly dramatizes is: what justifies or determines that we should go on in one particular way rather than another at any step in the production of any rule's extension?

It will not help here to say, with Baker and Hacker, that the rule and nothing but the rule will determine which step to take, and hence which extension to construct; for if the identity of a rule is logically dependent upon the identity of its extension, then to ask which extension accords with the rule just is to ask which rule it is that we are applying. And if we say instead that if a practice of employing the rule really is given, then so must be the technique for producing or constructing its correct extension, we do not avoid the problem; for to ask which extension accords with the rule just is to ask how the technique for producing its extension is to be employed. How can that question simply be dismissed as nonsensical—unless of course one thinks that a technique of use can effect its own implementation?

It seems plausible to interpret Malcolm as following this line of thought when he concludes that Baker and Hacker's reiteration of the givenness of a rule's extension can only signify an intuitionistic commitment to the idea that rules somehow contain their extensions—anticipating the future of their own unfolding, treating the production of a rule's extension as its reproduction. It will then seem that, for them, the beginning of the series 'add 2' 'is a visible section of rails invisibly laid to infinity' (*PI* 218), that it 'traces the lines along which it is to be followed through the whole of space' (*PI* 219). On the other hand, it is equally easy to see why, to Baker and Hacker, Malcolm's emphasis upon the need for a rule's extension to be produced appears to tend towards the opposite extreme, also condemned by Wittgenstein—the idea that a new decision is needed at every step in a rule's application. After all, it is not as if we do not know how to produce the extension, to implement the technique, of adding two beyond any given point in its application. As Wittgenstein is careful to acknowledge, anyone who understands that technique understands that—for example—'1,002' is what results from adding two to '1,000'; and the teacher in section 185 would be perfectly correct in saying that if, when first instructing the pupil to add two, she had been asked what he should produce when adding two to '1,000', she would have said '1,002'. Precisely because a rule and its extension are internally related, anyone who understands the relevant technique must be able to produce its extension, and to do so by applying or employing that technique; this is central to what they take themselves to be saying when they claim that the rule determines its own extension.

It seems fair to say that, from Baker and Hacker's point of view, Malcolm's belief that the question raised in section 185 must be taken seriously depends upon his acceptance of the idea that the development of a rule's extension amounts to constructing novel applications of it; for only then can they be seen as requiring a new decision from us. But this acceptance is too ready. 1,000 may be a number to which we have never previously added 2, but in doing so we apply exactly the same rule (exactly the same technique) as we employed in the past, and so are not making a new, or a new kind of, application of the rule.

So even though, *ex hypothesi*, I have never added 2 to 1,000, writing '1,002' *is* going on in the same way as before, doing the same as hitherto. It is no more a novel ('unprecedented') application of the rule for addition than calling a hitherto unseen red object 'red' is a novel ('unprecedented') application of the rule for the use of 'red'.

The point of the notion that in learning to add I grasp a rule is not that the rule mysteriously determines a unique answer for indefinitely many *new* cases in the future . . . Rather should we say that the point is that it is of the nature of stipulating rules that future cases (typically) *are old cases*, that each application of a rule is doing the same again.[18]

In other words, from Baker and Hacker's perspective, Malcolm is failing to absorb the lesson of Wittgenstein's remark that 'the use of the word "rule" and the use of the word "same" are interwoven' (*PI* 225). To arrive at a number as the result of adding two to a number never before encountered can be thought of as doing something new only if one forgets that one arrived at it by applying an utterly familiar technique. From the point of view of the rule (as it were), there is nothing novel about it.

34. What are we to make of this deadlock? Do the mutual recriminations of these most sophisticated of commentators show how difficult it is for followers of Wittgenstein to avoid seeing versions of the illusions he identifies in even the most nuanced and self-aware attempts to identify the platitudes which lurk beneath them? Or does their very insistence upon those platitudes suggest rather that both parties have indeed succumbed to the temptation to inform one another of something about which they could hardly fail to know already, and thus to

---

[18] G. P. Baker and P. M. S. Hacker, *Scepticism, Rules and Language* (Blackwell, Oxford: 1984) 87–8; hereafter *SRL*.

reproduce illusions essentially complementary to the ones they intend to castigate? What does it say about the nature of philosophical illusion, about its pervasiveness and its immunity to direct refutation, that neither party devotes much if any time to considering either of the above possibilities—that neither remains silent for long enough to hear the uncanny similarities between some of their own remarks and those of the interlocutors in the text about which they are disputing?

Two things, at least, do seem worth noting. The first is that, if Malcolm really has succumbed to decisionism and Baker and Hacker to intuitionism, certain features of the particular example of rule-following Wittgenstein has chosen to employ make these responses peculiarly difficult to avoid. The second is that, since these are features peculiar to this example of rule-following, and hence not obviously generalizable, this commentators' quarrel raises a fundamental question about Wittgenstein's apparent assumption that a technique of addition is genuinely exemplary of rules, and so of rule-following, more generally.

To begin with the first point. Against the background laid out in the last section, one critical characteristic of the technique of adding two stands out—namely, the fact that it is an iterated operation. As with any series of numbers produced by iteration, each step in the series generated by 'Add 2' appears as the result of using its predecessor as the base for the relevant operation, and hence as, one might say, successive or ordered. But then any step in the series will appear as at once new (derived from, and hence going beyond, its predecessor) and old (derived by the same operation which generated its predecessor). Seen under the first of these aspects, the example invites us to be struck by the fact that a question about how to go on with the rule's extension can be raised at any and every step of its production—hence Malcolm's (decisionistic?) objections to Baker and Hacker's supposed intuitionism. Seen under the second aspect, it invites us to be struck by the fact that any and every step taken in the expansion of the series is a matter of doing the same thing again, and hence suggests that there is nothing new to be met with, however far we go with its expansion—hence Baker and Hacker's (intuitionistic?) objections to Malcolm's supposed decisionism. Each party to the dispute presses the importance of one of these aspects, but neither gives much indication of perceiving the other—as if each occludes the other, like the two aspects of the duck–rabbit. As a result, neither party perceives either the interdependence of these two features or its root cause.

With respect to adding two, then, it is immediately clear why anyone would want to say both that we are doing something new, and that we are doing exactly the same again, in constructing the series. But Baker and Hacker's own comparison between adding two and using the word 'red' inadvertently makes it clear just how localized a normative phenomenon this dual-aspect impression of novelty and familiarity (exactly the same and yet completely different) really is. As we saw, they assert that there is no difference between (because nothing genuinely novel involved in) adding two to a number for the first time and describing a red object seen for the first time as red. Is this, however, entirely beyond question? To be sure, in both cases a given technique is (re)applied; but while it would not be unnatural to describe the former case as one in which we make a new application of an old technique, it surely would be unnatural to describe the latter as one in which we perceive a new instance of a familiar colour, or even a new instance of an object having that familiar colour. (Is my third red apple of the day a new instance of red? My first ever red pepper might be a new instance of a red object, but only because an object of that familiar kind having a colour of that familiar kind is new to me.)

Whereas I can see immediately why anyone would want to say that, in doing to 1,000 what we previously did to 998, we construct a new step in that sequence, I am not at all inclined to say that in describing a hitherto unseen object as red, I am constructing a new step in the sequence of applications of the word 'red'. (The idea of a new application would more properly be invited by someone's beginning to talk of 'being caught red-handed'; the idea of a decision needing to be made might seem appropriate when we meet an object whose colour appears as much purple as red, but here we have a hard case rather than a new one.) And the underlying problem is to understand what exactly might be meant by talking of constructing or producing (let alone deriving) the extension of (a grammatical rule for the use of) a colour-term. In applying colour-terms to the objects we encounter, are we extending a given sequence of applications? It is not obvious that the notion of an infinitely extendable ordered sequence of applications is called for with respect to the use of any word of ordinary (i.e. non-mathematical) language; but without it, the idea of novelty so clearly invited by our original mathematical context would not obviously be called for at all, and so the idea of familiarity or sameness that *is* called for in the everyday case cannot resemble the notion of reiteration that is at home (and that accounts for the simultaneous appearance of novelty and sameness) in mathematics.

If this is correct, what follows? Most immediately, it follows that, while Baker and Hacker are right to see a certain queerness in projecting the idea of novel applications invoked by the addition example into the context of ordinary language use, they are wrong to see no essential difference between non-mathematical and mathematical cases in this respect, and therefore wrong in how they appear to account for that queerness (it depends not upon the fact that we are applying the same rule once again, but upon the fact that the use of non-mathematical terms is not happily described as the production of an indefinitely extensible ordered sequence of applications). Malcolm, on the other hand, while right to see a certain naturalness in introducing the idea of novel applications in the addition example, is wrong to see no essential difference between mathematical and non-mathematical cases in this respect, and so wrong in how he appears to account for that naturalness (it depends not upon the open-endedness of any word's technique of use, but upon the fact that reiterative mathematical techniques such as addition generate indefinitely extendable ordered number sequences).

More generally, however, it follows that the distinctive features of addition which give rise to the philosophical illusions that threaten to engulf Wittgenstein's interlocutors and commmentators alike are not ones that all rules share—particularly not the rules governing the use of ordinary (non-mathematical) words, what we might be inclined to call rules of grammar. How, then, are we to understand Wittgenstein's decision to use such a rule as the focus of his study of rule-following in general—a study that seems so evidently intended to cast light upon how one goes on with words, and hence upon his idea of grammar? Is he simply unaware that his example cannot easily be made to generalize? And if he is not, how can he hope to make philosophical progress with such an unrepresentative example, and from cultivating an apparent ignorance of that unrepresentativeness? We must return to this.

35. The second focal point of the debate between Malcolm and Baker and Hacker is the question of whether and how sense might be made of the idea of an isolated rule-follower. Their opposing views on this second issue are, of course, linked to their opposing views on the first. Malcolm's claim that when a rule is given, its extension is not given entails that different people with similar training and equal intelligence could form different extensions in accordance with the same general expression; but if such divergence became frequent, then any understanding of what rules are, and of what following a rule is, would have disappeared. Hence following a rule is only possible against a background of quiet communal agreement on its correct application. By contrast, Baker and Hacker's claim that a rule determines its own extension leads them to reject the idea that communal agreement has

any essential role to play in rule-following. An isolated rule-follower must establish a normative practice or technique—which means that his behaviour must be sufficiently complex to manifest not only regularity but also signs that he is guiding and correcting his behaviour by reference to a rule—and this technique must be one that could in principle be shared with others; but there need not be any actual community of rule-followers with whom his generation of the rule's extension might or might not be in agreement.

The strength of Baker and Hacker's case in this second phase of their argument with Malcolm comes out most clearly in their discussion of the possibility of a Robinson Crusoe following rules. Malcolm says that the intelligibility of this story depends upon the assumption that Crusoe learned to follow rules in England before his shipwreck. Baker and Hacker dismiss the issue of Crusoe's background and upbringing as introducing the wholly extraneous question of how Crusoe acquired his rule-following abilities, when the real focus should be that of how it is or could be manifest in his behaviour on the island that what he then acquired was indeed the ability to follow rules: 'the criteria for whether [what Crusoe speaks or writes] is a language and for what the words of the language mean make no reference to what people did in London twenty years earlier' (MLR 174). The criteria for rule-following are criteria for the possession of an ability, and do not make reference to how the candidate creature might have acquired this ability; to think otherwise is to commit a form of the genetic fallacy.

On Baker and Hacker's view, those criteria presuppose not only a regularity in Crusoe's behaviour but also 'an array of circumambient normative practices or activities, eg of correcting mistakes, of checking what one has done for correctness against a standard, and—*if asked*—of explaining what one has done, justifying what one has done by reference to this rule, and teaching the rule and what counts as accord with it to others' (MLR 176).

Crusoe's island context cuts away any chance of his displaying explanatory, justificatory, or teaching activities since he has no opportunity to do so until others join him; and that makes it rather more difficult than Baker and Hacker sometimes appear to acknowledge to give content to the idea that he might be capable of engaging in such activities in the appropriate circumstances (for if our fictional narrative does not allow those circumstances to materialize, it is not easy to see how one might distinguish, even in principle, between a Crusoe who has those capacities although he does not manifest them and one who does not manifest them because he does not have them). Nevertheless, he may perfectly well make mistakes and correct them—that is, discriminate between what seems to him to be right and what is actually right in the application of his rules. To be sure, he could have no use for such phrases as 'This seems to me to be correct, but it is actually incorrect'; but he could perfectly well say, 'This seemed to me to be correct, but it is actually incorrect.' He could, for example, spend a day painting a decorative frieze on his cave walls, frequently referring to a sample pattern he drew earlier on the floor and occasionally repainting the sections on which he is working; he might then go back to the sequence the next day and correct one part of it—perhaps with expressions of irritation or contrition—after comparing it with the sample or with earlier parts of the sequence. Would this not constitute a circumambient array of normative behaviour, and so fulfil our criteria for judging that, in decorating his cave wall, Crusoe is following a rule—producing a sequence of applications from a general expression?

That Crusoe could ever have managed to develop such capacities in utter isolation might appear highly implausible; but whether or not he did is plainly not relevant to our judgement of what he can now do—and anyway, the mere idea that a being capable of manifesting these abilities might turn out never to have acquired them from others is surely not inconceivable. Nor could Malcolm argue that a Crusoe from birth could never distinguish between thinking that he had made a mistake and actually making a mistake. For Crusoe's ability to compare what he produces with his original pattern, and to reassess his earlier judgements about such comparisons, need not be any less reliable than our own; and if this problem were to be viewed as fatal to Crusoe's normative practice, it is not obvious why it should not be equally fatal to a community of rule-followers. For how might such a group distinguish between their collectively thinking that they have made a mistake, and their actually making a mistake? If the usual human capacities for reflection, checking, and rechecking are available to and sufficient for them, why should they not be available to and sufficient for Crusoe? In both cases, unrecognized errors may persist; but acknowledging that possibility supports rather than subverts the realization that the very idea of correctness and incorrectness is applicable to both.

If there is a weakness in Baker and Hacker's case here, it lies elsewhere. In defence of their claim to be offering Wittgenstein's view of the role of the community in rule-following, they emphasize that when he poses the question of the necessary multiplicity of agents (in section 199), he takes great care not to assert that it is impossible for an isolated individual to follow a rule. But they pay little attention in this context to the section that follows that one.

It is, of course, imaginable that two people belonging to a tribe unacquainted with games should sit at a chess-board and go through the moves of a game of chess; and even with all the appropriate mental accompaniments. And if *we* were to see it we should say they were playing chess. But now imagine a game of chess translated according to certain rules into a series of actions which we do not ordinarily associate with a *game*—say into yells and stamping of feet. And now suppose those two people to yell and stamp instead of playing the form of chess that we are used to; and this in such a way that their procedure is translatable by suitable rules into a game of chess. Should we still be inclined to say they were playing a game? What right would one have to say so? (*PI* 200)

In the first paragraph of section 199 Wittgenstein asks a two-part question—about the multiplicity of occasions and the multiplicity of agents; in the remaining paragraphs of that section he answers the first of those questions. Might it not be worth while considering the possibility that section 200 provides his answer to the second?

Are the yelling and stamping people playing a game of chess or not? Initially, we would probably be inclined to deny it—appearances are against them. But suppose it is pointed out to us that their yells and stamps can be mapped onto procedures licensed by the rules of chess. Would that give us the right to say that they are playing that game? The problem—the problem that these sections have been circling round since section 185—is that their yells and stamps could in principle be mapped onto an indefinite number of different, equally familiar procedures—a description of the wildlife observed on their last trip, or a recitation of the lyrics of All Saints' latest single, or a calculation of the decimal expansion of pi, or the Catholic liturgy of the Eucharist, and so endlessly on. We have no more and no less right to say that these yells and stamps are moves in a game than we do to say that they form part of any of those other procedures—and that simply means that here we can't talk about right. What we know and see gives no substance to the idea that these people are doing anything in particular other than yelling and stamping in a regular or patterned kind of way. It doesn't even, as it stands, give us any ground for saying that they are following rules—for the fact that a pattern of behaviour can be mapped onto a pattern of normative behaviour does not show that it is normative. All we have a right to say is that these people are yelling and stamping.

Against this background, let us think again about Crusoe and his wall-markings. Throughout my telling of his story (itself a retelling of Baker and Hacker's story) I talked of him as decorating those walls; and of course, in this respect appearances were with me, since human practices of interior decoration do look like this. But what right do I have to describe his actions in that way, given the information that my story provides? After all, as we saw with the 'chess-playing' tribesmen, appearances do not provide an adequate basis for such judgements. And is it not as true of Crusoe as it is of the yelling, stamping tribesmen that his behaviour might with equal facility be mapped onto an endless list of very different kinds of activity—perhaps the floor pattern is a short-hand record, and the wall-markings a more elaborate transcription, of his hunting successes and failures, or of a sonnet sequence composed on his previous trip across the island; or perhaps the floor pattern summarizes the rules for a game whose moves he enacts on the wall; or perhaps it is a religious ritual . . . We have no more and no less reason to describe his behaviour as decorating his walls than we do to describe it in terms of any of the items on that list; and that means that here we can't talk about right.

What Baker and Hacker call the circumambient array of his normative behaviour at least gives us reason to think of what he does as akin to rule-following rather than simply as a behavioural regularity. But even this is more questionable than it may appear. First, that 'circum-ambient array' is rather more skeletal than it would be in ordinary circumstances; lacking the scope for explanatory or justificatory behaviour, it consists purely in self-directed corrective behaviour, and so can at best amount to a primitive analogue to 'normative behaviour' proper. Second, as Wittgenstein points out in sections 233–4, behaviour that involves repeated reference to what seems to be a general expression of a rule might in reality be part of a practice of awaiting inspiration to guide one's responses to that general expression, a listening to one's inner voice that licenses differences in one's 'application' of that 'general expression', and that is therefore to be contrasted with normative behaviour; Crusoe's actions, as they have so far been characterized, give us no way of determining, even in principle, whether or not he is inspired or commanded by his floor pattern. If we take these points together with the further fact that the question of what rule (or even what kind of rule) Crusoe might be following lacks any real substance, then what substance remains to the claim that his behaviour really is normative?

In ordinary life these critical distinctions—between normative and inspirational practices, and between types of normative practice—are easily made, because the individual behaviour under judgement is manifestly related to the analogous behaviour of others as embedded in a complex array of specific practices, institutions, and customs. When other people are participating in his wall-marking practice, we can see whether or not behaviour radically divergent from Crusoe's own counts as a legitimate response to the 'sample', and so see whether this wall-marking technique is normative or inspirational; and by seeing the place of that technique within a complex form of life, in which religious, poetic, ludic, and reproductive concerns (among others) achieve their distinctive but interwoven articulations, we can see the particular kind of purpose to which his wall-marking behaviour gives expression. In other words, the significance of any given type of human behaviour is determined by its place within the variegated tapestry of a common culture and form of life; but the tale of Crusoe's wall-marking behaviour as I have told it (and as it is typically told in the literature) sketches in no such context, and hence makes the question of its normative significance virtually empty of content. Without massively enriching the tale so as to contextualize his behaviour in such ways, all that we can say is that Crusoe is making marks on a wall; and whatever rule-following amounts to, it amounts to more than the regular production of marks.

Even if this critique of Baker and Hacker is right, however, it does not vindicate Malcolm's opposing position. In part, this is because the critique does not depend upon agreeing with Malcolm that a Crusoe from birth would lack the capacity to distinguish correctly following his rule from merely thinking that he is correctly following his rule, and that a background of communal agreement is required to make any such distinction possible. In the main, however, it is precisely because Malcolm's position is the opposite of Baker and Hacker's; for he takes himself to be giving a different answer to the same question, and thus presupposes that this question is meaningful. But the force of Wittgenstein's remarks in section 200 is to deny that there is a genuine question here that needs to be answered one way or the other. For that question to have substance, we would have to be able to say the following: 'We have and follow rules in the ordinary circumstances of our lives. Could there be such rules in very different kinds of circumstance? What are the necessary conditions for there to be behaviour with the same grammar as that of "following a rule"?' Baker and Hacker think that there could be rules in Crusoe-type circumstances; Malcolm thinks that there cannot. But for there to be normative behaviour *just is* for there to be behaviour with a specific position in our lives and specific connections with other things in our lives. Our complex life with rules is not one thing and our concept of 'following a rule' something else, something that might or might not stand in a relation of logical or conceptual dependence to that complex life. And so Crusoe's life, in which what might appear to be a primitive version of rule-following behav-

iour in fact has a very different position in, and very different connections within, his life, just is a life in which there is no concept of 'following a rule'. The point of Wittgenstein's strategy is not to show that
something, some particular, concrete thing (say Crusoe's following a
rule) is or is not empirically or conceptually impossible; it is to show
that, when we thought that we were imagining something specific, we
were not imagining anything at all. And if this claim—a claim which is
(as we saw earlier) central to Diamond's reading of these passages—is
correct, then Malcolm's position is no less subject to criticism than
Baker and Hacker's.

RULES: FANTASIES, MYTHS, AND SYMBOLS

36. This emphasis upon the way in which rule-following must be understood in relation to the broader circumstances of our lives with rules
should immediately make us reconsider the significance of the fact that,
throughout his discussion of rule-following, Wittgenstein sticks resolutely with his original choice of a mathematical example. If we could
assume that all instances of rule-following share a common normative
essence, then his choice of example would be arbitrary. If, however (as
Wittgenstein earlier emphasized in his interpolated consideration of the
family resemblance structure of guidance and derivation), the very idea
of a common essence to normativity is questionable, and if (as he is now
emphasizing) the significance of any given technique is manifest in its
specific place in our form of life, in its specific connections with other
such techniques, and so in the differences between its place and that of
other techniques, then it is at least open to question whether examining normativity as such through the lens of a specifically mathematical
technique is not likely to mislead at least as much as it illuminates—
particularly when these risks are not exactly highlighted in his treatment
of the topic.

The potential difficulty here in fact goes even deeper. For in appearing, at least implicitly, to accept the mathematical as exemplary for normativity as such, Wittgenstein appears to exemplify our tendency to
sublime the logic of our language, to take mathematics and logic as normative for language—a tendency against which he firmly sets his face
in the discussion which effectively acts as a prologue to his rule-
following remarks. How, for instance, does his choice of example
hang together with the following comment?

F. P. Ramsey once emphasized in conversation with me that logic was a 'normative science'. I do not know exactly what he had in mind, but it was doubtless closely related to what only dawned on me later: namely, that in philosophy we often *compare* the use of words with games and calculi which have fixed rules, but cannot say that someone who is using language *must* be playing such a game. (*PI* 81)

Here, we are being warned against treating the forms of determination manifest in logic and mathematics as a kind of ideal or sublime picture of rules in general and of linguistic rules in particular. As Cavell comments:

Ordinary language will aspire to mathematics as to something sublime; that it can so aspire is specific to its condition. The idea of ordinary language as lacking something in its rules is bound up with . . . this aspiration . . . In this role of the normative, the mathematical is not a special case of a problem that arises for the ordinary; without the mathematical this problem of the ordinary would not arise. (*Conditions Handsome and Unhandsome*,[19] 92)

Why, then, does Wittgenstein appear to invite the accusation that his overarching strategy in the rule-following remarks takes it for granted that the mathematical is an apt picture of (at least the underlying essence of) ordinary language as such, and so that speaking a language is a matter of 'operating a calculus according to definite rules' (*PI* 81)?

Finding an answer to this question depends upon recalling that our sense of ordinary words as suffering in comparison with logic and mathematics is part of what one might call a philosophical picture, and upon recalling further the care with which Wittgenstein specifies the distinctive status of pictures at the very beginning of his book. This status is in fact very well illustrated by the attitude Wittgenstein's commentators have generally taken to the issue now under discussion—or more precisely, by the fact that almost without exception they have not taken it to be an issue, and have not discussed it. It is not as if they are virtually all *of the opinion* that the mathematical is exemplary of normativity as such, and hence *of the opinion* that Wittgenstein is right so to treat it; that he apparently so treats it is not mentioned in their commentaries, as if so treating it is so pervasive an assumption or attitude among us all that Wittgenstein's apparent exemplification of it is not even remarked upon, not seen as in any way philosophically questionable. This is precisely how a picture can shape our thinking.

If we were of the opinion that ordinary language is deprived of a sublimity which mathematics exemplifies, Wittgenstein might profitably have opposed or contradicted it; since, however, he rather takes it to be

---

[19] (University of Chicago Press: Chicago, 1990); hereafter *CHU*.

a fantasy or illusion under which we labour, something that shapes the particular opinions we might hold and to which our condition as creatures burdened with language makes us naturally vulnerable, then any such direct opposition would merely incite responses shaped by that picture and so reinforce its grip. What is rather needed is a way of loosening that grip, of freeing us from our captivation, of bringing about a kind of disillusionment. And the influence of a fantasy is best broken not by flatly denying its reality but by accepting the terms it sets, working through them from within and hoping thereby to work beyond them. Psychoanalysis would call it transference: the analyst suffers the analysand's projection of her fantasies, but does so precisely in order to put its mechanisms and motivations in question, to work with and upon the material rather than simply reiterating it.

Suppose, then, that we take Wittgenstein's apparently unquestioning use of a mathematical rule to exemplify normativity as such as in fact an exemplification of philosophical transference—the essential step in coming properly to terms with our fantasy of mathematics as normative for language as such. What does his enactment of it allow us to appreciate about its mechanisms and motivations?

37. Most fundamentally, it tells us that our aspiration towards the mathematical as the sublime itself depends upon a sublimation of the mathematical, upon an idealization of the qualities which genuinely distinguish mathematical from non-mathematical concepts—an idealization which is then projected onto ordinary language as a whole (whether as its deepest desire or as its hidden essence). In other words, one reason Wittgenstein dwells so insistently upon the realm of mathematical rules is that he thinks that if he can successfully question our fantasized picture of that realm, then we will no longer find attractive our further fantasy of the mathematical as normative for language as such.

The most obvious fantasy that Wittgenstein's example of a mathematical rule invites is the attribution of a kind of absolute abstractness and self-containedness. To know how to add two is, it seems self-evident, to know how to construct an utterly specific series of numbers from a general formula; the requisite actions seem so utterly minimal, so sublimely bare and schematic, that the skill they manifest appears comprehensible entirely independently of any broader background of skills, fellow practitioners, and culture. It is as if, in the mathematical context, rule-following as such has been pared down or refined to its pure essence. And if our life with language is understood as a matter of rule-following, then mathematical rule-following will naturally appear as revelatory of its essence too. In short, knowing how to go on with words will present itself as equally possessed of a context-independent, schematic, but utterly determinate essence—that of producing a more or less precise sequence of applications of the word.

This fantasy of mathematical rule-following as the bare production of a sequence of signs can be productively compared to the depiction of the yelling and stamping tribesmen of section 200. Precisely because their actions are so bare and schematic, they invite us to ask what makes them the right way to go on—in short, they invite interpretation; but once interpretation is invoked, their sublime bareness ensures that they are unable to avoid being overwhelmed by it, by an endlessly proliferating chain of different, but apparently equally valid, ways of putting flesh on their bones. And what this shows is that thinking of a sequence of minimally characterized actions—a display of yells and stamps, the moving of pieces of wood on a board, the production of a familiar-sounding sequence of marks or noises—as the essential skeleton of rule-following leaves us with nothing that we would want to describe as rule-following (even mathematical rule-following) at all. We are left with the stamps, the wooden pieces, the marks; but we are deprived of any suggestion that they form part of a particular rule-following practice.

Once again our impulse—an impulse which seems particularly strong in mathematical contexts—is to dig beneath the surface, to penetrate the phenomena, to pare away what we take to be the inessential surroundings of everyday normative human activities in order to find its underlying essence. And once again Wittgenstein invites us instead to rotate the axis of our investigation towards the horizontal plane—to see that grasping a rule is exhibited in what we call 'obeying the rule' and 'going against it' in particular cases (*PI* 201), and so in the differences between the various kinds of rule-following practice that are exhibited in those particular cases, and so in the complex tapestry of different kinds of customs, uses, and institutions within which any specific rule-following practice has its distinctive place. The essence of a (rule-following) technique is not best understood as a procedure for determining which number or move or noise to produce in response to another number or move or noise; it is rather made manifest in its specific location within a form of human life with language.

The deviant pupil is thus the embodiment of a particularly forceful contestation of this fantasy of the mathematical (and hence of language) as sublimely abstract. Wittgenstein's point is not to contest the very idea that mathematical rules are abstract, but to contest a particular picture of that abstractness, to bring it back to earth by showing how the distinctive qualities of such rules are grounded in specific aspects of human forms of life. The deviant pupil shows how the life or essence of even the most abstract rules, those most apparently redolent of universal, culture-transcendent canons of rationality, ultimately draws upon the particularities of their embeddedness in human culture, and upon an agreement in natural reactions. In other words, mathematics, in all its abstractness, is what it is because of its embeddedness in the human form of life; and by showing that our fantasy of mathematics works to resist this, Wittgenstein implies that our picture of ordinary language as aspiring to this condition attracts us by appearing to satisfy a desire to deny that all our words are grounded in our conditionedness by nature and culture.

38. Wittgenstein's most striking and pervasive way of inviting us to consider the other elements of fantasy in our picture of the mathematical is to suggest that the ways in which we talk about such rules (and so about rules as such), ways which we regard as descriptions of empirical or metaphysical verities, are in fact figurative or symbolic—more precisely, that they are mythological. It might be said that the terms of this diagnosis are already implicit in his discussion of the machine-as-symbol, with its emergent myth of rules as super-machines; but they are first made explicit when he returns to the words of his interlocutor to which the figure of the machine-as-symbol was a response—the (intuitionist) claim that, with a rule, all the steps in its expansion are already taken before we produce or construct them.

'All the steps are really already taken' means: I no longer have any choice. The rule, once stamped with a particular meaning, traces the lines along which it is to be obeyed through the whole of space.—But if something of this sort really were the case, how would it help?

No: my description only made sense if it was to be understood symbolically.—I should have said: *This is how it strikes me.*

When I follow a rule, I do not choose.

I follow the rule *blindly.*

But what is the purpose of that symbolical proposition? It was supposed to bring into prominence a difference between being causally determined and being logically determined.

My symbolical expression was really a mythological description of the use of a rule. (*PI* 219–21; translation amended)

Wittgenstein's characterization of his interlocutor's words as mythological is not a way of dismissing them as somehow insignificant or literally meaningless, but of capturing the particular way in which they are meaningful. According to him, they say how the phenomenon of rule-following strikes us, giving expression to the impression it makes on us; in other words, their apparent orientation towards the object of a subject's concern masks their real orientation towards the subject's response to that object. And Wittgenstein's response to this mythological expression is to provide a gloss upon it, and then to give his own mythological expression of that gloss—as if properly interpreting our responses to phenomena will return us to the phenomena themselves. The further implication is that philosophical writing can answer to his desires for it, fulfil his fantasy of it, only through its receptivity to such registers of the human voice and its ability properly to interpret their significance—an ability which is not separate from the ability to continue speaking in that same mythical register, to understand and make use of its powers as well as its limits.

By mythologizing the way in which rules govern our future actions in terms of lines laid to infinity, the interlocutor evokes a sense of choice as lost or taken away, but does so in terms which picture rules as ideal machines (their lines guiding us in the way that rails compel the train that rides them to travel in a certain direction). This invocation of the mechanical precisely obscures the difference it aims to capture, transforming the distinction between causal and logical determination into one between two species of causal constraint. Wittgenstein offers an alternative mythology: 'I follow the rule *blindly*.' His immediately preceding gloss implies that this maintains the original myth's orientation to the idea that choice is excluded, but invokes it differently. How, exactly?

Wittgenstein's alternative myth invokes two ideas, each of which varies an element in the original myth: the idea of sight as merely absent rather than entirely lost or taken away (someone who does something blindly fails to see or do something they could and should have seen or done, and hence is precisely not someone who is or has been made blind); and the idea of rules as followed rather than obeyed. This second contrast is not so much obscured as reversed in the Anscombe translation; she registers the difference between *befolgen* and *folgen* in these passages, but associates the former with 'following' and the latter with 'obeying'. This precisely inverts Wittgenstein's purposes here—purposes prepared by an association that he explicitly sets up in section 206: 'Following a rule (*Einer Regel folgen*) is analogous to obeying an order (*einen Befehl befolgen*). We are trained to do so; we react to an order in a particular way.' The analogy referred to here is very limited (we shall return to it); and any analogy drawn between two phenomena presupposes that they are different. Rules are not orders, and one way to see this is to recall that, typically, orders are obeyed, whereas rules are followed. Wittgenstein's German here marks that fact by introducing a distinction between *folgen* and *befolgen* that he keeps to virtually without exception for the rest of his discussion of rules, reserving the former verb for our responses to rules and the latter for our responses to orders. And yet in almost every context where he talks of following rules, Anscombe translates him as talking of obeying them.

This is not an entirely gratuitous decision on her part; indeed, there is even a sense in which Wittgenstein invites such a confusion when he inaugurates his discussion of rules by imagining someone who must derive a series from a rule-formulation when someone else orders him to do so (*PI* 143)—the story to which he repeatedly returns throughout the next hundred or so sections of the *Investigations*. But of course, the fact that we can obey an order to follow a rule does not mean that every time we follow a rule we are obeying it, as if obeying an order it issued to us. And yet, despite the fact that Wittgenstein never conflates this distinction, and indeed explicitly marks it, Anscombe systematically translates *folgen* as 'to obey'—as if even for such a scrupulous follower of Wittgenstein the invitation of his inaugural story is no sooner issued than blindly accepted, with fateful consequences for her teacher's reception in the English-speaking world. We could hardly have a more remarkable confirmation that the myth or picture that rules are really orders is an utterly natural, entirely unremarkable part of our philosophical repertoire.

The immediate consequence of this mythical mistranslation is that Wittgenstein's alternative mythology of rule-following takes on a highly undesirable inflection in English. Where he talks of blindly following a rule, Anscombe has him talking of blind obedience to it. This gives his talk of our blindness a rather cowardly or fearful cast, as it has when someone talks of 'merely obeying orders' or of 'blind terror' (here I recall that in section 212 Wittgenstein talks of how he might respond when 'someone whom I am afraid of orders me to continue the series'; it is as if Anscombe pictures us as all fearfully obeying rules). Talk of obedience implies that rules have authority or power over me, that they limit my freedom—as if normativity as such were a species of compulsion, a laying down of the law. Talk of blind obedience suggests that we have given away our freedom, displaced our responsibility for our actions onto the rule. Anscombe's Wittgenstein thus talks in terms congenial to the interlocutor he intends to subvert—as if he too thinks that, in accepting the guidance of rules, the self gives away its autonomy, its capacity to give a law to and from itself.

Wittgenstein himself, however, talks of following the rule blindly. A follower sounds more like a disciple—someone who has gladly chosen to follow in another's footsteps, to accept her as an authority, to take her word as law. Compulsion is here internalized, discipline is freely taken on or self-imposed, authority seen not as a matter of orders being issued but guidance being found attractive. Here, then, the self's giving away of its autonomy is itself autonomous, an expression of its freedom—not so much giving a law to itself as finding a law for itself. In this context, blindness suggests not a fearful submission but an absence of doubt or hesitation—a trusting certainty.

This is confirmed by Wittgenstein's gloss on his own myth. For him, it is not so much that, when we follow a rule, we can no longer choose, but rather that we do not choose. We could, for example, choose no longer to follow the rule—just as we originally chose to follow it; no one compelled us to do so, and nothing prevents us from changing our minds. Nevertheless, in committing ourselves to the rule, we do not leave ourselves with the task of choosing how to apply it; in applying it, we do not choose between interpretations of it or contemplate alternative ways of going on—we simply act upon it, as if every next step in its application were entirely natural, self-evident. As Wittgenstein will later say: 'The rule can only seem to me to produce all its consequences in advance if I draw them as a *matter of course*' (*PI* 238). One might say: we draw those consequences not mechanically but automatically—not because of a super-causal compulsion but in an immediate, unreflecting (unthinking but not thoughtless) way. We have, one might say, utterly absorbed or internalized the rule.

Picturing mathematical rules as stamping out lines to which we must be obedient is thus a way of attempting to avoid the self's responsibility for its own subjection to these rules—to avoid acknowledging that we are not compelled to follow a rule, and that the expansion of any rule is something we unhesitatingly construct (its authority grounded in the naturalness of our shared reactions). And in taking mathematical rules, thus mythologized, to be exemplary of language as such, we satisfy a desire to deny our own responsibility for our words—to think of the steps we take with them as really always already taken by the words themselves, as if the rules governing them also lay out infinitely long rails along which we simply travel, commanded beyond any question of dispute or wilfulness, beyond any sense that we might be staking the coherence of our own responsiveness when we unhesitatingly project our words into new contexts.

39. The myth of predetermined obedience is the myth of the intuitionists—those struck by the fact that adding two is a transparently simple

technique, a matter of reapplying an utterly familiar operation, endlessly doing the same again. The decisionists—those struck by the newness of every next step in the series produced by this operation, by our need to apply it anew each time—resort to a very different kind of mythological expression to which Wittgenstein also devotes much attention. Since each case of such a rule's application is utterly specific or determinate, and yet there is no end to the sequence they make up, we feel inclined to say that the rule must be showing us more than it could possibly say, that we can 'perceive something drawn very fine in a segment of a series, a characteristic design, which only needs the addition of "and so on", in order to reach to infinity' (*PI* 229), that it gives us an indication or hint of endless (but endlessly precise) consequence. This inclination finds the following mythological expression: 'the line intimates to me the way I am to go' (*PI* 222).

Wittgenstein subjects this mythology to the following diagnosis and reformulation:

'The line intimates to me which way I am to go' is only a paraphrase of: it is my *last* arbiter for the way I am to go.

Let us imagine a rule intimating to me which way I am to follow it; that is, as my eye travels along the line, a voice within me says: '*This* way!'—What is the difference between this process of following a kind of inspiration and that of following a rule? For they are surely not the same. In the case of inspiration I *await* direction. I shall not be able to teach anyone else my 'technique' of following the line. Unless, indeed, I teach him some way of hearkening, some kind of receptivity. But then, of course, I cannot require him to follow the line in the same way as I do.

These are not my experiences of acting from inspiration and according to a rule; they are grammatical notes. (*PI* 230, 232; translation amended)

'Intimation' suggests hearkening to the hints or indications of an oracle, a kind of inspiration or inner voice. It therefore implies attendance upon the source of the inspiration, and it allows for divergences between individual responses to it (between my own at different times, and between my own at a given time and those of others). There are indeed techniques for opening oneself to inspiration; but they cannot guarantee either that inspiration will enter all those open to it, or that it will move them all in the same way. Hence to talk of rules as intimating how we are to obey them would imply that we were on tenterhooks about what they will tell us, waiting upon their nod or whisper (*PI* 223), and that we would feel astonished or grateful—the recipients of an unlooked-for blessing—if we turned out to agree in our response to them (*PI* 234).

Wittgenstein's alternative mythology is: the rule is my *last* arbiter for the way I am to go. An arbiter, because its authority is juridical, akin to that of a court in the sense that its verdict has a universal application, demanding in exactly the same way of all those under its jurisdiction. A last arbiter, because it is akin to a court of last resort, a supreme court or court of final appeal; its authority is not dependent upon, and the import of its pronouncements are not subject to interpretation by, any other court. Wittgenstein's myth thus aims to bring out the fact that our responses to mathematical rules are shared and immediate; when following such a rule, what it requires is immediately obvious to us, and we expect it to be just as obvious to others.

What, though, of the decisionist's sense of the inexhaustibly specific guidance that such a rule can give us? Wittgenstein allows this impression to find another mythological expression.

'A series presents us with *one* face!'—All right, but which face? Clearly we see it algebraically, and as a segment of an expansion. Or is there more in it than that?—'But the way we see it surely gives us everything!'—But that is not an observation about the segment of the series; or about anything that we notice in it; it gives expression to the fact that we look at the mouth of the rule and *do something*, without appealing to anything else for guidance. (*PI* 228; translation amended)

The mythological idea here is that there is something ineffably particular about the guidance that a rule gives us; it is as if it has a face, a specific character, a unique physiognomy that cannot possibly be given full verbal expression but must rather be taken in—so that when we try to explain to another person what we understand in understanding a rule, we can only try to get him to guess the essential thing, to get the ineffable drift of our examples (*PI* 210). But this merely returns us to the confusion that the case of the deviant pupil first elicited (*PI* 187–8): understanding the rule involves more than we can possibly say only in the sense that we could not possibly produce a complete sequence of its applications, because nothing could count as completing such a sequence. But an unlimited sequence is not a sequence whose length reaches beyond every other length (*PI* 209); and mastery of the rule which generates it simply means being able to continue the sequence at any point, not having already worked out its continuation at every point.

The specificity of the rule's character, our sense of it as having a face, has two valid roots: first, the fact that it generates one specific sequence—that at every point it requires that we do *something specific*; and second, the fact that in each case we *do* that specific something—

immediately, without hesitation or act of interpretation, as a matter of course. We react as immediately and unquestioningly to it as a soldier would to a familiar parade-ground order (this is the highly specific analogy between following rules and obeying orders that Wittgenstein allows at *PI* 206). In short, the rule determines our actions in both senses of that phrase as they were outlined in section 189: it requires that we do something determinate, and it determines our actions—we act with certainty, and in concert.

Wittgenstein's myth of final arbitration aims to capture this sense of the specificity of the rule's demands as well, but without inviting the illusions encouraged by the myth of intimation's way of expressing the same point. For that myth displaces the rule's specificity onto the rule-follower's private perception of ineffable physiognomy or her private hearkening to an inner voice, and so gives expression to our utter absorption of, our unhesitating familarity with, the rule in a way which misleadingly singles out the individual rule-follower—as if it makes an impression on each of us to which others can have no necessary access, or says things that others can only guess at. The myth thereby satisfies our desire to deny our commonness with other rule-followers, to deny that in our compliance with its instructions we are utterly unexceptional, of no particular importance. And by interposing the idea of a private impression, it also allows us to deny the immediacy of our response to the rule; it covers over the fact that, in rule-following, reaction is more fundamental than reflection, deeds more fundamental than thoughts. It thus obscures the degree to which our normative behaviour informs and is informed by the body as much as the mind.

40. We saw earlier, when examining the first phase of the dispute between Baker and Hacker and Malcolm, that the features of mathematical rules which invited the intuitionist and decisionist responses—responses that find mythological expression in ideas of super-causal obedience and ineffable intimation—were aspects of the specifically mathematical idea of an iterative series. In taking these features as exemplary of linguistic rules as such, we are thereby attributing to our life with words an idea that has no obvious application to it. Cavell has expressed the contrast as follows:

I suppose that something that makes a mathematical rule mathematical—anyway that makes adding adding—is that what counts as an instance of it . . . is, intuitively, settled in advance, that it tells what its first instance is, and what the interval is to successive instances, and what the order of instances is. The rule extends to all its possible applications . . . But our ordinary concepts—for instance that of a table—are not thus mathematical in their application: we do not, intuitively within the ordinary, know in advance . . . a right first instance, or the correct order of instances, or the set interval of their succession. And sometimes we will not know whether to say an instance counts as falling under a concept or to say that it does not count . . . To say [this] is perhaps to say that the instances falling under an ordinary concept do not form a series. (*CHU* 89–90)

This passage correctly locates the pivotal role of the idea of a series of applications; but in talking primarily of mathematical rules as settling in advance what, in any context, counts as an instance of its application, Cavell appears to downplay an opposing implication of his sense of the successiveness of those instances, rather occluding the open-endedness (the essential incompleteness) of the rule in Wittgenstein's example, and hence the idea of the mathematical series as having to be produced—an idea that helps to invite the troublesome paradox of rule-following, and that motivates related ideas upon which Wittgenstein appears to place great importance: decisionist conceptions of rule-following, and myths of ineffable intimation. We are, of course, to be disillusioned of those ideas; but the feature of the mathematical technique that invites them is surely not simply to be denied or passed over— a conclusion reinforced by Wittgenstein's care to encode ideas of us having to act on what the rule tells us, to actually go on with it, to produce its extension, in his alternative myths.

The broader context of Cavell's treatment of the contrast between ordinary words and mathematical rules suggests that this occlusion hangs together with a general suspicion of the idea that our ways of going on with words can helpfully be pictured as governed by rules for their use at all, and of the idea that Wittgenstein might think otherwise. This suspicion finds expression when Cavell says that he cannot share the sense that 'the concept of a rule is fundamental to Wittgenstein's thought', or that he 'attaches salvational importance to rules' (*CHU* 66–7); it underlies his careful refusal to talk of Wittgensteinian criteria as rules, or of Wittgensteinian grammar as a framework of rules. If he is assuming that mathematical rules occlude open-endedness or newness, and that they are in this respect exemplary of rules as such, these suspicions and refusals would be well motivated—a way of preserving the sense that our ordinary ways with words possess a certain kind of provisionality or creativity, an openness to the future. But both assumptions are, it appears, put in question by Wittgenstein's text, which seems more fruitfully readable as inviting us to perceive the contrast between mathematical and non-mathematical forms of normative givenness and open-endedness as showing how rich and various our many ways of living our life with rules really are—as showing how different mathematical rules are from linguistic ones. Of course, this reading may itself be questionable; but to exclude it as a possibility altogether seems merely one more way of succumbing to the temptation to treat the mathematical as normative for the ordinary.

One reason to feel nevertheless tempted towards a Cavellian position here lies in Wittgenstein's apparently obdurate refusal to accept the idea of inspiration (and hence of creativity, provisionality, and newness) encoded in the myth of intimation as having any real bearing upon rule-following. Indeed, his discussion of the topic concludes with repeated attempts to contrast the idea of inspiration and that of following a rule—quite as if his sense of what goes to make up 'the physiognomy of what we call "following a rule" in everyday life' (*PI* 235; translation amended) importantly includes what in section 232 he calls its grammatical differences from what we call acting from inspiration (that is, the absence of any role for receptivity and the expectation of divergent responses). But before we take this proffered contrast to undercut his earlier willingness to acknowledge an element of open-endedness in rule-following, we should look more closely at the relevant passages.

First, given that Wittgenstein earlier declares that 'to understand a language means to be master of a technique' (*PI* 199), it is worth noting that he does not contrast acting from inspiration and following a rule in terms of the absence as opposed to the presence of a technique. Rather, he acknowledges that there could be a technique of acting from inspiration, that it could be taught to children, and that it amounts to a form of guidance; but he declares that agreement in our responses to that voice could not be taken for granted, regarded as a matter of course. He then goes on to ask whether it might be possible for there to be a practice of calculating whose participants regard their agreement at every step not as a matter of course but as a matter for astonishment and even gratitude. Can we say that this is beyond our imagination? Is it flatly obvious that the physiognomy of such a practice—its specific place in our form of life—would differ so much from practices of following rules that we would not be prepared to regard it as a (highly unusual) example of one? If it is not obvious, then the only difference between inspiration and following a rule appears to lie in differences between the normative techniques they embody—more specifically, in their differing relation to a certain attitude of receptivity, a passive waiting upon the source of guidance.

Here, it is worth remarking that the examples driving Wittgenstein's discussion of these grammatical differences suggest a very stark contrast—rule-following is exemplifed by calculation, and acting from inspiration is compared with composing. It seems clear that the idea of passive receptivity is ill suited to simple mathematical exercises, and that of unhesitating activity is ill suited to musical composition; but are we here responding to the nature of the specific examples invoked, or to a general distinction between all instances of the two general types those specific practices are supposed to exemplify? Some uses of some words are, after all, unhesitating: Wittgenstein instances that of identifying the colours of objects (*PI* 238). But there are other kinds of use of ordinary words: there are, for example, figurative or mythological uses of words—the medium of the very investigation whose deliverances we are now assessing. Is our grasp of how to go on from the myths of 'obedience to lines drawn in space', of 'inner voices intimating guidance', of 'blind following' and 'final courts of appeal' unhesitating and immediate? Would we take it for granted that all competent speakers would agree with our own ways of developing the significance of the words used in such ways? And yet, would we wish to deny that going on with these words in these ways is no less subject to precise and rigorous guidance from the words them-selves—a matter of recalling their logic or grammar? If not, then at least these kinds of uses of words belong rather more with composing than calculating—inviting the application of ideas of receptivity and the need to acknowledge possible disagreement.

When Wittgenstein chooses to characterize the general portrait of fol-lowing a rule built up in these sections as a picture of its 'physiognomy', and thereby reiterates a critical element of the myth of intimation (with its emphasis upon rules as having a face, a specific physiognomy), he not only underlines this self-subverting contrast between the apparent substance and the latent form of his investigation as a whole; he also suggests that we might make more of the concluding phases of that investigation if we think of it as continuing to operate in the mytho-logical dimension of language use. This would mean thinking of calcu-lating and composing not so much as two single and specific kinds of normative technique (an interpretation Wittgenstein seems to hinder by emphasizing that calculating is not a unitary phenomenon but a family of cases; *PI* 236), but as two concluding figures or symbols of norma-tivity that effectively reformulate Wittgenstein's earlier mythical contrast between rules understood as issuing orders and rules understood as offering hints (itself a reformulation of his even earlier mythical con-trast between rule-following as reproducing steps and rule-following as creating or inventing them).

Adam Phillips[20] has recently suggested that psychoanalysis can think of its patients' relation to the norms of human culture in terms of two

---

[20] See *The Beast in the Nursery* (Faber: London, 1998), esp. ch. 3: 'A Stab at Hinting'.

starkly contrasting myths—one in which those norms amount to commands, whose authority is unquestioned and to which submission is demanded, and another (far less common) in which they amount to formulations of hints, ways of offering guidance which invite questioning, further exploration, and the use of individual judgement. Phillips is not interested in arguing that either suggestion is correct—that norms are or can be either commands or hints but not both, that we must decide which, and that all right-thinking people must choose in favour of hinting. His claim is rather that norms necessarily invite both kinds of picture of themselves—that, as forms of authority that we impose upon ourselves and without which we cannot inhabit human forms of culture, they cannot but be both a constraint upon and an expression of freedom; that the myth of norms as commands is dominant, not only in psychoanalysis but in human culture more generally, and specifically in that culture's ways of bringing up its young; and that encouraging the myth of norms as hints is therefore an important corrective—a way of resisting the pervasive idea that the pleasure children take in curiosity, questioning, and play must be put aside if they are to attain adulthood, a way of allowing those qualities to continue to breathe in (to inspire) human culture.

I am tempted to say that Wittgenstein is engaged in a very similar project with respect to philosophy. From this perspective, his claim would be that the idea of mathematics as the abstract, self-contained essence of rule-following, and hence the sublime of ordinary language, is primarily in the service of mythologizing linguistic norms as orders, pure constraints upon freedom—a way of picturing them which occludes the degree to which they leave room for individual judgement, the willingness to explore disagreement, and to attend upon a word's capacity to tolerate and reshape the contexts into which we find ourselves wishing to project it. He attempts to undermine this subliming of the ordinary by showing that this minimalist idea of mathematics is itself a subliming—the result of a failure to see that even mathematical series have to be produced, exist only in their specific embeddedness in human culture, and are grounded upon shared natural reactions—the very features of rules to which myths of intimation respond. Desublimated, this particular version of human normativity will no longer act satisfactorily as an ideal towards which we can take linguistic normativity as such to aspire, and hence no longer allow us to aspire towards unconditionedness—towards a way of conceiving meaning as purified of the various formations of culture and of the human form of life.

Philosophical progress accordingly does not depend upon substituting the myth of intimation for the myth of command, but upon recognizing that the panoply of normative techniques that together make up the physiognomy of rule-following each contain features that invite both kinds of myth, but in differing degrees from case to case. The myth of command tells us that a norm, once chosen, is an impersonal authority, a constraint upon the will; the myth of intimation, with its talk of an inner voice (*eine innere Stimme*), tells us that our typically unhesitating agreement or attunement (*Ubereinstimmung*) in acting upon norms must be pictured (as Wittgenstein's German expression of the myth enacts) as the alignment of our individual voices rather than their elimination, and hence as requiring and enabling a moment of genuinely individual judgement. Wittgenstein's alternative myth—that of blindly following norms understood as the final arbiters of our actions— is similarly intended to give expression to the ways in which norms condition freedom (that is, at once trammel it and make it possible); by stressing the immediacy of their guidance, our typically taking it so completely for granted what they require, it pictures norms as informing rather than coercing our wills, and hence pictures us as having absorbed them, quite as if internalizing their authority makes us what we are— makes us human, fellow inhabitants of a culture. Thus, Wittgenstein's myth points towards its own further development in the idea of continuous seeing-as (part of a broader discussion which this study must take steps to examine), and points us away from the illusions of individuality eliminated and exalted, of the self as either coerced by rules or singled out by their nods and whispers, that are encouraged by the myths it aims to replace.

41. So far I have suggested that Wittgenstein's focus on the example of a mathematical rule is designed to turn us away from our desire to treat the mathematical as normative for language. But I want to end by recalling a critical respect in which mathematical and non-mathematical concepts do resemble one another—a kinship that is central to Wittgenstein's vision of language and philosophical method. Cavell specifies the comparisons and contrasts as follows: 'In precision, in accuracy, in the power of communication, ordinary concepts are the equal of mathematical. The ordinary (nonmathematical) concepts are by no means the equal of the (ordinary) mathematical in, let us say, abstractness, or universality, or completeness' (*CHU* 89–90). In his discussion of family resemblance Wittgenstein identifies these common features by negation, when contesting our intuition that the words of ordinary language are vague, inexact, or ill defined. ' "Inexact" is really a reproach, and "exact" is praise. And that is to say that what is inexact attains its goal less perfectly than what is more exact. Thus the point here is what

we call "the goal"' (*PI* 88). The purposes and interests served by mathematical concepts give point to one ideal of precision and accuracy, and those served by non-mathematical concepts give point to another—to a different but no less legitimate inflection of our concepts of 'precision' and 'accuracy'. A simple or complete refusal to associate non-mathematical ordinary concepts with mathematical ones would imply a refusal of that truth; Wittgenstein's reliance upon a simple mathematical rule to exemplify linguistic normativity as such can thus be read as inviting us rather to acknowledge it.

If, however, this association teaches us something critical about the precision and accuracy of grammar, it can hardly avoid teaching us something critical about the precision and accuracy of grammatical investigations; it must, in other words, be readable as teaching us how to read the text of which these remarks about rules and grammar are a part, as an invitation to acknowledge the form or mode of Wittgenstein's power of communication. Two remarks we have so far passed over, from the methodological prologue to the rule-following remarks, are particularly pertinent here: 'The concept of a perspicuous presentation is of fundamental significance for us. It earmarks the form of account we give, the way we look at things. (Is this a "Weltanschauung"?)' (*PI* 122; translation amended).

In other parts of Wittgenstein's writings he explicitly connects the idea of the perspicuous with the work of formal proofs—in mathematics, for example. Cavell has claimed that this coincidence of concepts is not accidental—that having once hit off the experience of the convincingness (perhaps the unity) of a formal proof with the concept of perspicuousness, Wittgenstein comes to hit off an experience of a unity or reordering of ordinary words of the kind which the *Investigations* contains with the same concept, as if discovering a new facet of that concept in discovering something new about the kinds of order to which ordinary language can be brought.[21]

In his methodological prologue Wittgenstein also claims that 'A philosophical problem has the form: "I don't know my way about"' (*PI* 123)—that philosophy begins in disorientation; so perspicuous presentation must be designed to provide reorientation. Recalling or imagining language-games is one way of overcoming such disorientation, but since it requires only that mastery of ordinary language which is common to all competent speakers, it places no particular pressure on Wittgenstein's language—sets him no specific task of writing. Sometimes, however, the

[21] In 'The *Investigations*' Everyday Aesthetics of Itself', in Mulhall (ed.), *The Cavell Reader*; hereafter IEA.

movement from being lost to finding oneself happens at a stroke, without the intermediary methods of grammatical investigations—as, for example, with the following sentences: 'The human body is the best picture of the human soul' (*PI* 178); 'Why can't my right hand give my left hand money?' (*PI* 268); 'If I have exhausted my grounds I have reached bedrock, and my spade is turned' (*PI* 217); 'Uttering a word is like striking a note on the keyboard of the imagination' (*PI* 6). These are ostentatiously literary gestures, but are they—as this study has in effect argued throughout—essential to the philosophical work of the book? As readers, we take pleasure in them, perhaps experience a certain shock of freedom and even exposure—as of the revelation of one's most private thoughts and fantasies; they liberate us by giving us a means of self-expression—a way of articulating experiences of estrangement, perversity, and torment, as well as moments of recovery, soundness, and peace. They contribute to the book's work because providing such expression is a means of overcoming disorientation, part of a therapeutic response to the human being's pervasive and recurrent lostness to itself—a demonstration that it need not remain unintelligible or unresponsive to itself and others.

Pleasure and liberation are also integral to our experience of the perspicuity of formal proofs; when first encountered, for example, Euclid's proof that the sum of the inner angles of a triangle equals 180 degrees can induce a kind of ecstasy as well as a kind of relief. Such proofs also create a sense of arrival or completeness, defining or locating a point at which a course of thinking is broken off—a thought separated, with finish and permanence, from the general range of experience. A not unfamiliar form of ordering of ordinary words to which these same predicates of pleasure and freedom, completeness and breaking off, are applicable is the aphoristic. For Cavell, the concept of the perspicuous is as surely invited by contexts of aphorism as it is by those of proof and of grammatical investigation; more precisely, he claims that the aphoristic supplies the only philosophically adequate way of displaying what grammatical investigations allow us to see.

The power of grammatical investigations in *Philosophical Investigations* is a function of their leading a word back from its metaphysical capture by the appeal to its everyday use (*PI* 116). The power of the aphoristic is a function of its granting the appeal, even in a sense the reality, of the metaphysical. It is a mode of reflecting the clarity brought by grammatical methods, one that in itself, as itself, exhibits this clarity, together with a satisfaction or acknowledgement of the obscurity from which clarity comes. To say that this exhibition is essential to the work of the *Investigations* is to say that appeals to the ordinary which fail this mode of reflection are not Wittgensteinian appeals, they do not take their bearing from the power to make philosophical problems completely disappear—hence appear (*PI* 133). They do not, accordingly, express our interest in these problems, and so leave us subjected to them without understanding what kind of creatures we are, what our form of life as talkers is, that we are thus fascinatable, that philosophy is seductive. (*IEA* 385)

The mathematical example which holds together Wittgenstein's remarks on rule-following is not, of course, a proof; but we have already seen that his discussion of addition aims to bring out its connections with certain notions of completeness and freedom, and the abstract orderliness of its succession of instances possesses a stately, musical beauty that is apt to evoke a calm pleasure. So it too invites the application of the predicates that Cavell takes to justify talk of perspicuity in mathematics, and so hits off a connection between the work of such rules and the work of Wittgenstein's prose. In doing so, it exemplifies the flexibility of grammar—the ways in which ordinary concepts (such as that of 'perspicuity') tolerate projection into new contexts, which elicit facets of significance that are neither fully determined by nor wholly unprepared for in our sense of their grammar, the sense in which words are open to the future rather than party to its foreclosure.

Of course, Cavell's reading further connects Wittgenstein's conception of philosophical writing with the idea of modernism; it shows how, beyond its composition in a numbered sequence of remarks, the irregular rhythm of its resort to an aphoristic register produces an inflection of the characteristically modernist sound of the fragment, the denial of system (which does not mean a denial of the systematic). More generally, it suggests that the compulsive desire of commentators (and translators) to downplay or pass over the pervasiveness of Wittgenstein's commitment to the symbolic or mythological dimensions of ordinary language amounts to a blindness to his sense of the importance of the figurative to what he means by the ordinary, and so to what he takes to ground the efficacy of his grammatical investigations. One might say: appeals to the *Investigations* that fail to acknowledge this mode of its work are not Wittgensteinian appeals; they do not express our interest in its words, and in the vision of words to which those words attempt to give expression.

THE PARADOX OF ASPECT-DAWNING

42. The text of the *Investigations* goes on smoothly from its remarks on rule-following to a consideration of the fantasy of a 'private

language'; and many of the themes touched upon in those earlier remarks certainly point in that direction. But we have seen that as they draw to a close, as Wittgenstein begins explicitly to interpret the mythological expressions to which we are attracted in thinking about rule-following, he encounters an outcropping of imagery—the idea of rules as possessed of a face or physiognomy, as having a particular atmosphere or intimating something so fine as to be beyond explanation, of seeing the rule's applications as the segment of an expansion, and of taking that expansion unhesitatingly for granted—that is most intensively studied in section xi of part II of the *Investigations*, as part of Wittgenstein's concern with seeing aspects. Following out this apparent displacement of part I's chain of figuration will ultimately return us to the notion of rules, and hence to Wittgenstein's notion of grammar, by further characterizing the physiognomy of following a rule in everyday life (*PI* 235). I first published an extended reading of this material over a decade ago; but it would be unwise to take my readers' familiarity with that work for granted, and I cannot demonstrate the ways in which the preceding reading of earlier portions of the *Investigations* makes it possible for me to extend, revise, and reinflect my initial conclusions (or indeed acknowledge the indebtedness of the preceding reading to those initial conclusions) without re-presenting the main points of that earlier interpretation here, even if in a heavily condensed form.[22]

Section xi begins with the following remark: 'I contemplate a face, and then suddenly notice its likeness to another. I *see* that it has not changed; and yet I see it differently. I call this experience "noticing an aspect"' (*PI* 193c[23]).

Wittgenstein thus introduces and characterizes noticing an aspect or experiencing the dawning of an aspect—we might even say that he defines the phenomenon—by reference to its inherent paradoxicality. We feel that the face or figure is altogether different after the change of aspect, as if it had altered before our very eyes; and yet we know that there has been no such change.

Wittgenstein reinforces this emphasis in his later definition of the counter-concept to aspect-dawning.

---

[22] See my *On Being in the World: Wittgenstein and Heidegger on Seeing Aspects* (Routledge: London, 1990).

[23] All references to section xi of *Philosophical Investigations* will be given in the form of a page number followed by a letter to indicate the position of the relevant remark on that page. The other main Wittgenstein texts to which reference is made here will be abbreviated as follows. *Remarks on the Philosophy of Psychology*, vol. i, trans. G. E. M. Anscombe, vol. ii, trans. C. G. Luckhardt and M. A. E. Aue (Blackwell: Oxford, 1980); hereafter *RPP*. *Last Writings on the Philosophy of Psychology*, i and ii, trans. C. G. Luckhardt and M. A. E. Aue (Blackwell: Oxford, 1982, 1992); hereafter *LW*.

The question now arises: Could there be human beings lacking in the capacity to see something *as something*—and what would that be like? What sort of consequences would it have?—Would this defect be comparable to colour-blindness or to not having absolute pitch?—We will call it 'aspect-blindness'—and will next consider what might be meant by this. (A conceptual investigation.) (*PI* 213f)

It quickly emerges that, although the aspect-blind as Wittgenstein imagines them do not experience the dawning of an aspect, this does not mean that they could not become aware of the likeness between one face and another: it means that they could not experience the dawning of that awareness as a matter of the observed face seeming to alter before their eyes. Such people might call the figure first one thing and then another, but they would not experience the change as a jump from one aspect to another (*PI* 123g); they would not feel inclined to say that the perceived figure was the same and yet not the same (*LW* i. 174), that after every change of aspect it was as if they saw a different object (*RPP* ii. 42), that two aspects might seem to be incompatible with each other (*RPP* i. 877).

In other words, to be aspect-blind is to have no sense that a paradox lies at the heart of a change of aspects; and Wittgenstein's discussion of aspect-dawning is, at least in the first instance, an extended response to the puzzlement which those paradoxical formulations perfectly naturally elicit in those who nevertheless feel impelled to employ them. The beginning of that extended response is a demonstration that the paradox cannot be accounted for by invoking a certain incoherent notion of 'visual impressions'. For Wittgenstein's interlocutor quickly suggests that we can banish the appearance of paradox if we assume that our feeling that the object in question has altered arises from the fact that there has indeed been a change—but in what we subjectively see, in our visual impression rather than the object itself. The idea is to separate out the intentional objects of the two contradictory claims whose conjunction creates our sense of paradox: instead of saying that the object both is and is not the same, we can say that the object is unchanged but our visual impression of it—our inner picture of that object—is not.

Can we, however, justify the claim that suddenly seeing a face in a puzzle-picture is a matter of experiencing a change in our visual impression of it—for example, in its organization? If it were, we should be able to make those changes manifest in the way we represent what we see; just as we can capture changes in perceived colour or shape by altering the colour or shape of our representation of what we see, so we should be able to capture changes in perceived organization by altering the organization of our representation of what we see. In the case of the puzzle-picture face, however, we can do no such thing; the change we experience is not expressible in our representation of what is seen (*PI* 196b). Unless, therefore, we want to think of our visual impression as a queerly shifting construction—one capable of alterations which cannot be registered in the very outer pictures upon which this hypothesized inner picture is modelled—then we must admit that the dawning of an aspect cannot amount to a change in what we subjectively see.

Could Wittgenstein's interlocutor invoke a change in our interpretation of our visual impression rather than a change in its properties? Could she claim, for example, that when we suddenly see a schematic figure as a three-dimensional cube, we immediately perceive an array of lines which we then interpret indirectly (perhaps according to habits formed by past visual experience) (*PI* 193g)? The problem Wittgenstein sees here is that calling a description of an experience 'indirect' only makes sense in circumstances where we can also give a direct description; 'This paint is the colour of blood' can intelligibly be called an indirect description because we can also describe the colour directly—'this paint is red'. However, in the case of 'I see the figure as a cube', no such more direct description of the experience involved is available; so it makes no sense to regard it as an indirect description. Indeed, if it were, then the experience to which it refers could not be one of aspect-dawning, since it is definitive of such experiences that the mode of representing the perceived change is not one of a number of possible ways of describing it, but is rather felt to be the only possible expression of our visual perception, an essential means of expressing exactly what we see—as if a new copy of the figure were required, even though we know that that isn't really the case (*LW* i. 493).

43. Wittgenstein's critique of the model of visual impressions as inner copies or pictures really is as swift as this summary suggests (which does not, of course, make it any less definitive). Its contours are also rather familiar: the key ideas it invokes (that representations of what is seen are the outward criteria of which any 'inner' process, event, or experience stands in need, and that forms of words can function as expressions of experience rather than descriptions of it) will be well known to anyone who has read even halfway through part I of the *Investigations*.[24] Furthermore, this critique can be mounted entirely without

[24] Marie McGinn, in her recent commentary on the *Investigations*, sees sections 398–401 as a particularly fruitful early rehearsal of these themes; see the final chapter of *Wittgenstein and the Philosophical Investigations* (Routledge: London, 1997).

reference to the unprecedented number of newly minted terms that Wittgenstein introduces in the course of his reflections on aspect-dawning. He talks of 'picture-objects', 'continuous seeing as', 'regarding as', 'aspect-blindness', and so seemingly endlessly on; but this extraordinary terminology has no obvious role to play in the considerations I have just outlined. Finally, even if the critique is entirely successful, if the model of visual impressions it targets really is incoherent, then that merely deprives us of one way of accounting for the air of paradox in aspect-dawning, and so leaves entirely untouched the sense of puzzlement which led us to call upon that theory in the first place. If we are to remove that philosophical bafflement, we need some other way of accounting for its genesis and persistence; but nothing we have seen so far gives any indication as to how we might go about that task.

It is therefore striking that Wittgenstein's commentators, having correctly seen that his response to the problem includes a demonstration of the incoherence of this model of visual impressions, appear almost without exception to think that it also exhausts it.[25] For them, the paradoxicality internal to aspect-dawning does not appear to survive that demolition—quite as if the air of paradox is produced by the incoherent theory of vision rather than being what produces it, as if they find nothing inherently puzzling in the dawning of an aspect. In other words, they see no need for anything other than that essentially negative moment in Wittgenstein's thought because they have no independent sense that a paradox lies at the heart of the experience of aspect-dawning. Their mistaking one small part of Wittgenstein's project for the larger enterprise to which it contributes thus implies not only that they are blind to the particular aspects of this problem that most interest Wittgenstein, but that they are themselves aspect-blind.

DISSOLVING THE PARADOX

44. In reality, Wittgenstein's detailed, ramifying discussion of the various phenomena for which he introduces his freight of new coinages embodies a set of reminders about our relation to pictures, photographs,

[25] Robert Fogelin's *Wittgenstein* (Routledge: London, 1976) and Malcolm Budd's *Wittgenstein's Philosophy of Psychology* (Routledge: London, 1989) are in this respect exemplary. They distinguish themselves from most general commentators by at least discussing aspect perception, and in accurate and meticulous ways; but the former devotes four pages to it, and the latter identifies Wittgenstein's problem and its solution using material drawn exclusively from the first ten pages of section xi.

and drawings which together form the necessary background against which the seemingly paradoxical experience of aspect-dawning can be seen as entirely unsurprising—as simply one specific manifestation of that broader relation to representational objects. In other words, his approach to this problem, as to any philosophical confusion, is to rotate the axis of our investigation from the vertical to the horizontal: instead of trying to penetrate to the supposedly hidden reality of the experience of aspect-dawning, Wittgenstein attempts to locate that experience in the wider context of our life with pictures.

We can see this shift or reorientation begin at the very beginning of section xi, in a long passage that is very often entirely overlooked. There Wittgenstein interrupts his developing critique of the erroneous theory of vision in order to introduce the Jastrow duck–rabbit figure, and thereby to introduce two of his key coinages.

I must distinguish between the 'continuous seeing' of an aspect and the 'dawning' of an aspect.

The picture might have been shewn me, and I never have seen anything but a rabbit in it.

Here it is useful to introduce the idea of a picture-object. For instance

would be a picture-face.

In some respects I stand towards it as I do towards a human face. I can study its expression, can react to it as to the expression of the human face. A child can talk to picture-men or picture-animals, can treat them as it treats dolls.

I may, then, have seen the duck–rabbit simply as a picture-rabbit from the first. That is to say, if asked 'What's that?' or 'What do you see here?' I should have replied: 'A picture-rabbit'. If I had been further asked what that was, I should have explained by pointing to all sorts of pictures of rabbits, should perhaps have pointed to real rabbits, talked about their habits, or given an imitation of them.

I should not have answered the question 'What do you see here?' by saying: 'now I am seeing it as a picture-rabbit'. I should simply have described my perception: just as if I had said 'I see a red circle over there'. (*PI* 194–5)

A dual-aspect figure such as the duck–rabbit is here presented as one genus of a broader species of highly schematic, minimally filled-out yet evidently representative figures that Wittgenstein calls 'picture-objects'. In these compressed remarks Wittgenstein stresses three things. First, when we see a picture-object, we see what it depicts—we describe our perception of it in terms of what it is a picture *of*, not in terms of an arrangement of marks. Second, our grasp of what a picture-object is typically comes out in the ways in which we unquestioningly relate it to that which it depicts—for example, by drawing no distinction between making references to other pictures of rabbits and making references to real rabbits and their behaviour when asked to explain what a picture-rabbit actually is. Third, we can and do relate to such picture-objects in the kinds of way in which we relate to the objects they depict—we can, for example, recoil from the malevolence of a picture-face, or feel cheered by its glowing happiness. (Here, once again, Wittgenstein finds himself introducing the figure of the child, her modes of play emblematic of aspects of adult speech and life that we otherwise tend to repress philosophically.)

Since this discussion of picture-objects is explicitly introduced to illuminate the distinction between aspect-dawning and continuous seeing as, we must assume that Wittgenstein means the latter term to capture these three points and their implications. And the most obvious implication of the fact that we describe picture-objects in terms of what they depict, explain what they are by grouping them together with what they depict, and react to them in the kinds of way that we react to what they depict is that we treat even highly schematic drawings (figures that seem hardly substantial enough to be capable of representation) in ways which take their representational status entirely for granted.

Wittgenstein reinforces this understanding of continuous seeing as as a specific kind of attitude in later stretches of his discussion of picture-objects. For example, at *PI* 203b he asks whether, when we look at a schematic drawing of an animal transfixed by an arrow, it is more correct to say that we *see* the arrow or that we merely know that certain lines in the drawing are supposed to represent parts of an arrow. He answers by suggesting that the concept of seeing is forced on us here when our immediate response to the question 'What are you seeing?' after being shown the drawing even for a moment would be to proffer a representation which involved reference to an arrow; we would describe what we saw as a picture of a transfixed beast, or draw a copy showing some sort of animal transfixed by some sort of weapon (*PI* 203f). Someone who merely knows that it is an arrow would need to read the drawing as we would a drawing designed (in the manner of a blueprint) to convey practical information, drawing conclusions about what it represents from its particular arrangement of lines, and happy to regard her response as one among several possible interpretations of what she had seen (*PI* 204h,c).

Here, however, we might object that Wittgenstein has simply distinguished a simple act of visual perception from one of interpretation. After all, a picture-object (like a picture) just *is* the sort of thing that is correctly described by describing what it represents; so someone who describes the schematic figure in animal terms is merely demonstrating the basic human capacity to perceive what is before her eyes. But Wittgenstein thinks that 'seeing' here carries a further range of significance: ' "To me it is an animal pierced by an arrow". That is what I treat it as; this is my attitude to the figure. This is one meaning in calling it a case of "seeing" ' (*PI* 205a). If what Wittgenstein means by 'seeing' here is not simply a capacity to perceive the schematic figure as a transfixed animal but an attitude, a way of treating what is perceived, then the crucial distinction between seeing and knowing cannot lie simply in the capacity to describe the figure in terms of what it represents. It must lie rather in the *immediacy* with which someone who sees the drawing in this way would reach for such a description—in the fact that it would be an instantaneous reaction to even a momentary view of the drawing, the first thing to jump to her eye, and that any faults in the description she gives would be (so to say) faults in the right pictorial space. She might, for example, misidentify the species of the animal or mistake the arrow for a spear; but she would not misidentify the array of lines in the drawing in ways that would give the depicted creature an anatomically nonsensical arrangement of limbs (*PI* 204a). She would, in short, respond to the drawing in ways that take it for granted that it is a depiction, and a depiction of something in particular.

This kind of seeing as opposed to knowing corresponds to what Wittgenstein means by continuous aspect perception; and he associates it with other fine shades of behaviour of the kind mentioned earlier. For example, when discussing the difference between seeing and knowing in relation to schematic figures of the kind employed in descriptive geometry (*PI* 203b), he invokes a particular kind of mastery of the practice of operating with such drawings. Someone who is seeing such a drawing three-dimensionally is distinguished by a certain kind of knowing her way about—for example, by moving her pencil around within the drawing as if she were moving it around within a three-dimensional model, or by indicating the three-dimensional relations between the picture-elements in her gestures. Someone who merely knows that the drawing is meant to represent such three-dimensional relations would operate more hesitantly in these respects; her behaviour would show that she was not taking the three-dimensionality of the figure for granted, that she did not stand towards the drawing in the kinds of ways we can stand towards what it represents.

Wittgenstein does not, however, restrict the application of the concept of continuous aspect perception to the domain of picture-objects. Much of his discussion focuses on fully fledged paintings, photographs, and drawings; he discusses cases of what he is inclined to call the dawning of an aspect of these representations (cases where, unlike the duck–rabbit, there is no other pictorial aspect with which to contrast it; *PI* 201c–e,g[26]), thereby reminding us that the role they play in our lives also presupposes a very specific attitude towards them on our part. As with picture-objects, we distinguish seeing from knowing what a picture represents in terms of the immediacy with which a description of what it represents is forthcoming even after only a glimpse of the picture, of whether that description is proffered as one among a number of possible interpretations, and of whether any faults in that description make sense in terms of what it depicts. Perhaps most forcefully, however, Wittgenstein reminds us that we often relate to a picture as we do to that which it depicts: 'Perhaps the following expression would have been better: we *regard* the photograph, picture or drawing as we do the object itself (the man, landscape, and so on) depicted there' (*PI*, 205e).

The echo of his earlier claims about picture-faces is clear; and the idea is plainly not that people who respond in such ways to pictures—by, for example, kissing a photograph of a loved one, or feeling ashamed under the gaze of a saint's icon, or being struck with awe at the immensity of the sky in Van Gogh's 'Starry Night'—are mistaking the picture for what it depicts, or that people always respond to pictures in such ways. The point is rather that such reactions to pictures are perfectly familiar parts of human experience, that they are intelligible only on the presupposition that the people concerned take it entirely for granted that the picture depicts a specific something or someone, and that this is in turn dependent on the very general fact that human beings relate to, treat, regard pictures as pictures (as representational objects).

We do not, of course, always feel so moved by seeing our spouse's face in a picture that we want to kiss it; but the very idea of such an action would never occur to us unless the general shape of our lives with pictures were not deeply informed by an unhesitating awareness of and responsiveness to what they depict. Such an action would certainly make

---

[26] Cases which therefore demonstrate the invalidity of Paul Johnston's claim (on pp. 243–4 of the appendix to his otherwise valuable book *Wittgenstein: Rethinking the Inner* (Routledge: London, 1994)), that the experience of aspect dawning is conceivable only when there is an alternative aspect to be seen.

no sense to those who merely know that pictures are meant to be representative, who perceive and describe them in terms of lines and colour patches; indeed, even those who do perceive and describe pictures in terms of what they depict need not necessarily be inclined to feel ashamed under the gaze of a saint's icon—they might find such a stylized representation inhuman and repellent. Such people, one might say, directly perceive what pictures depict, but that is a necessary rather than a sufficient condition for continuously perceiving pictures as pictures. What Wittgenstein has in mind when introducing that concept is the fact that human beings do manifest such further responses to pictures—that our form of life is pervaded with practices which exploit in various ways the fact that we treat pictures in terms of what they depict. In this respect, regarding pictures as we do the objects depicted is simply one extreme but exemplary manifestion of a more pervasive human attitude.

The bearing of these reminders on the sense of paradox implicit in experiences of aspect-dawning may now be more evident. For if, in general, we do not simply recognize *that* pictures depict and *what* they depict but rather take their specific pictorial identity (as a picture of *x* rather than *y*) for granted in our dealings with them, if we generally respond to pictures in terms of what they depict, then we will of course tend to regard a picture-duck as being as different from a picture-rabbit as a duck is from a rabbit. And we will accordingly be tempted to give expression to the sudden realization that the picture-object before us is both a picture-duck and a picture-rabbit in terms which suggest that the picture-object itself has altered—that a pictured duck has been transformed into a pictured rabbit, one sort of picture-object into another, very different sort. In short, against the background Wittgenstein encapsulates in his notion of continuous aspect perception, our paradoxical sense of the dual-aspect figure changing even though we know that it remains unaltered becomes entirely unsurprising; what else would one expect from people who relate to pictures and picture-objects in terms of what they depict?

One could go further. If someone is incapable of such experiences of aspect-dawning, if she has no inclination to utilize those characteristically paradoxical formulations when she notices a new aspect of a picture-object, that gives us grounds for doubting that her general attitude to pictures is one of continuous aspect perception. In other words, the capacity to experience the dawning of an aspect is simply one (admittedly striking) manifestation of—one criterion for—a person's general relation to pictures being one of continuous aspect perception; and hence aspect-blindness as Wittgenstein first defines it must be one (admittedly striking) manifestation of a general inability continuously to perceive an aspect. After all, if we can experience the dawning of an aspect as a bizarre fluctuation in the identity of the relevant picture-object only if we generally treat pictures in terms of the objects they depict, then those incapable of that experience must also have a different general relation to pictures. Someone who cannot, for example, see a schematic drawing of a cube first one way then another is someone who cannot continuously see the schematic drawing as a cube either way—she could not stand to such a picture of a three-dimensional object as she does to the object itself (*RPP* ii. 479).

On this reading of Wittgenstein's coinages, his treatment of aspect-perception *does* attempt to account for our sense of the paradox involved in any experience of aspect-dawning. He deploys this idiosyncratic vocabulary precisely in order to situate that experience within a broader framework of human practices and responses which makes clear the pervasiveness of a specific human attitude to pictures. Understood as simply one manifestation of a general tendency to treat pictures in terms of what they depict, the apparent paradoxicality inherent in the ways in which we give expression to experiences of the dawning of an aspect dissolves. But this therapeutic dissolution simultaneously suggests that, to grasp Wittgenstein's broader purposes, we must displace the experience of aspect-dawning from the dominating position it typically occupies in discussions of these matters. On this accounting of the matter, such experiences constitute only one striking manifestation of continuous aspect perception; and it is this concept—and the general attitude it characterizes—that is Wittgenstein's real concern.

ASPECTS OF MEANING

45. This has important implications when we turn our attention to a more explicit displacement to which Wittgenstein subjects his discussion roughly halfway through section xi—from the domain of visual perception to that of language.

The importance of [aspect-blindness] lies in the connexion between the concepts of 'seeing an aspect' and 'experiencing the meaning of a word'. For we want to ask 'what would you be missing if you did not *experience* the meaning of a word?'

What would you be missing, for instance, if you did not understand the request to pronounce the word 'till' and to mean it as a verb,—or if you did not feel that a word lost its meaning and became a mere sound if it was repeated ten times over? (*PI* 214d)

With experiences of meaning, a form of words standardly employed to report a speaker's intentions or to describe the technique of a given word's use (i.e. with reference to word-synonymy, explanations of meaning, and so on) is utilized as the expression of an experience undergone in very specific circumstances—we move from 'The word has this meaning' to 'I said the word in this meaning'. The original or primary employment of the term relates to questions of use and purpose, to the particular technique of using a word and the particular intentions of a speaker in a specific context; but in experiences of meaning, words are uttered in isolation, forming no part of linguistic interchange and divorced from specific purposes—and yet we are inclined to use the word 'meaning' here too.

Literature furnishes analogous experiences with language. A poem or a narrative can strike me as like a painting in words, and an individual word as like a picture (*PI* 215c); such words can seem to be a *manifestation* of their meaning, a living embodiment of the sentiment they express. And as these similes suggest, there is a general parallel here with experiences of pictorial aspect-dawning. There, too, a portrait can seem to come alive for me ('Her picture smiles down at me from the wall!'; *PI* 205h); and more generally, a form of words standardly employed to denote changes in a perceived object is used to give expression to a highly specific visual experience, one in which ambiguous schematic figures lacking a determining pictorial context nevertheless seem to *become* one sort of picture-object rather than another.

If this parallel is real, then we should expect experiences of meaning to be simply one striking example of a general human attitude to language which parallels that of continuous aspect perception—call it continuous meaning perception. And indeed, Wittgenstein's second opening example carries just this implication: for no one would be inclined to say that words can lose their meaning and become mere sounds when repeated too often if she standardly perceived them as mere sounds in the first place. The sound aspect of words can dawn on someone precisely because she directly perceives the written and spoken elements of language as meaningful words and sentences, not as sounds or marks standing in need of interpretation.

Taken on its own, of course, this might seem merely to register our capacity for perceiving what is shown or said to us (as opposed to having to interpret it). After all, words just *are* meaningful sounds or marks, so someone who responds to them as meaningful might be said simply to have correctly perceived what is there to be perceived, not to have manifested a distinctive attitude to language. Once again, however, for Wittgenstein, this perceptual capacity forms the core of a more distinctive assemblage of responses and practices, and so is a necessary but not sufficient condition for what we are calling 'continuous meaning perception'. For instance, the words we use to give expression to the experience of meaning in Wittgenstein's first example ('Mean "till" as a verb', 'Mean it as a noun', 'Say the word "bank" and mean it as a riverbank') presuppose a sense of words as having more than one meaning and a capacity to distinguish those meanings—to compare and contrast the word with neighbouring words and their differing techniques of use. So, someone undergoing the experience of meaning must not only regard her language as being organized in a certain way, with its individual elements having a precise location within it, but must have assimilated this awareness of linguistic structure to the point at which its every twist and turn informs her experience of the individuality of specific words outside the practical context of their ordinary meaningful use.

Wittgenstein recalls several other instances of such unhesitating familiarity with the specific identity of individual words. There is, for example, the way we choose and value words (*PI* 218g). We very often know immediately whether a given word is exactly the one we want; but what grounds those immediate judgements is the fact that it is possible to say a great deal about such fine quasi-aesthetic differences, to assess the extensive ramifications effected by each candidate word. The immediacy of such judgements shows the depth to which we have assimilated the principles of organization that structure our language and constitute the specificity of individual word-meaning.

Often, the exact ramifications of a word take us beyond directly linguistic differences, to include their links with non-linguistic phenomena with which their specific technique of use associates them. Wittgenstein instances our inclination to think that a name might fit or fail to fit its bearer ('The name "Schubert" fits Schubert's works and Schubert's face'; *PI* 215f). We know that names neither fit nor fail to fit their bearers in sound or appearance, but the techniques of a word's use ensure that it will habitually be encountered against a reasonably specific and recurring background of objects, persons, and circumstances; and if our assimilation of the word *as the bearer of a specific technique* is a deep one, then our sense of the non-linguistic background against which that technique locates the word will tend to be assimilated in its turn, and so will naturally help to define our sense of that word's specific identity.

For Wittgenstein, however, the key point is not so much our awareness of the specificity of a word's linguistic and non-linguistic contexts, but the pervasiveness and depth of that awareness; and that is shown by the fact that we are inclined to express our awareness by talking of a word being a portrait of its bearer (*LW* i. 70), or of a word having a familiar physiognomy: 'The familiar physiognomy of a word, the feeling that it has taken up its meaning into itself, that it is an actual likeness of its meaning—there could be human beings to whom all this was alien. (They would not have an attachment to their words.)' (*PI* 218f). We react to such associative and linguistic tie-ups as if they had been absorbed by the word, as if it made manifest every aspect of its meaning on its face. Mere awareness of those tie-ups would not entail the adoption of such an attitude, for one could admit their existence and still find the idea of a word's having absorbed them incomprehensible—in just the way that some people might find it incomprehensible to feel shame before the gaze of a saint's icon while being perfectly capable of perceiving which saint's icon it is. Our inclination to regard *the words themselves* as having a particular physiognomy in which those tie-ups are made manifest reflects the degree to which *we* have assimilated those words, the degree to which we are at home with them; our attachment to them indicates the pervasive depth of our familiarity with and mastery of them.

Against the background of our general sense of the physiognomy of words, the experiences of meaning with which we began appear not as paradoxical aberrations but as unusually striking manifestations of our capacity continuously to perceive the meanings of words. For of course, the instruction 'Say the word "bank" and mean a riverbank' will make sense to us only if our absorption of those techniques inclines us to regard a word as something that carries its meaning on its face. And to find it intelligible to pronounce a word in one or other of its meanings when the context lacks any features which might determine which technique of using that word was being employed, and thereby to exhibit in one's behaviour the sense that, beyond its visual and aural properties, a word has a physiognomy which manifests its meaning and which can be emphasized and experienced, simply reveals the degree to which we have assimilated those words as bearers of specific techniques of use. If we overlook that background, such experiences might lead us to think that linguistic meaning as such is something experiential—as if words are shells to be filled with and emptied of sense by the impress and receptivity of human consciousness; but when that background is recalled, we can see that the experiences that encourage such philosophical mythologies of meaning are in fact subversive of it, in that they register the depth to which our awareness of words is informed by our mastery of their techniques of use.

Experiences of meaning also manifest a sense of words as having physiognomies in a second way—in the way we give expression to them by using the word 'meaning'. As we saw earlier, our talk of meaning in these unusual contexts diverges radically from the term's standard use—to report a speaker's intentions or note differences in techniques of use. But as we also noted, we could not express what we are trying to express in these unusual contexts by using any word other than 'meaning', with all the implications it carries as a result of its familiar use: our forms of expression here track the differences in techniques of use that the term 'meaning' captures in its original home, we are inclined to use them precisely because they do so, and hence we reveal ourselves as inclined to presuppose that the word retains its original significance in this new context. In other words, in contexts of experiencing meaning it is the word 'meaning' *as well as* whatever word is being said in one its meanings that is being treated as if it had taken up its meaning into itself.

But then, any experience of aspect-dawning—whether linguistic or pictorial—is doubly dependent on the inclination to take over an expression from its standard technique of use and employ it as the immediate expression of an experience. Even in pictorial contexts the relevant words become an essential part of the expression of one's visual experience rather than of a perceptual report, but we are inclined to use them in the new context precisely because of their significance in the old; we act as if they carry their original implications into their new context, as if they have absorbed or assimilated their original technique of use. This is what happens when we express our realization that there is a face in a puzzle-picture by saying that we see a change in the picture's 'organization', even though we know that no actual rearrangement of its parts has occurred; and more generally, any talk of 'Now I'm seeing it as . . .', when we know that the relevant picture-object has not changed, modifies the concept of seeing in a way whose point depends upon a sense that its original meaning necessarily comes along with the word itself.

46. This parasitic relationship between linguistic techniques is an instance of what Wittgenstein means by primary and secondary senses.

Here one might speak of a 'primary' and 'secondary' sense of a word. It is only if the word has the primary sense for you that you use it in the secondary one.

The secondary sense is not a 'metaphorical' sense. If I say 'For me the vowel *e* is yellow' I do not mean: 'yellow' in a metaphorical sense,—for I could not express what I want to say in any other way than by means of the idea 'yellow'. (*PI* 216c)

As Wittgenstein's further example of finding Wednesday fat or lean makes clear (*PI* 216d), the primary–secondary sense model has three key features. First, secondary uses of a word do not illustrate but rather presuppose (even while transforming) its primary use; even those inclined to regard Wednesday as fat rather than lean could not explain the meanings of 'fat' or 'lean' by pointing to the examples of days of the week, but only in the usual primary way. Second, no other word would do to express my inclinations in the secondary contexts; it is the word 'fat', with all its usual implications and connotations, that aptly expresses my feelings with respect to Wednesday. Third, any candidate causal explanations for my inclinations in the secondary context are irrelevant; even if I am inclined to call Wednesday fat rather than lean because I was taught by a fat teacher on Wednesdays (*LW* i. 795), this does not explain away the inclination to treat the word as if it had absorbed this association, as if it had become part of its physiognomy.

Our inclination to construct new, expressive uses of language in ways that simultaneously presuppose and transform the primary senses of words is thus one further manifestation of continuous meaning perception—of our inclination to treat words as if every fine shade of their linguistic and non-linguistic ramifications as bearers of specific techniques were visible in their face. What the primary–secondary sense model particularly emphasizes, however, is that in so far as certain secondary uses of words are defining or criterial manifestations of certain experiences, reactions, and responses, then only those inclined to make use of words in this way can intelligibly be said to have the relevant experiences, reactions, and responses. Only those who are sufficiently at home with the primary sense of words to be capable of seeing their potential for secondary employment are capable of certain ranges of human experience. This restriction may not appear particularly significant if we focus exclusively upon coloured vowels and embodied weekdays. But the same basic structure of responsive absorption also underlies a multitude of expressive rituals (ranging from sticking pins into the effigy of an enemy to prizing a lock of one's dead child's hair) and some central linguistic practices (such as calculating in the head), as well as providing one major patterning principle that unifies the otherwise potentially overwhelming diversity of linguistic practices that make up a natural language.

Wittgenstein's model of primary–secondary meaning is in fact strongly reminiscent of his account of the concept of a gesture—an idea that governs much of his scattered remarks on aesthetic judgements (in music, architecture, and poetry), as well as on the nature of ritual behaviour, religious belief, and anthropology. In such contexts he emphasizes two features of the concept's grammar: the inseparability of a gesture's meaning from the gesture itself, and the importance of the context of the gesture in accounting for its impact on us. In a religious ceremony, for example (*RPP* i. 34–6), Wittgenstein notes that we are sometimes particularly struck by a certain gesture of the celebrant: even if we don't fully grasp its meaning, we feel that it is not only brimful with significance but that no other gesture would be capable of containing or manifesting that significance, that it is the best possible expression for what is expressed here. At the same time, however, he points out that we can come to understand the gesture's significance by exploring its surroundings—by, for example, altering some aspect of the surrounding ceremony and assessing what difference if any is thereby made to the import of the gesture; and this implies that the impact of the gesture is in fact dependent on its place in a wider context. His point is not that our sense of the inseparability of the gesture's significance from the gesture itself is a misapprehension; it is rather that we experience the gesture itself as if it had absorbed its own context—as if traces of the ceremony as a whole, and of the form of life of which it is a part, are inscribed in the gesture itself.

The connection with continuous meaning perception, with our sense that words absorb their specific place in the world of language, is evident; and it is reinforced by Wittgenstein's tendency to express our sense of the specific atmosphere or physiognomy of even humdrum words such as 'if' in terms not just of an 'if-feeling' but of an 'if-gesture' (*LW* i. 366–83). Furthermore, secondary extensions of word-meaning plainly possess the grammatical physiognomy of a gesture: only the given word will do as the expression of the feeling or inclination concerned, but it is this word understood as the bearer of a specific primary technique and so as located in a specific way in the linguistic field. We might say, then, that our feeling that words have a physiognomy is manifest in their availability for us as elements of a gesture language, as a means by which to articulate a further set of spontaneous reactions to the world and our experience of it. And if we recall here the degree to which the coinages and turns of phrase with which Wittgenstein's discussion of aspect perception is saturated first surface in the *Investigations* during the early discussion of rule-following, as part of his attempt to find the right mythological expression for our sense of having internalized the rules of grammar, taking their projection into new contexts as an unhesitating matter of course, then the most important general moral of the present reading may become clear.

As the case of the deviant pupil emphasizes, pre-linguistic natural reactions ground the human inheritance of language. But acquiring forms of linguistic behaviour does not just provide us with new instruments for achieving our practical purposes; it also shapes and informs our nature, making possible the genuine inhabitation of human culture, and the self-transformative potential that this talking form of life opens up. In particular, this mutual information of nature by culture can create a new realm of spontaneous *linguistic* reactions—responses to our experience that are possible only because we have acquired language, and that themselves form the basis of new language-games, a further extension of our range of linguistic behaviour. It is as if humans inherit language twice, and the second inheritance is made possible by—and so is expressive of—the depth of the first; for only when our first inheritance of language has come to inform our lives in such a way that each and every word of it is available to us as a unique gesture do we find ourselves possessed of the reactive substratum, the new natural reactions, that are essential for our inheritance of a further range of language and experience. In this sense, our attachment to our words, our tendency to assimilate them, shows that linguistic behaviour is second nature to us—that to acquire language is to acquire a second nature.

Wittgenstein's model of primary and secondary meaning is thus an emblem of the productive interaction of nature and culture, an exemplary instance of the ways in which the two aspects of our forms of life, their yoking together of the instinctual and the social, opens human beings to an undefined future. And our reinheritance of words as gestures appears as a fundamental medium of human individuation and intimacy: for the spontaneous linguistic reactions upon which it is grounded provide a terrain upon which the specificity of one person's inner life might find more and more fine-grained articulation, but in terms which can call forth an answering resonance in another person and which—precisely because they are not instances of the application of rules—thereby form touchstones of intimacy, the medium for a closer community or fellowship, a communion of souls. But of course, what can bring us together can also separate us; those same reactions can testify to a failure of intimacy, a mutual incomprehension. Little wonder, then, that Wittgenstein describes the aspect-blind person's uncomprehending queries about the justification of secondary uses of words as 'having a different racial origin, as it were' (*LW* i. 56)—for they are the questions of someone with a very different nature (and a very different culture); it is as if the aspect-blind are a different race of people, 'a different type of man' (*LW* ii. 2c). It is as if the double inheritance of language relates to a two-stage process of speciation. The first inheritance amounts to one's claiming membership of the species whose form of life is linguistic; and the second inheritance is of one's individuality, one's capacity to individuate oneself as a distinctive member of that species, with the distinctive patterns of our linguistic gestures tracing our filiations to and from other individuals.

We can imagine from a different angle what the general incapacity of those unable to take up that second inheritance would be like if we recall the difference (obliterated, in Wittgenstein's view, by Augustine; *PI* 32) between someone's relation to her mother tongue or native language and her relation to a second language that she acquired and mastered for most practical purposes in adulthood but never truly absorbed. Such a person might express the difference by saying that she still has to think her way through certain of its grammatical constructions, or that swearing and declarations of love don't seem truly effective in it, or that she can't properly appreciate its literature, or more generally that she doesn't feel completely at home in the second language. The formulations Wittgenstein has been employing to characterize the human attitude to language—a sense of words as portraits of their bearers, as having physiognomies, as being likenesses of their meaning, and a sense of language as a realm in which we know our way around—seem highly apt in such a context; and that in turn suggests that what Wittgenstein has in mind when imagining a linguistic version of aspect-blindness is a more generalized version of the attitude we often have to a second language. In this respect, the aspect-blind have no native language; for them, there is no mother tongue.

ASPECTS OF THE INNER

47. Recounting the grammar of the terms underpinning Wittgenstein's investigation of aspect perception has so far shown that what most fundamentally interests him is doubly distanced from that which most commentators attribute to him. His primary concern with the experience of aspect-dawning is not the difficulty it creates for an erroneous theory of vision but its striking manifestation of a more general human attitude to both pictures and words—to what he christens continuous aspect perception and continuous meaning perception. This, however, only takes us through two-thirds of the material in section xi of the *Investigations*; Wittgenstein concludes his exploration by devoting ten or so pages of remarks to issues arising in the philosophy of psychology. In what ways do the themes so far developed lead us naturally in that direction?

Analogues to experiences of aspect-dawning are not hard to come by in our relations with other persons: there are many occasions on which we are profoundly struck by the particular shade of consciousness manifest in someone's expression or behaviour—when we not only see that someone is fearful or joyful, but *see* the fear in his eyes, the joy in her face. But of course, the truly significant question is whether we can see anything analogous to continuous aspect perception. The most obvious signpost here is the central figure Wittgenstein has been employing to capture striking instances of meaning perception; for of course, the claim that words have a distinctive physiognomy— that their physical appearance encapsulates their individuality— displaces an expression that has its original home with respect to the human face and body. We might even think of the claim as a secondary use of the term 'physiognomy'—for what other word has the implications that this one carries with it from its primary use? Talk of the familiar physiognomy of a friend's face expresses our sensitivity to the unique identity of that person, our sense that we can see the finest shades of their thoughts and feelings in the fine shades of their expression and behaviour. Our knowing someone well comes out in the unhesitating way we judge the genuineness or insincerity of her expressive behaviour, even when the evidence to which we are responding would not convince—and might not even be noticeable by—another observer (*PI* 227d–h); and this capacity for right judgement involves being able to make the right connections—to see a particular expression as a manifestation of a precise state of mind, to link that inner state with something in the situation to which that person is responding (even if others would not), to foresee just how her future behaviour will reveal or repress that response, and what the consequences of such revelation or repression might be. In turning at last to the realm of psychology, then, we might say that Wittgenstein is returning the word 'physiognomy' from its secondary to its primary sense, from its mythological to its everyday home.

Within that realm the significance of judging connections aright in the case of specific individuals reflects their importance in the grammatical structure of psychological concepts more generally. Wittgenstein's work in this area constantly emphasizes the fact that psychological concepts are applied within certain characteristic surroundings of human behaviour—not just to a given type of behaviour but to that behaviour seen in relation to what occasions it and follows from it. These concepts, in effect, draw together a certain *Gestalt* of behaviour, utterance, and occasion, but the patterning here is not at all rigid. Human behaviour is not uniform: neither our circumstances nor our reactions to those circumstances are so inflexible as to give point to a conceptual structure which yoked such elements together as a matter of unvarying necessity; and different cultures will shape and give prominence to certain patterns in different ways. We must learn to know our way around with cultures as well as individuals; we have to find our feet with them, try to render what is initially enigmatic ultimately transparent—and we may, of course, fail (*PI* 223 f,g). Experience, familiarity, and responsiveness to fine detail is required properly to understand an individual's thoughts and feelings; but the capacity to apply such concepts to any given person will presuppose the capacity to perceive human life as 'the same occurring again, but with variations'—that is, to see, to respond to, or regard new combinations of behaviour, utterance, and circumstance as a variation on one of the loose patterns.

Wittgenstein reinforces these points when he hints at an analogy between blindness to the meaning of words and blindness to the meaningfulness of human behaviour.

... it is clear that the tendency to regard the word as something intimate, full of soul, is not always there, or not always in the same measure. But the opposite of being full of soul is being mechanical. If you want to act like a robot—how does your behaviour deviate from our ordinary behaviour? By the fact that our ordinary movements cannot even approximately be described by means of geometrical concepts. (*RPP* i. 324)

The suggestion seems to be: the aspect-blind regard a human being's behaviour as we would the behaviour of a robot, of a construction whose behaviour is mechanical and thus describable by means of geometrical concepts. Geometrically conceptualized behaviour would lack imponderable fine shades, variety, and flexibility of the kind we have been describing; such concepts would eliminate the loose weave of behaviour, utterance, and circumstance that makes up our understanding of genuinely human action and expression, and that makes it possible for culturally relative paradigms of expressive behaviour to be inflected by the irregularities and variations of texture that give individual style or character to a particular person's actions. For these reasons, the aspect-blind would be blind to the humanity and individuality of other persons; and that blindness would express itself in a certain rigidification or mechanization of their own behaviour in relation to those others—they would miss certain subtleties and complexities, stumble over irregularities in the patterns of occasion, behaviour, and consequences, hesitate where others take things for granted. And this stiffness or failure to find their feet with others would be reinforced by their failure to see the point of certain secondary, expressive uses of language, with their consequent exclusion from certain key ranges of experience, reaction, and response. In short, the behaviour of the aspect-blind would be as mechanical or robotic as their perception of the behaviour of others; their blindness to the humanity of others is paralleled by a dehumanizing rigidity in themselves.

REINHERITING THE IDEA OF GRAMMAR

48. We have followed Wittgenstein's chain of remarks as far as it goes in section xi of the *Philosophical Investigations*; indeed, our last step required divining the implications of a far from clear passage in the preliminary typescripts and manuscripts from which section xi was composed, and thus might already be criticized for failing to take seriously enough Wittgenstein's decision not to incorporate the thoughts it expressed in the more polished composition. A policy of combining interpretative valour with exegetical discretion at this point may seem warranted. Wittgenstein does not explicitly extend his account of aspect perception beyond the three specific domains of pictures, words, and people, and we should respect the implications of that self-restraint.

Indeed, some commentators have argued that Wittgenstein explicitly imposes restrictions on the generality of the phenomenon of aspect perception, and so on the generalizability of his account of it. In his *Wittgenstein Dictionary*[27] entry on aspect perception, for example, Hans-Johann Glock takes the passage quoted below, which immediately follows Wittgenstein's early introduction of the idea of picture-rabbits, to amount to a denial that continuous aspect perception is generalizable:

It would have made as little sense for me to say [of the picture-rabbit] 'Now I am seeing it as . . .' as to say at the sight of a knife and fork 'Now I am seeing this as a knife and fork'. This expression would not be understood.—Any more than: 'Now it's a fork' or 'It can be a fork too'.

One doesn't *take* what one knows as the cutlery at a meal *for* cutlery; any more than one tries to move one's mouth as one eats, or aims at moving it. (*PI* 195b–c)

---

[27] (Blackwell: Oxford, 1996).

However, this interpretation of that passage misunderstands Wittgenstein's intentions. It would be defensible only on the assumption that employing the form of words 'Now I'm seeing it as . . .' is a criterion for continuous aspect perception (for then its inappropriateness would justify our withholding the latter concept in the relevant contexts); but Wittgenstein repeatedly treats that form of words as expressive of aspect-dawning, not of continuous aspect perception. The former is a very specific visual experience with characteristic forms of verbal expression (or *Ausserungen*); the latter is an attitude whose presence is sometimes revealed in an individual's susceptibility to aspect-dawning experiences, but which also finds expression in a variety of other fine shades of verbal and non-verbal behaviour. This attitude is certainly not a continuous sequence of aspect-dawning experiences; and it is just such a misinterpretation that Wittgenstein is plainly attempting to ward off here. He is, in other words, simply denying the ubiquity of experiences of aspect-dawning; his remarks have no direct bearing on the ubiquity of continuous aspect perception.

There are, however, other reasons for doubting that the attitude of continuous seeing as is manifest in domains other than the three Wittgenstein explicitly discusses—reasons also invoked in Glock's account. For example, there is a clear sense in which pictures and words are both representative objects—entities with symbolic functions, phenomena which signify other phenomena; human beings are not representative objects in this sense, but they are meaningful in the different but related sense that their behaviour gives expression to their thoughts and feelings, their bodies picture their souls. Consequently, all three kinds of entity can be seen as offering a very sharp contrast between their material and their symbolic–expressive dimensions which is simply not available with respect to most other kinds of object—a contrast which simultaneously makes the interpretative model of perception highly attractive, and allows Wittgenstein to oppose that model by stressing our capacity directly to perceive the symbolic in the material.

We can, however, easily become unduly fixated on the peculiarity or uniqueness of symbolic or meaningful objects. After all, a picture just *is* the kind of entity one can describe by describing what it depicts, a word just *is* a meaningful mark, and a human being just *is* the kind of creature whose behaviour is expressive of mind; to know these things about them is simply to know what pictures, words, and people are. Indeed, to think that there is something highly distinctive about these kinds of entity, something that marks them off from all other kinds of object, is to think of their meaningfulness as something additional and alien to their materiality; it thus amounts to succumbing to the very conception of these entities that supports the interpretative model. If, by contrast, we emphasize that seeing a picture in terms of what it depicts is simply to see it as the particular kind of thing it is, then we might be less inclined to think that there is any fundamental difference between seeing a picture and seeing a hammer or a table or a computer; all involve relating to an object as one particular kind of object or another, and all are therefore capable in principle of being ready to hand for us as the kinds of object they are.

What matters most at this critical juncture is the fundamental priority of language in the triad of particular entities upon which Wittgenstein's discussion of aspect perception focuses. It becomes plain as section xi progresses that much of Wittgenstein's interest in the ways in which we relate to pictures and people lies in how those relations illuminate important dimensions of our relation to words; but if language is the key issue for Wittgenstein here, we need to recall that 'language' can be understood in two, very different ways. In one sense, the term refers to a body of words and sentences, and so to one particular kind of phenomenon among the many we encounter in the world, one species of symbolic or meaningful entity that we might employ to achieve some of our practical purposes. But it can also refer to a grammar, to the articulated network of discriminations that inform our capacity to word the world, to bespeak anything and everything we encounter within it.

49. Understood in the first sense, Wittgenstein's accounting of language crystallizes around our sense of words as having a physiognomy; and, as our returning of that expression to its primary home underlined, this invites us to think of words as soulful, as having the individuality that we attribute to people. If we put this together with Wittgenstein's famous claim that 'the human body is the best picture of the human soul' (*PI* 178), then we must ask how the body of words, the field of their human use, makes their soul manifest to us—what invites the application of that term. Since, as we saw earlier, Wittgenstein claims that 'the opposite of being full of soul is being mechanical' (*RPP* i. 324), that question can be reformulated as asking what it is about the field of human uses of language that resists the idea of the mechanical, the robotic. And if we take seriously the by now familiar thought that Wittgenstein's repeated invocations of mechanical human beings (shopkeepers, builders, sublimers of logic, reading-

machines, rule-followers), which here find their apotheosis in the construction of an image of aspect-blindness as robotic, are not only expressions of a primitive conception of human ways with words but also an expression of the primitive state to which those ways are presently reduced, the question can be further reformulated as asking by what means this reduction might be overcome.

To this multifaceted question Wittgenstein suggests two answers. The first emerges in the following remark: 'It would be possible to imagine people who had something not quite unlike a language: a play of sounds, without vocabulary or grammar. ("Speaking with tongues.")' (*PI* 528). Here Wittgenstein emphasizes the rhythms and intonation contours of speech, the shifting patterns of tempo, stress, and pitch that form a child's first approximations of human speech and that draw glossolalia within the field of application of the term 'language', the phenomena he elsewhere refers to as *Satzklang* ('one feature of our concept of a proposition is, *sounding like a proposition*'; *PI* 134). Without the logical multiplicity that these intersecting dimensions of variation provide, human speech would lack fluidity and flexibility; it would tend towards the empty, mechanical, soulless paradigm of words as uttered by computer voice-synthesizers, from which we would never receive an impression of words as full of soul—and hence, of anything we might want to call a genuinely human voice.

Wittgenstein's second answer refers to writing rather than speech, and emerges when he asks: 'Would one also get an impression of a group-picture [i.e. of sentences as a group of words each with an individual face] from sentences written in telegraphic style?' (*RPP* i. 325). What is lost when we compose a telegram are the connectives and definite articles, the expansive and idiosyncratic field of syntactic and semantic elements in which the whole history and specificity of the language reside, and from which the individual writer can select to construct her own personal idiolect and style. In a world of writing that refused such individual variation within parameters of cogency and correctness of expression, the idea of words as having an individual physiognomy—as differentiating themselves from, and so resisting substitution by, other words—would not easily arise.

These answers lead to the following general claim:

There might . . . be a language in whose use the 'soul' of the words played no part. In which, for example, we had no objection to replacing one word by another arbitrary one of our own invention.

We speak of understanding a sentence in the sense in which it can be replaced by another which says the same; but also in the sense in which it cannot be replaced by any other. (Any more than one musical theme can be replaced by another.)

In the one case the thought in the sentence is something common to different sentences; in the other, something that is expressed only by these words in these positions. (Understanding a poem.)

Then has 'understanding' two different meanings here?—I would rather say that these kinds of use of 'understanding' make up its meaning, make up my *concept* of understanding.

For I *want* to apply the word 'understanding' to all this. (*PI* 530–2)

These remarks amount to an implicit critique of Wittgenstein's own previous ways of accounting for language—a revision of his earlier pictures or figures for words. For the idea of words as tools which dominates part I of the *Investigations* precisely implies the substitutability of words; if a word is a tool, it is replaceable by any other tool that will fulfil the same purpose. Whereas the idea of words as gestures which implicitly dominates part II of the *Investigations* pictures words as saying themselves, as being veritable likenesses of their meaning, and so denies the idea that any other word could be an adequate substitute for them. We might say that our first inheritance of language is akin to the acquisition of a set of tools, but our second comes when the tool has come to take on the appearance of a work of art, an icon, a gesture. The transfiguration of Wittgenstein's imagery thus aims to capture the ways in which our absorption of language transmutes our attitude to words from the equipmental to the gestural.

50. What, though, of the second sense of the term 'language' that I specified a little earlier—the idea of language not as a body of words and sentences that we encounter within the world but as an articulated network of conceptual discriminations that inform our ability to word the world in all its phenomenal variety? Wittgenstein's term 'grammar' is meant to hit off this second sense of 'language'; and the discriminations to which it refers have implicitly been guiding our discussion of pictures, words, and people throughout these sections. Grammatical investigations presuppose that reminding us of what we say when about any given kind of object is a mode of access to the essence of that object—'essence is expressed by grammar' (*PI* 371); and Wittgenstein imposes no restriction on the kinds of object in relation to which a grammatical investigation is appropriate. If, then, we understand continuous meaning perception as Wittgenstein's attempt to characterize our typical relation to language in this grammatical sense,

as trying to capture the way in which we absorb or assimilate the grammatical articulations of our mother tongue as well as the meaningfulness of its individual words, then this assimilation will inevitably make itself manifest not only in our encounters with words and sentences as opposed to other kinds of entity, but also in our encounters with objects of any kind.

Wittgenstein does, after all, emphasize that a language is embedded in a form of life, and so implies that a full grasp of its grammatical articulations involves seeing the ways in which they inform and presuppose a wide array of reactions and responses, practices and practical activity—an array that will include specifically linguistic behaviour, but that will also range far more widely. If continuous meaning perception is an attempt to characterize what it is to have a mother tongue, to speak a language like a native, then we need to remind ourselves that linguistic behaviour typically hangs together with parallel forms of non-linguistic behaviour—that the native speaker's seamless, unhesitating assimilation of the resources of her mother tongue is shown not only in the handiness of its words but in the ways in which the objects of the world as that language articulates them are handy for her, are woven so seamlessly into her practical activity. It is only when seen against this broader background that the true physiognomy of native speech, of what it is to follow the rules of our mother tongue, properly emerges. And what emerges from this attention to the horizontal rather than the vertical axis of philosophical investigation is that the world is the native element of human beings, that we and it absorb one another. In short: to be at home in a language is to be at home in the world.

We need to note, however, that in reaching this conclusion, Wittgenstein has been forced to subject his guiding notion of 'grammar' to a certain kind of grammatical transformation. In part i of the *Investigations* that notion is implicitly tethered to the notion of a rule (although only after establishing a remarkable, highly specific but unusually flexible conception of the grammar of that latter notion). But in part ii Wittgenstein opens up territory that asks us to accept far more than the idea that what we might as well call rules of grammar should not suffer mathematicization, that they need not acknowledge logic as their sublimed ideal. This advance is implicitly flagged towards the end of Wittgenstein's discussion of rule-following, when he finds that our mythology of rules leads us to talk of them as having a face, or an indefinably particular atmosphere; he also talks of our capacity to see a series as the segment of an expansion, and he glosses our claim that rules are our last arbiter as a mythological expression for our capacity to take its correct expansion utterly for granted. We can now see that these are the marks of continuous meaning perception, expressed in terms of our relation to rules rather than words; and against this background the recurrent temptation to picture rules as sublime machines appears as an impulse to think of words as mechanical rather than full of soul, and so as an expression of aspect-blindness.

Wittgenstein's explicit study of continuous meaning perception tells us that the more sensitive we become to the souls of words (the more at home we are with the grammar of a language), the more their possibilities of signification transmute themselves from the equipmental to the gestural. And that transmutation, symbolized by the generation of secondary from primary senses of our expressions, takes our grasp of words beyond any simple grasp of rules and into realms of mutual intimation (or the failure of it), into a matching (or mismatching) of linguistic gestures, the attempted exchange of nods and whispers. We might say that the fullness of our inheritance of the rules of grammar is a capacity to find possibilities of meaning in the words they govern which are not themselves governable by (not simply projections, however unexpected, of) rules. In the mythical terms set up in *PI* 232–4 words come to inspire us rather than giving us orders; we go on with them as if composing rather than calculating, through a kind of receptivity to the music of language (see *PI* 527), awaiting their direction in the hope rather than the expectation that others will follow us.

In these dimensions of language Wittgenstein's notion of grammar, and so of the ordinary, might be said to find its own limits. But of course, just as the secondary sense of words can never entirely be cut free of their primary sense, so the gestural possibilities of language must not be pictured as taking us entirely beyond the realm of grammatical rules. It is rather that acknowledging those possibilities casts a new light on what is involved in understanding the grammar of words, by revealing that our capacity to master the projection of words in their primary senses cannot be disentangled from a capacity to be mastered by secondary modes of their projection, by the symbolic or mythological dimension of sense that intersects every step of their more impersonal trajectories. Recalling Wittgenstein's constant sense of the child within the adult speaker, and his specific sense of her modes of play with dolls as presiding over his account of aspect perception from the start, we might think of this as a dimension of the playfulness of words. Continuous meaning perception teaches us that, just as Wittgenstein's conception of understanding words is meant to accommodate both their tolerance and their intolerance of substitution, so his conception of the ordinary and its grammar is meant to include an acknowledgement of its own internal potential for transcending normativity.

But if his conception of grammar contains such an acknowledgement, then so must his conception of grammatical investigation. The internal relation between the object of Wittgenstein's concern and the method by which he gains access to it is, after all, one we have implicitly been tracking throughout this commentary. In part i of the *Investigations* Wittgenstein's denial of the idea that rules of grammar approximate to calculi with fixed rules—his sense of the play of language—finds its methodological expression in imagining language-games (conjuring up fictional contexts which invite the projection of our concepts in unpredictably controlled ways), in coining metaphors and similes, and in the liberating resonances of aphorism. This reflexivity culminated, at the culmination of his discussion of rule-following, in his uncovering of symbolic or mythological modes of meaning words—modes which part ii of the *Investigations* shows to be redescribable as secondary senses of terms (which must be distinguished from metaphorical uses of them). But of course, this redescription emerges from a grammatical investigation of aspect perception and its ramifications which is permeated and governed by a phalanx of new coinages—a body of terms whose sense trades upon and yet goes beyond their ordinary grammar—that itself exemplifies the phenomenon of secondary sense. In short, in a more systematic way than ever before, Wittgenstein here explores the capacity of language to generate secondary meanings, its openness to gestural or mythological senses, precisely by deploying it. And he shows thereby that, just as the grammar of our words can make possible modes of projecting meaning that go beyond the projection of rules, so a grammatical investigation can discover new ways of establishing philosophical self-possession, by allowing itself to be informed by a certain transfigured sense of the necessities and limits of grammar—one in which the word 'grammar' (and so the idea of grammatical structure) is discovered to tolerate projection into a context which is intolerant of the concept of rules. This suggests that grasping our second inheritance of language at once requires and makes possible our second inheritance of Wittgenstein's method; and it further implies that the way in which we take up that reinheritance is itself a touchstone of intimacy—with Wittgenstein, and with one another.

My attempts to capture Wittgenstein's vision of the physiognomy of native speech have more or less explicitly resorted to versions of

Heiddeggerian terminology—both from his early, phenomenological work ('readiness-to-hand', 'Being-in-the-world'[28]) and from his later writings ('gesture', 'myth', 'thinking as a handicraft'[29]). This raises a general question about the ways in which Heidegger's work—both early and late—might be read as displacing or displaced by, as transfiguring or transfigured by, Wittgensteinian themes and preoccupations. It is to the task of providing materials that might be used to begin such a reading that the next part of this book is devoted.

[28] My *On Being in the World* explores this specific set of connections in more detail.
[29] The key text here is *What is Called Thinking?*, trans. J. Glenn Gray (Harper & Row: New York, 1968); hereafter *WCT*.

OPENING: QUOTATION

1. *Being and Time*[1] begins with a two-chapter introduction, which is itself introduced by a foreword (as it is titled in the author's notes to the text), which opens with a citation from Plato's *Sophist*.[2] Heidegger's translation of the citation is translated by Macquarrie and Robinson as follows: 'For manifestly you have long been aware of what you mean when you use the expression *'being'*. We, however, who used to think we understood it, have now become perplexed' (*BT* 19). Why might Heidegger choose to begin his text with another's words? Why this other, and why these words?

Such a choice ensures that Heidegger's own opening words will appear as a response to those he has quoted—as if the philosophical work of his words is essentially responsive, not so much a matter of constructing theses but of engaging in dialogue with the words of others, always already finding an origin outside themselves. Heidegger's responsiveness, unlike that of Wittgenstein, is keyed to words in canonically philosophical texts; he gives no indication that his philosophy is called for by words that are offered neither as contributions to a philosophical enterprise, nor in a spirit recognizably related to such enterprises. In placing himself within the tradition of Western philosophy, however, Heidegger simultaneously distinguishes himself by choosing to cite a text of Plato's; he thereby dissociates himself from contemporary philosophical works (even those of the teacher to whom his book as a whole is dedicated, Husserl) and associates himself instead with the origins of philosophy in ancient Greece. This suggests that Heidegger thinks of his own philosophy as essentially historical, as making progress by engaging in dialogue with its inheritance—as if all genuine philosophy is history of philosophy; it further implies that every such dialogue is or should amount to a return to the origins of the subject, that every new philosophical beginning can and should amount to a new beginning for philosophy; and it hints that the texts produced by the history of philosophy since Plato are at best no more capable of inviting and bearing up under questioning that might truly engender a new beginning for the subject than are Plato's own—as if in order to make philosophical progress we must give up our assumption that any such progress has been made since Plato's time, or at least radically revise our conception

---

[1] Trans. J. Macquarrie and E. Robinson (Blackwell: Oxford, 1962); hereafter *BT*. References will specify section numbers, followed by the relevant pages of the English translation.
[2] Trans. N. White (Hackett: Indianapolis, 1993); hereafter *S*.

of what such progress might look like and where it might be found. For Heidegger, the subject has lost its way from the outset, been unable to live up to its own beginnings, become disoriented; beginning to achieve reorientation means returning to our beginnings.

2. So much is indicated by Heidegger's choice of an ancient Greek text with which to begin his book. But why these particular words from this particular Platonic dialogue?[3] How might their substance offer a new orientation for him and for us? The remainder of Heidegger's fore-word—two full paragraphs—provides the following guidance:

> Do we in our time have an answer to the question of what we really mean by the word 'being'? Not at all. So it is fitting that we should raise anew *the question of the meaning of Being*. But are we nowadays even perplexed at our inability to understand the expression 'Being'? Not at all. So first of all we must reawaken an understanding for the meaning of this question. Our aim in the following treatise is to work out the question of the meaning of *Being* and to do so concretely. Our provisional aim is the Interpretation of *time* as the possible horizon for any understanding whatsoever of Being.
>
> But the reasons for making this our aim, the investigations which such a purpose requires, and the path to its achievement, call for some introductory remarks. (*BT* 19)

According to these paragraphs, Heidegger takes the quotation from Plato to specify the state to which, above all or least before all, he wishes to bring his readers. They (and he—if we are to take his 'we' seriously) do not have an answer to the question of what the word 'being' means, and are not perplexed by that fact about themselves. So Heidegger's first task is to 'reawaken an understanding for the meaning of this question'—that is, to (re-)create a sense in us that the question of the meaning of 'Being' is itself meaningful, significant, weighty by (re-)creating a sense of perplexity about it. In other words, he wants to

---

[3] This dialogue was the subject of a lecture course offered by Heidegger in the years immediately preceding the final drafting of *Being and Time*. Those lectures have recently been published (*Plato's Sophist*, trans. R. Rojcewicz and A. Schuwer, Indiana University Press: Bloomington, 1997). However, much of this material concerns Aristotle rather than Plato; and the material that does concern Plato provides no more than a very general background for understanding one stage in Heidegger's rapidly evolving conception of the relation between his own project and that of his ancient Greek predecessor. Certainly, the lectures neither support nor undermine the conclusions that can—as we shall see—be drawn from Heidegger's decision to begin *Being and Time* with this particular quotation from the *Sophist* (apart, perhaps, from Heidegger's fervent rejection of the familiar idea that the dialogue's examination of the question of Being should be treated as its kernel, with the first half of the dialogue functioning only as an essentially dispensable dramatic frame for that examination).

transform us, his readers, so that we might overcome our tendency to identify ourselves with those addressed in the first of the quoted sentences from Plato, and instead earn the right to say of ourselves what the second quoted sentence says about the speaker and those for whom he speaks.

Heidegger thus identifies philosophizing with questioning, but distances it from (at least certain conceptions of) the business of establishing answers to questions. He describes the aim of his treatise as one of working out a question, not of working out an answer to it—as if what most concerns him is the proper articulation of the question rather than its definitive resolution, the raising of an issue rather than the laying of it to rest; and this articulation of his philosophical task itself emerges in response to a series of questions. Of course, he also provides answers to those questions—but answers that are so exaggeratedly definitive that they immediately raise more questions in their turn (do we really have no answers to the question of what 'being' means?; so why be perplexed at an illusory inability?), and so amount to the rearticulation of the original question. And he further implies that properly working out a question means properly working out its meaning or significance, which means becoming or being perplexed by it—as if proper questioning hangs together with a particular state of mind or mood, as if philosophizing not only begins in wonder or disorientation, but continues only in so far as the working out of its questions remains itself questionable or perplexing.

3. Such is the overt import of Heidegger's citation of these words of Plato. But a closer examination suggests that the full significance of Heidegger's choice of text here goes far deeper than its handy formulation of the question of the meaning of Being in conjunction with a mood of perplexity; for if its substance or content appears to carry Heidegger's endorsement, what of its form and location? Might not these aspects of the quotation carry their own weight of significance?

The two quoted sentences come from 244a of Plato's dialogue the *Sophist*, marking roughly the midway point of the extended exchange between Theaetetus and a Stranger from Elea. They are words spoken by the Stranger to Theaetetus, but they also form part of the Stranger's imagined dialogue with those he calls tellers of myths about Being—in particular, with those who claim that everything is made up of two beings or types of being (e.g. hot and cold, or wet and dry) that are married off and set up house together (*S* 242d). The Stranger takes this tale of domestic harmony as representative of any mythology that attributes multiplicity to Being, and as representatively vulnerable to the charge that they are incapable of explaining what they mean when they say such things as 'hot and cold exist'—that is, when they attribute being to that which they claim is or constitutes Being. Hence the ironic quoted attribution to these myth-makers of an awareness and freedom from perplexity that the Stranger claims to lack.

So, Heidegger opens his book by citing words that a philosophical author's fictional character imagines speaking to an imaginary group of fiction-makers; he places a further set of inverted commas around words that have already acquired two such sets, creating a triple quotation. But the citationality or embeddedness of these sentences is more complex even than this—it has, as it were, a horizontal as well as a vertical axis. For the Stranger's fictional interchange with his myth-makers is itself embedded within a dialogue he is having with Theaetetus about the intelligibility of claims concerning Being and non-Being, which is embedded within a dialogue between the two about the difference between philosophy and sophistry, which is itself initiated by Socrates as a means of identifying the true nature of the Stranger from Elea—is he human or divine, a genuine philosopher or a sophist?

Once the Stranger accepts Socrates' choice of topic, the transition from attempting to define sophistry to that of determining the intelligibility of talk about Being is clear (if not exactly straightforward): for the Stranger ultimately wishes to characterize the sophist as a maker of appearances, someone who makes false statements, who says that which is not—a strategy which faces the objection that it is not possible to say or think that which is not, and so not possible intelligibly to accuse someone of doing so; but if that which is not is not sayable, how can we say or think that which is? Hence the Stranger's imaginary interrogation of the myth-makers about Being. But in quoting from that interrogation, and so apparently identifying himself with the Stranger's diagnosis of his interlocutor's confusions, how far is Heidegger thereby identifying himself with the Stranger's ulterior motive for engaging in that interrogation, and how far is he thereby accepting the Stranger as an authority on these matters—as a genuine thinker or philosopher? In other words, how far does Heidegger's excision of his two sentences work to deny, and how far to acknowledge, any implication in their broader dialogical context?

4. We might (re)articulate this question by asking how the Stranger's performance in the dialogue as a whole grounds his claim to be a genuine philosopher—to be someone who is not merely a member of the Eleatic school founded by Parmenides but a genuine inheritor of Parmenides' claim to philosophical authority. To ask the question in

this way is to return us to the opening of the whole dialogue, to challenge us to begin again with Heidegger's opening by beginning with Plato's beginning; for Socrates' opening response to the Stranger's opening appearance—a response which at once determines that there will be a dialogue, between whom it will occur, and what its fundamental topic will be—is a barely disguised articulation of this very question. After noting that 'the genuine philosophers who haunt our cities—by contrast to the fake ones—take on all sorts of different appearances just because of other people's ignorance' (*S* 216c), he asks the Stranger whether the Eleatics think 'that sophists, statesmen and philosophers make up one kind of thing or two . . . or . . . three kinds . . . ?' (*S* 217a); and he further asks how the Stranger would prefer to explain the grounds for his answer—'by yourself in a long speech, or . . . with questions?' (*S* 217c). All that follows between Theaetetus and the Stranger unfolds without any further intervention from Socrates, but it nevertheless implicitly subserves his questioning of the visitor's authenticity; having given voice to philosophy's conscience, his subsequent silence allows that call to reverberate throughout the dialogue.

The subject of this questioning creates a positive initial impression by choosing to employ the method of questioning—the one that, as Socrates points out, was preferred by Parmenides himself; and he further strengthens his claim to a genuine philosophical inheritance by devoting the second half of his ensuing dialogue with Theaetetus to a critique of Parmenides' famous assertion that we should avoid the thought that that which is not may be (*S* 237a). The implication seems clear: the Stranger is devoted to Parmenides' method, not to the unthinking defence of every one of his specific conclusions—he is prepared to follow the path the dialectical method demands even when it involves criticizing the man from whom he learned to apply it.

However, other evidence internal to the dialogue points towards a less positive conclusion. Before making the transition to what is so often taken to be the main business of the dialogue (the analysis of the relations between speech, Being, and non-Being), the Stranger guides Theaetetus through no less than seven different definitions of the sophist—definitions primarily designed to differentiate him from the philosopher. After a warming-up exercise on defining angling, Theaetetus learns that employing the same dialectical method will tell us that sophistry is the hunting of rich young men by applying expertise in persuasion; that it is a species of exchanging words and learning about virtue and the soul, whether wholesaling or retailing the products of others or selling what the dealer has produced himself; that it is the moneymaking branch of debating; that it is an expertise in cleansing the soul by the discriminating assessment of its beliefs and opinions; and that it amounts to falsely claiming knowledge about everything, and so to the making of appearances that aren't likenesses. It is with this seventh definition that the Stranger confronts the problem of false saying or believing, and so of the utterability of non-being and being.

The striking thing about this perplexingly varied sequence of definitions is the degree to which its terms apply to the discourse and circumstances of the person generating it. The Stranger is, after all, applying his expertise in persuasion to the rich young men of Socrates' acquaintance, and if he is not clearly hunting them, he repeatedly describes his task in the discourse as one of hunting the wealthy men known as sophists (he says he wants to 'hunt down and deal with' them (*S* 218d), describes them as wanting to escape from his pursuit (*S* 231c), describes himself as not letting 'the beast escape' (*S* 235b), and as capturing a catch he wishes to hand over but which might slip down and away from him (*S* 235c)). Similarly, his three interlinked characterizations of the sophist as trading words and learning about the soul themselves utilize words for trading that reflect back on himself; his distinction between wholesale and retail is a distinction between trading between cities and trading within one, when he is himself trading words within one city that he picked up in and transported from another. When defining sophistry as the moneymaking branch of debating, he defines its non-moneymaking branch as mere chatter, unpleasant in style (*S* 225c–e), thus implicitly placing his pleasant and serious debating manner in the sophistical branch. His dialogue with Theaetetus is plainly supposed to be an exercise in soul-cleansing, in discriminating true from false belief. And, perhaps most striking of all, his discourse frequently relies upon utilizing and analysing fictions, myths, and tales of giants and men (*S* 242d, 244a, 246a), and so involves the making of appearances that are not likenesses of anything, that are multiply distanced from reality—the very crime of which he accuses the sophists.

It is, then, hardly surprising that, towards the end of this sequence of attempted definitions, the Stranger begins to display a certain sensitivity to the uncanny proximity of sophistry and genuine philosophy. After defining the class of discriminating soul-cleansers, he says:

STRANGER. I'm afraid to call them sophists.
THEAETETUS. Why?
STRANGER. So we don't pay sophists too high an honour.

THEAETETUS. But there's a similarity between a sophist and what we've
been talking about.

STRANGER. And between a wolf and a dog, the wildest thing there is and
the gentlest. If you're going to be safe, you have to be especially careful
about similiarities, since the type we're talking about is very slippery. Still,
let that stand. (*S* 231a)

If we really are careful about similarities here, if we pay close attention
to the similarities between what the Stranger presents as the defining
characteristics of sophistry and certain key features of his own activity,
between the content of his claims and their style or form, then we confront the following question: does the Stranger not stand condemned
from his own mouth as an inauthentic philosopher? Or is he rather a
living example of how easy it is to mistake the gentlest of dogs for the
wildest of wolves?

5. Against this background the precise form and location of the passage
from the *Sophist* that Heidegger chooses to quote appear highly significant. To begin with, as we have already noted, the two sentences function as quotations within the dialogue from which they have been
extracted—they form part of the Stranger's imagined interrogation of a
group of myth-makers, and their requotation thus underlines the fact
that the form of his supposedly soul-cleansing discussion with Theaetetus repeatedly engages in the kind of appearance-making that the
Stranger has attributed to sophistry, and has presented as its most per-
nicious characteristic. Heidegger could not have signalled more clearly
his awareness of the problem that leads Socrates to focus the dialogue
on the distinction between sophistry and philosophy in the first place:
is the Stranger a sophist or a philosopher? And in raising this question
with respect to this particular aspect of the Stranger's performance, Heidegger further implies that the distinction turns upon two interlinked
issues: whether or not the Stranger is an appearance-maker or a
likeness-maker—whether things appear as they are in what he says; and
whether or not he is as he appears to be—in other words, whether the
form of his discourse and mode of existence are consistent with the
message it proclaims.

By endorsing the Stranger's message that recovering a certain perplexity about the question of the meaning of Being is fundamental to
philosophy, but questioning his ability to live up to that message, Heidegger thus implicitly endorses the way in which Plato's dialogue nests
or embeds the question of the meaning of Being within the question of
what makes for genuine as opposed to inauthentic philosophizing.
For of course, any form of philosophical questioning is vulnerable to

sophistical distortion and hollowing out, to modes of corruption so difficult to distinguish from philosophical health that even the one corrupted may not be aware of what has happened. It follows that there can be no genuinely fruitful approach to the question of the meaning of Being without a penetrating working out of the question of the nature of questioning (and of the opportunities and ills to which it is heir), and so of the nature of human beings *qua* questioners (both genuine and sophistical). Put otherwise, any account of the meaning of Being is necessarily subject to the question of its own genuineness, and that above all means working out whether its form properly reflects or rather subverts its own content.

6. This brings us to a further layer of significance in the form of Heidegger's quotation—the fact that it is doubly citational. The relevant sentences are not only part of the Stranger's imagined dialogue with his myth-makers, they are also part of his dialogue with Theaetetus—they are, in short, part of a Platonic dialogue, words that Plato puts in the mouth of one of his fictional characters. Heidegger's decision to place inverted commas around these particular sentences thus highlights the question of how the content of the dialogue as a whole relates to its form; for if the Stranger resorts to fictional devices as part of his attempt to condemn sophistry as appearance-making, then so surely does Plato (and doubly so, since his drama involves the creation of a fictional character who resorts to fiction-making). How, then, are we to understand Plato's decision to mount what appears to be an attempt to defend this critique of sophistry against a forceful objection in the form of an imagined dramatic dialogue? Is he as oblivious to the self-condemnation that apparently results as the Stranger? Or does the fact that his dialogue imagines a character who appears as subject to such self-condemnation rather suggest that Plato is well aware of the potential problem, and in fact wishes his readers to realize thereby that appearance-making cannot and should not be subject to so simple and unqualified a critique? When the Stranger resorts to a fictional dialogue in order to dismiss myth-making as child's play (*S* 242c), does he simply represent an inadvertently self-subverting general hostility towards the fictive potential of human speech that Plato creates him to endorse, or is his self-subversion rather deliberately intended by its author to undercut his character's dismissal of the mythical—perhaps to suggest (as Wittgenstein suggests) that myth-making is one manifestation of the playfulness without which language would not be what it is, perhaps to suggest that a myth which knows itself to be such may be more truthful than a dialogue that represses its own

reliance upon the human capacity to create appearances with words?

Here we come up against another form of the problem of the Stranger's authority—or rather, we see that this problem is internally related to that of Plato's authorship and its strategies, and so to Plato's authority: is the Stranger simply Plato's mouthpiece, or rather a dramatization of what Plato takes to be a fundamentally erroneous perspective on the questions under debate? As I have already suggested, however, for Heidegger, working out the right question in the right way may be more important than finding an answer. So what matters most here is that his choice of citational source once again forces on us a double question: what is the nature of a philosopher's copy-making with words—is it a matter of constructing illusory appearances or genuine likenesses? and how might that question turn upon whether or not the form of a philosopher's words lives up to its content?

7. We can nevertheless infer something of how Heidegger wishes to position himself in relation both to Plato's and the Stranger's positions on sophistry and the meaning of Being from the position in the dialogue of the two sentences he chooses to quote. First, the passage occurs before the Stranger begins to develop his positive account of how one should understand statements about non-being and being, an account which allows him to deny that his critical definition of sophistry can be rejected as incoherent. In effect, then, Heidegger's choice of this passage rather than a later one is a choice not to endorse that positive account; it reinforces my earlier suggestion that what he values about the Stranger is his perplexed grappling with the question of the meaning of Being rather than his way of answering the question, and more fundamentally that he rejects the Stranger's implicit assumption that his perplexity constitutes a challenge to be overcome—that it is a stimulus for its own dissolution rather than a mood to be maintained. Moreover, by conspicuously failing to endorse the Stranger's answer to his question, Heidegger also deprives him of what he needs to block the sophist's accusation of incoherence, and thereby implies that that accusation still stands—that in Heidegger's view there is something self-undermining about the Stranger's position.

We have already seen in general terms what Heidegger thinks that self-subversion amounts to. But by choosing to quote a passage in which the Stranger is acknowledging the force of the sophist's counter to his most critical dialectical definition of his quarry, Heidegger adds something more specific to his diagnosis by effectively endorsing that acknowledgement. In doing so, he implies his agreement with the

Stranger's sense (carefully built up in the preceding parts of the dialogue) that philosophical critiques of sophistry must meet the challenge of accounting for the human capacity to say of that which is that it is, and of that which is not that it is not—the possibility of human knowledge of and discourse about reality; in other words, Heidegger endorses the idea that genuine philosophizing, in confronting its most intimate enemy, thereby confronts the challenge of scepticism. But Heidegger also implies that the Stranger is right to sense that the interlinked questions of grasping the meaning of sophistry and grasping the meaning of Being pose a fundamental challenge to his favoured philosophical technique or strategy—that of the dialectic.

As exhaustively demonstrated in the opening half of the dialogue, the Stranger's dialectical method involves locating any phenomenon in which he is interested within a particular category, and then recursively dividing that category into subcategories until the subcategory peculiar to that phenomenon is established. We might think of this as the phenomenon's particular branch of the tree of categories—the conceptual equivalent of definition by genera and species. When applying this technique to the sophist with respect to the seventh definition of him as an appearance-maker, however, the Stranger uses a different metaphor:

We'll divide the craft of copy-making as quickly as we can and we'll go down into it. Then if the sophist gives up right away we'll obey the royal command and we'll capture him and hand our catch over to the king. But if the sophist slips down somewhere into the parts of the craft of imitation, we'll follow along with him and we'll divide each of the parts that contain him until we catch him. Anyway, neither he nor any other kind will ever be able to boast that he's escaped from the method of people who are able to chase a thing through both the particular and the general. (*S* 235c)

I noted earlier that the Stranger frequently characterizes his own activity as a form of hunting. According to this rather venomous and hubristic passage, his dialectical method is the weapon without which he could not pursue his prey; as he puts it elsewhere, his hunting takes the distinctive form of trying to 'hem in [the sophist] with one of those netlike devices that words provide for things like this' (*S* 235b). It is worth noting that this remark embodies a virtual citation of an earlier passage in the very first of the Stranger's dialectical definitions—the supposedly arbitrary preliminary example of angling.

STRANGER. And all hunting of underwater things is fishing.
THEAETETUS. Yes.

STRANGER. Well then, this kind of hunting might be divided into two main parts.

THEAETETUS. What are they?

STRANGER. One of them does its hunting with stationary nets and the other one does it by striking.

THEAETETUS. What do you mean? How are you dividing them?

STRANGER. The first one is whatever involves surrounding something and enclosing it to prevent it from escaping, so it's reasonable to call it enclosure.

THEAETETUS. Of course.

STRANGER. Shouldn't baskets, nets, slipknots, creels, and so forth be called enclosures?

THEAETETUS. Yes.

STRANGER. So we'll call this part of hunting enclosure-hunting or something like that. (*S* 220b–c)

Since this preliminary example prepares the ground for the Stranger's first definition of sophistry as a kind of hunting, and since the baskets, nets, and creels it mentions are in effect a kind of filtering, straining, or winnowing device of the sort the Stranger invokes in his sixth definition of sophistry as a kind of soul-cleansing (*S* 226b), the Stranger's characterizations of his own method imply in more than one way that it will prove to be a misbegotten approach to the fundamental philosophical questions of the dialogue as a whole. And so it proves: for by invoking the problem of articulating claims about being and non-being, the sophist slips from the method's clutches—'escap[ing] neatly into an impossibly confusing type to search through' (*S* 236d).

In other words, by quoting the Stranger's acknowledgement of his perplexity about the meaning of Being, and thus at once endorsing his sense of the problem that his dialectical method faces and failing to endorse his attempt to overcome that problem, Heidegger suggests that neither sophistry (and hence genuine philosophy) nor being (and hence non-being) can properly be understood by enclosure-hunting—by chasing them through the traps and nets of the particular and the general. In short, neither phenomenon should be thought of as a category—as a branch in the tree of concepts. I suggested earlier that the Stranger's main claim to philosophical authority lay in his loyalty to the dialectical method he inherited from Parmenides over any of Parmenides' specific doctrines—more precisely, in his willingness to employ that method to criticize those doctrines about Being. Heidegger's careful citational strategy undermines this claim by implying that true philosophical questioning must, if necessary, extend even to putting one's methodological inheritance in question. In the context of questions concerning sophistry and Being, the kind of filtering, winnowing, and straining to which the Stranger continues to cleave amount to no more than sophistry; genuine philosophizing must find another kind of discriminating response to the most fundamental of its concerns.

THE MEANING OF BEING: GENUS AND SPECIES

8. The teaching implicit in Heidegger's decision to open *Being and Time* with words of Plato is beginning to take shape. That decision tells us that his substantive concern will be with the question of the meaning of Being. It also tells us that he doubts the efficacy both of the Stranger's particular answer to that question and of the dialectical method with which he approaches it, but is happy to agree that any proper approach must acknowledge the internal relation between this question and that of the nature of sophistry, and hence of the distinction between authentic and inauthentic philosophizing. It further indicates that authentic philosophizing has a particular mood, is essentially responsive to the history of philosophy, seeks to make a new beginning by working out its questions and their meaning rather than answering them, and must confront the interrelated challenges of scepticism and of philosophy's hostility to and dependence upon copy-making—upon the human capacity to make reality appear in speech, and to create appearances (in myth, in fiction, in figuration) to which nothing real appears to correspond.

In the *Sophist* these themes or questions are articulated in one particular way, in accordance with Plato's interpretation of their meaning and interconnection. As the second paragraph of the foreword to *Being and Time* makes clear, its two introductory chapters are intended to lay out Heidegger's interpretation of them. That these chapters are prefaced by a quote from the *Sophist* suggests that Heidegger's sense of the interconnection of these issues is profoundly indebted to that of Plato; that *Being and Time* is presented as in dialogue with that dialogue suggests that Heidegger finds Plato's articulation of the issues questionable, and hence in need of rearticulation. In short, the introduction to *Being and Time* neither repeats nor repudiates Plato: it returns to his words in order to find a new beginning, to render a reading that is also a recounting.

This recounting begins with Heidegger's response to what he describes as a dogma that sanctions the complete neglect of the question of the meaning of Being. 'It is said that "Being" is the most universal and the emptiest of concepts. As such it resists every attempt at definition. Nor

does this most universal and hence indefinable concept require any definition, for everyone uses it constantly and already understands what he
means by it' (*BT* 1.21). As this passage makes clear, the three versions
of this dogma rest on a common assumption—namely, that 'Being' is
the most universal concept. Given this assumption, an understanding of
it is implicit in understanding anything which one apprehends (the first
version), and can be taken to be self-evident or to go without saying
(the third version); but this understanding is not susceptible to definition, since the most general concept in our family of concepts cannot,
by definition, be defined as all concepts are defined—namely, by nomi-
nating a more general concept under which it falls and a concept on the
same level from which it can be differentiated (the second version). Heidegger attacks all three versions by attacking their common assumption.
'. . . the "universality" of "Being" is not that of a *class* or *genus*. The
term "Being" does not define that realm of entities which is uppermost
when these are articulated conceptually according to genus and species
. . . The "universality" of Being "*transcends*" any universality of genus'
(*BT* 1.22). The clarity, self-evidence, and indefinability of 'Being' is itself
clear and self-evident only if one accepts that the sole legitimate way of
defining the meaning of a term is by characterizing it as one species of
a given genus—in other words, by locating it within a conceptual and
ontological family tree of concepts, in effect by employing the dialectical method beloved of Plato's Stranger. But this definition of 'definition'
is itself questionable: Heidegger points out that Aristotle, for one,
attempted to define the universality of 'Being' as transcendental, as a
unity of analogy rather than a universality of genus. What such a mode
of definition might ultimately amount to is here less important than the
possibility it exemplifies—that there might be an alternative way of
defining the meaning of a term; and the possible existence of such an
alternative renders questionable the assumption that all definition must
be dialectical.

It follows that it is not self-evident that 'Being' is indefinable. What
is self-evident is that 'Being' is indefinable in terms of genus and species,
the terms applicable to entities and types of entity; but that may simply
show the inappropriateness of that model of definition to this case—
in other words, it may show that 'Being' is not an entity. And yet it is
undeniable that 'Being' is involved in some way whenever we apprehend entities (whenever we perceive that the sky *is* blue, or that he *is*
merry, and so on). But this means that we do not know how to articulate an essential aspect of our comprehending grasp of anything and
everything we encounter. In other words, rather than having an implicit
understanding of Being in everything we do and say, it might rather be

the case that 'In any way of comporting oneself towards entities as entities—even in any Being towards entities as entities—there lies *a priori* an enigma. The very fact that we already live in an understanding of Being and that the meaning of Being is still veiled in darkness proves that it is necessary in principle to raise this question again' (*BT* 1.23). Note that the enigma here lies not just in the question of the meaning of Being but in the nature of the questioner: if those who live in an understanding of Being lack an understanding of its meaning, then they also lack an understanding of the meaning of their lives. To this extent, they are an enigma to themselves; for them to raise the question of the meaning of Being is to reawaken a sense of their own Being as questionable.

THE STRUCTURE OF QUESTIONING

9. Since Heidegger's aim is to reawaken our sense that the meaning of Being is questionable, since he claims that we take ourselves to know what we mean when we talk of 'Being' when in fact we do not, he cannot begin his inquiry either by telling us what Being is (i.e. by giving us even the beginnings of a systematic answer that we—including he— are not supposed to possess) or by taking it for granted that we even know how to pose the question of Being aright in the first place (since any articulation of a question about Being presupposes a particular understanding of what 'Being' means). How, then, can he begin? What starting-point is available to him that is not vulnerable to the charge that it implicitly begs the very question that he aims to pose?

Heidegger's response (in section 2 of his first chapter, 'The Formal Structure of the Question of Being') is to turn the full force of this hovering anxiety about presuppositions to his own advantage. For if it were to be worked out in a truly radical way, that anxiety would suggest that any articulation of a question about Being not only presupposes a particular understanding of what 'Being' means but also a particular understanding of what questioning is. This, after all, was what gave rise to the various attempts to dismiss Heidegger's reposing of the question of Being in the previous section; those dismissals all rested on the assumption that the appropriate way to articulate the question of Being was that suited to the questioning of beings, the dialectical articulation of genus and species. So, any genuine attempt to make Being and its meaning questionable must not take it for granted that we know what genuine questioning is—whether it is questioning about Being or about anything else; it must, in short, treat questioning as itself questionable. 'We must . . . explain briefly what belongs to any question whatsoever, so that from this standpoint the question of Being can be made visible as a *very special* one with its own distinctive character' (*BT* 2.24).

According to Heidegger's provisional account, there are three fundamental characteristics of questioning or inquiry in general. First, any inquiry is an inquiry about something: it must, on pain of emptiness, have a direction or orientation of some sort, however provisional, from the outset—some conception of what is sought. Second, inquiring has a threefold internal structure: it asks about something (the issue which first motivates the inquiry); in asking about this something, something else—some entity or body of evidence—is interrogated; and something results—is found out or discovered—from the asking. Third, any inquiry is an activity engaged in by an inquirer: it can thus proceed in a distinctive variety of ways that are themselves conditioned by the distinctive nature of the being who engages in that activity—as Wittgenstein might put it, the grammar of this activity is internally related to the grammar of agency.

The first of these three characteristics gives Heidegger the leverage he needs to address the worry about presuppositions. For if any and all questioning must, in so far as it is a question about something in particular, be guided at the outset by some provisional, not yet fully analysed conception of its object, then the idea of an utterly presuppositionless inquiry makes no sense—and hence, no inquiry can be criticized for failing to attain such an utterly pure, self-originating starting-point. The very idea of such a beginning is an illusion, the sign of an unquestioned conception of questioning. Genuine questioning does not seek to deny its own conditionedness, to slough off its prior understanding of its object, but rather to question it—to unfold that pre-understanding with the utmost vigilance, in order to reject, modify, and refine its elements in accordance with what emerges from the inquiry itself.

Hence, for Heidegger, genuine questioning of the meaning of Being must begin within the horizon of a vague, average understanding of Being; after all, we cannot even ask 'What *is* "Being"?' without making use of the very term at issue. But as we have seen, this pre-understanding of Being is indefinite, fluctuating, and obscure. It does not amount to genuinely knowing what 'Being' means—and of course, it may well be sedimented with the distortions of earlier theorizing and ancient prejudices. But the way to move beyond those indefinitenesses and obscurities is not to look for a starting-point elsewhere. That might remove the obscurities, but it would also remove us from that which they obscure—the preliminary object of our inquiry, that which, even in its indefiniteness, gives our inquiry what definition it has. What is needed is rather to subject those obscurities to questioning—to take our inquiry forward by subjecting previous answers and previous articulations of the question to further questioning.

The second characteristic of questioning, its tripartite structure, determines Heidegger's explicit initial articulation of the question of the meaning of Being. What he is asking about is Being—'that which determines entities as entities, that on the basis of which entities are already understood, however we may discuss them in detail' (*BT* 2.25–6). Being is thus not an entity (as we have already observed), but it always appears as the Being of entities and hence is encounterable only in so far as we encounter entities; so what Heidegger's inquiry interrogates will be entities themselves, with regard to their Being. And of course, what this inquiry is to uncover is the meaning of Being. It is the second of these three interrelated elements that poses the problem, that remains so far rather too indefinite:

Everything we talk about, everything we have in view, everything towards which we comport ourselves in any way, is being: what we are is being, and so is how we are. Being lies in the fact that something is, and in its Being as it is; in Reality; in presence-at-hand; in subsistence; in validity; in Dasein; in the 'there is'. In *which* entities is the meaning of Being to be discerned? From which entities is the disclosure of Being to take its departure? (*BT* 2.26)

Here we return to the problem of establishing the right beginning, or more precisely, to that of establishing our right to begin with some particular entity in some particular way—of avoiding the accusation that the place and form of this beginning has no real justification.

Has, then, Heidegger's posing of the question of the nature of questioning really made no progress, been nothing more than a digression—a simple deferral of the question of how to begin? Such a conclusion overlooks the third characteristic of questioning—its status as an activity we engage in. Our difficulty is to determine which entity should be interrogated in our questioning and how to achieve genuine access to it. But

Looking at something, understanding and conceiving it, choosing, access to it—all these ways of behaving are constitutive for our inquiry, and therefore are modes of Being for those particular entities which we, the inquirers, are ourselves. Thus to work out the question of Being adequately, we must make an entity—the inquirer—transparent in his own Being. The very asking of this question is an entity's mode of *Being*; and as such it gets its essential character from what is inquired about—namely, Being. This entity which each of us is himself and which includes inquiring as one of the possibilities of its Being, we shall denote by the term '*Dasein*'. If we are to formulate our question explicitly and transparently, we must first give a proper explication of an entity (Dasein), with regard to its Being. (*BT* 2.26–7)

The question of Being gets its essential character from its object; but it is also conditioned by the fact that questioning as such and the posing of this question in particular is an activity performed by a particular being, and hence is determined in its nature by the nature of that being. Accordingly, Heidegger suggests that any indeterminacy in our preliminary grasp of how to pose our question might be diminished by inquiring further into the nature of ourselves as inquirers—that we can, in effect, only properly pose our question about Being and its meaning by first putting our own Being as questioners in question.

In one sense, this is simply the culmination of a single, radically reflexive movement of thought, the starting-point to which Heidegger is compelled by his attempt to render the grounds or presuppositions of his inquiry into Being and its meaning as minimal, as explicit and as transparent as possible—by working out in a preliminary way his preconception of Being (as that which determines entities as entities, that on the basis of which entities are always already understood), of questioning, and of the being who questions (i.e. ourselves). In doing so, the task of inquiring into the Being of the being who questions appears as an essential preliminary to the task of inquiring into Being and its meaning—a prologue or introduction to, and hence essentially separable from, Heidegger's central inquiry. Furthermore, that preliminary inquiry's only two presuppositions about its object are that questioning is one possibility of its Being, and that its Being is our Being—in other words, that in questioning Dasein with regard to its Being, we are questioning ourselves about our ability to question. The term 'Dasein' thus does have a positive content that goes beyond its non-identity with the myriad other terms that the history of philosophy and human culture have generated for the Being of human beings; but it is difficult to see how an inquiry which finds (and cannot avoid finding) its initial orientation in the aim of reawakening our ability to question could presuppose a more minimal preconception of human being. Heidegger's distinctive gift lies in his capacity to allow that tiny seed to germinate, elaborating from the idea of Dasein as questioner an articulation of his inquiry that will provide him with food for thought not only throughout *Being and Time*, but far beyond it.

In fact, these two explicit presuppositions of Heidegger's promised inquiry into Dasein offer more definite guidance than might at first appear. For if, in questioning Dasein with regard to its Being, we are questioning ourselves about our ability to question, then we can further say not only that Dasein's ability to question includes an ability to question beings with regard to their Being, but also that Dasein is capable of questioning itself with regard to its Being. In other words, Dasein is the kind of entity who can relate questioningly to the Being of other entities, and who can relate questioningly to its own Being: in short, Being (its own and that of others) is an issue for it. Furthermore, we can say that, since Dasein is an 'entity which each of us is himself' (both author and readers), Heidegger's inquiry into the Being of Dasein is a realization or enactment of Dasein's capacity to make its own Being an issue for it. It follows that whatever emerges from that inquiry must have application to the inquiry itself; in particular, the form of the text in which that inquiry is enacted must, on pain of self-subversion, acknowledge or authenticate its content. In the remaining two sections of his opening chapter Heidegger draws out some of the implications of these further presuppositions.

THE PRIORITY OF DASEIN

10. Section 3, 'The Ontological Priority of the Question of Being', develops the idea that the Being of entities is an issue for Dasein. For Heidegger, in everything that human beings do, they relate to the objects, processes, events, and other phenomena around them in ways that reveal an implicit understanding of those phenomena as existent and as possessed of a specific nature—'both with regard to the fact that it is, and with regard to its Being as it is' (*BT* 2.24). Different aspects of this implicit understanding can each become the theme of a rigorous scientific investigation—can become, as Heidegger would say, an issue for us, become explicitly questionable. Historians, physicists, sociologists, linguists, and so on each delimit certain definite areas of subject-matter, articulating bodies of 'ontic' knowledge which emerge from, but can also refine, modify, or even reject, our pre-scientific ways of experiencing and interpreting the relevant things. But these ontic sciences themselves presuppose certain basic 'ontological' concepts and structures, by means of which their specific field is articulated and explored, and these too can become questionable—when the science experiences a foundational crisis, as with the advent of relativity theory in physics or of structuralism in the human sciences. Since the methods peculiar to the discipline presuppose these articulations, they cannot be

employed to answer any questions raised about them without begging those very questions.

Here philosophy steps in, claiming its peculiar authority to address questions that arise from other disciplines but transcend their ability to answer them—questions that are ontological rather than ontic, and which remain philosophical even if asked and answered by individuals who are physicists or literary theorists by profession rather than philosophers. But there remains a respect in which even philosophy's ontological inquiries can remain unquestioning:

Ontological inquiry is indeed more primordial, as over against the ontical inquiry of the positive sciences. But it remains itself naive and opaque if in its researches into the Being of entities it fails to discuss the meaning of Being in general. And even the ontological task of constructing a non-deductive genealogy of the different possible ways of Being requires that we first come to an understanding of 'what we really mean by this expression "Being"'. (*BT* 3.31)

A philosophy which questions the ontological conditions for the possibility of a given ontic science, but which fails to question the conditions for the possibility of the ontological conditions themselves, cannot be said to have properly engaged in ontological questioning at all. Even articulating a question (let alone an answer) about the Being of mathematical or theological or biological entities in each case presupposes a specific understanding of the term 'Being', but does not in itself make an issue of that understanding; and to that degree, 'it remains blind and perverted from its ownmost aim' (*BT* 3.31)—that of bringing the human capacity to comprehend and question the Being of entities to its fullest possible, its most radical, thoroughgoing and transparent, development. Only this deserves the title 'fundamental ontology'.

11. In section 4, 'The Ontical Priority of the Question of Being', Heidegger develops the idea that Dasein's own Being is an issue for it.

Dasein is an entity which does not just occur among other entities. Rather it is ontically distinguished by the fact that, in its very Being, that Being is an *issue* for it. But in that case, this is a constitutive state of Dasein's Being, and this implies that Dasein, in its Being, has a relationship towards that Being—a relationship which itself is one of Being. And this means further that there is some way in which Dasein understands itself in its Being, and that to some degree it does so explicitly. It is peculiar to this entity that with and through its Being, this Being is disclosed to it. *Understanding of Being is itself a definite characteristic of Dasein's Being.* Dasein is ontically distinctive in that it *is* ontological. (*BT* 4.32)

Unlike sticks and stones, bees and cats, Dasein stands in a relation to its own Being that is both comprehending and questioning (as is Dasein's relation with any entity in its Being); and this means that every moment of its existence embodies at once a particular answer to the question of its Being (enacting one interpretation of how to live) *and* a reposing of that same question. This is because Dasein understands itself in terms of possibilities. In so far as it exists at all, its existence realizes one possibility of its Being; but that present actuality exists only as a possibility for the next moment of its existence, as one way in which Dasein may, but need not, continue to exist. So whether or not Dasein actualizes that possibility in the future is a question for it—not a given, not a necessity flowing from its essential nature or determined by its membership of a particular genus and species. Dasein must choose how to live, and indeed whether to continue living at all; it thus relates questioningly to its own existence, just as it does to the Being of any entity—both as fact (answering the question 'whether?') and as form (answering the question 'how?').

In so far as Dasein does continue to exist, it must actualize certain possibilities from the range available to it—whether by positively seizing one such possibility or by unquestioningly continuing with the consequences of its previous choices—and in doing so it determines its own identity or essence: by its answers to the question 'how?', it also answers the question 'who?' As Heidegger puts it, Dasein's Being is disclosed to it in and through its Being; in actualizing certain activities, lifestyles, and conceptions of the good (and thereby not actualizing others), Dasein at once reveals and enacts its own conception of what it is to be a (flourishing) human being. Its relationship to its Being is thus itself one of Being; Dasein comes to terms with the question of its existence only through existing. Since, however, each enacted moment also reposes the question of whether and how to go on living, no past answer to that question, no enacted understanding of its Being, ever makes any future relation to itself necessary, beyond question. In other words, its Being is also always a (questioning) relationship to its Being; even to treat its mode of Being as beyond question is to answer the question of its existence in a particular way.

In this respect, Dasein's relation to its own Being is fundamentally analogous to its relation to the Being of other entities—both involve questioning the fact and the form or mode of the relevant being; and this means that there is a fundamental disanalogy between Dasein's relation to its own Being and the relationship in which other entities stand to their own Being. For, while the fact and the form of its existence is a question for Dasein, it is not a question for other entities: whether to continue existing, and if so how to exist, are simply not an issue for stones and snakes. Furthermore, as we have seen, Dasein's answers to the questions 'whether?' and 'how?' issue in answers to the question 'who?'; the Being to which it relates itself through its existence is its own Being, its to own, the Being which it itself is. In other words, in answering the question of existence through its existence, Dasein can individualize itself (or, of course, can fail to do so—if, instead of seizing its existence, it neglects it; *BT* 4.33).

Heidegger honours Dasein's distinctiveness grammatically, by using the terms 'existentiell' and 'existential' to denote the distinction between particular existential possibilities enacted by Dasein and the structural conditions for the possibility of such enactments—a distinction that he denotes with respect to other entities by discriminating between 'ontic' and 'ontological' levels of characterization. The same concern drives his restriction of the term 'existence' to Dasein alone: entities other than Dasein do not exist, in the sense that the form and fact of their continued existence is fixed by their nature or essence—by what Heidegger calls their 'what-being'. Since Dasein's Being is a question for it, a question answered by its enacted self-interpretations, its essence is rather fixed in and through its existence. In short, Dasein cannot be defined dialectically—in terms of properties characteristic of a particular species and genus.

These distinctions are critical because they confer a threefold priority on Dasein over all other entities for the purposes of Heidegger's investigation. First, unlike every other entity, every ontic (or rather, existentiell) state of Dasein embodies a relationship to its own Being—in so far as it exists, it relates itself to its Being as a question. Second, every such relationship embodies a comprehending grasp of its Being—a particular answer to the question that its Being poses; its every existentiell state is thus implicitly 'ontological', making manifest an understanding of Dasein in its Being, and so an understanding of Being. Third, in enacting any given existentiell state Dasein necesssarily relates itself to the world of entities around it—I can't decide to take a shower or rob a bank, to mow the lawn or meditate on the meaning of Being, without engaging with the tools of my chosen task; Dasein is thus always already relating itself comprehendingly (and so questioningly) to other entities as the entities they are—in their Being. If, then, our concern is to locate an entity to interrogate with a view to disclosing the meaning of 'Being', Dasein's threefold intimacy with beings in their Being makes it the obvious choice. If we can come to understand the only Being for whom Being is an issue, we will have grasped what it is to understand beings in their Being; and since what is understood in an understanding of

Being is Being, then to grasp the existential structure of that understanding (that which permits it to take the Being of beings as its 'object')
will amount to grasping the grammatical structure of that which is
understood (what it is for Being, in any and every one of its ways, shapes
and forms, 'to be').

Hence, providing an existential analytic of Dasein turns out not to be
a preliminary to the task of articulating the question of Being and its
meaning but rather to lie at its heart; 'the ontological analytic of Dasein
in general is what makes up fundamental ontology' (*BT* 4.35). Heidegger's development of the implications of his minimal introductory characterization of Dasein (as the being who questions) has thus shown it
to yield rather more substantial guidance than at first appeared—an
exemplary instance of his conception of how acknowledging rather than
denying the essentially conditioned nature of human questioning can
allow for a virtuous as well as a vicious hermeneutic circularity, engaging a reflexivity that deepens and clarifies the question to which it is a
response rather than begging it, turning Dasein's ineliminable indebtedness to pre-ontological understandings into a creditable and productive resource for the future.

12. Towards the end of section 4 (and so of his first chapter), however,
Heidegger forcibly reminds us of an implication of this circular movement of thought which can easily be passed over—the fact that the
project of *Being and Time* is itself a form of questioning, and so that
its results must be understood to have a reflexive application. '. . . the
roots of the existential analytic . . . are ultimately *existentiell*, that is,
ontical. Only if the inquiry of philosophical research is itself seized upon
in an existentiell manner as a possibility of the Being of each existing
Dasein, does it become at all possible to disclose the existentiality of
existence and to undertake an adequately founded ontological problematic' (*BT* 4.34).

Philosophical research is a mode of inquiry, and so an existential possibility of the being whose Being involves questioning. It can therefore
be seized, taken hold of, or neglected: Dasein can engage in the
project of an existential analytic of Dasein, and hence in that of fundamental ontology, in such a way as to acknowledge that in doing so its
own Being as a questioner is at issue, or it can avoid doing so; it can,
in short, philosophize questioningly or unquestioningly. To do so
questioningly, it must take responsibility for the fact that it is philosophizing and for its manner or method; it must not take its starting-point
and approach for granted, as if beyond question. It must also acknowledge that, in answering the question of whether and how to philoso-

phize, it is in part answering the question 'who?'; in choosing to engage in this project, it does not simply choose a profession or a pastime, but rather makes concrete a certain interpretation of itself and of its world, and so individualizes itself (or fails to). Philosophizing is not an alternative to, or a deferral or transcendence of, existing, but a mode of doing so.

Hence Heidegger, as the author of a book which recounts his enactment of his project and which is itself accordingly a (re-)enactment of that project, must strive to ensure that the form of his text realizes the questioning comprehension which its content attributes to the Being of the being that he himself is. And he will expect his readers, as beings whose Being that book aims to characterize, also to be capable of striving to ensure that their engagement with the text enacts the same questioning comprehension—the same refusal to take any particular aspect of it (say, its starting-point or its form) as beyond or beneath question. But then, any author who takes the fact and form of his own authorship as an issue must acknowledge that his words are ordered for the comprehension of readers, and so must acknowledge a responsibility to address them in ways that acknowledge rather than deny his book's recognition that reading is a possibility of the being whose Being is Dasein. Heidegger's words must therefore work to invite a comprehension that is also a questioning—they must, that is, avoid encouraging their readers to neglect rather than to seize upon the reading of these words as a possibility of their own Being, as an act which answers the questions 'whether?', 'how?', and 'who?', an act through which they can each either realize or repress their own individuality. Heidegger's words cannot, therefore, encourage an unquestioning acceptance of his own views or doctrines—indeed, Heidegger cannot consistently think of his book's purpose as one of uncovering and presenting theses whose authority is beyond question, or as presenting such a conception of philosophizing. We should rather expect the form of his writing to reflect the view that philosophizing is a radicalization of Dasein's Being as questioner, and a way in which each individual being whose Being is Dasein (including himself as author and each of his readers) confronts his or her own existence as an issue.

Here, I would suggest, we can begin to see Heidegger's provisional way of articulating the Platonic connection between the question of Being and its meaning and the question of the distinction between genuine philosophizing and sophistry. By characterizing the Being of Dasein as questioning, and underlining the constant but enigmatic possibility that Dasein can neglect that most fundamental possibility of its Being, Heidegger redefines both the significance of his inquiry into the meaning of Being and the nature of the criticisms to which it must be subject. On the one hand, genuine philosophy (that is, fundamental ontology) appears as a radicalization of what is distinctively human about our existence; on the other, its achievement or realization (in other words, its avoidance of sophistry) appears as almost impossibly difficult—as requiring not just (or not so much) the attainment of truth but the concrete realization of a kind of existential truthfulness in both the formal and material aspects of its recounting (in its relation to itself, and in its relation to others). Plato's Stranger is emblematic of the perplexing but exhilarating dangers of this reconceived philosophical enterprise—a thinker at once so sensitive to the requirements of genuine philosophizing, and yet so far from bringing the form of his discourse and existence in line with its content. After Heidegger philosophy has never looked so vulnerable to its most intimate enemy; but the prize for its overcoming of that uncanny threat has never seemed more valuable.

DASEIN, TIME, AND HISTORY

13. The second chapter of Heidegger's Introduction to *Being and Time* rearticulates a number of the other Platonic themes raised by his opening quotation from the *Sophist*, but once again presents them as always already implicit in his introductory characterization of Dasein as the being whose Being is questioning. That led us to the idea that the Being of Dasein is an issue for it, and thence to the idea that Dasein understands itself in relation to the possibilities of its Being that it realizes or passes over in its existence. In section 6 Heidegger focuses on a further implication of this account.

Whatever the way of being it may have at the time, and thus with whatever understanding of Being it may possess, Dasein has grown up both into and in a traditional way of interpreting itself: in terms of this it understands itself proximally and, within a certain range, constantly. By this understanding, the possibilities of its Being are disclosed and regulated. Its own past—and this always means the past of its 'generation'—is not something which *follows along after* Dasein, but something which already goes ahead of it. (*BT* 6.41)

Dasein's existentiell answers to the question its existence poses are always situated or contextualized by its past; its present array of choices is conditioned not only by its past choices and the 'who' it has thereby become, but also by the range of existentiell possibilities established and maintained by past generations of its culture and society. Dasein's future is thus marked by its past, it lives out its past; as Heidegger puts it, Dasein historizes its own way of Being out of its future at each moment of its existence (*BT* 6.41).

This historicality is only the most obvious of the ways in which Dasein's Being is essentially temporal—in which its existence, and hence its questioning comprehension of its own and others' Being, is conditioned by the horizon of time. Thus Heidegger provisionally works out the most fundamental horizon of his book, the connection between Being and time. But if Dasein's Being is essentially historical, if it has always already grown up both into and in a traditional way of interpreting itself, then the same must be true of any and all of its modes of questioning, including that of philosophical investigations into fundamental ontology. In effect, then, the preliminary understanding within which Heidegger's exercise in fundamental ontology must necessarily find its orientation will be that of the philosophical tradition of investigations into Being and its meaning. His philosophizing thus will and must be essentially historical (no philosophy without the history of philosophy, as his opening quotation implied): it will begin by questioning what the philosophical tradition has, proximally and for the most part, found it possible to say about Being. And it turns out that the most common reflex in that tradition is to invoke the concept of time.

'Time' has long functioned as an ontological—or rather an ontical—criterion for naively discriminating various realms of entities. A distinction has been made between 'temporal' entities (natural processes and historical happenings) and 'non-temporal' entities (spatial and numerical relationships). We are accustomed to contrasting the 'timeless' meaning of propositions with the 'temporal' course of propositional assertions. It is also held that there is a 'cleavage' between 'temporal' entities and the 'supra-temporal' eternal, and efforts are made to bridge this over . . . Hitherto no-one has asked or troubled to investigate how time has come to have this distinctive ontological function, or with what right anything like time functions as such a criterion; nor has anyone asked whether the authentic ontological relevance which is possible for it, gets expressed when 'time' is used in so naively ontological a manner. 'Time' has acquired this 'self-evident' ontological function 'of its own accord', so to speak; indeed it has done so within the horizon of the way it is ordinarily understood. And it has maintained itself in this function to this day. (*BT* 5.39)

Turning to the philosophical ontological tradition thus underwrites a key implication of Heidegger's working out of his definition of Dasein as questioner; it too relates the question of Being to that of time, and so reinforces Heidegger's independent sense that his existential analytic must follow out the same connection with respect to the Being of Dasein. No one can now complain that this fundamental horizon of Heidegger's analysis is merely dogmatic or arbitrary; for the aspect of Dasein upon which it chooses to concentrate is that in terms of which Dasein typically understands itself, not only whenever it relates comprehendingly to its own Being but also whenever it radicalizes that self-questioning in philosophizing.

However, Heidegger's relation to this ordinary or everyday self-understanding is itself questioning. It aims to make an issue of that which is so often taken for granted, and which thereby blinds and perverts ontological inquiry—namely, what exactly is meant when time is invoked as an ontological criterion; in other words, in asking the question of the meaning of 'Being', he is simultaneously asking the question of the meaning of 'time'. Thus, he neither rejects the guidance which the tradition can offer (which would amount to leaving his inquiry entirely without orientation) nor takes it for granted (which would place it beyond questioning); he looks upon it as an inheritance from which a more positive future for philosophizing can emerge if it is comprehended questioningly.

This is why Section 6 is entitled 'The Task of Destroying the History of Ontology': but the term 'destruction' here must be understood to mean 'de-struction' (a kind of de-structuring or reconstruction) or 'de-construction' (a dismantling that frees living philosophical resources for building anew). Hence much of Heidegger's larger project will take the form of reading highly influential works of the tradition—those of Descartes, Kant, and Aristotle particularly—in order to stake out the positive possibilities it continues to guard and hold out for the future of that tradition. And hence those readings typically take the form of shaking up our sense of the necessity of the categories which have articulated and guided that tradition's development. For just as Dasein can establish a truly questioning relationship to its own Being only if it recognizes that none of its possibilities of Being are necessities or essences, determinative of its existence beyond any question, so Dasein can truly question the meaning of Being only by recognizing that none of its time-hallowed ontological categories are self-evidently necessary, any less marked and conditioned by their historicality than are their creators. So Heidegger's philosophizing aims constantly to 'demonstrat[e] the origin of our basic ontological concepts by an investigation in which their 'birth certificate' is displayed' (*BT* 6.44); in other words, his deconstruction of the history of ontology is always genealogical in form.

PHENOMENOLOGY: APPEARANCE AND REALITY

14. In Section 7 Heidegger spells out his conception of 'the phenomenological method of investigation' in a manner that is not only highly distinctive in itself, but rearticulates two further themes implicit in his opening quotation from the *Sophist*. Rather than relate his conception of phenomenology to that of its founder, Edmund Husserl, thereby grounding his claim to inherit that more immediate tradition of philosophizing, Heidegger offers an etymological birth certificate for the term. Uninterested in the history of the word as a label for philosophical schools (*BT* 7.50–1), he focuses in obsessive detail on the history of the two Greek words from which that word is composed or synthesized. In effect, he aims to derive philosophical instruction from the historicality of Dasein as that is manifest in and through the historicality of Dasein's language—to find the future of Western philosophizing in the Greek history of present German technical terms.

The first of the two component terms is 'phenomenon', which Heidegger traces back to a Greek term for that which shows itself in itself. He then itemizes a number of different ways in which such showing or manifestation might occur: entities can appear as something that they are not (semblance), as an indication of the presence of something else that does not show itself directly (symptoms), or as the manifestation of something else that cannot ever show itself directly (for example, Kantian phenomena and noumena). Since, however, all such appearances show themselves in themselves, in accord with their true nature, Heidegger counts them all as types of the ordinary notion of 'phenomenon'. He then goes on to contrast the phenomenological sense of 'phenomenon' with these modes of appearance. He recalls the Kantian notion of space and time as forms of sensible intuition—that is, as not themselves entities or properties of entities, and so not encounterable as part of the content of experience, but rather as constituting the form or ordering of any experience of entities whatsoever. On this account, space and time are real, foundational but unthematized aspects of everyday experience, but they can be brought to explicit attention by careful and nuanced philosophical investigation. They thereby exemplify what Heidegger understands by the phenomenological sense of 'phenomena': 'that which already shows itself in the appearance as prior to the "phenomenon" as ordinarily understood and as accompanying it in every case, can, even though it thus shows itself unthematically, be brought thematically to show itself; and what thus shows itself in itself ("the

form of the intuition") will be the "phenomena" of phenomenology'
(*BT* 7.54–5).

The fit between this definition and Heidegger's provisional conception of the Being of beings is obvious. But the more interesting implications of this etymological exercise from the perspective afforded by
Plato's *Sophist* derive from Heidegger's bewildering initial discrimination between types of 'appearance'. Indeed, the first such connection is
suggested by his explicit and repeated emphasis on just how bewildering the terrain through which we are moving really is—he talks of bewil-
derment as being 'unavoidable', and as 'essentially increasing' (*BT*
7.53); for in invoking this mood, he recalls the perplexity first invoked
in this book by the quoted words of the Stranger of Elea to his myth-
making interlocutors, and hence the mood that the Stranger implies is
an essential aspect of genuine philosophizing. Heidegger's implicit citation of the Stranger here thus all but declares that a genuinely philosophical reading of this subsection should tarry awhile over this idea of
appearance.

And if we do, we find a further echo of the *Sophist*: for the first sense
of appearance that Heidegger lays out is that of semblance or seeming,
of encountering an entity showing itself as something that in itself it is
not; and this, of course, is the concept used by the Stranger in his most
incisive critical definition of the sophist and his use of words—a definition which immediately invites the response that no sense can be made
of such a possibility, and thus forces the Stranger to investigate the possibility of intelligible discourse about Being and non-Being. Against this
background what Heidegger has to say about the relation between semblance and the Greek-based ordinary meaning of the term 'phenomenon' carries an extra layer of significance:

> If we are to have any further understanding of the concept of phenomenon,
> everything depends on our seeing how what is designated in [its] first signifi-
> cation . . . ('phenomenon' as that which shows itself) and what is designated in
> the second ('phenomenon' as semblance) are structurally interconnected. Only
> when the meaning of something is such that it makes a pretension of showing
> itself—that is, of being a phenomenon—*can* it show itself *as* something which
> it is *not*; only then *can* it 'merely look like so-and-so' . . . the primordial signi-
> fication (the phenomenon as the manifest) is already included as that upon
> which the second signification is founded. (*BT* 7.51)

Since, as we have just seen, Heidegger later argues that the primordial ordinary sense of the term 'phenomenon' is itself founded on the
phenomenological sense of the term ('that which shows itself in the
appearance as prior to the "phenomenon" as ordinarily understood and

as accompanying it in every case . . . will be the "phenomena" of phenomenology'; *BT* 7.54–5), then the implicit thrust of this etymological analysis is as follows. There can be no adequate understanding of semblance without an adequate understanding of what it is for any entity to show itself, and no adequate understanding of that without a grasp of Being and its meaning. Hence Plato's Stranger correctly intuits a critical connection between the problem of sophistry, semblance, and scepticism on the one hand and that of Being on the other; but only a Heideggerian approach to the latter problem will provide the resources needed to resolve it, and hence to resolve the problem of how it is possible for something and someone to appear as what they are not. In other words, the question of Being is indeed intimately bound up with the question of the nature of appearance-making, of the human relation to reality, and of the difference between inauthentic and authentic philosophizing; but it will take at least the whole of *Being and Time* to lay out a more adequate articulation of these questions than that of the Stranger.

This sense that Heidegger conceives of his text as in effect a more truthful continuation of Plato's dialogue, a rewriting of it from the point at which his opening citation of it breaks off, is reinforced by his companion etymological analysis of the other component of the term 'phenomenology'—that of *logos*. Heidegger acknowledges the multiplicity of meanings embodied in this Greek term; but he claims that its root signification is that of 'making manifest what one is "talking about" in one's discourse' (*BT* 7.56). When our 'discoursing' takes the form of speaking, of letting something be seen by pointing it out, then it has a certain synthetic structure; it involves 'letting something be seen in its *togetherness* with something—letting it be seen *as* something' (*BT* 7.56). And of course, this makes it possible both to speak truly—to let something be seen as it really is—and to speak falsely—to pass something off as what it is not. Once again, then, we reach the problem of falsehood and of fictionality or appearance-making more generally; and once again, Heidegger's claim is that any adequate grasp of these phenomena requires that we explore the conditions of their possibility— namely, the human capacity to disclose or uncover entities, to let them be seen, to make them manifest: the capacity marked by the Greek idea of truth as *aletheia* (unhiddenness) and covered over by more contemporary notions of truth as correspondence. And, as the synthesizing of 'phenomenon' with *logos* in the term 'phenomenology' suggests, this capacity amounts to that of understanding and questioning beings in their Being; it can be understood only by reposing the question of the meaning of Being. Once more, then, Heidegger implicitly presents his text as an attempted solution to the reticulation of problems that gives the *Sophist* its distinctive structure. It is by uncovering the positive possibilities of that founding text in the Western philosophical tradition that *Being and Time* hopes to forge a new beginning for its philosophical generation.

And by using these etymologies to characterize his own method as 'to let that which shows itself be seen from itself in the very way in which it shows itself from itself' (*BT* 7.58), where that which is meant to show itself 'is something that for the most part does not show itself; but at the same time . . . is something that belongs to what thus shows itself, and . . . belongs to it so essentially as to constitute its meaning and its ground' (*BT* 7.59), Heidegger signals an awareness (that Plato's Stranger appears to lack) of the imbrication of his own method in the ambivalent business of appearance-making. For of course, the phenomena he aims ultimately to uncover through his phenomenological exercises typically lie hidden in what shows itself; the structures of Being form the self-concealing ground of the unconcealment of entities, and so the project of discovering those structures at all carries a critical risk of falsifying them in their essential nature. As Heidegger puts it: 'Within a "system", perhaps, those structures of Being—and their concepts—which are still available but veiled in their indigenous character, may claim their rights. For when they have been bound together constructively in a system, they present themselves as something "clear" . . .' (*BT* 7.60). What such a form of presentation would lack is any formal reflection of the essential veiledness of the structures that it works to unveil, any sense that these structures 'must first of all be *wrested* from the objects' (*BT* 7.61). Hence the 'awkwardness and "inelegance" of expression in the analyses to come' (*BT* 7.63) is itself an attempt to ensure that the objects of these analyses show themselves as they are in themselves—as un-veiled (just as Wittgenstein's aphoristic prose attempts to acknowledge the seductive metaphysical obscurity from which grammatical clarity comes).

Paradoxically, however, this self-critical awareness of the need to match the form of the analyses with every aspect of their object—this radical commitment to copy-making as likeness-making in Platonic terms—takes as its vehicle a method which tends more towards the making of copies that are not likenesses but mere appearances. For in general, phenomenology can only work as a mode of philosophical discourse in so far as it aims to conjure up in words 'the things themselves' when those things are plainly not at that moment there before author or readers; Heidegger's famous examples of the hammer, the car indicator, fear, and angst, without which his analyses would lack any grounding, are not, after all, copies of phenomena presently available to the senses of author or reader (in their studies and libraries) but rather recountings of the ordinary or the everyday in its present absence. To this degree, Heidegger is committed to discovering entities in their Being through an essentially fictional exercise. To cite one of his concluding introductory remarks: 'so much semblance, so much "Being"' (*BT* 7.60). Little wonder that the challenge of distinguishing sophistry from genuine philosophizing appears far more problematic, and hence even more vital, in *Being and Time* than it did to Plato's Stranger.

EVERYDAYNESS: THE AVERAGE, THE PRIMITIVE, AND THE THEOLOGICAL

15. The first chapter of the first division of *Being and Time* begins by emphasizing not only the theme, but also the key or pitch, of the impending analytic of Dasein. Heidegger returns to his earlier discovery that Dasein's questioning relation to its own Being gives a central role to the issue of its authenticity, entailing that any and every existentiell state of Dasein is either authentic or inauthentic: '. . . because Dasein is in each case essentially its own possibility, it *can*, in its very Being, "choose" itself and win itself; it can also lose itself and never win itself; or only "seem" to do so. But only in so far as it is essentially something which can be *authentic*—that is, something of its own—can it have lost itself and not yet won itself' (*BT* 9.68). Following out the etymological link between that which is authentic (*eigentlich*) and that which is one's own (*eigen*), Heidegger claims that inauthenticity must involve Dasein's disowning of itself, being oblivious to its mineness (to the fact that it is in each case mine and not yours to live), and (utilizing another etymological connection) implies that this indifference to itself is realized in an essentially undifferentiated existence. Authentic modes of existence thereby appear as essentially differentiated.

On this account, however, inauthentic modes of Dasein's existence might be rather more suitable starting-points for an existential analytic than authentic ones. For the aim of such an analytic is to uncover the existentiality of Dasein's existence (the existential structures that condition its every existentiell state); and the differentiatedness or specificity of those states of Dasein in which a definite existential possibility has been genuinely realized or appropriated may encourage us to confuse what is particular to that existentiell state with that which it shares with any and all such states. Furthermore, Heidegger considers that such existential differentiation is relatively rare; proximally and for the most part, Heidegger claims, our existence is undifferentiated. 'This undifferentiated character of Dasein's everydayness is *not nothing*, but a positive phenomenal characteristic of this entity. Out of this kind of Being—and back into it again—is all existing, such as it is. We call this everyday undifferentiated character of Dasein *"averageness"*' (*BT* 9.69). Such average everydayness may be undifferentiated, but its underlying existential structures are neither vague nor essentially distinct from authentic modes of existence; being indifferent to one's Being, even fleeing in the face of it, constitutes a very definite way in which Dasein addresses the issue of its Being. Hence, in its average everydayness, Dasein genuinely shows itself as it is in itself, and so provides a perfectly appropriate starting-point for Heidegger's phenomenological analytic of Dasein.

This means that, throughout division 1 of *Being and Time*, Heidegger is elucidating the existentialia of Dasein through the phenomenology of an inauthentic existentiell state. In other words, while the ontological structures that can be made to stand out from such a phenomenology are unquestionably integral to Dasein's distinctive mode of Being, that from which they stand out must not be thought of as somehow more real or genuine than other existentiell states—as if more intimately oriented to Dasein's Being and hence to Being itself; or as if, in choosing to focus upon it, Heidegger intends to commend such a state to his readers as more authentic than other states. If anything, its methodological virtue rather resides precisely in its inauthenticity, in the fact that it exemplifies Dasein's capacity to flee from or repress what is most its own.

But in emphasizing that Heidegger's initial interest is in *average* everydayness, in what one might call the ordinary as the inauthentic, we also confirm the proximity of Heidegger's perspective to that of Wittgenstein. For on my reading, Wittgenstein's conception of ordinariness is no less receptive to the idea that its structures may become fixated or frozen, expressive of the human flight from ordinariness as it might otherwise be, than is Heidegger's. As if to confirm this Wittgensteinian tone, Heidegger says of average everydayness that its very ontic familiarity is what makes an adequate ontological accounting of it so difficult—an inflection of Wittgenstein's thought about ordinary language and life that 'the aspects of things that are most important for us are hidden because of their simplicity and familiarity. (One is unable to notice something—because it is always before one's eyes)' (*PI* 129).

Furthermore, he underlines that paradox by quoting Augustine, who declares in book x of the *Confessions* that the self's very closeness to itself makes it into a land of labour and inordinate sweat to the explorer. In this act of citation, from the book which serves as a pivot between the *Confessions'* 'autobiographical' books and its 'philosophical' ones, Heidegger declares a further set of desires that he apparently shares with Wittgenstein—that of inheriting the Augustinian idea that the autobiographical can be a genuine mode of access to the philosophical, and of characterizing the individual's lostness to itself and its world as the beginning of philosophy ('A philosophical problem has the form: "I don't know my way about" ("Ich kenne *mich* nicht aus"'; *PI* 123 (my emphasis)).

It can then seem like rather more than coincidence that Heidegger chooses to end his first chapter by giving expression to a sense of the uncannily intimate distance between everydayness and the idea of the primitive—the very idea with which Wittgenstein attempts to epitomize both the emptiness and the truthfulness of Augustine's picture of language. '*Everydayness does not coincide with primitiveness*, but is rather a mode of Dasein's Being, even when that Dasein is active in a highly developed and differentiated culture—and precisely then. Moreover, even primitive Dasein has possibilities of a Being which is not of the everyday kind, and it has a specific everydayness *of its own*' (*BT* 11.76). This emphatically declared non-coincidence of (average) everydayness and primitiveness overtly means that there are primitive and non-primitive forms of average everydayness, and of its overcoming or modification; inhabiting a 'sophisticated' culture is no more incompatible with existing inauthentically than inhabiting a 'primitive' culture is incompatible with overcoming inauthenticity; ordinariness can be inflected either way in either circumstance. But if inauthenticity is characterized by undifferentiatedness, and cultural sophistication by developed differentiation, then the realization of inauthenticity in a non-primitive culture amounts to its primitivization—to the hollowing out of its pretensions to sophistication. Our allegorical reading of Wittgenstein's early tale of the builders is here uncannily close.

However, Heidegger's citation of Augustine does more than indicate parallels with Wittgenstein's sense of the ordinary and its vicissitudes; it also emblematizes Heidegger's sense (itself not exactly denied by Wittgenstein's own opening citation of Augustine) that the philosophical tradition of conceptualizing human existence that he aims to inherit is pervasively inflected by Christian theology. When differentiating fundamental ontology from anthropology, psychology, and biology, he

claims (using citations from Calvin and Zwingli to underwrite his position) that the biblical vision of humans as made in God's image has
ensured that philosophical conceptions of human being take it for
granted that we are creatures at once rational (possessors of the originally divine *logos*), and (hence?) transcendent (reaching yearningly
beyond ourselves) (*BT* 10.74]. Heidegger sees traces of this theological
inheritance in philosophy's sense of our rationality and transcendence
as a supplement to our animality, and more broadly in its sense of
human beings as essentially compound—as composed of body, soul, and
spirit and hence comprehensible through decomposition, by studying
each element or aspect of human being separately (hence the constitution of distinctively biological, psychological, and anthropological
modes of the human sciences). Heidegger rejects this approach: '. . . the
question of man's Being . . . is not something we can simply compute by
adding together those kinds of Being which body, soul and spirit respectively possess—kinds of Being whose nature has not yet been determined. And even if we should attempt such a procedure, some idea of
the Being of the whole must be presupposed . . .' (*BT* 10.74). Heidegger will therefore question not only our taken-for-granted conceptions
of body, soul, and spirit, but also our conception that humanity is a
whole compounded from them; in this sense, his term 'Dasein' names
neither one of those elements nor the whole they supposedly compound,
but rather his desire to question their true significance for human being.
But such questioning is not a simple rejection of them—any more than
Heidegger's desire to deconstruct the philosophical tradition is a desire
to destroy or deny it. He aims rather to free from its fixations the
resources that will allow genuine philosophical progress; and since his
own analyses do not reject but rather radically rethink the idea of
human existence as informed by the *logos* and as transcendent, and
hence find a certain insight in the biblical vision (as if its image of the
human is as much a likeness as it is a semblance), we must say that fundamental ontology detaches itself no more from its theological than
from its philosophical horizons. (And we might wonder whether the
same can or must be said of Wittgenstein's *Philosophical Investigations*,
given their originating and pervasive engagement with Augustine.)

THE CARTESIAN SUBJECT: INVITING SCEPTICISM

16. In the first chapter of division I, Heidegger refers at an early stage
to Descartes's conception of human beings as thinking things, treating

it as exemplary of the ontotheological assumptions about human exist-ence that he wishes to question (*BT* 10.71); and he ends that chapter by suggesting that a vital part of this questioning will be working out the idea of a natural conception of the world—a working out that the new wealth of comparative anthropological data provides only a semblance of facilitating, and that philosophy finds disturbing (*BT* 11.76–7). This implies that Cartesian conceptualizations of human being somehow block or turn away from, even that they refuse to achieve, a proper understanding of human relations to the world, of human openness to reality as such—an implication that already recalls the centrality of the sceptical problematic in the *Sophist*. It can then seem striking that the final chapter of division I, in drawing together the threads of Heidegger's detailed analysis of Dasein's worldliness, concludes by spelling out how the resources provided by this conception can overturn sceptical conclusions about the human capacity to encounter the world. It thus appears that the general trajectory of Heidegger's project in these first six chapters begins and ends in relation to scepticism, as if continuously responsive to it.

It is therefore chastening for me to acknowledge that a detailed reading of *Being and Time* that I published five years ago was largely oblivious to this responsiveness—in large part because it passed over the way in which the book's opening is fundamentally shaped by its citation of the *Sophist*. Coming to perceive division I's continuous relation to the threat of scepticism does not exactly require me to with-draw anything I claimed about it in that earlier reading, as if showing it to be false in any particular (indeed, those claims importantly prepare the way for grasping the full implications of that new perception); but it does illuminate certain remarks, passages, and matters of organiza-tion or form that I previously saw as obscure or marginal, and it alters my sense of the underlying significance (call it the specific mood or attunement) of every step Heidegger takes within this division. Hence, while the compressed but unavoidable re-presentation of those steps in the sections of commentary to come cannot help but seem familiar to those acquainted with my earlier book, the present context—as deter-mined not only by my preceding remarks on Heidegger's opening words but also by the reading of Wittgenstein that precedes it—should also make its pitch or tone seem unfamiliar (as if taking on another aspect altogether).

Heidegger chooses to open the second chapter of division I in a way which (even if indirectly) confirms my new impression of his continu-ous sensitivity to the sceptical problematic. It begins by developing a preliminary sketch of Dasein's worldliness that most immediately derives itself from further etymological reflections. Heidegger claims that the verb from which our talk of ourselves as being 'in' the world derives invokes ideas of residence, inhabitation, or dwelling, and is itself derived from terms which further invoke a sense of familiarity with and a concern or care for that alongside which we dwell. In a sense, everything that emerges in chapters 3–5 of division I—each of which articulates one interlinked aspect of Dasein's worldliness—can be seen as a phenomenological recounting or underwriting of this etymological invocation of the world as the human habitat, as an environment in which Dasein is or can be thoroughly at home.

In the philosophical tradition, however, Heidegger claims that this vision of at-homeness is systematically repressed. That tradition's dominant account of human existence in the world is one according to which one entity called 'man' (understood as the juxtaposition of a spiritual with a corporeal substance) is juxtaposed with another entity (or set of entities) called 'world' in a relationship that is most fundamentally cognitive (in that Dasein's other modes of relating to the world all presuppose it). However, by picturing that cognitive relationship as one holding between a 'subject' and an 'object' (that is, by modelling the Dasein–world relationship in general on the way in which entities other than Dasein relate to one another within the world), the modern philosopher (as exemplified elsewhere in Heidegger's text by Descartes) places the very phenomenon to which he wishes to attribute such fundamental significance—that of knowledge—beyond our comprehension. In short, for Heidegger, the Cartesian enthrones cognition in such a way as to ensure its abdication.

The problem is simple, as Heidegger indicates when he points out that such a conception of cognition inevitably 'becomes the "evident" point of departure for problems of epistemology or the "metaphysics of knowledge"' (*BT* 12.86). For the knowledge this relationship generates plainly belongs to the knowing subject, and to that aspect of the subject that is not corporeal or bodily—to its mind or soul or spirit. It is thus essentially distinct in its nature from that to which it is directed and against which it is measured—the objects of its knowledge, the world. But then, how can the knowing subject ever come directly into contact with its object? How can it make the transition from its own realm to the wholly distinct one to which it claims to have access without leaving itself open to sceptical anxieties? The classical expression of this epistemological and metaphysical problem is the 'closet of consciousness' myth, in which the distinctness of subject from object is interpreted as the subject's interiority or extensionless inwardness as opposed to the exteriority or extendedness of the material objects of its knowledge, with that knowledge pictured as modifications of inwardness (ideas, concepts, representations) which correspond to that which is exterior to it. In this form, Cartesianism invites the question: how can such a subject ever check the supposed correspondence between its ideas and their objects? Indeed, since its every attempted foray outside itself can only result in further internal modifications of itself, how can such a subject even be sure that there is anything external to itself and its ideas?

The history of philosophy since Hume reinforces Heidegger's belief that these sceptical anxieties are unassuageable if we restrict ourselves to the resources the Cartesian conception makes available. If so, we must conclude that this conception has pictured the specific subject–object relationship which it regards as the condition for the possibility of all such relationships in such a way as to undermine the conditions of its own possibility; it has rendered unintelligible the very phenomenon that is supposed to make all other phenomena intelligible. It thus exemplifies what Heidegger means by an ontological investigation that is blind and perverted from its ownmost aim; it meets its nemesis precisely because it takes for granted the ontological or existential category that forms the basis of its own questioning. '. . . if one does no more than ask how knowing makes its way "out of" [the subject] and achieves "transcendence", it becomes evident that the knowing which presents such enigmas will remain problematical unless one has previously clarified how it is and what it is' (*BT* 13.87).

17. For Heidegger, what makes scepticism (or its logical culmination, solipsism) not only possible but unavoidable on the Cartesian account of knowing is its representation of cognition as a relation between two spatially contiguous but essentially distinct kinds of entity—as if the knowing subject relates to its object in the way a chair relates to the wall against which it is placed, in the mode of what Heidegger calls presence-at-hand or sheer occurrence. On that model, the human subject stands in no more need of objects, ontologically speaking, than the chair stands in need of the wall; Dasein could exist as the kind of being it is in the absence of objects—its directedness towards objects, its residence in the world of objects, appears as a merely contingent or secondary fact about it. Furthermore, the subject appears as a floating mirror of its objects: they are essentially objects of representation, a focus of speculative contemplation—the static complement of an essentially immobile consciousness.

Taken together, these two aspects of the Cartesian model of Dasein as present-at-hand repress a fundamental dimension of the sense in which Being is an issue for Dasein. Dasein would not be the kind of being it is if it did not relate itself to itself in and through relating itself to other entities (and vice versa), and if those relations were not a matter of concern to it—if they didn't matter. Each moment of Dasein's existence is the realization of an existential possibility, and so answers the question its own existence poses for it; but each such realization also necessarily makes concrete a particular relation to other entities, an engagement with them in terms of some or other possibility of their Being, and so embodies a particular understanding of them in their Being—an answer to the question that their Being poses.

We might say that Dasein's existence has to be enacted, made concrete, and hence that Dasein is essentially an agent or actor; so Dasein's world is essentially an arena for action, for practical activity, and its relations with the objects of that world must be understood accordingly—must be grasped in a way that discovers rather than represses the conditions for the possibility of their availability as objects of concernful praxis. Against this background the relation of knowing beloved of Cartesian philosophers appears as something that Dasein does, as one mode of its concernful practical activity—but as a deficient mode, one of holding oneself back from the manipulation or utilization of objects in order to encounter them in the way they look (that is, as present-at-hand).

Thus understood, the reality of the world appears immediately resistant to any intelligible expression of scepticism. For if cognizing entities as present-at-hand is even a deficient mode of Being-in-the-world, and so an understanding of Dasein as inherently worldly is presupposed in grasping its nature, then there is no way of making the reality of the world questionable by questioning the reliability of our knowledge of it. On the contrary, once the ontological presuppositions of knowing are articulated, then the self-defeating nature of any such sceptical anxiety—its reliance in its questioning upon a concept one of whose preconditions constitutes a condition for the impossibility of asking that very question—becomes manifest. For when Dasein comprehends an entity, it does not have to get out of its own distinct inner sphere, penetrate external reality, and return inside with its spoils; rather, it is always already actively engaged with entities in the world.

Accordingly, whereas the Cartesian's apparently anti-sceptical commitment to the reliability of human cognition of the world (founded as it is upon a conception of knowledge which invites and renders unanswerable the expression of sceptical anxieties about the world) is in reality a further expression of scepticism, Heidegger's conception of knowledge as a deficient mode of Being-in-the-world makes scepticism inexpressible. We might think of this as Heidegger's first attempt to rearticulate the Platonic interconnections between Being, sophistry, and the threat of scepticism: an inadequate or sophistical conception of the Being of Dasein, and hence of Being, annihilates the possibility of human discourse about reality, whereas a genuinely adequate conception annihilates the possibility of sophistical arguments that such discourse is impossible. In this sense, Heidegger's project as developed in division 1 is in continuous confrontation with scepticism; its extended phenomenological underwriting of his opening etymological vision of Dasein's at-homeness in the world at once opposes and is given point by scepticism's otherwise irresistible eviction of Dasein from its habitat.

QUESTIONS OF METHOD: CONSTRUCTION AND HYPHENATION

18. Heidegger's account of knowing also provides a condensed diagnosis of the origin and plausibility of Cartesian misconceptions of it. For if knowing is a deficient mode of Being-in-the-world, a kind of disengagement of oneself and the relevant object from any particular field of practical activity, then it will evidently be experienced ontically as an isolated contemplative relationship between one entity and another. And since someone investigating the nature of our relationship to the world is very likely to take knowing as exemplary of that relationship (the philosopher in her study saying to herself 'What is the nature of our relationship to the world? What, for example, is involved in my knowing that there is a book on my desk?'), then a single object of theoretical contemplation will naturally come to stand for the world and the human knower of that object will naturally appear as a pure perceiver, with the two poles of the relation present-at-hand to one another (see *BT* 12.85–6).

It is, however, vital to see that Heidegger does not endorse this appearance. When he refers to knowing as a *deficient* mode of Being-in-the-world, he does not mean that it possesses a lesser degree or kind of Being than non-deficient modes such as producing or manipulating; he is not according ontological priority to the practical over the theoretical on the grounds that theoretical relations with objects really are somehow stripped of structures of Being that condition more active modes of practical engagement with the world. Indeed, in so far as he describes knowing as a deficient mode of *Being-in-the-world*, he could not consistently intend any such thing; knowing (like any other possibility of Dasein's Being) is inherently worldly or environed, and hence articulated by the existential structures that articulate any of Dasein's existentiell possibilities. If we are to understand knowing properly on an ontological level, therefore, we must explore its worldliness; we must grasp the significance of that aspect of Dasein's existentiality.

Knowing is a deficient mode of Being-in-the-world only in the sense that it is a mode of recontextualizing one's relations with objects that can easily present itself as a decontextualization. It appears to require the detachment of both subject and object from their embeddedness in specific practical tasks, purposes, and concerns, and so seems to present itself as what remains when these matters are stripped away—as their core or foundation. Knowing therefore naturally tends not only to cover over its own preconditions, but also to suggest that it is itself the precondition of all other modes of practical engagement with the world; it not only conceals or hides its own Being to an unusual degree, but appears in disguise, as a semblance of the Being of practical activity.

If the existentiell state of knowing really were ontologically revelatory, it would imply that investigations into the structures of Being (and so, those structures themselves) take a very particular form. First, the axis of the investigation would be vertical: essence is pictured as that which remains once surface appearance is penetrated, as that which is hidden within or beneath Dasein's everyday experience. Second, its prosecution involves decontextualization: a phenomenon can be understood in its essence without making reference to any other phenomena, however closely related they are to it in appearance or experience. Third, it involves disarticulation: the phenomenon under analysis is itself taken to be composed of elements each of which is comprehensible independently of those with which it is compounded. And fourth, its focus is singular or atomic: the essence of the phenomenon is pictured as belonging to one of its many elements, to a single, core structure or relation. In effect, then, this method is essentially constructive, and it secretes an essentially constructive conception of the Being of human existence. Dasein's existence appears as a juxtaposition of discrete phenomena, each a function of the elements from which it is combined together with their mode of combination, and each essentially founded on a single core element.

For Heidegger, such constructive philosophical investigations are the exact opposite of phenomenological investigations; they negate every element of what he takes to be the only adequate approach to structures of Being, and so constitute a paradigm of pseudo-philosophy, of sophistry. For him, the axis of investigations into Being is horizontal: increasing the clarity and transparency of our understanding of a phenomenon in its Being requires that we contextualize it, seeing its specific place among related phenomena, and that we see the phenomenon itself as an articulated whole—with the significance of each of its elements determined by their place in an interrelated totality. There is no single such element which, taken in isolation, embodies the foundational essence of that whole, and which must be uncovered by stripping its other components away; on the contrary, each such element means what it does only in the context of the phenomenon as a whole, and to grasp the phenomenon in its Being involves seeing it as an articulated whole with a specific place in a broader context. The Wittgensteinian resonance here is striking: we might say that to give a phenomenological account of Dasein is to recount its form of life without subliming the logic of its articulations.

Hence, Heidegger begins his account of Being-in-the-world with the following remarks:

The compound expression 'Being-in-the-world' indicates in the very way we have coined it, that it stands for a *unitary* phenomenon. This primary datum must be seen as a whole. But while Being-in-the-world cannot be broken up into contents which may be pieced together, this does not prevent it from having several constitutive items in its structure. Indeed the phenomenal datum which our expression indicates is one which may, in fact, be looked at in three ways. If we study it, keeping the whole phenomenon firmly in mind beforehand, the following items may be brought out for emphasis . . . (*BT* 12.78)

In other words, these three items, each of which form the topic of one of the following three chapters of division I (in-the-world, the being whose Being is Being-in-the-world, and Being-in) are not distinct elements in Being-in-the-world but rather three aspects of, or ways of looking at, that whole. They are not conceptual atoms from which an understanding of the whole can be constructed, but rather can be studied separately only provisionally, and only with the essentially unitary phenomenon of Being-in-the world kept as constant background to the analysis. This is the critical methodological and substantial issue lying behind Heidegger's apparently obsessive use of compound terms; and it is also a salutary lesson in reading the chapters concerned. It tells us that we should interpret their separateness as purely provisional and perspectival, and so think of the division they form as an essentially unitary writing phenomenon.

Hence, when Heidegger opposes the Cartesian conception of knowing and the ontological significance attributed to it, he is also opposing a fundamental misconception of philosophical method—a pseudo-phenomenology. He needs to demonstrate that this conception of cognition overlooks an essential condition of its own possibility, one that it shares with all modes of Dasein's Being, but which is especially well hidden in its case; and he also needs to show that it is essentially incapable of being the condition for the possibility of other, more obviously practical, modes of Dasein's engagement with the world—that it cannot be used as the basis for constructing an adequate understanding either of practical activity or of the world in which such practical activities occur. Both aims require that he turn to examine in more detail instances of more obviously practical modes of Dasein's existence. For the worldliness of such activities is less difficult to bring out than in the case of knowing; and in bringing it out, Heidegger can clarify exactly what the Cartesian thinks can be constructed from his conception of knowing, and exactly why any such constructive enterprise is doomed to failure.

DASEIN'S WORLDLINESS

19. Heidegger therefore turns to entities which we encounter not as present-at-hand, the objects of bare perceptual cognition, but as ready-to-hand—as objects we grasp in both senses of that term: we cognize them as they are, but we also physically take a grip on them, put them to use. He uses a term for them that is translated as 'equipment', but we could as happily talk of gear or stuff (as in DIY gear or gardening stuff—hence Heidegger's famous hammer).

A truly phenomenological investigation into the Being of equipment finds that its goal is best subserved not by isolating one specific piece of equipment and analysing its elements or parts, but rather by placing it in the broader practical and conceptual context without which it would not be the thing it is: the analytical axis is horizontal, not vertical. For to begin with, the idea of a single piece of equipment makes no sense: nothing could function as a tool in the absence of what Heidegger calls an 'equipmental totality'—a pen exists as a pen only in relation to ink, paper, writing-desks, and so on. Further, the utility of a tool presupposes something *for which* it is usable, an end-product—a pen is for writing letters, a hammer for making furniture. This directedness is the 'towards-which' of equipment. Such work also presupposes the availability of raw material: a hammer can make furniture only in conjunction with wood and metal upon which to work and from which the hammer itself can be made—that 'whereof' it is constituted. Finally, the end-product of the work will have recipients, people who will make use of it in turn, and so whose needs and interests will shape the worker's labour. Here, the context of the individual working environment appears as itself environed, part of the larger social world.

A piece of equipment is thus essentially something 'in-order-to': its being ready-to-hand is constituted by the multiplicity of reference- or assignment-relations which define its place within a totality of equipment and the practices of its employment. Properly grasped, therefore, an isolated tool points beyond itself, to a world of work and the world in which that work takes place; hence Heidegger talks of our implicit understanding of that circumambient network as circumspection. Here again, however, the self-concealing tendency of Being is revealed; for of course, anyone concentrating on the task at hand will be focusing her attention primarily on the goal of her labours, the correctness of the final product, and the tools she is employing to achieve this will be caught up in the production process, rendered invisible by their very handiness.

This handiness does, however, reveal itself at certain points within the work-world—paradoxically, when tools become unhandy in various ways when damaged, misplaced, or otherwise obstructive. Such unhandy equipment can easily become present-at-hand, as our attempts to circumvent the difficulty focus more exclusively on the occurrent properties of the tool with which we must now concern ourselves. Here is another root of our tendency to understand all objects in terms of presence-at-hand; but here also is a possible source of phenomenological illumination—of what Heidegger calls the 'dawning' or 'lighting up' (*aufleuchten*) of an aspect of Dasein's Being. For the unhandiness of missing or damaged objects forces us to consider with what and for what they were ready-to-hand, and so to consider the task, and everything that hangs together with it, that we cannot at present perform. (A Wittgensteinian might say: everydayness first stands out or announces itself through its loss, and hence as something that is to be returned to.)

When an assignment to some particular 'towards-this' has been thus circumspectively aroused, we catch sight of the 'towards-this' itself, and along with it everything connected with the work—the whole 'workshop'—as that wherein concern always dwells. The context of equipment is lit up, not as something never seen before, but as a totality constantly sighted beforehand in circumspection. With this totality, however, the world announces itself. (*BT* 16.105)

What Heidegger means by 'the world' here is a totality of assignment-relations; but any such system of relations, in defining the serviceability of a given manifold of equipment, has a terminus. Any given ready-to-hand entity, being involved in a specific task, points beyond itself; and in so far as that task is nested within other, larger tasks, it points further beyond itself; but sooner or later these reference-relations invoke a goal or purpose, a 'for-the-sake-of-which', that pertains to a possibility of Dasein's Being. The handiness of a hammer is for building a roof, which is for the sake of sheltering Dasein; the handiness of a pen is for the sake of communicating with others. Thus, the ontological structures of worldhood are and must be existentially understood; the world is a facet of Dasein's Being—Dasein's Being is Being-in-the-world.

This returns us to Heidegger's guiding conception of Dasein as the being for whom Being is an issue, or rather an inextricably intertwined set of issues. For as we saw earlier, Dasein's ability to realize in action its answers to the question that its own existence poses presupposes that it can and does encounter material objects as a field for practical activity, which amounts to its answering the question that their Being poses by making concrete its understanding of them as ready-to-hand. Accordingly, if circumstances force or invite it to hold back from such practical dealings in order to focus upon the occurrent properties of these no-longer-handy objects, such apparent decontextualization must be understood as a recontextualization, a new way of understanding those objects (as present-at-hand) that presupposes and is presupposed by a new way of understanding itself (as a being engaged in more or less explicitly theoretical modes of questioning—a tool repairer or a molecular chemist). Being-in-the-world thus appears as a condition for the possibility of Dasein's having Being as an issue for it; it provides a further articulation of the full significance of that characterization. And in particular, it appears as a condition for the possibility of encountering entities as present-at-hand—as the objects of bare perceptual cognition and hence of the theorizing built upon such cognition: even present-at-hand entities are encounterable as such only within a world, against the horizon of a particular, environing system of assignment-relations (even if a deficient one).

THE WORLDHOOD OF THE WORLD

20. Any mode of Dasein's existence thus presupposes the idea of the world; but what might it mean to understand the world existentially—as an aspect of the Being of Dasein? Here Heidegger turns to the one type of tool that is precisely designed to indicate the worldly context within which practical activity takes place (rather than merely revealing it retrospectively when it fails to fulfil its function)—the sign. Heidegger's example is that of a car indicator. In one sense, a sign is simply one more piece of equipment, a tool whose proper functioning presupposes its place in a complex equipmental totality—one including the car, road markings, conventions governing how to alter the direction of a car's travel without disrupting that of other cars, and so on. Only within that social or cultural context can the sudden appearance of a flashing amber light on the right rear bumper of a car signify that it intends to turn right. But such a flashing light also lights up the environment within which the car is moving. When other drivers and pedestrians encounter it, they are recalled to the pattern of roads and pavements, crossings and traffic lights within which they are moving together with the signalling car, and to their position and intended movements within it. In short, the light indicates the present and intended orientation not only of the signalling car, but also of those to whom its driver is signalling; it is a focal point around which a traveller's awareness of a manifold of equipment, and of its structuring of the significance of the environment through which she is moving, can crystallize. As Heidegger puts it: '*A sign is . . . an item of equipment which explicitly raises a totality of equipment into our circumspection so that together with it the worldly character of the ready-to-hand announces itself*' (*BT* 17.110).

What the world thereby announces itself *as* is clearly neither something present-at-hand nor something ready-to-hand. It is not itself an entity, but rather a web of socially or culturally constituted assignments of significance within which entities can appear as the particular entities they are, and which must therefore always be laid out or disclosed (however implicitly) in advance of any particular encounter with an object. These assignments are social in that they are not restricted to a single, or to any particular, individual; they are cultural in that their significance can vary from culture to culture—drivers in Rome use and understand car indicators in ways very different from drivers in Rejkjavik (and Heidegger speculates (*BT* 17.112–13) that the inhabitants of 'primitive' cultures, within whose magical or fetishistic practices 'signs' do not indicate other objects so much as coincide with or go proxy for them, could not be said to use signs as tools or equipment at all); and they are assignments of significance or meaning, determining that and how objects matter to Dasein. Growing up in, or otherwise coming to inhabit, a specific culture is a matter of acquiring a practical grasp of the widely ramifying web of concepts, roles, functions, and functional interrelations within which that culture's inhabitants orient their interactions with the objects in their environment.

Heidegger casts further light on the nature of this web and the orientation it confers by contrasting an essentially worldly being's everyday experience of spatial orientation with the kind of orientation allowed for in a Cartesian account of space. For the Cartesian, space is essentially mathematicized: spatial location is fixed by imposing an objective system of coordinates upon the world and assigning a sequence of numbers to each and every item in it, and Dasein's progress through this fixed array of present-at-hand items is a matter of measuring off stretches of a space that is itself present-at-hand. For Heidegger, this utterly fails to capture Dasein's everyday understanding of objects as near or far, close or distant—an understanding that is internally related to its practical purposes. The spectacles on my nose are further away from me than the picture on the wall that I use them to examine; the friend I see across the road is nearer to me than the pavement under my feet; my friend's appearance at my side would not bring her any closer to me, and moving right up to the picture would in fact distance it from me. Objects are in the world around us, disclosed to us as embodied beings: not just in the sense of being to hand or not to hand, but of being on the right hand or the left hand (or neither). This is a distinction that is sometimes of critical circumspective importance (for example, with gloves as opposed to hammers—although a craftsman's right-handedness might well make a hammer within reach of his left hand unhandy; *BT* 23.143), but one that is inexpressible in Cartesian coordinates.

As this reappearance of the human hand in Heidegger's discourse underlines, closeness and distance in his sense involve equipmentality; the spatial disposition of the manifold of objects populating my environment is determined by their serviceability for my current activities, and hence in relation to possibilities of my Being. Cartesian space is thus an abstraction from our understanding of space as a region or set of regions, an interlinked, ramifying totality of places and objects that belong to equipmental totalities and an environing work-world; the former is a deficient mode of the latter, not its essence or basis. For Dasein, spatial relations are not mathematical functions but rather coordinations of significance; naturally enough for the being for whom Being is an issue, its situatedness in a world of objects is conditioned by whether and how those objects and their relations with one another relate to it, matter to it.

21. Heidegger's particular emphasis upon this issue of orientation at least raises the question of its reflexive significance—of its implications for our grasp not only of his concept of the world, but also of his own philosophical achievement. For of course, a failure to understand Dasein's spatiality in existential terms would not only make it impossible for us to understand Dasein's capacity to orient itself, to place itself in a world of objects and projects; it would also leave us philosophically disoriented (not knowing our way about, as Wittgenstein might put it), unable to situate ourselves within the articulated totality of Being-in-the-world as Heidegger lays it out—lacking a sure grasp of the way its various aspects relate themselves to one another, and of course to ourselves. For such ontological disorientation would amount to being unable to place ourselves in relation to the Being of the being that each of us is; it would signify a kind of lostness to ourselves, a disorientation with respect to the issue that our own Being is for each one of us. For how far can we properly confront the question of our own existence ontically when its ontological elucidation so systematically eludes us?

What matters more for our purposes, however, is that this contrast between conceptions of spatial orientation brings out a key element in Heidegger's more general critique of Cartesian conceptions of Dasein's worldliness—their implicit dependence upon a mathematical paradigm. As we saw earlier, Cartesians would attempt to understand the world in its worldhood as a construct from an essentially cognitive relation to entities, as something established by projecting particular human values and interests upon present-at-hand entities. Setting aside for the moment Heidegger's view that the very idea of presence-at-hand presupposes that of the world and can hardly therefore account for its possibility, his central objection is most clearly articulated in the following passage:

The context of assignments or references, which, as significance, is constitutive for worldhood, can be taken formally in the sense of a system of Relations. But one must note that in such formalizations the phenomena get levelled off so much that their real phenomenal content may be lost, especially in the case of such 'simple' relationships as those which lurk in significance. The phenomenal content of these Relations and Relata—the 'in-order-to', the 'for-the-sake-of', and the 'with-which' of an involvement—is such that they resist any sort of mathematical functionalization . . . They are rather relationships in which concernful circumspection as such already dwells. (*BT* 18.121–2)

Heidegger happily admits that, when entities are encountered as present-at-hand, they can have their properties defined mathematically in purely functional concepts; this is a key feature of Descartes's characterization of objects as pure substance, matter extended in space, and is indeed central to any natural-scientific understanding of reality. But, he claims, the network of relations that makes possible our engagement with objects (whether as ready-to-hand or as present-at-hand) essentially resists such mathematical systematization.

To think that a set of relations can be represented mathematically presupposes that the nature, extent, and number of those relations can be given a clear, determinate, and self-contained specification—so that the network they constitute might be calculable from those specifications, in the way that a function can mechanically generate a set of coordinates in space. But what is grasped by someone who grasps that a hammer is for hammering is not specifiable in terms of a finite list of tasks (she knows that a hammer can hammer nails into surfaces, pegs into holes, two dovetailed planks into one another, a pole into the ground, and so seemingly endlessly on). She will know that each such task presupposes a subtly different kind of equipmental context (certain kinds of preparation, certain kinds of other tools, and so on), each of which might be provided from an indefinite number of different arrays of objects. She would also know that each such hammering task could be performed by an indefinite number of other objects—that, in certain circumstances themselves not listable in advance, iron bars, lumps of granite, car jacks, and so on might all be used as (might become) hammers; and she would further know that hammers can be used for an indefinite number of tasks other than hammering (to prop open doors, to repel intruders, to play games of 'toss-the-hammer' and so on).

Knowing what it is for something to be a hammer is, among other things, knowing all this; and knowing all this is, therefore, an inherently open-ended capacity. It cannot be exhaustively captured by a finite list of precise rules whose application from context to context is transparent. For our practical activities always engage with specific situations, but there is no such thing as a determinate set of all the possible situations we might encounter in which our knowledge of a hammer and its capacities might be pertinently deployed. Hammering know-how is in critical part a capacity to improvise—to respond appropriately to new contexts and opportunities as they emerge in ways that make concrete an entity's handiness for hammering. Such know-how neither is nor is a function of knowing that—it is not reducible to a grasp of determinate propositions or rules. For any such knowledge must be applied to the situations the competent agent faces, and this process must itself either be based on propositional knowledge or essentially ungrounded. The former threatens an infinite regress; the latter raises the question why the original practical ability itself cannot be ungrounded.

The sophistical constructive model of ontological investigation inherently tends towards representing structures of Being as mathematical functions, because that fits with its conception of itself as uncovering the foundations of phenomena by decontextualizing them and disarticulating their component elements; the systematicity it seeks involves treating any whole as a function of its independently given parts. The worldhood of the world resists such representation for a number of reasons. First, in so far as it is the condition for the possibility of an inherently flexible and open-ended grasp of entities as ready-to-hand, it must itself be flexible and open-ended; it is not an always already articulated space of possibilities of significance, but rather a horizon within which such spaces of possibilities can be articulated, questioned, and revised in conditioned but essentially unpredictable ways. Hence any ontological articulation of it must itself be provisional, flexible, open to question and revision; it must eschew fixity or formalization of the kind it denies to that which it claims to articulate. Furthermore, in so far as Heidegger does provisionally lay out the worldhood of the world, it is as an articulated totality that is itself an aspect of a greater articulated totality (Being-in-the-world); in other words, it is at once a context for its own constitutive structures and itself essentially contextualized. Accordingly, any explicit articulation of it—containing as it does elements that are themselves internally structured and being itself part of broader structures—will always implicitly ramify beyond its own limits. Hence, both the world in its worldhood and any adequate ontological account of it will have an ineliminable provisionality and inexhaustibility: like Wittgenstein's notion of grammar, each will always be open to further articulation and to being articulated otherwise—inviting further questioning and being themselves questionable.

WORLD, LANGUAGE, AND DISCOURSE

22. The fact that the worldhood of the world involves assignments of significance, and that it announces itself most clearly through a system of symbolic expression and representation, suggests very strongly that there must be some kind of inner connection between worldhood and meaning; and Heidegger's account of interpretation, language, and meaning in general appears to confirm this intuition. Although that account is deferred until the later stretches of chapter 5, it is tempting to follow up this connection immediately in the context of a reading that takes division I to be fundamentally concerned with the issue of scepticism. This is because Heidegger's concluding examination of scepticism in chapter 6 appears to depend solely upon his account of worldhood, language, and discourse; and if this impression were to prove well founded, it would at once clarify the core of Heidegger's full response to the sceptic, and imply that (contrary to my overarching claim) significant elements of his existential analytic had no real relevance to that issue. In order to demonstrate the strength of the case for this opposing interpretation, I propose to continue this commentary by, as it were, succumbing to the temptation to pass over chapter 4 and the early stretches of chapter 5; the costs of this reading strategy (of allowing the active or projective dimension of Dasein's Being to occlude its receptivity or thrownness)—a strategy from which my earlier commentary on *Being and Time* did not sufficiently distinguish itself—will be made clearer a little later.

As we have seen, the smooth course of our everyday activities is sometimes disrupted—when we have to repair a broken tool, say, or adapt an object for a certain task. In so reorienting ourselves, in making the structures of our comprehending engagement with objects our explicit concern, we engage in what Heidegger calls 'interpretation'. This is not something superimposed upon our practical comprehension but rather a development of it—the coming to fruition of a possibility inherent in that everyday circumspection. It amounts to a comprehending grasp of our comprehension: our understanding takes a practical interest in how it guides practical activity, and discovers the following: 'That which has been circumspectively taken apart with regard to its "in-order-to" and taken apart as such—that which is explicitly understood—has the structure of *something as something*' (*BT* 32.189). The Wittgensteinian resonance of this talk of a seeing as structure should be clear; but there are also more immediate echoes of Heidegger's introductory etymological connection between the *logos* of phenomenology and the capacity to see something as something, upon which he there simply asserted that both semblance and truth-telling depend (*BT* 7.55–8). Heidegger now begins to make good on that claim by showing that seeing as (or seeing aspects) is the fundamental structure of the totality of assignment-relations that make up the worldhood of the world. The types of category 'as which' we see things (as doors, hammers, pens) are specifications of the ways in which they can be woven into Dasein's practical activities, referred to possibilities of its Being; but they are also specifications of how objects make themselves intelligible to Dasein, how Dasein grasps the issue of their Being. Thus, Dasein's twofold comprehending relation to its own Being and that of other beings is grounded in a unified field or framework of meaning; and that field is not a projection upon an essentially meaningless world but rather an ineliminable aspect of it.

For Heidegger, just as interpretation is grounded in understanding, so linguistic assertion is grounded in interpretation. Considering how to repair a tool involves making explicit the structure of our understanding of it in use; and if we describe our difficulty—by asserting that 'The hammer is too heavy'—we pick out the object as having a certain character, and so conceptualize it in terms recognizably related to the structure of our wordless attempts to modify it. Ultimately, therefore, the structure of comprehension made explicit in assertions is rooted in the circumspective understanding of practical activity; indeed, both assertion and interpretation can illuminate hitherto unnoticed aspects or potentialities of the objects we are examining which can be embodied in, and hence reshape, our practical concerns with them. On the other hand, however, assertions also narrow down and level out the focus of our concerns, restricting it to a specific occurrent property of an object. In effect, then, assertions are proto-theoretical; they transform our relation to the object by severing it from its place in a work-world of practical concern, situating it solely as a particular thing about which a particular predication can be made; in a single movement what is ready-to-hand is covered up and what is present-at-hand is discovered.

This account doubly distances linguistic meaning (as manifest in assertions) from meaning per se—the field of significance that grounds the human understanding of the world. True, just as interpretations grasp the structures of pre-interpretative understanding, so assertions articulate what concerns us in our interpretations; they may allow the significance-structure of interpretation to dwindle or simplify itself, but they do not annihilate it altogether—and they might even deepen its future serviceability. As a mode of Being-in-the-world, asserting cannot be entirely disoriented or dislocated. Nevertheless, its tendency towards reductiveness, levelling, and decontextualization makes it a very misleading blueprint for genuinely phenomenological investigations.

23. However, immediately after establishing this negative conclusion, Heidegger introduces the term *Rede* (which is translated as 'discourse', but could more happily be taken to mean 'talk') to refer to something that is at once the existential foundation of language (including assertions) and the articulation of intelligibility. Indeed, he claims that 'the intelligibility of Being-in-the-world . . . expresses itself as discourse' (*BT* 34.204). Some aspect of language therefore appears as genuinely disclosive of beings in their Being, something that avoids, while nevertheless underpinning, the reductiveness of assertoric utterance. But what?

Even in making an assertion about an object, we use a linguistic term to categorize it as a particular kind of thing (e.g. a hammer); and in employing that categorization, we articulate our seeing it as something—which is, of course, the foundational structure of significance or meaning, and so of practical understanding and interpretation. So the concepts and categories of language—the articulations that make subject–predicate characterizations of entities possible—correspond to the articulations of the field of meaning. Indeed, given the rootedness of even assertoric utterances in the comprehending grasp that interpretation takes of our circumspective understanding of things, one might think of recountings of the articulations of language as a fruitful thematization of—a realization of a possibility inherent in—the otherwise inexplicit articulations of meaning.

We might, then, see Heidegger's distinction between assertion and discourse as a phenomenological appropriation of the familiar distinction between a type of speech-act and the conceptual framework upon which any speech-act must draw. Discourse is thus an enabling condition of utterance, determining the sense of the words we employ to do certain things; but it can therefore also be thought of as an articulation of the intelligibility of things. Whether or not we are right to assert that a hammer is too heavy must be settled by reference to the facts about the tool concerned; and any investigation we might engage in to make that determination must itself be guided by a grasp of what it is for something to count as an instance of a hammer, and as a heavy one. But this understanding can be thought of as at once a grasp of how to use the words 'hammer' and 'heavy' *and* as a grasp of what a hammer is and of what heaviness is. For to know how to use the word 'hammer' just is to know what must be true of an entity if it is to count as a hammer, to appreciate the characteristics without which it would not be what it is—in short, to grasp that type of being in its Being. At this level, linguistic meaning and the meaning of entities are one and the same thing: the former discloses the latter.

In so far as it does, however, discourse thereby articulates the field of meaning, and hence the worldhood of the world; so it must be understood as an *existentiale* of Dasein—which means that its articulations cannot be conceptualized as a system of mathematical functions. Our grasp of hammers in their Being as hammers is inherently open-ended—a holistic, provisional, and inexhaustible kind of know-how; hence, its articulations must be seen as themselves flexible, capable of projecting themselves into new and unpredictable situations in ways that are neither entirely arbitrary nor utterly mechanical—ways that are justifiable, but only retrospectively. In short, they are always capable of putting themselves in question, revealing potentialities never previously actualized, and so always disclosing themselves to Dasein against a future horizon of undisclosed possibilities. Furthermore, both their present actualizations and their future projections are part of a larger totality—that of Dasein's Being and so of Being in general. Hence their meaningfulness is always contextualized, the full significance of their articulations itself ramifying into broader ontological articulations that can never be grasped as a definitive or fixed whole. From a phenomenological perspective, therefore, talk of discourse as a kind of conceptual or grammatical framework must always place the traditional idea of a 'framework'—with its implication of a fixed or formalizable system of relations—in question (in just the way that Wittgenstein inflects his talk of the grammar of words).

SCEPTICISM: THE SCANDAL OF PHILOSOPHY

24. This connection between worldliness and discourse can seem (did seem to me) enough taken on its own to determine Heidegger's concluding response to scepticism in chapter 6 of division i. In section 43 he reiterates and deepens his view that we cannot render intelligible the sceptic's request for a proof of the existence or reality of the external world: 'the "scandal of philosophy" is not that this proof has yet to be given, but that *such proofs are expected and attempted again and again*' (*BT* 43.249). For even to formulate the 'problem' we must take for granted the existence of the human subject and ask whether any of our beliefs about a world existing beyond the present moment of our

consciousness can be justified. But this presupposes that the question of the human subject's existence can be separated off from the question of the existence of the world in which it dwells—in short, it assumes that Dasein's Being is not Being-in-the-world. If, however, Dasein's Being is grasped as Being-in-the-world, then the sceptical 'problem' is not coherently statable: in positing the human subject as existing, the sceptic also posits the world whose reality she claims to doubt.

In other words, Heidegger aims not to answer the sceptic but to show that her doubts are inarticulable—that she cannot intelligibly ask her sceptical question, because the relation between subject and world cannot, on any adequate ontological understanding of Dasein, be made an issue for us. We might say that this false appearance of questionability rests on a misunderstanding of knowledge or cognition; for 'knowing is a founded mode of access to the Real' (*BT* 43.246)—a relation in which Dasein can stand to a given state of affairs, but not towards the world as such. Dasein can know that a lake is deep or doubt that a chair is comfortable, but it cannot know that the world exists. The world is not a possible object of knowledge, because it is not an object at all—not an entity or set of entities. It is that within which entities appear, a field or horizon of assignment-relations; it is the condition for the possibility of any intra-worldly relation, and so is not analysable in terms of any such relation. In short, the Cartesian conception of subject and world opens the door to scepticism because it interprets both subject and world as entities (or sets of entities)—as if the world were a great big object, a totality of possible objects of knowledge, rather than that wherein all possible objects of knowledge are encountered. In Heideggerian terms, the Cartesian creates the condition for the possibility of scepticism by assuming that a specific existentiell stance of the subject might go proxy for the *existentiale* which makes all such stances possible: she conflates the ontic and the ontological.

If, however, the world is ontologically grounded in the Being of Dasein, must it not follow that when Dasein does not exist, neither does the world? And what objective reality is left to a world that is dependent for its own existence upon the continued existence of human creatures within it? In thus subjectivizing reality, does not Heidegger's analysis amount to a further expression of scepticism?

Heidegger rebuts the charge as follows:

Of course, only as long as Dasein *is* (that is, only as long as an understanding of Being is ontically possible), 'is there' Being. When Dasein does not exist, 'independence' 'is' not either, nor 'is' the 'in-itself'. In such a case this sort of thing can be neither understood nor not understood. In such a case even entities within-the-world can be neither uncovered nor lie hidden. *In such a case* it cannot be said that entities are, nor can it be said that they are not. But *now*, as long as there is an understanding of Being and therefore an understanding of presence-at-hand, it can indeed be said that *in this case* entities will still continue to be. (*BT* 43.255)

Even by Heidegger's standards, this is a syntactically tortuous passage. But the outbreak of italicization and quotation marks acts as an emphatic reminder to his questioners that the issue they aim to raise can be worthy of a response only if it can intelligibly be articulated; and that is itself questionable.

When Dasein encounters material objects, it does so as phenomena which exist independently of its encounters with them. This is one key respect in which we distinguish them from illusions and hallucinations: when we claim to see a table, we mean that we see something which will (*ceteris paribus*) continue to exist when we can no longer see it; and part of what we mean when we talk of the real world is a realm of objects that existed before the human species developed and that is perfectly capable of surviving our extinction. Hence, to ask whether material objects exist only as long as Dasein exists, to regard this as an open question, is to betoken confusion about what such entities are—about what it is to encounter beings in their Being as material objects, about what we mean by the term 'material object'. Anyone capable of grasping such entities as entities understands that they would not count as material objects if their existence were conditional upon that of Dasein. Thus, there seems to be no real question here deserving of an answer—only the appearance of one.

If Dasein were to vanish, what would then vanish from the world on Heidegger's view is not beings but the capacity to understand beings in their Being, the capacity to uncover them as existing and as the entities they are. In such circumstances, it could not be asserted either that entities exist or that they do not—there could be no comprehending grasp of them at all. Nothing whatever can be said of entities (and hence nothing about the relation between their existence and that of Dasein) in a world-without-Dasein; but in so far as anything whatever can be said of entities (i.e. in so far as Dasein exists), then the only thing that can intelligibly be said about entities-in-a-world-without-Dasein is that those entities will continue to exist. Since the very asking of the sceptical question is an act of a being whose Being is Dasein, and hence presupposes that Dasein exists, its only intelligible answer is self-evident.

25. As Heidegger's emphasis upon the intelligibility of the sceptic's utterances suggests, his treatment of the 'problem' of the external world ultimately depends upon his views on language and truth. For him, the question of what it would be true to say about entities-in-a-world-without-Dasein must not be conflated with the question of whether that truth could conceivably be uttered in such a world. In effect, then, he is claiming that the existence of Dasein is a condition for the possibility of truth—not just because judgements require judgers, but also because there can be no question of a judgement's corresponding (or failing to correspond) with reality without a prior disclosure of that reality, and there can be no such disclosure without Dasein.

Heidegger's example in section 44 is of someone who judges that 'the picture on the wall is askew'—a representation of the properties of a representation. (We might already feel moved to ask: but might not this picture be non-representational, and thus exemplify Dasein's capacity to articulate or communicate in the absence of any correspondence with reality? Or are we rather likely to ask: when we see a representational picture, do we perceive something that corresponds to what it depicts— a landscape, say—or do we just perceive what it depicts? Do pictures correspond to reality or disclose it?) Heidegger points out that what confirms the truth of such a judgement is our perceiving that the picture really is the way the judgement claims that it is, and that this presupposes our capacity to encounter the picture as a picture and as it is in itself.

> To say that an assertion 'is true' signifies that it uncovers the entity as it is in itself. Such an assertion asserts, points out, 'lets' the entity 'be seen' in its un-coveredness. The *Being-true* of the assertion must be understood as *Being-uncovering*. Thus truth has by no means the structure of an agreement between knowing and the object in the sense of a likening of one entity (the subject) to another (the Object).
>
> Being-true as Being-uncovering is in turn ontologically possible only on the basis of Being-in-the-world. This latter phenomenon . . . is the *foundation* for the primordial phenomenon of truth. (*BT* 44.261)

Here we need to recall the distinction between assertion and discourse. Whether or not an assertion is true is determined by reality —by whether things are as it claims them to be. But only meaningful propositions can be true or false; to determine the truth of a claim that a picture is askew, we must grasp the meaning of its constituent terms, which means grasping what a picture is and what it is for a picture to be askew—we must, in other words, grasp a certain articulation of discourse. It is the opening up of just such a space of intelligibility that Heidegger means by his talk of uncovering, drawing upon the Greek concept of truth as *aletheia* (unconcealing). And in his view, while one can intelligibly ask whether a proposition corresponds with reality, one cannot do so with respect to the articulations of discourse.

In part, this is because an infinite regress threatens: if the intelligibility of assessing correspondence-relations depends upon a grasp of discourse, then assessing the correspondence between discourse and reality would presuppose the existence of a super-discourse that founded this correspondence-relation, for which the same question would arise; and so endlessly on. A deeper reason emerges if we think of the linguistic aspect or dimension of discourse, and bear in mind that the articulations of a conceptual or grammatical framework, being specifications of meaning, are akin to rules rather than to assertions. Articulating the grammar of a word is not a matter of advancing hypotheses or claims about reality, but rather of determining what must be the case if a given aspect or element of reality is to count as an instance of a given type of phenomenon. Such determinations—Wittgenstein calls them criteria—no more claim that something is true of the world than the rules of chess governing the movements of the queen describe how that piece is as a matter of fact moved. The chess rule rather specifies how the piece should be moved, how it is to be moved; it determines that only certain patterns of movement count as valid moves in a chess game, and so that a piece moved in ways other than those specified are not ways of moving the queen in chess. In just the same way, the grammar of a word does not make claims about the phenomena of the world; it rather specifies that if a given phenomenon satisfies certain conditions, then the relevant word is applicable to it, it counts as a certain kind of thing—and if it does not, then it is not so applicable and it does not so count. In short, grammatical criteria, like rules, neither correspond nor fail to correspond with reality; as determinants or norms of meaning, they are neither true nor false, but rather articulate a space (a clearing) within which true and false claims can be made and assessed.

The articulations of discourse nevertheless determine the essential nature of phenomena, in that they manifest the necessary feature of any given type of thing—those without which they would not count as a thing of that kind at all; in Heidegger's terms, they articulate the Being of beings. If, however, those articulations cannot be thought of as true or false to reality, then reality cannot be thought of as inherently and independently possessed of an articulated essence to which the articulations of language might (or might not) correspond, and which might exist in the absence of language-wielding creatures. In other words, whereas the truth about beings must continue to hold in the absence of Dasein, their Being or essence cannot. The Being of beings is not simply one more fact about them, one more aspect of the truth about reality that human beings come to know but which is independent of their coming to know it. Essence is not empirical, not a function of how things are in the world but of how the field of discourse is articulated, and hence a function of the Being of Dasein as Being-in-the-world. In short, ' "there is" truth only insofar as Dasein "is" and so long as Dasein "is" ' (*BT* 44.269): Dasein is the condition for the possibility of truth.

Does this relativity signify that all truth is subjective? If one interprets 'subjective ' as 'left to the subject's discretion', then it certainly does not. For uncovering, in the sense which is most its own, takes asserting out of the province of 'subjective' discretion, and brings the uncovering Dasein face to face with the entities themselves. And only *because* 'truth' as uncovering, *is a kind of Being which belongs to Dasein*, can it be taken out of the province of *Dasein's discretion*. Even the 'universal validity' of truth is rooted solely in the fact that Dasein can uncover entities in themselves and free them. Only so can these entities themselves be binding for every possible assertion—that is, for every possible way of pointing them out. (*BT* 44.270)

So by the end of this concluding rearticulation of Heidegger's response to scepticism, we can see again his way of forging Plato's connections between Being, scepticism, and sophistry. Heidegger accepts that a proper understanding of the sceptical challenge presupposes that we understand the ontological preconditions for the human capacity to speak truly and falsely of what is the case—in other words, that we must come to grips with that fundamental dimension of the Being of Dasein, and hence of Being more generally. The Cartesian approach to human subjectivity makes it possible to give an intelligible articulation of sceptical doubts, and impossible to allay them; this is because it allows itself to take knowing's semblance of penetrating ontological revelation to be a genuine appearance of that which is hidden. By contrast, a genuinely contextual phenomenology of knowing and of Dasein's Being in its worldliness makes it plain that the expression of sceptical doubts has only the appearance of intelligibility—that it rather indicates the sceptic's disorientation, her lostness in the ontological realm and hence her lostness to herself. In this opacity of the self to itself, Heidegger sees once more a sign that the being to whom an understanding of Being most closely belongs is also capable of distancing itself from that understanding, and so from itself. How and why such distancing might be overcome or de-severed becomes an increasing preoccupation of Heidegger's text. But the touchstone of such reorientation is already evident: it lies in grasping how and why Being is not a fitting subject for assertoric utterance, is not articulable in language in the ways in which entities and their properties are articulable (not, for example, as the most universal genus). For Being is neither true nor false, but rather that which makes truth and falsehood possible; so talk of Being neither corresponds nor fails to correspond to reality—is neither hypothesis nor description. Some other mode of speech is required to wrench the articulations of intelligibility from their hiddenness in a way that does not at once disguise them.

AVERAGE EVERYDAY BEING-WITH-OTHERS: THE 'THEY'

26. In section 22 I succumbed to the temptation to conclude that Heidegger's concluding treatment of scepticism could be grasped as exclusively dependent upon the connections he forged between worldliness, language, and discourse. Now I want to explore the benefits of resisting that temptation. After all, the way Heidegger actually structures division I suggests that chapter 6's analysis of scepticism can be brought off only after establishing the conclusions reached in chapters 2, 4, and 5 put together—in other words, only after grasping the ways in which worldliness hangs together not only with discourse, but with the social dimension of Dasein's Being (its Being-with) and with its articulation into both projective understanding and thrown state-of-mind (Being-in). My overarching question is thus: how might grasping these further aspects of Dasein's Being enrich our understanding of scepticism and of Heidegger's attitude to it?

As Heidegger's sense of the internal relation between worldhood and language would anyway suggest, he conceives of Dasein's worldliness as inherently social or shared. Dasein's world is a with-world: its ontological structures make implicit but essential reference to the Being of other beings like itself, in three interrelated ways. First, other Dasein form one more class of being that Dasein encounters within its world. But Dasein does not relate to them simply as it does to any and every entity, as if 'encountering' a new intra-worldly phenomenon—whether present-at-hand or ready-to-hand. For (second), others typically provide what Dasein works upon and make use of what Dasein's work produces; the 'whereof' and the 'towards-which' of equipmental totalities implicitly relate the work-world to others—grasped not as components of the totality that Dasein can comprehend or make use of, but as like Dasein in that they too comprehend, make use of, and produce entities. After all (third), the readiness-to-hand of objects for a particular Dasein could not conceivably be understood as their readiness-to-hand for that Dasein alone; any object that is genuinely handy for a given task must be handy for any Dasein capable of performing it. In short, Dasein's Being-in-the-world is a Being-with-others: it shares its world with beings that genuinely are its Others—beings capable of inhabiting or dwelling within that same world, creatures who are ontically distinguishable yet ontologically identical.

Hence, I can say of my Others that their Being is my Being, but they are not me; and I can say of the world we inhabit that it is theirs but that it is mine too—that is, that it is ours. Such a world is no less mine because it is also yours; having the world in common is not the denial of what talk of Dasein's subjectivity ought to mean, and of what Heidegger's talk of Dasein as having its own Being as an issue for it does mean, but rather its further specification. If Dasein's essentially worldly Being is essentially Being-with, then its questioning relation to its own Being is realizable not only in and through its questioning relation to the Being of other intra-worldly entities but also in and through its questioning relation to the Being of Others. In fact, it is Heidegger's concern in chapter 4 of division 1 to show how the matter of Dasein's mineness or individuality—its capacity to be 'something of its own' (*BT* 9.68), to be authentic (or of course to fail to do so)—is inextricably tangled up with the question of its relations to its Others.

27. For Heidegger, Dasein's average everyday way of relating to itself is determined by its sense of how it differs from Others. We understand those differences either as something to be eliminated at all costs, or as something that must at all costs be emphasized. Both are forms of conformity, since even the latter (less common) choice amounts to allowing the choices of Others to determine how we live by negation: we live an apparently non-conforming life not because of the life it is but because of the life it is not—because it is not the life of Others. Either way, Dasein subjects itself to Others—but not to a definite Other or Others, because in so far as those Others have the Being of Dasein, then they too will typically and for the most part stand in subjection to Others. Hence this sovereign 'Other' is not a collectivity of genuinely individual human beings whose shared tastes dictate the tastes of every-

one else (a group of definite Others), and not a supra-individual being (a definite group-Other). It is not a being or set of beings to whom mineness or differentiation belongs, but a neutered 'who', a collective hallucination of genuine Otherness that is both the cause and the consequence of our each giving up the capacity for genuine self-relation and an authentically individual existence. If a given Dasein's thoughts and deeds are (determined by) what *they* think and do, its answerability for its life has been not so much displaced as misplaced; it has vanished, projected onto an everyone that is no one by someone who is, without it, also no one, and so has only the illusion of a genuinely inhabited and inhabitable world. As Heidegger puts it, 'everyone is the other and no-one is himself. The *"they"*, which supplies the answer to the question of the "who" of everyday Dasein, is the *"nobody"* to whom every Dasein has already surrendered itself in Being-among-one-another' (*BT* 27.165–6).

Hence, inauthenticity is undifferentiated—an indifferent mode of its Being-with that finds expression not only in Dasein's self-relation but also in its mode of Being-in-the-world, in Dasein's relation to or disclosure of the entities it encounters in the form of idle talk, curiosity, and ambiguity. In idle talk, our concern for the object of our claims is eclipsed by our concern for the claims: rather than trying to achieve access to things as they are in themselves, we take it for granted that what is said about them is so, simply because it is what is said about them, and we pass it on—disseminating the claim, allowing it to inflect our conversations about the relevant things, lubricating its social circulation without any attempt to ground it in the reality of its ostensible subject. Idle talk thus closes off its objects, and forecloses any future investigations of them: we take ourselves to understand them perfectly because we know what everyone knows about them. The apparent completeness of this understanding encourages us to turn our attention away from the everyday towards the exotic and alien; Dasein focuses upon the novel and attends primarily to its novelty, seeking new objects not in order to grasp them as they really are but to stimulate itself with their newness—and since that novelty evaporates on contact, the stimulation we seek demands ever-renewed sources. Such curiosity thus introduces new 'knowledge' to the social circulation of idle talk, but with increasing velocity; increasingly distracted by new possibilities, Dasein increasingly uproots itself from its environment, floating rather than dwelling, losing orientation. Hence it loses its grip on the distinction between genuine and counterfeit understanding; superficiality takes on the appearance of depth, and real comprehension appears marginal and eccentric. Such ambiguity is the hallmark of the understanding bequeathed by the they-self, signifying that Dasein is typically absorbed or entangled in its world, and hence oblivious to its own alienation from the issue that its Being (and that of other beings) poses for it: Heidegger calls this frictionless turbulence 'falling'.

28. Heidegger further claims that falling is 'a definite existential characteristic of Dasein itself' (BT 38.220)—a claim that echoes his earlier assertion that the they-self as such is 'an essential *existentiale*' of Dasein (BT 27.168). In other words, inauthenticity is not merely a common ontic or existentiell possibility for Dasein, but rather a 'primordial phenomenon [which] belongs to Dasein's positive constitution' (BT 27.167), a part of its ontological structure—as if Dasein is inherently inauthentic. Once again, the true import of this startling claim flows from Heidegger's understanding of Dasein's worldliness; it betrays the fact that there is something inherently public or impersonal about the worldhood of the world, something that no more acknowledges the individuality of those who inhabit it than a public transportation system acknowledges the individuality of its passengers or a newspaper that of its readers. Heidegger emphasizes that Others appear to Dasein as producers, suppliers, field-owners and farmers, booksellers and sailors—as bearers of social roles; and they are judged in terms of how well they carry out their roles. Their identity is given primarily by their occupation, by the tasks or functions they perform; who they are to us is a matter of what they do and how they do it. But these matters are defined purely impersonally: given the necessary competence, which individual occupies the role is as irrelevant as are any idiosyncrasies of character or talent that have no bearing on the task at hand. In effect, then, Others appear in our common world not as individuals but as the essentially interchangeable occupants of impersonally defined roles; and we appear to them in exactly the same way.

This reflects the fact that the world, understood in its worldhood, is a widely ramifying web of socially defined concepts, roles, functions, and functional interrelations within which alone human beings encounter objects as meaningful. And just as those objects must be understood primarily in relation to purposes and possibilities-of-Being embedded in cultural practices, so we must understand ourselves primarily as practitioners—as performers of socially defined tasks whose nature is given prior to our own individuality, and which will typically be unmarked by our temporary inhabitation of them. It must be possible for others to occupy exactly the same role as ours, to engage in exactly the same practice; the continuation and inheritability of society and culture requires it, and the very idea of a practice embodies the idea of its own reiterability. Hence the Being whose Being is Being-in-the-world must relate to itself as the occupant of roles in practices, and so begin to confront the issue of its own Being in the terms those roles lay down—terms which refer not to a particular person but to a set of functions, and so which specify not what you or I must do in order to occupy the role but rather what one must do, what must be done. The role-occupant thus specified is an idealization or construct, an abstract or average human being rather than anyone in particular—it is, in other words, a species of the they-self.

In this important but limited sense, the 'they' is an essential *existentiale* of Dasein. But of course, the individual who occupies impersonally defined roles need not always relate to them purely impersonally. A social role can be a vital element in an individual's self-understanding (as a vocation, for example); it can, therefore, be appropriated authentically, even if its essential nature does not ensure or even encourage such appropriations. Hence, for Heidegger, authenticity remains a real possibility for Dasein, but only as an existentiell modification of the 'they'—as an achievement that is a breaking or turning away, a reorientation or recovery from disorientation with respect to one's mode of Being-with-Others. Dasein always begins from a self-relation in relation to Others from which it must break away (the they-self), and this turning away is always also a turning towards, a modification rather than a transcendence of Being-with-Others; but such turning away is never ontologically foreclosed.

As they-self, the particular Dasein has been *dispersed* into the 'they', and must first find itself . . . If Dasein discovers the world in its own way and brings it close, if it discloses to itself its own authentic Being, then this discovery of the 'world' and this disclosure of Dasein are alway accomplished as a clearing-away of concealments and obscurities, as a breaking up of the disguises with which Dasein bars its own way. (*BT* 27.167)

These last sentences, with their talk of unconcealment clarifying the enigmatic and deconstructing disguises, recall Heidegger's introductory characterization of his phenomenological method and of the obstacles it faces. For if Dasein's average everyday mode of existence is that of the they-self, then that must be the average everyday mode of Dasein's philosophizing. The being to whose Being an understanding of Being belongs is capable of having established and maintained a fundamentally misconceived tradition of ontological inquiry precisely because those inquiries are typically expressive of Dasein's fallenness. Driven by curiosity, maintained by idle talk, and mired in ambiguity, the currency of philosophical inquiry will be as inauthentic, as indicative of lostness in the 'they', as any other aspect of human culture; more specifically, philosophy's repeated attempts to understand Dasein in terms appropriate to intra-worldly entities simply reflect Dasein's typically fascinated absorption in its world. Any attempt to retrieve an authentic ontological understanding will accordingly be a modification of philosophical fallenness; it will be experienced as subverting obvious and self-evident truths, its turning us towards Being as a turning away from common sense and ordinary language. In short, genuinely phenomenological questioning will, in its contesting of the disguises Dasein has imposed upon its own worldliness, appear as at once strange and strangely familiar, as returning to us that which we have repressed—in short, as uncanny.

BEING-IN: THROWN PROJECTION

29. If the world that Dasein discloses is a with-world, chapter 5 emphasizes that Dasein's openness to that world has two aspects or dimensions. 'Understanding' (which we examined earlier) picks out the ontological condition for Dasein's capacity to enact its existence, to project itself upon one of the existentiell possibilities that its personal and cultural circumstances make available and thereby actualize it (together with a specific grasp of the objects in its environment). *Befindlichkeit* (translated by Macquarrie and Robinson as 'state-of-mind') picks out the companion ontological condition for the situatedness of Dasein's projections of itself, for the fact that they always emerge from a particular way in which Dasein is affected by things, in which it finds that it and the entities it encounters already matter to it. In Heidegger's terminology *Befindlichkeit* registers the thrownness of Dasein's understanding—the passive or necessitarian aspect of Dasein's disclosure of itself and its world.

The phenomenon of *Stimmung* (translated as 'mood') is the most obvious existentiell indication of this existential affectivity. Depression, boredom and cheerfulness, joy and fear, are inflections of Dasein's temperament that are typically experienced as 'given', as states into which one has been thrown. We talk of moods and emotions as passions, as something passive rather than active, something that we do not inflict but rather suffer—where 'suffering' signifies not pain but submission, as when we talk of Christ's Passion or of his suffering little children to come unto him. Moreover, our affections do not just affect others but mark our having been affected by them; we cannot, for example, love and hate where and when we will, but rather think of our affections as captured by their objects, or as making us vulnerable to others, open to suffering.

Such affections are a pervasive condition of human existence. We can, of course, sometimes overcome or alter our prevailing mood, but only if that mood allows, and only by establishing ourselves in a counter-mood (tranquillity is no less a mood than ecstasy); and once in their grip, moods can inflect every aspect of our existence. In doing so, according to Heidegger, they determine our grasp upon the world, inflecting Dasein's relation to the objects and the possibilities among which it finds itself. Thus, a particular mood at once discloses something (sometimes, everything) in the world as mattering to Dasein in a particular way—as fearful, boring, cheering, or hateful—and discloses Dasein to itself—as afraid, bored, cheerful, or hateful.

Here, however, Cartesian thinking threatens to recur. For it is easier to accept the idea that moods disclose something about Dasein than that they reveal something about the world. The claim that someone is bored or cheerful may be said to record an objective fact about them (about their subjective state); but such a mood does not itself pick out a simple fact about the world—it is simply a subjective response to a world that is in itself essentially devoid of such significance. The idea, in other words, is that moods merely colour the world; they are projections upon it, not receptions of it. Heidegger wholeheartedly rejects this position—but not by simply contradicting the Cartesian claim, not by arguing that moods are objective rather than subjective in the Cartesian understanding of that opposition. His concern is rather to question that understanding of subjectivity and objectivity, to show that Cartesianism is blind to the true ontological significance of the categories it deploys. And he does so by invoking his analysis of Dasein's worldliness: 'A mood is not related to the psychical . . . and is not itself an *inner condition* which then reaches forth in an enigmatical way and puts its mark on things and persons . . . It comes neither from "outside" nor from "inside", but arises out of Being-in-the-world, as a way of such Being' (*BT* 29.176).

30. Heidegger's questioning of these categories occurs on two levels: first, he questions our unthinking interpretations of both the 'subjective' and the 'objective' dimensions of moods, in so far as they are directed towards objects in the world; and second, he places the applicability of the distinction itself in question, in so far as moods are directed towards the world as such. Of course, these two levels of investigation

are internally related, since a mood's capacity to disclose objects is ultimately comprehensible only because moods can disclose a world; but an analytical separation of these issues may make their full implications clearer.

The first level of the investigation is grounded in a detailed analysis of the specific mood of fear. Heidegger sees this as having three basic elements: that in the face of which we fear, fearing itself, and that about which we fear. That in the face of which we fear is the fearful or the fearsome—something in the world which we encounter as detrimental to our well-being. Fearing itself is our response to something fearsome; and that about which we fear is of course our well-being or safety—in short, ourselves. Thus fear plainly has a subjective dimension: it is a human response to the world, and one which has the existence of the person who fears as its main concern. This reflects the fact that Dasein's Being is an issue for it; more precisely, it reveals yet another facet of the meaning of that characterization—the way in which the sheer continuance of one's existence as well as its form or mode can become questionable for us, can suddenly be threatened, and hence matter absolutely to us. In this sense, moods exemplify Dasein's disclosive self-attunement. But fear also has what might be called an objective dimension: for what puts Dasein's Being at issue here is something in the world—a gun, a virus, a rabid dog—that can pose a genuine threat. In this respect, Dasein's capacity to respond to things as fearful is attuned to something real, to (aspects of) things that really are capable of affecting Dasein.

For Heidegger, since Dasein's Being is Being-with, the self-disclosive aspect of moods—their subjectivity—must be understood as importantly intersubjective or social. He is, for example, happy to talk of moods as themselves social: Dasein's membership of a group might well lead to it being thrown into the mood that grips that group, finding itself immersed in its melancholy or hysteria. More fundamentally, however, the range of moods into which Dasein can be thrown—the articulation of its affective possibilities—is itself socially and culturally inflected (as is the range of existentiell possibilities upon which it can project itself).

Charles Taylor has developed this point using Heidegger's tripartite analysis of mood.[4] Taylor argues that an emotion such as shame is essentially related to a certain sort of situation and to a particular response to it: a feeling of shame just is one that finds expression in distinctive forms of behaviour (hiding or covering up) in distinctive situations

---

[4] See his *Philosophical Papers*, i (Cambridge University Press: Cambridge, 1985).

(shameful or humiliating ones). Hence, such feelings can fit or fail to fit their context, but they cannot be identified at all in the absence of the types of situation that give rise to them. But the significance of the term we employ to characterize the feeling and its context is partly determined by the wider field of terms for such emotions and situations in which it plays a part. Describing a situation as 'fearful' will mean something very different depending upon whether or not the available contrasts include such terms as 'terrrifying', 'worrying', 'disconcerting', 'threatening', 'disgusting'; the wider the field, the finer the discriminations. Accordingly, the significance of the situations in which an individual finds herself, and the import of her emotions, is conditioned by the range and structure of the vocabulary available to her for their characterization.

For Heidegger, this range and structure reflects the articulations of the field of meaning which underlies the worldliness of Dasein. No one in late twentieth-century Europe can experience the pride of a Samurai warrior; but that is not just because a certain set of Japanese words or their equivalent is unavailable, or rather it is because that unavailability is part of a wider absence—that of a complex web of assignment-relations grounded in a field of assumptions, customs, and institutions. Suddenly inventing or importing words will not alter the social conditionedness of Dasein's moods: thinking or saying alone does not make it so. Moreover, not any definition of our feelings can be forced upon us, just as some we gladly take up turn out to be inauthentic or deluded; Dasein's Being is thrown projection, not just thrownness—is conditioned rather than entirely determined. But such words, together with the totality of cultural relations within which they have their significance, do not simply match or fail to match a pre-existing array of feelings in the individual; we often experience how access to a more sophisticated vocabulary and culture can make our emotional life more sophisticated. There is rather a potentially creative (and hence potentially debilitating) play between Dasein and its world here, as there is elsewhere in Heidegger's analysis; his hyphenation of Being-in-the-world indicates internal relations rather than simple identity, and hence embodies a complex and situated notion of subjectivity.

His companion notion of objectivity—of the way in which moods disclose the Being of other beings—is equally nuanced. For example, it incorporates elements central to a position developed by John McDowell.[5] For McDowell, any adequate account of the fearfulness

---

[5] See 'Values and Secondary Qualities', in his *Mind, Value and Reality* (Harvard University Press: Cambridge, Mass., 1998).

of certain things must invoke both certain subjective facts—features of human beings and their responses—and certain facts about the object of fear. A rabid dog is fearful because of the dangerous properties of its saliva; that saliva is, of course, only dangerous because it interacts in certain ways with human physiology, so invoking the human subject is essential in spelling out what makes the dog fearful—but that does not make its fearfulness any less real, as a bite from it would confirm. We need, in other words, to distinguish two different senses in which something might be termed 'subjective': it might mean 'illusory' (in contrast with veridical), or it might mean 'not comprehensible except by making reference to subjective states, properties, or responses'. Primary qualities are not subjective in either sense; hallucinations are subjective in both senses; and fearfulness (together with, on the standard—if questionable—account, secondary qualities) is subjective only in the second sense. In short, whether something is really fearful is in an important sense an objective question—as the fact that we can find some things fearful when they do not merit that response shows (e.g. house spiders). Accordingly, in so far as our capacity to fear things permits us to discriminate the genuinely fearful from the non-fearful, then that affective response reveals something about worldly phenomena.

MOODS: DECONSTRUCTING KANT

31. What fundamentally motivates these recountings of traditional answers to the question of the nature of subjectivity and objectivity is Heidegger's desire to put in question the traditional distinction between subjectivity and objectivity. In doing so, he implicitly deconstructs Kant's highly influential attempt to explicate and anchor that distinction in the *Critique of Pure Reason*;[6] and he does so by turning to his own advantage the aspect of the Being of moods that appears most seductively to invite the traditional interpretation of them as mere subjective colourings of the world—the fact of their givenness and hence of our apparent passivity in relation to them, our sense that we can be thrown into them without warning or control, without their onset or dissolution necessarily being triggered by any particular thing in our minds or in the world.

---

[6] Trans. N. Kemp Smith (Macmillan: London, 1929).

Kant begins his Second Analogy by noting that we distinguish in our experience between the order in which our senses represent different states of an object (the subjective temporal order) and the order of those successive states in the object itself (the objective temporal order). For example, when I successively perceive the various parts of a house, I do not judge that my perception of its basement must either succeed or precede my perception of its roof; but when I perceive a ship sailing downriver, I do judge it necessary that my perception of it upstream precede my perception of it further downstream. Since, according to transcendental idealism, I never apprehend objects in themselves but only successive representations of objects, I can judge that certain sequences of representations represent changes of state in the object (that is, I can experience an event) only if I can regard their order as irreversible—only, that is, if I subject them to an a priori temporal rule (the schema of causality). As a condition of the possibility of the experience of an objective succession, the schema is also a condition of the succession itself (as an object of possible experience). In short, the schema has 'objective' reality; its application alone makes possible both the experience of an objective temporal order and (of course) the experience of a merely subjective temporal order. In its absence, the very distinction between inner and outer orders of experience would have no ground.

However, Heidegger's emphasis upon moods as assailing us entails that those aspects of our experience are not tractable by this distinction. As Stanley Cavell has put it, discussing Emerson:[7] 'The fact that we are taken over by this succession, this onwardness, means that you can think of it as at once a succession of moods (inner matters) and a succession of objects (outer matters). This very evanescence of the world proves its existence to me; it is what vanishes from me' (*SW* 127). Kant claims that the possibility of distinguishing an objective from a merely subjective order of experience is anchored in an irreversibility or necessity of succession imposed on the manifold of inner sense by its subsumption under a rule. But when we experience an alteration of mood—our present cheerfulness assailed by the onset of depression, or fearfulness resolving into boredom—we experience that alteration as something to which we are irreversibly or necessarily subjected. According to Kant's argument, therefore, we must regard it as both a subjective succession (something to which we are subjected) and an objective one (something imposed upon us from without).

[7] See his 'Thinking of Emerson', in *The Senses of Walden* (North Point Press: San Franscisco, 1981); hereafter *SW*.

Staying with the terms of this opposition, we would have to conclude that the successions of our moods track transformations in the world as well as transformations in our orientation within it, or rather that the two kinds of transformation are internally related—not a surprising conclusion if the worldhood of the world is that which orients us. When, for example, our apprehension of the world as a cheerful place is annihilated by a sudden apprehension of it as dreadful, we find ourselves inhabiting a new world as well as a new stance towards that world; as Wittgenstein once put it, the world of the unhappy man is not that of the happy man. As Heidegger puts it: 'It is precisely when we see the "world" unsteadily and fitfully in accordance with our moods, that the ready-to-hand shows itself in its specific worldhood, which is never the same from day to day' (*BT* 29.177). The evanescence of our mood—our inability to credit our lost sense of good cheer—is matched by the evanescence of the cheerful or cheering world it revealed; and this mutual exclusion of moods and of worlds itself reveals something about both—that the world and our moods are mutually attuned, and that both can slip from our grasp.

One way of expressing this attunement would be to say that moods must be taken as having at least as sound a role in advising us of reality as any sense-experience has—that judging the world to be boring or dreadful may be no less objective (and of course, no less subjective) than judging an apple to be red or green. As Cavell puts it: 'sense-experience is to objects what moods are to the world' (*SW* 125). The problem with the Kantian attempt to ground the distinction between subjective and objective orders of experience is that it is exclusively geared to sensory experiences of objects and not to experiences such as moods; and by relying upon an impoverished conception of experience (a one-sided diet of examples), it is fated to generate a correspondingly impoverished conception of the reality which that experience reveals. In particular it accommodates the fact that our experience is of objects while failing properly to accommodate the fact that those objects are met with in a world.

In part, Kant's myopia resembles that of the Cartesians who model Dasein's relation to the world upon a relation in which Dasein stands to specific states of affairs encountered in the world; there is, in other words, a conflation between ontic and ontological levels of analysis—a tendency to treat the world as a great big object or a totality of possible objects of experience. Since the Being of the world is essentially distinct from that of objects, it should be no surprise that a definition of the distinction between subjectivity and objectivity that is attuned to our experience of objects should break down when we attempt to apply it to orders or aspects of our experience which are rather attuned to that which makes our experience of objects possible. Since, however, the world in its worldhood can only be understood existentially, it is not surprising that we should tend to think that those aspects of our experience which are attuned to it must be categorized as subjective rather than objective. It is Heidegger's implicit purpose to show that, just as the dual-aspect disclosedness of moods should prompt us to question what we take subjective (and hence objective) experience to be, so the existential basis of the world should prompt us to question what we take objective (and hence subjective) experience to be.

Ultimately, however, the questions that Heidegger raises for Kant's object-based conception of objectivity go deeper. For the basic principle of transcendental idealism is that 'the conditions of the *possibility of experience* in general are likewise conditions of the *possibility of the objects of experience*' (A 158/B 197), and the twelve categories of the understanding give us those conditions. But the implication of Heidegger's (and Cavell's[8]) accounts of moods is that these categories—functioning as they do to relate our representations of objects to one another—articulate our notion of 'an object (of nature)' without articulating our sense of externality. More precisely, they articulate my sense of each object's externality to every other (making nature a whole, showing it to be spatial), but not my sense of their (internally related) externality to me (making nature a world, showing it to be habitable). Instead, that idea of objects as being in a world apart from me is registered in Kant's concept of the thing-in-itself; and the problem is that that concept (or the concepts which go into it—the concepts of externality or world) do not receive a transcendental deduction. Kant fails to recognize that these concepts should be seen as internal to the categories of the understanding, as part of our concept of an object in general; and by dropping those concepts into the concept of the thing-in-itself, he makes it impossible to resist the sceptical conclusion that he is positing the existence of things, somethings or other, that we cannot know. Heidegger, by contrast, aims to overcome scepticism by providing something like a transcendental deduction of the concept of a world; and in doing so, he reveals that there are more ways of making a habitable world—more layers or aspects to it—than Kant's twelve categories allow.

[8] See *CR* 53–4.

AN UNCANNY EMBLEM OF
BEING-IN-THE-WORLD: ANXIETY

32. In chapter 6 of division I Heidegger begins by drawing together the various strands of analysis laid out in the preceding three chapters (dealing with Dasein's worldliness, its Being-with, and its Being-in respectively). As his terms for these elements of Dasein's Being insist, they are interrelated elements in the ontological totality or whole of Being-in-the-world; but he thinks that his successive treatment of each disguises their equiprimordiality and their unity, and so he requires a way of making that equiprimordial unity apparent—a way of making the form of his representation of Dasein's Being reflect that which it represents.

Heidegger is clear on the wrong way to go about this:

> it is beyond question that the totality of the structural whole is not to be reached by building it up out of elements. For this we would need an architect's plan. The Being of Dasein, upon which the structural whole as such is ontologically supported, becomes accessible to us when we look all the way *through* this whole *to a single* primordially unitary phenomenon which is already in this whole in such a way that it provides the ontological foundation for each structural item in its structural possibility. Thus we cannot interpret this 'comprehensively' by a process of gathering up what we have hitherto gained and taking it all together. (*BT* 39.226)

Heidegger rejects a constructive or atomist conception of ontological analysis as pseudo-philosophical—as sophistry. Ontological structures are not founded upon or composed from independently given and meaningful parts, as houses are built from bricks and timber, and rest on foundations; rather, each analytically separable element or substructure has its significance only as part of a whole, of a horizontally extended web of interrelations. So the unity of such wholes is not compositional, and a grasp of that unity cannot take the form of grasping its supposedly separate components and running or holding them together—of synthesizing a pre-given manifold in Kantian manner; hence Heidegger's attempt to represent that unity in his orderings of words must avoid any such synthetic form.

The correct phenomenological approach is rather to let a being be 'seen from itself in the very way in which it shows itself from itself' (*BT* 7.58); so he must allow the equiprimordial unity of Dasein's Being to show itself in and through a specific ontic or existentiell mode of its Being. He must locate a particular existentiell state that we can see as indicating the very ontological structures that it also presupposes—that can be read as a sign of the ontological (just as Heidegger takes car indicators to light up the worldhood of the very environments without which they could not function). If an understanding of its own Being belongs ineliminably to the Being of Dasein, there must be states of its Being in which it discloses itself in a far-reaching and primordial manner, even if the range and elementality of such disclosure simplifies what is disclosed in a certain sense (*BT* 39.226). Choosing to concentrate on states in which we are fully preoccupied either with intra-worldly entities or with pure introspection could be rich in detail; but each, in their opposing fixations on objects and the subject respectively, would tend to occlude the articulated worldliness of Dasein's Being—the very phenomenon we are trying to get into focus. Only a far less common kind of state, in which our ordinary concern with specific objects or psychological states fades out and the background conditions for such concern are highlighted (and thus at once more clearly disclosed and yet dangerously simplified), will give Heidegger's analysis the grounding in ontico-ontological reality that authentic philosophizing requires. And hence, only a portrayal of such a state that succeeds in conjuring up the ontological in the ontic could function as an epitome or emblem of everything that precedes it in *Being and Time*.

33. The state whose emblematic portrait Heidegger chooses to paint is the mood he calls *Angst* (anxiety or dread). Anxiety is not fear: both are responses to the world as unnerving, hostile, or threatening, but whereas fear is a response to something specific in the world (a weapon, an animal, a gesture), anxiety is in this sense objectless. Its distinctive oppressiveness lies precisely in its not being elicited by anything specific, or at least in its being entirely disproportionate to the circumstances which appear to have triggered it; either way, it cannot be accommodated by responding to those circumstances in any concrete way (e.g. by running away). He calls this anxiety's 'indefiniteness' (*BT* 40.231), thus echoing his opening characterization of average everydayness as 'undifferentiated' (*BT* 9.69)—as if indicating in advance the feature of this unusual mood that discloses a critical dimension of the medium of his analysis hitherto. For according to Heidegger, what oppresses us in anxiety is not any specific object or totality of objects but rather the possibility of such a totality: we are oppressed by the world as such— by the worldliness of our existence. Anxiety makes Dasein aware that it is always already delivered over to situations of choice and action which matter to it but which it does not itself fully choose or determine; it confronts Dasein with the determining and yet sheerly contingent fact of its own Being-in-the-world.

But Being-in-the-world is not only that in the face of which the anxious person is anxious; it is also that for which she is anxious. Dasein is anxious about itself—and again, not about some concrete existential possibility, but about the fact that possibilities are the medium of its existence, that its life is necessarily a matter of realizing one or other existential possibility. In effect, then, anxiety plunges Dasein into an anxiety about itself in the face of itself. In such a state particular objects and persons within the world fade into insignificance and the world as such occupies the background; we turn away from our typical absorption in the specific existential possibility and worldly array that confronts us, and are turned instead towards ourselves—thrown back upon the fact that our own Being is an issue for us.

In confronting Dasein with the fact that its relation to its own Being is questionable, anxiety at once highlights the fact that Dasein typically leaves that relation unquestioned and questions the necessity of doing so. In other words, anxiety indicates that authentic individuality remains a possibility for us despite our tendency to turn or fall away from that fact. Anxiety thus lays bare the basis of Dasein's existence as thrown projection fallen into the world. Dasein's thrownness (exemplified in its openness to states-of-mind) shows it to be already in a world; its projectiveness (exemplified in its capacity for understanding) shows it to be at the same time ahead of itself, aiming to realize some existential possibility; and its fallenness shows it to be preoccupied with the world. This overarching tripartite characterization reveals the essential unity of Dasein's Being to be what Heidegger calls *Sorge* (care): ahead-of-itself-Being-already-in(-the-world) as Being-alongside(-entities-encountered-in-the-world).

The process of progressive simplification (or rather condensation) here could not be clearer. Five chapters of detailed ontological analysis are compressed into a brief phenomenology of anxiety, whose results are then encapsulated in a single, sentence-long hyphenated phrase, which is in turn embodied in a word. Just as the project of *Being and Time* as a whole unfolded from a questioning introductory articulation of the simple idea of Dasein as the being who questions, and the project of division I unfolded from a questioning etymological articulation of the simple idea of Dasein as existing 'in' the world, so everything in Heidegger's text up to now is being folded back into the space of a single word. The gesture declares Heidegger's sense of the open-ended ramifications of discourse, the density of implication in each node of the grammatical articulations of intelligibility.

34. One implication folded into the idea of care is that of Dasein's uncanniness. Anxiety forces the realization that human life is always

conducted in the midst of objects and events, and that typically we bury ourselves in them—in flight from acknowledging that our existence is always capable of being more or other than its present realizations, and so that, for all our worldliness, we are never fully at home in any particular world. This uncanniness highlights the finitude of Dasein's freedom; Dasein is responsible for choosing its mode of life, but must do so without ever fully controlling the circumstances in which that choice must be exercised, and without ever being able entirely to identify itself with the outcome of any particular choice. It is always haunted by the choices it didn't make, the choices it couldn't make, and its inability to choose to live without the capacity to choose—the conditions of freedom for a finite creature, one that must inhabit a spatio-temporal world.

In effect, then, the uncanniness of anxiety reveals the world as one component of Dasein's finitude. By revealing the conditionedness of human freedom, anxiety demonstrates the externality of the world to its human denizens; for those conditions reflect the fact that human existence is essentially worldly or environed, that the natural world of objects and events is one which we inhabit, and so that the world must be thought of as both intimately related to us and yet separate from us. Furthermore, anxiety elucidates the relative autonomy of the world in the terms that we saw Cavell lay out earlier—as a matter of its being at once evanescent and permanent. The uncanniness anxiety induces shows that each particular arrangement of objects and events will be succeeded by others, so no such arrangement can be thought of as exhausting the significance of the world as such, which exists rather as the horizon of possibilities within which actuality is encountered. And yet, in so far as Dasein can be absorbed in the present arrangements of its existence to the point at which it loses its sense of itself as free to live otherwise than it does, anxiety also teaches us that the world answers to our conceptions of it—that its successions can be fixed or frozen, and so that the world is such that it constantly and obediently becomes what we make of it. In short, according to Heidegger's acccount of anxiety, the world's externality must be understood as its inexhaustible capacity to be all the ways our moods tell us it can be—its capacity to be apart from us and yet be a part of us.

Since the worldhood of the world is grounded in the structures of intelligibility that Heidegger labels discourse, anxiety's revelation of the world's relative autonomy also discloses the relative autonomy of discourse. If we look at the linguistic dimension of the articulations of discourse, this dependence becomes clear. For on the one hand, the grammar of our words individuates phenomena in ways that express human interests and human nature; the ways in which criteria tell one kind of object from another reflect the distinctions that matter to their users, their shared sense of what is natural and what outrageous, what useful and what pointless. Hence the worldhood of the world is internally related to human culture and forms of life—an articulation of Dasein's answers to the question posed by its own Being and that of other beings. Since, however, grammatical articulations neither correspond nor fail to correspond to reality (since, like rules, criteria cannot coherently be assessed in terms of truth or falsity), then their rootedness in what matters to human beings cannot undercut the world's independence from its human inhabitants. On the contrary: the world's autonomy finds expression in precisely that which the articulations of grammar make possible—namely, in reality's capacity to falsify putative descriptions of it, in the role it plays as the independent object of meaningful human assertions and hypotheses.

If, however, the nature of discourse accounts for the relative autonomy of the world, and if the world in its worldhood impresses itself on us through the evanescent permanence of our moods, then there should be a way of articulating a connection between moods and discourse—of seeing not only the discursive basis of moods but also the mooded or affective aspect of discourse. The discursiveness of moods is easy to see: for, as an aspect of Dasein's openness to beings in their Being, moods must be structured by the articulations of the field of meaning. The affectivity of discourse is less evident, but emerges if, for example, we recall that Wittgenstein's term for the mode of our ordinary agreement in the articulations of discourse is *Übereinstimmung*—a word that contains Heidegger's word for moods (*Stimmung*) and which invokes exactly the same notion of attunement to the world. For as Cavell has pointed out (see *CR* 31–2), the idea of agreement Wittgenstein thereby invokes is not that of coming to an agreement on a given occasion (say, to a contract), but that of being in agreement throughout (like being in harmony); human beings who agree in the language they use are mutually voiced with respect to it, mutually attuned from top to bottom. And since the criterial articulations of discourse register the distinctions that count for or matter to their users, then we can say that the mode of our attunement in discourse is a matter of passion as well as action—that it is internally related to Dasein's affectivity or *Befindlichkeit*.

We might think of this as Heidegger's concluding insistence upon the unity and the equiprimordiality of moods and discourse in Dasein's Being. If, however, discourse is essentially 'mooded', then the same must be true of the philosophical method which relies upon recounting the articulations of discourse—it must be true of Heidegger's phenomenological investigation. In other words, authentic phenomenological philosophy has an essentially passive or receptive aspect. It must take as given the discursive articulation of Dasein's Being-in-the-world, the network of mutual attunements that govern our access to beings in their Being. Those articulations are flexible and open-ended: each node can contain a multiplicity of structures, the relations between nodes extend beyond any surveyable context, and any philosophical articulation of a given aspect of that network can and must itself be questioned and subject to rearticulation. In other words, the precise nature and extent of these articulations is always an issue for Dasein, always open in various ways to its own determinations. Nevertheless, Dasein always finds itself already immersed in this field of significance, already oriented towards beings in their Being (including itself and other beings whose Being is Dasein) in accordance with some prior articulation of them, however provisional—on pain of utter disorientation and unintelligibility. Hence, when philosophizing, Dasein must always project its phenomenological investigations from within that of which it aims to give an account, and is accordingly always already indebted, essentially incapable of determining its own trajectory and resources *ab initio*. Phenomenology cannot be fundamentally self-originating or spontaneous; it is always essentially reconstructive and deconstructive rather than constructive.

This suggests a contrast with Kant's vision of the power of thinking. For Kant, experience is a function of combining concepts and intuitions, where concepts are based on the spontaneity of thought, and sensible intuitions on the receptivity of impressions. Thinking is therefore understood as a matter of synthesizing impressions, of the understanding taking up the given manifold of experience and constructing or imposing an organization upon it; the intellectual hemisphere is active and the intuitive hemisphere passive. In short, for Kant there is no intellectual intuition. For Heidegger, by contrast, true thinking is passive or receptive. Just as one can only overcome scepticism by recognizing that the world is not to be known or grasped in cognition but accepted or acknowledged as the condition for the possibility of knowledge claims, so more generally one can make philosophical progress only by recalling the structures of discourse, by accepting them—if only for the purposes of radical questioning. In effect, for Heidegger there is only intellectual intuition; and this phenomenological receptivity is a reflection of the fact that human beings are creatures who lead their lives in a world which matters to them, a world which is at once evanescent and permanent, and revealed as such by the mutual attunement of moods and world.

A SCEPTICAL MOOD

35. We can now at last ask how this ontological recounting of the links between worldliness, Being-with, and Being-in, as emblematized in anxiety, gives us a deeper understanding of scepticism. As we have already seen, at the conclusion of chapter 6, Heidegger claims that scepticism is essentially inarticulable—a confusion of discourse rooted in a confusion about discourse. In the course of justifying this diagnosis, Heidegger shows that a proper conception of Dasein's worldliness makes the sceptic's question inexpressible; in other words, he shows that a proper conception of the world shows its permanence—its being beyond even our most radical attempts to deny its beyondness or externality to us. On the other hand, his sense of scepticism as a threat that still requires diagnosis, as a seemingly perennial scandal, taken together with his demonstration that, on a Cartesian conception of our worldliness, sceptical doubts are not only articulable but irrefutable, implies that there is something inherently evanescent about the world—that it is capable of answering even to our conception of it as beyond our grasp, and so of vanishing from our grasp (in an apotheosis of self-concealment).

We might think of this as Heidegger's discovery of the simultaneous evanescence and permanence of scepticism: the sceptical impulse is at once self-subverting (its doubts annihilating a condition for the possibility of their own intelligibility) and self-renewing (an apparently ineradicable human possibility which affects those possessed by it with unutterable conviction). As a human possibility, however, it should itself be analysable in terms of the existentialia Heidegger discerns in Dasein; and its uncanny replication of the permanent evanescence of the world—its implicit responsiveness to the world in its worldhood—more specifically suggests not only that scepticism illuminates Dasein's worldliness but that it does so because it is inflected by a characteristic mood.

And of course, it is so inflected: the true sceptic, rather than the straw-stuffed figure of epistemology textbooks (and as Heidegger says, 'perhaps such sceptics have been more frequent than one would innocently like to have true when one tries to bowl over 'scepticism' by formal dialectics'; *BT* 44.272), is beset by doubts, she is in the grip of anxiety—scepticism just *is* how angst makes itself manifest in philosophy. But Heidegger characterizes anxiety as a fundamentally revealing existentiell state, 'one of the *most far-reaching* and *most primordial* possibilities of [Dasein's] disclosure' (*BT* 39.226), in which Dasein reveals itself as a worldly being whose Being is an issue for it; so sceptical anxiety must embody exactly that illumination.

The 'external world' sceptic feels an abyss to open up between herself and the world, a sense of its insignificance or nothingness; she experiences a hollow at the heart of reality, and an essential uncanniness in her own existence—a sense of herself as not at home in the world. The 'other minds' sceptic feels an abyss to open up between herself and others, as if their thoughts and feelings were withdrawing unknowably behind their flesh and blood, as if she were truly confronted by hollowed out bodies, mere matter in motion; she experiences a sense of herself as alone in the world. In either mode scepticism finds itself opposed to common sense, to the truths that average everyday human existence, with its absorption in phenomena and in the opinions of others, appears to confirm us in taking for granted; and in this opposition the sceptic both falsifies and discloses the underlying realities of human existence. For on Heidegger's account, we are essentially worldly, but we are also uncanny; we are essentially Being-with, but we are also individuated. Hence, the intellectual (call it the traditional philosophical) expression of scepticism, both in its denials of our worldliness and commonality and in our denials of those denials, conceals the truth of Dasein's Being; but the anxiety of which it is the expression, in its aversiveness from worldly absorption and its existential solipsism (its *solus ipse*, as Heidegger has it, at once recalling and revising Descartes *BT* 40.233), reveals that truth.

Furthermore, the inarticulacy to which the sceptic's thwarted desire for connection with reality drives her makes manifest both the fundamentality and the contingency of the discursive attunements upon which Dasein's capacity to grasp beings in their Being depends. For the fact that the sceptic can unknowingly repudiate criteria shows that human attunements to discourse can become discordant, that they exist only if Dasein continues to invest its interest or concern in them, and that Dasein can effect such withdrawals of interest in the guise of the most passionate investment of that interest. The sceptic's self-subversion thus shows that human responsiveness to the articulations of discourse, in which the issue of Dasein's own Being is most fundamentally at stake, is not something to which Dasein is fated or with which it is automatically endowed (as if part of a pre-given essence that determines its existence) but is rather an inheritance for which Dasein must take (or fail to take) responsibility in and through its existence. In all these ways, then, in her sense of uncanniness and the eloquence of her inarticulacy, the sceptic suffers the truth of her existence as Being-in-the-world, even if she does not properly question or make a cognitive issue of how her passion might best be understood.

For Heidegger, what one might call the truth in scepticism finds its emblematic expression when someone gripped by anxiety says that what makes her anxious 'is nothing and nowhere' (*BT* 40.231). As we shall at least begin to see later, he will make this emerging sense of Dasein as fundamentally related to nullity and not-at-homeness utterly pivotal to his new beginning in division II (and if this appears fundamentally to oppose his intuition of human relations with the world to that of Wittgenstein, with his wish to return us and our words from metaphysics to the everyday, we should recall that if the everyday is that to which we must be returned, then Wittgenstein's philosophy no less than Heidegger's stakes itself on a perception of us as always already away from home, disoriented by and in our ordinariness). It seems, then, that Heidegger's decision to conclude his initial analysis of Dasein's Being by giving pride of place to anxiety is intended not only to affirm his general sense of phenomenology's methodological affectivity but also to declare that his method is inflected by a specific mood long associated with philosophical scepticism. There is, after all, no such thing as a concrete existentiell state of Dasein that is not itself informed by some mood or other—and that includes the concrete existentiell state of engaging in phenomenological investigations of Being. If the phenomenological investigator opens herself to sceptical angst, if, rather than dismissing it as utterly insignificant, she not only subjects it to serious phenomenological analysis but also allows its unpredictable advent in her existence to inform her sense of what matters in the field of her practical activity, then she will be receptive to the most far-reaching and primordial existentiell disclosure of the Being of Dasein; and what could be more likely at one and the same time to facilitate her attempts to seize upon the object of her investigation and to seize upon her own act of investigating—to make the exploration of Dasein's Being her own as a possibility of her Being?

It is, however, critical that the phenomenologist adopt a questioning attitude to her sceptical mood—in particular, that she not take scepticism's interpretation of its own significance for granted. She cannot, for example, accept the sceptic's over-anxious claim to know that the world is not knowable without acknowledging that the world cannot therefore be doubtable either; neither can she accept its account of the world as beyond our grasp, except in so far as the possibility of giving such an account confirms the permanent evanescence of that world. And this is not just a matter of intellectual error: after all, in so far as Dasein's Being is Being-in-the-world, any authentic attempt to live out one's scepticism about the reality of the world will inevitably turn back upon the sceptic, as if such despair about reality covers over a despair about oneself. As Heidegger puts it: 'if any sceptic of the kind who denies the truth, factically *is* . . . and has understood himself in this Being, he has obliterated Dasein in the desperation of suicide; and in doing so, he has also obliterated truth' (*BT* 44.271). Self-murder is here the annihilation of Dasein understood as a being who questions Being, who grasps beings as they truly are; the sceptic obliterates within herself the condition for the possibility of her sceptical questioning.

In other words, authentically sceptical phenomenology needs to wrest the disclosures made possible by its own mood from its self-concealments and dissemblings—it needs to overcome scepticism from within, to be sceptical about its own scepticism, to dwell in this mode of Being-in-the-world without being at-home in it. We might, indeed, regard this as an illuminating characterization of everything that Heidegger has been hoping to achieve in the first division of *Being and Time*; for we have begun to see that his thinking in those chapters is magnetized by—is sometimes dismissive of, sometimes scandalized by, but always responsive to and hence oriented by—anxieties about sceptical angst. In effect, then, for Heidegger, there is something fundamentally truthful about scepticism; phenomenological philosophy is and must be indebted to it, even if it must discredit scepticism's self-understanding in order to draw upon it.

THE ONTOLOGICAL MYTH OF CARE

36. I suggested earlier that Heidegger attempts to fold the whole of the teaching of division I into his not quite concluding tripartite characterization of Dasein's Being as 'care'. But of course, this systolic pressure prepares a diastolic response. The idea of 'care' not only incorporates what Heidegger has already established but embodies implications whose elaboration will take him into new territory; in this sense, the end of division I incubates the new beginning of division II. We have seen how the final sections of chapter 6 unfold one consequence of viewing Dasein through the lens of anxiety—a deeper understanding of scepticism, and a new sense of Dasein's uncanny nullity. Another obvious implication is a shift in emphasis from inauthenticity to

authenticity. Just as that mood breaks into Dasein's average everyday commitment to the they-self and opens the possibility of its overcoming, so Heidegger's analysis of that mood underlines his text's hitherto unquestioned restriction to the domain of Dasein's average everyday experience, and prepares us for his shift in division II to more explicit questions about Dasein's capacity to become itself. But the most fundamental shift in focus between the divisions depends upon an aspect of the definition of care that remains implicit in Heidegger's account until he quickly and briefly shifts its register from ontological analysis to myth.

Before reintroducing his obsessive concern with scepticism, Heidegger tells us that there is an ancient fable which embodies Dasein's interpretation of itself as 'care', and quotes the relevant Latin text. His translators' English version of that text runs as follows:

Once when 'Care' was crossing a river, she saw some clay; she thoughtfully took up a piece and began to shape it. While she was meditating on what she had made, Jupiter came by. 'Care' asked him to give it spirit, and this he gladly granted. But when she wanted her name to be bestowed upon it, he forbade this, and demanded that it be given his name instead. While 'Care' and Jupiter were disputing, Earth arose and desired that her own name be conferred on the creature, since she had furnished it with part of her body. They asked Saturn to be their arbiter, and he made the following decision, which seemed a just one: 'Since you, Jupiter, have given its spirit, you shall receive that spirit at its death; and since you, Earth, have given its body, you shall receive its body. But since 'Care' first shaped this creature, she shall possess it as long as it lives. And because there is now a dispute among you as to its name, let it be called '*homo*', for it is made out of *humus* (earth). (*BT* 42.242)

Heidegger claims that he cites this document purely to show that his apparently strange definition of Dasein in terms of care is in fact well grounded in pre-ontological human experience—that it has been part of Dasein's ontic interpretations of itself, even if not of its ontological investigations. But the text is plainly more than illustrative; it also makes more concrete certain aspects of the care-structure that Heidegger's more theoretical definition of it leaves implicit. For example, if Cura is Dasein's creator, then Dasein is the creature of Care: and any creature is doubly conditioned—it is created rather than self-creating, and conditioned by its mode of creation. Thus in saying that Dasein is indelibly marked by its maker, the fable implies that care is the unifying origin of the various limits that characterize Dasein's distinctive mode of existence. In effect, it emblematizes the conditionedness of human existence—the human condition—as fundamentally a matter of being fated to a self and to a world of other selves and objects about which one cannot choose not to be concerned. Similarly, the precedence the tale accords to Cura over Jupiter and Earth underlines the essentially unitary nature of Dasein's Being, its transcendence of decomposition, and so its resistance to any compositional or atomistic understanding of its nature.

Moreover, the fable offers guidance for the future that is not so easily to be drawn from the theoretical definition it is supposed merely to confirm or underwrite. To begin with, by characterizing Cura's creation of Dasein as 'thoughtful' and 'meditative', Heidegger's fable associates philosophizing with care—emphasizing that genuine thinking about Being not only takes care as its object but is itself a radical ontic realization of the care-structure. The fable also relates competing ways of understanding Dasein's Being to the question of Dasein's openness to death. When Saturn restricts the rights of Jupiter and Earth over man's spirit and body to the end of that creature's life, the fable implies that to grasp spirit and body independently of one another is equivalent to annihilating the existence of the creature they supposedly constitute; but it further acknowledges that subjection to death (and hence to birth) is part of Dasein's creatureliness, and hence that an understanding of Dasein's existence is impossible without an understanding of the mortality of that existence.

The topic of the first chapter of division II begins to emerge here, as does the basic concern of division II as a whole. For, as Heidegger underlines by pointing out that the ultimate arbiter, Saturn, is the God of time, the fable suggests that the Being of Dasein is under the sway of time, and thus indicates that division II will be devoted to a deepening of division I by rearticulating the structures of care in terms of temporality. In this sense, Heidegger's fable is the pivot of his whole book, explicitly conjoining Being and time in the manner promised by its title but only implied by his sentence-long articulated definition of care.

37. A further moral of the tale concerns the relation between language and essence—the question of how the name of a being relates to its Being. For although Saturn declares that Cura will possess the creature in life, he also declares that its proper name is 'homo'—an adaptation of the name for one of the elements from which it is made and into which its death will decompose it. It is of no little interest that the clay provided by Earth is deemed a more fitting source of Dasein's name than the spirit given by Jupiter; but most interesting of all is that Dasein's proper name consequently does not have its origin in Dasein's Being. According to this fable, then, the naming relation invites constituents or stuffs or entities as its object: as Augustine assumes, names refer to

things, and so cannot be taken as a clue to the Being of those things, or a fortiori to Being more generally. If language, then, is to recount beings in their Being, it must do so otherwise than by denotation—than by a careful accounting of the matter and properties of things.

How, then, is it to achieve such a recounting? The source of Heidegger's citation of the fable is its citation in an article by Burdach entitled 'Faust und die Sorge'—in other words, it is cited from a discussion which sites Heidegger's master-word at a confluence of literature and myth (Burdach's concern is with Goethe's indebtedness to Herder for the Cura myth which he works up into the second part of his great poem); and Heidegger introduces the fable into his text as a way of removing an appearance of strangeness in his more theoretical analysis of care. In other words, he implies that what may appear unfamiliar to philosophers is in fact the return in reflection of that which is entirely familiar to Dasein outside ontological inquiry. He thereby characterizes his provisional phenomenological results as uncanny (the return of the repressed familar), and as reintroducing us to that with which literature has long been familiar. It is as if philosophy is fated to struggle in order to recover that which literature always already possesses, even if not in a properly reflected form. And as we have seen, this fable not only provides an emblematic condensation of his preceding labours, but also contains the germ of his future inquiries—providing the second division of his book with an essential preliminary orientation. This would suggest that genuine philosophy progresses not only by putting literary texts in question, but by allowing such texts to put philosophical results in question.

This becomes more evident if—prompted by Heidegger's declared indebtedness—we look more closely at the ways in which Goethe's *Faust* incorporates, questions, and is questioned by the myth of Cura.[9] Towards the end of part II of that poem Faust commits his culminating crime: in order to acquire a unifying view of his newly colonized domain, he orders Mephistopheles to remove an old couple from their smallholding on a nearby hill; but his 'servant' exceeds his orders and burns them alive in their hut. Faust's rash command brings four Grey Hags to his door—Want, Guilt, Need, and Care. Care alone is able to gain entry to his palace; she and Faust argue over the nature and scope of her power over human affairs, until Care departs, cursing Faust by breathing on him and inducing blindness. He responds by redoubling his building work, but he dies very soon after, not knowing that

---

[9] J. W. Goethe, *Faust Part Two*, trans. P. Wayne (Penguin: London, 1959); hereafter *F.*

Mephistopheles intends the new colony to be handed over to Neptune rather than to the hard-working colonists of Faust's imagination. The drama ends almost immediately, with the elevation to heaven of Faust's immortal soul.

The general relevance of this myth of the human impulse towards epistemic overreaching, of a man who sells his soul for knowledge that reaches beyond all human conditions, to Heidegger's battle with scepticism is obvious; the confrontation between Faust and Care underlines it, when, for example, the latter talks of those whose 'resolve is lost in doubt' (*F* 266). However, other issues are also at stake. To begin with, Faust regards Care as his final or fundamental temptation, a figure representing a view of existence whose rejection he regards as the epitome of wisdom. In this scene Care paints a baleful portrait of her influence on human beings—an influence that the usual (non-Heideggerian, perhaps Augustinian) meaning of the word 'care' perfectly captures. She talks of careworn people as harbouring darkness in their souls: they lose all capacity to act, unmoved by the prospect of pleasure or pain, halting the passage of time ('for him no sunset or sunrise'; *F* 458); they are neither resigned nor despairing but 'swept along in pained let-live' (*F* 479), in thrall to the imperatives of others who are equally enthralled. And this thwarted straying, their uselessness and that of their world, is all due to the fact they are 'always on the future waiting, nothing ever consummating' (*F* 465–6)—in other words, they are paralysed by turning towards the future and away from past and present.

In effect, Goethe's Care dramatizes Heidegger's conception of the they-self, of how Dasein's care-structure is inflected when it flees from its world and the issue of its own Being; and it connects that flight to a specific mode of occupying time—one which looks ahead, curious for the next new thing, and away from the possibilities in the present that are opened up by the past. This is the diagnosis of inauthenticity that Heidegger will advance in division II. Faust opposes Care by emphasizing that human wisdom means rooting one's existence in 'the earthly round of men' (*F* 441): we must recognize that 'what's beyond is barred from human ken', and focus on enacting our own existence, acting on the knowledge that 'things he perceives are his to realize' (*F* 448)—only thus, he thinks, can we know the 'worth of being man' (*F* 450). Here we see at least some elements of a characterization of what Heidegger would acknowledge as authentic human existence.

However, Faust—unmindful of the fact that Care alone of the four Hags found entry to his palace through its keyhole, that she is the key to his inhabitation of the world—takes such authenticity or wisdom to require not (as Heidegger would have it) the modification or inflection of care, but its utter rejection: ''tis hard, I know, of daemons to be rid, the spirit-bond is difficult to sever; but you, O Care, in stealing action hid, creep with a power I will acknowledge never' (*F* 491–4). The action which brings Care to his door expresses a similarly unqualified denial, since the old couple on the hill whose death he causes are introduced by Goethe as having cared for a needy wayfarer, and thus as embodying the positive inflection of care (as solicitude) that Heidegger affirms. Hence Faust is immediately cursed: Care asserts her power over him, and does so by blinding him. Loss of vision is the most apt punishment for one whose overweening desire for a perfect view of his domains led to the death of the old couple; and that desire, expressing Faust's ineradicably sceptical wish (against his own best judgement) for a perspective on his world which is not from within it—for an Archimedean surview of the human condition from beyond its limits—suggests that only by acknowledging Care could he ever truly plant his feet on the earth, and live out the life of authentic Dasein.

Since Care affirms her possession of Faust by blinding him, she implies that the proper medium for acknowledging her presence is not sight; and her opening introduction of herself (containing the claim that 'outward ear will never hear me, yet the listening heart will fear me'; *F* 424–5) explicitly declares that she speaks inwardly to her creatures, in a manner that is silent (to the outward ear) but nevertheless audible through inward suffering. The lineaments of Heidegger's coming analysis of the silent voice of conscience, first adumbrated in Socrates' silent overseeing of Plato's dialogue, are here discernible. And Goethe further implies that properly attuning one's inner ear to Care, properly acknowledging her power, would mean acknowledging her sisterhood— the three other Hags with whom she is affiliated, and their brother (see *F* 390). That would mean acknowledging the internal relation between Care and Want, Need, Guilt, and Death.

Faust is already committed to the importance of Want understood as desire: before acquiring wisdom, he says, he 'stormed through life . . . desire, fulfilment, then desire again' (*F* 437–8); but even afterwards, he claims that 'In forward-striving pain and bliss abide, he finds them who is never satisfied' (*F* 451–2). But he shows no sign of appreciating that this endless cycle of desire is fuelled by lack or need, and associated with guilt—a German term that connotes indebtedness, and hence a deficiency for which reparation must be made; indeed, his response to Care's curse is to commit himself anew to a frenzy of action, to a furious absorption in his colonizing work-world that Mephistopheles has always already undermined. One might say that Faust enacts a conception of care as needy or addictive desire—a conception that Heidegger distances himself from by repeatedly distinguishing his own conception of care from that of 'willing and wishing, or urge and addiction' (*BT* 41.238). Faust thereby avoids the connection between care and absence or nothingness, which is one aspect of the connection between Care and death—a connection that Mephistopheles unknowingly makes Faust's epitaph, when he declares over his dead body that he is 'gone, to sheer Nothing, past with null made one' (*F* 598).

Heidegger might, therefore, question Goethe's concluding affirmation of Faust's interpretation of want or desire (when the angels bear his immortal soul to heaven declaring that 'he whose strivings never cease is ours for his redeeming'; *F* 936–7); but Goethe's preceding dramatization of Care—his questioning encounter with the Latin myth—introduces a family of concepts (death, conscience, guilt, nullity) that go beyond the original myth itself, and that will be central to Heidegger's rearticulation of care in division II. Indeed, by choosing to invoke those concepts by conjoining himself to a specifically German tradition of dialectical encounter between philosophy, literature, and myth, he implicitly prefigures a further constellation of concepts in division II: that relating the fate of authentic intellectual inquiry to the destiny of a culture and a political community.

In effect, then, Heidegger's citation of Burdach's citation of Goethe's citation of Herder's citation of the myth of Cura (its multiple nesting recalling that of his opening citation from Plato) appears to declare philosophy's indebtedness to what one might call the literary rather than the denotative dimension of language. Even the word of power into or out of which he enfolds the results of his ontological inquiry—'care'—invokes a totality of relations rather than naming a thing or a property of things; and only when he breathes life into that word by relating it to its fabular or fictional personification as a creator of human life, and to primordial (or primitive?) literary appropriations of that persona, does his inquiry uncover the full range of the word's provisional guidance for the next phase of his investigations. We knew from the beginning that the object of ontological inquiry is neither an entity nor a property of entities; so if Being is to be made to reveal itself, its ramifying articulations must (in critical part) be made to appear through a questioning relation to the fabular, the mythological, and the figurative more generally. No more fundamental disagreement with Plato's Stranger and his hostility to mere appearance-making could be imagined. For Heidegger, a fable can be closer to the truth philosophy seeks than any attempt to represent the literal likenesses of things.

CONSCIENCE: THE SILENT CALL

38. We might, then, think of Heidegger's philosophical and literary analyses of 'care' as both the end of division I of *Being and Time* and the beginning of division II. The latter enacts a second turn around the hermeneutic circle first opened up by the former's provisional conception of Dasein as Being-in-the-world. Heidegger's aim is to deepen the analysis of that structural totality by revising or rearticulating it in terms of temporality—a concept or set of concepts that is at once new and yet emergent from the concepts that turned out to be implicit in the idea of Dasein's worldliness. The two chapters which open division II are thus at once a new beginning and a confirmation of what has already been established. They prepare the ground for Heidegger's explicit and detailed accounts of Dasein and temporality in later chapters by offering a more explicit and detailed account of certain key implications of Heidegger's previous analysis of anxiety and care—the notions of mortality and conscience in particular. Since these concepts also turn out to have a reflexive dimension, applying to the project and text which discovers them, they provide a suitable conclusion to this account of *Being and Time*'s indebtedness to Plato's *Sophist*, and its overarching concern with overcoming philosophical inauthenticity.

Heidegger's account of anxiety presented it not only as unifying his own analysis of Dasein's Being but as the pivot around which Dasein itself could transform its lostness in the they-self into a genuinely individual mode of existence. In revealing the ontological unity of Dasein's care-structure, anxiety also revealed the possibility of Dasein's recovery from the undifferentiated self-dispersal or dissemination characteristic of inauthenticity, and its achievement of the kind of articulated unity or selfhood that Heidegger means by 'authenticity'. The question Heidegger faces in chapter 2 of division II is: how can this ontological possibility be brought to concrete fruition in the life of a being whose individuality is always already fallen—lost in the 'they'? For in the absence of such attestation, Heidegger's theoretical declaration of that possibility lacks any true phenomenological underwriting. So: what existentiell state, if any, can and does disclose to fallen Dasein its own fallenness and the realizable possibility of its overcoming?

Heidegger's answer is: the call of the voice of conscience. As the ideas of 'call' and 'voice' suggest, he thinks of this phenomenon as a mode of discourse—a way in which Dasein discloses itself and its world to itself, but one which disrupts the idle talk of the they-self to which it is typically attuned. The voice of conscience must therefore do without novelty and ambiguity, and provide no foothold for curiosity. Otherwise its voice will be taken as an occasion for endless self-examination or narcissistic soliloquies, and so will be entirely perverted—one more victim of the they-self's repressions. Accordingly, its call must be essentially devoid of content: or rather, its transformative potential depends upon its calling to Dasein in a manner that goes beyond articulating a specific response to specific occasions of moral or spiritual challenge, beyond any concrete view of how to think or act in specific circumstances (the ontic dimension of conscience upon which we tend to focus our everyday attention, and which is of primary interest to theologians, psychoanalysts, and sociobiologists). As well as saying something in particular, there is a register of the voice of conscience that says nothing in particular, that addresses us by saying nothing: as Heidegger puts it, 'Conscience discourses solely and constantly in the mode of keeping silent' (*BT* 56.318).

If our hearing is attuned to this register, then we do not respond to it as a Dasein that has a specific public role or status, committed to a particular way of living, and with a specific identity in the eyes of others. Or rather, in addressing us with specific guidance about our concrete existentiell situation, conscience also addresses us as beings capable of and condemned to such situatedness—as beings whose Being is an issue for them, and is in each case mine: in other words, as beings for whom genuine individuality is a possibility. The voice of conscience summons Dasein before itself, short-circuiting its fallenness in the world by holding up every facet of its existence for trial before its capacity to be itself. Fundamentally, then, the voice of conscience calls forth Dasein to its ownmost possibilities without venturing to dictate what those possibilities might or should be.

This means not only that the voice of conscience addresses Dasein non-specifically, but that its own source or origin is non-specific. The one who calls or speaks in and through this voice has no identity beyond that of caller or speaker; that which summons Dasein to itself exists only as summoner. But phenomenally speaking, Dasein hears this voice within itself, and understands it as an aspect of itself; so must we not say that, in the voice of conscience, Dasein speaks to itself? Heidegger's endorsement of this thought is importantly qualified: 'Indeed the call is precisely something which *we ourselves* have neither planned nor prepared for nor voluntarily performed, nor have we ever done so. "It" calls, against our expectations and even against our will. On the other hand, the call undoubtedly does not come from someone else who is with me in the world. The call comes *from* me and yet *from beyond me.*' (*BT* 57.320). Dasein-as-addresser and Dasein-as-addressee must differ from one another, for the Dasein to whom appeal is made is lost in the 'they', whereas the Dasein who makes the appeal is not and could not be (if its silent voice is to disrupt the discourse of the they-self). Hence we experience the voice of conscience as placing demands on our will, as Categorically Imperative, as originating beyond ourselves; for the self it addresses has lost its hold not only on the concrete possibilities it enacts and confronts but also on its loss of hold ('the "they" even hides the manner in which it has tacitly relieved Dasein of the burden of explicitly *choosing* these possibilities'; *BT* 54.312). Conscience can thus give voice only in and as a differentiation within Dasein—a differentiation between Dasein understood as the bearer of expectation and will, and Dasein understood as suffering a call or summons: in short, between Dasein's active and its passive aspects or dimensions.

As Heidegger's emphasis upon the *voice* of conscience implies (*Stimme*, voice, recalling *Stimmung*, mood), the call of conscience is something we suffer; it gives voice to Dasein's thrownness—its always already being delivered over to the task of existing, placed in a situation that it did not choose to occupy but from which it must choose how to go on with its life. Thus, in the voice of conscience Dasein's uncanniness speaks: Dasein is recalled to the awareness that the state in which it finds itself is never all that it is or could be, and so never something with which it can fully identify or to which it should reduce itself. Dasein's lostness in the 'they' is manifest in its utter self-domestication, its feeling fully-at-home with whatever form of life and world it finds itself inhabiting, its refusal of any sense of itself as other or more than it presently is. The voice of conscience is experienced as coming from beyond me because it is the silent redisclosure of the possibility of the self's beyondness to itself.

39. The short-circuiting or non-specificity of Dasein's relation to itself in the voice of conscience resembles its self-disclosure in anxiety; hence we can think of the voice of conscience as the call of care, as the disclosure of the care-structure of Dasein's Being. And just as anxiety, in wrenching us from our absorption in the they-self, confronts Dasein with the not-at-homeness of its relation to the world, so the voice of conscience, in saying nothing, really says 'Nothing'; it discloses an essential nullity in Dasein's Being—a nullity Heidegger labels Being-guilty. We might think of his phenomenological exploration of this nullity as not only uncovering the existential grounding of a familiar existentiell state but also revealing the truth in scepticism; it is his attempt to attend to the sceptic's 'nothing and nowhere' as a call to authenticity in philosophy.

The word 'guilt' speaks of indebtedness: a guilty person seeks atonement, aims to make reparation for a deprivation she inflicted on others—which in turn presupposes that she is lacking or deficient in some way, and responsible for that deficiency. In other words, being guilty is a matter of being the basis of a nullity; and for Heidegger, that notion reflects the fundamental basis of Dasein's care-structure.

Dasein is always thrown into a particular state of self and world; its capacity for projective commitment must always be deployed from within a context over which it does not have complete control. Moreover, in projecting upon one particular existential possibility, Dasein thereby negates all other possibilities: the realization of one is the non-realization of all others. Hence, Dasein's existence as thrown projection amounts to the null Being-the-basis of a nullity: Dasein as such, beyond its ontic guilt for specific actions (which specific acts of atonement might eradicate), is guilty. This is what the reticent, anxious voice of conscience discloses: it invites Dasein to project itself upon its ownmost Being-guilty—to be, in Heidegger's terms, resolute.

This means (not overcoming or transcending guilt but) taking responsibility for the particular basis into which one is thrown and the particular projections one makes upon that basis, to make one's necessarily guilty existence one's own rather than that of the they-self. Resoluteness returns Dasein to its particular place in the world, to its specific concernful relations with entities and solicitous relations with others, in order to discover what its possibilities and necessities in that situation really are. According to the previous chapter's account of Dasein's mortality (its relation to death understood as a possibility of its Being rather than as a future event), any such discovery requires seeing those circumstances as those of a mortal being. A mortal being is one whose existence is contingent (its present modes of life no more than the result of past choices), whose non-existence is an omnipresent possibility (so that each of its choices might be its last), a being with a life to lead (its individual choices contributing to, and so conditioned by, the life of which they are a part), and one whose life is its own to lead (so that its choices should be its own rather than that of determinate or indeterminate others). Only thus can our sense of what is changeable and what unchanging in our circumstances be tested; only thus can we discover whether and how we have treated as necessary what might be otherwise, or incoherently yearned to be released from that which conditions our existence.

Resoluteness cannot, therefore, be treated simply as a matter of generating concrete answers to existentiell questions. More fundamentally, it gives existential definition to a context that has hitherto been volatilized by the ambiguity, curiosity, and novelty-hunger of the

they-self; it constitutes Dasein's place in the world as a genuine existential 'Situation', one in which it can pose definite questions to which
Dasein can give (or fail to give) an answer. Resoluteness thus means not
only projecting upon whatever existential possibility is most authentically one's own, but projecting one's context as possessed of a definite
range of existential possibilities in the first place. Resoluteness constitutes the context of its own activity.

Likewise, the voice of conscience does not primarily seek a response
in which we adopt some particular schedule of moral rights and wrongs,
some specific calculus of spiritual debt and credit: it seeks the response
of responsiveness, the desire to have a conscience, a willingness to be
appealed to by its voice. To live resolutely, as mortal, as Being-guilty, is
thus to put oneself in servitude to one's capacity for individuality: it is
to choose oneself—to choose the uncanniness of self-differentiation or
beyondness to oneself rather than self-identity, to choose selfhood as
opposed to its absence. Heidegger's concern is thus not with the usual
questions of moralists and moral philosophers (who, in addressing questions about what it is right and wrong for individuals to do, take it for
granted that there really are individuals in the world for whom their
answers might have pertinence), but with one of their presuppositions.
His text gives voice to an issue that is both within and beyond morality, attempting to induce an anxious differentiation between moral
thinking as it is and as it could and should be.

LOCATING THE VOICE OF CONSCIENCE

40. A certain anxious reticence is, however, present in these pages in
ways that go beyond this. For it is questionable whether Heidegger's
analysis of conscience succeeds in answering the question that first
prompted it, concerning an existentiell attestation of Dasein's capacity
to attain authenticity. Heidegger tells us that the voice of conscience is
the call of Dasein's repressed but not extinguished capacity for genuine
individuality; but if that capacity is genuinely repressed, how can it possibly speak out? To do so, its repression must already have been lifted;
but it is just that lifting which the call of conscience is supposedly
invoked to explain.

Heidegger thinks of Dasein as doubly ontologically split or doubled
with respect to its own individuality. On the one hand, any Dasein is
capable both of being authentic and (hence) of being inauthentic; on the
other, he conceives of authenticity in terms of the self's differentiation

from itself, its relating to itself as always more or other than it presently is—a self-relation that goes into eclipse in inauthentic states, when the self's falling into fascinated absorption with its world ensures that it thinks of itself as coinciding with itself, as being all that it could be. To hear the voice of conscience is to recover one's sense of one's own un-canniness or non-self-coincidence; but that is in itself an indication of having attained an authentic relation to one's Being, and so can hardly function as the means of that attainment.

Heidegger's problem originates with his emphatic declaration that 'the call [of conscience] undoubtedly does not come from someone else who is with me in the world' (*BT* 57.320). For this commits him to the view that the transition from inauthenticity to its opposite is and must be brought about by the self's own resources. But the coherence of this vision of the self-overcoming of self-imposed darkness is questionable; for only two possibilities are thereby left open. Either the very capacity of the self which is in eclipse brings about its own emergence from eclipse; or the capacity at present eclipsing the self's capacity for authen-ticity might place itself in eclipse. Both operations seem essentially self-subverting; neither seems intelligible.

The problem disappears once we put in question what Heidegger uncharacteristically assumes is beyond question—the idea that the call of conscience does not come from someone else in the world, from a third party. After all, Dasein's Being is essentially Being-with, and Heidegger's earliest discussion of this structure identifies a mode of solic-itude for Others in which, rather than taking over from the Other that with which it is most properly to concern itself, Dasein helps the Other to become transparent to itself in, and to free itself for, that self-concern (*BT* 26.158–9). Moreover, Heidegger specifically notes in passing that 'Dasein . . . can become the conscience of Others' (*BT* 60.344), and refers to the voice of conscience as 'the voice of the friend whom every Dasein carries with it' (*BT* 34.206). What, then, if the call of conscience is articulated by someone else, a friend who diagnoses us as lost in the they-self and has an interest in our overcoming that inauthenticity and freeing our capacity to live a genuinely individual life?

The intervention of such a person would disrupt the hermetic, self-reinforcing dispersal of Dasein in the they-self from without, recalling the self to its own possibilities without requiring an incoherent process of internal bootstrapping. Ontologically speaking, there is no self–other differentiation in the they-self, and so no internal self-differentiation in its members; each Dasein mirrors every other Dasein by conflating its existential potential and its existentiell actuality, repressing its uncanni-ness. When, however, it encounters an authentic friend, her mode of existence disrupts the undifferentiated mass of the 'they'; her selfhood is not lost in a slavish identification with (or differentiation from) others, so she cannot confirm Dasein in its anonymity by mirroring it, and she prevents Dasein from relating inauthentically to her. For Dasein could mirror another who exists as separate and self-determining, and who relates to others as genuinely other, only by relating to her as other and to itself as other to that other—that is, as a separate self-determining individual. This amounts to Dasein acknowledging the mineness of its existence, and so its internal self-differentiation (the uncanny non-coincidence of what it is and what it might be). In short, an encounter with a genuine other disrupts Dasein's lostness by awakening otherness in Dasein itself; the relation that that other establishes with Dasein instantiates a mode of Dasein's possible self-relation—a relation to itself as other, as not self-identical: the otherness from, in, and of which the voice of conscience speaks.

The sheer fact of the friend's existence can thus disrupt Dasein's lost-ness in the they-self, and create in those to whom she relates herself the conditions for the audibility of her call to individuality. Such a friend would, in a sense, be speaking from outside or beyond us; but if her aim is to help us recover our capacity for selfhood, our autonomy, she could not consistently wish to impose upon us a specific blueprint for living, or in any other way substitute a form of servitude to herself for our present servitude to the 'they' (any more than Wittgenstein could present himself as advancing theses, or as drawing upon a specific exper-tise unavailable to his readers, or as founding a philosophical school). On the contrary: her only aim would be that of recalling us to the fact of our capacity for individuality and urging us to listen to the specific demands it makes upon us. In doing so, she would function as an exter-nal representative of an aspect of ourselves, her voice going proxy for the call of our ownmost potential for authenticity, a call that is at present repressed but which nonetheless constitutes our innermost self; in that sense, she would be speaking from within us. Hence, such a voice would perfectly fit the (transferential and counter-transferential) phenomenol-ogy of the voice of conscience as Heidegger defines it—its origin at once beyond and within me.

THE VOICE OF PHILOSOPHY'S CONSCIENCE

41. These further implications of the idea of the voice of conscience give further specificity to my earlier claim that Heidegger thinks of the

sceptic's 'nothing and nowhere' as a philosophical inflection of the 'Nothing' of and through which the voice of conscience always speaks. They suggest, for example, that we might think of philosophical scepticism as differentiated from itself, as always already split between its doctrinal or systematic realization and the anxious mood of which those doctrines are the intellectual expression; its philosophical authenticity resides in its beyondness to its own self-image, in the uncanniness that speaks silently before and beyond its assertions. They further suggest that we might think of scepticism as representing an aspect of ourselves, both in its anxious receptivity to our uncanny individualization and in its intellectualized flight from that apprehension. If so, then authentic, phenomenological philosophizing must mean being prepared to acknowledge the sceptic within us—which means being prepared to give voice to the anxieties that we typically repress by projecting them outside ourselves, to let them find their natural expression, and then of course to find a way beyond those expressions, to find a way of articulating them otherwise.

There is, however, another, more general reflexive register to Heidegger's account of conscience whose anxious reticence we ought to overcome. For of course, his conception of Dasein as split, with its capacity for authenticity eclipsing or being eclipsed by its capacity for inauthenticity, is intended to apply to his readers. As students of philosophy, we will be immersed in the prevailing modes of that discipline; and since philosophizing is a mode of Dasein's Being, its everyday enactments will be as imbued with inauthenticity as will those of any human activity. In short, Heidegger conceives of the readers of *Being and Time* as inauthentic, although capable of authenticity. Since, however, outlining an insightful fundamental ontology of Dasein would necessarily be an achievement of authentic philosophizing, and since that is precisely what *Being and Time* claims to develop, Heidegger implicitly presents himself as having achieved an authentic mode of human existence (while not being immune to the temptations of inauthenticity). Furthermore, since providing such a fundamental ontology to his readers amounts to an attempt to facilitate their transition from inauthentic to authentic philosophizing, the form of Heidegger's relation to his readers precisely matches the modified model of conscience that I have just articulated. Heidegger thus appears as the voice of conscience in philosophy, offering himself as an impersonal representative of the capacity for authentic thinking that exists in every one of his readers, presenting them not with specific philosophical or ethical answers but with a portrait of themselves as mired in unquestioning inauthenticity, in order to recall them to knowledge of themselves as capable of authentic thought, and thereby to encourage them to overcome their repression of that capacity by asking questions for themselves. In short, Heidegger's words offer themselves (just as Wittgenstein's words offer themselves) as a pivot for their reader's self-transformation, at once a mirror in which their present disorientation is reflected back to them and a medium through which they might overcome it.

Perhaps one might more accurately say that Heidegger's words hold out the possibility of being taken in this way—that they secrete a possible conception of their own task, and hence a possible self-conception for their author, to which both author and words do not always attain. For of course, Heidegger emphatically denies that the voice of conscience is ever the voice of an actual other, a third party; and in doing so he maintains his attachment to the idea that a given individual can manage the transformation from inauthenticity to authenticity with his own resources—that Dasein can originate its own rebirth. But of course, as the author of a genuine fundamental ontology of Dasein, Heidegger lays claim to authenticity as a philosopher, and hence to having managed the transition from inauthenticity. So his unmodified model of conscience allows him to present himself as having done so entirely out of his own resources, as having single-handedly created his fundamental ontology and his deconstruction of the philosophical tradition of the West.

His achievement thus appears as his alone—an appearance enhanced not only by his inconsistently observed reticence about the truth in philosophical expressions of scepticism (as opposed to his lengthy and systematic indictments of its falsehood), but also by his decision (in his introductory chapters) almost entirely to repress the role that his teacher Husserl played in the origination of his own thinking, to repress the voice of conscience that Husserl clearly represented for him. It is the depth of Heidegger's need to think of himself as self-originating (a particularly striking inflection of the inauthentic assumption of self-coincidence) that leads him to deny that his model of conscience can also account for the relation in which he stands to his readers; for how can he explicitly declare that, while others require the intervention of his voice to reactivate their potentiality for authenticity, he alone stood in no such need—that he benefited from no one in the way his readers will benefit from him?

42. However, to say that Heidegger's actual text does not always live up to its own best possibilities is not to say that it always fails to do so. We have already seen traces, even within his account of conscience, of an acknowledgement of the resources it contains for its own modifica-

tion; and elsewhere in division II of *Being and Time* those hints are transformed into a far more explicit and detailed enactment of that modification. Perhaps unsurprisingly, this realization of Heidegger's beyondness to himself is made concrete through another extended act of citation, with consideration of which this recounting of *Being and Time* can come to a provisional conclusion.

The citation occurs in section 77, with which Heidegger concludes chapter 5 of division II—a chapter that focuses on the way in which the temporality of Dasein's Being is made manifest both in the historicality of Dasein's existence and in its engagement in the study of history. Heidegger's central concern is with the interconnection of these two themes. According to his account, true historical inquiry allows past, present, and future reciprocally to question and illuminate one another: to disclose a past possibility as it really was is to reveal it as something other than it is typically taken to be in a present controlled by the they-self, and to reconceive the future (one's fate as an individual and the destiny of one's community) in its light. Hence, true history (historiology) is both a preparation for and a manifestation of Dasein's resoluteness. Since she is herself an essentially historical (or historizing) being, the historian can only do her job authentically if she is herself authentic; her capacity to grasp the particular past possibility which embodies the best destiny of her community presupposes that she has a resolute grasp of her own present and future in the light of her past. But her capacity so to disclose her own fate depends in critical part on the possibilities opened up for her and her community by historical inquiry.

If historiology and historizing thus form a circle of mutual presupposition, it is always either vicious or virtuous. Either the absence of authentic historizing blocks off the possibility of authentic historiology and is reinforced by doing so, or its presence brings about authentic historiology and thereby reinforces its own reality and wider dissemination. But this circularity suggests a paradox similar to our earlier difficulty with conscience (indeed, identical with it, since conscience calls for authenticity from and to Dasein in its historicality): if authentic historizing presupposes authentic historiology, but only an authentically historizing Dasein can engage in authentic historiology, how can authentic historiology ever get started?

In sections 76 and 77 Heidegger resolves the paradox by silently but deliberately committing himself to the modified model of conscience I articulated earlier. For in that section he suddenly (and, within the precincts of *Being and Time*, uniquely) introduces a cluster of predominantly respectful references to other thinkers. At the end of section 76 Nietzsche takes the stage as someone whose analysis of the 'use and abuse of historiology for life' contains in embryo the core of Heidegger's own analysis; and the whole of section 77 is devoted to an admiring discussion of Wilhelm Dilthey's and Count Yorck von Wartenburg's conceptions of the human sciences in general and the science of history in particular.

Taken in isolation, much about this section appears deeply puzzling. First, and assuming the accuracy of Heidegger's account of Dilthey and Yorck, it adds nothing to the conclusions already established earlier in the chapter; at best it shows only that they were in some very dim and indirect ways presaged in the work of these two men. Second, despite the fact that Heidegger interprets Yorck as clarifying the underlying message of Dilthey's work, the copious quotations Heidegger assembles from Yorck's letters to Dilthey have a continuously critical tone. Third, the discussion focuses upon what seem very marginal texts: instead of examining Dilthey's more famous works, Heidegger's attention is on Yorck—and on Yorck's letters at that. And finally, Heidegger's own voice virtually disappears from these concluding pages; his purported discussion of Dilthey's and Yorck's thought is in fact little more than a sequence of quotations from Yorck.

Placed in the context of his earlier analysis of conscience, these difficulties disappear; for what Heidegger is offering is an example of how the voice of conscience can break in upon historiology. Yorck's letters to Dilthey are his attempt to point out for his friend's benefit how he might break free from a broadly inauthentic understanding of historiology and historicality by developing those aspects of his views that are closest to what Yorck sees as the truth of these matters. His questioning is thus not coercively and futilely external—there is no failure to respect his friend's autonomy; it is rather calibrated to those aspects of Dilthey's own world-view that have the most potential for positive internal development. And by presenting himself as disclosing points already implicit in Dilthey's own work, as in effect his friend's best interpreter, Yorck shows that his own position is not based upon superior expertise. On the contrary, he implies that he could not have attained the position from which he criticizes his friend without standing on his friend's shoulders—that his position is nothing more than Dilthey's own best possibility, that of himself which goes beyond himself, his unattained but attainable self (as Cavell might put it[10]).

Heidegger's citation thereby implies more generally that progress towards authenticity in any part of human existence is essentially historical. Yorck's further progress towards the existential truth about

---

[10] *CHV.*

the science of history and human existence is itself produced by a questioning appropriation of possibilities disclosed by the past. In Heidegger's terminology, his position is the result of repeating the past in a moment of vision about the present that is oriented towards the best destiny of himself *qua* historian, the discipline of which he is a member, and the culture of which that discipline is such an important component. Thus, the final implication of Yorck's example is that for the practitioner of any discipline to be authentic is for her to act as the voice of conscience to the past (and thus to the present and future) of her discipline and culture—to question the past from the perspective of its own best possibilities with a view to galvanizing the present from the perspective of its destined future.

By placing this account of Dilthey and Yorck at the end of his own investigation of historiology and historicality, Heidegger presents Yorck's position as an unresolved precursor of his own, and thereby places Yorck in exactly the position that Yorck places Dilthey (a position structurally reminiscent of that in which Augustine is placed by Wittgenstein). Heidegger offers an implicit critique of Yorck, but one that presents itself as internal, devoted to developing Yorck's own best possibilities, and so as one to which Heidegger himself could not have attained without Yorck's own help and example. He thus offers himself as the voice of conscience to Yorck, as an example of authentic historiology (someone capable of recovering the discipline's destiny even from such unpromisingly marginal documents as private correspondence), and as attempting thereby to befriend his culture—to turn it away from its present forgetfulness of its past and towards its best future. But in doing so, Heidegger silently acknowledges that his own best insights did not spring fully formed from his own intellect. He presents Dilthey and Yorck as the voice of conscience that awakened him from inauthenticity, and thus rescues from self-subversion his implicit claim to be the authentic voice of philosophical conscience to his readers by withdrawing his earlier implication that he occupies a position of personal superiority or expertise over that of his readers.

But this reticent section of *Being and Time* does more than embrace the modified model of conscience; it elaborates that model by historizing it. This can be seen as prompted by the worry that the idea of the friend as resolving the problem of bootstrapping inauthentic Dasein into authenticity might appear simply to displace that problem onto the friend: for if inauthentic Dasein's transformation to authenticity presupposes a friend, how did that friend attain authenticity? Heidegger's discussion of Dilthey and Yorck suggests the following answer: through the intervention of another friend—Yorck can befriend Heidegger because he was befriended by Dilthey. One might, however, reiterate the question: surely such historical chains of friendship must have a beginning, a first link; and a first friend would necessarily be an unbefriended friend, someone who managed the transformation into authenticity unaided. But it was the impossibility of such a self-overcoming of self-imposed lostness that caused our problem in the first place.

The air here of a Kantian antinomy to do with uncaused causes, the sense that a fundamentally non-historical notion of origination underlies this anxiety, is not misleading. For a first or self-befriending friend would be required only in a world in which human inauthenticity was universal and absolute; and Heidegger's conception of human existence neither entails nor permits such a possibility. He does claim that lostness in the they-self is Dasein's typical position, even that it inherently tends towards fallenness because of the essential impersonality of its social roles; but this makes authenticity a rare and fragile achievement, not an impossible one. And no community of beings to whom an understanding of their own Being necessarily belongs could utterly lose a sense of themselves as capable of authenticity. Traces of this repressed self-understanding may be discoverable only in marginal or eccentric institutions, individuals, and texts or in the unquestioned margins and apparent eccentricities of central institutions, individuals, and texts; but some vestiges of it will survive for as long as the Being of human beings is Dasein, and will thereby ensure that chains of friendship are always already there to attract new members.

* * * * * *

43. Although the question of how to read Heidegger's philosophical writings as a whole has long been bedevilled by the search for a turn (or *Kehre*) in his thinking, a decisive break between the philosophy of *Being and Time* and everything that came after some supposed reorientation in the 1930s, more recent commentators—perhaps prompted by the increasing availability of the various texts Heidegger produced during the 1920s and 1930s and for decades thereafter—have preferred to multiply these hypothesized turning-points, at once increasing the number of analytically separable phases of Heidegger's thought and acknowledging the indebtedness of each such phase to its predecessors. This allows them to take seriously Heidegger's often expressed later view that, while he would not and could not take up the provisional conceptions of *Being and Time* as a fruitful starting-point for his present thinking, neither could that thinking be understood except through an adequate appropriation of the new philosophical beginning that *Being and Time* represented.

But of course, this view of thinking as at once both new and renewed, of the necessary situatedness of any philosophical originality, was always already implicit in *Being and Time* itself. Its second division is explicitly presented as at once a reappropriation and a radical revision of its first—a new beginning inherently indebted to the beginning that preceded it; while the originality of division 1 was itself explicitly presented as a radical return to the beginnings of the Western philosophical tradition, and to the potential for a new beginning that each great contribution to that tradition implicitly harboured. Since *Being and Time* thereby all but declares that to philosophize is a matter of endlessly beginning again, of opening new beginnings for thinking by reopening the possibilities bequeathed by (one's own and others') past thinking, then Heidegger's lifelong attempts to begin his philosophizing anew represent one fundamental respect in which his career as a thinker remains with a conception of thinking that is indebted to *Being and Time*.

Because of this, any attempt to take the full measure of *Being and Time*'s worth as a new philosophical beginning must question the worth of the new beginnings it makes possible in Heidegger's later work. But of course, any one of those new beginnings can be authentic (according to the terms established by *Being and Time*) only if it relates questioningly to itself and hence to its own indebtedness to Heidegger's first beginning; each must in its own way make an issue of its own point of origin, which means in part making an issue of the idea of beginnings and of beginning again. So the new beginnings that *Being and Time* made possible demonstrate the full worth of their origins only by submitting them to radical criticism; only by turning away from what they turn towards can they properly acknowledge their indebtedness.

These issues of originality and indebtedness are particularly sharply posed in the case of the renewed beginning enacted in the series of lectures translated under the title *What is Called Thinking?*; for they were originally delivered in 1951–2, at a highly charged transitional moment in Heidegger's career. They were the first lectures he had been permitted to give at the university of Freiburg since 1944, when he had been drafted by the Nazis into the *Volkssturm* (the people's militia), after which the French occupying powers had forbidden him to teach; they were also the last course of lectures he would deliver before his formal retirement from the university. In and through their delivery Heidegger returns to the responsibilities for teaching and thinking to which he had committed his existence and from which political issues had turned him away; and he does so as a representative of an institution whose founding claim is to represent those responsibilities. He is therefore doubly compelled to return to the underlying reasons for his banishment—to the political (and not merely political) judgement that he had betrayed his calling as teacher and thinker through his all too recent entanglement with the Nazi party's grasp on German society and culture.

How, then, are we to think about the fact that these lectures also mark Heidegger's turning away from any formal identification with the institution of the university? Does it symbolically underwrite the judgement that he had irrevocably betrayed his vocation? Or does it rather resonate with his judgement that the institution of the university has irrevocably betrayed its claim to represent the claims of teaching and thinking? Neither interpretation accommodates the fact that Heidegger's turning away from the university as a site for teaching and thinking takes place on that very site and so amounts to a turning towards it, that his refusal of the claim of the university is how he takes up the responsibilities of a teacher and thinker within its precincts. This suggests that, even though Heidegger's manner of teaching and thinking may subvert the institution's prevailing conceptions of those tasks, it is not intended entirely to reject either those conceptions or that institution. What seems rather implied is that true teaching and thinking is at once a turning towards and a turning away from prevailing conceptions of teaching and thinking—that the calling of the teacher, like the calling of the thinker, calls for the enactment of a transition from what thinking and teaching are to what they might become. In other words, the true thinker, like the true teacher, is always in the process of becoming what she is; she turns towards teaching and thinking as it really is by turning away from what she presently takes teaching and thinking to be.

BEFORE THE BEGINNING: A WORD-CHAIN

44. How, then (or more precisely, where), does *What is Called Thinking?* begin? The first lecture of this series devotes five paragraphs to what appears to be a prologue—a chain of thoughts designed to show that thinking must begin ('before all else', as Heidegger has it) with what is most thought-provoking, and hence with the assertion that '*Most thought-provoking is that we are still not thinking—not even yet, although the state of the world is becoming constantly more thought-provoking*' (WCT 4). The implication would appear to be that this sentence is the location of Heidegger's present attempt to begin

thinking anew. This implication is not, of course, simply to be denied; but when—a few pages further into the text—Heidegger tells us that we 'shall take a few practice leaps [into the neighbourhood where thinking resides] right at the start, though we won't notice it at once' (*WCT* 12), we might all at once notice that Heidegger's thought-provoking assertion is not in fact right at the start of his series of lectures, and so feel the need to ask whether, rather than leaping over Heidegger's supposedly preparatory but genuinely opening sentences in order to reach the official site for the commencement of thinking, we should instead turn back to them and attend to the possibility that we have already turned away from his first invitation to take a few practice leaps into thinking.

Lecture I actually begins with the following sentences:

We come to know what it means to think when we ourselves try to think. If the attempt is to be successful, we must be ready to learn thinking.

As soon as we allow ourselves to become involved in such learning, we have admitted that we are not yet capable of thinking.

Yet man is called the being who can think, and rightly so. (*WCT* 3)

The most obvious implication of these sentences is that the topic of learning and so of teaching will be central to Heidegger's enterprise; the main body of the first lecture and its summary provides abundant confirmation of this. A less obvious but equally important implication is built into the first of this sequence of sentences—a silent declaration that it is the first sentence in a set of (transcribed) lectures with a very specific title and subject-matter, and hence that one arrives at it only by a leap from elsewhere. For by making a claim about what is involved in coming to know what it means to think, it implicitly identifies its readers or auditors as people who think that they need to be told what is involved in thinking; and it can do so because its author knows that the 'we' he addresses would only have put ourselves in a position to be so addressed if we had been attracted by the title he has given his project. If we felt certain of what it means to think, if we really felt that we knew what is rightly to be called thinking or that what gets called thinking really is worthy of that name, then a set of lectures entitled 'What is Called Thinking?'—a title which promises to treat the matter as questionable—would not have interested us; we would not have picked up the book or attended the lecture.

Hence the opening sentence of Heidegger's opening lecture implicitly acknowledges its own belatedness or secondariness; by presenting itself as the beginning of an answer to a prior question, it makes it manifest that a condition for the possibility of its own orientation and existence is a prior initiating event, a seductive encounter between reader or auditor across a title that takes the form of a question. It thereby eschews any claim to truly originating status; and it suggests that philosophical thinking is something to which we must be attracted, that it originates more properly in being attracted to a question or to questioning what may seem beyond question than to the provision of an answer, and that a properly philosophical attitude towards such answers as may emerge in response to such questions is to put them in question by making an issue of their enabling conditions. Moreover, the particular enabling condition it underlines allows it to contextualize or situate itself in a particular way—as a moment in an encounter between an author or speaker and a reader or listener, an encounter between individual human beings who bear responsibility for their choices (of words and their orderings, of deeds and their consequences—particularly the choice of attending to another's orderings of words), an encounter that is itself mediated by individual, institutional, and cultural circumstances. The thinking that these words aim to encourage is not that of pure reason, not the cause or consequence of transactions between disembodied consciousnesses or with Platonic Ideas; thinking is something done by human beings—one of the many existential possibilities they may or may not realize.

The sentences following this first one develop Heidegger's diagnosis of the consequences of our having allowed ourselves to be attracted by his title. They stress that our presence to them declares that we lack any certainty about our capacity to think, that we are ready to try to think again, to learn what thinking might really be; our presence is an admission that we might not yet, not at present, be thinking or even be capable of thinking—that we are capable of thinking of ourselves as not yet capable of thinking, despite being the kind of being who is rightly characterized or marked by their possession of the capacity to think. Heidegger thereby diagnoses those he addresses as not having realized an essential part of their nature; and since he thinks of his orderings of his words as having 'allowed us' to admit this about ourselves, he further diagnoses us as ignorant of that fact, and as needing to overcome ourselves in order to become aware of it—in other words, as having repressed our present incapacity to think. We are not only not transparent to ourselves; we are divided against ourselves—capable of turning ourselves away from our own essential nature, eclipsing our own most authentic possibility.

Against the background of his hostility in *Being and Time* to the idea that human beings are possessed of an essence, Heidegger's willingness to talk of thinking as belonging to our essential being may give us pause for thought. And this hesitation is compounded by his seemingly untroubled citation, in his third opening paragraph, of a very traditional philosophical formulation of that point—one that the author of *Being and Time* would surely have thought ripe for interrogation. 'Man is the rational animal. Reason, *ratio*, evolves in thinking. Being the rational animal, man must be capable of thinking if he really wants to . . . [But] we are capable of doing only what we are inclined to do. And again, we truly incline only toward something that in turn inclines towards us . . . by appealing to our essential being . . .' (*WCT* 3). In fact, however, the sentences following the first in this quoted sequence do amount to a questioning of it. When Heidegger says that 'Reason, *ratio*, evolves in thinking', he implicitly raises the question of whether reason and thinking are distinguishable phenomena, whether the latter is rightly called reason or rationality at all; and by talking of reason as evolving in thinking, he claims that what we mean by the word changes over time—that the notion has historical roots (in, for example, the notion of 'ratio') and hence is indebted to a specific sequence of cultural formations within which it accrued the complex significance that it carries into the present.

But Heidegger's talk of evolution here has a further significance; for it resonates with a typically eclipsed implication of the traditional definition of human being, with the fact that a rational animal is the subject of evolution, is embedded in natural processes, because of its animality. Heidegger thereby implies that his account of human beings as beings who can think is a radical rereading of the traditional account; it is intended to embed human rationality within human animality, to show how the human capacity to think is an aspect of and so is indebted to their creatureliness. Philosophy typically distinguishes sharply between mind and body, between the timeless truths of reason and the spatio-temporal limitations of flesh and blood, between the spirit's active expression in the will and its inability to avoid undergoing the vicissitudes of sensation, emotion, and mood. Heidegger's aim is to prompt philosophy to evolve beyond that opposition, to allow itself to admit the embodiedness of the thinker into its thinking.

As an exemplary exercise in such thinking, the rest of his third paragraph develops by developing one implication of the thinker's creatureliness. Philosophy's dissociation of mind from body typically associates the body with desire, with the press of creaturely impulse and our dependence upon its satisfaction. Call this our capacity to 'want'—the capacity that Augustine, and Wittgenstein after him, make central to our inheritance of language and of philosophy. Heidegger begins his denial of philosophy's denial of the body by declaring that wanting is an essential condition for thinking, that our capacity to think depends upon our wanting to think, and hence that our not thinking is traceable to our not wanting to think. He then turns the notion of 'want' into that of 'inclination': he thereby announces a theme (of inclination and aversion, turning away and turning towards) that will play a critical role in the rest of the lecture, and since he finds the notion of 'appeal' within that of 'inclination', he simultaneously recalls the implication of his opening sentence that trying to think depends upon being attracted to it, upon finding it appealing and thereby admitting to an absence of present satisfaction, a lack.

Once sensitized to this unfolding chain of words, would it be going too far to think that Heidegger's third paragraph ends by invoking the ideas of 'memory' and 'gift' because of the former's invocation of re-membering, of knitting together or repairing the limbs of an organism, and the latter's invocation of givenness, of the mind's dependence upon the deliverances of the senses, its need to suffer the world's impress? How far can we trust the impression that these connections are not a fabrication, a projection upon language of our own wilfulness, but rather a revelation of the fact that words are always already knit together in language beyond our will and knowledge, and in ways from which we might derive genuine guidance if we can allow ourselves to learn from them? If we allow ourselves to think of this impression, not only as a rearticulation of *Being and Time*'s notion of the open-ended articulations of discourse, but also of that early text's impression of their moodedness or givenness, then we might further recollect Heidegger's early intuition that moods subvert the (traditional) distinction between subjective and objective experience, and ask ourselves whether our impression of the necessity in Heidegger's unfolding of his chain of words is not intended to make us question our understanding of the supposedly opposing attitudes to language here invoked—to raise the possibility of a way of reading words that is neither a merely wilful projection upon them nor a mere suffering of their thrownness, that is both an invitation to found a new community and a rededication of an old one.

What is undeniable is that, within the ten or so pages of Heidegger's first lecture, the notion of inclination generates in turn the notions of interest, of provocation, of being drawn and being withdrawn, of pain and suffering; in other words, the implications of the questioning first set in motion by his opening association of animality with wanting provide that lecture with such unity as it possesses, and indicate the kind of unity and progress, the kind of evolution, to which Heidegger's thinking aims to aspire. He tries to encapsulate the nature of this method very early in the first lecture: 'Let us look . . . closely, and from the start allow each word its proper weight. Some things are food for thought in themselves, intrinsically, so to speak innately. And some things make an appeal to us to give them thought, to turn toward them in thought: to think them' (*WCT* 6). He is also aware from the outset that allowing ourselves to think of words in their mutual neighbouring as genuine food for thought is not something that will attract us in our present unthinking state. He even voices the objections that are likely to come to mind: 'If we, as we are here and now, will not be taken in by empty talk, we must retort that everything said so far is an unbroken chain of hollow assertions . . .' (*WCT* 7). To those in the grip of thought-lessness, each link in the chain of words that Heidegger attempts from the outset to recollect or remember will appear hollow, empty, weight-less; and it is the first step in overcoming our present state to acknowledge that this is how they impress us. But the second step is to attempt to overcome this desire to regard such a fast retort to Heidegger's design as definitive, as a reason to turn away from his words once and for all. He must undertake to justify his proposed evolution in our conception of what deserves to be called thinking; but we should withhold judgement on its attractiveness until we have allowed him the time and space to make his case as forcefully as he can, and allowed ourselves to weigh each link of the chain of words he lays out—to ask whether our sense of their weightlessness might not be a wilful projection of our own hollowness.

One other aspect of Heidegger's 'prologue' is worth noting before we move on. Just before turning to his thought-provoking thought, he attempts to illustrate what he means by claiming that human beings learn to think by giving their minds to whatever essentials are addressed to them: 'What is essential in a friend, for example, is what we call "friendly". In the same sense we now call "thought-provoking" what in itself is to be thought about . . . [And] we will call "*most* thought-provoking" what remains to be thought about *always*, because it is at the beginning, before all else' (*WCT* 4; my italics). It would be easy to leap over this illustrative example—this passing reference to the essence of friendship. But those who recall the pivotal analysis at the beginning of division II of *Being and Time*, in which Heidegger characterizes the silent call of conscience as the voice of the friend whom every Dasein carries with it and silently identifies his own voice as that of philosophy's conscience, might be brought to think that Heidegger is here recollecting or remembering that aspect of his earlier work. The implication would be that he continues to think that it is of the essence of philosophical friendship to provoke one's other to thought, to distract them from their repression of their capacity to think and instead attract them towards what might be of genuinely human interest in reclaiming and exercising that which—properly understood—remains of their essence. In this respect, his choice of example is exemplary of the fact that, in learning to read Heidegger's words, we must never allow ourselves to think that any of its details, whether of form or of content, might be purely illustrative. In Heidegger's transformation of thinking, the merely ornamental can be the cornerstone of his edifice, the essence of the edification he aims to provide.

HEIDEGGER'S MOST THOUGHT-PROVOKING THOUGHT

45. If the chain of words we have begun to uncover provides the skeleton of Heidegger's lecture series, its overt focus lies in the thought with which his first lecture officially commences, italicized variants of which punctuate its entire course. The canonical formulation of that thought is as follows: 'Most thought-provoking in our thought-provoking time is that we are still not thinking' (*WCT* 6). 'Still not' crystallizes the diagnosis of those he addresses that is first adumbrated in his prologue: those who are not yet thinking are those who (like their culture or time) are mired in an unthinking state but are nonetheless essentially capable of authentic thought. Heidegger further emphasizes what his prologue also claimed—that at least some of the responsibility for this thoughtlessness lies with us; we are not at present thinking because we have failed to hold on to, to gather, what is most deserving of thought in our memory. But he goes on to claim that this inability exists 'by no means only because man does not sufficiently reach out and turn to what is to be thought' (*WCT* 8); for if we can truly incline only towards what inclines towards us, then our existing disinclination to think also holds sway 'because the thing itself that must be thought about turns away from man, has turned away long ago' (*WCT* 7).

Our present inability to think is not an accidental or temporary derangement, as if curable by an act of will or a resolution to be more thoughtful in future; if it were, it would not be what is most thought-provoking about our thought-provoking time—it would not be what always remains to be thought about. However, if what must be thought 'keeps itself turned away from man since the beginning' (*WCT* 7), how could human beings ever have fulfilled the capacity for thinking that is of their essence, and how might they in the future? Heidegger responds by distinguishing between absence and withdrawal. That which turns away from us is not thereby nothing, but rather

draws us along by its very withdrawal, whether or not we become aware of it immediately, or at all. Once we are drawn into the withdrawal, we are drawing towards what draws, attracts us by its withdrawal. And once we, being so attracted, are drawing towards what draws us, our essential nature already bears the stamp of 'drawing towards'. As we are drawing toward what withdraws, we ourselves are pointers pointing toward it. We are who we are by pointing in that direction . . . (*WCT* 9)

The attractiveness of thought, our capacity to be provoked to thought, is here characterized as a matter of being provoked *by* what is to be thought—a matter of seduction. That which is meant to elicit our inclination towards it does so by inclining itself away from us; for what is thought-provoking, turning away is turning towards. And if its turning away from us always already turns us towards it, if it draws us whether or not we take ourselves to be so drawn, then what appears to be our turning away from it in fact bears the stamp of turning towards it; for us, turning away from what is most thought-provoking is turning towards. What may give the impression of our withdrawal from thought in reality carries the impress of the withdrawal of what is most worthy of thought; our aversion from thought is a sign that it is the withdrawal or aversiveness of what is thought-provoking, as much as what thereby withdraws, that is its most thought-provoking feature.

46. However, by characterizing the thought that we are still not thinking as 'most thought-provoking', Heidegger underlines the fact that it is a thought; and since he presents his audience with that thought, he thereby presents himself as thinking—as having been provoked to thought. This reinforces the implications of the institutional fact that he is not attending these lectures but giving them; the position or office he occupies is not that of someone needing to learn what thinking is but someone who claims to be able to teach those who need to learn this, someone who must, therefore, have avoided succumbing to the unthinking state in which he finds his students. Heidegger is taking thought and attempting to encourage others to do the same; he thereby diagnoses himself as realizing the essential human capacity to think, and so as having gone beyond the unthinking state of his audience.

The arrogance of this implication raises a number of questions. The first is what one might call a problem of reflexivity or origination—of the applicability of Heidegger's diagnosis of the prevailing form of human culture to itself, understood as one event within that culture.

For why should Heidegger, alone among those attracted to the discipline of philosophy, be capable of responding authentically to what is most thought-provoking? What dispensation from the broader cultural thoughtlessness has he been granted, and why? The second problem refers not to the relation between the content and source of his thoughts, but to that between their content and their audience; it might be called a problem of audibility or destination. For in so far as he takes himself to be addressing people whose capacity to think has been eclipsed by the prevailing interest in 'philosophizing', why does he bother to attempt to convey his thoughts to them? How can he coherently expect his own lectures to be comprehended by his students—to elicit genuine thought rather than superficial, transient intellectual interest?

Another, seemingly contradictory, implication of Heidegger's formulation of his guiding thought further complicates these difficulties. For that formulation uses the first-person plural pronoun: if '*we* are still not thinking', then neither he nor his audience are as yet thinking. Indeed, he explicitly emphasizes this point in the 'summary and transition' passage appended to his first lecture: 'we are still not thinking; none of us, including me who speaks to you, me first of all' (*WCT* 14). How, then, can Heidegger present himself as a teacher of thinking, as exemplary of that of which he thinks neither he nor his students are yet capable? This difficulty immediately takes a further turn: for Heidegger claims to have been provoked to thought by the specific thought that neither he nor anyone else is thinking. But if what that thought claims is true, then neither he nor anyone else could have been provoked to thought by it; and if it is false, it can contain no provocation to genuine thought.

A firmer foothold amidst these currents emerges if we acknowledge that, through this apparent paradox, Heidegger is implicitly citing and engaging in a dialogue with the Western philosophical tradition. It was, after all, Socrates (the figure Heidegger draws into his thinking at the end of the first 'summary and transition' passage) who, when told that the Delphic oracle had described him as the most knowledgeable of all the Greeks, concluded that the oracle could only mean that he at least knew that he knew nothing. And Descartes inaugurated philosophical modernity by attempting to demonstrate that one's own non-existence was in fact absolutely unthinkable by any thinking being. Against this background we might interpret Heidegger as attempting to demonstrate that the thought of our own absolute non-existence as thinking beings is and must be false, because it could only be true if it were thinkable, but if it is thinkable then it must be false. In other words: the fact that we can think that we are still not thinking proves that our aversion to thought is not absolute. Our uttermost withdrawal from thought therefore cannot definitively turn us away from thinking because it will always be possible for us to be provoked to thought by it, to think our inability to think. Hence, thinking must remain possible as an event in a culture which has withdrawn from thought; for if that withdrawal cannot be absolute, it can itself be the pivot around which the culture can return to the claims of thinking. Indeed, by turning towards our own withdrawal from thought in thought, we turn not only towards thinking but towards what is most thought-provoking—our own capacity to turn away from what is to be thought, and the capacity of what is to be thought to turn away from us: the mutual aversiveness of thinker and object of thought. Hence, turning away is turning towards; or as Heidegger puts it: 'Once we are so related and drawn into what withdraws, we are drawing into what withdraws, into the enigmatic and therefore mutable nearness of its appeal. Whenever man is properly drawing that way, he is thinking—even though he may still be far away from what withdraws, even though the withdrawal may remain as veiled as ever' (*WCT* 17).

So much for the question of origination; what of that of destination? On this account, the only difference between Heidegger and his students is that, whereas both he and they are not thinking, he has begun to think that he and they are not thinking. This difference is, however, inessential—an accident of timing; for, like Socrates in relation to his fellow Greeks, Heidegger is not posssessed of either a provocation to thought or a capacity for thought that his students lack. His thought would in fact have no object at all if he had not been as mired in thoughtlessness as they, if he could not think his own thoughtlessness. So that which gives him food for thought is equally available to all; and since only those capable of inclining towards thought can avert themselves from it, he can be sure that they retain the capacity to think about their aversiveness. By presenting himself to his students as having been provoked to thought by his own aversion to thought, he represents to them a possibility that each of them possesses; he exemplifies the fact that, even in this darkest and most thought-deprived of times, human beings can turn away from thoughtlessness by turning thoughtfully towards it.

TRANSITION: THINKING AND TEACHING

47. The main elements of this recollection of the task of authentic philosophical writing, indebted to and hence differing from their first

articulation in *Being and Time*, are encapsulated in the discussion of teaching that dominates the first 'summary and transition', in which Heidegger explicitly denies the non-Socratic (and non-Wittgensteinian) implications of the institutional division between lecturer and student. The true teacher does not have a store of information that the student lacks—she knows nothing that her students do not know; her authority in relation to her students derives neither from expertise nor office. On the contrary:

Teaching is far more difficult than learning, because what teaching calls for is this: to let learn. The real teacher, in fact, lets nothing else be learned than—learning. His conduct, therefore, often produces the impression that we learn nothing from him, if by 'learning' we now suddenly understand the mere procurement of useful information. The teacher is ahead of his apprentices in this alone, that he has to learn to let them learn. The teacher must be capable of being more teachable than the apprentices. (*WCT* 15)

The student needs to learn about the subject-matter of the lecture course, and the teacher needs to learn how to let her do this; but learning, as Heidegger reiterates, means 'to make everything we do answer to whatever essentials address themselves to us at a given time... depending on the realm from which they address us' (*WCT* 14). Accordingly, a teacher of thinking must let the student learn how to make everything she does answer directly to the essentials of thinking. Such a teacher does not, therefore, impose her views or personality upon her student, but directs the student's attention away from herself and onto the realm of thinking; and the best way of doing that—of turning away from those who turn towards her in such a way as to turn them away from her and towards thinking—is for her to exemplify in her own activity what it is to be a student of thought, what it is to answer to the essentials of the realm of thought. But to answer to the essentials of any given realm is to think about it; so to exemplify what it is to be a student of thinking is to exemplify thinking about thinking. To teach thinking one must therefore exemplify it, by letting oneself learn how to think and how to maintain oneself in the draft of thinking. In other words, the true teachers of thinking are the true students of thinking—the thinkers; for the true thinker is always (even if not only) a thinker about thinking.

The true teacher of thinking is thus both a midwife and a sign, both a transitional and a representative figure; in so far as she exemplifies thinking about thinking, she points away from herself and towards the essentials of the realm of thought. But this implies that thinking is, in its essence, a matter of pointing towards thinking—that thinking is essentially transitional, a matter of always letting oneself learn to go beyond prevailing conceptions of thought and its objects in favour of ones which more authentically answer to the essentials of that which they address. In this sense, the true thinker can act as midwife to others' capacity for genuine thought because the genuine thinker continuously acts as midwife to herself; thought about thinking is truly thoughtful only when it facilitates the emergence of one's future self as thinker from one's existing self-conception—it is a matter of endlessly giving birth to oneself as a thinker, endlessly turning away from what one has hitherto taken thinking to be and towards whatever one has learned to think that thinking might become.

There are many traces of such an aversive relation to the thinking of *Being and Time* in Heidegger's first lecture, with its accompanying summary and transition. For example, Heidegger cites words of Hölderlin to reopen his questioning of the Stranger from Elea's unqualified opposition between genuine philosophizing and myth-making. He points out that Plato's Stranger is speaking from a point at which such a distinction and opposition, and hence a conception of rationality marked by that evaluation, has evolved; in other words, it is not a timeless deliverance of reason nor a truly originary step in the development of philosophy, but rather a belated, dependent, and hence questionable re-membering of Western culture.

The *mythos* is that appeal of foremost and radical concern to all human beings which makes man think of what appears, what is in being. *Logos* says the same; *mythos* and *logos* are not, as our current historians of philosophy claim, placed into opposition by philosophy as such; on the contrary, the early Greek thinkers . . . are precisely the ones to use *mythos* and *logos* in the same sense. *Mythos* and *logos* become separated and opposed only at the point where neither *mythos* nor *logos* can keep to its original nature. In Plato's work, this separation has already taken place. (*WCT* 10)

Heidegger then reinforces this rearticulation of his early suspicions about thinking, truth, and appearance-making by pointing out that the idea of 'memory' which forms one link in the chain of ideas unfolding from his re-embodiment of human reason itself embodies the name of Mnemosyne, daughter of Heaven and Earth, bride of Zeus, who in nine nights becomes the mother of the Nine Muses. This suggests that 'poesy is the water that at times flows backward towards the source, towards thinking as a thinking back, a recollection' (*WCT* 11)—an association between thinking and poetry that he later specifies as identity in difference, as a cleaving one to the other that is also a cleft between them (thereby specifying his thought by allowing two cleanly divided meanings to cleave to one another in one word, an exemplification of his 'chain of words' method which links it with what might be called a poetic receptivity to language; WCT 20).

Another familiar figure from *Being and Time* re-emerges when Heidegger characterizes thinking as a handicraft. He thereby discovers another link in the chain of ideas connecting thinking to creatureliness, picturing thinking as an activity of the whole human body—an activity whose metonymic figure is the craft of the hand. To this degree, his new mode of thinking does not diverge from his earlier one, given the latter's opening refusal to treat the human body as distinct from mind, and its central distinction between readiness-to-hand and presence-at-hand, with everything that flows from it. But his development of this new formulation suggests an implicit criticism of his earlier self:

But the craft of the hand is richer than we commonly imagine. The hand does not only grasp and catch, or push and pull. The hand reaches and extends, receives and welcomes—and not just things: the hand extends itself, and receives its own welcome in the hands of others. The hand holds. The hand carries. The hand designs and signs, presumably because man is a sign. Two hands fold into one, a gesture meant to carry man into the great oneness. The hand is all this, and this is the true handicraft. (*WCT* 16)

It is difficult to deny that the hand of *Being and Time* is mainly pictured as catching, pushing, and pulling (in the manner that Heidegger now associates with the actions of paws, claws, and fangs)—gripping tools and heaving obstacles out of the way; indeed, Heidegger traded on the polyvalence of the idea of grasping to connect practical activity to human comprehension as such. And even if his conception of Dasein as Being-with prevents the utter repression of the hand's interactions with other hands, it was recessive in comparison with his early interest in subject–object relations. Now he takes it that a proper weighing of this metonymy should highlight the hand's relation to language, to the call of religion, and perhaps most fundamentally (via the image of the hand, receiving, welcoming, and carrying) to the idea of receptivity. This reformulates his opening suggestion that the traditional philosophical distinction between mind and body was aligned with a distinction between the active will and the body's suffering of sensation, emotion, and mood. In re-evaluating the hand as a figure for human thinking, Heidegger thereby suggests that this must include a re-evaluation of thinking as a fundamentally passive or receptive mode of activity—a path that, he implies, *Being and Time*'s emphasis upon the moodedness of human existence opened up but did not sufficiently or adequately explore.

48. It is worth remarking that the idea of thinking as transitional is also encoded into the very form and structure of Heidegger's lecture series— particularly in the way that he progresses from one lecture to another via a 'summary and transition'. The reader soon realizes that the purported summary elements of these passages are not simple restatements of claims to correct attractive but misleading interpretations and foreground unobvious implications. In effect, the essential work of the course occurs at least as often in these 'transitional' passages as in the lectures they link, so that the lectures can often appear to be merely transitions between the 'summaries'; in other words, the very distinction between lecture and summary soon loses its grip in favour of the conviction that each phase of Heidegger's thinking is essentially a transition to the next—a movement which typically involves recounting a past step, but in such a way as to propel us beyond it in unexpected ways.

The idea of self-midwifery is also formally underlined by the peculiarly distanced and impersonal way in which Heidegger relates to his own initiating thought. From the moment of its introduction in the first lecture (italicized, as if quoted), Heidegger develops its implications and complexities as if he were reading another's words: he makes interpretative starts which turn out to be false, justifies inferences about the implications of the thought solely by references to the precise form and content of its linguistic expression, and consistently refuses to utilize the authority over determining the meaning of a speech-act that we typically attribute to its author. In part, this amounts to a lesson in how to read, how to weigh words; in part, it exemplifies Heidegger's implicit identification with his students—standing as an encouraging or attractive enactment of his belief that the thinking to which he aspires is something that they too can actualize. But beyond this it suggests that the best way to learn from one's own thoughts is to treat them as one would the thoughts of another—that they can best bear fruit for the future if one takes them as an expression of a self-conception, and so an aspect of oneself, from which one has already departed or become distanced. In other words, this mode of writing itself enacts the doubled or split conception of the self to which his prologue alludes (itself an allusion to a key idea of *Being and Time*), and to an enactment of which he wishes before all to attract his audience. For Heidegger, genuinely to take thought is to become other to oneself, to use oneself to go beyond oneself, relating to one's actual understanding of the realm of thought as that from which one's more authentic, unattained, but attainable understanding of that realm can and must be born.

If, however, Heidegger truly takes himself to be representative of true thinking to his students, and so to be the standard by reference to which they might turn away from thoughtlessness, then who or what taught him this? Who was the representative of genuine thinking who drew his hitherto unthinking attention to the fact that he was still not thinking, and so seduced him into beginning to think the very thought he presents in his lectures as the pivot of both his and his students' lives as thinkers? Who, in short, was Heidegger's friend? According to his own view, his teacher could only be a thinker, and a thinker about thinking; and according to the development of his lecture course, that thinker was someone who had a vanishingly small but nonetheless similar role in *Being and Time*—Nietzsche.

NIETZSCHE: THE BLOSSOMING OF SCEPTICISM

49. Most obviously, Heidegger presents his thought that we are still not thinking as a citation or recounting of Nietzsche's thought that 'the wasteland grows . . . woe to him who hides wastelands within'. This thought is given expression in *Thus Spake Zarathustra*, which, according to Heidegger, advances the idea of the superman as a counter to the wasteland; and the superman is neither superhuman nor subhuman, but rather the man who goes beyond, who passes over, man as he is—the overman. 'Man, unless he stops with the type of man as he is, is a passage, a transition; he is a bridge; he is "a rope strung between the animal and the superman"' (*WCT* 60). Zarathustra himself is the overman in the process of becoming, and exemplary precisely because he exists in transition, as transitional. To be genuinely human just is to be in transition, to be passing over from the type of human being one is to the type one is yet to be, and to be passing beyond that unattained state of oneself, once attained, in favour of some further unattained state. To be is to point beyond oneself, and thus to represent the standard of genuine humanity to others—to show that they too must become transitional, that humanity is achieved and maintained precisely not by achieving and maintaining some particular self-understanding or other, but by achieving and maintaining transitionality—by seeing any particular self-understanding as essentially self-overcoming, as a shell from which another, more authentic self-understanding can and must emerge.

According to Heidegger, this aspect of the content of *Thus Spake Zarathustra* is reflected in its subtitle: 'A Book for Everyone and No-One'.

'For Everyone'—that does not mean for everybody as just anybody; 'For Everyone' means for each man as man, for each man each time his essential nature becomes for him an object worthy of his thought. 'And No-One'—that means: for none among these men prevailing everywhere who merely intoxi-cate themselves with isolated fragments and passages from the book and then blindly stumble about in its language, instead of getting underway on its way of thinking, and thus becoming first of all questionable to themselves. (*WCT* 50)

The book declares itself to address everyone *qua* genuine thinker and so *qua* genuine human being, and it does so by refusing to address anyone *qua* hider of the wasteland within, anyone in so far as they are disinclined to thought. Nietzsche's thinking aims to attract its readers to self-overcoming, to enacting for themselves the self-overcoming Zarathustra exemplifies, by resisting their satisfaction with themselves and their self-conceptions; in short, it seduces by repul-sion, aiming to turn its readers towards the genuine thinking it repre-sents by turning themselves away from themselves in so far as they represent the absence of thought. It does so by making their assump-tion that they are already thinking (itself an expression of their thought-lessness) questionable, and by expressing its revulsion for that thoughtlessness; its aversiveness to them thereby exemplifies the self-aversiveness that it aims to inculcate in them. And Heidegger claims that the essential impersonality of this aversive seduction is further reflected in one of Nietzsche's last messages before succumbing to madness: 'After you had discovered me, it was no trick to find me: the difficulty now is to lose me . . .' (*WCT* 55). Here Nietzsche declares that his aim is not to ensure that his readers think his thoughts—accept every element of his particular views or follow some concrete existen-tial blueprint that they claim to identify in Zarathustra's preaching, for example; that would be merely a further expression of their own thoughtlessness, a way of exchanging their fixation on one self-concep-tion by a fixation on another. What he wishes to inculcate is rather the overcoming of fixation, the capacity to go on from any and every given self-conception, to achieve genuine humanity by achieving genuine tran-sitionality; and that can only be done by leaving one's teacher behind—by learning how to learn from his thinking without simply reproducing it, by uncovering that in his thinking which harbours its own overcoming.

50. Heidegger is plainly aware of the reflexive implications of this element of his reading of Nietzsche—of his need to demonstrate that he has found and lost the essentials of his mentor's thinking.

Only a dialogue can answer, then, to Nietzsche's thought which is a transition—a dialogue whose own way is preparing a transition. In such a transition, Nietzsche's thought as a whole must, of course, take its place on the one side which the transition leaves behind to move to the other . . . but for that very reason [the transition] cannot pass it over in the sense of disregarding it. In the course of the transition, Nietzsche's thought, the entire thought of the West is appropriated in its proper truth (*WCT* 51–2)

The truth that Heidegger finds through his thoughtful appropriation of Nietzsche is the motivational taproot of a philosophical conception of thinking that gives intellectual expression to the wasteland of thoughtlessness we inhabit. This conception pictures thinking, judgement, and experience as a process of forming ideas or representations of things in the world. At times he links this notion of thinking with a certain kind of politico-scientific-industrial cultural formation; he refers at different moments to the supersession of craftwork by factory-based industrial processes, to cybernetics and logistics, to the Second World War and the moral rearmament of the cold war, and connects these various events to the advent and dominance of the age of technology. On his account, a technological approach to the world finds its theoretical apotheosis and underpinning in a picture of thinking as forming ideas.

Heidegger finds that the essence of this picture of thinking is identified by Nietzsche when, in *Thus Spake Zarathustra*, he tells us: '*The spirit of revenge*, my friends, has so far been the subject of man's best reflection; and wherever there was suffering, there punishment was also wanted' (*WCT* 85). Heidegger sharpens his sense that representational theories of thinking are essentially expressions of revenge in the following series of deliberately questionable rhetorical questions: 'Could it be that this manner of forming ideas at bottom sets upon everything it sets before itself, in order to depose and decompose it? What manner of thinking is it that sets all things up in such a way that fundamentally it pursues and sets upon them?' (*WCT* 84). This chain of ideas points forward, towards the details of the second part of Heidegger's lecture series; but it also points back to Heidegger's earlier, extraordinary discussion of the blossoming tree.

He takes it that those of us who understand thinking to be a process of forming ideas will also take the sciences of psychology and neurophysiology to be the best way of investigating the nature of this process. Accordingly, when, for example, we perceive a tree in bloom, we will be inclined to investigate the nature of our experience by exploring whatever events are then taking place in our minds or brains.

But—while science records the brain currents, what becomes of the tree in bloom? What becomes of the man—not of the brain but of the man, who may die under our hands tomorrow and be lost to us, and who at one time came to our encounter? What becomes of the face-to-face, the meeting, the seeing, the forming of the idea, in which the tree presents itself and man comes to stand face-to-face with the tree? (*WCT* 42)

In Heidegger's view, what becomes of the tree is that it is declared to be unreal. It is transformed into 'a void, thinly sprinkled with electric charges here and there that race hither and yon at enormous speeds' (*WCT* 43), a sprinkling that becomes what we think of as a tree only in our consciousness; the earth on which it spreads its branches exists only in our head, its meadow only in our soul. In short, the representational theory of thinking 'drops the blooming tree'; it 'never lets the tree stand where it stands' (*WCT* 44). Such theories both depose and decompose the tree: they decompose it into hypothesized constituents (whether electrons or psychic atoms) from which the human subject must then reconstitute the thing itself, which is thereby deposed from its proper place in the perceptual relation; it loses its authority as an independent being whose existence makes possible and whose nature governs our perception of it, and becomes instead an inner construct— one whose existence and nature depend upon the subject's determining constitutive activity.

Heidegger cites a passage from Schopenhauer to drive home his central point: 'however immeasurable and massive the world may be, yet its existence hangs by one single thin thread: and that is the given individual consciousness in which it is constituted' (*WCT* 40). In other words, if (as Schopenhauer elsewhere puts it) 'the world is my idea', then the very existence of that world and everything in it is subject to scepticism; but this subjection is not a discovery about reality, about the way things are really set up between human beings and their world—it is rather created by a particular conceptualization of it. We set up the world and its objects in such a way that we set upon them; sceptical doubts assail us because we have assailed the independent reality of things by decomposing and thereby deposing them.

Thus far, Heidegger's account of scepticism does not differ in essentials from his general approach in *Being and Time*; but he goes beyond that old beginning in taking Nietzsche to have seen that this attack is fuelled by the spirit of revenge; in other words, he takes scepticism about the external world to be a punishment we impose on reality for some species of suffering that we take it to have inflicted on us. And since vengeance typically aims to give or take like for like, an eye for an eye,

Heidegger further implies that our decomposition and deposition of the world aims to inflict upon reality the kind of suffering that we take reality to have inflicted on us. By means of the representational theory of thinking, and more generally by the technological cultural formations it exemplifies, we take revenge upon the world for what we experience as its attack upon our independence and reality, its attempts to decompose and so depose us. We do not allow the tree to stand where it stands, because we take ourselves to have suffered from the tree's refusal to let us stand where we stand. But how might we have come to think that— to experience our encounter with a tree in bloom as one in which we suffer decomposition and deposition?

Heidegger takes Nietzsche to point towards an answer when he goes on, in *Thus Spake Zarathustra*, to define the spirit of revenge as follows: 'This, yes, this alone is *revenge* itself: the will's revulsion against time and its "It was"' (*WCT* 93).

Thought against the backdrop of temporality established in *Being and Time*, an encounter with a blossoming tree can be seen to invite human revulsion in at least two important senses. First, it exemplifies the worldliness of our existence, the fact that we are always already environed, and so always already standing outside ourselves before the reality of other existent beings. An encounter with the tree thus forces us to attend to the fact that our experience is given to us, that it is something we suffer rather than dictate—the experience of a finite creature; it tells us that the earth does not exist in our heads but that we exist on earth, and so points to the earth's existence beyond us—to the fact that it will continue to exist beyond our deaths, that it will survive our own going whereas we could not survive its extinction. Second, in so far as it is blossoming or in bloom, the tree's thraldom to the seasons and to processes of growth and decline exemplifies the need for all existent beings to alter with the passage of time; an encounter with it therefore forces us to attend to the temporality of existence, to its transitionality or becoming.

The notion that human being is both being-in-the-world and becoming is not new for the author of *Being and Time*; but Nietzsche's example initiates a deeper understanding of the roots of our resistance to that notion, for it allows Heidegger to stress that a full acknowledgement of it—in the face of the blooming tree—would doubly decompose our sense of ourselves. Rather than underwriting an idea of integral self-sufficiency or unconditionedness, it underlines a double articulation in human being—between the human being and her world, and between the human being as she is and as she can be. It is Heidegger's intuition that, rather than accept such a disarticulation, rather than acknowledge that we must suffer the world's otherness to us and our otherness to ourselves, human beings have disarticulated the world; they have preserved their own sense of independence by assailing that of the world, at once decomposing and deposing it by making its reality conditional upon our supposedly constitutive consciousness.

However, just as revenge understands itself to inflict that which it has suffered, so Heidegger understands revenge to suffer that which it inflicts. As he puts it: 'The revulsion of revenge remains chained to this "It was"; just as there lies concealed in all hatred the abysmal dependence upon that from which hatred at bottom always desires to make itself independent—but never can, and can all the less the more it hates' (*WCT* 103–4).

The vengeful will takes itself to have restored its authority by decomposing and deposing reality, but its underlying dependence upon that reality cannot be undone—human existence can never not be being-in-the-world and becoming; so the punishment the will inflicts on reality is necessarily a species of self-punishment, a suffering inflicted upon that which is internally related to itself (what in *Being and Time* was described as a form of suicide). Since the punishment was decomposition, the will's self-punishment takes the same form; and Nietzsche's Zarathustra offers us a glimpse of its effects.[11]

I see and have seen . . . things . . . so monstrous that I should not wish to speak of all of them; but of some of them I should not wish to be silent: and they are men who lack everything except one thing, of which they have too much—men who are no more than a great eye or a great mouth or a great belly or something else great—I call such men inverse cripples . . .

Truly, my friends, I walk among men as among the fragments and limbs of men!

The terrible thing to my eye is to find men shattered in pieces and scattered as if over a battle-field of slaughter. (*Thus Spake Zarathustra*,[12] 160)

Thoughtless men hiding the wasteland within are both monstrous and fragmented, at once reduced to a single part and to a scattering of many parts, because they cannot overcome their dependence upon that upon which they wish to avenge themselves. For, being essentially worldly, their decomposition of the world must effect a self-decomposition, a disarticulation of the internal relation between human being and world; their revenge on the world fragments them. And being essentially transitional, creatures whose worldly existence is one of endless becoming,

[11] Heidegger does not cite the following passage of Nietzsche's text, but it has recently been drawn to our attention by Stanley Cavell, 'Counter-Philosophy and the Pawn of Voice', *PP* 76.

[12] Trans. R. J. Hollingdale (Penguin: London, 1961); hereafter *TSZ*.

their denial of worldly transience effects a denial of their own transience, their otherness to themselves. The articulation between themselves as they are and as they might become is recomposed as a single, fixated state (what Heidegger earlier called the they-self) in which they have turned away from self-transformation in favour of the undifferentiated state they presently occupy; their revenge on time deforms them into a single, monstrous part or fragment of themselves.

51. This diagnosis is the core of what Heidegger takes to be the truth in Nietzsche's account of the wasteland of thought and culture; and the terms it specifies also secrete a general sense of how we might begin to overcome this masochistic thoughtlessness. Heidegger encodes his version of that counter-conception in another of his early, apparently throwaway examples—in this case, one designed to illustrate the peculiarity of the temporal dimension implicit in his thought that we are still not thinking.

This 'still not' is of a unique kind, which refuses to be equated with other kinds. For example, we can say, around midnight, that the sun has still not come up. We can say the same thing in the early dawn. The 'still not' is in each case different. But, it will be objected, it is different here only regarding the time span, the number of hours that pass between midnight and dawn; while the daily rising of the sun is certain. Certain in what sense? Perchance the scientific sense? But since Copernicus, science no longer recognizes sunrises and sunsets. Scientifically, it has been unequivocally established that these things are illusions of the senses. By the common assumption of the customary view, this 'still not' concerning the rising sun retains its truth at midnight and at dawn; but this truth can never be scientifically established, for the simple reason that the daily morning expectation of the sun is of a nature that has no room for scientific proofs. When we wait for the sun to rise, we never do it on the strength of scientific insight. It will be objected that men have become habituated to the regularity of these phenomena. As though the habitual went without saying, as though it were understood! As though there could be anything habitual without habitation! As though we had ever given thought to habitation! (*WCT* 35–6)

If not by simple equation, then at least by analogy, Heidegger's talk of awaiting sunrise tells us much about how he imagines the turn towards genuine thought. He makes his own the Platonic image of the sun as the object of all our strivings, inviting its sense that only the return of what is to be thought about can illuminate and nourish our existence, but further implying that we cannot act so as to bring about that return but must rather await it in anxious hope or expectation. By focusing on the annihilation of sunrise by sciences in the grip of technology, he figures every such denial of the phenomena of ordinary life as a refusal of the fact that human beings are earthlings—creatures who dwell on the earth just as blooming trees are rooted in meadows spread out on the earth (*WCT* 43). They are to be thought of not as one organism on one planet in a particular solar system, as if seen from a perspective beyond all embodiment or particular habitation, but rather as beings who inhabit a world that lives and dies by the light of the sun, and who measure their life by the transitions between sun and moon, night and day—who are, in short, diurnal beings, creatures of the daily or the everyday. What genuine thinking aims to achieve is thus a new habitation of the ordinary, a reinhabitation of the world.

If Nietzsche is of critical importance in specifying that aim, Heidegger also believes that his account suffers from its indebtedness to the very traditions it intends so radically to criticize; and he traces this to Nietzsche's assumption that our vengefulness is an expression of the will, and of the will's revulsion against time. In this, Heidegger sees a debt to the long tradition of metaphysical thinking, with its modern apotheosis in the Schellingian claim that 'Willing is primal being'—more generally, in the idea that the Being of beings appears as the will. By envisaging human deliverance from revenge as a reorientation of the will (imagining the overcoming of our doubled self-fragmentation and self-deformation as a function of our willing the eternal recurrence of the same), Nietzsche fails in Heidegger's eyes to escape from this tradition, and so remains turned towards the essentially technological and representational orientation to beings that it crystallizes. If such an escape is to be possible, it must begin by turning away from even the most radicalized, apparently anti-metaphysical, versions of the idea that willing is primal being. It must imagine our self-overcoming not as a function of our willing anything in particular, but rather as our deliverance from prevailing conceptions of the will and of ourselves as essentially willing beings.

THINKING, LANGUAGE, HISTORY

52. In the first half of the second part of his lecture series, Heidegger prepares the ground for this deliverance by returning to the real starting-point of his efforts—by going back beyond his thought that we are still not thinking to the title under which that thought was introduced: the question 'What is called thinking?' This single question is in fact fourfold: it asks what is designated by the word 'thinking', what

our prevailing theory of thought understands thinking to be, what is required to think aright, and what commands us to think. In focusing anew on the first of these meanings, Heidegger renews his commitment to thinking about language, and claims that our prevailing theories of language are no more responsive to the reality of words than our prevailing theories of thought answer to the realities of thinking.

Both theories are essentially representational. The (Augustinian) theory of language which Heidegger rejects claims that words are names coordinated with things; language is a simple medium or means of expression, an intermediary between thought and things. Since this picture implies a simple, unambiguous one-to-one correspondence between words, the ideas they stand for, and the objects that both represent, it can be seen as a variant of the approach that Heidegger earlier referred to as one-sided or one-track thinking. 'For it is only on the plane of the one-sided uniform view that one-track thinking takes its start. It reduces everything to a univocity of concepts and specifications the precision of which not only corresponds to, but has the same essential origin as, the precision of technological process' (*WCT* 34). As one might expect, and as we have already seen, Heidegger's approach to language looks rather for multivocity or polyvalence; it aims to weigh the full and multiple depths of meaning—the unfolding chains of association and connotation—that a proper receptivity to language can reveal (and that what Wittgenstein would call 'taking mathematics and logic as a normative ideal for language' would conceal).

Heidegger's response to the representational theory of language is thus not to deny that words are names but rather to attend to the true multivocity of the concept of 'naming'.

To name something—that is to call it by name. More fundamentally, to name is to call and clothe something with a word. What is so called, is then at the call of the word. What is called appears as what is present, and in its presence it is brought into the keeping, it is commanded, called into the calling word. So called by name, called into a presence, it in turn calls. It is named, has the name. By naming we call on what is present to arrive . . . All naming and all being named is the familiar 'to call' only because naming itself consists by nature in the real calling, in the call to come, in a commending and a command. (*WCT* 120)

If words call the things they name, if they command their appearance and commend their essential nature into our thoughtful keeping, then words are not a means for thinking or a medium for the expression of thoughts but are rather themselves thoughtful. We do not speak and think with words—rather, words speak of and for the things they name, and so provoke (call out) thought about those things, commanding us as thinkers to attend to them and commending us into the keeping of their essential nature. On Heidegger's view, such a properly responsive attention to (what Wittgenstein might call the physiognomy of) words involves a responsiveness to their etymology— to the history of their composition and decomposition, their transformations and translations. Thinking about words means thinking about them as essentially transient or temporal, as endlessly becoming—endlessly moving on from what they were to what they might be without ever losing all the eggshell pieces of their past modes of significance. Hence Heidegger's dismissal of abbreviations: they are weightless words, lacking a history of their own, no sooner minted than made obsolete.

What might such an attentiveness to the word 'thinking' reveal? First, a connection in Old English between *thencan* (to think) and *thancian* (to thank)—the idea of thought as the expression of grateful thanks, presumably for something unlooked for received and accepted, as if thought were a gift whose giver thereby earns the devotion of a thoughtful disposition towards both gift and giver. This idea is in turn connected to memory, since according to Heidegger 'memory' essentially means a constant concentrated abiding with something (whether past, present, or yet to come), a steadfast intimate concentration upon the things that essentially speak to us. And this in turn returns us to the idea of thinking with which the lectures series began, where Heidegger claimed that to think is to be inclined towards that which in turn inclines towards us, and thereby gives us not only particular things to think about but the very capacity for thinking that constitutes our essence. As Heidegger puts it: 'Original thanking is the thanks owed for being' (*WCT* 141). And of course, this linking of thinking, thanking, and memory governs the process by which it is uncovered. Heidegger establishes those links by thinking about words (by a steadfast intimate concentration upon the things that essentially speak to us) and by recalling their history (by an act of linguistic remembrance); in short, he uncovers it by an act of memory, which is, according to his own discoveries, an example of the grateful thanking by which thinking proceeds. And what this reflexivity suggests is that Heidegger takes language to be the most appropriate object for thankful thought—that we best give thanks for being by letting words speak. What he goes on to do in the final phase of his lectures is to give an extended, virtuoso enactment of how one might take the lesson to heart—by reading words that speak to us from the beginnings of philosophy in the West, words set down at a time when *mythos* and *logos* said the same thing, and which must therefore be heard as mytho-logical speech (a linguistic register in which Wittgenstein too places great faith).

PARMENIDES' WORDS

53. Recounting two or three elements in Heidegger's rereading of the famous saying of Parmenides (in which he departs from its standard translation as 'One should both say and think that Being is', transfiguring it into 'Needful: the saying also thinking too: being: to be') will suffice to give some sense of how that rereading both confirms and amplifies his preceding claims.

The second element of Parmenides' thought contains words traditionally translated as 'saying' and 'thinking'. Heidegger reads the first of these as indirectly connected with speaking or stating, but as primarily invoking an idea of laying—of things laid before us or laid out for us; speaking of something is just one way of laying it before us, and obscures the fact that something may lie before us without our first having laid it out, whether linguistically or otherwise. In reality, our laying something out in speech—the telling or tallying of things to which all speech aspires—presupposes and is essentially responsive to what appears in so far as it comes forward or comes into presence of itself.

Heidegger's claim is that this idea of telling as laying out contains an idea of setting up or instating, rather than standing in contrast with it; 'that which has set itself up, has settled, and as such lies before us' (*WCT* 200). In this respect, the Greek idea of a statement or hypothesis embodies a notion of letting-lie-before-us, of thoughtful receptivity to what is, that has been stood on its head in the modern philosophical tradition (at least until the advent of phenomenology as practised in *Being and Time*).

What is set up is released into the freedom of its station, and is not the effect of our doing and thus dependent on us. Because of the subsequent employment made of the terms thesis, antithesis and synthesis—especially by Kant and German Idealism—we hear in the word thesis only the spontaneous action and movement of the idea-forming subject. (*WCT* 201)

For Heidegger, the Kantian notion of experience as a product of the synthesis of the manifold according to the categories of the understanding epitomizes a vengeful picture of thought and experience as setting up the world by setting upon it; it presents the things of the world as the product of a grasping, clutching mode of human handicraft.

The second word in this second element of Parmenides' thought also stands in opposition to the Kantian picture. Standardly translated as 'thinking', Heidegger translates it as a mode of perception that is a matter of taking something to mind and to heart. Since what is taken to heart must first have been laid out and allowed to lie before us, 'letting-lie' is given priority in Parmenides' thought over 'taking-to-heart'; but since nothing can be said to have been fully or properly permitted to come before us as it is if its true nature has not been taken to heart by us, then the order of Parmenides' words cannot signal a simple logical priority. Rather: 'the letting-lie-before-us and the taking-to-heart enter upon and into one another, in a give-and-take. The relation . . . is not a patchwork of things and attitudes otherwise alien to one another. The relation is a conjunction, and what is joined here is, each of itself, related to, that is, connatural with the other' (*WCT* 209). This conjunction reiterates that taking is not grasping but letting what lies before us come forth as itself; and it further emphasizes that acknowledging things as they are in themselves involves taking them to heart, suffering their presence and reality rather than resenting or revenging oneself upon its seeming incomprehensibility, its autonomous otherness. As Heidegger spells out:

Thinking, then, is not a grasping, neither the grasp of what lies before us, nor an attack upon it . . . what lies before us is not manipulated by means of grasping or prehending. In the high youth of its unfolding essence, thinking knows nothing of the grasping concept (*Begriff*) . . . [When] what is problematical becomes merely questionable, the questionable then appears as something uncertain, weak, and fragile, something that is threatening to fall apart. We now need some assurance that will put everything together again in comprehensible security. This reassuring combination is the system . . . The systematic and system-building way of forming ideas through concepts takes control. (*WCT* 212–13)

The very word for the idea of a concept which has dominated human thought about thinking after the Greeks spells out the distortion it facilitated; the echo of *greifen* in *Begriff* says that to think is to grasp or clutch at things, to paw or claw at their reality rather than taking it to heart. And the commitment to system-building in philosophy (itself emblematized by Kant's concern for the architectonic of his thought, a concern from which *Being and Time* never turned away) is itself a thoughtless turning away from our real need—that of letting the *logos* of phenomena lie before us, of articulating things in their essence with the unsystematic rigour, the sensitivity to their ramifying inwardness with one another, that thinking requires.

Heidegger also takes the third and fourth elements of Parmenides' saying, each being a different form of the word standardly translated as 'Being', as needing to be read in conjunction with one another. The participial form of the third element confirms this, since participles participate in both the nominal and the verbal meaning of a term; Heidegger takes this to show that Parmenides is pointing out a duality in Being—the fact that a being has its being in Being, and that Being persists as the Being of a being. This duality returns us by a new path to a familiar thought of *Being and Time*; and it allows Heidegger to reject the Platonic understanding of that duality as a mode of participation—an interpretation which places being and Being in different places, which thinks the separation between the two grammatical forms as a difference in existence, and so constructs the difference between beings and Being in a way which, because it presupposes a comprehension of what it is to be, takes for granted the very duality it claims to be constructing.

The alternative Heidegger proposes involves a radical rereading of the metaphysical assumption that Being should be understood in terms of presence. Kant's definition of beings as objects of experience makes sense only because beings do present themselves to us, and endure in that encounter; but the Kantian interpretation of that self-presentation leads to an understanding of being as that which is objective in objects, and thereby prepares the way for our age of technology (in which we at once posit and dispose of nature by grasping it in terms of the energies we can wrest from it, as an environing energy supply). What Heidegger takes the Greek idea of 'presence' to say is very different.

What is present has risen from unconcealment . . . But this rise from unconcealment does not specifically come to the fore in the presence of what is present. It is part of presence to hold back these traits, and thus to let come out only what is present. Even, and in particular, that unconcealment in which this rise and entry takes place, remains concealed, in contrast to the unconcealed present things. (*WCT* 236–7)

This sense of presence as an illumined, radiant self-manifestation was not something that the Greeks explicitly attended to, because it was not problematic for them but rather the horizon within which their specific questionings were pursued. It was not thought by the metaphysical tradition, because the conditions for the possibility of the presence of things that it implies were progressively covered over (a process encouraged by the inherent self-concealment of Being) by interpretations of Being that took thought away from its true object. If the resulting wasteland of thoughtlessness is to be recultivated, made habitable, we must follow out the clue to the nature of Being that this concealment of Being embodies, and continue along the path of thought that *Being and Time* opened and that Heidegger has reopened by his retranslation of Parmenides' words. We must, in other words, think anew the thought that 'Useful is the letting-lie-before-us, so (the) taking-to-heart too: the presence of what is present'.

THE DRAW OF PARATACTIC READING

54. There is, however, at least as much to learn from the form of Heidegger's presentation of these thoughts as from their content or substance. For the way he reads Parmenides' words does not simply produce certain results (readings that in many ways echo and refine thoughts from *Being and Time*); it also exemplifies the responsiveness to language that he takes to be essential to genuine thinking—to set the standard to which he wishes us to make us aspire (a standard almost wholly alien in form, if not in spirit, to the systematicity of *Being and Time*).

What, then, most fundamentally characterizes this mode of reading? Heidegger offers us the following, unobtrusively reflexive, trope for true reading: 'We normally understand by reading only this, that we grasp and follow a script and written matter. But that is done by gathering the letters. Without this gathering, without a gleaning in the sense in which wheat or grapes are gleaned, we should never to able to read a single word, however keenly we observe the written signs' (*WCT* 208). Other scattered remarks further specify what he takes this harvesting of the sense of language to require. It means, first, acknowledging a connection between language and gaming: 'We are here venturing into the gambling game of language, where our nature is at stake' (*WCT* 128). The stake in our readings of words is our nature as thinking beings, the wager is that the hand of words (the cards or the lot) that we draw will gift us the resources we need to draw again when the round is over, to continue in the game of allowing words to determine our destiny as thinkers. 'Heidegger further claims that words must be understood as wells. Words are not terms, and thus are not like buckets and kegs from which we scoop a content that is there. Words are wellsprings that are found and dug up in the telling, well-springs that must be found and dug up again and again, that easily cave in, but that at times also well up when least expected' (*WCT* 130). To think of words as marks which human beings fill with or empty of sense (the mark of aspect-blindness, on Wittgenstein's account) is to think of them as vessels from which meaning can be scooped, as if by a paw or claw; it is to set up words to be set upon, to handle them unthinkingly. To think of them as well-springs is to think of their meaningfulness as theirs to preserve and dispense, to view linguistic meaning as always already laid out before us in the landscape of language; we have to uncover the wellspring, but the water that then pumps out does so under its own pressure—it gives itself to those who can divine its subterranean presence. And, as the context of Heidegger's image makes clear, this actively passive responsiveness to word-meaning involves a sensitivity to words as historical entities—a receptivity to the etymological traces of their past significance and of the losing and winning gambles of their translation from one language or culture into another (the exchanging of one linguistic card for another).

Heidegger draws out the connection with reading as gleaning by associating the wellshafts of historical interpretation with the furrows of ploughed fields. He does so by citing and reading a line of Hölderlin's:

'It is useful for the rock to have shafts | And for the earth, furrows.' . . . Shafts are no more necessary to the rock than furrows to the earth. But it belongs to the essence of welcome and being at home that it include the welling of water and the fruits of the field. 'It is useful' says here: there is an essential community between rock and shaft, between furrow and earth, *within* that realm of being which opens up when the earth becomes a habitation. (*WCT* 190–1)

This commentary associates thoughtful reading with the establishment of a dwelling-place in the wasteland (and hence with his earlier image of the dawn of thinking, of human beings as earthlings needing to rehabituate themselves to diurnality); and it does so by associating words as wellsprings with words as furrows—reminding us that lines of words on a page are raked or ploughed in parallel straight lines, and so can (if properly irrigated from the wellsprings of their own history) bloom and bear fruit that can then be gleaned, as Heidegger gleaned his tale of the blooming tree, as he is gleaning the words of Parmenides, and as he invites us to glean the furrows of his own prose.

His emphasis upon the historicality of words is further inflected by his invocation of memory—the process of devoted gathering together by means of which reading as gleaning is made possible. And of course, remembrance embodies re-membering, the putting together of disarticulated fragments into a whole. Taken against the background of Nietzsche's talk of inverse cripples, Heidegger is here saying that a reading which is also a remembering will deliver us from our vengeful, self-maiming state; we will redeem time and thereby redeem ourselves by knitting words together as pregnancy knits together a child's limbs. Redemptive reading is thus the means by which the thinker acts as midwife to others and to herself, giving birth to the thinker that she and they are yet to become.

We might here recall that the book we are presently reading is itself an act of remembrance or commemoration—a written re-collection or gathering together of the original verbal delivery of this series of lectures. We might thereby find materials with which to question the common impression that in these lectures—most egregiously, in his early declaration that Socrates was the purest thinker of the West because he wrote nothing (*WCT* 17)—Heidegger prioritizes speech over writing. Setting aside the question of whether Heidegger declares that Socrates' purity resides in his writing nothing or rather in his writing nothing out of thoughtfulness, and passing over his careful discrimination of purity from greatness (*WCT* 26), we might take the generic form of Heidegger's text as a whole as an attempted problematization of the very opposition between speech and writing that is being invoked. For does his decision to publish the text of a set of spoken lectures declare that the work of those lectures was so important that it was worth attempting to preserve it in written form for those not privileged enough to hear the original delivery; or does it rather imply that their work could only be completed or brought to fulfilment in the form of a written text, a form that allows the fullest possible exploration of the polyvalence of its constituent words? Since Heidegger appears to have worked hard to preserve traces of his original spoken delivery of these words in their printed record, we might do better to consider the possibility that he thinks of the work of the lectures as requiring a form that is at once spoken and written, as if its words ask to be both heard and seen, inviting a mode of listening that is also a mode of reading. In that case, the originariness of the lectures is undecidably distributed between speech and writing; if their original form must be either one or the other, then they have no original form—no pure origin and thus nothing that is purely secondary. What matters to Heidegger about his orderings of words is not that they present themselves as either written or spoken, but that they give expression to a recognizably human voice rather than marking its absence.

But the notion of remembering most forcefully refers us to the gesture with which Heidegger initiates his reading of Parmenides' words—that of inserting three colons 'to give a sharper articulation to its word-structure' (*WCT* 182). He thus begins by disarticulating or dismembering the traditional translation into four parts, and calls this paratactic as opposed to syntactic reading.

In our saying, the words follow upon one another without connection. They are lined up side by side ... the word order of our saying is paratactic and not, as the usual translation represents it: 'One should *both* say and think *that*.' By this 'both' and 'that' the words are put in a specific order. The connection co-ordinates them, puts them together in an order ... by inserting connecting words. In regard to its word-order, the translation is syntactic. (*WCT* 183)

Syntactic translation imports connections into Parmenides' thought that are not there in the original language; the autonomous reality of his words is denied, an order originating in the reader being imposed upon them in order to make them conform with superficial notions of completeness or sophistication in thought or expression. For Heidegger, this is simply one more example of the way inauthentic thinking is grasping or coercive; syntactic reading, like synthetic thinking, imposes an alien order on its objects because it presupposes that the elements of which that object appears to be made are fragments or precursors of a more sophisticated integrity or wholeness. Just as the first moment of the Kantian transcendental synthesis is an apprehension of the given as a manifold, an aggregation of elements suitable for the reintegrating functions of the understanding, so syntactic readings of a text must begin by imposing a suitable fragmentation if they are later to impose a reintegration.

Heidegger's paratactic reading minimizes the order it imposes upon Parmenides' words by restricting itself at the outset to acknowledging their spatial order, the line or furrow they trace out on the page. Any further connections it elaborates are driven purely by an intensive gleaning of the historical wellspring represented by each individual word; in effect, the connections it posits well up from the words themselves, the neighbourliness that their meanings establish. And in fact, each of Parmenides' words does turn out to support and be supported by its neighbours. Just as the separate words in the second, third, and fourth phrases ('letting-lie-before-us', 'taking-to-heart', and 'the presence of what is present') are interwoven with their fellow words, so the three phrases are internally related to one another and with the phrase that precedes them ('It is useful'); all four hang together by pointing us towards other links in the lexical chain set up by ideas of the hand, of memory, and of thanking. What results from a paratactic approach is thus the kind of re-membering that recounts an existing neighbourliness in language—an endless chain of transitions that is the linguistic equivalent of the transitionality of human existence—rather than one which must obliterate any pre-existing connectedness by means of a disarticulation along lines that will facilitate the kind of reintegration it always already wanted to impose.

The full power and range of the neighbourliness of words as Heidegger conceives of it is given perhaps its most striking demonstration in the way that each of the readings he offers in his series of lectures—not only that of Parmenides, but also that of Nietzsche and of his own thought-provoking thought—is held together with its neighbours by a network of resonance struck from a single key phrase in his first lecture: his claim about the draw or draught of thought.

A glance at a dictionary reveals the polyvalence of the word 'draw'. We talk, of course, of our attention or desire being drawn, whether by an object or a person—the meaning with which Heidegger begins. But we also talk of drawing conclusions, drawing or dragging something by grasping or pulling at it, drawing and quartering something, drawing a weapon, and drawing a troop of soldiers (thinking as clutching or setting upon). We talk of drawing a cheque, drawing a bow, and drawing something out (the thinker as self-indebted self-transformer, the endlessly becoming being who shoots the arrow of her longing beyond herself). We talk of the draught of a vessel, drawing water from a well, and a draw or channel in the land, as well as drawing lots, drawing a hand of cards, and drawing a game (the being of language). Finally, we even talk (or once did) of drawing words—of rendering one expression or passage into another writing style or another language (reading as gleaning). In other words, the main turns of Heidegger's lecture series, its seemingly arbitrary and unmotivated offshoots of imagery and metaphor, can in the end be read as the result of drawing upon the wellspring of one word.[13] As Heidegger asks himself—as if dazed by the wealth he has uncovered: 'Is it only by accident that these meanings come together under the common roof of the same word-sound?' (*WCT* 205). Or is what this piece of language lays before us a place in which we might continue to dwell as thinkers?

[13] That we can read these unifying ramifications in an English rather than a German word might be thought to confirm Heidegger's thought that translation is a gamble that thinking can win, a gleaning from which thinking can gather a rich harvest.

THE HORIZON OF CHRISTIANITY

55. In these ways, Heidegger's lectures effect a transition not only from Nietzsche's thought but from his own earlier thinking; they engage in a dialogue with those bodies of words that allow him to go beyond them by going through them—by following in the directions they indicate. How, then, might we effect a transition from Heidegger's lectures? In what ways do his words point beyond themselves, turning us towards genuine thinking by turning us away from themselves as they happen to be?

Heidegger offers a clue when discussing the point of his own departure from Nietzsche. He tells us that Christian dogma knows of a way, very different from Nietzsche's own, in which we can attain deliverance from the 'it was', from time and transience—by repentance, and the establishment of a relation to God. And in a remark which he tells us will have to remain just a remark, he adds: 'If Nietzsche does not take the Christian road of repentance, it is because of his interpretation of Christianity and what it means to be a Christian . . . And Nietzsche's interpretation . . . is based on the fact that he thinks of all things in their relatedness to Being as will' (*WCT* 105). Heidegger's point is that Nietzsche is thereby committed to thinking of Christian repentance as involving a relation to the eternal will of the redeeming God. How, then, might we go beyond this? By going beyond Christianity, on the grounds that it is imbued with a metaphysics of the will? Or by going beyond such a metaphysical interpretation of Christianity—recognizing that this religion can be understood in terms other than the metaphysically imbued ones with which Nietzsche thinks it?

It does not seem too much to say that *Being and Time* is drawn to the second possibility. Quite apart from its frequent resort to theological terminology (falling, conscience, guilt), I noted earlier that the opening chapter of division ɪ establishes the book's theme with a patchwork of citations from Augustine, Calvin, Zwingli, and Genesis; and it identifies the Christian anthropology of human beings (as made in God's image) as a frame for traditional philosophy that any authentic phenomenology of Dasein must revise rather than reject—reclaiming *logos* (understood as discursive articulation) and 'transcendence' (understood as ecstasis: Dasein's standing out into the world, and beyond its attained state, in the ecstases of temporality) as fundamental to Dasein's Being. If we allow ourselves to think of *What is Called Thinking?* as so drawn, then a number of Heidegger's more puzzling themes and images can suddenly appear to point towards the story of Christ's Passion.

To begin with, the Passion is a form of suffering that is also sufferance or passivity, a dying that represents a capacity to die to the demands of the self in favour of acknowledging the reality and worth of others; Heidegger's interconnected emphases upon receptivity, letting things lie before us, and taking things to heart offer a powerful inflection of this image. The Passion is also a gift, a function of grace, since its motivation is God's wholly gratuitous love for mankind; Heidegger's sense of the givenness or giftedness of beings in their Being here finds one source or origin. The Passion further links pain or suffering to language, just as Heidegger puzzlingly uses a Hölderlin hymn to link a loss of speech to an inability to feel pain ('We feel no pain, we almost have | lost our tongue in foreign lands'; *WCT* 12); for the being who suffers crucifixion is also the Word of God, and most fully the Word in so far as he accepts his painful death on the cross. In fact, this aspect of Christ's nature places him in direct competition with the figure of Socrates, the purest thinker of the West because he wrote nothing; for of course, Christ too wrote nothing, and had no need to do so precisely because he is the living Word, the truth that is also life—a being to whom Hölderlin's further remark that 'we are the sign that is not read' might most fitly be applied.

Going beyond the specifically Christian aspects of Heidegger's imagery, we might also recollect his obsessive return to the example of the blooming tree—which he identifies as an apple tree (*WCT* 173)—and ponder whether it gives expression to an Augustinian sense that we inhabit our present wasteland of representational thinking because we ate the knowledge-endowing fruit of just such a tree, that our existence is an exile from the Garden in which it grew. And of course, as part of his revised conception of the thinking as a human handicraft, Heidegger is careful to include a reference to the way in which, in prayer, 'two hands fold into one, a gesture meant to carry man into the great oneness' (*WCT* 16).

Should we think of this horizon of imagery as akin to Nietzsche's indebtedness to a metaphysics of the will, and so as something to be turned away from by any genuinely aversive thinking? Or should we rather think of it as the unattained but attainable thought to which his own present thinking points, a way of re-membering otherwise disarticulated elements in his thought? Only a genuinely responsive or receptive thinking of Christian rebirth, a capacity to let its vision make an impression on us, can determine which way to turn here. But it is striking that Heidegger explicitly refuses to attend to the most obvious exemplar of such a reading in his intellectual neighbourhood—the writings of Kierkegaard. Of him, Heidegger curtly announces: 'No discerning mind would deny the stimuli produced by Kierkegaard's thought that prompted us to give renewed attention to the "existential". But about the decisive question—the essential nature of Being— Kierkegaard has nothing whatever to say' (*WCT* 213). This dismissal simply replicates the equally brusque negative references to Kierkegaard that are to be found relegated to the footnotes of *Being and Time*; and it is no less questionable. For how could someone be thought to have nothing to say about the decisive questions of thinking if his words were what prompted Heidegger himself not only to a concern with specific concepts (such as angst) but also to a renewal of attention to questions of existence—the very heart of the domain of thinking as he lays it before us both in *Being and Time* and later? If the out-throw of religious imagery in Heidegger's writings is not to remain a sign that is not read, we must turn to a more detailed weighing of Kierkegaard's own orderings of words.

PART THREE

KIERKEGAARD'S VISION OF RELIGION

Reading *Philosophical Fragments,*
Fear and Trembling,
and *Repetition*

THE SELF-ASSESSMENTS OF JOHANNES CLIMACUS

1. It is striking how easily one can fail to be struck by how much of the scholarly attention devoted to Kierkegaard's philosophical pseudonym Johannes Climacus has been unquestioningly directed at the Postscript to his *Philosophical Fragments* rather than at the *Fragments* itself—beginning and ending with what declares itself to be an addendum to his writing project rather than its main body, and hence with its end (or rather, that which outruns its end) rather than its beginning (or rather, that in which its beginning is brought to a formal end). True, the Postscript is some six times longer than its parent text, and it appears to focus in a more extensive and unremitting manner on recognizably philosophical concerns; but quantity does not reliably track quality or significance, and appearance sometimes disguises reality. Perhaps these commentators would argue that Climacus inserts the truly significant philosophical material into his voluminous and rambling Postscript rather than the main text to poke fun at their profession, and at Hegelian ideals of a systematic, self-contained presentation of the Truth. But that would imply that the *Fragments* itself contains little or no material of philosophical significance, that its form is somehow more acceptable to, or less subversive of, philosophical expectations than that of the Postscript, and that it is somehow incomplete or inadequate without its Postscript—that the central point of Climacus' authorship would have been missed in its absence. The first two assumptions are extremely implausible; and the third not only appears to miss the further joke implicit in the idea that a fragment or collection of fragments could somehow be made complete by appending one more piece (however large), but runs flatly contrary to a number of remarks made by Climacus himself in both the *Fragments* and its Postscript. The origin of this reading lies in the assumption that those remarks should be taken seriously.

2. The only evidence internal to the *Fragments* which suggests that it could even accommodate (let alone require) a postscript is Climacus' concluding comment that 'in the next section of this pamphlet, if I ever do write it, I intend to call the matter by its proper name, and clothe the issue in its historical costume' (*Philosophical Fragments*,[1] 109). Although this implies that the pamphlet is not yet complete, it also implies that any such sequel would be supererogatory, since Climacus

[1] Trans. H. V. and E. H. Hong (Princeton University Press: Princeton, 1985); hereafter *PF*.

sees no *need* to write it; and this is confirmed in his introductory remarks to the Postscript he eventually composes. There, he begins by stating that 'I have not felt bound by that promise, even though it was from the beginning my intent to fulfil it and the prerequisites were already on hand concurrently with the promise' (*Concluding Unscientific Postscript to the Philosophical Fragments*,[2] 9). But this suggestion that the Postscript was always already a part of the *Fragments* project is immediately given a self-subverting interpretation: 'As far as my promise is concerned, its casual form was not in the least accidental, because the promise, essentially understood, was no promise, inasmuch as it had been fulfilled in the pamphlet itself' (*CUP* 10). In other words, the prerequisites for the Postscript were on hand concurrently with the promise because they were part of the text in which the promise was so casually made; the Postscript is not an addendum to the *Fragments*—the provision of essential elements missing in that text—but a re-presentation or recounting of it.

Climacus is even more specific about this, as he goes on to describe the structure of the Postscript.

The objective issue, then, would be about the truth of Christianity. The subjective issue is about the individual's relation to Christianity. Simply stated: How can I, Johannes Climacus, share in the happiness that Christianity promises? . . .

In order to make my issue as clear as possible, I shall first present the objective issue and show how that is treated. The historical will thereby receive its due. Next, I shall present the subjective issue. That is really more than the promised sequel as a clothing in historical costume, since this costume is provided merely by mentioning the word 'Christianity'. The first part is the promised sequel; the second is a renewed attempt in the same vein as the pamphlet, a new approach to the issue of *Fragments*. (*CUP* 17)

According to this account, although the forty pages of part I of the Postscript fulfil his promise in *Fragments*, that promise could as well have been fulfilled by uttering the word 'Christianity'; and since in fact he did just that immediately after making the promise (by pointing out that 'it is not difficult to perceive what the historical costume of the next section will be. As is well known, Christianity is the only historical phenomenon that despite the historical—indeed, precisely by means of the historical—has wanted to be the single individual's point of departure for his eternal consciousness, has wanted to interest him otherwise than

[2] Trans. H. V. and E. H. Hong (Princeton University Press: Princeton, 1992); hereafter *CUP*.

merely historically, has wanted to base his happiness on his relation to something historical'; *PF* 109), the text of *Fragments* plainly fulfils its own promise. As for the remaining 570 pages that constitute part II of the Postscript: this goes beyond fulfilling the promise made in the *Fragments*, and is a new approach to the issue that the *Fragments* addresses, but it is also a renewed attempt in the same vein as that pamphlet. It follows that neither the topic nor the tone, neither the content nor the form, of the Postscript attempts anything that is not attempted in the *Fragments*.

According to Climacus' own account, then, even if the Postscript is not entirely superfluous to the *Fragments* project as a whole, it introduces nothing that should be unfamiliar to the readers of the main text; 'it is much more frivolous of him to complete the more difficult part, and then to promise a sequel, especially the sort of sequel that any attentive reader of the first part, provided that he has the requisite education, can easily write on his own—if he should find it worth the trouble' (*CUP* 10). We therefore have good reason to reject the hypothesis that the Postscript is the true heart of the project; as Climacus says, 'it is therefore quite in order that [the promise regarding the sequel] be fulfilled in a postscript, and the author can scarcely be accused of the feminine practice of saying the most important thing in a postscript, that is, if the whole matter is of any importance at all' (*CUP* 11). Further, we may suspect that those attracted to that erroneous hypothesis place the wrong value upon their education, finding it worth the trouble to exercise their learning and erudition. For 'in essence, there is no sequel. [But] in another sense, the sequel could become endless in proportion to the learnedness and erudition of the one who clothed the issue in historical dress. Honour be to learning and knowledge ... But the dialectical is nevertheless the vital power in the issue' (*CUP* 11). In short, if Climacus' project can be said to have a centre of gravity, it lies in the dialectic of the *Fragments* itself.

3. Elsewhere in the Postscript, however, Climacus implies that, although it may be necessary to master the dialectic of the *Fragments* if we are to understand it and him, it is definitely not sufficient. For when commenting upon a German reviewer of the *Fragments*, he has this to say.

His report is accurate and on the whole dialectically reliable, but now comes the hitch: although the report is accurate, anyone who reads only that will receive an utterly wrong impression of the book ... The report is didactic, purely and simply didactic; consequently the reader will receive the impression that the pamphlet is also didactic. As I see it, this is the most mistaken impression one can have of it. The contrast of form, the teasing resistance of the imaginary construction to the content, the inventive audacity (which even invents Christianity), the only attempt made to go further (that is, further than the so-called speculative constructing), the indefatigable activity of irony, the parody of speculative thought in the entire plan, the satire in making efforts as if something [altogether extraordinary, that is new] were to come of them, whereas what always emerges is old-fashioned orthodoxy in all its rightful severity—of all this the reader finds no hint in the report. (*CUP* 274–5)

This litany of criticism tells us, not only that Climacus regards the form of his book as at least as important as its dialectical content, but also that this form must be seen as contrasting with that content, and doing so by the incessant deployment of irony, parody, and satire. How many readings of the *Fragments* might be subject to the same critical litany? And how might this reading avert it?

Climacus' review of his reviewer continues as follows.

And yet the book is so far from being written for nonknowers, to give them something to know, that the person I engage in conversation in this book is always knowledgeable, which seems to indicate that the book is written for people in the know, whose trouble is that they know too much. Because everyone knows the Christian truth, it has become such a triviality that a primitive impression of it is acquired only with difficulty. When this is the case, the art of being able to *communicate* eventually becomes the art of being able to *take away* or to trick something away from someone. This seems strange and very ironic, and yet I believe I have succeeded in explaining exactly what I mean. (*CUP* 275)

The person Climacus engages in conversation in the *Fragments* is the interlocutor who intervenes at the end of each chapter, the character Climacus describes as his 'dear reader' (*PF* 89), and so presents as the text's internal representation of its intended audience. Climacus then suggests that his relation with this doubled reader is strange and ironic— 'ironic' because his text appears to be designed to communicate a certain kind of knowledge (the dialectic so ably captured by the German reviewer), and yet in reality aims to reduce or remove that knowledge; and 'strange', because it does so by estranging us from it, by defamiliarizing it. For

when a man is very knowledgeable but his knowledge is meaningless or virtually meaningless to him, does sensible communication consist in giving him more to know, even if he loudly proclaims that this is what he needs, or does it consist instead of taking something away from him? When a communicator takes a portion of the copious knowledge that the very knowledgeable man knows and communicates it in a form that makes it strange to him, the communicator is, as it were, taking away his knowledge, at least until the knower manages to assimilate the knowledge by overcoming the resistance of the form. (*CUP* 275)

In other words, *Philosophical Fragments*, by employing a non-didactic form that resists its dialectical content, attempts thereby to resist being assimilated by its readers as an addition to their store of knowledge. Its satirical presentation of old-fashioned orthodoxy as something new and extraordinary is intended to ensure that a certain portion of its readers' existing store of knowledge—their knowledge of the Christian truth— might be properly assimilated rather than taken for granted, that it might become genuinely meaningful to them. In short, this text's author pictures his readers as having a purely cognitive or epistemic relation to Christianity; they know what it is, but it means nothing to them—it is pure information, not something that informs their lives.

Of course, on the (not unreasonable) assumption that this approach is a constant feature of the Climacus authorship, certain conclusions follow for the way in which the Postscript to the *Fragments* is usually read.[3] For our purposes, however, what matters is the direct advice it provides concerning how to read the *Philosophical Fragments* proper. Any adequate reading must show how this text does not provide new information but rather takes it away, and how its incessant irony, parody, and satire encourage the genuine assimilation of its dialectical content—how overcoming the resistance of its form might serve to make that content more meaningful for its readers.

4. If, however, we are not to begin our reading of Climacus' project with that portion of it which outruns its own end, might we not be well advised to turn instead to that portion of it which precedes its official or public beginning? For although the *Fragments* and its Postscript make up Climacus' collected works, another text which bears his name— *Johannes Climacus*; or, *De Omnibus Dubitandum Est*—was earlier composed by the man identified as editor of his writings, Søren Kierkegaard. It provides a short biography of Climacus, and a longer

---

[3] James Conant's reading of the Postscript—uniquely among Kierkegaard commmentators, as far as I am aware—operates on this assumption; indeed, it was his work which led me to speculate on the possibility of developing a parallel reading of the *Fragments*, and hence to the fundamental interpretative trajectory of this part of the book. See 'Must we Show what we Cannot Say?', in R. Fleming and M. Payne (eds.), *The Senses of Stanley Cavell* (Bucknell University Press: Lewisburg, Pa., 1989); 'Wittgenstein, Kierkegaard and Nonsense', in T. Cohen, P. Guyer, and H. Putnam (eds.), *Pursuits of Reason* (Texas Technical University Press: Lubbock, 1993); and 'Putting Two and Two Together', in T. Tessin and M. von der Ruhr (eds.), *Philosophy and the Grammar of Religious Belief* (Macmillan: London, 1996).

(unfinished) treatment of Climacus' attempts to take modern philosophy seriously. Kierkegaard never published this text, and since it does not constitute part of his pseudonymous authorship as a whole—let alone that part of it authored by Climacus himself—its pertinence to the task of understanding the *Fragments* and its Postscript can legitimately be questioned. Nevertheless, certain important features of Climacus' orientation to modern philosophy are likely to be underplayed if we ignore Kierkegaard's early biography of his pseudonym altogether.

In particular, the *Fragments* and its Postscript tend to focus almost exclusively on Hegelianism as representative of the practice of modern philosophy; and commentators have generally tended to follow this lead, assuming that Climacus thinks of Hegel as his emblematic philosophical opponent (except in the 'Interlude', with its focus on doubt, belief, and scepticism). In *Johannes Climacus*, however, our young hero begins his philosophical studies with Descartes and the method of Cartesian doubt—and the unfinished text leaves him still grappling with the question of how properly to apply that method. Against this background I take the lack of extensive overt reference to Descartes in the *Fragments* to be suspicious; hence the second originating assumption of this reading is that Climacus' text can best be understood as being in continuous but implicit dialogue with Cartesian philosophy.

My third originating assumption grows from the second, and has been all but explicit in the preceding paragraphs; for I further take it as not accidental that the Descartes with whom the young Climacus is presented as grappling represents not just the founding figure of modern philosophy but also the presiding genius of Climacus' own attempts to step over the threshold of philosophy, understood not just as a discipline but as a form of life. Climacus' dialogue with Descartes is thus, in both form and content, concerned with what it means, philosophically speaking, to begin—which means (among other things) with what it means to begin philosophy, to begin speaking (and writing) philosophically, and hence to begin a life in and of philosophy, in the condition of modernity. One line of implication is clear: there can be no authentic modern philosophy that does not find the matter of its own beginning questionable, and find its own beginning (and hence its own goal or end) in such questioning, a questioning that is provoked by and endlessly responsive to the words of another. It then follows, however, that the beginning of Climacus' philosophical project cannot be found in orderings of words about him (even those of his editor), but only in words of his own ordering, words of his own—in the text in which he first, beyond question, finds his own philosophical voice.

SUBVERTING DESCARTES: THOUGHT AND EXISTENCE

5. Against this background it is unsurprising that Climacus should begin his thought-project in chapter 1 of the *Fragments* by engaging in a dialogue—questioning (as Heidegger's later writings question) a question of Socratic origin about the nature of teaching and learning, and developing thereby a contrast between a Socratic conception of the teacher (as a dispensable means of awakening knowledge always already possessed or possessable by the pupil) and a contrasting, non-Socratic conception (the teacher as indispensable, conveying both the truth and the condition for grasping it to the pupil). In doing so, however, he appears to engage in a further, more specific and less honourable, mode of citation, as the chapter's concluding dialogue with his interlocutor makes explicit. For he accuses Climacus of plagiarizing the non-Socratic model of teaching and learning—accusing him, in other words, of passing off another's words as his own, of lacking originality. Climacus claims that this charge is misdirected; it presupposes that he is parading as his own invention the ideas of another, which implies that the interlocutor regards these non-Socratic ideas as the intellectual property of some particular human being or at least of the human race as such—that is, as ideas that are well within the scope of human invention. This is not what believers in the non-Socratic hypothesis would say; for it is part of that hypothesis that human beings can only receive the truth which the hypothesis embodies through an encounter with the god. They would regard the texts Climacus cheerfully admits to plagiarizing (the Holy Bible and other texts of the Christian tradition) as divinely inspired—and it is not obvious that human beings can steal anything from God, let alone his words or his Word; indeed, since, Christianly speaking, the Word of God *is* God, this plagiarism would have to be what its etymology suggests—a form of kidnapping. Climacus, however, appears to think that the divine authorship of the hypothesis need not be taken on trust, but can be demonstrated from its content alone.

Is it not curious that something like this exists, about which everyone who knows it knows that he has not invented it, and that this 'Go to the next house' does not halt and cannot be halted, even though one were to go to everybody? Yet this oddity enthrals me exceedingly, for it tests the correctness of the hypothesis and demonstrates it. It would indeed be unreasonable to require a person to find out all by himself that he does not exist. But this transition is precisely the transition of the rebirth from not existing to existing. Whether he understands it later certainly makes no difference, for simply because someone knows how to use gunpowder, knows how to analyze it into its components, does not mean that he invented it. (*PF* 22)

This passage suggests that the non-human authorship of the non-Socratic hypothesis follows from the fact that one of its key elements is an idea of rebirth—of a transition from non-existence to existence (itself an idea central to Augustine's conception of conversion). According to that hypothesis, human beings are not only in ignorance of the truth but lack the necessary condition for understanding it, until they receive both from the god. We could not have been created in that state of untruth (since we would not then have been created human), so we must somehow have lost or been deprived of the truth; this could not have been effected by the god (since it would conflict with his original creative intention, and with his goodness), nor could it have resulted from an accident (since we would then have possessed as essential attribute of our natures only contingently), so it must have been our responsibility. In short, we must have forfeited, and be continually forfeiting, existence in the truth; our state is what Climacus suggests we call 'sin'. Having used our freedom to place ourselves in servitude to unfreedom, we cannot free ourselves; but when the god frees us, we are restored to the state for which our original creation intended us. Climacus comments:

Inasmuch as he was in untruth, and now along with the condition receives the truth, a change takes place in him like the change from 'not to be' to 'to be'. But this transition from 'not to be' to 'to be' is indeed the transition of birth. But the person who already *is* cannot be born, and yet he is born. Let us call this transition *rebirth*, by which he enters the world a second time just as at birth . . . (*PF* 19)

However, this final element of the non-Socratic model raises a fundamental difficulty (with which Heidegger's lectures on thinking also engage).

This matter of being born—is it thinkable? Well, why not? But who is supposed to think it—one who is born or one who is not born? The latter, of course, is unreasonable and cannot occur to anyone, for this notion cannot occur to one who is born. When one who is born thinks of himself as born, he is of course thinking of this transition from 'not to be' to 'to be'. The situation must be the same with rebirth. Or is the matter made more difficult by this—that the non-being preceding the rebirth has more being than the non-being that precedes birth? But who, then, is supposed to think this? It must, of course, be one who is reborn, for it would be unreasonable to think that one who is not reborn should do it, and would it not be ludicrous if this were to occur to one who is not reborn? (*PF* 20)

The idea of being born can only occur to those who have already been born, for two main reasons. First, only existing beings are capable of thought as such. Second, someone can think of themselves as unborn only if they can think of themselves as non-existent; but Descartes's most famous contribution to modern philosophy was to argue that it is impossible for any thinking being to doubt its own existence, to even think it possible that 'I do not exist'—a thought that he also took to reveal that thinking was essential to our nature as existent beings. Those who *are* born do not, of course, face this problem, since in order to think of themselves as born they need only think of themselves as having been non-existent in the past (to think 'I did not exist').

According to Climacus, the non-Socratic hypothesis raises exactly the same difficulty, because it embodies the idea of a radical change in one's being, from a wilful repudiation of one's intended orientation to the truth (and so of one's true humanity) to one in which that true nature is genuinely fulfilled—a change paralleling that from non-existence to existence. It follows that this idea of rebirth is thinkable only by those who have been reborn, and for the same two reasons. First, only reborn beings are capable of genuinely truth-oriented thinking; and second, someone can think of themselves as un(re)born only if they can think of themselves as non-existent—which is, on the Cartesian principles which guide modern Socratic philosophers, unthinkable. The reborn avoid this difficulty, because they are required only to think of themselves as having been non-existent—and 'I did not exist' is perfectly thinkable.

To those who would argue that the two cases of birth and rebirth are not parallel, since the state preceding rebirth which the non-Socratic hypothesis characterizes as a mode of non-existence is what we standardly think of as full-blooded existence, Climacus' riposte is simple: who is in a position to think that thought, to make the requisite comparison between the non-existence preceding birth and that preceding rebirth? Only those who can think of the state preceding rebirth as one of non-existence: but for those existing in that state, this would again mean thinking of themselves as non-existent—whereas those who have been reborn need only think of themselves as having been non-existent. And to those who would argue that, if they can understand the non-Socratic hypothesis as Climacus has outlined it, then it must have been possible for them—or indeed any human being—to have invented it, Climacus deploys his analogy with gunpowder. Someone capable of analysing the chemical structure of gunpowder does not thereby provide any grounds for believing either that she did or that she could have invented it; the two capacities are no more interchangeable or necessarily connected than those of the literary critic and the author. In the same way, Climacus implies, even if the Socratic follower really can follow his analysis of the logical structure of the non-Socratic hypothesis, it would give us no reason for thinking that she might have invented the structure herself. On the contrary: any modern follower of Socrates who claimed that the non-Socratic hypothesis was a human invention would be committed to claiming that she can not only think, but could also have thought up, what she is committed to regarding as unthinkable.

SUBVERTING DESCARTES: CREATION AND DEPENDENCE

6. In the second chapter of the *Fragments* Climacus sounds the same anti-Cartesian note, but in a different key, and with reference to a different element of the non-Socratic hypothesis. If the first register or dimension of his philosophical voice was that of logic, within which the conceptual skeleton of a thought-project could unfold, the second is that of poetry, within which an imaginary erotic tale is told. It, too, concerns itself (at least figuratively) with a mode of birth, a transition to a new existence—but one undergone by the god rather than by those the god encounters. In narrating the story of a king besotted with a lowly maiden, Climacus argues that—according to the non-Socratic hypothesis—the god is motivated to bring about an encounter with his human learners because he desires a fully reciprocal loving and comprehending relationship with them. This means that the relation must be between equals, even though the two involved are as unequal as it is possible to be; the learner must understand her complete dependence on the god without this destroying her self-confidence, thus rendering their relationship an unbearable sorrow to them both. Raising the learner to the god's level would not solve the problem. If she was exalted, the lover would have changed the beloved and implied that his love required that change; if he elicited her adoration by appearing in his full glory, he would imply that his glory was what made him lovable, and so make her lowliness a cause for despair. The only solution is for the god to descend to the learner's level: not merely to take on a human guise—since that would be the mere appearance of equality—but to become fully human. In short, there must be an Incarnation.

Once again, the key lesson of this poetic venture emerges in Climacus' concluding dialogue with his interlocutor. The charge of plagiarism is again raised, and again denied by denying that the venture can be thought of as having human origins.

But then my soul is also gripped with new amazement—indeed, it is filled with adoration, for it certainly would have been odd if it had been a human poem. Presumably it could occur to a human being to poetize himself in the likeness of the god or the god in the likeness of himself, but not to poetize that the god poetized himself in the likeness of a human being, for if the god gave no indication, how could it occur to a man that the blessed god could need him? This would indeed be the worst of thoughts, or, rather, so bad a thought that it could not arise in him, even though, when the god has confided it to him, he adoringly says: This thought did not arise in my heart—and finds it to be the most wondrously beautiful thought. (*PF* 36)

For Climacus, then, what betrays the divine authorship of the idea of the Incarnation is its implication that the blessed god needs human beings—that he becomes fully human because he needs to disclose his love for them without either deceiving or destroying them, and needs to elicit their freely given and self-confident love. But why is this idea of a creator dependent on his creatures beyond human invention?

Here we might recall that in the course of his meditations, after establishing the certainty of his own existence and thereby establishing the principle that whatever is clearly and distinctly perceived is true, Descartes next claims to have a clearly and distinctly perceived idea of God as a perfect being. By contrast, he perceives himself as an imperfect, conditioned, and dependent being, and takes this to demonstrate that he cannot conceive of his own existence as self-grounding, but rather as sustained by the actions of a perfect, infinite, and unconditioned being—by God. In other words, he assumes that his idea of God as free of imperfections or limitations is as indubitable a truth as that of his own existence while thinking; and he utilizes the contrast between divine perfection and human imperfection to prove God's existence by proving our dependence upon him as our creator.

On Climacus' account, the non-Socratic conception of the god precisely inverts this Cartesian line of reasoning. Its distinctive doctrine of the Incarnation makes sense only on the supposition that the god is essentially dependent: not only does he take on the dependences inherent in the finite human nature he exemplifies, he also needed to make himself incarnate, because the fulfilment of his love depends on establishing a mutually loving and comprehending relationship with human beings. For a Cartesian, this thought is not thinkable: the idea of a dependent or needy divine being is a contradiction in terms, and we could have no reason to think of any idea that incorporates it as an idea of God at all. If, however, the very idea of a dependent god could not—according to Cartesian principles—be thought by the unaided human intellect, it could hardly be thought up or invented by it; the existence of that idea is thus explicable only as the product of divine authorship. We are, it seems, dependent on the god for our idea of him as dependent on us.

SUBVERTING DESCARTES: METAPHYSICS AND DIFFERENCE

7. Against this background it is hardly surprising to find Climacus ask the following question at the heart of his third chapter: 'Is it not here as it is with the Cartesian dolls? As soon as I let go of the doll, it stands on its head' (*PF* 42). Climacus' translators, the Hongs, claim that this is a double error on Climacus' part: misremembering a kind of eccentrically weighted tumbler doll that rolls to its feet when released, Climacus misnames it for a 'Cartesian devil' (a hollow glass figure that moves in a partially filled container of water when the pliable top of the container is pressed). It seems much more likely that Climacus is deliberately using an inverted version of the tumbling doll to allude to his argumentative strategy of inverting the founding moves and principles of the Cartesian meditations.

We should not, however, interpret that strategy as an attempted proof of the non-Socratic hypothesis—as if Climacus aims not only to defamiliarize our knowledge of Christianity by presenting it as a mere imaginative exercise, but also to provide anti-Cartesian demonstrations of God's existence from the existence of our idea of him (since the non-Socratic idea of God presupposes the humanly inconceivable and so necessarily divinely inspired ideas of his dependence and our non-existence). For first, the damage done to the Socratic hypothesis depends only on the existence of the non-Socratic hypothesis *qua* hypothesis—its reality as an idea; it need not correspond to anything real for it to prove a stumbling-block to its opponents. Second, the non-Socratic hypothesis entails that followers of Socrates must lack the condition for understanding the truth; so the fact that they confront a paradox shows only that the non-Socratic hypothesis has avoided an internal inconsistency—it does not demonstrate its truth. And third, Climacus himself emphasizes in his third chapter that no proofs of God's existence are possible. His underlying point seems reminiscent of the Kantian claim that 'existence is not a true predicate'. Logical or deductive links hold only between concepts, as part of the unfolding or interrelating of ideas or essences; such connections can be elaborated from an existential pre-supposition (by, for example, showing that any object with one property must have another property), but they cannot by themselves deliver an existential conclusion, since that amounts to determining whether a given idea has application to the world (whether a certain empirical possibility is actual) and the contrary of any matter of fact is always logically possible. In short, logic cannot adjudicate existential claims; the abyss between the realm of essence and that of factual being is not bridgeable in thought.

Nevertheless, his two preceding exchanges with his (plainly Socratically minded) interlocutor show that she has a hubristic misconception of her relationship with the non-Socratic hypothesis. For this modern representative of Socrates is prone to imagine that the non-Socratic hypothesis might have been invented by a human being, and so to presuppose that it falls within the realm of human conceivability—that it can be grasped by and in thought (and then, of course, rejected). But the reality appears to be that its key elements are not thinkable on Cartesian principles, and so that the hypothesis as a whole is beyond the powers of human invention or construction. All paradoxes present themselves as a challenge to the understanding; but this paradox really is absolutely beyond its scope.

In a terribly compressed metaphysical analysis in this third chapter Climacus tries to demonstrate the hubris attendant upon any claim by the understanding to be able to construct an adequate idea of that which is beyond it. If this idea of the unknown or the unknowable truly is to be something that thought cannot think, then it must be absolutely different from thought; there must be no trace within it of anything by reference to which thought might be able to grasp it, and so no mark by which the unknown is distinguished from other known or knowable things—since the unknown would then at least be knowable as the opposite or negation of that knowable thing, and so the supposed beyond of thought would be thinkable by way of negation.

Defined as the absolutely different, [the unknown] appears to be at the point of being disclosed, but not so, because the understanding cannot even think the absolutely different; it cannot absolutely negate itself, but uses itself for that purpose and consequently thinks the difference in itself, which it thinks by itself. It cannot absolutely transcend itself and therefore thinks as above itself only the sublimity it thinks by itself. (*PF* 45)

If all distinguishing marks must be erased from the absolutely different, that must include whatever distinguishes it from the understanding;

the understanding must therefore negate itself absolutely, negate even its grasp of the difference as absolutely different from itself, since that too amounts to a relation between it and the difference (by way of self-negation), and so negates the absoluteness of its difference. But if the understanding negated even this relation to the idea of the absolutely different, it would not stand in any relation to it at all—in other words, it would be absolutely ungraspable. Instead, surreptitiously but necessarily, the understanding continues to think absolute difference by using itself—that is, by thinking of the unknown as absolutely different from itself, and so as the negation of itself in some respect or other. Climacus characterizes this as a dispersion of the unknown—the dissemination of a number of ideas of the unknown which differ according to which aspect of the understanding has been negated to produce it: the unknown as the ridiculous, as the prodigious, and so on. But then, our choosing to develop any particular one of these ideas is entirely arbitrary—each is as little and as much an idea of the absolutely different as any other; and of course, all are ultimately constructions of the understanding, which knows deep down that it has capriciously produced its idea of the unknown god itself, and so knows that it is not truly an idea of the absolutely different at all.

Hence, every idea of the unknown which the understanding can grasp must be one in which the supposedly absolute difference between the unknown and the understanding has in fact absolutely collapsed. 'If the difference cannot be grasped securely because there is no distinguishing mark, then, as with all such dialectical opposites, so it is with the difference and the likeness—they are identical. Adhering to the understanding, the difference has so confused the understanding that it does not know itself and quite consistently confuses itself with the difference' (*PF* 45). This is why paganism has produced such a variety of gods resembling human beings in so many different ways; and it is also why the understanding tends to generate misleading conceptions of the non-Socratic hypothesis of divine incarnation. For it will interpret that hypothesis as requiring that a human being who behaves in just the way all other human beings behave is and can be known to be the god.

How do I know that? Well, I cannot know it, for in that case I would have to know the god and the difference, and I do not know the difference, inasmuch as the understanding had made it like unto that from which it differs. Thus the god has become the most terrible deceiver through the understanding's deception of itself. The understanding has the god as close as possible and yet just as far away. (*PF* 45–6)

Any idea of god constructed by the understanding is made in its own all too human image, and is (therefore?) also an image of a terrible deceiver, an evil demon—since an incarnate god who was indistinguishable from any other human being would have made it impossible for anyone even to imagine that he was, let alone to encounter him as, the god. The closest that the understanding can come to an idea of the absolutely different inevitably fails to respect its absoluteness, and so places itself as far away as possible from the god. The absolute paradox of divine incarnation constitutes the downfall of the understanding.

But for Climacus, collision with such a paradox is exactly what the understanding most fundamentally desires; the ultimate paradox of thought is its desire to discover something that thought cannot think, to will its own downfall. This is once again a Kantian diagnosis; it reiterates the famous opening declaration of the first *Critique*, that it is the fate of human reason to set itself questions that it is capable neither of answering nor of dismissing. The first half of that *Critique* (the Transcendental Analytic) presupposes that the understanding attains true maturity only when it determines for itself the limits of its legitimate employment—mapping the limits of the comprehensible from within; and the second half (the Transcendental Dialectic) studies the various deformations of reason which can result from the paradoxical impulse to violate those limits—a taxonomy of the perversions to which thought is unavoidably heir. The Kantian bequest to modern philosophy is thus the idea that reason is both inherently obliged to explore its own limits, and inherently inclined to violate them. So when Climacus says that anything which presents itself to thought as a limit simultaneously torments and incites the understanding, that thought needs to discover a boundary beyond which it cannot go but can never stop wanting to go beyond any such boundary, he is adapting that Kantian vision (and anticipating its Wittgensteinian adaptation) to account for the understanding's fascination with the paradox of the incarnate god. For the paradox really is beyond the scope of the understanding, and so fixes its limits from the outside, as it were; but precisely because of that the understanding will never cease wanting to grasp it, and never cease claiming to have succeeded—even though it knows at bottom that it can never succeed, that the absolute paradox represents its own nemesis. In effect, the paradox of the incarnate god and the understanding's paradoxical desire for its own downfall are made for one another; only the absolute paradox can elicit and satisfy the passion of the understanding to its fullest possible extent.

In this way, the third dimension of Climacus' philosophical voice (call it its metaphysical register, since this third chapter is called 'a metaphysical caprice') draws upon both its logical and its poetic possibilities: the understanding represents the claims of logic, and desire or passion represents the innately erotic bent of poetry. In the Postscript to the *Fragments* Climacus brings to centre-stage the resulting picture of the absolute paradox and the perverse understanding as a marriage made at once in heaven and in hell; but in the appendix to this third chapter he restricts himself to presenting its sadomasochism as a drama of contested copyright. He defines all passion as a kind of suffering, and the passion of the understanding's unhappy love for the paradox of the unknown god (what Climacus calls 'offence', as opposed to what he will later call the happy love of 'faith') as one in which the understanding—subject to an acoustical illusion—continually protests its own authorship of the paradox, is wounded by its own inevitable failure to validate that claim and to accept that everything it knows of the paradox originates from the paradox itself rather than its own creative resources, and yet continually returns to the cause of its endless suffering—to that which wounds it by its very existence. In this context, the understanding's struggle to avoid acknowledging its own perversity appears as itself perverse—as one more sadomasochistic twist in that spiral of self-injury. It confirms Climacus' suspicion that the modern followers of Socrates—committed to the essential transparency and truthfulness of human nature—ought to consider (as did their master) the possibility that human beings are in fact as bizarre and mysterious in their nature as winged horses, gorgons, and other monsters.

SUBVERTING THE SUBVERSION: SOCRATIC ORIGINS

8. Climacus himself, however, takes his metaphysical caprice one step further than its identification of a certain capricious perversity in the understanding, by insisting that it directs us towards a paradox that appears to confront more than just the modern followers of Socrates.

. . . if a human being is to come truly to know something about the unknown (the god), he must first come to know that it is different from, absolutely different from him. The understanding cannot come to know this by itself (since, as we have seen, this is a contradiction); if it is going to come to know this, it must come to know this from the god, and if it does come to know this it cannot understand this and consequently cannot come to know this, for how could it understand the absolutely different? . . . If the god is absolutely different from a human being, then the human being is absolutely different from the god—but how is the understanding to grasp this? At this point we seem to stand at a paradox. (*PF* 46)

Followers of the Socratic hypothesis have just been charged with erroneously thinking that they can think the unthinkable—construct a contentful idea of that which is beyond the understanding. But even if we assume divine authorship and delivery of an appropriately constructed idea of the absolutely different, it would still *ex hypothesi* be ungraspable by the human understanding. So it should not be graspable even by those who want to use it in elaborating the non-Socratic hypothesis, or defending it against the intellectual hubris of their Socratically minded opponents.

Of course, according to the non-Socratic hypothesis, the reborn would be able to grasp it; for an encounter with the god is supposed to give us both the truth and the condition for understanding it—to transform our corrupted understanding so that it can grasp the truth. But if only transformed human beings can grasp the non-Socratic hypothesis, anyone offering to explain and defend that hypothesis would not only be presumptuously presupposing their own redemption, but embarking on a futile task—since the only people for whom an explanation and defence of the hypothesis might be useful would be unable to grasp it.

Might we perhaps distinguish between thinking the unthinkable and thinking that the unthinkable is the unthinkable? At one point Climacus remarks in passing that 'we do not say that [the learner] is supposed to understand the paradox, but is only to understand that this is the paradox' (*PF* 59); perhaps, then, only the transformed human understanding can think the unthinkable paradox, but the untransformed human understanding can at least grasp that the paradox is unthinkable—and so can usefully be led to appreciate this. Interestingly enough, Descartes uses a distinction of this kind when defending his own conception of God's absolute freedom to abrogate even the laws of logic, and thus to create a logically impossible world.[4] He distinguishes between knowing that God is the author of everything (including logic) and conceiving or grasping it; just as we finite creatures cannot embrace a mountain but can only touch it, so our imperfect understanding cannot embrace God's omnipotence in thought but can touch

---

[4] James Conant has examined this matter in some detail, in 'The Search for Logically Alien Thought', *Philosophical Topics*, 20/1 (Fall 1991), to which the following paragraphs are indebted.

it. So perhaps the untransformed understanding can frame a thought about that which lies beyond the thinkable because it can conceive of something inconceivable without conceiving that inconceivable something; the latter task can be performed only by the transformed understanding. Could we not, then, touch the absolutely different in our thought without actually embracing it; and so is there not room for explanation and even defence of the non-Socratic hypothesis by and for the unreborn?

We must surely, however, ask the same question of this claim that Climacus has just insisted on asking the followers of Socrates: is the idea of absolute difference invoked here really absolute? If even the most minimal relation between the understanding and the idea of absolute difference undermines its absoluteness, then understanding that something is the absolutely different (even it if is not equivalent to understanding the absolutely different) presupposes some kind of relation between that idea and the untransformed understanding. If the untransformed understanding could not even touch the idea of the absolutely unthinkable in its thought, the non-Socratic hypothesis would be neither explicable nor defensible; but if it so much as touches that idea, even if it restricts itself to thinking that the unthinkable is the unthinkable, then it is not an idea of the absolutely unthinkable.

9. Thus, the paradox to which Climacus's commentary on his metaphysical caprice appears to direct us is that the anti-Socratic line of argument developed thus far in the *Fragments*, in both its logical and its poetic registers, is hoist by its own petard. It criticizes the Socratic hypothesis for presuming to think the unthinkable, generating an interpretation of the god as the absolutely different in order to underline this presumption; but that criticism must help itself to the same, supposedly unthinkable notion, and so displays the presumption it castigates. For if the idea of absolute difference is humanly unthinkable, how can the idea that absolute difference is humanly unthinkable—the idea just employed to explain the non-Socratic model and criticize its opponents—be humanly thinkable? According to its own analysis, either the anti-Socratic position must be itself unthinkable or it must be surreptitiously helping itself to an idea of something other than the absolutely unthinkable—thus collapsing the distinction between human beings and the absolutely different.

Climacus thinks of this collapse as a confusion of difference and likeness; and he diagnoses its cause as follows: 'in defining the unknown as the different, the understanding ultimately goes astray and confuses the difference with likeness' (*PF* 46). In other words, the problem lies with our definition of the unknown as the absolutely different. In fact, Climacus' discussion of the paradox in chapter 3 begins by referring to a frontier of thought, and his metaphysical caprice properly gets under way only when he shifts from the idea of a frontier to the idea of difference: the unknown, he says, 'is the frontier that is continually arrived at, and therefore when the category of motion is replaced by the category of rest it is the different, the absolutely different' (*PF* 44). Moreover, he later remarks that the fatal dispersion of the idea of the absolutely different comes about only 'if the unknown (the god) is not solely the frontier' (*PF* 45). This suggests that the understanding goes astray the moment it shifts from picturing the unknown as a frontier to picturing it as the different.

But how momentous could such a (merely) figurative shift be? Well, the idea of the frontier allows Climacus to develop the following thought: 'The paradoxical passion of the understanding . . . has correctly perceived the unknown as frontier. But a frontier is expressly the passion's torment, even though it is also its incentive. And yet, it can go no further, whether it risks a sortie through *via negationis* (the way of negation) or *via eminentiae* (the way of idealization)' (*PF* 44). When, by contrast, we think of the unknown god as the absolutely different, it presents itself as something lying beyond the frontier of thought; so when we attempt to think that difference, we find ourselves assuming that we can somehow get beyond that frontier—that we can know the unknown (*qua* absolutely different). The followers of Socrates attempt this via a combination of negation (defining the unknown by self-negation) and idealization (idealizing their powers of understanding); their opponents deploy a similar combination (constructing an idealized understanding by negating our familiar one). And both fail, because their attempts illicitly and ironically render what is supposedly unknown and unknowable as in fact knowable.

Any true frontier of the thinkable can never be crossed by thought, but—as Climacus says—can only be arrived at and engaged with; for anything beyond such a frontier would be unthinkable. But the idea of the absolutely different attempts to mark that frontier from the outside, to pick out some specific thing that thought cannot think. It therefore presupposes that there are two types of thought—the thinkable thoughts and the unthinkable ones; whereas an unthinkable thought is not a peculiar kind of thought—it is no thought at all. More generally, it presupposes that we can delineate the limits of thought by thinking both sides of the limit; but if we could think both sides of this boundary, it could not be the boundary of the thinkable, but at best a boundary within the boundary of the thinkable—a division within the realm of thought. The echoes of Wittgenstein's diagnosis of our tendency to misinterpret the limits of thought (from the preface of the *Tractatus* to his later philosophy) are clear; Climacus expresses the same vision by saying that the understanding 'thinks as above itself only the sublimity that it thinks by itself' (*PF 45*).

Trying to supplement the non-Socratic distinction between transformed and untransformed modes of human understanding with a further Cartesian distinction between ideas touchable by thought and ideas embraceable by thought merely deepens the problem. If a transformed understanding might grasp ideas that are beyond the capacities of an untransformed understanding, then the limits of the untransformed understanding are not the absolute limits of the thinkable, but rather constraints that can conceivably be transcended; the unthinkable is only contingently unthinkable, as it were. And if the untransformed understanding can touch the ideas that only a transformed understanding can embrace, then the contingently necessary limits of the thinkable are not even contingently necessary—the boundary can be crossed even by untransformed thought, and so must mark a division within the realm of the thinkable. The limits of the thinkable are thus transgressable by the unreborn as well as the born; they are doubly displaced or devalued, doubly non-absolute.

Could the anti-Socratic critique be rescued by reformulating it in terms of a frontier rather than of absolute difference? Climacus does appear to think that its problems begin when the picture of a frontier is left behind. Sensitized by his own warnings, however, we may be less sanguine; after all, no matter how much he stresses that the frontier of thought can only be arrived at, that it cannot be crossed, the image itself can accommodate the thought that (as with territorial borders) there is a realm beyond the frontier to which we are being denied access. Whatever the truth of this matter, however, in so far as the anti-Socratic critique developed earlier utilizes the idea of the god as that which thought cannot think, it commits the very error of which it accuses its opponents (that of violating the limits of the thinkable), and it hides its violation in exactly the same way—by illicitly de-absolutizing those limits, picturing them as a boundary drawn within a wider realm and so as thinkable from both sides. Thus, the anti-Socratic claim to have more respect for the proper limits of the understanding itself transgresses them—its fervent warning against the hubris of the mind merely a further expression of that hubris. What greater proof could there be of the understanding's perverse tendency for self-deception and self-ironization—its all but unappeasable desire for its own downfall—than its impassioned construction of an idea of the god that demands that it nail itself to a cross of perpetual torment?

10. This self-subversion of the anti-Socratic critique strongly suggests that its interpretation of the god's paradoxicality, as something that thought cannot think, is driven by the perverseness of the understanding rather than the nature of the god. And in fact, once we notice the further reflexive implications of Climacus' metaphysical caprice, their consequences engulf virtually every aspect of his earlier development of the non-Socratic hypothesis.

First of all, according to his analysis, any attempt to grasp the unthinkable by negating some or other aspect of the understanding will go awry, collapsing the very distinction it aims to comprehend. But in the previous two chapters those opposed to the Socratic model attempted to demonstrate its incoherence by presenting key elements of the non-Socratic hypothesis as negations of Socratic conceptions of the limits of the understanding. This at first appeared to be a particularly powerful way of criticizing the understanding; but now it appears as simply one more instance of the understanding attempting to think the unthinkable by negating some aspect of its own self-conception, and thus as exemplifying exactly the same inability to think the unthinkable of which the modern followers of Socrates were accused. And once suspicions are raised about constructions by negation, then the whole of Climacus' elaboration of the non-Socratic hypothesis is placed in the dock. For he repeatedly insists that that hypothesis is constructed by negating every element of the Socratic hypothesis. Only thus, we were told, could its originality be maintained—its claim to have gone beyond Socrates. But according to the metaphysical caprice, constructions of the understanding that operate by self-negation remain indebted to that which they negate; so no such construction could be anything other than Socratic in its essence.

This suggests that Climacus' project is misbegotten from the outset. But of course, the reiterated operation of negation that produces the anti-Socratic hypothesis is not the real starting-point of Climacus' presentation—as the label 'anti-Socratic' suggests, and as our initial interest in the interlocutor's charge of plagiarism led us to overlook hitherto. For that hypothesis is explicitly introduced as an alternative to a prior Socratic competitor, and both are introduced as responses to a prior question, with the articulation of which the first chapter properly commences: 'Can the truth be learned? With this question we shall begin' (*PF* 9). As Climacus immediately points out, this is 'a Socratic question'; in other words, he structures his elaboration of the Socratic and non-Socratic hypotheses from the outset as alternative solutions to a Socratic paradox. And the profoundly questionable nature of this starting-point is signalled by that part of the text of chapter 1 that precedes even its opening sentences—the *propositio* (proposition or hypothesis) which forms its title or heading, and hence its formal origin: 'The question is asked by one who in his ignorance does not even know what provided the occasion for his questioning in this way' (*PF* 9). The question referred to can only be that which immediately follows this *propositio*—the Socratic question of how the truth can be learned. Since Climacus asks this question of himself and us, the *propositio* in effect describes him as someone ignorant of what leads him to ask the question, and ignorant of his ignorance; it suggests that Climacus never questions the importance and correctness of his procedure, but in fact lacks the fully transparent self-knowledge whose reality the very asking of the Socratic question presupposes.

Suppose he (and we) were to ask (as Heidegger and Wittgenstein each begin their own journey of thinking by asking) what occasioned his investigation, to take up the invitation of the chapter's formal opening to begin its project again by questioning its beginnings, what answer might emerge? What does this starting-point tell us about his motivation? First, that it is a response to a paradox—that learning the truth is not possible, since those who know the truth have no need to acquire it, and those who do not know what it is cannot look for it. As we are reminded in chapter 3, this is exactly the starting-point we would expect for a meditation by a follower of Socrates; 'the paradox is the passion of thought, and the thinker without the paradox is like the lover without passion: a very mediocre fellow' (*PF* 37). After all, Climacus often says that he is not himself a Christian, not one of the reborn or one who propounds the non-Socratic hypothesis as the truth; he is a humorist and a philosopher who is trying to make sense of the possibility for eternal happiness that Christianity claims to offer.

It should not therefore surprise us that his perspective on his material is Socratic through and through; but the implications of that fact are fundamental. For it entails that, despite its overtly anti-Socratic thrust, his presentation of the non-Socratic hypothesis will manifest every weakness and incoherence of which his anti-Socratic critique accuses its opponents. Indeed, according to the appendix to chapter 3, any Socratically inflected presentation of the god is an expression of the understanding's unhappy love for the paradox—an expression of offence rather than faith. So we should expect this presentation to manifest the distinguishing marks of offence: 'Offense is the erroneous accounting, the conclusion of untruth, with which the paradox thrusts away. The one offended does not speak according to his own nature, but according to the nature of the paradox, just as someone caricaturing another person does not originate anything himself, but only copies the other in the wrong way' (*PF* 50–1). If Climacus' thought-project produces a caricature of the god, then his Socratic interlocutor's constantly reiterated charge of plagiarism is (unsurprisingly) precisely the reverse of the truth; the problem is not that Climacus presents the words of a (divine) other as his own, but that he presents his own words as those of a divine other. This is the opposite or negation of plagiarism—a species of ventriloquism, an acoustical illusion (of the kind to which the title of the appendix carefully draws our attention): we have taken Climacus' voice, echoing back from the frontier of thought, as that of the unknown god, and allowed him to remake the god in his own Socratic image. But in what sense is that image an erroneous copy or caricature of the non-Socratic god?

Since Climacus' orientation entails that the non-Socratic hypothesis is presented primarily as a second possible solution to a Socratic paradox, divine incarnation emerges as one solution to a Socratic question about the transmission and acquisition of knowledge. It also entails that the non-Socratic hypothesis emerges by negation from the Socratic hypothesis, and so embodies an interpretation of the divine incarnation as beyond the limits of human understanding, as the absolute negation of thought and reason. In every respect, therefore, this interpretation of the god casts him in terms of his relation to the understanding. He appears as one element in a hypothesis, an intellectual structure designed to solve an intellectual problem; and whether we are offended by him or not, it is our understanding—our capacity for thought—that is engaged by him, our understanding that suffers and is wounded by his existence. If, then, we really are to live up to Climacus' warning against interpreting the unknown god in Socratic terms, we must surely reject as a caricature of the truth the idea that our relation to him is best interpreted in terms of the understanding—as if the only kind of challenge that the incarnate god poses to the followers of Socrates is an intellectual one, a challenge to thought. We must, in short, recognize that the understanding's self-constructed crucifixion is a blasphemous, intellectualized parody of the real challenge that the god's crucifixion sets us.

LOGIC, POETRY, AND THEOLOGY

11. Climacus claimed in the Postscript that his aim in the *Fragments* was to re-present our knowledge of Christianity in such a way that it is no longer meaningless to us. This claim explicitly denies that the non-Socratic hypothesis is literally unknowable or unthinkable; it says rather that it has come to mean nothing to us—that we cannot see how or why we might think of ourselves and our lives in the particular terms it proposes. In short, the real problem for Climacus is to get us to see the existential or spiritual point of Christianity—to appreciate once again the true nature of the challenge it poses. The Socratic interpretation of the incarnate god as the key element in a non-Socratic solution to a Socratic problem of knowledge merely continues the original problem, by disguising the existential challenge of Christianity as an intellectual challenge. Even the supposedly anti-Socratic insistence that the god is beyond our intellectual capacities implies that this intellectual insight is an essential prolegomenon to any proper relation to Christianity—something that must be cleared up before an appropriate relation with the god can be established. However, even explaining that the god is absolutely inexplicable is, after all, a kind of explanation; and this type of assumption is identified by Climacus as one of the characteristic signs of offence: 'When the understanding wants to have pity upon the paradox and assist it to an explanation, the paradox does not put up with that but considers it appropriate for the understanding to do that, for is that not what philosophers are for— to make supernatural things ordinary and trivial?' (*PF* 53). But this suggests not only that the blasphemous parody of the god with which the offended understanding presents us in *Fragments* trivializes the divine, but also that the paradox will not put up with that trivialization—that it will nevertheless find a way of getting its true nature across despite the parody. After all, a caricature is not an entirely inaccurate portrait of someone; a good caricature exaggerates the true features of its subject, and may even give a clearer picture of it than a more faithful representation can convey.

We must therefore ask how Climacus' intellectualized caricature of the god might nevertheless indirectly convey the true existential challenge embodied in Christian vision and terminology—might contain at least an echo of the voice of the god as it is reflected by the offended understanding. The necessary shift of aspect is not hard to identify in general terms. Both his thought-project and his poetic venture present the non-Socratic vision as a rigorously elaborated conceptual chain or network, first as a mapping of pure logic and then as a mapping of pure desire; at various points in both elaborations Climacus notes in passing that particular nodes of the network might be labelled with tags from Christian theology, but implies that these are at best marginal aide-memoires. If we are to reclaim the true significance of Christianity, we need to invert the terms of this ironical presentation—to recognize that it is those seemingly dispensable tags (which even Climacus' caricature cannot entirely eliminate from his subject-matter) that embody the real substance of the Christian vision. Some guidance for effecting this inversion in properly existential terms emerges if we recall that the chapter which invites us to take on that task is written in such a way as to draw upon both the logical and the poetic registers of Climacus' (and so the human) philosophical voice—registers hitherto sharply segregated. For that implies that accepting its invitation would mean recounting Christianity in a voice of poetic understanding—one that, by acknowledging the passion informing its concepts, might succeed in putting flesh on its bones: one that, by re-embodying Christianity in human life, might succeed in picturing its soul.

This is certainly what Climacus' concluding remarks in chapter 3 suggest. There, immediately after hinting that his metaphysical caprice implies that the anti-Socratic critique is self-subverting, he goes on to explain how the god's difference from human beings might be perfectly adequately understood.

... if the god is to be absolutely different from a human being, this can have its basis not in that which man owes to the god (for to that extent they are akin) but in that which he owes to himself or in that which he himself has committed. What, then, is the difference? Indeed, what else but sin, since the difference, the absolute difference, must have been caused by the individual himself. (*PF* 47)

Here, the absolute difference is not a cognitive distance but a moral or spiritual one; human beings are sinful and the god is not—it is not their understanding but their soul that is inadequate as it stands, and their encounter with the god gives them a consciousness of their own self-willed falling away from goodness. In other words, the transition of rebirth, which the thought-project in chapter 1 presents as embodying the anti-Cartesian intellectual challenge of thinking of oneself as non-existent, is here presented as the existential challenge of thinking of oneself as spiritually non-existent, as living a life that is oriented away from the good. The key issue is not negating the cogito, but overcoming our resistance to thinking of ourselves as radically or originally sinful creatures.

Climacus elaborates this alternative interpretation by switching attention from sinner to saviour: 'Only the god could teach [consciousness of sin]—if he wanted to be teacher. But this he did indeed want to be, as we have composed the story, and in order to be that, he wanted to be on the basis of equality with the single individual, so that he could completely understand him' (*PF* 47). This is the aspect of the non-Socratic hypothesis that was elaborated in chapter 2; what was originally presented as an anti-Cartesian point about divine dependence or imperfection now appears as a point about god's love for mankind. The difficulty is not the intellectual one of recognizing divinity in imperfection, but the practical one of recognizing oneself—a sinner—as nevertheless lovable by god, as having something of the divine that an incarnate god might redeem.

Combining these two elements, Climacus immediately derives a spiritual version of the absolute paradox that was the topic of his third chapter. 'Thus the paradox becomes even more terrible, or the same paradox has the duplexity by which it manifests itself as the absolute— negatively, by bringing into prominence the absolute difference of sin, and positively by wanting to annul this absolute difference in the absolute equality' (*PF* 47). But what might it mean, existentially speaking, to perceive oneself in these terms—as a sinner redeemed by one's relation to God?

APPENDIX AND INTERLUDE: CAPTION AND PERFORMANCE

12. The appendix to chapter 3 begins to elaborate the conceptual resources needed to provide a genuine answer to this question. Its account of the understanding's unhappy love has three central themes. First, the understanding suffers through its relation to the god; it must, indeed, undergo a self-inflicted crucifixion if it is to maintain that relationship. Second, an acoustical illusion is central to that relationship— the understanding is unwittingly but ineliminably indebted to the paradox for its words about the paradox. And finally, the understanding needs to step aside—to resign its self-given position of importance in relation to the paradox; 'the understanding surrenders itself and the paradox gives itself' (*PF* 54). Those familiar with the Postscript will recognize each of these elements; for Climacus there anatomizes Christianity (religiousness B) as incorporating and transcending an absolute orientation to the absolute good (religiousness A), and he anatomizes

this orientation in terms of three aspects or moments: resignation, suffering, and guilt (a term which also signifies indebtedness). The overt interpretation placed on those elements in the appendix may trivialize their demands; but part of the theological skeleton of the Christian vision is visible in the caricature.

Two things are not yet visible, however: first, the rest of that skeleton—the ways in which a consciousness of oneself as sinful transcends as well as incorporates a sense of oneself as guilty; and second, a clearer indication that these theological terms require existential application. After all, if the true challenge posed by the god is existential rather than intellectual, more must be involved in meeting it than simply shifting our terminology from cognitive paradoxes to theological ones; Climacus' caricature must show that the Christian vision of sinful but redeemable humanity is meant to find application to human life—to secrete an existential imperative. But the second half of the *Fragments* can be seen to do just that—in its usual self-subverting way.

The Postscript's brief analytical account of how sin-consciousness transcends guilt-consciousness focuses almost exclusively on the Christian conception of the divine incarnation—on the idea that since, in religiousness B, the absolute good to which religiousness A asks us to orient ourselves enters time, it asks us to orient ourselves to the absolute good in time, to the incarnate deity. Sure enough, the fourth and fifth chapters of the *Fragments* appear to do just that: they confront the redoubled absurdity involved in relating oneself *qua* temporal being to the eternal made temporal. Equally predictably, however, they interpret this difficulty as an intellectual one—that of comprehending the nature of any relation to such a deity—and they take this comprehension to be an essential preparation for properly relating oneself to the god.

The 'Interlude', in particular, presents itself as a virtuoso metaphysical analysis of the concepts of existence, necessity, and history designed to demonstrate that the absurdity of the idea of an incarnate deity is such as to collapse any religiously significant difference between different generations of Christian believers. Faith in Jesus as the incarnate god is neither strengthened nor weakened by temporal propinquity, since not even a lifetime's close observation of him could determine his divinity. In short, a believer's interest in the historical event of the Incarnation is not essentially historical, and so is essentially unaffected by considerations pertinent to historical beliefs.

We might say: according to the 'Interlude' between 'The Contemporary Follower' and 'The Follower at Second Hand', there is no religiously significant interlude between the contemporary follower and the follower at second hand. But then how religiously significant can the 'Interlude' be? Climacus describes himself as having 'thought to fill the intervening time by pondering the question set forth' (*PF* 72); he tells us that, although 'how long the intervening period should be is up to you', he has assumed as large a passage of time as possible (1,843 years); and he remarks that 'the most recent philosophy ... seems to suffer from a strange inattention, confusing the performance with the caption' (*PF* 73). But the metaphysical analysis tells us that historical distance is no barrier between the individual and the god, that there is no religiously significant time gap to fill between Climacus himself and the god; whatever challenge the god poses for us, he poses it as immediately now as he did during his lifetime. And yet Climacus does not engage with that challenge, but rather allows time to pass (and as large a passage of time as possible) by musing about metaphysical questions—as if the first challenge posed by the god is an intellectual one. Instead of relating to the god, he relates to the idea of relating to the god; he focuses on the caption rather than the performance.

But his own metaphysical performance explicitly stresses that no coming into existence, and so no action, performance, or event, is ever necessary. In particular, 'belief is not a knowledge but an act of freedom, an expression of will' (*PF* 83); so faithfully believing in the incarnate deity is doubly expressive of the individual's free will, since it involves willing to believe in the coming into existence of a historical event, and willing to believe in the divinity of that which comes into existence. In short, it is an event that is also an action, just like the Incarnation; it means undergoing an existential transformation, a change from one mode of existence into another—a change which must therefore itself be both an event (induced by the god) and a freely willed action. Nothing will ensure that this transition comes about—not even the god's presence, but particularly not the presence of some piece of knowledge, even if it purports to be knowledge about the transition; and yet only through that transition can the individual be reborn.

The would-be believer must therefore maintain a continued relation to the god: as the titles or captions of these chapters emphasize, she must become a follower of the god. To believe in the god is to follow the god; and to follow him is not to follow him around but to live as he did, to imitate him—he did, after all, say 'I am the Way, the Truth and the Life'. Focusing on the incarnate god as someone to follow means focusing on his way of living—the life that was sufficiently different from everyday human life to ensure that the incarnate deity did not entirely obscure his divinity, and yet not beyond the power of ordinary human beings to imitate. Climacus describes him as 'so absorbed in the service of the spirit that it never occurs to him to provide for food and drink' (*PF* 57), and as being essentially a teacher; but that means that he *is* his teaching—that his life, and particularly his death, are what he calls those who would follow him to imitate. In short, the crucifixion he requires of us is not a crucifixion of the intellect but of the heart; the challenge he poses is to live in the way that he was willing to die—to keep body and soul together according to a conception that the self will experience as tearing them asunder.

TEACHER AND TEACHING: OWNING INDEBTEDNESS

13. If this really is the message that the *Philosophical Fragments* aims to convey, why does Climacus choose such a perversely indirect way of doing it? Why construct a text that develops a progressively more baroque parody of Christianity to the point where its implications subvert its own foundations and bring down the whole edifice, leaving only marginal adumbrations of the true Christian vision for those with eyes to see them?

Climacus' general answer appears in the concluding exchanges with his interlocutor in the appendix to chapter 3. He is accused once again of plagiarism—of having woven his descriptions of the understanding's unhappy love for the paradox from the words of other authors (ranging from Tertullian to Shakespeare); but he seems, as usual, untroubled by the charge.

... have not all these men talked about a relation of the paradox to offense, and will you please notice that they were not the offended ones but the very ones who held firmly to the paradox and yet spoke as if they were the offended ones, and offense cannot come up with a more striking expression than that. Is it not peculiar that the paradox thus seems to be taking bread from the mouth of the offense ... as odd as an opponent who absent-mindedly does not attack the author but defends him? ... Yet offense has one advantage: it points up the difference more clearly ... (*PF* 54)

By citing these authors' words, Climacus implies that this description of them applies to him; he therefore identifies himself as holding firmly to the paradox despite speaking as if he were offended by it, and he implies that this does the paradox the service of pointing up the difference— the paradox—more clearly. But how does his performance do this, and why in this indirect way? Two reasons suggest themselves.

The first involves his readers' philosophical predilections. Since Climacus thinks of the understanding as an obstacle to establishing a proper relation to the paradox (the god), and as inherently prone to violate its own proper limits, he is bound to expect that even the best attempts to understand these ideas are likely to be unconsciously but radically distorted—especially by philosophers, those well-known followers of Socrates. They in particular will be prone to think that his insight about the superfluity of the understanding is itself a matter for the understanding—and to regard direct warnings to this effect in the same, radically inappropriate way. Consequently, Climacus instead develops his idea in a way which is gradually but increasingly distorted by the perversity of the understanding, but in such a manner that the attentive reader gradually becomes conscious of the distortion. By enacting the error to which he thinks that his readers are prone, but in a way that allows them to become conscious of it as an error, he is in effect trying to inoculate them against it—to make them see how easily they can fall into it, and how important it is that they avoid this trap. In short, he offers his own text (as Heidegger and Wittgenstein offer theirs) as a mirror in which his readers might see an aspect of their own perversity, and thereby avoid its baleful consequences.

His second justification for indirection reflects his sense of the centrality of an unmediated god-relationship. If the god really is to go beyond Socrates, then—as we have seen—he must be both teacher and teaching; if his message can be separated from his person, then our true focus as learners would have to be the teaching rather than the teacher, who would then be a Socratic midwife—a mere occasion for our learning that which we could have learned some other way. If, however, our relation to the teacher is essential to his teaching, if he is the Truth, then we must owe everything to him and we must know that we are so indebted. How, then, can someone who believes that the teacher is the teaching pass on that teaching?

If . . . that ardent learner, who did not, however, go so far as to become a follower, spoke ever so frequently and emphatically about how much he owed that teacher, so that his eulogy had almost no end and its gilding was almost priceless—if he became angry with us as we tried to explain to him that the teacher had been merely the occasion—neither his eulogy nor his anger would benefit our reflections . . . By talking extravagantly and trumpeting from the housetops as he does, a person hoodwinks himself and others that he actually does have thoughts—since he owes them to another. (*PF* 61)

If the message this learner preaches really is that any learner owes the teacher everything, that only a relation to the teacher is a relation to the teaching, then he cannot convey that teaching directly to other would-be learners; that would suggest that his teacher was only an occasion for him, and that he himself will do as well as his teacher as an occasion for others to learn. If he has properly absorbed what his teacher teaches, he can help others to learn that lesson only by helping them to learn from his teacher; he must not even present himself as an occasion for them to learn, but rather find a way of removing himself entirely from the scene—a way of bringing other learners to the teacher without allowing them to assign any kind of authority to him, not even the authority of one who prepares the way to the teacher (for the teacher *is* the way).

Paradoxically enough, one such way is for Climacus to trumpet his message from the housetops with exaggerated intensity—to present his claim that he owes the god everything as a carefully elaborated metaphysical hypothesis of his own devising; for he then makes it almost impossible to ignore the contradiction between the form and the content of his communication, which in turn makes it almost impossible for his readers to avoid seeing that a full appreciation of its content requires the avoidance of that kind of contradiction. This means, of course, that they should not attempt to communicate it to others in similarly inappropriate ways; such communication is something they do (an existential act), and the message of the god is most fundamentally that they live a certain form of life, so Climacus' caricature simply emphasizes that there should never be any contradiction between what they profess to believe and how they live. In short, Climacus produces a caricature that invites his readers' repudiation precisely because repelling his readers from any reliance upon him as an example or an authority is required by what he takes himself to have learned; it is what is required of a writer who is also a follower.

And yet, who could deny that this extremity of writerly self-abnegation, this attempt utterly to avoid the claim to authority apparently inherent in the act of authorship by owning that one's every word is owed to another, is itself a form of philosophical and theological originality? In its repeated return to ideas of plagiarism and contested copyright, and its compulsive resort to quotation, this text all but declares its author's conviction that finding a philosophical voice of one's own is to be understood not as finding one's way to words hitherto unspoken but as finding a way to mean what one says when one utters even the most common or familiar of words. With respect to words rather than the Word, what is yours is mine, and what is mine is yours; human individuality lies in the acknowledgement of the commonness of language rather than its denial.

* * * * * *

DE SILENTIO, BY JOHANNES CLIMACUS

14. According to Johannes Climacus, Johannes de Silentio's little book *Fear And Trembling* is one in a series of recently published texts each of which took their words right out of his mouth. As he tells us in one of several appendices to his Postscript to the *Fragments* (the one at the centre of that enormous body of words, entitled 'A Glance at a Contemporary Effort in Danish Literature'), having overheard an old man, standing over the grave of his son who had been led astray from faith by philosophy, extract a promise from his grandchild never to follow in his father's footsteps, Climacus was inspired to embark on the project of trying to understand why and how Christianity and modern speculative thought had come into such a dubious relation. He resolved to begin by examining the existence-relation between the aesthetic and the ethical—and at once *Either/Or* was published. Since this text left unexplored the relation between the ethical and the religious, and in particular the terror involved in coming to experience the ethical as a temptation and in being unable to give intelligible expression to that experience, Climacus resolved to begin again by examining that hidden terror, that terrible hiddenness—and at once *Fear and Trembling* was published.

The comedy in this narrative of pseudonymous superfluity, baulked inspiration, and deferred beginnings survives even the suspicion that Climacus' tale of eavesdropping in the graveyard may be a little too good to be true. Whether real or invented, however, its implications betray Climacus' status as an unreliable narrator rather more comprehensively than we may at first suspect. For if the grandfather might be well advised to harbour doubts about the propriety of extracting a promise from a young child to treat philosophy as a temptation, a mechanism for seducing oneself from true faith in Christ, he would be in no doubt whatever that anyone who responded to that warning by conceiving an ambition to make intellectual sense of philosophy's threat to faith—in other words, by committing himself not to a life of faith but to a life in which he devotes his best intellectual endeavours to urging that one should not allow intellectual endeavours to distract one from a life of faith—has utterly failed to avoid philosophy's seductiveness. Moreover, what should a would-be (an alternative or shadow) author of *Either/Or* make of someone who claims suddenly to have found meaning in his life by committing himself to a project whose realization requires a particular talent, and which can therefore be realized by anyone who possesses that talent (as Climacus' successive pseudonymous pre-emptions comically imply)? Any such attempt at founding significance on contingencies is surely a paradigm case of an aesthetic orientation to human existence—one which does not even break through to the ethical.

Any reader would accordingly seem well advised to hesitate before treating Climacus' account of the import of any pseudonymous text as reliable. After all, he doesn't hesitate to treat these texts, each authored by a different pseudonym, as providing an easily summarizable and extractable conceptual element in a single overarching project that he happily attributes in the last resort to one Magister Kierkegaard—despite the fact that his own Postscript ends with a 'First and Last Explanation' signed by Kierkegaard in which he claims that

in the pseudonymous books there is not a single word by me. I have no opinion about them except as a third party, no knowledge of their meaning except as a reader, not the remotest private relation to them . . . A single word by me personally in my own name would be an arrogating self-forgetfulness that, regarded dialectically, would be guilty of having essentially annihilated the pseudonymous authors by this one word. (*CUP* 626)

and despite the further fact that (as we noted earlier) he devotes a long and savagely critical footnote in this very appendix to a German reviewer of the *Philosophical Fragments* precisely because he extracts a didactic content from that text.

If Climacus' reading of *Fear and Trembling* really is analogous to the German reviewer's reading of *Philosophical Fragments*, then it must be an 'accurate' account of the book's substance that nevertheless conveys an 'utterly mistaken impression' of the book as a whole (*CUP* 274–5 n). In one sense, therefore, Climacus must be utterly mistaken in seeing an expression of his own misbegotten intellectual project in Silentio's text, and hence seeing himself in the other Johannes; to do so must annihilate that author's true intentions, and hence his autonomous reality. On the other hand, the same analogy implies that Climacus' account of the *substance* of Silentio's book is accurate, and that an accurate impression of *Fear and Trembling* as a whole can be obtained only by reading that text against itself in just the way that is required by Climacus' own writings (that is, by reading the resistance posed to its content by its form as the fundamental point of the book). If so, then Climacus is in a certain sense right to see himself in the other Johannes: for not only is his reading of the substance of *Fear and Trembling* not false—de Silentio's authorial strategy is in general terms precisely analogous to that of Climacus.

We already know from the *Philosophical Fragments* that Climacus is a self-subverting author; what we can now see is that his reading of this and other pseudonymous texts is part of that strategy of self-subversion (overtly attributing a purpose to those texts, and simultaneously providing the evidence needed for the reader to see the erroneousness—or at least the incompleteness—of that attribution), and invites us to find a similar strategy in those other texts. It is, therefore, striking (to say the least) that Climacus' overt reading of *Fear and Trembling*, as intended to delineate the hiddenness and terror of the religious in contrast with the ethical, is one which virtually every commentator takes to be unquestionable—as if they are happy to stand to Silentio's text in just the way that the German reviewer stands to Climacus' text. What, on my reading, Climacus invites us to consider is whether and how we might interpret this reading as at once accurate to the substance of the text and yet utterly mistaken about its fundamental purpose—whether and how we might see the two Johanneses as different and yet the same.

ABRAHAM WITHOUT WORDS

15. If we do not question the assumption that Johannes de Silentio's central claim is that the religious differentiates itself from the ethical in its hiddenness and in its capacity to find the ethical a temptation, then we will take it that the heart of *Fear and Trembling* beats in de Silentio's development of 'the dialectical aspects implicit in the story of Abraham' and his willingness to sacrifice Isaac to God (*Fear and Trembling*,[5] 53). In other words, we will ground our reading of his text in the three problemata that occupy its concluding two-thirds—beginning at its end, as it were. The first problema argues that, if Abraham is to be a father of faith, there must be a teleological suspension of the ethical—it must be possible for an individual to encounter the demands of the ethical realm as a temptation to disobey God's commands. The second argues that, if Abraham is a father of faith, one's duty to God must be absolute, and hence one's ethical duties must be merely relative or conditional. The third argues that, if Abraham is a father of faith, then it must be defensible for him to have concealed his intention from Sarah (his wife), Eliezer (his faithful servant), and Isaac (his son); in other words, it must be possible for him to be obliged to keep his inten-

---

[5] *Fear and Trembling*, in *Fear and Trembling & Repetition*, trans, H. V. and E. H. Hong (Princeton University Press: Princeton, 1983); hereafter *FT*.

tions hidden or enclosed, or more precisely, to be incapable of giving ethically intelligible expression to his intention—indeed to find himself beyond the demands of intelligibility altogether.

It is not difficult to see why problema I (and, to a lesser degree, problema II) has tended to catch the imagination of de Silentio's readers far more firmly than problema III. The idea that what ethical judgement would regard as murder might be required of a religious believer under the aspect of sacrifice, and the implication that respecting the most fundamental of ethical prohibitions might legitimately be regarded as a spiritual temptation by such a believer, is far more interesting (because far more likely to make us shudder) than a claim about the inexpressibility of Abraham's intention in thought and language. But the author of this text seems to think something like the reverse: he takes problema III to develop the most fundamental, and hence the most intellectually significant, dialectical aspect of Abraham's position.

This is evident not only in terms of the relative amounts of space allotted to, and hence the complexity of, the development of each problema (the first two occupy less than fifteen pages each, the third almost forty). It is also manifest in the fact that the issue of hiddenness is made to emerge as a consequence of the issue of conflict with the ethical within the development of both problema I and problema II, and with accelerating speed. In problema I the idea of a teleological suspension of the ethical is shown to be a paradox, and hence 'impervious to thought' (*FT* 56), within three pages, and shown thereby to entail the inexpressibility of Abraham's position within four more pages ('Abraham . . . cannot speak'; *FT* 60). In problema II the idea of an absolute duty to God is linked to the idea that faith is essentially interior, essentially beyond external manifestation or expression, within a single page (*FT* 69).

This linkage between the three problemata depends upon de Silentio's understanding of universality. The ethical exemplifies the universal in two ways: first, its demands are exceptionless, made upon everyone at all times (problema I); and second, they apply not only to one's outward behaviour but to one's inner life, and hence forbid any incommensurability between outer and inner—any aspect of interiority that could not find legitimate public articulation or realization (problema II). Thought and language exemplify the universal in different, but related, senses: for nothing can be thought or said without the employment of concepts, which means categorizing the particulars of experience in terms of general categories and acknowledging the logical relations between concepts; and anything thinkable or sayable must be intelligible to anyone capable of thought or speech (problema III).

The connection between these two aspects or dimensions of the universal is given theoretical expression in the Kantian and Hegelian equations of the moral and the rational—whether in the idea that the moral law is pure practical reason, or that individual human existence acquires ethical substance only through participation in the rationally ordered life of human community. So understood, an inability to express or justify the maxims of one's will in ethical terms does not simply indicate a local failure of language—as if one's actions, while not morally intelligible, might nevertheless make some other kind of sense; rather, it reveals that one lacks rationality and hence intelligibility as an agent altogether, that one's practical existence amounts to a negation of reason.

Since the religious believer gives absolute priority to her relation to God, all other demands on her can be at best of relative importance: it must therefore be possible, from her perspective, that she be called upon to violate the demands of ethics (violating what ethics regards as her duty, and thereby placing an aspect or dimension of her interiority beyond its sway) and the demands of rationality (acting out of motives that violate the laws of thought and language, that can only find expression in nonsense). Abraham's intention to sacrifice Isaac exemplifies this double possibility. By killing Isaac, he violates a father's duty to love his son (and hence violates ethics, and—on Kantian and Hegelian conceptions of the matter—reason); but he also violates reason more directly, since his actions imply that he simultaneously believes that God will make him the father of many generations and that this same God wants him to kill the only being through whom he could become the father of many generations. In Isaac, then, both aspects of the universal are exemplified: he is the fruit of Abraham's loins, and himself the possessor of fruitful loins—both son and potential father. Abraham's willingness to sacrifice his son therefore provides an extreme example of the way in which, on de Silentio's account, religious belief individualizes the believer. It isolates him from, by placing him beyond, the realm of the universal; and this isolation finds its most fundamental expression in the believer's exile from the *logos*—from the realm of articulate thought and speech.

This is why problema III forms the centrepiece of de Silentio's text: 'Was it Ethically Defensible for Abraham to Conceal his Undertaking from Sarah, from Eliezer and from Isaac?' These interlocutors represent the claims of the ethical realm (of which family life is, de Silentio tells us, the highest expression for Abraham; *FT* 112), and those of human interlocution as such; Abraham cannot disclose his undertaking to them because, ethically speaking, it could only be described as murder, and because his belief that Isaac will nevertheless be returned to him is not articulable at all (because absurd, paradoxical, nonsensical). As de Silentio puts it: 'Speak he cannot; he speaks no human language. And even if he understood all the languages of the world, even if those he loved also understood them, he still could not speak—he speaks in a divine language, he speaks in tongues' (*FT* 114). Well might the other Johannes feel that de Silentio is taking the very words from his mouth: this vision of the language of God or of religious belief as not humanly intelligible, of its medium as that of the absurd or the paradoxical, of the individual believer being condemned to run his head up against the limits of language—these formulations would fit very smoothly into the text of the *Philosophical Fragments* and its Postscript.

ABRAHAM'S WORDS: SAYING NOTHING?

16. In the context of *Fear and Trembling*, however, de Silentio's claims carry an absolutely fundamental problem on their face: for it simply is not true that, in the biblical account of Abraham's journey to Mount Moriah with Isaac, he is presented as being unable to speak. On the contrary, he speaks at least three times: to God (at the beginning of his ordeal and at its climax, when he acknowledges God's address to him in identical words: 'Here I am'); to the servants who accompany him to the mountain (to whom he says 'Abide ye here with the ass; and I and the lad will go yonder and worship, and come again to you'); and to Isaac (to whom, when he inquires about the whereabouts of the lamb for the sacrifice, Abraham replies, 'My son, God will provide himself a lamb for a burnt offering'). His intercourse with God might be dismissed as irrelevant, since it is not an instance of human interlocution (although, of course, it is about the murder–sacrifice and it is reported in words that appear perfectly intelligible). However, the other two instances both involve speaking to other human beings about the undertaking that de Silentio presents as beyond human articulation. Indeed, if we follow de Silentio in speculating that Eliezer would very likely have been one of the servants accompanying Abraham on his journey (see Exordium iv: *FT* 14), then we can say that, according to the Bible, Abraham speaks both to Eliezer and to Isaac about his undertaking. In short, of the three representatives of ethics and language nominated by de Silentio himself and with whom he represents Abraham as being incapable of intelligible communication, in fact only Sarah does not explicitly engage in dialogue with Abraham.

To be sure, De Silentio does confront one aspect of this issue in the concluding pages of problema III. But our sense that he might have any real sensitivity to the problem it poses for the general shape of his account is hardly strengthened by the fact that he introduces his discussion of it with a kind of parody of a paradox, an absurdly contradictory attempt to have his cake in one sentence only to eat it in the next: 'So Abraham did not speak. Just one word from him has been preserved, his only reply to Issac, ample evidence that he had not said anything before' (*FT* 115). He then suggests that Abraham's reply to Isaac is in fact the very heart of the matter, that what and how he speaks is the element that holds everything in the story together, and hence is deserving of the most careful analysis. 'Without these words, the whole event would lack something: if they were different words, everything perhaps would dissolve in confusion' (*FT* 116). His claim is that this apparent volte-face is really consistent with his general approach because Abraham speaks to Isaac in such a way as not to say anything.

De Silentio's argument (see *FT* 118–19) is that Abraham's reply to his son perfectly reflects the double movement of spirit which is the essence of his faith. On the one hand, he has resigned himself to Isaac's loss: without in any way relinquishing his love for his son, he is entirely willing to sacrifice him to God. On the other hand, he continues to have faith in Isaac's return, continues to believe against reason that God will restore Isaac to him. His words must therefore be truthful both to his resignation and his faith, to his knowledge that he will sacrifice Isaac if that should be required and to his knowledge that God might bring it about that something entirely different happens. His reply achieves this with beautiful elegance and economy: for it is so constructed that the fulfilment of either of his and Isaac's possible futures (more precisely, the fulfilment either of their possible future or of their impossible future) will, with equal legitimacy, render it true. Since his words exclude some possible futures (those in which God will not provide a lamb for the sacrifice), they are not empty—they do say something; but since what they predict is equally consistent with two very different ways in which that lamb will be provided, they can also be said to say nothing about their apparent topic. In effect, then, in his situation Abraham can only speak truthfully (true to what he knows about the future, to his beliefs about God, and to his own intentions) and intelligibly (in both the general and the moral sense of that term) not only by saying something that says nothing, but by this particular way of saying something that says nothing. This is why de Silentio can claim to understand 'Abraham's total presence in that word' (*FT* 118).

One cannot but admire the elegant economy of de Silentio's reading; it may involve attributing to Abraham an elegantly economical way with the truth that is ethically dubious, but then he is supposed to be finding the ethical a temptation. Nevertheless, problems remain. To begin with, de Silentio's reading characterizes Abraham's reply as ironic: 'His response to Isaac is in the form of irony, for it is always irony when I say something and still do not say anything' (*FT* 118). De Silentio thereby associates the father of faith with someone he has just (on the previous page) described as an intellectual tragic hero—Socrates. A few words are required from such individuals because, de Silentio tells us, 'the meaning of a hero's life is oriented to spirit' (*FT* 117); there is an analogy here between Socrates' comments on his own death sentence and Abraham's reply to his son because the latter 'as the father of faith . . . has absolute significance oriented to spirit' (*FT* 117). Intellectual or not, however, the tragic hero is a category from which de Silentio has hitherto tried to distinguish the father of faith. According to his earlier claims, the tragic hero (such as Agamemnon or Brutus) is someone who sacrifices one ethical value for a higher ethical value, and therefore does not exile himself either from the ethical realm as such or from the realm of speech and thought; in short, the tragic hero does not confront the paradox with which the father of faith must grapple. Consequently, by associating Abraham with Socrates even by analogy, de Silentio undercuts a central element of his own dialectical endeavour.

Furthermore, and regardless of whether or not saying something while saying nothing is well characterized as an ironical mode of speech, we have good reason to doubt that Abraham's words are rightly characterizable as not saying anything—even on de Silentio's interpretation of their significance. For that interpretation in fact shows that what Abraham says is capable of being taken in two different ways—that it is ambiguous, or rather, sufficiently indeterminate to be consistent with more than one eventuality. But this indeterminacy is determinate: it is in fact very precisely determined by Abraham's need to avoid untruth without actually saying anything that would falsify his knowledge of God and of himself, which means that it must be consistent with two very different but very specific possibilities. To be sure, Abraham could have said something rather more specific (and hence less ambiguous or misleading) than he did—perhaps by explaining in more detail what he did and did not know. But it doesn't follow that what he did say amounted to saying nothing at all—to an empty or nonsensical form of words. If it did, de Silentio could not have provided such an elegant and economical elucidation of its presuppositions and implications, and their fitness for use by someone in Abraham's difficult position.

This determinate indeterminacy of Abraham's words—call it their invitation to interpretation—casts a very different light on the supposedly counterfactual possibility with which de Silentio immediately contrasts his analysis of Abraham's utterance.

> This becomes still more evident when we consider that it was Abraham himself who should sacrifice Isaac. If the task had been different, if the Lord had commanded Abraham to bring Isaac up to Mount Moriah so that he could have his lightning strike Isaac and take him as a sacrifice in that way, then Abraham plainly would have been justified in speaking as enigmatically as he did, for then he himself could not have known what was going to happen. But given the task as assigned to Abraham, he himself has to act; consequently, he has to know in the crucial moment what he himself will do, and consequently, he has to know that Isaac is going to be sacrificed. If he had not known this for sure, he would not have made the infinite movement of resignation; then his words certainly are not untruth, but he is also very far from being Abraham, and he has less significance than a tragic hero—indeed, he is a man devoid of resolution who cannot make up his mind one way or the other and for that reason always speaks in riddles. A vacillator like that, however, is merely a parody of the knight of faith. (*FT* 118–19)

Is it, however, so obvious that God's actual words are inconsistent with de Silentio's counterfactual recounting of the tale? If we go back to the biblical account of them—words which de Silentio quotes in (what the Hongs call 'a free, but essentially accurate'; *FT* 341) Danish translation at the beginning of his four false versions of the story in the Exordium, as if establishing indisputable ground from which his imagination is going to take flight—what we find is this: 'And God tempted Abraham and said to him, take Isaac, your only son, whom you love, and go to the land of Moriah and offer him there as a burnt offering on a mountain that I shall show you' (*FT* 10).

Both the English Authorized Version and the King James Version actually have 'offer him there *for* a burnt offering'. This looseness might encourage us to look back in the book of Genesis to the previous burnt offering that Abraham sacrifices to God (on the occasion of his confirmation of his initial promise to make Abraham the father of many nations), where we find that the process involved Abraham bringing sacrificial animals to the altar and dividing them in two thereon, but the fire that consumes them (described as a smoking furnace and a burning lamp) is provided by God. It might then appear significant that, although Abraham takes fire as well as wood with him as he climbs the mountain, he does not actually set the fire to the wood upon which Isaac is laid. Put these points together with the correction to de Silentio's translation, apply to God's opening words the template of determinate indeterminacy developed by de Silentio for Abraham, and we appear to have a second possible way of interpreting them, one that Silentio considers only to reject but which is as consistent with everything in the biblical account as his own preferred reading. On this alternative interpretation, God commanded Abraham to bring his son to Mount Moriah for the purpose of making a burnt offering of him, but did not command him to carry out the sacrifice itself (as with their last sacrificial encounter, that would be his affair)—and Abraham so understood God's command, bringing fire only for the journey and reaching for the knife to prepare the lamb for the sacrifice rather than to complete it.

If so, de Silentio tells us, 'Abraham plainly would have been justified in speaking as enigmatically as he did' because he would not have been certain what was to happen on the mountain; in other words, he would not have been exiled from the ethical realm (let alone the realm of reason)—he would not even have made the first movement of infinite resignation, which presupposes the complete acceptance of the loss of one's beloved object. De Silentio carefully tells us that this would have made of Abraham 'a vacillator . . . merely a parody of the knight of faith' (*FT* 119). If, however, the biblical text at the very least allows for an interpretation of the story along just those lines, which is the parody of faith—and who is the parodist?

If the above speculation seems too ingenious to carry conviction, a further, entirely independent reason for querying de Silentio's interpretation of the tale can be found in the simple fact that, despite the care his Abraham takes to balance his utterance between two possible futures—one in which Isaac is the lamb which God provides for the sacrifice, and one in which God provides a lamb to be used for the sacrifice in place of Isaac—neither of them is in fact realized. Isaac, of course, turns out not to be the envisaged lamb; but God provides as an alternative not a lamb but a ram (caught in a thicket by his horns). In the most obvious, literal sense, therefore, Abraham's prediction or prophecy is simply wrong. He may have tried his utmost to avoid untruth with respect to his beliefs and intentions, but his reply fails accurately to identify the sacrificial animal that God in fact provides; so he has failed to avoid falsehood altogether, and it cannot be said—as de Silentio says—that he knew for sure what will happen.

Is this objection not just a little too pedestrian to be convincing? Does it matter that the animal God provides is a mature rather than a young member of the species Abraham specifies? As we shall see, from the perspective of Christianity, it would not be an exaggeration to say that absolutely everything turns on the fact that God's actions on

Mount Moriah do not literally fulfil Abraham's prophecy. But from the perspective of de Silentio, with which we should continue a little longer, it is not obvious that there could be a worse error in a reading of the Genesis narrative than literal inaccuracy; for throughout *Fear and Trembling* it is deviations from the literal that attract his deepest scorn.

LANGUAGE AND THE LITERAL

17. We can, in fact, trace this theme of language, literality, and interpretative fidelity back from the dialectical climax upon which we have been focusing, through virtually every phase of de Silentio's text, to the preface. It crops up most explicitly in problema II, when de Silentio compares our refusal to recognize the reality of Abraham's violation of ethics with our refusal to accept the literal significance of a well-known New Testament text—Luke 14: 26: 'If anyone comes to me and does not hate his own father and mother and wife and children and brothers and sisters, yes, and even his own life, he cannot be my disciple.' De Silentio notes that theologians claim that the Greek word translated here as 'hate' should be understood as meaning 'love less, esteem less, honour not, count as nothing'; but he regards this as an evasion.

The context in which these words appear, however, does not seem to confirm this appealing explanation. In the following verse we are told that someone who wants to erect a tower first of all makes a rough estimate to see if he is able to finish it, lest he be mocked later. The close proximity of this story and the verse quoted seems to indicate that the words are to be taken in their full terror in order that each person may examine himself to see if he can erect the building. (*FT* 72)

De Silentio is well aware of one reason why people are reluctant to take this text, and that of Abraham, at face value. We are, he says, afraid to let people loose, afraid that the worst kinds of barbarities and outrages will happen as soon as the single individual feels licensed to behave in ways that are unjustifiable in universal ethical or rational terms. De Silentio feels that this worry fails to take account of the fact that genuinely religious singularity will manifest itself in fear and trembling rather than the indulgence of selfish appetite (see *FT* 75). But he is insistent that, whatever difficulties it creates, there is only one legitimate way to read texts such as these: 'It is easy to see that if this passage is to have any meaning it must be understood literally' (*FT* 73).

This note is first sounded in the Problemata section of the book rather earlier than problema II—in the 'Preliminary Expectoration' (perhaps more happily translated as 'Preamble from the Heart') with which it begins. For the Preamble itself begins with a tale about the kind of attitude to the Abraham story prevalent in Christendom which provokes de Silentio to write his book in the first place. Preachers tell the story, but they recite it in clichés, or more precisely in generalities: 'the great thing was that he loved God in such a way that he was willing to offer him the best'. As de Silentio points out, while this is not false, it is certainly vague, and such vagueness has consequences:

So we talk, and in the process of talking interchange the two terms, Isaac and the best, and everything goes fine. But just suppose that someone listening is a man who suffers from sleeplessness—then the most terrifying, the most profound, tragic and comic misunderstanding is very close at hand. He goes home, he wants to do just as Abraham did, for the son, after all, is the best. If the preacher found out about it, he perhaps would go to the man, he would muster all his ecclesiastical dignity and shout, 'You despicable man, you scum of society, what devil has so possessed you that you want to murder your son.' And the pastor, who had not noticed any heat or perspiration when preaching about Abraham, would be surprised at himself, at the wrathful earnestness with which he thunders at the poor man. (*FT* 28–9)

The preacher fails to see that the supposedly demonic listener is simply putting into practice the behaviour that the sermon had held up to him as exemplary of religious faith. In other words, he fails to appreciate the literal import of his own words, and hence, the literal significance of the biblical narrative upon which he has been preaching; and so he finds himself, 'like a cherub with a flaming sword', having to place himself 'in front of the person whose actions would give the lie to the old saying that things do not go in the world as the preacher preaches' (*FT* 29).

In effect, then, de Silentio condemns the preacher for failing to take the literal meaning of his own words, and those of the Bible, seriously. Where the preacher contents himself with vague clichés, moving away in his sermonizing from the concrete details of Abraham's situation by substituting more general or universal terms for the less palatable ones the biblical text actually employs, de Silentio implicitly advocates a model of reading which reverses this process—one in which these preacherly generalities are exchanged for (translated back into) the linguistic and experiential particulars from which they originated.

Venturing into the realm of generality ourselves, then, we might say that the kind of reading to which de Silentio objects in the Problemata is one that dilutes the meaning of texts by a process of linguistic exchange—whether one in which terms with very different meanings are treated as synonymous, or one in which terms with very specific significance are substituted by terms of more general import (species by genera, particular by universal). What he advocates by contrast is the refusal of such linguistic transactions: reading a text should mean staying with its actual significance, tarrying to extract the full resonance and implication of its terms rather than moving hastily on to other words, whatever their claims to equivalence in meaning. The focus of his readings is actuality rather than possibility; their key resource is a capacity to attend to what is there in the text rather than to what might have been but is not.

The figurative terminology with which he introduces his Preamble to the Problemata—when he claims that, spiritually speaking, only one who works gets bread—confirms this. This adage, he tells us, is false of the external world, in which the law of indifference reigns, and he who has the world's wealth has it regardless of how he got it. In the world of spirit, however, the rain does not fall on the just and the unjust alike: only the one who was in anxiety finds rest, only the one who draws the knife gets Isaac. 'There is a knowledge that presumptuously wants to introduce into the world of spirit the same law of indifference under which the external world sighs. It believes that it is enough to know what is great—no other work is needed. But for this reason it does not get bread; it perishes of hunger while everything changes to gold' (*FT* 27–8).

The Midas touch aptly symbolizes value as understood within systems of thought governed by the law of indifference because they evaluate things in terms of the wealth they represent, representing them as commensurable with (and ultimately indistinguishable from) one another, rather than in terms of their intrinsic and distinctive qualities (their use value, one might say). De Silentio immediately connects this critique of exchange value with a critique of linguistic exchange: 'The story about Abraham is remarkable in that it is always glorious no matter how poorly it is understood, but here again it is a matter of whether or not we are willing to work and be burdened. But we are unwilling to work, and yet we want to understand the story. We glorify Abraham, but how? We recite the whole story in clichés . . .' (*FT* 28). Then follows the tale of the preacher. The point is clear: to gain spiritual bread from biblical texts, we must refuse to treat its orderings of words as part of a system of linguistic exchange or equivalence. We must rather labour to appreciate their incommensurability with other words, and hence with other tales that might be told by their means; we must use what we have been given rather than subjecting it to transformation.

This lesson is central to what precedes the Problemata—the Exordium (perhaps better translated as 'Attunement', with all its Wittgensteinian and Heideggerian connotations). Here, de Silentio imagines four variations on the original biblical account of Abraham's ordeal: while leaving unchanged God's original command and his eventual intervention, he recounts four different ways in which Abraham might have reached that end from that beginning. The clear implication is that each such variation would have made Abraham less or other than a father of faith; in other words, de Silentio's seemingly inexhaustible capacity to imagine the tale otherwise than the Bible (a capacity exercised throughout the book as he unfolds innumerable variations on tales of tragic heroes of myth, legend, and reality in order to emphasize Abraham's transcendence of that category) paradoxically works to focus our attention upon every detail of the narrative as Genesis records it. These endlessly proliferating alternative narrative possibilities are designed to bring the one narrative actuality into stark and literal life—to make us, as readers and spiritual beings, refuse to trade the tale we have been given for ones of our own (and our own culture's) imagining, to recognize that its significance is not expressible in other terms.

The same figurative foreshadowing of de Silentio's hostility to linguistic terms of trade that opens the Problemata also appears in what precedes the Exordium, and hence might be said to open his book as a whole. For the preface begins by suggesting that the status of spiritual goods in the world of ideas might profitably be compared with that of material goods in contemporary Denmark: 'everything can be had at such a bargain price that it becomes a question whether there is finally anyone who will make a bid' (*FT* 5). De Silentio places the immediate blame for this upon Hegelian philosophy's dominance of the world of ideas: it has established terms of trade for religious belief (particularly with respect to ethical and philosophical goods) that significantly undervalue it. But such intellectual exchanges in effect establish a set of conceptual equivalences, and hence are not detachable from linguistic terms of trade—a point that de Silentio underlines when he characterizes his own text in explicitly commercial terms: '[The present author] writes because to him it is a luxury that is all the more pleasant and apparent the fewer there are who buy and read what he writes' (*FT* 7).

If his writing is a kind of luxury good, then the terms in which it clothes the religious ideas it discusses must set a very high price for them—the very reverse of a bargain basement clear-out. Indeed, the

general drift of the passage is such as to suggest that his writing will
have attained a certain kind of perfection or fulfilment when its would-
be consumers vanish altogether—in other words, the terms of trade he
would ideally propose are such as to price religious goods beyond any
exchanges or transactions at all. He wants his words to leave us with
no alternative but to allow the words of the Bible, in all their literal
specificity, to work upon our spirits.

DE SILENTIO: PHILOSOPHER OR POET?

18. If, then, from the very begining of *Fear and Trembling* de Silentio
regards fidelity to the literal meaning of the Genesis narrative as his
interpretative ideal, the fact that his concluding interpretation of
Abraham's relation to language depends not only upon arguing that
when Abraham literally says something he does not really say anything,
but also upon failing to see that what Abraham says is literally false,
can hardly be dismissed as a minor inconsistency. De Silentio's presumption that the words 'lamb' and 'ram' are synonymous, like his presumption that determinate indeterminacy of meaning is the same as
meaninglessness, are rather undismissable symptoms of a far more fundamental split in the integrity of his text's understanding of the relation
between faith and language—a division manifest in the way his polemic
begins by stressing Abraham's utter alienation from words (an emphasis central to the early 'Eulogy on Abraham', in which de Silentio lauds
Abraham for his refusing all incitements to speech, whether in doubt,
in lamentation, or in prayer), and yet somehow ends by stressing
Abraham's 'total presence' in his words (*FT* 118), by arguing that he
'consummates himself' as a father of faith through his reply to Isaac (*FT*
117). Is de Silentio confused, and unaware of his own confusion? Or is
his confusion rather intended as a signal, all but unmissable, that he
expects his readers to work a little harder to earn their bread? Just who
is Johannes de Silentio?

   Is he a philosopher? He denies it in his preface, twice, in exactly the
same words: 'The present author is by no means a philosopher' (*FT* 7).
And yet, in the Preamble he tells us: 'I for my part have applied con-
siderable time to understanding Hegelian philosophy and believe that I
have understood it fairly well; I am sufficiently brash to think that when
I cannot understand particular passages despite all my pains, he himself
may not have been entirely clear' (*FT* 33). Which claim should we
believe?

Is he a poet? The subtitle to his book implies it (even 'a dialectical lyric' is a lyric); he explicitly claims as much in its preface ('[the present author] is *poetice et eleganter* [in a poetic and refined way] a supplementary clerk'; *FT* 7); and the structure of his Eulogy turns on the contrast between Abraham (understood as the hero) and himself (understood as his poet or orator). Indeed, the Eulogy goes so far as to say that 'the poet is, so to speak, the hero's better nature' (*FT* 16)—his loving and admiring words the only thing that stands between the hero and oblivion, his praise creating and preserving a sacred bond between human generations that would otherwise succeed one another with as little meaning as the successive generations of trees in a forest, their individual members leaving as little a mark as the wind in the desert.

In fact, however, this self-identification causes problems—for de Silentio gives us more than one reason to be suspicious of a poet's perceptions of a father of faith. How, for example, can a poet be the better nature of someone whom the poet himself defines as essentially transcending the domain of language, his position undisclosable in words? Are such a person's agonies expressible even by the greatest of poets? De Silentio raises this question himself a little later in his book:

Thanks to you, great Shakespeare, you who can say everything, everything, everything just as it is—and yet, why did you never articulate this torment? Did you perhaps reserve it for yourself, like the beloved's name that one cannot bear to have the world utter, for with his little secret that he cannot divulge the poet buys this power of the word to tell everybody else's dark secrets. A poet is not an apostle; he drives out devils only by the power of the devil. (*FT* 61)

If even Shakespeare did not and perhaps could not articulate this torment, whence de Silentio's lyric? What is the dark secret by means of which de Silentio purchases his apparent power to tell Abraham's secret when Abraham himself cannot? What devilish power permits him to drive out the devilish misunderstandings of Abraham that he sees around him?

Suppose that de Silentio's self-identification as a poet is his way of telling us that he has a dark secret—the silence of which his name speaks; and suppose further that the disclosing of this secret is the essential work that he expects his readers to perform if they are to receive the bread he has to give them. It would then be our task as readers to find and expel the devil in his text, to locate the subtext or context through which the true naming of de Silentio's beloved hero is accomplished in implicit subversion of the apparent themes of his text as we have so far understood them. We must, in other words, recast our account of de Silentio's *Fear and Trembling*—begin our reading of it again, from the very beginning.

LANGUAGE AND THE FIGURATIVE

19. Where, however, does this text begin? As Edward Mooney has pointed out, it is not obvious that it has a single point of origin. On the contrary, it appears to begin four times: with the preface, of course, but then again with the Exordium, and again with the Eulogy, and again with the Preamble to the Problemata.[6] Each beginning is new because it approaches Abraham from a different angle, in a different mode of language; each is nevertheless a renewal of one and the same project, that of comprehending Abraham. Our rereading must therefore refound itself by returning to each of these beginnings.

We must, however, begin by questioning Mooney's view that the preface is the first of de Silentio's beginnings. For between the book's title-page and the first page of its preface there is a small intervening text, an epigraph consisting of a short quotation from a letter written by Johann Hamann to Johannes Lindner, in which Hamann cites elements of a tale recounted by Valerius Maximus concerning Tarquin the Proud. In English translation the quoted German passage runs as follows: 'What Tarquinius Superbus said in the garden by means of the poppies, the son understood but the messenger did not.'

The broader context of the tale from which this quoted citation is drawn concerns Tarquin's war with Gabii. An early king of Rome, Tarquin arranged for his son to flee to Gabii under the pretence of paternal mistreatment, its inhabitants making him their military leader as a consequence. By striking off the heads of the tallest poppies in his garden before the eyes of his son's messenger, Tarquin managed to convey to the son that he should eliminate the elders of the city. His son followed this advice, and Gabii quickly surrendered to Tarquin's forces. Why should de Silentio think that a recounting of Hamann's recounting of Valerius Maximus' account of a tale told about Tarquin might offer us guidance in reading the text that follows?

Tarquin's message to his son is a command that he execute the elders of Gabii; it thus echoes God's command to Abraham that he execute

---

[6] E. Mooney, 'Art, Deed and System: The Prefaces to *Fear and Trembling*' in R. L. Perkins (ed.), *International Kierkegaard Commentary*, vi: *Fear and Trembling & Repetition* (Mercer University Press: Macon, Ga., 1993).

Isaac. However, the threat posed by father to son in the tale's preamble is in fact fictitious, part of a deception to accomplish quite different ends; are we to think the same of Abraham's (and God's) apparently murderous intentions? Moreover, the true command to kill is conveyed from father to son: should we then think of Abraham as a son of God (when he is only ever described as a father), or should we rather think of Tarquin's response to the question posed by his son's messenger as analogous to Abraham's reply to Isaac's question? Then again, the epigraph's message is conveyed from father to son via an uncomprehending intermediary: does this intermediary then represent the angel who intervenes on the mountain (even though the angel's command is that an execution should not take place, and he does comprehend it), or Abraham—who would then be conveying a message from God to his son, a message whose true import is something to which Abraham himself is oblivious? Two further aspects of the tale might then become significant. First, Tarquin communicates with his son without saying a word; in effect, the epigraph recounts an instance of what can, literally, be said to be saying something without speaking—something that can be said of Abraham's utterances only metaphorically or figuratively (thus further opposing any identification of Abraham with Tarquin). Second, Tarquin's son shows his understanding of his father's message not by cutting off the tallest poppies in his own garden, but by executing the elders of his city; in other words, he grasps that its true import is metaphorical or allegorical rather than literal. It might then strike us that any and all of the interpretative possibilities canvassed above depend upon regarding the epigraph's relation to the main text in figurative or symbolic rather than literal terms.

Suppose, then, that we take heed of de Silentio's prefatory sarcasm about readers who prefer conveniently to skim books during their after-dinner nap (*FT* 7–8). Rather than assuming that the epigraph presents Tarquin as analogous to Abraham because both issue death threats and communicate with their sons by saying nothing, we might instead consider it as inviting us to interpret Abraham as an oblivious messenger between God and Isaac, someone who fails to see that God's words about his son, and the words that God's words constrain him to use in reply to his son, are to be understood figuratively or allegorically rather than literally. And given that the epigraph as a whole invites such figurative or allegorical interpretation, we might also consider that the author who utilized it as his text's first beginning is also inviting us to interpret him figuratively or allegorically—to think of his emphasis upon the literal as exemplary of an obliviousness to the true nature of religious uses of language, an oblivion that his readers are intended to overcome in the end, just as Abraham eventually overcomes his own misunderstandings on Mount Moriah.

20. As we have already seen, *Fear and Trembling*'s second beginning (its preface) opens by invoking economic exchange as a symbol both of Hegelian conceptual systematicity and of linguistic equivalences, and closes by implicitly proposing to invert philosophical attempts to drive down the price of spiritual goods by working out a mode of writing which will represent them as luxury goods—purchasable only at the highest possible price. It should surely strike us, however, that luxury goods are available only to those with a great deal of purchasing power, those with the wealth of the world regardless of how they got it. De Silentio's image therefore appears to locate his interpretation of religious faith within the external world and its law of indifference—a world he condemns without reservation in his subsequent 'Preamble from the Heart'. Moreover, the price of goods can be manipulated in ways that bear no relation to their intrinsic worth or to the desires of those who consume them—by, for example, manipulations on the supply side. In fact, de Silentio's Epilogue opens by conjuring up just such a piece of sharp economic practice: that of dumping cargoes of spices in the sea in order to raise the price of what remained. He then comments: 'This was an excusable, perhaps even necessary, deception. Do we need something similar in the world of the spirit?' (*FT* 121). Are de Silentio's tactics for making faith a luxury good part of an excusable, perhaps even necessary, deception? Or does the deception lie rather in the fact that, by exchanging the image of a bargain for that of a luxury, de Silentio hardly escapes the metaphor of economic exchange: a luxury good is still a good, still purchasable and hence still commensurable with other goods in the system. Perhaps a proper evaluation of the goods of the spirit rather requires an escape from the imagery of economic exchange altogether, and thus from the idea that every form of language use can always be evaluated in terms of a single dimension of meaning—say, the literal.

21. The third beginning of de Silentio's book is its Exordium, which (as Mooney notes) opens by recounting an old man's recollection of tales told in his childhood about the biblical tale of Abraham. It thereby recapitulates the fourfold citational nesting of the epigraph—a gesture whose significance only becomes clear at the opening of his fourth beginning, to which we shall turn below. The significance of other aspects of de Silentio's portrait of a man who becomes increasingly obsessed with the tale of Abraham are more easily disclosed.

In particular, we learn that the central cause of his obsession is that 'life had fractured what had been united in the pious simplicity of the child' (*FT* 9). And yet, the mode of his obsession with Abraham repeats that fracturing rather than overcoming it; we are told, for example, that his only concern is to experience Abraham's journey to Mount Moriah—a journey that he distinguishes sharply from the broader context (geographical, cultural, and personal) within which it is located by the biblical text. The reason, says de Silentio, is that 'what occupied him was not the beautiful tapestry of imagination but the shudder of the idea' (*FT* 9). But perhaps, just as the pious simplicity of his child-hood understanding of the tale might precisely have depended upon a child's inability to distinguish imagination from thought, so our under-standing of Abraham's journey might critically depend upon the personal and cultural assumptions he inevitably brought to bear in understanding his own situation. Perhaps, in short, de Silentio's man is meant to guide us by indirection to a way of reading Genesis that contextualizes that text.

Two other aspects of this man's attitude might also make us hesitate. First, he is not an exegetical scholar: 'He did not know Hebrew; if he had known Hebrew, he perhaps would easily have understood the story and Abraham' (*FT* 9). Even before reading de Silentio's detailed dis-cussion of translation problems in the New Testament (*FT* 72–5), we might wonder whether this ironic dig at scholarship in comparison with pious simplicity might nevertheless contain a literal truth. After all, if our goal is to understand the biblical text in all its concrete specificity, how could it not be relevant to understand the meanings of the words in which it was originally composed? Can problems of translation simply be dismissed as a distraction? 'The second cause for hesitation is that the man's obsession is such that he forgot everything else because of it; his soul had but one wish, to see Abraham, but one longing, to have witnessed that event' (*FT* 9). In other words, he focuses exclusively on his relation with Abraham rather than his relation with God. From Abraham's own point of view (as from Climacus'), this must be a fun-damental error. Attempting to make oneself present to a climactic episode in another person's relationship with God does not amount to making oneself present to God; rather, it provides a potentially inex-haustible distraction from that task, and implies not only a mistaken sense of priorities but a complete lack of clarity about the only real point of reading the Bible. Can we really expect this mode of reading to clarify the true nature of religious faith?

Next come the four false starts or variations on the biblical account. We have already noted the overt strategy here: de Silentio attempts to highlight the significance of every small detail of the Genesis narrative by showing how different its impact would be if each such detail had altered. In variation I Abraham fails to maintain his silence with respect to Isaac, and is consequently forced to manipulate his son into a God-relation (hardly a strategy of which God would approve). In variation II Abraham is unable to allow God's rescinding of his command to wipe out the significance of the command itself; his conception of God is polluted, and he cannot accept his son back in the joy and pride with which he originally accepted him (he cannot perform what de Silentio will later call the movement of faith). In variation III Abraham (sensitized by the memory of his maltreatment of his first, illegitimate son) doubts the perfection of his love for Isaac, and hence doubts whether the command to sacrifice him really is a divine suspension of the ethical rather than a temptation to violate it (we will come back to this initially rather obscure point, as does de Silentio). In variation IV Abraham despairs even as he reaches for the knife: he cannot manage what de Silentio will later call the movement of infinite resignation, and because he cannot conceal this inability from Isaac, his son loses faith in God, and thereby ensures the non-fulfilment of God's covenant (Abraham has fathered faithlessness rather than faith).

By negation, we can infer that, for de Silentio, what makes Abraham a father of faith is his ability to make the double movement of resignation and faith, the perfection of his love for Isaac, and his capacity to bear up under the strain of non-communication. This is, of course, exactly the ground covered in later sections of the book. But this interpretation leaves entirely unaccounted for the parallel sequence of short texts that de Silentio attaches to each of his four variations, as if providing a gloss on the narratives from which they depend—as if implying that the main text of his book as a whole harbours a subtext, a message that must be unearthed by subjecting its surface meaning to interpretative transformation.

Each gloss appears to transpose one counterfactual narrative about Abraham into a narrative about a mother weaning her child. Thus, Abraham's presentation of himself as an idolatrous father is compared to a mother blackening her breast to discourage her child; Isaac's loss of a joyful father to the child's loss of the mother when she conceals her breast; Abraham's loss of conviction in his love for Isaac to the mother's loss of closeness to her weaned child; and the despair which deprives Isaac of his faith to a mother's need to provide stronger sustenance for her weaned child. Summarized thus, the moral they are intended to derive seems clear: the vicissitudes of the child represent those suffered by Isaac as a consequence of Abraham's various fallings away from exemplary faithfulness in the main texts.

If this reading is correct, however, two other consequences appear to follow.[7] First, the events preceding the confrontation on Mount Moriah are to be understood as modes of weaning, and hence as having the prime purpose of bringing a child closer to the autonomy of adulthood, of educing maturity. If this child is Isaac, then how exactly does his experience represent the gaining of maturity (of body, mind, or spirit), and why should de Silentio resolutely avoid emphasizing the significance of Abraham's ordeal for his son throughout the remainder of his book? Or is de Silentio's emphasis meant rather to suggest that Abraham is the child, and that his ordeal is a process of spiritual maturation? Second, Abraham's fatherhood is re-presented in the parallel texts as a mode of motherhood. Might this be designed to remind us that his title 'father of faith' has a less honorific and more productive (or rather, reproductive) sense—that to call him a father of faith means not so much that he is exemplary of faith as that true faith is something that he fathered, something represented not so much in him as in his offspring (both immediate and ultimate)? And might not this more developed faith be best understood in terms associated with the female rather than the male, with the maternal rather than the patriarchal?

22. The fourth beginning of *Fear and Trembling* is the 'Eulogy on Abraham'. As we have seen, its portrait of the poet's relation to his hero not only emphasizes Abraham's hiddenness but makes it difficult to avoid the apparent contradiction between de Silentio's claim that Abraham is essentially alienated from language and the claim that the being who sings his praises can be thought of as his better nature, without whom he would be as nothing. But the opening of the Eulogy also helps to make sense of the formal gesture with which two of the three preceding beginnings of the book are themselves opened.

I noted earlier that the fourfold nesting of the Exordium repeats the fourfold nesting of the epigraph—each telling tales about tales told by others, each opening a perspective into distant reaches of human history. But these literary gestures exemplify the function of the poet as de Silentio represents it in the opening of the Eulogy:

if there were no sacred bond that knit humankind together, if one generation emerged after another like forest foliage, if one generation succeeded another like the singing of birds in the forest, if a generation passed through the world

---

[7] Mooney notes both implications, but does not develop them in the ways essayed here.

as a ship through the sea, as wind through the desert, an unthinking and unproductive performance, if an eternal oblivion, perpetually hungry, lurked for its prey and there were no power strong enough to wrench that away from it—how empty and devoid of consolation life would be! But precisely for that reason it is not so, and just as God created man and woman, so he created the hero and the poet or orator. (*FT* 15)

The tale of Tarquin the Proud, with its revisions, inflections, and reinterpretations, is one such sacred thread; and the tale of Abraham is another. Without its endless recounting, Abraham's ordeal would have been devoured by eternal oblivion, his exemplarity utterly powerless to affect his posterity. It might be hubristic for de Silentio to claim that the poet is the hero's better nature; but faith's ability to establish and maintain itself in human existence does depend inextricably upon its capacity to make itself manifest in discourse—in sacred texts, in rituals, in communal memory. Indeed, since de Silentio compares hero and poet to man and woman, making Abraham as father poetically real comes to look like a maternal function, a matter of incarnating the father's spirit or better nature in words (incarnating the Word?). In this sense, there can be no ultimate discontinuity or alienation between faith and language, and so no essential hiddenness in Abraham.

Amidst de Silentio's endlessly unfolding, productive cascade of imagery (itself exemplary of the generative and regenerative function of language that it describes), the image of generational change that it conjures up has an obvious application to these ideas of fatherhood and motherhood in faith. It confirms that the productivity of that fatherhood (in its conjunction with the productivity of motherhood) is to be seen not so much in the life of the father himself but in the way in which his existence is productive in the future—in the influence his recounted example secures, and in the spiritual fruitfulness of the future generations of which he is the father, both immediately and unforeseeably into the future. In other words, this passage at once reinforces and develops the idea that emerged earlier—that what makes Abraham a father of faith may be something or someone that he fathers, with whom his life has a sacred bond.

ABRAHAM'S POSTERITY: PARABLE AND PREFIGURATION

23. The same point is reiterated in revised form at the opening of the fifth beginning of *Fear and Trembling*—the Preamble. While explaining

why the law of indifference does not apply in the world of spirit, de Silentio declares: 'Here it does not help to have Abraham as father or to have seventeen ancestors. The one who will not work fits what is written about the virgins of Israel; he gives birth to wind—but the one who will work gives birth to his own father' (*FT* 27).

This wind recalls the Eulogy's reference to the unproductive and unremarked passage of wind through the desert; and the idea that avoiding such idleness amounts to giving birth to one's own father deepens the idea that what establishes Abraham's fatherhood of faith is what happens after him, what is done by his offspring. He fathers faith only if those he fathers are faithful, accepting the burden of spiritual work. Accordingly, we may need to look far beyond the story of Abraham himself to understand what makes him a father of faith. And since this passage makes his fatherhood dependent upon another's acceptance of motherhood, it confirms the suggestion of the Exordium that the maturity of faith is reached in identification with femaleness rather than maleness.

Further developments of these covert interwoven chains of imagery unfold in the three problemata themselves. In problema I, for example, de Silentio's overt hostility to non-literal interpretations is formulated in terms that nevertheless point beyond Abraham himself.

The story of Abraham contains just such a teleological suspension of the ethical. There is no dearth of keen minds and careful scholars who have found analogies to it. What their wisdom amounts to is the beautiful proposition that basically everything is the same. If one looks more closely, I doubt very much that anyone in the whole wide world will find one single analogy, except for a later one, which proves nothing if it is certain that Abraham represents faith and that it is manifested normatively in him . . . (*FT* 56)

Since we already have reason to doubt that Abraham represents a properly mature faith, perhaps we should look more closely at the mysterious exception de Silentio allows to his general rejection of analogical interpretations of Abraham's tale. To what, or to whom, might this offhand reference to a later analogy be intended to direct us? Perhaps to one of Abraham's offspring, a more or less remote descendant of the nation he founded through his fatherhood of Isaac? If so, two references towards the end of problema I become important.

The first reiterates the Exordium's implicit linkage of mature faith with maternity. For de Silentio chooses to utilize Mary as exemplary of the kind of greatness that he wishes us to see in Abraham: 'To be sure, Mary bore the child wondrously, but she nevertheless did it "after the manner of women", and such a time is one of anxiety, distress and paradox' (*FT* 65). The terrors of Abraham are here compared to those of childbirth; and of course, the child to whom Mary gave birth was not only the son of God but also the distant offspring of Abraham— Jesus Christ, the figure to whom de Silentio immediately turns in his quest for another example of anxious, agonizing greatness of the kind Abraham exemplifies.

Sweet sentimental longing leads us to the goal of our desire, to see Christ walking about in the promised land. We forget the anxiety, the distress, the paradox. Was it such a simple matter not to make a mistake? Was it not terrifying that this man walking around among the others was God? Was it not terrifying to sit down to eat with him? Was it such an easy matter to become an apostle? (*FT* 66)

De Silentio thereby equates Abraham's greatness with the greatness of following in Christ's footsteps, which he in turn equates (via Mary, and via the reference, implicit in talk of sharing his meal, to partaking in Christ's Eucharist) with the incarnation of Christ in human form, allowing him to inform and be informed by one's fleshly, embodied existence. In doing so, for the first time in his book, de Silentio allows the Old Testament tale of Abraham to be contextualized in New Testament terms—by introducing a distinctively Christian religious perspective, which of course thinks of itself as the fulfilment or maturation of that understanding of God and faith whose origins lie in the books of the Old Testament. The implication would seem to be that Christ is the later analogy in terms of which we must attempt to understand Abraham's ordeal. But how precisely are we to do this?

Problema II offers further guidance, when de Silentio returns to the New Testament to specify his sense of how biblical texts should properly be read. As we saw earlier, he rejects any idea that we might legitimately weaken the meaning of Luke's attribution to Christ of the command that following him requires that we hate our father and mother, because of the context of that attribution.

In the following verse we are told that someone who wants to erect a tower first of all makes a rough estimate to see if he is able to finish it lest he be mocked later. The close proximity of this story and the verse quoted seems to indicate that the words are to be taken in their full terror in order that each person may examine himself to see if he can erect the building. (*FT* 72)

If we do follow this advice, however, we will not conclude, with de Silentio, that 'if this passage is to have any meaning it must be understood literally' (*FT* 73). For of course, the story of the tower is a parable, as is the story preceding the verse in question (the parable of the great supper) and the discourse in which all three passages play their part—hardly surprising, since the characteristic tenor of Christ's discourse throughout the Gospel stories is parabolic. And by definition, parables are not to be taken literally; they can be understood only by analogy, by understanding the symbolic significance of the events they literally describe. Of course, understanding the literal sense of such utterances is an essential prerequisite for their interpretation: we must, for example, know whether or not the Greek transliteration of the original Hebrew term is accurate (as biblical scholars would deny in the case of the term translated into English as 'hate'—*pace* de Silentio's earlier sarcasm about Hebrew exegesis). But we must then go further, and aim to understand how those terms are intended to signify non-literally. If we accept de Silentio's suggestion that the task of reading the New Testament is exemplary for reading the Old, this would mean looking beyond the literal significance of the tale of Abraham's ordeal in search of its symbolic or allegorical meaning.

24. The issue comes to a head in problema III, which tells us that, if only we 'would read the New Testament, maybe [we] would get some other ideas' (*FT* 112), and that 'there are . . . places in the New Testament that praise irony, provided that it is used to conceal the better part' (*FT* 111). De Silentio here inverts his argument about Abraham's alienation from language, claiming that the words he speaks to Isaac are ones in which he is totally present, in which he consummates himself as a father of faith. If we attempt to read those words again, bearing in mind the alternative interpretative perspective we have slowly been assembling from de Silentio's self-subverting hints and asides, what emerges?

What emerges is a prophetic dimension of significance in Abraham's words of which he is oblivious. When he states that 'God will provide himself a lamb for the burnt offering, my son,' what he predicts turns out to be literally false, since God provides a ram rather than a lamb for the sacrifice on Mount Moriah; but it remains prophetically true, since God later provides the Lamb of God, his only Son in whom he is well pleased, for the sacrifice on Golgotha. In short, Abraham's ordeal prefigures the Atonement—the Incarnation, Passion, Death, and Resurrection of Christ, God's sacrifice of himself to overcome human sinfulness. God's substitution of a ram for Isaac thus prefigures his substitution of his own Son for human offspring, so that the sins of the fathers are no longer visited upon the sons; and Isaac's unquestioning submission to his father's will (his carrying of the wood of his own immolation to the place of sacrifice) prefigures Christ's submission to his own Father. In this sense, Isaac's receptive passivity represents the maturation of Abraham's activist conception of faith—a transition from an understanding of God as demanding the sacrifice of what is ours to an understanding of God as demanding the sacrifice of the self. Against the background of his historical and cultural context, Abraham found no difficulty in conceiving of his God as capable of demanding human sacrifice; but God's refusal to accept that sacrifice—his substitution of an animal for a human being—is designed to wean Abraham away from such conceptions of deity, to transform his self-understanding as a father of faith in the direction represented by his son, and hence to allow Isaac's incarnation (in fear and trembling) of the idea of self-sacrifice to give birth to his own father.

It should not be surprising to find that this analogical, symbolic, pre-figurative interpretation of the Abraham story presents it as a drama of symbolic substitution and transfiguration. God substitutes the ram for Isaac and for Abraham's 'lamb', for which he later substitutes his own Lamb. Abraham stands for God the Father, and Isaac for God the Son; and Isaac also stands for Mary, exemplar of the work of incarnating Christ, and thence both for Abraham (in his fathering of himself) and for Abraham's mother (whom Genesis never names). It seems an apt apotheosis of a life in which Abraham's relation to God began with God's renaming of him, and with God's dedication of himself to Abraham's offspring early and late.

ETHICS AND FAITH: AFTER ABRAHAM, AFTER HEGEL

25. The previous paragraphs simply encapsulate the most orthodox Christian interpretation of Abraham's ordeal. Why, then, should de Silentio's overt interpretative trajectory have taken him so far from these familiar reference points? There are two obvious switching-points in *Fear and Trembling*—two pivotal moments at which, in retrospect, we can see de Silentio going off the rails.

The first concerns his hostility to Christendom's tendency to avoid or otherwise downplay the concrete details of the Abraham tale. Its origin lies in his contempt for pastors who sermonize about Abraham in generalities which allow them to avoid the specificities (and in particular, the specific horrors and anxieties of Abraham's and Isaac's experience). Thus far, de Silentio seems absolutely right: the orthodox Christian interpretation of the tale must be earned by following the specific twists and turns of the Genesis narrative. It does contextualize that narrative within Abraham's specific culture and the broader framework of the New Testament, but only in order to reveal levels of meaning in the details of the original text that would otherwise be missed. Such broadenings of focus are thus ultimately in the service of attention to the particular (thereby conforming to Wittgenstein's picture of what is involved in understanding a gesture).

However, somewhere between this initiating experience and problema III de Silentio's legitimate desire to return contemporary believers to a careful reading of the biblical texts is transformed into the principle that the only legitimate mode of interpreting those texts is in accordance with its literal meaning. The temptation to accept this transformation without question is real and strong: the belief that taking a sacred text seriously must mean taking it literally, that reading the word of God allegorically, symbolically, and figuratively amounts to hollowing it out (as if the figurative dimension of language is a seduction, a means of veiling or even voiding truth), is hardly unfamiliar in contemporary religious culture. Nevertheless, it is this transformation that leads to the all but unmissable contradiction between de Silentio's talk of Abraham as incapable of speech and his admission of the centrality of what he does say to the import of his tale and his life. And there is, of course, no reason why he (or we) should regard this transformation as legitimate. Any interpretation of a text—whether literal, analogical, metaphorical, allegorical, or otherwise symbolic—can claim validity only in so far as it answers to the details of the text itself. Interpretation by analogy does not presuppose, as de Silentio seems sometimes to assume, that 'basically everything is the same' (*FT* 56); on the contrary, it contends that the specificity of a text, the full depth of its distinctiveness and difference from other texts, emerges only when we move from the level of literal meaning to that of the figurative.

The second pivotal moment of de Silentio's disquisition occurs when, in order to preserve the distinctiveness of the religious and the ethical realms, he applies Hegelian dialectics to Abraham's ordeal. De Silentio constructs what he regards as the dialectical heart of his polemic, the Problemata, in terms of three interrelated dilemmas for a Hegelian understanding of religious belief. Problema I tells us that if the ethical is the universal, then Hegel must condemn Abraham as a murderer; problema II tells us that if one's only duties to God are ethical duties, then Hegel must condemn Abraham as altogether lost to duty; and problema III tells us that if the individual must always be capable of full self-disclosure, then Hegel must condemn Abraham as having succumbed to the temptation of having placed self before duty.

In effect, in his desire to contradict the Hegelian equation of the religious and the ethical, de Silentio constructs a depiction of Abraham (and hence of faith) by simply negating three Hegelian claims about the ethical. But he thereby leaves the accuracy of those original claims unquestioned; his rejection of Hegelian claims about the realm of faith takes for granted the truth of Hegelian claims about the ethical by asserting that they have no application to faith—that faith is the negation of the ethical (as Hegel understands that realm). Thus, as his claim to have immersed himself in Hegel's philosophy might lead us to expect (*FT* 33), de Silentio's supposedly anti-Hegelian account of the religious realm remains implicitly indebted to Hegel's understanding of the ethical realm (as his reliance upon the characteristically Hegelian operation of negation to power his supposedly anti-Hegelian dialectic would anyway suggest). As with Climacus and Socrates, de Silentio's declared hatred of all things Hegelian leads him to characterize the religious realm as a kind of mirror-image of Hegel's view of ethics. He never stops to consider that Hegel's illicit equation of the ethical and the religious realms might be as much a consequence of his misinterpretation of the ethical realm as it is of the religious realm—that the equation depends upon a misunderstanding of both relata.

More particularly, de Silentio's idea that Abraham cannot speak, that his faith is an offence against the *logos* (as manifest in reason and in discourse), merely inverts and hence implicitly presupposes the Hegelian notion that the domain of the ethical and the domain of the universal are one and the same—that the ethical is reason made practical and concrete, and hence that any form of practical existence lacking a recognizably ethical articulation is an offence against reason. In depriving Abraham of speech, de Silentio takes himself to be defending the specificity of faith in relation to the ethical; in reality, he is distorting his account of faith in a way which precisely corresponds to Hegel's distorted characterization of the ethical realm as exhaustive, as the only intelligible form, of spiritually meaningful human existence.

26. Since de Silentio carefully ensures that these two fundamentally misleading interpretative presuppositions converge upon the glaring inconsistencies of his climactic treatment of Abraham's silent speech, and since both our objections to those presuppositions and our sketch of an alternative interpretation that seems more responsive to the Genesis narrative are constructed from materials supplied by de Silentio himself, I think we are justified in concluding that his strident advo-

cacy of those presuppositions is not designed to vindicate them but rather to encourage his readers to experience their seductiveness, initially accept their veracity, and only later discover their invalidity and begin to uncover more responsive and responsible ways of approaching the Abraham story. De Silentio wants his readers to work for their spiritual bread, and in doing so to realize the ease with which that work can be misdirected or avoided, and in particular the difficulty of realizing that even those whose overt aim is to clear the way for their readers to relate directly to Abraham's text in all its specificity might nevertheless come to interpose themselves between reader and text.

It should now be clear what kind of work he expects us to do if we are to attain a properly Christian understanding of Abraham's ordeal; but it may be less clear exactly how that understanding revises or qualifies the Hegelian interpretation of the relation between the ethical and the religious realms. We have been led to see that Hegel is wrong to equate the ethical and the religious, but that de Silentio is wrong in the ways in which he denies that equation. What, then, might be the right way to deny it? In particular, must we jettison that most interesting of de Silentio's claims—the idea that faith incorporates the possibility of a teleological suspension of the ethical—or must we rather reinterpret its significance?

If the allegorical or analogical reading of Abraham's ordeal as a prefiguration of Christ's Atonement is correct, then we must reject the idea that God could conceivably require a form of worship that involves murder; for the maturation of faith that the ordeal symbolizes is precisely a shift towards a conception of God as willing to shed his own blood rather than eager to spill the blood of others—as concerned not only to transcend the primitive idea of human sacrifice by substituting a ram for Isaac, but also to transcend the idea of sacrificing one's possessions to God in favour of an idea of sacrificing oneself (the act and attitude by means of which one incarnates God by imitating his essentially self-sacrificial nature).

This means that faith could never require the violation of ethical duty, although it might require its transfiguration. There can be no teleological suspension of the ethical in the sense that ethical requirements might ever be made null and void; from a Christian perspective, any voice in our heads that demanded such a thing would thereby declare itself to be that of a devil rather than of God. Indeed, de Silentio's account of such a teleological suspension all but declares that Hegel's equation of the ethical and the religious is and must be right, at least in a certain sense.

This emerges in his discussion of what criteria, if any, might allow someone to recognize when the demands of the ethical have become a temptation. He twice emphasizes that Abraham is open to such a possibility only because he is God-fearing, and because he loves his son more than himself.

If it fell to my lot to speak about him, I would begin by showing what a devout and God-fearing man Abraham was, worthy of being called God's chosen one. Only a person of that kind is put to such a test, but who is such a person? Next I would describe how Abraham loved Isaac. For that purpose I would call upon all the good spirits to stand by me so that what I said would have the glow of fatherly love. I hope to describe it in such a way that there would not be many a father in the realms and lands of the king who would dare to maintain that he loved in this way. But if he did not love as Abraham loved, then any thought of sacrificing Isaac would surely be a spiritual trial. (*FT* 31)

And again, a little later:

The absolute duty can lead one to do what ethics would forbid, but it can never lead the knight of faith to stop loving. Abraham demonstrates this. In the moment he is about to sacrifice Isaac, the ethical expression for what he is doing is: he hates Isaac. But if he actually hates Isaac, he can rest assured that God does not demand this of him, for Cain and Abraham are not identical. He must love Isaac with his whole soul. Since God claims Isaac, he must, if possible, love him even more, and only then can he *sacrifice* him, for it is indeed this love for Isaac that makes his act a sacrifice by its paradoxical contrast to his love for God. (*FT* 74)

De Silentio here returns to the issue underlying variation III in his Exordium, in which Abraham's troubled memory of his mistreatment of Ishmael leads him to doubt whether his love for Isaac was sufficiently pure for his intention to sacrifice him not to be sinful. But the second passage all but declares what the first passage implies: that a voice in one's head inciting one to kill one's son can only be the voice of God if one's love for one's son is perfect. Any imperfection, the slightest grain of impurity in one's attachment to the Isaac in one's life, and one's attempts to carry out that command would align one with Cain rather than Abraham, revealing the voice in one's head as that of an evil demon.

On the understanding (assumed by de Silentio throughout) that Isaac here symbolizes the demands of the ethical as such, this means that only an ethically perfect being (one who lives out the demands of the ethical without exception, one whose soul is permeated and informed by the ethical) could ever be in a position to judge that an impulse to suspend the demands of the ethical might be the manifestation of a divine command. And who could conceivably measure up to this standard? De Silentio appears to imply that Abraham at least does, and that therein lies a vital part of his claim to greatness as a father of faith—even though this would entail that his ordeal was a spiritual trial of his commitment to the ethical realm as much as to that of the divine. But de Silentio also gives us reason to think that events in the spiritual realm after Abraham's time make such claims to greatness no longer conceivable.

Here, we need to examine in more detail the third of de Silentio's four variations on hiddenness that together comprise his long introduction (by negation) to his portrait of Abraham's alienation from language in problema III: the tale of Agnes and the merman. De Silentio offers several versions of this third tale, all of which originate in the merman's impulse to seduce the maiden, but in which he varies the degree of innocence or guilt imputed to Agnes and considers various ways in which the merman's project of seduction might fail. The most important concerns the merman's choices when his impulse to seduce her has been crushed by the invincibility of her innocent love for him, and he must decide whether repentance for that impulse requires isolation and hiddenness or whether it might coexist with his retaining Agnes. One form of hiddenness (in which he tries to convince Agnes that he never really loved her, and thereby free her from her love) de Silentio says is demonic, the other (in which he simply withdraws from Agnes and trusts in God to save her from her sorrow) he says is not. If, however, he allows Agnes to save him, for example by marrying her, then he will have disclosed himself—and what he values in the world will have been returned to him through what de Silentio calls the paradox of the single individual attaining an absolute relation to the absolute.

At this point de Silentio intervenes into the main body and the subtext of his own text.

Now here I would like to make a comment that says more than has been said at any point previously.* Sin is not the first immediacy; sin is a later immediacy. In sin, the single individual is already higher (in the direction of the demonic paradox) than the universal, because it is a contradiction on the part of the universal to want to demand itself from a person who lacks the *conditio sine qua non* ... An ethics that ignores sin is a completely futile discipline, but if it affirms sin, then it has *eo ipso* exceeded itself. ...

As long as I move around in these spheres, everything is easy, but nothing of what is said here explains Abraham, for Abraham did not become the single individual by way of sin—on the contrary, he was a righteous man, God's chosen one ...

* Up until now I have assiduously avoided any reference to the question of sin and its reality. The whole work is centred on Abraham, and I can still encompass him in immediate categories—that is, insofar as I can understand him. As soon as sin emerges, ethics founders precisely on repentance; for repentance is the highest ethical expression, but precisely as such it is the deepest ethical self-contradiction. (*FT* 98–9)

De Silentio here explains why Abraham at least might think of himself, and be thought of by others, as capable of realizing ethical perfection: the concept of sin has no application to his life. If, however, we begin to think of our lives in terms of sinfulness, the idea of ethical perfection is utterly lost: repentance is not capable of entirely eradicating the stain of past wrongdoing because even the smallest past misdemeanour reveals our absolute difference from Absolute Goodness, and hence our inability to save ourselves by our own powers (thereby opening us to the possibility and necessity of divine redemption). And of course, the notion of sinfulness—together with the notion of original sinfulness, that apotheosis of the idea of the sins of the fathers being visited on the sons—is introduced to us through Christianity.

The advent of Christianity thus entails the dissolution of the category of a spiritual trial in which the ethical might function as a temptation; for such a trial is only possible if the one in the dock can be certain of the perfection of his ethical being, and the category of sin makes any such self-conception inconceivable. Whereas Abraham, according to de Silentio, did not become the single individual by way of sin, Christianity teaches that the only way to God is through sin—through recognizing our sinfulness and our inability to overcome it through our own resources. The Atonement is precisely God's response to our neediness, his loving sacrifice of himself to redeem our sins. It is this shift in religious sensibility that Abraham's prophetic utterance on Mount Moriah, his vision of a lamb for the sacrifice, foretells; and its human form is adumbrated parabolically in de Silentio's tale of a merman's rescue by way of sin, repentance, and the love of a woman named after the Lamb of God.

This vision of recovering a capacity to aim for ethical ideals by means of grace is the covert message of de Silentio's talk of the teleological suspension of the ethical. Acknowledging our sinfulness means acknowledging our inability to live up to the demands of the ethical realm; acknowledging Christ means acknowledging that those demands must nevertheless be met, with help from a power greater than our own. In other words, faith returns the ethical to us, but our existence within that realm has shifted its centre of gravity: we are no longer self-supporting, but rather suspended from an external, absolute, divine point of reference or telos. De Silentio himself provides the necessary image—while claiming to be talking about something rather different:

In learning to go through the motions of swimming, one can be suspended from the ceiling in a harness and then presumably describe the movements, but one is not swimming. In the same way I can describe the movements of faith. If I am thrown out into the water, I presumably do swim (for I do not belong to the waders), but I make different movements, the movements of infinity, whereas faith makes the opposite movements: after having made the movements of infinity, it makes the movements of finitude. (*FT* 37–8)

Suppose that one is thrown into the sea of ethics still in the harness, and one makes swimming movements: one would then be in a very different position from those swimming in the ocean unsupported, but would one not therefore be swimming? Surely one's position would be the marine equivalent of the knight of faith so poetically characterized in de Silentio's Preamble to the Problemata—the bourgeois philistine or tax-collector who is capable of turning the leap into life into walking, whose existence absolutely expresses the sublime in the pedestrian (*FT* 41). In short, those who live teleologically suspended in the ethical live in the ethical rather than elsewhere: they do not need to contemplate its violation.

They may, however, need to contemplate its intensification, and hence its transfiguration. For their goal of incarnating Christ in their own lives means that those lives must manifest an understanding of love as self-sacrificial; and genuinely to die to the self goes beyond the ethical in the sense that it will involve going beyond certain concepts that are typically taken to be central to an ethical self-understanding. If the knight of faith's capacity for self-sacrifice is truly to resemble that of his Master, it must, for example, encompass the ability to refrain from making claims upon others even when he is, ethically speaking, justified in doing so—even, indeed particularly, when the ethical realm would consider the making of such claims (say, claiming one's rights) integral to the maintenance of one's own dignity or self-respect. Such self-denial, imitating the example of Christ on the cross, is rooted in recognizably ethical principles of concern for others, but develops them to a point that appears ethically (rather than logically) absurd or paradoxical, when from the perspective of Christianity it appears as their perfection or telos. Thus the distinctive mark of those who have re-founded their ethical being in Christian terms is the room they make in their lives for the concept of sacrificing oneself rather than another. The Christian faithful whom Abraham fathered, the sons and daughters of the Son, are their own Isaacs.

* * * * * *

CONSTANTIUS, BY JOHANNES CLIMACUS

27. According to Johannes Climacus, he might as easily have written Constantin Constantius' little book *Repetition* as de Silentio's *Fear and Trembling*; for it too takes a step along the intellectual path opened up to him by his graveyard encounter. Indeed, since these pseudonymous texts were published simultaneously, their appearance must in retrospect have struck him as a kind of interior doubling or repetition of his own voice—as if his words were capable of being thrown back at him from two different places at once. And since he sees the two books as complementary, each making good the other's lack with respect to their shared preoccupations, he hears himself giving voice to something different in each place—as if his thoughts were not only as common as bread or water, but also as subject to dispersal or dissemination.

More specifically, Climacus tells us that, while *Repetition* mirrors *Fear and Trembling* in its concern with faith as a movement by means of the absurd, with teleological suspensions of the ethical, and with the notion of a spiritual trial or ordeal, it also repairs an omission in its twin. For his reading of *Fear and Trembling* led him to think

that by way of precaution it would be good to see to it that what was attained would not come to nothing through a *coup de main*, so that hiddenness would come to be something that is called hiddenness, a bit of the aesthetic, and faith would come to be something that is called immediacy, *vapeurs*, for example, and the religious paradigm something that is called a prototype, a tragic hero, for example.

What happens? During that same time, I receive a book from Reitzel titled *Repetition*. (CUP 262)

On this account, *Repetition* is a cautionary tale: the surprise stroke of the Young Girl's marriage to another reveals the Young Man's silence towards and withdrawal from her as a poetic artefact, his newly forged devotion to Job as dependent upon a misreading of him (and of himself) as a tragic hero, and his eager anticipations of a whirlwind of his own as irreligious vapourings.

Such a recounting of *Repetition* seems plausible; but the implication that it can be reduced to a precautionary supplement to *Fear and*

Trembling is far less credible, even on Climacus' own interpretative terms. For if there is any element of de Silentio's text that stands least in need of elaboration, it is its near-obsessive concern that we not confuse the religious paradigm with the prototypical tragic hero, and that we sharply distinguish religious from non-religious forms of hiddenness and immediacy. In other words, if Climacus' implied reading of *Repetition* were accurate, it would entail that de Silentio and Constantius were merely one another's doubles, each reiterating the other's central thought and hence each entirely dispensable in relation to the other. *Repetition* (or, of course, *Fear and Trembling*) would then not amount to a step beyond its twin in the unfolding of Climacus' project, but rather to a retaking of its supposedly distinctive step—to a mere repetition.

Our unreliable commentator emphasizes three other aspects of *Repetition*, two of which are (closely related) matters of substance. The first is that the critical issue in the life of its hero is an engagement, or more precisely the possibility of breaking it off; Climacus notes approvingly that, whereas novelists would think that a breach of promise could interest their readers only if it involved additional moral crimes (making the woman pregnant, abandoning her and her child, marrying another), the author of *Repetition* uses dialectic 'to make it as terrible as possible, and the hero becomes a hero through the very passion with which he interprets the terror in himself and as decisive for his life' (*CUP* 266). Interpreting a broken pledge as an ordeal is, he claims, the book's second substantial merit; for it allows its readers to appreciate the contrast between religious and ethical views of spiritual trials or ordeals, in which the ethical becomes a temptation.

An ordeal is the religious paradigm's highest earnestness, but for the purely ethical an ordeal is a jest, and to *exist on trial* is by no means earnestness, but a comic motif, which incomprehensibly enough no poet has yet used to depict lack of will to an almost insane degree, as if someone wanted to marry on trial etc. But that the highest earnestness of the religious life is distinguishable by jest is like saying that the paradigm is the irregularity or particularity, and God's omnipresence his invisibility, and revelation a mystery.[8] (*CUP* 263)

Climacus' third emphasis falls on one of Constantin Constantius' virtues as a writer; his mastery of what Climacus calls a 'doubly reflected communication form'. Here, *Repetition*'s subtitle is deemed significant: for Climacus, any book calling itself 'an imaginary psychological construction' (more literally, 'a venture in experimenting psychology')

---

[8] Since Christianity would endorse all three of this sentence's concluding claims, we should recognize that when Climacus connects religious earnestness and the jest, he is not jesting.

aims to create an opposition, establishing 'a chasmic gap between reader and author and fixing the separation of inwardness between them, so that a direct understanding is made impossible' (*CUP* 263). It does so by avoiding didacticism, preferring instead to employ 'a confusing contrastive form' (*CUP* 263).

At this point, however, the unreliability of our commentator once more becomes impossible to overlook. For Climacus' praise of those who avoid didacticism is the culmination of a highly didactic summary of the intellectual skeleton of Constantius' putative project—a repetition of the mode of reading that so incensed Climacus himself when it was enacted by a German reviewer of his own text. And if we allow this blatant inconsistency to lead us to reconsider Climacus' other claims about *Repetition*, we might notice that they focus exclusively on the narrative of the Young Man's engagement; they studiously overlook the fact that Constantius is as much a character in his own text as the Young Man (if not more). Is this avoidance Climacus' way of respecting Constantius' inwardness? Or does he rather intend to imply that Constantius' casting of himself in the role of the Young Man's reflective, nostalgic, and confessional older friend really does serve the purpose of distancing himself from, rather than revealing himself to, his readers?

The moral for readers of *Repetition* seems clear. The confusingly didactic form of Climacus' comments imply that his reading of *Repetition* is accurate in its substance, but nevertheless conveys an utterly mistaken impression of the book as a whole, because it fails accurately to interpret the resistance posed to its content by its form. Climacus' self-subversion thereby invites us to appreciate the self-subversions of Constantin Constantius—to go beyond what seem to be uncontroversial claims about the content of his book in order to work out the implications of its author's choice of form, and in particular his performance of a role in the drama he is narrating.

PROLOGUE: CITATION, QUESTION, AND GENRE

28. How and where might we begin this work? The work of *Repetition* itself begins at its beginning, where Constantius tells us that his concern is with a question—that of determining whether repetition is possible. But the form of his answer to that question is determined by the citation with which he precedes his articulation of it, and which

begins the text proper: 'When the Eleatics denied motion, Diogenes, as everyone knows, came forward as an opponent. He literally did come forward, because he did not say a word but merely paced back and forth a few times, thereby assuming that he had sufficiently refuted them' (*Repetition*,[9] 131). Constantius then picks up the most obvious implication of this tale—Diogenes' refusal to answer the Eleatics in their own terms (those of dialectical argument), his attempt to bring out a contradiction between the argumentative claims and the conditions of concrete existence to which all, including the Eleatics themselves, are subject—and suggests that his own approach to his self-posed question will repeat Diogenes' strategy, by attempting to repeat an earlier journey he made to Berlin. He thereby implies that his deepest response to that question will lie in his apparently digressive tale of that return trip, and so not in the apparently more central narrative of the Young Man's romantic and poetic travails (the very reverse of the emphasis that Climacus reads into the book). But Constantius leaves unacknowledged at this point a further implication of the tale of Diogenes, to which his tale about Berlin will later recur: the idea that philosophical progress might take the form of taking steps, of discovering edification in the pedestrian, in the achievement of a certain inflection of the ordinary human gait.

The second and final stage of what might be called the prologue to *Repetition* takes the form of an extended explanation of the significance of repetition in the constitution of human identity. '. . . what would life be if there were no repetition? Who could want to be a tablet on which time writes something new every instant or to be a memorial volume of the past?' (*R* 133). Here, the possibility of repetition represents the possibility of genuine individuality, of a mode of existence in which one's selfhood is neither endlessly redefined nor eternally fixed—in which an individual, by repeating what she has been, thereby makes what she has been into something new, forging a narrative unity between past, present, and future (see *R* 149). Constantius then passes over the further implication of his own imagery that there is a connection between achieving individuality and the idea of writing and reading, and begins his book again by beginning the story of the Young Man.

These opening pages thus appear to be plain sailing—until one reaches the end of the book, when Constantius directly addresses what he calls his real reader and warns him repeatedly that the import of his writing is not so easily discerned. He talks, for instance, of 'writing in

---

[9] *Repetition*, in *Fear and Trembling & Repetition*, trans. H. V. and E. H. Hong (Princeton University Press: Princeton, 1983); hereafter *R*.

such a way that the heretics are unable to understand it' as a 'very proper' strategy (*R* 225); and he concludes his concluding remarks by warning us that 'At times you may be distracted by an apparently pointless witticism or an idle defiance, but later you perhaps will be reconciled to those things' (*R* 231). Taken together, these words raise the possibility that we will only understand Constantius' aims as a writer if we treat the apparently pointless elements or dimensions of his text as central to its work. Constantius thereby implicitly reiterates his opening suggestion that his apparently digressive account of returning to Berlin is in fact at the heart of his response to the book's guiding question, suggesting now that it is the apparently inessential or distracting elements of that digression that will turn out to be most important. But how might we reconcile ourselves to such a claim about that account?

Perhaps by taking seriously another question that Constantius implicitly poses in his concluding address to his reader, when he imagines how a reviewer might answer the question of what kind of drama is narrated in *Repetition*: 'The book may provide an ordinary reviewer the desired opportunity to elucidate in detail that it is not a comedy, tragedy, novel, short story, epic or epigram' (*R* 226). Would an extraordinary or exceptional reviewer contest one of these negative characterizations? Or would a real reader rather see that this apparently exhaustive list of possible literary genres is not in fact complete? Climacus obligingly points us in the latter direction by citing Constantius' own one-word characterization of his ordering of words (a word he does not provide in *Repetition* itself): he wrote (Climacus tells us that he tells us) 'a droll book' (see *CUP* 263). Drollery is not (or not simply) comedy: it tends towards the mocking or the burlesque; it is (so the *OED* tells us) another word for farce. And Constantius does in fact tell us a great deal about the genre of farce in *Repetition*, when, in recounting his return trip to Berlin, he recalls the evenings he spent during his first trip there at the Königstadter Theatre, whose company specializes in performances of that very particular kind.

THEATRICALITY AND SELFHOOD

29. The Danish word (which is also the German word) for that theatre's version of the genre is Posse. The Hongs summarize it as 'a light dramatic composition that often includes songs and music and is characterized by broad comedy, with a latitude of situations and relations, and

not infrequently by a satirical slant' (*R* 367 n. 55). This might easily be mistaken for a description of *Repetition* itself. The Young Man's initial attempts to extricate himself from an unwise engagement, his antithetical expectation of a Job-like thunderstorm to make him a suitable spouse, and his happy acceptance of life as a poet when his beloved marries another provide broad enough strains of satire and comedy even without the interwoven tale of Constantius' fanatically detailed and repeatedly unsuccessful attempt to repeat the pleasures of his time in Berlin; and both tales are punctuated by recurrent outbreaks of lyric poetry set against the background melodies of a coach-horn. However, the self-mocking narrator of these events takes pains to elaborate an even more particular understanding of the genre, and hence to set a more demanding standard for its applicability to his own narrative.

To begin with, Constantius associates farce with what he calls 'the magic' of theatre in general: he talks of any normally imaginative young person as 'swept along into that artificial actuality in order like a double to see and hear himself and to split himself up into every possible variation of himself, and nevertheless in such a way that every variation is still himself' (*R* 154). Theatre appeals to the young because their individuality is not yet fixed: its actual shape is only invisibly present and thus casts a variety of shadows, all of which resemble it and can equally claim to be it. This shadow-existence is not genuine personality, but it is genuine and hence demands satisfaction: so it benefits a person to live out this shadow-existence in youth, but it is tragic or comic if she lives out her life in it—and it verges on the demonic if she lives it out in order to evade the responsibility of having an actual self.

Constantius' Young Man is plainly at just the age at which the shadow-play of theatre in general is most likely to cast its spell—'just as a grape at the peak of its perfection becomes transparent and clear, the juice trickling from its delicate veins, just as the peel of a fruit breaks when the fruit is fully ripe' (*R* 135). His personality is not yet discernible, so he casts a number of shadow-shapes upon the scenes of his own existence, each of them demanding satisfaction; and while the flat avoidance of those demands cannot help his development as a genuine individual, neither can he consecrate himself as an individual exclusively to meeting them. This reading casts the Young Girl essentially as a means towards the Young Man's (not necessarily conscious) end of at once achieving and transcending these essentially transitional satisfactions. His love for her is one of the shadows cast by his invisible personality, and hence being her spouse has as much claim upon that personality as any other possibility; but it has no more claim than any other possibility that her existence serves to excite—particularly that of being a poet—and once it becomes clear that one of those others is the main shoot of his spirit (*R* 154), then he must give up the satisfactions of the shadow-play and accept the moral consequences of doing so. *Repetition* then appears as an account of the Young Man's struggle to comprehend his situation, to achieve this transcendence, and to become whom he chooses to be.

On this interpretation, Constantin Constantius invites us to consider him as a mature individual whose soul has integrated itself in earnest, but who is sometimes in the mood to return—at least temporarily—to the state in which the Young Man finds himself, and who is therefore particularly well equipped to help him through his rite of passage towards selfhood. *Repetition* is his report of that intergenerational generosity, of the doubts and hostility that it understandably but unfairly arouses, and of the happy accident (the Young Man's misreading of Job inducing a period of inactivity in which the Young Girl has time to act for herself) that allows the Young Man to accept the poetic vocation that Constantius knew from the start was really his (*R* 230). At the same time, however, Constantius notes the danger that anyone as familiar as he with the seductiveness of existential shadow-play may devote his existence as a whole to cultivating its pleasures, and hence tend towards a demonic avoidance of the satisfactions and responsibilities of selfhood. And Constantius cannot hide the fact that his initial exchanges with the Young Man have a touch of the demonic about them.

True, it is the Young Man's despair that first leads him to play a deceptive role in relation to the Young Girl he no longer loves: he 'proceeds with a fabrication', using 'all his poetic originality in order to delight and amuse her', implying thereby that 'she was and remained the beloved, the one and only adored' (*R* 138). But Constantius' response to this development is to encourage it—indeed, to invite the Young Man to transform his deceptive impulse into a life plan, to bend all his poetic abilities to the task of convincing the Young Girl that he is and has been a callous deceiver. Both men initially delude themselves that this is in the Girl's best interests, a means of extricating her from the misrelation without offering her the insult of telling her that she was only the occasion for the Young Man's discovery of his poetic calling; the project would thus constitute the apotheosis of his respect, if not his love, for her. But Constantius repeatedly emphasizes that the Young Man's reluctance to confess the truth initially springs from 'pride on her behalf' (e.g. *R* 138)—a dubious enough motive even when it is not groundlessly imputed to another. Moreover, the Young Man himself eventually refuses to carry out the plan, because (as he later states) it would amount to 'hex[ing] the beloved into a lie' (*R* 190), and to running the risk of 'chang[ing] places with the character you were using for your pious deception' (*R* 192)—that is, of actually becoming a callous seducer. Even Constantius himself admits after the collapse of his plan that confessing the truth to the Girl would have been 'a respectable thing to do' (*R* 145). And if the demonic aspect of the plan (with its call for the hiring of a seamstress for a year to pretend to be the Young Man's mistress) were not sufficiently clear, Constantius gives the game away by talking of himself as having held the stage ropes of the affair in his hands (*R* 145)—quite as if its enactment could have taken place in the theatre, with Constantius the stage manager of another's despairing denial of selfhood.

FARCE AND SELFHOOD

30. We might think of the above interpretation as a developmental reading of *Repetition*: the Young Man experiences the seductiveness of shadow-play to the unformed personality, and Constantius thinks of himself as guiding the Young Man towards the maturity that lies beyond this seductiveness—without fully realizing that his supposedly integrated individuality is in fact a demonic continuation of the Young Man's temporary bewitchment. This would be a way of understanding Constantius' narrative as essentially self-subverting—providing us with the tools to diagnose the form and the source of its opacity to itself. But this diagnosis requires only the idea of *Repetition* as essentially theatrical, as a literary version of shadow-play; it makes no use of the more specific idea of *Repetition* as farce. If we are to justify the intuition that Constantius' disquisition on the Königstadter Theatre, its repertoire, and its company is also meant to have reflexive application, we must look more closely at its details.

According to that disquisition, Posse provides a particular inflection of what Constantius calls 'the shadow-play of the hidden individual' (*R* 156), one that can satisfy a need felt even by those whose soul has integrated itself in earnest:

Yes, although the art may not then be sufficiently earnest for the individual, he may at times be disposed to return to that first state and resume it in a mood. He desires the comic effect and wants a relation to the theatrical performance that generates the comic. Since tragedy, comedy and light comedy fail to please him precisely because of their perfection, he turns to farce. (*R* 157–8)

What Constantius appears to mean by 'perfection' here is a kind of completion or self-possession involving a relation to a pre-existing ideal or telos. A tragedy or a comedy are constructed in accordance with traditional aesthetic conventions of which its spectators are well aware, and this generates a relation of mutual respect between theatre and audience—a distancing and impersonal self-consciousness. By contrast, 'Every general aesthetic category runs aground on farce . . . Because its impact depends largely on self-activity and the viewer's improvisation, the particular individuality comes to assert himself in a very individual way and in his enjoyment is emancipated from all aesthetic obligations to admire, to laugh, to be moved etc. in the traditional way' (R 159). In farce, the audience and its responses are an ineliminable part of the performance; the world that the characters inhabit is not autonomous or self-subsistent, not one that the audience simply observes, as if from elsewhere. Farce therefore makes very peculiar demands on its audience: it asks them to come in a state which is not a single mood but the possibility of any and all moods, and to allow the performance to determine that indeterminacy unmediated by conventions or the responses of others. In short, farce individualizes its viewers by addressing their capacity for genuinely self-reliant responsiveness.

According to Constantius, however, farce makes equally peculiar demands on its performers; and what makes the Königstadter Theatre company so superb is their capacity to bear up under those burdens. Any such company must include at least two actors who are capable of overcoming reflection and allowing themselves to be empowered by the natural power of laughter, as its momentum alters from moment to moment on stage and in interaction with the audience; they must, in short, themselves be capable of a self-reliant responsiveness. Constantius claims that the Königstadter company possesses two such actors in Beckmann and Grobecker; but he stresses that these two *farceurs* embody rather different, if essentially complementary, aspects of such talent.[10]

Beckmann has two main claims to fame. First, he is able not only to walk convincingly on stage but to come walking with the whole scenic setting of his character in tow; it is as if he walks out of his character's world onto the stage, and thereby brings it with him—his gait implies

---

[10] T. F. Morris has noted the general lineaments of these two actors' personae in 'Constantin Constantius' Search for an Acceptable Way of Life', in R. L. Perkins (ed.), *International Kierkegaard Commentary*, vi: *Fear and Trembling & Repetition* (Mercer University Press: Macon, Ga., 1993); but his interest in this aspect of the text is very different from my own.

that world. Second, he is capable of letting loose the lunatic demon of comedy that dwells within him, of abandoning himself to it.

In this respect, B.'s dance is incomparable. He has sung his couplet, and now the dance begins. What B. ventures here is neck-breaking, for he presumably does not trust himself to create an effect with his dance routines in the narrow sense. He is now completely beside himself. The sheer lunacy of his laughter can no longer be contained either in forms or in lines; the only way to convey the mood is to take himself by the scruff of the neck, as did Munchhausen, and cavort in crazy capers. (*R* 164)

Grobecker, by contrast, tends towards the ludicrous rather than the lunatic, and reaches it via sentimentality or bathos.

I remember seeing him in a farce in which he played an estate overseer who, because of his devotion to his master and mistress and his belief in the importance of festive arrangments in embellishing life for their lordships, thinks of nothing but having a rustic festival in readiness for their lordships' very important arrival. Everything is ready. Grobecker has chosen to portray Mercury. He has not changed his overseer's uniform but has simply attached wings to his feet and put on a helmet. He takes up a picturesque pose on one leg and is about to begin his speech to the master and mistress. (*R* 165)

Grobecker's powers depend upon standing rather than walking, and upon a certain kind of resistance to self-abandonment; he is best suited to characters who are somehow incapable of stepping outside themselves.

When all these factors come together as they did on Constantius' first trip to Berlin, he finds himself transported by the experience in just the way that he associates with the brook that runs past his father's farm— his constant companion in childhood, his comforter in the weariness and melancholy of his middle age.

Then I lay at your side and vanished from myself in the immensity of the sky above and forgot myself in your soothing murmur! You, my happier self, you fleeting life that lives in the brook running past my father's farm, where I lie stretched out as if my body were an abandoned hiking stick, but I am rescued and released in the plaintive purling!—Thus did I lie in my theatre box, discarded like a swimmer's clothing, stretched out by the stream of laughter and unrestraint and applause that ceaselessly foamed by me . . . Only at intervals did I rise up, look at Beckmann, and laugh so hard that I sank back again in exhaustion alongside the foaming stream. (*R* 166)

It is hardly surprising that Constantius associates the happier self of his self-abandonment and self-forgetfulness with the laughter provoked by Beckmann's lunacies. But he knows that such blissful ecstasy nevertheless lacks something; and he finds it in his perception of one member of the theatre audience—a young girl. Every time he is exhausted by the current of laughter, the sight of her friendly gentleness allows him 'to climb out of the pool and return to himself' (*R* 167). And 'when in the farce itself a feeling of greater pathos burst forth, I looked at her, and her presence helped me to yield to it, for she sat composed in the midst of it all, quietly smiling in childlike wonder' (*R* 167). The girl's wonder is his touchstone for pathos; her responsiveness to moments of Grobeckian sentiment acts as the counterbalance to his moments of Beckmannian ecstasy. Through her Constantius can synthesize self-abandonment with self-constancy, just as his secret observations of a young girl's unself-conscious enjoyment of and refreshment by her untroubled nights of sleep can soothe the frenzies of his insomnia—her bright dawns overcoming his white nights (see *R* 167–8).

31. Constantius' general remarks about theatre suggest that the magic of its shadow-play speaks to the self's sense of its existence within a medium of possibilities, its awareness of itself as always capable of being more or other than it presently is—an awareness that can (although, as Heidegger shows, it need not) run counter to the awareness that genuine selfhood also requires self-integration, the making concrete over time (that is, the repeated actualization) of one of these many possible modes of existence. Beckmann and Grobecker each represent an extreme or heightened version of one of these two essential aspects of selfhood. Beckmann represents the self's transcendence of itself: his lunacy or ecstasy, his being completely beside himself, figures the self's capacity to carry itself away from its present state towards another possible state, to abandon its actual state in favour of realizing another mode of existence that is attainable but as yet unattained, and that can be attained only if it takes itself by the scruff of its own neck (acting as its own Munchhausen). Grobecker represents the self's faithfulness to itself: his ludicrousness or bathos lies in his constancy to his present state, and his inability to slough off his actual identity even in play figures the self's need for self-constancy, its ability to resist the call to self-abandonment in order to maintain its concreteness or actuality.

When Constantius tells us that his abandonment to Beckmann's lunacy lacked something—that it required correction or supplementation by a young girl's composed responsiveness to Grobeckian pathos— he is in effect saying that genuine selfhood is a matter of marrying the Beckmann and the Grobecker in all of us. On its own, Beckmann's walking explodes into a dance of cavorting, crazy capers; on its own, Grobecker's walking freezes into a ludicrous one-legged pose. If either wishes to achieve and maintain a recognizably human gait, he must open himself to the genius of the other—which means openness to the thought that being human means taking steps, that each step takes us to a place at which either a stand or another step can be taken, and that each stand or step taken in that spirit is like a movement in a dance that each dancer must improvise for himself. As an image of selfhood, such a synthesis teaches us that individual maturity or integration means finding a balance between self-abandonment and self-constancy, knowing when to keep faith with the attained state of oneself and when to allow oneself to be seduced by one's unattained but attainable state. Genuine individuality means improvising a path between a Beckmannian eclipse of the rightful draw of the attained and a Grobeckian eclipse of the rightful draw of the unattained.

REPETITION AS FARCE: DOUBLING, DYNAMISM, AND THERAPY

32. The most immediate reflexive application of this picture of the doubledness of the self in farce is the parallel between the roles of Beckmann and Grobecker in the Königstadter company and those of the Young Man and Constantius in the farce of *Repetition* (a parallel indicated by Constantius' passing remark that no farce is complete without a pleasant, engaging, friendly, and winsome sweetheart (R 163)—someone just like the Young Girl). In the first part of the book Constantius (true to his name, which might be rewritten 'Steadfast Self-possession') exhibits a degree of composure in the face of his friend's fluctuating moods and intentions that the Young Man will later describe as a kind of monstrous self-possession. 'Is it not, in fact, a kind of mental disorder to have subjugated to such a degree every passion, every emotion, every mood under the cold regimentation of reflection! Is it not mental disorder to be normal in this way—pure idea, not a human being like the rest of us, flexible and yielding, lost and being lost!' (R 189). Constantius confirms the Young Man's diagnosis when he exhibits such zeal to provide a practical proof that repetition is possible through his return trip to Berlin, and when he reacts to (what he takes to be) his discovery that repetition is impossible by establishing a 'monotonous and unvarying order . . . in [his] whole economy. Everything unable to move stood in its appointed place, and everything that moved went its calculated course' (R 179). He continues to walk, but according to such a measured pace and rigid orientation that he thinks

of himself as a living fossil, a human relic disinterred by archaeologists of the unknown future. Grobecker's one-legged pose as Mercury could hardly be more ludicrous.

By contrast, the Young Man as portrayed in part I of *Repetition* no sooner abandons himself to love than he finds himself abandoned to its abandonment in favour of poetry; and he ends by abandoning his beloved by taking flight to a neighbouring country. Constantius is quick to see the Beckmannian madness in this, describing the young man in his first appearance on the narrative scene as 'quite beside himself' (*R* 134). This ecstasy is, however, superseded in part II by a Grobeckian attachment to stasis that outdoes even the living death of Constantius' new domestic economy. For his reading in exile of the book of Job leads him to believe that divine intervention might shatter his personality in such a way as to make him a suitable husband; in other words, he yearns for self-constancy, and prepares himself for it by attempting to attain an extreme of passivity or patience, a suffering endurance of his present state that he describes in Grobeckian terms as a daily regrowing of the beard of his ludicrousness (*R* 214). The extremity of this reversal invites us to recollect that Constantius' self-possessed stance in relation to the Young Man has a taint of demonic inconstancy that leads him (among other things) to suggest a project that takes his friend's lunatic self-abandonment to an unmanageable extreme, and that is enacted within an almost obsessive sympathetic identification with his original state or condition of self-abandonment: 'I could not resist stealing an almost enamoured glance at him now and then, for a young man like that is just as enchanting to the eye as a young girl' (*R* 135). And of course, this bewitchment is matched by the Young Man's inability to break off relations with Constantius throughout the events of the narrative—their mutual obsession being perhaps most starkly expressed in part II, in the Young Man's inability to stop writing to Constantius and Constantius' inability to stop reading those letters even when he cannot reply to them.

In other words, both Constantius and the Young Man oscillate between lunacy and the ludicrous, between Beckmannian ecstasy and Grobeckian pathos, between the two extremes of self-abandonment and self-constancy. Each more or less consciously sees in the other the aspect of genuine selfhood that he lacks, but neither sees the essential complementarity of those extremes; hence their relationship constantly fluctuates, shifting from absolute identification to absolute alienation without ever attaining equilibrium. But their endless oscillation allows the reader to see the possibility of a balance or harmony that the characters never attain, to extrapolate from the doubling between the Beckmann–Grobecker double and the Young Man–Constantius double an implicit vision of an improvisatory self-reliance that is the ground of genuine individuality.

33. But the repetition of the Beckmann–Grobecker double in the Young Man and Constantius introduces something new to the old pattern— a dynamism or movement. The opposition between Beckmann and Grobecker in the theatre is one of generic ideals that is resolved (if at all) not through the mechanism of the play and its plot but in the mind of the audience (a point Constantius makes when, after observing the young girl in the audience, he recognizes that he must be responsive to both the ecstasy and the pathos of the farce he is viewing). When Constantius and the Young Man instantiate those ideals in existential guise, however, they induce mechanisms of projection, identification, and alienation in one another's psyches—processes of seduction and repulsion which empower the narrative as a whole.

Their interaction is, of course, presented as fundamentally unproductive. The Young Man is initially seduced by Constantius' self-possession and Constantius by the Young Man's poetic passion; the Young Man's momentary impulse to deceive the Young Girl is consequently brought forth by Constantius and reflected back in so intensified a form that it repels the Young Man from both beloved and interlocutor, propelling him towards a mirror-image or simple negation of his earlier state that is no less distant from the maturity he seeks. Even so, he continues to need Constantius as a confidant, but by ensuring that interlocution is impossible (by omitting a return address from his letters), he excludes any possibility of either man being helped by the other to move beyond their new one-sidedness except by events off stage beyond their control.

We might say that *Repetition*, uncannily anticipating one cultural future for its key concept, here presents itself as the account of an unsuccessful therapeutic relationship. Constantius thinks of himself as a highly appropriate analyst for the Young Man; indeed, he all but declares this fact in his concluding letter to his readers when he says:

You will now understand that the interest focusses on the young man, whereas I am a vanishing person, just like a midwife in relation to the child she has delivered . . . My personality is a presupposition of consciousness that must be present in order to force him out . . . So he has been in good hands from the very beginning, even though I frequently had to tease him so that he himself could emerge. (R 230)

Unfortunately, Constantius is deceived as to the success of his treatment. For his identification with the Young Man as a revenant of his younger self induces a counter-transference that precisely corresponds to the Young Man's transference to Constantius as instantiating true maturity. These transferential interactions combine to engender an intensification of the Young Man's worst impulses (with the analyst encouraging what the Young Man only proposes because it is what he imagines the analyst would do), a mutual repulsion between analyst and analysand, and finally a repetition of the analytical relationship that is rendered futile by its epistolary form—as if the Young Man, infuriated by Constantius' impassivity but still captivated by it and dimly aware that a version of such unresponsiveness is what he needs to achieve his own emancipation, attempts to re-create a less damaging version of it, but only succeeds in creating a more damaging paralysis (a vacuum which he then fills by finding a new analyst with whom to (mis)identify—Job).

In effect, then, *Repetition*'s portrayal of imbalanced interactions between individual representatives of the self's self-constancy and its self-abandonment not only implies a vision of what their integration within a self might make possible; it also indicates that, and how, one's relationship with another person can facilitate the attainment of that internal integration. Since Constantius fails to perform that role for the Young Man because he suffers from the very problem the Young Man needs to overcome, the implication of that failure is that only someone who has achieved that overcoming is in a position to help others to achieve it also. More specifically, it suggests that a successful therapeutic process will involve two stages: first, making the analysand aware of his imbalanced state by reflecting that imbalance back to him, but in such a way that it induces him to recognize it rather than enact it more intensively; and second, to instantiate for him the overcoming of that imbalance—to exemplify what it might mean to take a step away from one-sidedness, and thus attract him to his unattained but attainable self. In a sense, the two steps are one, since to gain a perspective on oneself as reiterating a settled state of the self is already to have gone beyond that state, to have seen that staying with that state is taking a stand on it, is a matter not of suffering a condition of one's existence but of maintaining it as it is—something one might choose to do or not to do. The point, therefore (one appreciated by both Heidegger and Wittgenstein), is not to dictate what that neighbouring state of himself might be, but rather to awaken him to its existence by exemplifying the doubled structure of selfhood that it presupposes—which means exemplifying that the self is always both attained and unattained, that existence is a matter of taking steps and taking a stand.

THERAPY TRANSPOSED: WRITING AND READING

34. At this point another step in our reading presents itself. To see it, we need to recall the stages through which Constantius' supposedly therapeutic relationship with the Young Man passes. In part I of *Repetition* they interact in the flesh, meeting constantly—at some points on an almost daily, or rather nightly, basis. In part II this conversational interaction becomes epistolary and one-sided; Constantius has only the Young Man's letters to interpret, and cannot convey his conclusions to him—he becomes, in short, the Young Man's reader. And in what deserves to be called part III, after reading the Young Man's final letter announcing the Young Girl's marriage and his own rededication to poetry, Constantius himself writes a letter—one addressed 'to Mr. X Esq., the real reader of this book' (R 223). He thereby implicitly identifies himself with the Young Man (a point confirmed when he signs himself off as 'Your devoted', the Young Man's favoured epistolary self-description), and us—his readers—with himself.

The point of this identification is reinforced when Constantius uses this final letter to hint that the Young Man may not in fact be real.

A poet is ordinarily an exception. People are usually pleased with someone like that and with his compositions. I thought, therefore, that for me it might be well worth the trouble to bring someone like that into being ... I can do no more, for the most I can do is to imagine a poet and to produce him by my thought. I cannot myself become a poet ... (R 228)

These sentences remain ambiguous, since they could refer to the processes by which Constantius attempts to draw out the Young Man's personality, to assist at his birth into genuine individuality as a poet. And even if we take them otherwise, as a confession that the Young Man is Constantius' literary creation, then none of our questions and conclusions thus far about the two men's motivations and symbolic significance would be undermined. They would rather become questions and conclusions about Constantius' reasons for presenting himself as conducting a relationship of the kind he has described with such a Young Man. The second interpretation would, however, foreground Constantius' role as a writer, someone we know only through his orderings of words on these pages. And this, taken together with his implicit transposition of the structure of his relationship with the Young Man onto our relationship with him, implies that

he (once again, like Heidegger and Wittgenstein) wishes us to conceive
of the relation between his writing and its readers as itself therapeutic
in nature.

The more specific consequences of this implication are, however, less
easy to divine. If we think of ourselves as in Constantius' position and
of him as in that of the Young Man, that would make us the analysts
and his text the analysand. But only the concluding seven pages of his
book take this epistolary form; and he tells us there that, just as he tried
to help the Young Man, so 'I now try to help you, dear reader, by once
again taking another role' (*R* 228). In other words, the role he takes in
addressing us by means of a letter both is and is not the role he plays
in the rest of the text: he is performing it once again, but it is another
role—that is, a new analysis or interpretation of that earlier role, an
attempt to exemplify how his earlier exemplification of it might be taken
a step forward.

We do, after all, know that such a step is needed. Constantius himself
has given us the clues we need to penetrate beneath his presentation
of himself as a mature and wise doctor of souls to the reality this
occludes—to the fact that he is a rather incompetent analyst, and
incompetent precisely because he is labouring under the illusion that he
stands in no need of analysis himself. He has also indicated that the first
step in a competently conducted analysis is to present the analysand
with a picture of themselves as they presently are, subject to whatever
illusions stand in need of therapeutic attention. Perhaps, then, in inviting us to identify ourselves with him, and in presenting himself as thinking of himself as a competent analyst when he is not, he is reflecting
back to us our delusive picture of ourselves as readers—as beings
capable of subjecting the texts we meet to analysis, and hence as standing in no need of it ourselves.

He does, after all, warn us from the outset of this concluding letter
that real reading 'is an art', that it takes time to acquire, and that the
readers he is actually addressing are 'fictional', that is, unreal—as if
we have opened a letter addressed to the reader in us that we have not
yet become. And by issuing the invitation to identify with him from
the position of one who is not reading but is rather being read, Constantius further implies that real reading is a matter of allowing oneself
to be read by the text one wishes to read. In other words, attaining
to the presently unattained state of real readers of a text depends
upon inverting that picture of ourselves—upon coming to think of ourselves as in need of therapeutic treatment and of the text as being in a
position to provide it. In short, he is urging us to think of therapeutic
reading as a matter not of interpreting a text but of being interpreted

by it—as taking a stand on our sense of ourselves, and as needing to take a step beyond it.[11]

JOB'S TESTAMENT: THE WHIRLWIND'S NATURE

35. If we are to take that step, then we must ask how *Repetition* invites us to take a step beyond its portrayal of the various ways in which selves can fail to attain a balance between self-constancy and self-abandonment, towards a more concrete sense of how this balance—and hence a genuine repetition of the spirit (in which one's individuality synthesizes old and new, moving forward from what has been and thus avoiding both a pure reiteration of the past and a pure recreation from the future; see R 133)—might be attained. The text's overt exemplar of such balance is, of course, Job; and unsurprisingly, the question of how best to relate to him presents itself as a question of how best to read the narrative of his vicissitudes.

Job's self-constancy is the most evident aspect of the biblical tale: faced with the satan's divinely licensed attacks upon everything he holds dear in the world, he maintains his conviction in his own righteousness despite the increasingly hostile comments of his comforters, and even desires to defend himself against God in a court of law. His self-abandonment is less evident, but it is equally critical to the narrative in two main ways. First, he does not devote himself to recollecting his previous states as if incapable of letting them go—his primary concern amid the ashes is not with his previous wealth, and he does not allow his time on the ash-heap to taint his experience of the redoubled return of his wealth; and second, he allows the experience of the Whirlwind to bring about the utter abandonment of his previous sense of God's injustice. The change induced by his repentance amid dust and ashes pivots around the constancy of his commitment to God, and leads to a repetition of the most rewarding kind.

The Young Man's reading of Job focuses upon these ideas of constancy and repetition, and results in the following conclusion: 'Was Job proved to be in the wrong? Yes, eternally, for there is no higher court than the one that judged him. Was Job proved to be in the right? Yes, eternally, by being proved to be in the wrong *before* God. So there is a repetition after all' (R 212).

[11] This invokes a model of reading that Stanley Cavell has developed, in relation to other authors, in various places—see 'The Politics of Interpretation', in *Themes out of School* (North Point Press: San Francisco, 1984).

Is this, however, the kind of reading of Job upon which we ought to take a stand as readers? The Young Man describes himself as having read this text with the eyes of his heart; every word is food and clothing and healing for his wretched soul. He finds his joy in repeatedly transcribing everything Job has said; he regards it as unbecoming to make Job's words his own in the presence of another, to quote him; but 'when I am alone, I do it, appropriate everything' (R 204). This idea of total appropriation suggests that the Young Man has read himself into this text rather than allowing himself to be read by it: every word Job says merely confirms his sense of suffering, injury, being misunderstood; nothing Job says is allowed to put his sense of who he is and what he deserves into question. Consequently, he draws a peculiar moral from the tale: having moved from an extremity of self-abandonment to an extremity of self-constancy, in which all that matters to him is finding a way of fulfilling his engagement with the girl, he takes Job's story to license the expectation of a whirlwind which will remould his personality in such a way as to fit him for marriage—in other words, to make it possible for him to fulfil what he takes to be his deepest desire, and to appear before the world as having been in the right all along. Instead, his whirlwind takes the form of the young girl's decision to marry another, and that utterly non-divine dismissal frees him to become the poet he has appeared to be all along.

Constantius is very clear from the beginning that the Young Man has misread his text—misunderstood what a genuinely religious response to the difficulties of his situation might have been. According to him, if the situation had gained religious meaning

he would have acted with an entirely different iron consistency and imperturbability . . . he would have won a fact of consciousness to which he could constantly hold, one that would never have become ambivalent for him but would be pure earnestness because it was established by him on the basis of a God-relationship. Immediately the whole question of finitude would have become a matter of indifference; in the more profound sense, actuality itself would make no difference to him. Then he would have religiously emptied that situation of its frightful consequences. He would not be essentially changed if actuality manifested itself some other way, no more than he would be more terrified than he already had been if the very worst were to happen . . . A religious individual . . . is composed within himself and rejects all the childish pranks of actuality. (R 230).

Constantius plainly regards faith as a kind of heightened Stoicism; it expresses an essential indifference to actuality and the realm of consequences more generally. This is a rather peculiar moral to draw from the tale of Job, in which its protagonist is incensed by what he takes to be the religious significance of his calamitous experiences, and in which his reward for repentance is that his worldly wealth is returned to him twofold. And Constantius' misreading agrees with that of the Young Man in taking Job's self-constancy (his iron consistency and imperturbability) as the key feature of the tale. It is as if neither of them take the Whirlwind's intervention, and Job's self-abasing response to it, as in any sense putting his previous stance in question. In doing so, they collude in occluding the significance of self-abandonment in Job's achievement of repetition.

36. Herbert Fingarette has famously argued that the book of Job is best understood as inviting its protagonists (and hence its readers) to take a step beyond an understanding of God's relation to human beings as essentially juridical—to be comprehended in terms of commandments, punishment, rights, and wrongs.[12] For the disagreement between Job and his comforters is based on an underlying agreement—that God ensures that those who obey his Law prosper and those who violate it suffer. Job's comforters infer from his suffering that Job is unrighteous; Job retains his conviction that he is righteous, and therefore concludes that God has been unjust—not only to himself but to all those other good men who suffer reverses in life, and to all those evildoers who prosper. He is thus entirely consistent in wishing to plead his case against God in a court of law—even though the framework of thought that leads to this conclusion also condemns it as blasphemous. On this reading, the voice from the Whirlwind not only does not provide an answer to Job's question about unjust suffering (this is obviously the case, much to many commentators' puzzlement), it does not intend to; it is God's attempt to change the subject—to reject the terms of the original question in favour of other, very different ones.

... the Voice out of the whirlwind, whose words constitute one of the great poems of literature, reveals to us ... in direct poetic revelation, the glories, the wonders, the powers, the mysteries, the order, the harmonies, the wildness and the frightening and amazing multifariousness of untamable existence, and its inexhaustible and indomitable powers and creativity. The Book of Job shatters, by a combination of challenge and ridicule and ultimately by direct experiential demonstration, the idea that the law known to human beings reflects law rooted in the divine or ultimate nature of being, and the idea that the divine or ultimate nature of being is in its essence lawlike ...

We are nothing as measured against the whole; we are puny, vulnerable, and transient. As mere beings we can only be humble. But as beings who are

---

[12] See 'The Meaning of Law in the Book of Job', in S. Hauerwas and A. MacIntyre (eds.), *Revisions* (University of Notre Dame Press: Notre Dame, 1981); hereafter MLBJ.

conscious of this miracle, who participate however humbly in it, we are tran-
scendently elevated and exhilarated. (MLBJ 269)

The new terms that the Voice proposes do not ask us (as Constantius
appears to think) to become indifferent to actuality; they ask us to revel
in its glories, to acknowledge that the wealth of God's creation exceeds
anything we might have thought or imagined, and in particular to
acknowledge that its bounty is not expressible or containable in terms
of either natural or moral law. The point of the shattering intervention
of the Whirlwind is not, as the Young Man's lawcourt imagery implies,
to allow Job to continue to think of his relation to God and his creation
in juridical terms, even if differently systematized (to think that Job is
not simply in the right, but both in the wrong and in the right). The
point is to shatter Job's reliance upon juridical terminology altogether—
to stop him picturing the realm of experience and existence as answering to human moral worth, to take a step beyond the idea of God as
exercising his Will through the natural order, as if nature were simply
and solely responsive to human good and evil, an appendage to our own
spiritual drama.

When Job says 'I abhor myself and repent' (more literally, 'I melt
away, and I repudiate my words'), he expresses his willingness to die to
any expectation that how his life goes will reflect his spiritual worth, to
repudiate words suggesting that the universe answers to his own conceptions and needs. In abandoning those words, he abandons the
attained state of his soul; he turns away from it, allowing it to melt
away, and turns towards what the Voice reveals as its unattained but
attainable state. He learns that religious progress depends upon seeing
that the stand he has taken is one from which he must take a step, that
of reconceiving suffering not as a punishment but as effecting a decentring of the self, a decentring that is but a dim reflection of the divine
self-abnegation, the withdrawal that God makes from nature in order
to let nature exist in all its wondrous excess.

The medium of this transformation is not argument or logic, and not
the dialectic of question and answer. What shows that the question is
improperly articulated, expressive of a spiritual confusion and hence
in need of dissolution rather than resolution, is poetry. The Whirlwind's
voice effects a shift in perception by bodying forth in verse the marvels
of creation and eliciting a sense of wonder thereby; to take its effects
seriously would amount to shattering one's sense of how such
shattering changes might legitimately be effected—to take a step in one's
conception of how to make progress in comprehending matters of the
spirit. In this sense, the Young Man's poetic powers make him far more

capable of appreciating the message of the book of Job than do Constantius' powers of detached reflection, as his belief in reading the text by the eyes of his heart suggests; but neither of them is prepared to have those poetic powers turned upon their own souls, to emulate Job in allowing himself to suffer being read by the shattering poetry of the Whirlwind.

CHRIST'S TESTAMENT: PRODIGAL FORGIVENESS

37. If *Repetition* invites us to take a step beyond the Young Man's and Constantius' readings of Job, it also invites us to take a step beyond the book of Job itself, towards another religious text and paradigm that implicitly refers back to Job's poetic drama—as if presenting itself as the neighbouring, unattained but attainable, stage of the spiritual trajectory to which Job abandoned himself.

This further step is first adumbrated in Constantius' reminiscences about the Königstadter farces. What we have not remarked thus far, in our concern with the genre of farce itself and with the composition of the Königstadter company, is the particular farce that the company performs during Constantius' first stay in Berlin. He tells us several times that it is called *The Talisman* (a three-act farce by Nestroy). The term 'talisman' normally nowadays refers to good-luck charms, vessels of superstition; but it is originally constructed from a Greek word signifying a consecrated object or a religious rite, or more specifically the performance or completion of a religious rite. With this in mind, we might then recall that Constantius first introduces us to the theatre as it appears from the window of his lodgings in Gensd'arme Square, as paired with a pair of churches—as if offering a competing or perhaps complementary site for ritual (R 151). And Berlin itself appears to be engaged in a very particular religious ritual on the day of Constantius' second arrival there:

I became completely out of tune, or, if you please, precisely in tune with the day, for fate had strangely contrived it so that I arrived in Berlin on the *allgemeine Busz und Bettag* [Universal Day of Penance and Prayer]. Berlin was prostrate. To be sure, they did not throw ashes into one another's eyes with the words: *Memento o homo! quod cinis es et in cinerem revertaris* [Remember, O Man! that you are dust and to dust you will return]. But all the same the whole city lay in one cloud of dust . . . in Berlin at least every other day is Ash Wednesday. (R 152–3)

Constantius then carefully stresses that he sees no connection between this dusty atmosphere and his project of attaining repetition; but the prominence of his denial actually presses upon us the connection between repetition and repentance, and between Job's heap of ashes and the mark of ashes on the forehead that initiates the Christian season of Lent.

The latter connection is of course intentional, part of Christianity's understanding of itself as a fulfilment of Old Testament understandings of God. The ashes distributed on Ash Wednesday are the cremated palms used to celebrate Palm Sunday—the day of Christ's arrival in Jerusalem for his Passion and Death. The idea of repentance encoded in the season of Lent which Ash Wednesday initiates thus incorporates the Christian belief in Christ's Atonement (his self-sacrifice, his abandoning of himself to the Cross in order to suffer the punishment due to the human race for its sinfulness) and ultimately his Resurrection. Christianity thereby claims to take Job's embodiment of repentance and repetition to a new level, by taking the idea of self-abandonment and self-constancy to a new level.

Constantius underlines this recounting of Old Testament conceptions in the way he begins and ends part I of *Repetition*. In his concluding peroration to the coach-horn, he remarks in passing: 'Why has no-one returned from the dead? Because life does not know how to captivate as death does, because life does not have the persuasiveness that death has' (*R* 176). Here, Constantius' later affirmation of indifference to life's vicissitudes is traced back to his lack of faith in Christ; without the Resurrection, one might say, there is no hope—Easter's repetition is what gives sense to the repentance embodied in Lent, and the Atonement embodied in the Cross. And indeed, in his opening peroration to repetition in the prologue to *Repetition* Constantius explicitly contrasts any genuinely modern understanding of that concept with one which incorporates any element of hope.

Repetition's love is in truth the only happy love. Like recollection's love, it does not have the restlessness of hope, the uneasy adventurousness of discovery, but neither does it have the sadness of recollection—it has the blissful security of the moment. Hope is a new garment, stiff and starched and lustrous, but it has never been tried on, and therefore one does not know how becoming it will be or how it will fit. Recollection is a discarded garment that does not fit. Repetition is an indestructible garment that fits closely and tenderly, neither binds nor sags. Hope is a lovely maiden who slips away between one's fingers; recollection is a beautiful old woman with whom one is never satisfied at the moment; repetition is a beloved wife of whom one never wearies, for one becomes weary only of what is new . . . He who will merely hope is cowardly; he who will merely recollect is voluptuous; he who wills repetition is a man . . . (*R* 131–2)

To affirm hope might also mean affirming other virtues, like faith and love. And is there not a certain cowardice in Constantius' aversion from adventurousness, his rejection of a lustrous new garment simply because he cannot know in advance how it will fit? Certainly, if hope is a maiden, we can begin to understand his obsessive but paralysing interest in the observation of young girls—the one to whom he gives a ride in his carriage (*R* 147–8), the one in the theatre, the one in the enclosed garden (*R* 167–8), and the Young Girl of the Young Man's dreams. Even his sense that the Young Man is as pleasing to his eye as a young girl (*R* 135) might then be traceable to his sense of that youth's potential—his openness to a future from which, in the end, Constantius can only avert his gaze, and consign himself to a living death in the mausoleum of his own home. After all, if there is no hope, there is only despair.

38. In what sense, however, does Christ's self-sacrifice exemplify a stance to life that takes us a step beyond Job's willingness to acknowledge that the universe does not owe him a living? The answer emerges from another task of reading, one to which we are implicitly invited by Constantius' concluding letter to his real reader (whose sign, let us recall, is that of the Cross). Perceiving in the Young Man's struggle a battle between the universal and the exception (with the Young Man refusing to accept his guilt over his breach of promise), he claims:

On the one side stands the exception, on the other the universal, and the struggle itself is a strange conflict between the rage and impatience of the universal over the disturbance the exception causes and its infatuated partiality for the exception, for after all is said and done, just as heaven rejoices more over a sinner who repents than over ninety-nine righteous, so does the universal rejoice over an exception . . .
   If heaven loves one sinner more than ninety-nine who are righteous the sinner, of course, does not know this from the beginning; on the contrary, he is aware only of heaven's wrath until he finally, as it were, forces heaven to speak out. (*R* 226–7)

This repeated reference to the ninety-nine righteous is a citation of words of Christ as recorded in the fifteenth chapter of Luke's Gospel, where they form a preface or introduction to one of Christ's most famous parables—that of the Prodigal Son. When the younger son of that story, having taken his inheritance and squandered it on sinful

living, comes upon hard times and returns to his father to beg his forgiveness, the father welcomes him with a celebratory meal, giving him
the best robes and killing the fatted calf. This incenses the elder son,
who has remained working for his father throughout:

Lo these many years do I serve thee, neither transgressed I at any time thy commandment: and yet thou never gavest me a kid, that I might make merry with
my friends:

But as soon as this thy son was come, which hath devoured thy living with
harlots, thou hast killed for him the fatted calf.

And he said unto him, Son, thou art ever with me, and all that I have is thine.
It was meet that we should make merry, and be glad: for this thy brother was
dead and is alive again; and was lost, and is found. (Luke 15: 29–32)

The elder son wants to make a stand on his rights. He has been
dutiful, mindful of his father's commandments; he has committed
no transgression. He deserves to be rewarded, he merits the fatted
calf if anyone does; instead, his father gives it to the brother who
has no such claim—who has in fact merited punishment for violating
his father's commandments. His father, however, has never thought of
his relationship with either son as a matter of his setting and their
observing commandments; for him, the relationship is one of love, in
which questions of what is mine and what thine are beside the point.
He wants the elder son to learn that genuine love means dying to a
sense of oneself as having rights, legitimate claims, or demands that
others must meet on pain of injustice; it means being reborn to a world
in which one's self does not occupy its centre of gravity, but in which
one rather decentres oneself in favour of the needs of others (including
those who have done wrong, and particularly those who have done
wrong to oneself).

The forgiveness at the heart of this parable thus takes a step beyond
the lesson of Job's whirlwind; Christ asks us not only to die to a sense
of the natural world as answering to our needs and conceptions, but to
any sense that the human world—the realm of law, rights, and responsibilities—owes us something. Christianity, having inherited Job's step
beyond a conception of the natural order as responsive to spiritual
worth, sets us the task of constructing a human order in which love
rather than justice, forgiveness rather than punishment, is primary. And
of course, the counterpart of forgiveness is the willingness to be for-
given—to present oneself as in need of another's ability to overcome her
sense of what one deserves. It is this capacity for humility that Job and
the younger son possess, and of which both the Young Man and Con-

stantius prove signally incapable—the Young Man continuing to avoid asking for the Young Girl's forgiveness by groundlessly imputing his sense of pride to her, Constantius by dismissing such a request as merely 'respectable' and by continuing to harbour grave suspicions about the young girl's innocence in the matter.

In conveying this message about the centrality of forgiveness and love, Christ takes a step beyond the poetic medium of Job's whirlwind; his voice is parabolic, still and small by comparison, a kind of diurnalization of that earlier rhetorical force—the creation of an everyday habitation for this shattering moral appeal. Its domesticated appearance—in ordinary tales of farming, housekeeping, and wedding parties—makes the new spiritual world it envisages seem right next to the world we inhabit, always there and always only a step away. But by contextualizing our attained array of moral reactions within that new world (in the form of the elder son and his various equivalents) and showing their mutual incomprehensibility, these tales also make clear how much allowing ourselves to take that step is likely to cost us.

In this respect, the Young Man's agonies in part II of *Repetition*—his sense that the seemingly trivial case of a breach of promise can be the means to break through to a radically new spiritual understanding of himself and his world, together with his concluding sense that this religious substratum was never more than possible, never something whose advent was destined as opposed to attainable—are exemplary. God was never asking him to violate the ethical in the name of faith; but he was asking him to suspend his present understanding of the ethical, to take a step beyond it in the name of its further fulfilment.

39. We might think of these sightings of Christ beyond Job beyond the Young Man and Constantius as ways of reading through the attained state of the selves in this narrative to the unattained but attainable states which neighbour them, states that we can see as intimately implicit in the present stances of these characters but to which they are blind. But it is not as if the logic of *Repetition*'s serial self-abandonings is immediately obvious to its readers. On the contrary, even if we do not stop at the first, developmental reading of Constantius' relation to the Young Man, we might easily stop with Constantius' apparently untroubled sense that he has attained a perspective on the issues of self-abandonment and self-constancy that is unavailable to his younger friend. And even when we do perceive Constantius' inability to see his own lack of attainment, and to register the receding horizon of Old and New Testament religious understandings of self-attainment, we might

then fail to see that our grounds for this perception lie in clues carefully made available to us throughout the text of *Repetition* itself—a text we know to be authored by Constantius himself.

Then we might see that the text's subversion of its narrator is something its narrator makes it possible for us to appreciate, and so perceive our own blindness—our own delusion of access to a perspective on the text not available to anyone within that text. We might, in other words, see that the text is structured so as to let us see that the diagnoses it applies to its characters also apply to us—not only because, as selves, we participate in the structures of self-abandonment and self-constancy that the text describes, but also because those structures are active in and determinative of our relation to the text and its characters. In short, the text encourages us to relate to it in the inadequate terms it lays out on a first reading, and then encourages us repeatedly to overcome those inadequacies on later perusals—to take steps in our reading that are themselves ways of acknowledging both our proneness to blind ourselves to unattained but attainable aspects of ourselves, and our capacity to overcome those oversights.

CONCLUDING DOGMATIC POSTSCRIPT

Biblical Origins:
Hereditary Sin and the Body of
the Victim

And when the woman saw that the tree was good for food, and that
it was pleasant to the eyes, and a tree to be desired to make one
wise, she took of the fruit thereof, and did eat, and gave also unto
her husband with her; and he did eat.

And the eyes of them both were opened, and they knew that
they were naked; and they sewed fig leaves together, and made
themselves aprons.

(Genesis 3: 6–7)

1. I noted earlier that, in both the *Philosophical Fragments* and its
Postscript, Johannes Climacus emphasizes that the pivotal difference
between belief in God and belief in the Christian God (between religiousness A and religiousness B) is the conviction that human beings
exist in the condition of original sin. He is, however, unforthcoming
about the detailed content of, and the justification for, this seemingly
paradoxical conviction (which, as its alternative title of 'hereditary sin'
underlines, apparently conceives of guilt as a biological inheritance
beyond any exercise of individual responsibility), and thus leaves unde-
veloped what he presents as the critical manifestation of faith in Jesus
Christ as the Son of God. Does Climacus intend this striking lacuna to
tempt us to supplement his words by turning to what is often taken to
be the immediate source of this Christian doctrine—the Genesis narrative of Adam and Eve, and their transgression of God's command concerning the fruit of the tree of the knowledge of good and evil? If so,
that tale's talk of forbidden apples and aprons of shame is very likely
to suggest that a belief in original sin amounts to an opening of one's
eyes to the inherent evil of human sexuality and sensuality, and hence
to the taintedness of human existence as such. Nietzsche would call it
a libel against the body.

Climacus' *Postscript* rather suggests that we should resist this temptation. For in his appended 'Glance at a Contemporary Effort in Danish
Literature', he includes among the pseudonymous works that have taken

projected words from his mouth a book by one Vigilius Haufniensis, entitled *The Concept of Anxiety: A Simple Psychologically Orienting Deliberation on the Dogmatic Issue of Hereditary Sin*.[1] Haufniensis certainly presents his account of the concept as a reading of the Genesis tale of the Fall; but neither its form nor its content resemble the familiar, let us say Nietzschean, reading of that text. On the contrary: Haufniensis explicitly denies its central tenets, presenting it as a libel of the understanding against the Christian conception of the human body (and hence of the human soul). To understand Climacus' view of original sin, therefore, we should approach the Genesis account of human origins through his own words—as uttered by Haufniensis.

Climacus identifies Haufniensis' reading as an attempt to present anxiety (understood as the presupposition of original sin) as the state of mind of those undergoing a teleological suspension of the ethical—thus linking his work (as does Haufniensis himself; *CA* 17–19 n.) to that of de Silentio and Constantius. But Climacus also notes that Haufniensis' text seems significantly more didactic in form than that of his pseudonymous peers—as if its author conceives of us as actually lacking information, rather than (as the other pseudonyms assume) needing to be disabused of the assumption that more information will help our lack of understanding. But we know that Climacus regards a didactic representation of his own words as expressive of the worst possible misunderstanding of their significance. So should we conclude that he hears a true echo of himself in Haufniensis' didactic words, when he finds only distortion in those of a reviewer? Or is his implicit purpose rather to suggest that the apparently didactic form of Haufniensis' text is no more to be taken at face value than Climacus' apparently didactic presentation of it?

2. Haufniensis argues that the prevailing understanding of hereditary sin places too much stress on heredity and not enough on sin. By treating the Genesis narrative as an explanation of human sinfulness, it implies that individual human beings commit sins because of the sinful nature they inherit from Adam; but this at once negates individual responsibility for sin (and hence human freedom and individuality), and makes Adam's sin inexplicable (since he could not have possessed the sinful nature his sin bequeathed to us all). On this account, Adam's descendants are all species and no individual, and Adam is all individual and no species; the father of us all is placed outside the human race.

---

[1] Trans. R. Thomte and A. B. Anderson (Princeton University Press: Princeton, 1980); hereafter *CA*.

For Haufniensis, the truth Genesis articulates is rather that every human being (including Adam) is both the individual and the species. In Adam's case, this is literally true; in everyone else's case, it means that each individual not only inherits the developments of the species over time but also makes her own contribution to those developments for the benefit of future generations. This (he claims) distinguishes us from non-human animals, where there is no such dialectic between specimen and species; and it preserves individual human responsibility for sins—allowing us to say that, while each individual's leap or fall from innocence into sin (like that of Adam) contributes to the sinfulness inherited by future generations of the human species, each such sinful act is no more determined by factors outside the leap itself than was Adam's original leap or fall. Since our only difference from Adam—the fact that he did not inherit a sinful nature, that he was created rather than procreated—cannot explain why he sinned, it cannot explain why we sin either. The doctrine of original sin tells us that sin entered into the world by sin; this is not an attempted explanation of individual sinful acts, but an expression of the enigmatic fact that no individual sinful act can be explained—that sinful acts presuppose sinfulness, and sinfulness presupposes sinful acts. The Genesis narrative thus gives expression to a paradox—the paradox of human freedom.

If the qualitative transition into sin cannot be explained, Haufniensis nevertheless considers himself capable of identifying its key presupposition—anxiety. Unlike fear, anxiety is objectless, or rather has nothing for its object; it is also essentially ambivalent about that nothing, being what Haufniensis calls an antipathetic sympathy and a sympathetic antipathy. It grips the innocent individual precisely because such a being, while neither incapable of freedom nor yet conscious of it, nevertheless dreams or suffers an intimation of its possibility. So to project its freedom as possible means projecting the possibility of existence in the realm of possibility, its capacity to be able (to act or not to act, hence to enact good or evil, hence to be a good or evil individual). Its own possible freedom thus at once attracts and repels it, as a fulfilment of itself that is also a condemnation to prohibition, judgement, and punishment. Hence it projects its innocence as ignorance—as the enormous nothingness of a non-necessary ignorance of good and evil whose overcoming the dreaming spirit or consciousness can neither reject nor accept.

That the step from dreaming to wakeful spirit in the human being (which Haufniensis thinks of as the point at which its synthesis of mind and body in spirit becomes actual) is a fall into sin remains beyond external determination, but it becomes less mysterious if considered as an expression of the dreaming spirit's attempt to flee from what it cannot avoid, of its falling entanglement in its own freedom. And this presupposition of our sinfulness helps us also to understand its consequence for our self-understanding.

In innocence, Adam as spirit was a dreaming spirit. Thus the synthesis is not actual, for the combining factor is precisely the spirit, and as yet this is not posited as spirit. In animals the sexual difference can be developed instinctively, but this cannot be the case with a human being precisely because he is a synthesis. In the moment the spirit posits itself, it must first pervade it differentiatingly, and the ultimate point of the sensuous is precisely the sexual. Man can attain this ultimate point only in the moment the spirit becomes actual. Before that time he is not animal, but neither is he really man. The moment he becomes man, he becomes so by being animal as well.

So sinfulness is by no means sensuousness, but without sin there is no sexuality, and without sexuality, no history. (*CA* 49)

Genesis recounts Adam's flight or fall as coinciding with his awakening to a knowledge of sensuousness and sexual difference—to a specific judgement of, and by, the apple and the aprons. He was created without sin, hence embodiment as such and sinfulness cannot be identical; but his becoming human, his positing himself as spirit, and hence as an individual embodied mind, is a positing of himself (and hence his desires, both sexual and non-sexual) as sinful. Each sinful act by his descendants reproduces and reinforces this equation, and hence bequeaths a heightened sense of its self-evidence to future generations— a foreboding presentiment which cannot determine that each new individual will fall into sin and reproduce the equation, but which makes the nothingness upon which their anxious innocence dreamily fixes loom ever larger. And his hereditary sinfulness is figured by sexuality as such, and by female sexuality in particular, precisely in so far as they signify reproduction or natality. Eve's birth, her derivative creation from the rib of a dreaming Adam, prefigures human procreation as such and implies that her later dealings with snake and apple externalize his innocent anxiety over his own potential freedom. And in giving birth, Eve and all her daughters not only experience an apotheosis of anxiety (their spirit's capacity enduringly to synthesize mind and body taken to its furthest extreme), but also make both the reproduction of the species and the production of new individuals (and hence the dialectic of inheritance and bequest between species and individual) possible.

Haufniensis concludes by pointing out that if anxiety is a presupposition of sin's appearance in the world, it is also a consequence of it. For once spirit posits itself as such, and the individual has fallen from innocence, her concrete knowledge of good and evil, and hence of the evil enacted by her species and herself, occasions renewed anxiety. Most typically, the awareness of good undone or repressed makes the sinful individual demonically anxious: she flees from her capacity to overcome her actual sinfulness, repelled by the good which she cannot simply reject. More rarely, anxiety can be roused by evil, and can itself arouse the individual to overcome her sinfulness in a moment of vision, by repenting of it and grounding her positing of herself as capable of the good in faith. For just as hereditary sin cannot explain individual sinful acts, so it cannot exclude individual acts of repentance; both are enigmatic, both rooted in powers (anxiety and grace) experienced as external, but neither are impossible.

3. Taking Haufniensis' claims at their didactic face value, we might wonder if they avoid the vices of imbalance and conceptual conflation of which they accuse their opponents. For example, in stressing the need to preserve the individual's responsibility for making the leap into sinful acts, does not Haufniensis lay insufficient stress on the dogmatic idea of sin as inherited? If, as he puts it, the sinfulness of our nature accumulates merely quantitatively, and can never by itself determine an individual's qualitative transition from innocence to a sinful act—if Adam's decendants resemble Adam in each bringing sin into the world as if for the first time—then in what sense is it sin, or even a settled disposition towards sin (as opposed, say to the mere capacity for sin), that we inherit *qua* member of the human species? Or again: in order to distinguish between identifying sensuousness with sinfulness and positing sensuousness as sinful, Haufniensis relies upon the Genesis narrative's presentation of Adam as originally sinless, and hence its projection of a lost mode of sinless embodiment. But his reading also projects that lost state as one in which spirit is not posited as such, and hence in which there is no psychophysical synthesis of individuality; in other words, prelapsarian Adam is, while not exactly animal, not exactly human either—and so it remains unclear how Christianity might conceive of an embodied spirit that is at once fully human and without original sin (and thus reject Nietzche's talk of a Christian libel against the human body).

Heidegger's inheritance of this concept of anxiety in *Being and Time* works hard to bequeath to us a secularized analogue of Haufniensis' teaching that avoids corresponding versions of these apparent weaknesses. By showing how the essentially impersonal intelligibility-structures of worldliness determine flight from authenticity, average everydayness, as Dasein's inevitable starting-point but not its fate,

Heidegger regrounds angst's capacity to pivot us from lostness in the they-self to the recovery of our genuine, finite individuality. He seems less consistently clear that the voice of conscience might require external representation if it is to make itself heard within Dasein's self-dispersion, but his sense of Dasein's world as essentially interpersonal can certainly accommodate its silent irruption into individual existence. These revisions depend not only upon Heidegger's reconception of human existence as essentially worldly (a dimension omitted in Haufniensis' talk of mind–body–spirit syntheses), but also upon retuning his account of anxiety primarily to death rather than to birth. For Dasein can be anxious about the possibility of its own impossibility, can relate itself to that impossibility as possible (and hence attain authenticity), only from within that which death makes impossible—its actual, finite existence; whereas anxiety about the possibility of one's own possibility (as Haufniensis has it) rather implies adopting a perspective upon one's life as if from before it, anyway outside it, thus projecting a vision of authenticity (figured by the prelapsarian Adam) as always already lost to, or to be found beyond, and hence as an impossibility for, finite human existence.

Despite this, however, *Being and Time*'s phenomenology of Dasein has often been accused of eliding or denying human embodiedness, and so of publishing a libel upon the body that continues this supposed mainstay of the Judaeo-Christian tradition rather than subverting it; and Heidegger's account of death is seen as its most revealing expression. For there he separates human from all other forms of life in terms of a distinction between dying and perishing (*BT*, section 49). Animals do not die but rather perish: only Dasein can die—can relate existentially to its own end; even when the end of its life is measured by physiological or medical criteria, we must talk not of Dasein's perishing but of its demise. Does not the term 'Dasein' here fall back towards marking an aspect or dimension of human existence that escapes the life of the body, as if in flight from the embodiedness of human finitude towards Haufniensis' equally sharp refusal of spirit to the beasts?

Heidegger confronts this challenge in his 1929–30 lectures *The Fundamental Concepts of Metaphysics*,[2] where he restates his understanding of Dasein's abyssal kinship with the animal realm in the following theses: 'The stone is *worldless*; the animal is *poor in world*; man is *world-forming*' (*FCM* 42. 177). These formulations hardly appear promising. For by attributing impoverished worldliness

---

[2] Trans. W. McNeill and N. Walker (Indiana University Press: Bloomington, 1995); hereafter *FCM*, cited by section and page numbers.

to animals, Heidegger implies that they have at least a diminished capacity to grasp beings as beings. He thus tries to distinguish animality from humanity in a way that presupposes their essential continuity (betraying an anthropocentric perspective that fails to grasp animal existence in itself, as such); and yet the need to reinforce this anthropocentrism leads him explicitly to contradict this central implication of his thesis—declaring, for example, that 'When we say that the lizard is lying on the rock, we ought to cross out the word "rock" in order to indicate that whatever the lizard is lying on is certainly given *in some way* for the lizard, and yet is not known to the lizard *as* a rock' (FCM 47. 198).

These suspicions intensify when Heidegger further claims that animal existence is one of captivation (*Benommenheit*)—that they relate to themselves and their environment as if fascinated, dazzled, dazed, benumbed. The instincts that drive them also ring them or fence them in: objects forcibly impinge upon them solely as disinhibitors of drives (as food or mate, predator or prey), and so as not only withholding other objects (until circumstances allow those other objects to disinhibit other drives in the ring) but also as withholding themselves *qua* objects. But even if such talk of disinhibition is well earned, to characterize animal existence as dazed benumbment once again appears to take human existence as normative; after all, *Benommenheit* is a term Heidegger uses several times in *Being and Time* to characterize Dasein's average everydayness (and once to characterize its anxious relation to its own uncanniness—that is, its route to authentic everydayness).[3]

4. Such suspicions treat Heidegger's words as prey rather than food for thought. They refuse the invitation, encoded in his advice about how to take his talk of the lizard's 'rock', to read the phrase 'world-poverty' under erasure—as if placing animals at once within and without the reach of the term 'world', as if animals place the limits of its reach in question; and they overlook his repeated and pivotal questioning of his own formulations. In sections 49 and 50, for example, he interrogates his very ability to form those theses, arguing that far from presupposing a human capacity for self-transposition into three different domains of otherness, they rather show that the capacity gestured at by this label

---

[3] See *BT* 149, for an example of the former use, and *BT* 68. 394 for an example of the latter use. David Farrell Krell lists these and other occurrences of the term in *Being and Time* in the introduction to his *Daimon Life* (Indiana University Press: Bloomington, 1992), a powerful example of recent attempts to convict Heidegger's phenomenology of Dasein on the charge of anthropocentrism.

is in fact elicited only by the animal realm (since the otherness of stones neither invites nor resists the transpositions of a self, and the otherness of other humans is always already internal to selfhood and its powers). More precisely, Heidegger claims that animality is 'essentially a potentiality for granting transposedness, connected in turn with the necessary refusal of any going along with' (*FCM* 50. 211), that human beings always already find themselves transposed into the animal as having a mode of access to and dealing with the world from which they are excluded. Animal dealings with objects are thus accessible to humans, but only as resistant to human accessibility; to grasp animality is to grasp it as a mode of being from which human beings are fenced out, that they can grasp only as beyond them.

How, then, does this sense of humans as excluded from the intersecting rings of animal comportment become the thesis that animals are excluded from human modes of being? If humans are fenced out from animality, why declare that animals are fenced out from humanity? In part, because—despite the space occupied in his account by the behaviour of bees, lizards, and amoeba—Heidegger's intuitions are importantly guided here by what he calls the 'striking example' of domestic animals.

We do not describe them as [domestic animals] simply because they turn up in the house but because they belong to the house, ie., they serve the house in a certain sense . . . We keep domestic pets in the house with us, they '*live*' *with us*. But we do not live with them if living means: being in an animal kind of way. Yet we *are with* them nonetheless. But this being-with is not an *existing-with*, because a dog does not exist but merely lives. Through this being with animals we enable them to move within our world . . . [The dog] eats with us—and yet, it does not really 'eat'. Nevertheless, it is with us! (*FCM* 50. 210)

Domestic animals belong to our domiciles, we dwell with them; their lives are not only conducted alongside ours, but intertwined with ours; they move not only through our world but within it. These expressions of our kinship with pets invoke ways in which an animal's encircling ring can intersect with, or be encompassed by, the human world; then there opens up the possibility of disrupting and expanding both ring and world, a vision of animal being as becoming more fully itself within a human world which is itself enriched thereby. Hence the thought that for us to be fenced out of the animal's encircling ring is for it to be fenced within it; talk of the animal's refusingly responsive poverty in world might then express a sense that the otherness of animality answers to something deep within our world, that animal and human beings can acknowledge their intimate otherness, and that its denial constricts both the encircling ring of their being and the horizon of our world.

Such thoughts are far more richly developed in Vicki Hearne's Cavellian (and hence both Heideggerian and Wittgensteinian) account of her life with animals in *Adam's Task*.[4] For her, the disciplinary rigours of training dogs and horses are justified because it permits these creatures to reinherit their nature, to discover and explore through obedience to human authority the true potential of their non-human being (for hunting, tracking, and jumping). But such human authority is legitimate only when it is itself obedient—not only to the animal's individual development of its species potential, but also to the demands that its assumption (its solicitation of the animal's trust) entails: consistency, honesty, and perseverance in its exercise, and trust in the animal under training—the humility necessary if the creature is to teach its teacher of possibilities in their relationship, ways of projecting its grammar, not previously imagined.

Hearne's account of the ways apes and wolves can, and cannot, be brought into human worlds frames her central tales of training domesticated species in order to show that this focus does not imply that wildness is accidental to animality as such, but rather that the wildness of wild animals is a matter of degree, and to be established not by a priori judgement but by experiment—essays in establishing stable, even if attenuated, projections of more familiar human–animal grammars. She sees a mythical expression of this in Genesis:

Adam gave names to the creatures, and they all responded to their names without objection, since in this dominion . . . there was no gap between the ability to command and the full acknowledgement of the personhood of the being so commanded . . .

Then Adam and Eve themselves failed in obedience, and in this story to fail in obedience is to fail in authority. Most of animate creation, responding to this failure, turned pretty irrevocably from human command . . . One may say that before the Fall, all animals were domestic, that nature was domestic. After the Fall, wildness was possible, and most creatures chose it, but a few did not. [They] agreed to go along with humanity anyway, thus giving us a kind of second chance to repair our damaged authority, to do something about our incoherence. (*AT* 47–8)

Here is another projection of significance in talking of animals as poor in world. It registers a sense of the responsive refusal of domestic animals to humanity as figuring the potentially rich but actually

---

[4] (Heinemann: London, 1986); hereafter *AT*.

impoverished refusing responsiveness of animality as such—a responsiveness lost because of a self-impoverishing human refusal of responsiveness. Picturing the wolf as fenced in upon itself is how we fence ourselves out from its being, further attenuating its intersection with our world.

5. Another articulation of the meaning of Heidegger's theses emerges in section 63, when he continues his self-interrogation, pre-empting his critics by accusing himself of characterizing animal not-having of world in terms which imply that they do have world. His response is to recall two key features of his broader project. First, his primary concern is properly to characterize the worldliness of human being; hence his characterization of animals as world-poor, while identifying one of the essential determinations of animality as such, is itself determined by his decision to regard the animal in comparison with humanity. Let us assume that this is not simply an admission (or not a simple admission) of anthropocentrism; then we can allow it to guide us towards reviewing the third of Heidegger's theses, that man is world-forming.

Unlike the formulations of *Being and Time*, which talk of Dasein as worldly or as Being-in-the-world, this thesis implies a more active human contribution to shaping the world—and perhaps more faintly invokes the idea of a plurality of such worlds (as if the human world can always be formed otherwise—perhaps so as to constrict, or to redraw more expansively, the encircling ring of an animal). This invocation is more explicit in the final pages of the lectures, when Heidegger glosses the idea of world-forming as projection, which is a *'turning towards that is a removal'* (FCM 76. 363)—carrying us out and away from ourselves, removing us into whatever has been projected, in such a way that we simultaneously turn towards ourselves. Heidegger explicitly glosses this reflexive removal as a 'raising away into the possible . . . in its possibly being made possible', as binding us 'not to what is possible, nor to what is actual, but to *making-possible*' (FCM 76. 363)—thus recalling projection as *Being and Time* understands it (and anxiety as Haufniensis understands it). But 'reflexive removal' is also an implicit transposition of the idea of human self-transposition, and one that brings out its psychoanalytic resonance; it thus implies that world-forming can be a defensive operation, the externalization of rejected elements of ourselves. Perhaps, then, projecting a world in which animality is fenced in upon itself is a projection of an aspect of ourselves from which we feel fenced out; perhaps the thesis that animals are world-poor is a projection of our own rejected animality.

6. Can Heidegger really be asking us to treat his own core theses as symptomatic? How does he understand the basic inflection or formative context of his questioning? His second response to self-criticism in section 63 is to recall that his lectures begin by claiming that contemporary human society discloses its world through the fundamental mood or attunement of boredom. But then, any authentic questioning must be receptive to that mood (see *FCM* 37. 160); hence 'we constantly already question concerning the essence of world [and hence the essence of animality] from out of this attunement' (*FCM* 63. 272). If the Dasein whose questioning these lectures report is in the grip of boredom, then the theses it advances in response must be advanced out of boredom—must be informed and pervaded by it. How, then, does Heidegger understand that mood?

Beneath or within such experiences as being marooned for hours at a railway station, or the self-induced emptiness of yet another pleasant dinner with friends, Heidegger detects the more profound possibility of encountering the world as a whole in such terms; fundamental boredom is 'Dasein's being delivered over to beings' telling refusal of themselves as a whole' (*FCM* 31. 139), a discovery of beings as indifferent to us, and hence of us as indifferent to them. This is not the nothingness of worldhood as anxiety's objectlessness reveals it; it is a suspension among beings, as if between life and death or of death in life, a limbo which indicates that Dasein's existence depends not only upon the realm of possibilities that its worldliness makes possible, but also upon its desire or drive to inhabit that realm, to be drawn or gripped by it—that Dasein can project only out of thrownness. Fundamental boredom means being entranced or benumbed by a time that is beyond flowing or standing still, indifferent to past, present, and future—by a temporal horizon whose unarticulated unity reveals the moment of vision, in its vanishing, as Dasein's originary extremity—that from which it can alone become itself in the midst of beings.

Heidegger's analysis concludes by emphasizing that the emptiness of Dasein uncovered by beings' self-refusal is not nothingness but 'emptiness as lack, deprivation, *need*' (*FCM* 38. 162). Fundamental boredom is not therefore overcome by, but is rather given expression in, identifying specific social, political, or aesthetic needs and trying to meet their demands; for what we lack is a neediness essential to our Dasein as a whole. Fundamental boredom is 'the absence of any essential oppressiveness' or mysterious demand, and of 'the inner terror that every such mystery carries with it, and that gives Dasein its greatness' (*FCM* 38. 163–4). This deprivation can be met, our entrancement by our needy deprivation of need can be disrupted, only through a moment of vision which discloses '*that Dasein as such is demanded of man, that it is given to him—to be there*' (FCM 38. 165); and it is just such a disclosure that genuine questioning within the attunement of boredom must seek. '. . . to question concerning *this fundamental attunement* . . . means . . . to liberate the humanity in man, to liberate the humanity of man, i.e., the *essence* of man, *to let the Dasein in him become essential*' (FCM 38. 166).

In what sense do Heidegger's theses envision Dasein's being-there, its thrownness, as an oppressive demand? The second thesis claims that animals exhibit a responsive refusal to humanity—their seductive self-withdrawals thus exemplifying the world's revealing refusal to go along with the essentially mooded comprehension of human beings. But it further claims that animals suffer deprivation in that they are entranced or benumbed by the world, their existence a hermetic ring of enraptured seduction by one drive-disinhibitor after another. This transposes to animality as such the predicates Heidegger previously attributed to humans in the grip of boredom—entranced by time's inarticulate horizon, and covering over the oppressive absence of a genuinely demanding world in which they can take an interest by an endless round of bustling attempts to manufacture and satisfy specific needs. This casts such boredom as tending to reduce the human to the animal; but because Heidegger further characterizes properly attuning oneself to that mood—questioning its discovery of the world—as disrupting the circle of our needy deprivation of need, he further implies that letting the Dasein in human beings become essential is a matter of liberating the humanity in man *from his animality*.

This does not imply a simple opposition between humanity and animality; it characterizes the realization of Dasein in human beings as a disruption from within of their animality. Dasein's existence is always a transcendence of animality, a disruption of it—but a disruption from within, because the thrownness from which Dasein's distinctive projection always emerges is a modification of desire or need, and hence of Dasein's embodiedness or animality. Realizing Dasein's mooded comprehension of its world thus neither negates nor reiterates animality; it is a demand made upon a particular species of it, a radicalization of animality as such. Hence Heidegger's early diagnosis of contemporary philosophies of culture, with their simple opposition between life and spirit within man, as further expressions of our boredom rather than questioning appropriations of it (FCM 6. 18). Hence also his concluding peroration on man's *enraptured* transition towards the blissful astonishment that is authentically human questioning. He characterizes this irruption as 'being seized by terror' (FCM 76. 366) because, whereas fear is attuned to danger and horror to the monstrous, terror is a response to violence, to that which might violate one's flesh and blood— and to let Dasein be is to do the most intimate, uncanny violence to one's animality, but thereby to answer the most originary demand our particular inflection of embodiedness (our form of subjection to desire) makes upon us.

No wonder we defend ourselves against this demand by projecting what embodies it within us upon those beings most closely akin to us— transposing our emptiness onto their self-sufficiency, seizing upon their indifference to us to cover over our terrifying indifference to ourselves. But we cannot wholly repress the knowledge that the abyss separating us is also a certain fulfilment of our kinship, and hence that non-human animal species are in a sense deprived of something into which human animals are thrown. 'In the end we do not first require the Christian faith in order to understand something of the saying of St. Paul (Romans VIII, 19) concerning . . . the yearning expectation of creatures and of creation, the paths of which, as the Book of Ezra . . . says, have become narrow, doleful, and weary in this aeon' (*FCM* 63. 272–3). We see in animal eyes the doleful weariness of our present self-stupefactions, and our yearning expectation of their overcoming; and perhaps we also see that this overcoming critically depends upon overcoming our refusal to allow animals to inhabit our world, to dwell with us as fellow creatures, and hence to acknowledge our own animality.

7. Does this acknowledgement merely transpose an abyssal distinction within living beings into one between living and merely material beings? Does Heidegger's first thesis that 'the stone is worldless' defensively fence off the animate from the inanimate? He denies it: 'when Dasein is determined in its existence by *myth*, and . . . in the case of *art*', man animates purely material things, and such animation is neither fantasy, nor metaphor, nor mere exception (*FCM* 49. 205). Wittgenstein's depiction of the myth or fantasy of a private language also has recourse to stone, when articulating his interlocutor's resistance to the claim that 'only of a living human being and what resembles (behaves like) a living human being can one say: it has sensations; it sees; is blind' (*PI* 281). Why is the animal body the privileged locus of awareness? Couldn't I imagine feeling pain and turning into a stone while I did so (*PI* 283)? But would the pain be the stone's? Could I imagine ascribing pain to a stone—say one seen on a beach or in a forest? Only if I could imagine reacting to it with pity, or trying to comfort it; and if its surfaces (perhaps startlingly cleft or abraded) do not entirely forbid such responses, they will not respond to them. Hence, denying the

distinctive natural expressivity of living bodies means denying our
natural responsiveness to them, the distinctive ways in which another's
stricken gaze or favouring of a limb calls forth our pity and comfort.
Imagining that we might turn to stone while our pain goes on is, then,
not only a way of repressing the specificity of animal otherness, but also
a mythological expression or accounting of its costs. For this fantasy of
petrefaction figures our denial of animation's rootedness in animality as
a denial of our own animality—as if our fellow creatures place demands
upon us so terrifying that we prefer to render ourselves absolutely insen-
sible to them. Rather than acknowledge that their bodies and ours are
mutually attuned, we would (Medusas to ourselves) turn our own flesh
into stone.

8. Does Heidegger's citation from St Paul allude to Haufniensis' citation of the same phrase in his account of what he calls objective
anxiety—the way in which Adam's sin cast a sinful shadow not only
over succeeding generations but also over nature? If so, he must contest
Haufniensis' sense that this notion of 'a reflection of possibility and a
trembling of complicity' with Adam in nature 'belongs in dogmatics'
(*CA* 58), and hence that those who would incorporate this eager longing
into non-theological modes of thought are spiritually confused. For
Paul's words express what Haufniensis calls the repentant anxiety of
good over evil—that undergone by one who sees himself as imperfect,
longs for 'the redemption of our body', 'the glorious liberty of the children of God', and knows himself incapable of achieving it on his own.
This stands opposed to demonic anxiety—the anxiety of evil over good.
Those possessed by it find the immediate presence of goodness incarnate an unbearable torment, and yearn to be cast out into non-human
animals, whose lives they then destroy (see Matthew 8: 28–34). Its criteria further include: enclosing reserve and unfree disclosure (telling
refusal?); the sudden or the discontinuous (moment of vision?);
contentlessness (self-emptying?); and boredom. Since Heidegger's
redemption of human animality attunes itself to the unfree disclosure of
boredom while spurning any reference to Christ (as if struck dumb by
his example; Luke 11: 14), Haufniensis is unlikely to find its tone or
mood attractive.

What, then, is the mood or attunement of Haufniensis' account? Here
we must recall his introductory words about the nature of any psychological deliberation about sin (and hence, presumably, his own). He tells
us that any science presupposes a mood, and any error in its modula-
tion can be as serious as one in the development of the thoughts it

informs. Hence, when the concept of sin is treated in the wrong place, its appropriate mood is replaced by false ones.

If sin is dealt with in psychology, the mood becomes that of persistent observation, like the fearlessness of a secret agent, but not that of the victorious flight of earnestness out of sin. The concept becomes a different concept, for sin becomes a state. However, sin is not a state. Its idea is that its concept is continually annulled . . . The mood of psychology would be antipathetic curiosity, whereas the proper mood is earnestness expressed in courageous resistance. The mood of psychology is that of a discovering anxiety, and in its anxiety psychology portrays sin, while again and again it is in anxiety over the portrayal that it itself brings forth. When sin is dealt with in this manner it becomes the stronger, because psychology relates itself to it in a feminine way. That this state has its truth is certain; that it occurs more or less in every human life before the ethical manifests itself is certain. But in being considered in this manner sin does not become what it is, but a more or a less. (*CA* 15)

The mood of Haufniensis' analysis of anxiety as a whole is thus itself anxious—and in such a way that it makes sin stronger. Notwithstanding the internal consistency of its dialectical or didactic thought-content, in so far as its readers wish to orient themselves towards an understanding of hereditary sin, they will be 'submitting to the service of a misplaced brilliance' (*CA* 14)—not even attaining the threshold of the ethical, let alone the religious. For the analysis presents sin as a state, and hence as something quantitative (recall our first suspicions about Haufniensis' conclusions earlier)—something that either endures or can be completely annulled—when it is to be overcome, and always to be overcome anew, and impossible to overcome without help (thus signalling the shipwreck of ethics and its ideal of self-sufficiency).

We cannot finesse this problem by citing Haufniensis' claim that the issue with which psychology *can* legitimately occupy itself 'is not that sin comes into existence, but how it can come into existence' (*CA* 22)—with the condition for the possibility of sin, rather than its actuality. For the very notion of hereditary sin invokes an idea of our sinfulness as actual—of us as always already existing in untruth. Hence, his claim entails that there could not be a psychologically orienting deliberation on hereditary sin. Why, then, should Haufniensis give his writing the form, and hence the mood, of that science—one which he declares in advance is discordant with its topic?

. . . if someone wants to observe a passion, he must choose his individual. At that point, what counts is stillness, quietness and obscurity, so that he may discover the individual's secret. Then he must practice what he has learned until he is able to delude the individual. Thereupon he fictitiously invents the passion and appears before the individual in a preternatural magnitude of the passion. If it is done correctly, the individual will feel an indescribable relief and satisfaction, such as an insane person will feel when someone has uncovered and poetically grasped his fixation and then proceeds to develop it further. (*CA* 55–6)

Haufniensis' anxiety is a magnified representation of the passion he diagnoses in his readers—an anxiety about the possibility of sin that leads them to observe its varieties without engaging in earnest resistance to its production and reproduction, and hence reproduces itself; and an anxiety about the possibility of salvation which, regarded as a mere expectation, simply redoubles that anxiety. By reflecting his reader's state back to her, Haufniensis hopes that she will recognize her fixation in his, and see what is needed to break that fixation.

What is needed, as Haufniensis repeatedly declares, is dogmatics— say theology, or more precisely faith. What is absent from Haufniensis' otherwise compelling reading of the Genesis narrative? The voice of God prohibiting the fruit of the tree: 'one need merely assume that Adam talked to himself. The imperfection in the story, namely that another spoke to Adam about what he did not understand, is thus eliminated' (*CA* 45). This absence figures the true imperfection in Haufniensis' understanding of Genesis and hence of original sin— the absence of God's Son (that is, of the Christian God). Haufniensis reads Genesis (as Heidegger reads Paul and Haufniensis) without reference to Christ, as if the Christian dogma of original sin can simply be read off the tale of Adam and Eve's transgression. But for a Christian, the reality of original sin is revealed, and hence can be seen to be revealed in this ancient tale of the origins of humanity, only in the light of Christ's revelation of himself as God. Only in revealing himself as the Way, the Truth, and the Life does he reveal us as existing in Untruth (and make it possible for us earnestly to resist and overcome that state). A Christian understanding of human beings as originally sinful cannot, therefore, be attained apart from understanding what it might mean to think of Jesus Christ as God incarnate, and hence as the fulfilment of the Old Testament and its truths; and by the same token, grasping what it might mean to think of Jesus as God is inseparable from appreciating what it might mean to think of ourselves as originally sinful. The first Adam's true significance is properly unveiled only by the second Adam; in Haufniensis' terms, the Adam who begets original sin must also be the Adam for whom Christ atones (*CA* 28).

9. According to Karl Barth,[5] Christ's self-revelation as God occurs through the Resurrection, but its full significance is made manifest in the forty days between his Resurrection and his Ascension. This implies that Christ's divinity prior to his death was veiled, that only his disciples' encounters with him after the Crucifixion make them capable of appreciating that his life from birth until death was one of veiled divinity. But what, in those forty days, attests to divinity unveiled? What is gained by a Barthian stress upon this second historical narrative, or rather upon the fragments of such a post-Resurrection narrative that the Gospels and the Acts of the Apostles provide, beyond the sheer fact of Christ's Resurrection?

Luke's collocation of these fragments makes up the final chapter of his Gospel, which has the form of a triptych. First, the women discover the empty tomb and are told by two angels that Christ is risen, and the other disciples confirm their tale by finding only discarded linen in the sepulchre. The chapter's centrepiece tells of two disciples walking to a village outside Jerusalem called Emmaus, three days after the crucifixion. They are joined by Jesus, whom they do not recognize, and to whom they express their sense of Jesus' death as having undermined their trust in the goodness and godliness of his life. Jesus rebukes their despair, retelling his first history as the fulfilment of scriptural prophecy. They invite him to eat with them, and recognize him at the breaking of bread, at which point he vanishes. The chapter ends with an account of Christ appearing to the other disciples in Jerusalem while they are being told of the events at Emmaus; he invites them to view and touch his wounded body, eats some fish and honey, opens their minds to the true meaning of scripture, and commissions them to preach in his name to all nations. After promising that they will soon receive the Holy Spirit, he leads them to Bethany and ascends before their eyes into heaven.

Luke thereby tells us that Jesus' resurrection is bodily, a mode of incarnation; his body is transfigured, but not discarded—either at the tomb or upon his return to God—and hence annihilated neither by death nor by participation in the divine. It continues to bear the marks of finitude (not only capable, but in need, of ingesting sustenance), and of the central experience of his first history (the physical traces of the Crucifixion). His disciples recognize him, hence the essential continuity between his crucified and his resurrected embodiment is made manifest, in two main ways: through his presentation of his body as bread, and as word. As bread, his body is broken in order to sustain his followers,

[5] *Church Dogmatics* (T. and T. Clark: Edinburgh, 1932–69), esp. iii/2. 440 ff.

and to unite them into one body of believers; as word, he not only comprehends but embodies the truth of scripture—he is the Word who was with, and who is, God. In thus making himself present to his disciples, Jesus reveals himself as having always been present throughout human history, and as always present in the future, through his own and his Spirit's embodiment in the church and through that Spirit's embodiment of the promise of his Second Coming. Jesus, as God, is thus the God who is, who was, and who is to come—whose mode of presence is both having-been and yet-to-come. His time, as God, is eternal; he is time's fulfilment—but that fulfilment is declared through his second history, his second mode of incarnation, which is itself presented as the fulfilment of—the unveiling of the true significance of—his first such mode of incarnation. Hence, divine time appears not as the annihilation but as the complement of embodied human time; Christ's incarnate life after death unveils the implicit divinity of the incarnate life of which that death was the fulfilment.

We might say: Christ's Resurrection and Ascension unveils the divinity of his Incarnation by transfiguring our understanding of his Crucifixion as its fulfilment rather than its negation. If the crucified body is resurrected and glorified, then the meaning of death—even a death full of pain and humiliation, even one experienced by its victim as Godforsaken—must be reconceived. Death need not be the measure of life, always capable of rendering meaningless whatever is truthful, beautiful, and good in human existence (as the disciples walking to Emmaus presume); on the contrary, a certain kind of life, embodying a radically new understanding of what human truth, beauty, and goodness might be, can give death new meaning by incorporating it, remaking it in its own flesh and blood. (We might think of this as Christianity's way of acknowledging that human existence is always Being-towards-death while denying Heidegger's assumption that no other can die in our place, can atone for us.)

10. In what ways, then, does Christ's first history incorporate this radically new understanding of death, and why does any human life which refuses such incorporation appear as originally sinful—as not just lacking the truth but existing in untruth? If we think of the basic principle of this understanding as the first or greatest of divine commandments, then this very question is addressed in all three of the Synoptic Gospels—perhaps most clearly in Mark.

And one of the scribes . . . asked him, Which is the first commandment of all?
    And Jesus answered him, The first of all the commandments is, Hear, O Israel; The Lord our God is one Lord:

And thou shalt love the Lord thy God with all thy heart, and with all thy soul, and with all thy mind, and with all thy strength: this is the first commandment.

And the second is like, namely this, Thou shalt love thy neighbour as thyself. There is none other commandment greater than these. (Mark 12: 28–31)

In the other Gospel accounts, this answer is presented as a reading of the Jewish law, and hence as Christ's fulfilling interpretation and embodiment of scripture. It is equally plain in all three contexts that the two commandments are not distinct; the second is like the first, it is another way of articulating the first's demands: to love God is to love one's neighbour as oneself, and vice versa. In Luke, Jesus' questioner asks for further clarification: who is my neighbour? Jesus responds with the parable of the Good Samaritan, who—unlike the priest and the Levite—stops to help a man assaulted by thieves, binding his wounds, taking him to and paying for his recuperation at a nearby inn, and pledging his credit against any debts the victim runs up. Jesus then asks: 'Which now of these three, thinkest thou, was neighbour unto him that fell among thieves? And he said, He that shewed mercy on him. Then said Jesus unto him, Go, and do thou likewise' (Luke 10: 36–7). The parable tells us nothing more about the man who fell among thieves than that he was travelling from Jerusalem to Jericho: he could be anyone—his tribe, social status, and occupation are entirely undetermined. What makes him the Samaritan's neighbour is his victimhood: he is simply another human being in need. And what makes the Samaritan this victim's neighbour is his compassionate response to him, and the unstintingness with which he embodies that response in action. Everything the Samaritan has—wine and oil, beast of burden, money, time, and energy—is available for the victim; at the last, the Samaritan even pledges himself for debts that the other might accumulate in the future—as if enslaving himself to the other, placing him at the centre of his own life.

In effect, then, Jesus teaches that our neighbour is anyone who has been made a victim, anyone whose suffering can be relieved by our actions; and that to acknowledge someone as one's neighbour means acknowledging oneself as their neighbour, which means sacrificing oneself in order to help them. To love one's neighbour thus amounts to denying oneself, without putting limits in advance upon what that self-denial might require. It is to make oneself as nothing in relation to the neighbour—to die to self (the lesson that Constantius encodes in his apparently casual citations of the parable of the Prodigal Son). This is how loving God, following his commandments, can amount to incorporating death into one's life, diurnalizing its forbidding presence and transfiguring its meaning. To love one's neighbour as oneself is to live as if dead to oneself.

11. Jesus drives home the shock of this demand, his raising of the spiritual stakes, by talking of this self-denying love for one's neighbour as a transposition of one's love for oneself. This formulation certainly cultivates an air of paradox. After all, surely one can love one's neighbour as oneself only if one loves oneself; and is not self-love precisely what Jesus intends to counsel against, rather than something to be generalized—a template for one's relations to others? His point is rather to challenge us to reconceive our sense of what self-love might be. For the Samaritan's active compassion quickly goes beyond anything we might think that the victim has a right to expect; by the point at which he offers to pay the victim's future debts, we might rather think that he had a perfect right not to mortgage himself to another's actions—even, perhaps, that his offer amounts to a failure to respect his own autonomy, to respect that in us which is (as Rawls, in his most Kantian vein, puts it) the 'self-originating source' of our moral claims on others. Jesus' claim is that to take such a stand on one's rights in the face of another's need is not an expression of human dignity or self-respect but a form of self-love; true human dignity asks us to regard our own dignity as nothing in comparison with the violated dignity of others, to ensure that where ego was, the other shall be.

So formulated, a further dimension of Jesus' teaching begins to emerge. For his picture of us as presently constituted by a self-love which we picture to ourselves as self-respect, and his advice to reconstitute ourselves in terms of a picture of self-denial or self-sacrifice ultimately epitomized by his Crucifixion, implies that selfhood is a matter of self-relation—of the self's relating to itself in one mode or another. In the terms proposed by his second commandment: we can be asked to stand to our neighbour as we stand to ourselves because the human self is inherently a neighbour to itself. As Jesus' interlocutor implies, the question is not, do I have a neighbour? but, who is my neighbour? Jesus' teaching is that the self either has itself as its neighbour (in which case it exists in self-love), or it has the other as its neighbour (in which case it exists in self-sacrifice or self-overcoming). There is no middle ground, because the self cannot but neighbour itself; human existence is neighbouring.

The perfectionist idea of a split or doubled self—an idea we have already encountered in the work of Kierkegaard's pseudonyms, in Heidegger's early and later writings, and in Wittgenstein's picture of us as needing to overcome our lostness to ourselves—thus finds one source in Christian reconceptions of faith. As if to confirm the connection, Jesus' construction of the Good Samaritan parable ends by drawing upon one critical aspect of that model—the fact that perfectionist pictures of self-relation are meant to apply to and work upon the relation between the texts that elaborate them and their readers. For Jesus ends by asking his interlocutor to identify the true neighbour; and that neighbour is, of course, a Samaritan—a member of a tribe looked upon with contempt by many Jews of the time. By being forced to acknowledge the Samaritan as having loved his neighbour, and hence as having acted as neighbour to the victim of robbery, Jesus' interlocutor is thereby invited to acknowledge the Samaritan as his neighbour—not only as a victim whose needs he has not acknowledged, but also as *his* victim, a victim of his own violence and self-love. He is challenged to recognize himself in the robbers of the tale, to see a connection between the behaviour that brought about the wounded body at the roadside and the behaviour that makes an outcast of the one who stops to bind those wounds. He is then further challenged to 'Go, and do thou likewise'; that is, to take the Samaritan as his spiritual exemplar—to see his hitherto unacknowledged victim as exemplifying a state of the self to which he should aspire, and hence as representing an attainable but unattained, a further or neighbouring, state of himself. In short, the parable implicates its hearer in the victimizing it depicts, and invites him to implicate himself in what the parable takes to be necessary for its overcoming; only by doing so, by seeing the Samaritan as his neighbour and by neighbouring him as he neighbours the victim, could he be said to love his neighbour as himself.

The fact that the parable's exemplar of neighbouring is himself in need of neighbouring, that it portrays the true neighbour of a victim as a victim, has further implications. It suggests, to begin with, that the spiritual challenge of victimhood is to absorb one's victimization rather than reproducing it in one's relations with others. The Samaritan does not become another link in the chain of violence and exclusion; he breaks it—he suffers his suffering without the all too human relief of inflicting it upon others. The connection between the parable's hero and its teller, between, say, taking on another's debts and the Atonement, is not far to seek. But it also suggests that acknowledging victimhood in others and experiencing victimhood oneself are somehow internally related. This suggestion includes the idea that experiencing victimhood might make one more sensitive to its presence and more inclined to respond to it; but since the tale's teller, who lives a life of identification with victims, himself ends as an exemplar of victimhood, it further intimates that an identification with victims might itself elicit victimization.

If we put together the ideas that loving one's neighbour means identifying with victims, that such identification involves overcoming one's capacity for victimizing, that this capacity is acquired from others, and that its overcoming amounts to a reconstitution of the self, then we have the essential structure of the Christian understanding of original sin.

12. James Alison has recently formulated this understanding in terms provided by the work of René Girard, and his conception of human self-hood as constituted mimetically.[6] Human beings become individuals by incorporating gestures, language, modes of consciousness, and activity from those around them; this mimicry or incorporation of the other is not something that a pre-given self does, but what goes to make up a self in the first place—and hence makes a self always already other to itself, structured in terms of neighbouring. Taking desire as a metonym for this process (as do Wittgenstein and Augustine in their tales of human constitution), we might say that human desire is not linear (a matter of subjects fixing directly upon objects), or reflexive (a matter of desiring another's desire, wanting the other to find oneself desirable), but rather triangular or mediated (we desire what another desires, according to the desire of the other).

This mimetic structure leads to conflict: individuals find themselves desiring the same object, and hence become rivals. This creates pressures within the social group that are only relieved when its members come to identify one of their number (or one subgroup) as marginal, abnormal, or otherwise threatening, and re-establish the social bond by combining to cast out their arbitrarily chosen scapegoat. Each such violent exclusion can only give temporary relief, however, since mimetic desire inevitably regenerates internal rivalry, and so the scapegoating process is repeated. The scapegoat thus appears as both cause and cure of the conflict, a fundamental threat and a miraculous source of healing, good, and evil. His corpse thereby becomes a focus of hugely conflicting currents of thought and feeling that may find expression in rituals of prohibition and worship, but whose true significance must nevertheless remain repressed if the scapegoating process is to continue performing its critical function.

Only a forceful intervention into these mechanisms of rivalry and victimizing can bring us to see what is happening, which means seeing that the victim is hated without cause, seeing our own complicity in that arbitary violence, and seeing the possibility of reconstituting ourselves

---

[6] *The Joy of being Wrong* (Crossroad Herder: New York, 1998).

around the incorporation of a kind of non-envious or unobstacled desire. Christ's first history amounts to just that disruption. By not only identifying with the guiltless objects of our victimage, but accepting the victimage that this identification brings upon himself (even unto death on a cross) without ever victimizing others in imitation or recompense ('Father, forgive them, for they know not what they do'), he exemplifies a mode of non-rivalrous desire—a desire for the satisfaction of the other's desire as if it were one's own—that can be incorporated by others without inevitably leading to rivalry and thence to further scapegoating.

The conflict, victimizing, and self-love thereby disrupted are not attitudes adopted by the self, who might profitably be advised or forced to abandon them, but rather constitute the self who responds to such advice or coercion. Since human selfhood is mimetic, becoming a human individual in an environment of rivalrous desire means becoming rivalrous—it means inheriting (and then bequeathing) a victimizing self. Hence, the pre-Christian tale we tell ourselves of the origins of humanity takes rivalrousness for granted. We project Adam and Eve's entry into the realm of desire as an appropriation of what is proper to God, picturing God as having proclaimed his identity over against theirs by a prohibition; since human selves are always already rivalrous, attempting to blame one another or their fellow creatures, and bequeathing murderous rivalry to their offspring by exemplification, their original exemplar must also be so constituted.

Nevertheless, the very mechanism of self-constitution which drives victimization so deeply into human being also provides the means for its overcoming—the possibility of a non-victimizing countermimesis from beyond the self, an exemplar of non-rivalrous human desire and existence. To be confronted with another human being who is capable not only of making the victim's desires his own, but of accepting the extremity of victimage that such self-sacrifice attracts without responding in kind, is to realize how human existence is presently constituted and how it might be constituted otherwise. The ambivalent status of the scapegoat is thus at once intensified and subverted from within. Attending to Jesus' crucified body at once uncovers the pervasiveness of scapegoating to human culture and individuation, and its contingency; for by initiating the establishment of a community in which the victimizing mechanism is turned upon itself, in which individuals attempt to construct and bequeath a culture of identification with the victim and hence of negating that within them which is of the victimizer, Jesus shows that what appears to be most deeply 'me' is an illusion.

Christianity's talk of original sin aims to encapsulate this Christ-derived sense of ourselves as both always already sinful and yet open to salvation. Sin is original to us, it is hereditary, because specifically human desire in us mimetic animals is awakened by the perception of another desiring, and thus constitutes the self—desiring what the other desires—in opposition or rivalry to that other. However, the very same irruption into this self-reinforcing chain of human reproduction that reveals its true functioning also reveals that it might function otherwise; for Christ's Incarnation exemplifes a mode of human selfhood that constitutes itself by substitution for the other. Hence the traditional Catholic distinction between original sin and concupiscence: desire as such is not sinful, and hence neither is human sexuality and sensuality—call it the body; to recognize oneself as originally sinful is to recognize that embodied human existence can be otherwise, while acknowledging that human beings could not have attained that recognition (let alone have become capable of acting upon it) by themselves.

If we were to encapsulate these ideas by saying, after Cavell after Wittgenstein, that the crucified human body is our best picture of the unacknowledged human soul,[7] then we must further say that it is also our best picture of how the human soul finds acknowledgement. But can philosophy acknowledge religion and still have faith in itself?

---

[7] See *CR* 430.

ACKNOWLEDGEMENTS

As this book's focus upon interrelated ideas of the self as structured by thrown projection or ecstatic constancy would imply, the intellectual project I pursue within it frequently revisits and revises earlier work of mine. The most important of these recountings are as follows:

Introduction. A version of this material was first published as 'On Refusing to Begin', *Common Knowledge*, 5/2 (Fall 1996).

Part One
Sections 42–8. A version of this material, under the title 'Seeing Aspects', is forthcoming in H.-J. Glock (ed.), *Wittgenstein: A Critical Reader* (Blackwell: Oxford, 2001).

Part Two
Sections 16–17, 19–20, 22–3, 26–7, 29, 38–41. These passages draw on interpretations first advanced in my *Heidegger and* Being and Time (Routledge: London, 1996).

Section 31. An earlier version of this argument first appeared under the title 'Can there be an Epistemology of Moods?', in A. O'Hear (ed.), *Verstehen and Humane Understanding* (Cambridge University Press: Cambridge, 1997).

Part Three
Sections 1–13. An earlier version of this reading of the *Philosophical Fragments* first appeared under the title 'God's Plagiarist', *Philosophical Investigations*, 22/1 (Jan. 1999).

I would also like to thank those colleagues and friends who read through the manuscript of this book, in whole or in part, and commented on it: James Conant, Peter Hacker, Philip Wheatley, and three readers for the Oxford University Press. I would never have contemplated beginning such a project without the stimulating interest, encouragement, and intellectual vitality of my colleagues in the Philosophy Department at the University of Essex; and I would not have been able to bring it to completion without the generosity of the Warden and Fellows of New College, Oxford, who gave me two terms of sabbatical leave at a crucial time.

As always, my thanks go to Alison Baker for her forbearance and support during the unusually long gestation of this unusually long book.

BIBLIOGRAPHY

ALISON, J., *The Joy of being Wrong* (Crossroad Herder: New York, 1998).

AUGUSTINE, *Confessions,* trans. H. Chadwick (Oxford University Press: Oxford, 1991).

BAKER, G. P. and HACKER, P. M. S., *Wittgenstein: Understanding and Meaning* (Blackwell: Oxford, 1980).

——*An Analytical Commentary on the* Philosophical Investigations, vol. i (Blackwell: Oxford, 1980).

——*Scepticism, Rules and Language* (Blackwell: Oxford, 1984).

—— *Wittgenstein: Rules, Grammar and Necessity* (Blackwell: Oxford, 1986).

——'Malcolm on Language and Rules', *Philosophy*, 65 (1990).

BARTH, K., *Church Dogmatics* (T. and T. Clark: Edinburgh, 1932–69).

BUDD, M., *Wittgenstein's Philosophy of Psychology* (Routledge: London,1989).

CAVELL, S., *Must we Mean what we Say?* (Cambridge University Press: Cambridge, 1969).

——*The Claim of Reason* (Oxford University Press: Oxford, 1979).

——*The Senses of Walden* (North Point Press: San Francisco, 1981).

——*Themes out of School* (North Point Press: San Francisco, 1984).

——*Disowning Knowledge* (Cambridge University Press: Cambridge, 1987).

——*Conditions Handsome and Unhandsome* (University of Chicago Press: Chicago, 1990).

——*A Pitch of Philosophy* (Harvard University Press: Cambridge, Mass., 1994).

——*Philosophical Passages* (Blackwell: Oxford, 1995).

CONANT, J., 'Must we Show what we Cannot Say?', in R. Fleming and M. Payne (eds.), *The Senses of Stanley Cavell* (Bucknell University Press: Lewisburg, Pa., 1989).

——'The Search for Logically Alien Thought', *Philosophical Topics*, 20/1 (Fall 1991).

——'Wittgenstein, Kierkegaard and Nonsense', in T. Cohen, P. Guyer, and H. Putnam (eds.), *Pursuits of Reason* (Texas Technical University Press: Lubbock, 1993).

——'Putting Two and Two Together', in T. Tessin and M. von der Ruhr (eds.), *Philosophy and the Grammar of Religious Belief* (Macmillan: London, 1995).

DIAMOND, C., 'Rules: Looking in the Right Place', in D. Z. Phillips (ed.), *Wittgenstein: Attention to Particulars* (Macmillan: London, 1989).

FINGARETTE, H., 'The Meaning of Law in the Book of Job', in S. Hauerwas and A. MacIntyre (eds.), *Revisions* (University of Notre Dame Press: Notre Dame, Ind., 1981).

FLEMING, R., *The State of Philosophy* (Bucknell University Press: Lewisburg, Pa., 1993).

FOGELIN, R., *Wittgenstein* (Routledge: London, 1976).

GLOCK, H.-J., *A Wittgenstein Dictionary* (Blackwell: Oxford, 1996).

GOETHE, J. W., *Faust Part Two*, trans. P. Wayne (Penguin: London, 1959).

HEARNE, V., *Adam's Task* (Heinemann: London, 1986).

HEIDEGGER, M., *Being and Time*, trans. J. Macquarrie and E. Robinson (Blackwell: Oxford, 1962).

—— *What is Called Thinking?*, trans. J. Glenn Gray (Harper & Row: New York, 1968).

—— *The Fundamental Concepts of Metaphysics*, trans. W. McNeill and N. Walker (Indiana University Press: Bloomington, 1995).

—— *Plato's Sophist*, trans. R. Rojcewicz and A. Schuwer (Indiana University Press: Bloomington, 1997).

JOHNSTON, P., *Wittgenstein: Rethinking the Inner* (Routledge: London, 1994).

KANT, I., *Critique of Pure Reason*, trans. N. Kemp Smith (Macmillan: London, 1929).

KIERKEGAARD, S., *The Concept of Anxiety: A Simple Psychologically Orienting Deliberation on the Dogmatic Issue of Hereditary Sin*, trans. R. Thomte and A. B. Anderson (Princeton University Press: Princeton, 1980).

—— *Fear and Trembling & Repetition*, trans. H. V. and E. H. Hong (Princeton University Press: Princeton, 1983).

—— *Philosophical Fragments*, trans. H. V. and E. H. Hong (Princeton University Press: Princeton, 1985).

—— *Concluding Unscientific Postscript to the Philosophical Fragments*, trans. H. V. and E. H. Hong (Princeton University Press: Princeton, 1992).

KRELL, D. FARRELL, *Daimon Life* (Indiana University Press: Bloomington, 1992).

McDOWELL, J., *Mind, Value and Reality* (Harvard University Press: Cambridge, Mass., 1998).

McGINN, M., *Wittgenstein and the* Philosophical Investigations (Routledge: London, 1997).

MacINTYRE, A., *After Virtue* (Duckworth: London, 1981).

MALCOLM, N., *Essays on Wittgensteinian Themes*, ed. G. H. von Wright (Cornell University Press: Ithaca, NY, 1996).

MOONEY, E., 'Art, Deed and System: The Prefaces to *Fear and Trembling*', in R. L. Perkins (ed.), *International Kierkegaard Commentary*, vi: *Fear and Trembling & Repetition* (Mercer University Press: Macon, Ga., 1993).

MORRIS, T. F., 'Constantin Constantius' Search for an Acceptable Way of Life', in R. L. Perkins (ed.), *International Kierkegaard Commentary*, vi: *Fear and Trembling & Repetition* (Mercer University Press: Macon, Ga., 1993).

MULHALL, S., *On Being in the World* (Routledge: London, 1990).

——*Stanley Cavell: Philosophy's Recounting of the Ordinary* (Oxford University Press: Oxford, 1994).

——*Heidegger and* Being and Time (Routledge: London, 1996).

——(ed.), *The Cavell Reader* (Blackwell: Oxford, 1996).

NIETZSCHE, F., *Thus Spake Zarathustra*, trans. R. J. Hollingdale (Penguin: London, 1961).

PAYNE, M., 'Introduction', *Bucknell Review*, 32 (1989).

PHILLIPS, A., *The Beast in the Nursery* (Faber: London, 1998).

PLATO, *Sophist*, trans. N. White (Hackett: Indianapolis, 1993).

RHEES, R., *Discussions of Wittgenstein* (Routledge & Kegan Paul: London, 1970).

RUNDLE, B., *Wittgenstein and Contemporary Philosophy of Language* (Blackwell: Oxford, 1990).

SCHLEGEL, F., *Lucinde & The Fragments*, trans. P. Firchow (University of Minnesota Press: Minneapolis, 1991).

STATEN, H., *Wittgenstein and Derrida* (Blackwell: London, 1984).

TAYLOR, C., *Philosophical Papers*, vol. i (Cambridge University Press: Cambridge, 1985).

WITTGENSTEIN, L., *Philosophical Investigations*, trans. G. E. M. Anscombe (Blackwell: Oxford, 1953).

——*Remarks on the Philosophy of Psychology*, vol. i, trans. G. E. M. Anscombe, vol. ii, trans. C. G. Luckhardt and M. A. E. Aue (Blackwell: Oxford, 1980).

——*Last Writings on the Philosophy of Psychology*, i and ii, trans. C. G. Luckhardt and M. A. E. Aue (Blackwell: Oxford, 1982, 1992).

INDEX

Adam's Task 423–4
algorithms 96–7, 103, 232
Alison, J. 436–8
amentia 16–18, 57, 60, 109, 120, 217, 295, 302
animality 218, 289–90, 298, 307, 380, 417–20, 421–7, 428, 438
anxiety 257–65, 272, 274, 377–8, 380, 416–19, 424, 428
aphorism 19–21, 152–3, 181
Aristotle 80–1, 197
articulation 22, 100, 134, 178–9, 187, 196, 201, 224–6, 231–3, 235, 239, 241, 251, 260, 263–4, 272, 279, 290, 304, 312, 316, 369
Ascension 431–2
aspect blindness 155, 157, 162–3, 173, 314
aspect dawning 153–63, 164, 172, 175, 227
aspect-seeing 127–8, 150, 219, 225, 234, 255
Saint Augustine 9, 29–55, 57–8, 109, 171, 217–18, 267–8, 269, 283, 289, 308, 318–19, 330, 436
authenticity 215, 217–18, 244–8, 251, 257, 272–8, 420, 421
autobiography 19, 30–2, 217
axis of investigation 92–3, 224

Baker, G. P. 37, 52, 123–35, 145
Barth, K. 431–2
Beethoven, L. 11–12
beginnings 1–2, 2–6, 11–13, 23–5, 29, 38, 42, 158, 170, 181, 185–6, 196, 206–8, 214, 218, 272, 283–4, 285, 286–95, 303, 323, 327–8, 343–4, 354, 356, 370, 390–1
Being-with 243–8, 277–82
Being and Time 185–284, 285–6, 295–6, 297–8, 299, 303–4, 305, 310, 312, 313, 318, 420
Blake, W. 22
body 415–16, 418, 419, 428, 431, 435, 438
boredom 425–7
Budd, M. 157n.
builders 52–8, 217

care 258, 265–72, 275
caricature 345, 346, 349, 353
Cavell, S. 1–25, 29n., 48n., 49, 56–8, 60, 72, 78–80, 136, 145–7, 150–3, 253–5, 259–60, 282, 405, 438
Christianity 217–18, 318–20, 324–5, 334, 346–8, 351, 363–4, 378, 383, 386, 409–14, 428–30, 431–2, 436–8
citation 30–1, 185–6, 188, 192–3, 271, 281, 329, 351, 353, 370, 372, 375–6, 390–1
The Claim of Reason 1–25, 39–40, 255
Climacus, J. 321–54, 355–6, 388–90
Conant, J. 327n., 339n.
The Concept of Anxiety 416–19, 428–30
Concluding Unscientific Postscript 323–7, 338, 348–9, 354, 359, 415
Confessions 30–6, 45, 49–50, 217
conscience 189, 270, 272–85, 420
Constantius, C. 388–412
continuous seeing as 157, 158–62, 172, 175
conversion 32–3, 38, 42–3, 50, 276–84, 284–5, 330, 424
criteria 7, 17, 54, 56, 58, 68, 93–7, 98–102, 103, 107, 146–7, 162, 241, 263

Dasein 201–85, 420, 425–7
de Silentio, J. 354–88
death 271, 420, 431–2
decision 113–14, 118, 121, 125, 127–8, 143, 145
definition 39–42, 59–61, 62, 72, 78, 95–6, 189, 196–8, 205, 254–5
Derrida, J. 65
Descartes, R. 13, 23, 73, 218–23, 230, 238, 263, 294–5, 328, 329–38, 339–40
desire 51, 62, 67, 71, 120, 137, 270–1, 289–90, 338, 347, 425, 426, 436–8
diachrony 70, 74, 85–7, 110
dialectic 189–90, 194–5, 196–8, 205, 325, 327, 366, 381, 408
Diamond, C. 99–102, 134–5
Dilthey, W. 282–3
drama 11–16, 19, 23, 392–9
duck-rabbit 127, 158, 161, 162

Emerson, R. W. 2
essence 87–97, 137–8, 179, 224–5,
    241–2, 289, 330, 426
ethics 380–8, 412, 434
etymology 211–15, 220, 309, 314
existentiell (vs. existential) 205, 237, 246
experience of meaning 163–7

false necessity 82, 210, 275, 342, 350,
    417, 437
family resemblance 81–7, 90, 91–2,
    94–5, 106–7, 110
farce 392–3, 395–9, 409
fear 250, 257
Fear and Trembling 354–90
fiction 213–15, 265–72, 404
figurative 36, 57–8, 86, 88, 119–20, 148,
    152, 154, 172, 178, 196, 257, 271,
    332, 341, 366, 370–6, 381
Fingarette, H. 407–8
Fleming, R. 6 n.
Fogelin, R. 157 n.
fragments 15, 153, 301, 305–6, 316, 323
Frege, G. 29
friend 277–8, 283–4, 291, 300, 390
Fundamental Concepts of Metaphysics
    420–7
fundamental ontology 203, 206

games 58–61, 73, 75–81, 82–7, 91–2,
    132
genealogy 81–7, 203, 210
Genesis 32, 51, 57–8, 318–19, 359, 362,
    373, 380, 415, 416–18, 423, 430, 437
gesture 168–9, 178, 381
Girard, R. 436
Glock, H.-J. 174–5
God 9, 33–4, 405–7, 430
Goethe, J. W. 268–72
grace 386, 419
grammar 54, 56, 58, 73, 84, 93, 97,
    101–2, 111, 120, 128, 129, 146, 148,
    151, 176–81, 233, 241, 258, 423
guilt 270, 275–6, 349, 351–3

Hacker, P. M. S. 37, 52, 123–35, 145
hand 72, 230–1, 298, 311, 314
Haufniensis, V. 416–19, 428–30
Hearne, V. 423–4
Hegel, G. W. F. 323, 328, 358, 367,
    381–2, 383
Heidegger, M. 182, 185–319, 329, 330,
    344, 352, 367, 398, 402, 404, 419–27,
    428, 430, 432, 434
hermeneutic circle 23–4, 206, 272

history 69–70, 71, 85–7, 96, 121–2, 177,
    208–9, 281–6, 324–5, 349–50
Husserl, E. 185, 211, 280

idea 36–7, 302–3
imagination 55–8, 65, 83, 110, 119,
    147, 367, 373
individuality 170–1, 263, 273–8, 353,
    358, 391, 393–4, 396, 398–9, 405,
    417
inheritance 13, 48–51, 54, 63, 66, 85–6,
    170–1, 178, 180–1, 185, 188, 195,
    206, 208–9, 217–18, 246–7, 261,
    263–4, 268, 284–5, 307, 349, 351–3,
    369–70, 376, 394, 418, 423, 433, 437
inner (vs. outer) 43–6, 90, 171–4, 175,
    220–1, 249–56, 357, 427–8
internal relations 76, 110, 119, 147,
    367, 373
intuition 113, 117, 118, 121, 125,
    127–8, 142–3, 145, 254–6
irony 361, 379

Jastrow, J. 158
Job 402, 405–9
Johnston, P. 161 n.
judgement 114, 118, 149–50, 165, 172

Kant, I. 211–12, 252–6, 284, 310–12,
    334, 337, 358
Kierkegaard, S. 319–20, 321–414,
    416–19, 428–30, 434
Krell, D. 421 n.
Kuhn, T. 37, 42

language-games 61–70, 81–7, 91–2
limits 89, 180–1, 337–46, 352, 357, 359
logic 88–93, 96
lyric 11–16, 19, 23

McDowell, J. 251–2
McGinn, M. 156 n.
MacIntyre, A. 80
Malcolm, N. 123–35, 145
mechanical 1, 43–6, 90, 108, 118–22,
    137, 173–4, 176–7, 180, 237
metaphor 20, 167–8
midwifery 296–7, 299, 315, 352, 401
modernism 12–23, 153, 328, 396
mood 187, 248–65, 274, 289, 298, 425,
    428–9
Mooney, E. 370
Moses 86
motherhood 374–5, 377–80
music 11–13, 21–3, 147–8

myth 18–21, 118, 119, 139–53, 166, 169, 180, 187–8, 190, 192–3, 265–72, 297, 309–10, 427

natural history 70–5, 86
nature 72, 86, 103, 122, 139, 170, 407–8
neighbouring 413, 433–4, 436
Nietzsche, F. 281–2, 300–7, 315, 318, 415
nonsense 41, 60, 68, 117, 135, 361
nullity 264, 271, 273–6, 299, 417

ontic (vs. ontological) 202–3, 238, 254
ordinary 43–52, 57, 88–90, 133–5, 145–6, 149, 151, 181, 215–18, 245, 307, 353, 391
orientation 37–8, 40–2, 43, 61, 90–3, 174–80, 230–3, 234, 236, 242, 245, 247, 254, 261, 264, 265, 280, 307, 328, 331, 348–9, 399
original sin 51, 348, 386, 410, 415–19, 429–30, 436–8
originality 10–13, 69, 71–86, 115, 148, 185, 196, 199, 233, 247, 284–5, 288, 315, 329, 334, 338, 343, 353, 427

parable 378–9, 411–12, 433–4
paradigms 37, 40, 42
parataxis 316–18
Parmenides 188–9, 310–13, 314–16
parody 362–3, 403, 407, 408
Payne, M. 6 n.
perfectionism 18, 109, 111–12, 152–3, 206–8, 276–8, 286, 296–7, 299, 402, 434–5
phenomenology 211–15, 225, 236, 247, 256–7, 261–2, 264, 268
Phillips, A. 148–9
Philosophical Fragments 323–54, 359
Philosophical Investigations 29–182
physiognomy 144–5, 147, 148, 150, 154, 166–7, 169, 172, 176–7, 179, 309
pictures 36–43, 85–6, 98–9, 136, 175–6, 240
picture-objects 158–9
plagiarism 329, 332–3, 338, 345, 351, 353
Plato 185–98, 207–8, 242–3, 297, 306
play 49–51, 64–6, 69, 72, 76, 86–7, 149, 159, 180–1, 192
poetry 265–72, 314, 319, 332–4, 338, 346–7, 369–70, 394–5

possibility 209, 222, 236, 250, 257–8, 273, 360–1, 366, 396, 398, 417, 424
presence-at-hand 221–2, 228, 279
primitive 52, 55–8, 60–1, 83, 119–20, 217–18, 230, 326
projection 54, 68, 83, 125, 142, 153, 169, 180, 234, 248, 249, 290, 401, 423, 434–5
psychoanalysis 137, 148, 278, 401–2, 404, 424, 434

questioning 7, 22, 53, 101, 113, 116–17, 149, 185, 187, 191–2, 198–202, 203–5, 244, 258, 264–5, 287, 307–8, 328, 337, 343–4, 390–1, 408, 425

Rawls, J. 16–17, 433
readiness-to-hand 226–9, 244
reading 106–12, 325–7, 310–18, 352, 365–6, 373, 383, 403–5, 414, 430, 435
reading-machines 108, 119, 177
regarding as 161
remembering 9–23, 32, 290, 297–8, 309, 314–15, 317, 391, 410
Repetition 388–414
Resurrection 410, 431
Rhees, R. 52–3, 63, 75–81, 82–4
Rojcewicz, R. 186 n.
rules 76–9, 87, 92–3, 97–8, 102–6, 112–53, 179–81, 232–4
Rundle, B. 84–7
Russell, B. 29, 86

Saint Paul 427–8
scepticism 44–6, 194, 213, 219–23, 234, 237–43, 255, 269, 270, 279, 300–7
Schelling, F. 307
Schlegel, F. 15
Schopenhauer, A. 303
Schuwer, A. 186 n.
secondary sense 167–9, 170, 180
seduction 293, 301, 354, 381, 383, 385, 394, 401, 426
self-abandonment 396–8, 400, 407–8, 413
self-constancy 396–8, 400, 406
self-sacrifice 380, 383, 387, 408, 410, 411, 433
sign 257, 229–30, 296–8, 320
sin 330, 347, 385–6, 411, 419, 429
social contract 17
Socrates 188–9, 191, 270, 294–5, 315, 319, 329, 361

song 21–3
Sophist 185–99, 211, 272
sophistry 188–96, 207–8, 213–15, 223,
  225, 242–3, 256
Staten, H. 111 n.
style 33–6
sublime 87–93, 94–6, 101, 104, 119,
  135–6, 137–9, 149, 335
synchrony 70, 85–7, 109
synthesis 256, 261–2, 310–11, 316

Taylor, C. 250–1
temporality 208–10, 267, 269, 281, 304,
  306–7, 309, 349–50, 425, 432
Theatetus 67, 81
theatre 392–5
the 'They' 243–8, 269, 272–4, 425
thinking 286–318, 335–46
thrownness 234, 248–56, 258, 274, 425
Tractatus Logico-Philosophicus 36–7,
  342
transitionality 295–301, 304, 309, 317,
  329–30, 347, 350, 393
truth 240–3

univocity 85, 308

victimhood 433–8
virtue 80–1
voice 10, 17, 18, 23, 46, 140, 143–5,
  150, 177, 272–8, 315–16, 328, 332,
  338, 345, 347, 359, 383, 384, 388,
  407–8, 420, 430

What is Called Thinking? 284–320
Wittgenstein, L. 2–5, 9, 10, 16, 29–182,
  185, 192, 199, 214, 216–18, 225,
  227, 231, 233, 234, 237, 254, 260,
  264, 278, 280, 283, 289, 296, 308,
  309, 310, 337, 342, 344, 352, 367,
  381, 402, 404, 423, 427–8, 434, 436,
  438
women 22–3, 270, 325, 359, 374–5,
  377–80, 397–8, 411, 418, 429
worldhood 229–34, 254, 260

Yorck (von Wartenburg) 281–3

Zarathustra 300–2, 305